THE DRAMATIC WORKS OF Richard Brinsley Sheridan

R. B. SHERIDAN
by Thomas Gainsborough
By courtesy of the Frick Art Reference Library

THE DRAMATIC WORKS OF Richard Brinsley Sheridan

EDITED BY
CECIL PRICE

VOLUME I

OXFORD
AT THE CLARENDON PRESS
1973

Oxford University Press, Ely House, London W. 1

GLASGOW NEW YORK TORONTO MELBOURNE WELLINGTON
CAPE TOWN IBADAN NAIROBI DAR ES SALAAM LUSAKA ADDIS ABABA
DELHI BOMBAY CALCUTTA MADRAS KARACHI LAHORE DACCA
KUALA LUMPUR SINGAPORE HONG KONG TOKYO

Printed in Great Britain
at the University Press, Oxford
by Vivian Ridler
Printer to the University

TO CEINWEN

WHO INTRODUCED ME TO

THE CRITIC

ACKNOWLEDGEMENTS

IN this work I continue a study of Sheridan's life and achievements that found first expression in an edition of his letters, published in 1966. The list of acknowledgements printed on that occasion was a long one: I shall not repeat it now, but should like to express once again my real gratitude for all the help that has been given me.

Some particular assistance must be mentioned more specifically. Mr. Robert H. Taylor has the finest collection of Sheridan texts in existence, and has very generously allowed me to work on them for this edition. Dr. M. L. Poston and Mr. R. C. Stretton very amiably gave me the use of the Sheridan manuscripts in their possession. Mr. F. W. Bateson placed me considerably in his debt by lending me his notes on the text of the plays. Mr. D. M. Davin not only suggested this edition but has also encouraged me to keep going at a period when my time was largely taken up elsewhere.

I am obliged to the President and Council of the University College of Swansea for allowing me sabbatical leave to enable me to complete my text. I warmly appreciate the grant given me by the Henry E. Huntington Library and Art Gallery, and the kind aid of its Director, Dr. James Thorpe, and his staff. I have also been fortunate enough to spend further periods at the Folger Shakespeare Library (under Dr. Louis B. Wright and, more recently of Dr. O. B. Hardison, Jr.), and to enjoy much friendly assistance. Dr. Towner and Mr. James M. Wells made it possible for me to make use of the excellent holdings of the Newberry Library.

To Mr. Joseph E. Jeffs and the late Father Repetti I am grateful for help so cordially given on the number of occasions I have called at the Georgetown University Library. For similar kindness I am also indebted to Miss Helen Willard of the Harvard College Theatre Collection; Miss Marjorie Wynne and Mr. H. W. Liebert of Yale University Library; and Mr. Alexander Wainwright and Mr. Earle Coleman of Princeton University Library.

For other favours I am grateful to the Marchioness of Dufferin and Earl Spencer, Dr. Rex Alston, to the late J. O. Bartley and Roland Baughman, to Dr. L. W. Conolly, Mr. J. Fleming, Professors Philip Highfill, Jr., Patricia Hernlund, F. W. Hilles, Gwyn Jones, and J. D. Jump, Mrs. George Hull, Mr. W. R. LeFanu, Professor D. F. McKenzie, Dr. J. G. McManaway, Dr. Robert F. Metzdorf, Professor T. F. Mustanoja, Miss M. Pollard, Miss Felicity Ranger, Professor Claude Rawson, Mrs. Norma Russell, Mrs. A. P. Vlasto and Mr. David Woolley.

My warm thanks are due to Miss Helen Frick for so readily allowing me to use a photograph of the Gainsborough portrait as frontispiece; and to Mr. Arthur Crook, editor of *The Times Literary Supplement*, for permitting me to reprint portions oı an article on 'The Composition of *The School for Scandal*'. I also confess obligations to previous writers on Sheridan: G. H. Nettleton, R. C. Rhodes, Iolo Williams, and R. L. Purdy.

My debt to my wife is very great, and is inadequately acknowledged in the dedication.

I must acknowledge too the privilege of being allowed to use material in the following collections: the Bodleian Library, the British Museum, Butler Library of Columbia University, the Duke of Devonshire's Library at Chatsworth, the Folger Library, Huntington Library, Indiana University Library, Library of Congress, the Morgan Library, National Library of Scotland, Newberry Library, Royal Irish Academy, Somerville College Library, Swansea University College Library, Trinity College Library, Dublin, Victoria and Albert Museum Library, Widener Library, and Houghton Library, Yale University Library, New York Public Library, and the University of California at Los Angeles Library. I owe much to the helpful co-operation of their directors and staffs.

C. P.

NOTE

WHILE the present work was in the press, the Sheridan papers of the late Clare Sheridan came up for auction. A brief summary of their attractions, as far as they bear on Sheridan's plays, is to be found on pages 831, 834, 837, and 841.

CONTENTS

LIST OF ILLUSTRATIONS

ABBREVIATIONS USED IN THE NOTES

Here and throughout, place of publication is London unless otherwise noted

Add. MS.	Additional MS., British Museum.
Anderson Cat.	Sale catalogue of John J. Anderson, Jr., the Anderson Auction Co., and the Anderson Galleries, New York City.
Black	Clementina Black, *The Linleys of Bath* (rev. edn., 1926).
Boaden, *Kemble*	James Boaden, *Memoirs of the Life of John Philip Kemble, Esq.* (1825, 2 vols.).
Chatsworth MS.	Manuscript owned by the Duke of Devonshire, Chatsworth, Derbyshire.
Dowden	*The Letters of Thomas Moore* (ed. Wilfred S. Dowden, Oxford, 1964, 2 vols.).
Dufferin MS.	Manuscript owned by the Marchioness of Dufferin and Ava.
Egerton MS.	Egerton MS., British Museum.
Folger MS.	Manuscript in the Folger Shakespeare Library, Washington, D.C.
Frampton Cat.	*Catalogue of A Collection of Books Relating to English and Foreign Literature Forming The Library of Richard Brinsley Sheridan at Frampton Court* (Privately printed, 1884). Owned by Dr. R. Alston.
Garrick Corr.	*The Private Correspondence of David Garrick* (ed. J. Boaden, 1831–2, 2 vols.).
Garrick, *Letters*	*The Letters of David Garrick* (ed. D. M. Little and G. M. Kahrl, Cambridge, Mass., 1963, 3 vols.).
Harvard MS.	Manuscript in the Theatre collection of Harvard College Library.
Hodgson Cat.	Sale catalogue of Messrs. Hodgson, Chancery Lane, W.2.
Huntington MS.	Manuscript in the Henry E. Huntington Library, San Marino, California.
Kelly	*Reminiscences of Michael Kelly* (2nd edn., 1826, 2 vols.).
LeFanu MS.	Manuscripts owned by Mr. W. R. LeFanu.
Letters	*The Letters of Richard Brinsley Sheridan* (ed. C. Price, Oxford, 1966, 3 vols.).
The London Stage	*The London Stage, 1660–1800: Part 4, 1747–1776* (ed. G. W. Stone, Jr., Carbondale, Ill., 1962, 3 vols.).
MacMillan	*Catalogue of the Larpent Plays in the Huntington Library* (comp. D. MacMillan, San Marino, California, 1939).

M.L.N.	*Modern Language Notes* (Baltimore, Md., 1886–1969, 84 vols.).
Moore	Thomas Moore, *Memoirs of the Life of the Right Honourable Richard Brinsley Sheridan* (2nd edn., 1825, 2 vols.).
Moore, *Journal*	*Memoirs, Journal, and Correspondence of Thomas Moore* (ed. Lord John Russell, 1853–6, 8 vols.).
Nettleton and Case	*British Dramatists from Dryden to Sheridan* (ed. G. H. Nettleton and A. E. Case, 1939).
P.B.S.A.	*Papers of the Bibliographical Society of America* (New York, 1906–69, 63 vols.).
P.M.L.A.	*Publications of the Modern Language Society of America* (Baltimore, Md.,—Menasha, Wis., 1884–1968, 83 vols.).
Purdy	*The Rivals, A Comedy. As it was first Acted at the Theatre-Royal in Covent-Garden. Written by Richard Brinsley Sheridan Esq. Edited from the Larpent MS. by Richard Little Purdy* (Oxford, 1935).
Rae	*Sheridan's Plays now printed as he wrote them and his Mother's unpublished Comedy A Journey to Bath* (ed. W. Fraser Rae, 1902).
Rae, *Sheridan*	W. Fraser Rae, *Sheridan, A Biography* (1896, 2 vols.).
R.E.S.	*The Review of English Studies* (Oxford, 1925–69, 45 vols.).
Rhodes	*The Plays and Poems of Richard Brinsley Sheridan* (ed. R. Crompton Rhodes, Oxford, 1928, 3 vols.).
Sichel	W. Sichel, *Sheridan* (1909, 2 vols.).
Sotheby	Sale catalogues of Messrs. Sotheby, London, and of the varying names of the firm from 1814 to 1969.
Speeches	*Speeches of the late Right Honourable Richard Brinsley Sheridan* (ed. 'A Constitutional Friend' [Sir John Philippart?], 1816, 5 vols.).
T.L.S.	*The Times Literary Supplement*, 1902–69.
Williams	Iolo A. Williams, *Seven XVIIIth Century Bibliographies* (1924).
Wm.	Dated watermark (or countermark) in the paper on which a manuscript is written.
W.T.	Typescript copies of letters and other MSS. of the Sheridan circle, formerly in the possession of Sophie, Lady Wavertree. These copies contain a number of obvious typing errors, and I have silently corrected them when quoting from the typescripts.
Yale MS.	Manuscript in the Yale University Library.

SOME DATES IN SHERIDAN'S LIFE

4 November 1751. Christened 'Thos. Brinsley Sheridan' at St. Mary's Church, Dublin.

1762–*c.* 1767–8. At Harrow School.
September 1770–August 1772. At Bath.
August 1772–March 1773. At Waltham Abbey.

13 April 1773. Married Elizabeth Linley at Marylebone Church.

17 and 28 January 1775. *The Rivals* acted at Covent Garden Theatre.

2 May 1775. *St. Patrick's Day* acted at Covent Garden Theatre.

21 November 1775. *The Duenna* acted at Covent Garden Theatre.

21 September 1776. Opened Drury Lane Theatre as principal manager.

24 February 1777. *A Trip to Scarborough* acted at Drury Lane Theatre.

March 1777. Elected a member of the Literary Club on the motion of Samuel Johnson.

8 May 1777. *The School for Scandal* acted at Drury Lane Theatre.

15 October 1778. *The Camp* acted at Drury Lane Theatre.

12 September 1780. Elected M.P. for Stafford.

27 March–1 July 1782. Under-Secretary of State for Foreign Affairs.

21 February–18 December 1783. Secretary to the Treasury.

7 February 1787. Made a celebrated speech on the Begums of Oude in the proceedings against Warren Hastings, and others (3–13 June 1788) on his impeachment.

November–December 1788. Confidential adviser to the Prince of Wales in the Regency crisis.

28 June 1792. Death of his first wife at Bristol Wells.

21 April 1794. Opened the rebuilt Drury Lane Theatre.

27 April 1795. Married Esther Ogle, daughter of the Dean of Winchester.

24 May 1799. *Pizarro* acted at Drury Lane Theatre.

November 1806. Succeeded Charles James Fox as M.P. for Westminster.

May 1807. Defeated in the Westminster election but became M.P. for Ilchester.

24 February 1809. Drury Lane Theatre destroyed by fire.

Autumn 1812. Defeated at the Stafford election, so losing a seat in Parliament.

7 July 1816. Died at Savile Row.

13 July 1816. Buried in Westminster Abbey.

INTRODUCTION

THE SHERIDANS AND THE MANUSCRIPTS

SHERIDAN aimed at perfection: he wrote the finest comedies and made some of the most brilliant speeches of his day. These were considerable achievements, but his contemporaries always expected more from a man of such surpassing talent. He was called 'the modern Congreve', but the compliment was double-edged: like Congreve, he had written his best plays by the time he was thirty and, after that, wanted to be known as a gentleman. In fact, Lord Thanet recalled that 'Sheridan, at no part of his life, liked any allusion to his being a dramatic writer.'[1]

He wrote comparatively little, and much of that remained unfinished. He took considerable trouble over preparation, though as William Wyndham said of his speeches, it was 'not from want of fertility or quickness that he *prepared* so much, but an over-desire of polish and correctness'.[2] The result was noted by Lord Holland when describing Sheridan's eloquence: 'the over-strained notions he had of perfection were very favourable to his style of oratory in giving it a certain elevation of tone and dignity of thought'.[3] The plays seem to have been written with less elaboration and more dispatch, but with the same care for words and figures of speech.

To give greater intensity to these sessions of thought, he worked to a certain ritual. Moore mentions that he surrounded himself with lights.[4] Tierney gives more detail, saying he 'worked very hard when he had to prepare himself for any great occasion. His habit was, on these emergencies, to rise at four in the morning, to light up a prodigious quantity of candles around him, and eat toasted muffins while he worked'.[5] These occasions do not appear to have been frequent. Something in his own nature prevented him from completing his corrections and publishing his work. His younger son said that 'what he wanted was self-denial; the power of overcoming the inclination of the moment'.[6] Besides, he was not fond of being alone: it brought out all the melancholy in his nature. He tended therefore to give more time to his multifarious activities in the business of the theatre and political life at Westminster, or to those social hours when friends were gathered around him and he could amaze them with his wit or trouble them by his silence.

[1] Moore, *Journal*, iii. 233.
[2] Ibid. ii. 315.
[3] Ibid. ii. 186–7.
[4] Extra-illustrated copy in the Widener Library, of Moore, *Memoirs of Sheridan*, vi, 25.
[5] Moore, *Journal*, ii. 226.
[6] Rae, ii. 279.

He could be very thorough in his preparations for writing, or he could leave everything to the inspiration of the moment. He knew his own faults very well, as is evident in some remarks he made about composing poetry: 'I believe I shall give up all attempts to versifying in future, for my Efforts in that way always bring me into some foolish Predicament. What I write in a Hurry I always feel to be not worth reading, and what I try to take Pains with, I am sure never to finish.'[1] There was an obvious conflict in his temperament between indolence and an exacting judgement.

When he could muster up enough determination, he worked hard and furiously. Of the composition of *The Rivals*, he noted: 'I had not written a line of it two months ago, except a scene or two, which I believe you have seen in an odd act of a little farce.'[2] With some drafts before him, he also completed *The School for Scandal* in two months.[3] He usually needed a stimulus, some challenge to his vanity or his pride. The circumstances in which he finished *The Critic* are well known, but are worth looking at again for what they reveal of Sheridan's habits as a writer:

> Two days previous to the performance, the last scene was not written; Dr. Ford and Mr. Linley, the joint proprietors, began to get nervous and fidgetty, and the actors were absolutely *au désespoir*, especially King, who was not only stage-manager, but had to play Puff; to him was assigned the duty of hunting down and worrying Sheridan about the last scene . . .
>
> At last, Mr. Linley, who being his father-in-law, was pretty well aware of his habits, hit upon a stratagem. A night rehearsal of 'The Critic' was ordered, and Sheridan, having dined with Linley, was prevailed upon to go; while they were on the stage, King whispered Sheridan that he had something particular to communicate, and begged he would step into the second green-room. Accordingly, Sheridan went, and there found a table, with pens, ink, and paper, a good fire, an armed chair at the table, and two bottles of claret, with a dish of anchovy sandwiches. The moment he got into the room, King stepped out, and locked the door; immediately after which, Linley and Ford came up and told the author that, until he had written the scene, he would be kept where he was.
>
> Sheridan took this decided measure in good part; he ate the anchovies, finished the claret, wrote the scene, and laughed heartily at the ingenuity of the contrivance.[4]

This is quoted by Kelly as proof of Sheridan's quickness in writing, but it is also a response to a challenge. He would show them he could write a brilliant scene on the spur of the moment. If it has not the sustained verve of the earlier scenes, it is still a remarkable piece of improvisation, and perhaps it is a pity that Sheridan was not locked up in the green-room more often.

[1] *Letters*, i. 121–2.
[2] Ibid. 85.
[3] See p. 297. Many of the points made in this introduction are elaborated in my prefaces to the particular plays in this edition.
[4] Kelly, ii. 308–9.

The knowledge that he could brace himself when necessary and provide whatever was wanted, probably made him procrastinate even more. He was not perturbed by the irritation of the members of the company, for he knew that they had entire confidence in his mastery of theatrical effect and ability to fill the playhouse. He even took advantage of their rapidity in learning their parts by sometimes scribbling out lines for them on scraps of paper during rehearsals.[1]

While Sheridan felt that what he wrote in a hurry did not really do him justice, he took it for granted from the first that he could improve on his work after the opening performance. He says as much in the preface to *The Rivals*: 'For my part, I see no reason why the Author of a Play should not regard a First Night's Audience, as a candid and judicious friend attending, in behalf of the Public, at his last Rehearsal.'[2] Even allowing for the element of excuse in this, we can find evidence to show that the attitude is characteristic of him. After the first nights of *St. Patrick's Day*, *The Duenna*, *The Critic*, and *Pizarro*, the newspapers criticized certain phrases or speeches, and these were deleted or revised before the second performances.[3] They were not the thorough corrections that followed the first presentation of *The Rivals*, but it is probable that Sheridan intended, at some future and unspecified date, to give the plays still further polish and bring them nearer his ideal standard.

His skill as a 'play-doctor' was shown in the revision of scripts sent to, or already at, Drury Lane Theatre. Tom Sheridan indirectly acknowledged this when writing about a farce he had prepared, to John Bannister: 'My Father must see it before it is acted. . . . I really think with a touch or two from my Father it will succeed, and I shall write to him so strongly, as to make it out of the question his not attending to it.'[4] Sheridan touched up a number of plays during his managerial career, usually for the better.[5]

That he was not satisfied with most of the published texts of his own plays, is evident from a letter that he wrote to his second wife:

> I hate anything thus surrept[it]iously publish'd to be attributed to me—I never yet own'd or allow'd the printing of anything Play Poems or Speeches but two things to both which I put my name viz. The Critic and a Political Pamphlet on the affairs of India—I put Pizzarro out of the Question—[6]

R. C. Rhodes challenged the truth of the statement, saying that it was 'undoubtedly incorrect, for *The Rivals* was first printed with a preface by Sheridan, who also must have revised the Third Edition Corrected of the same comedy'. He went on to assert that 'though the greater number of the early editions [of Shepidan's plays] were unauthorised, and

[1] See p. 754. [2] See p. 70. [3] See pp. 152, 210, 480, 635.

[4] The letter is undated, and the original is in the extra-illustrated copy of *The Poetical Works, Letters and Journals of Lord Byron*, vol. ix, in the British Museum (pressmark C. 44e). [5] See pp. 775–92. [6] *Letters*, iii. 202.

sometimes of abbreviated versions, there is no reason otherwise to doubt the authenticity of any of these texts'.[1] Both arguments seem to me to misunderstand what Sheridan meant. Surely what the dramatist intended to say was that he had put his name to only one play, *The Critic*, because it was the one that met, finally, with his approval. It is a fair assumption that he still intended to work on *The School for Scandal.* He seems to have been a little ashamed of some of the rest,[2] but was willing to do what he could to improve them.[3]

Support for my argument comes from a letter by Thomas Wilkie, written to Sheridan on 11 July 1801. He was the son of the original publisher of *The Rivals*,[4] had been a publisher himself, and seems to have known the background of the plays well. He declared:

In this age so famous for fine printing, I have very much regretted that your comedies are not to be had either correctly or uniformly printed.

I have entirely done with the printing and bookselling business as a profession, but as I should be very happy to give any encouragement in my power to the art; I take the liberty of troubling you with these few lines to say that I shall feel a great pleasure in offering to the public a splendid and correct edition of your plays . . .[5]

He went on to make certain proposals.

If any further proof were required that a correct edition of Sheridan's plays was needed, it would be found in another anecdote given by Michael Kelly. On this occasion Sheridan was startled to see how remarkably bad one of the current texts was, particularly when it had been used in the preparations for a performance[6] of *The Duenna* at his own theatre in Drury Lane:

It was customary with me, when I played at night, to read my part over in the morning, in order to refresh my memory. One morning, after reading the part of Ferdinand, I left the printed play of 'The Duenna', as then acted, on the table. On my return home, after having taken my ride, I found Mr. Sheridan reading it, and with pen and ink before him, correcting it. He said to me, 'Do you act the part of Ferdinand from this printed copy?'

I replied in the affirmative, and added, 'that I had done so for twenty years.'

'Then,' said he, 'you have been acting great nonsense.' He examined every sentence, and corrected it all through before he left me; the corrections I have now in his own hand-writing. What could prove his negligence more, than correcting an opera which he had written in 1775, in the year 1807; and then, for the first time, examining it, and abusing the manner in which it was printed?[7]

[1] Rhodes, i, pp. ix–x.

[2] See pp. 56, 153.

[3] Always excepting *Pizarro*, which he appears to have looked on as being in a special category because it was based on a translation.

[4] John Wilkie (d. 2 July 1785) was a successful bookseller, who became treasurer of the Stationers' Company. His business was taken over by his sons, George and Thomas.

[5] Birrell and Garnett Catalogue, no. 16 (1927), item 675.

[6] Probably on 15 May 1807.

[7] Kelly, ii. 219–20.

What seems even more striking to me is that Sheridan tried, thirty-two years after writing *The Duenna*, to correct it from memory. Unfortunately the corrections are not extant and we cannot tell how accurate they were. Sheridan's memory was an unusually good one, but, like Macaulay, he tended to rely on it too implicitly and to be betrayed into minor errors of detail. The real effect of this can best be seen when the manuscript versions of *The School for Scandal* are examined: corrections that appear in some are not carried on to others, and some obvious errors remain in them all.

One illustration, previously unnoticed, may be convincing. In Act III, Sc. i, Charles Surface describes himself as 'an extravagant young fellow, who want money to borrow'. The clause is in the copy of the text sent to the Lord Chamberlain for licensing[1] and in most of the later manuscript versions. It is evident, too, that it was in the Drury Lane prompt copies from which the actors learned their parts for, fifteen years later, a newspaper correspondent complained about the lines: 'Why in such polished dialogue as *The School for Scandal* have we such blots as, "I am an extravagant young fellow who want money to borrow?" an uncouth phrase!'[2] Thomas Moore tried to explain the expression away by suggesting that Sheridan 'had been tempted by an antithesis into an inversion of phrase by no means idiomatic'. He was accurate when he said that 'in the Collection of his Works [i.e. the Murray edition of 1821] this phrase is given differently[3]—but without authority from any of the manuscript copies'.[4]

On looking back through the manuscripts, I find the real source of error in the earliest draft of one of the sketches[5] that formed the basis of the comedy. The clause appears there, in this way:

> come no ceremony—I'm an extravagant young that want
> to borrow
> money—you I take to be a usurer an old Fellow that have

Sheridan was composing rapidly: he left out 'fellow', and inserted 'to borrow' as an after-thought. We might be justified in assuming that he intended the two words to be spoken before 'money', in spite of their rather ambiguous position. Unfortunately this scene is missing from the second stage in the development of the text, the draft that covers most of the play and is in Sheridan's hand. The phrase 'want money to borrow' appears in the next transcription, the text sent to the Lord Chamberlain for licensing, and was repeatedly to occur in that form for the next forty years. Even in the corrected manuscript copy that he presented to Mrs. Crewe, it remained unaltered.

[1] See pp. 336–7.

[2] 'Thespis', in *The Oracle*, 17 Sept. 1792.

[3] As 'who wants to borrow money' (*Works*, ii. 82). The phrasing of the Dublin piracies is 'that wants to'.

[4] Moore, i. 237 n.

[5] See pp. 333–7.

Sheridan was rather less than consistent in the correction of his texts, and we can form safe judgements on them only by accepting his suggestion that, apart from the first edition of *The Critic* (and presumably *Pizarro*), they were not finished versions.

He had every incentive to finish them, for his expensive tastes normally left him short of money. We may assume that he did not do so because he could not summon up all his powers to complete the task: his many interests, general dilatoriness, and desire for perfection of phrase, all stood in the way.

The point may be illustrated from the history of *The School for Scandal*. Nine days after its first performance, the *Morning Chronicle* reported that Sheridan did not intend to publish the play. No reason was given but we learn, elsewhere,[1] that he still wished to correct it to his own liking. He was equally strict about the acting copyright, and lent the text to other managers only as a special privilege, for one night only.[2] Provincial actors, who were not favoured in this way, concocted versions of their own that were much less accurate than the text given at Drury Lane.[3] The Irish managers were even more determined to present this much-discussed comedy by their own countryman. Sheridan recognized[4] that he had little legal protection there, because the Lord Chancellor of Ireland had recently declared that acting was not publication. Astutely (and generously), Sheridan presented a copy of the text to his sister Alicia, and she was able to sell it to Ryder, an Irish manager whose actors were busily copying down the play during performances at Drury Lane. Naturally, Ryder did not want to part with this treasure, and only pirated texts appeared in Ireland until 1799.[5] In the meantime, Ridgway, a London publisher, approached Sheridan and bought the copyright from him. He was unable to obtain a corrected text because the playwright said that he had not yet satisfied his own taste in the matter, though he claimed to have spent nineteen years on the task.[6]

When Drury Lane Theatre was burnt down on 24 February 1809, Sheridan was left without any source of ready money. He therefore arranged (in return for an advance) to supply Thomas Wilkie with authentic copies of the plays:

Memorandum of agreement between the Rt. Honble. Rich: Brinsley Sheridan, and Thomas Wilkie of Salisbury.—that in consideration of the sum of £600 to be now paid on account by the said Thomas Wilkie, to the said Richard Brinsley

[1] See pp. 316, 329. [2] See p. 327. [3] See pp. 327–8.

[4] Thomas Harris, manager of Covent Garden Theatre, had sought an injunction in the Court of Chancery of Ireland to prevent John Vandermere and partners (of the Fishamble Street Theatre, Dublin) from 'printing, publishing, or acting' *The Duenna*. The Lord Chancellor confined himself to acting, and refused to grant the injunction. His decision was reported in *The Gazetteer*, 3 May 1777: see p. 215 below.

[5] See pp. 326, 347. [6] For further details see p. 329.

Sheridan; Mr. S. engages to furnish Mr. Wilkie on or before the fifteenth day of November next with correct copies of all his dramatic Works, with a preface and dedication to each; and he hereby also engages to authorize Mr. Wilkie to print and publish the same either in Volumes or seperately for such further consideration as shall be agreed between them, or settled upon a fair and honourable arbitration, consisting of two Persons to be appointed by the above Parties:—Mr. Sheridan either selling outright, Title and interest in the said dramatic Pieces to Mr. Wilkie, or retaining a proportioned interest in them, for the benefit of the Family, as shall be agreed on, or recommended by the above arbitration.

It is further agreed between the said Parties that in case Mr. Wilkie is not furnished by Mr. Sheridan with the said corrected copies of his dramatic works at the time agreed upon, Mr. Wilkie is hereby authorised to print and publish the said Works from such Copies as he may be enabled to obtain, in the same manner as if they had passed through Mr. S.'s hands:—Mr. Wilkie of course to concert with Mr. Sheridan the manner of printing and embellishing the said works, that they may come forth in the handsomest form.

Mr. Sheridan gives Mr. Wilkie for his further security a counter acceptance for *£600*, not to be used unless the above conditions are forfeited on the part of Mr. Sheridan.

In case of Mr. Sheridan's death this agreement to be binding upon Mr. Thomas Sheridan, and Mr. Sheridan's Executors:—

Dated this fourth day of July one thousand eight hundred and nine

Signed
R.B.S.
T.W.[1]

Witnessed
Richard Peake
C. W. Ward.

Some disagreement appears to have occurred between them, and later in the year Sheridan wrote to the Treasurer of Drury Lane Theatre, Richard Peake, saying: 'send to Bully Raymond *immediately* tell him as much as you please of the past treaty and sound if he can advance a £1000, and pay off the Mayor [i.e. Wilkie]'.[2] Wilkie was not paid off, but was to claim his due soon after Sheridan's death.

James Grant Raymond was an actor who had decided to go into auctioneering and bookselling,[3] and his offer to Sheridan is to be found in the following note:

Dear Sir
As follows Mr. Sheridans poem and Dramatic Works——
£200 In cash when the pieces are put into Mr. Raymonds hands—
£100 In cash on the day of publication
£200 In notes at 6 and 9 months after the day of publication, which shall be before the 1st of Jany.

[1] W.T. Cf. draft in Egerton MS. 1975, ff. 61–2.
[2] *Letters*, iii. 69.
[3] A. Mathews, *Memoirs of Charles Mathews*, ii (1838), 25.

£100 In cash when 2500 are sold
and
one third of the clear profits, when 5000 Copies shall be sold a number, which will barely pay the expence of printing and publishing without one shilling profit.

J. G. Raymond[1]

An agreement embodying these proposals and dating them 'Nov. 1809' is rather more detailed in some of its statements. Sheridan agreed to sell 'the whole of his Dramatic and Poetical works' and was to be paid £200 in cash 'when the s[ai]d works (specified hereafter) shall be delivered to the s[ai]d J. G. Raymond with one general Preface containing one sheet and upwards of Octavo letter-press'.[2] It also carried at its foot an instruction in Sheridan's hand to the prompter of Drury Lane company to deliver the manuscript of *The School for Scandal* to Raymond. This brief note is of considerable importance because it reveals that Sheridan now regarded the prompt copy as the correct copy, suitable for publication. It may be argued that this only demonstrates Sheridan's indolence and inconsistency, but the fact remains that this is the last known wish that he expressed concerning the text of his masterpiece. Then Raymond gave up the notion of becoming a bookseller,[3] and nothing came of their agreement.

The matter seems to have languished for some years, until Sheridan discovered that his expectations of ready money from the new Drury Lane Theatre were to be sadly disappointed. Once again he turned to the idea of publishing his works: on 15 October 1814 he wrote to his wife to say 'this Winter I am determined to give my Friend Rogers full Power to put together and publish all my Scrib[b]lings—and he offers to ensure me four thousand Pounds if done by my Authority'.[4] Sheridan was surrounded by money difficulties, and had every reason to come to a decision—or series of decisions—that would bring him such a handsome reward. Yet the subject was not mentioned again until over fifteen months later, when Lady Holland noted that 'Lord Byron and Mr. Rogers have undertaken to publish forth a preface of Sheridan's plays and poetry, in order to give him a little Money of which alas! poor fellow he stands in great need'.[5] At about the same period[6] Samuel Rogers approached John Murray to try and raise money by publishing Sheridan's speeches. Murray's reaction is significant:

[1] From the manuscript owned by the present editor.

[2] Egerton MS. 1975, f. 21.

[3] He became acting manager of the English Opera instead: see the *European Magazine*, lxxii (1817), 433–5.

[4] *Letters*, ii. 202.

[5] To Grey, 4 Feb. 1816 (Correspondence of Charles, 2nd Earl Grey, deposited in the University of Durham). Cf. *Letters*, iii. 243–4 n.

[6] I reach this conclusion because of Sheridan's search for the manuscripts of his Begums speech: see *Letters*, iii. 242–3.

If you will pledge your word to the creditors for £300, I will pledge mine to you for £300, as soon tomorrow as Mr. Sheridan signs a regular instrument of assignment to me of the 'Speeches in Westminster Hall', or upon any other considerable security that you can suggest, without which even your long friendship with Mr. Sheridan would not, I think, advise me to proceed.[1]

In view of Sheridan's record, Murray's caution is understandable.

By this time Sheridan was seriously ill but when he recovered he wrote to an unidentified acquaintance and referred to a 'conversation on the subject of publishing all I had written. . . . I am now recovering fast and eager to pursue my object—could you favour me with a call between three and four tomorrow? perhaps Mr. Longman[2] would accompany you?'[3] Nothing seems to have come of this meeting, and Sheridan's desperation increased as his health grew worse and his debts mounted. On 15 May 1816, he wrote to Rogers: 'I am absolutely undone and broken-hearted. I shall negotiate for the Plays successfully in the course of a week, when all shall be returned.'[4] What progress he had actually achieved in preparing his works for the press or making a definite engagement is not clear; but some attempt was made, on his behalf, to collect his original manuscripts. His brother-in-law, William Linley, contributed an interesting relic:

. . . the little book with delineations of character for 'Affectation', I was the first to discover, and to dislodge from an old Chest full of nothing but the coverings of old letters, though poor Sheridan used to accuse me of having purloined from it sundry *notes of hand* and *bonds* to an immense amount. This scrap book together with the contents of the Chest Mr. C. Sheridan received from me a short time only before his father died.[5]

On another occasion Linley claimed,

I *had* in my possession two very curious Common Place books in Mr. Sheridan's own hand writing.—The one containing a rough sketch of some of the Scenes and Characters in the *Critic*.—The other still more valuable—being various outlines of Characters intended to be introduced in the Comedy he never finished—and thought to be Called *Affectation*, as that title appears written by himself in the beginning of the book. When Mr. Sheridan was on his Death bed He was exceedingly anxious to have every document and paper belonging to him collected and brought to him, and Mr. Charles Sheridan applying to me, in the name of his Father, for a Chest of Papers which was then in the possession of my Mother, tho' containing no documents of the least consequence, I conceived that I ought, also, to deliver over to his Charge the *Manuscripts* in question.[6]

[1] P. W. Clayden, *Rogers and his Contemporaries* (1889), i. 140–1.
[2] For Longman's earlier connection with Sheridan, see *Letters*, ii. 252.
[3] *Letters*, iii. 243–4.
[4] Ibid. 246. Cf., also, iii. 243–4.
[5] A. R. Bailey, 'A Note on Sheridan', *Notes and Queries*, 11th ser., x (1914), 62.
[6] In a letter to Wilkie of 16 Aug. 1818 (Add. MS. 29764, ff. 26–7).

It seems unlikely that Sheridan was able to do much work on these manuscripts in the closing months of his life. In collecting them, he probably had other objects in view. He was always devoted to the welfare of his sons and though Charles was already provided for,[1] Tom was short of money,[2] ill with tuberculosis, and had to maintain a wife and several children. I imagine that Sheridan hoped that the publication of his collected papers would benefit Tom and his dependants.

His other ambition was that his writings should appear to the world in a form chosen by himself. This is clear from a letter written at a later date by Charles Sheridan, in which he stated that he intended to give the publishers all his 'Father's MSS, for them to publish his entire works according to a Programme drawn up by himself'.[3] Sheridan's wishes, then, were known when he died on 7 July 1816, and it fell upon his wife and son to try to accomplish what he had never achieved.

On 5 August Hester Sheridan received a letter from Wilkie, in which he expressed his hope that she would consider proposals from him for a correct edition of Sheridan's works.[4] He also enclosed a copy of the agreement of 4 July 1809.[5]

On 24 October she wrote to Sheridan's sister Alicia to say:

> Our dear Sheridan has left an incredible quantity of private papers.[6] The effort I made to collect them all under the Bishop of London's roof in St. James's Square . . . almost kill'd me, and after I had examin'd about a 20th part of them . . . I was *order'd* out of town. I have taken a small house in Grosvenor Place . . . and as soon as I have got thro' the above-mention'd papers, I shall give my whole thoughts to a biographical account, and the publishing his works. It is a subject on which I am on fire, and I shall have no peace till I see something given to the public whether by the hand of a friend, or many friends simple clear just and eloquent.
>
> . . . One thing only I want, honor glory and *truth* for Sheridan.[7]

[1] By the settlement made when Sheridan married Hester Ogle (as his second wife) in 1795. She was provided for, too.

[2] Tom Sheridan was the only child of the first marriage, to Elizabeth Linley. When he died, he left bonds on Drury Lane Theatre worth £7,000, but if they were sold they would bring in only £1,000, to set against claims upon the estate for £1,500. His widow and four children had to live on £100 a year and the bounty of relatives. See Douglas Kinnaird's letter to the Duke of York, 4 Dec. 1817, in Hist. MSS. Comm. Rep., Bathurst MSS. (1923), pp. 443–4.

[3] To Thomas Moore, 20 Dec. 1823 (Yale MS.). Cf. p. 15 below.

[4] W.T. For the original, see Sotheby's Catalogue, 28 Feb. 1955, lot 422.

[5] He added, 'I was in hopes that he [Sheridan] would have been able to have accomplished the object of it long before this time, but various causes from that moment to the present, have retarded its execution' (W.T.).

[6] 'Sheridan was in the habit of putting by, not only all papers written by himself, but all others that came into his hands' (*Recollections of the Table Talk of Samuel Rogers*, 1856, p. 69).

[7] W.T.

This is the first mention of a justificatory biography, and the only one for the time being. The *Scots Magazine*, in a notice of the same year, confined itself to the better-known project:

We understand that the friends of Mr. Sheridan design to collect his scattered works, and to publish them by subscription. They are chiefly in the hands of an eminent literary friend, whose regard for his memory will secure to the public a complete edition of his writings; and whose labours will be further recommended by their being gratuitously exerted for the benefit of Mr. Sheridan's family.[1]

The friend seems to have been Samuel Rogers, but for some unexplained reason he did not go on with the task. So an approach was then made to Thomas Moore who, as Whig, Irishman, and man of letters, was sympathetically disposed towards Sheridan.

By this time (Nov. 1817), both Hester and Tom Sheridan were dead, and negotiations with the family were conducted through Charles Sheridan, an undergraduate at Trinity College, Cambridge. Wilkie wrote to him about Moore, and after some delay, Charles Sheridan replied on 19 November:

. . . Nothing could give me greater pleasure than Mr. Moore's writing a life of my Father; and any materials of which I may be in possession and which can be of service to him, I shall be most happy to contribute. The Copy of the School for Scandal, of which You speak and which is in my Father's own handwriting, is, I believe, at present in Mr. Rogers's house; and I am writing to him on the Subject by this day's post. I know not whether it can be found without my coming to Town to look for it among many other papers, and, unless its *immediate* production should be of consequence to the publication, I should be desirous of not coming up for this purpose till after the 16th of December, as by so doing I may perhaps lose my Term. . . .[2]

Wilkie's claim upon the Sheridan estate was admitted, as was Ridgway's ownership of the copyright of *The School for Scandal*.[3] They now joined with John Murray in the plan of publishing Sheridan's works. From Murray's list of books 'preparing for immediate publication' in April 1818, we can see that Moore's task was to be the writing of a prefatory essay. The advertisement reads:

The DRAMATIC WORKS complete, with the POEMS, &c., of the late Right Hon. Richard Brinsley Sheridan. To which will be prefixed an Essay on the Life and Genius of the Author By Thomas Moore, Esq., Author of Lalla Rookh. 4 vols. 8vo.[4]

[1] *Scots Magazine*, lxxviii (1816), 524–5.

[2] Add. MS. 29764, ff. 15–16.

[3] We may safely accept the idea that Sheridan had not paid back the earlier advances.

[4] The four-page list is bound with the fourth edition of Byron's *Beppo*, in a volume of Byron's poems, owned by the present editor.

Charles Sheridan's part in all this is outlined in his letter from West Cowes to Wilkie, on 20 July 1818:

I had conceived that every thing had been finally settled at Mr. Rogers's relative to the publication of my Father's Works—and that on receiving from the family all the MSS. and every assistance, which they had in their power to offer You were to allow for the Benefit of Mr. T. Sheridan's Widow and Children One Guinea on each Copy actually Sold. I believe you are aware of what materials we can supply. There is the original MSS. of the School for Scandal the Speech on Hastings's Trial some of Affectation, and various Scraps of Verse &c. Mr. Henry Ogle informed me that you considered the arrangement as Incomplete, which has induced me to trouble You with this Letter. Mr. Moore has got all the papers likely to be of use to him. . . .[1]

There is an interesting docket, on this letter, reading, 'the family will settle with Mr. Ridgway and Mr. Rogers'. This would seem to suggest that the Sheridan family had decided to meet any claim upon the estate by Ridgway or Samuel Rogers themselves, so that Tom Sheridan's dependants might have as much profit as possible from the publication of the works.

Moore thought the whole matter confused, and complained to Wilkie about it in a letter of 25 August 1818:

. . . I own I do not feel quite satisfied at the way in which we stand with respect to the Sheridan family—For there does not appear to have been any thing definitive arranged between you and Charles Sheridan, and my friend Mr. Rogers has not yet given me the papers that were in his possession—so that I am in fact, making use of materials for you upon which you have not yet established your claim—there being not only claims of the family yet to settle, but a *lien* of Mr. Rogers's on the property also—to say nothing of Ridgway's, which I know not how you have settled, but which has nothing whatever to do with *my* part of the business, though it [*The School for Scandal*] would be a material and vital omission in the works—indeed it would be like the old story of the play of Hamlet with the character of Hamlet left out—so that I trust you will not *think* of publishing, *without* the School for Scandal.[2]

Moore had a long talk with Rogers in October, and learned that in making 'a second search through the papers, they have found the Acts of "The Foresters" '.[3]

Moore worked at his task for the next two months, then found that the ownership of the manuscripts was likely to be challenged by new claimants, Sheridan's creditors. They were called together by Henry Burgess, Sheridan's former solicitor, 'to resist any exclusive property' in the publication of the Works. Moore's diary entry for 25 November explains the position:

[1] Add. MS. 29764, ff. 22–3.
[2] Ibid. 30–1: printed by Dowden, i. 462–3.
[3] Moore, *Journal*, ii. 191. See also pp. 805–8 below.

[Burgess] finding by the agreement of the booksellers with Mrs. T. Sheridan, that there are *thousands* talked of, is resolved to have a finger in the pie. Very natural, but very likely to upset the whole concern. Burgess told Murray there was but one creditor urgent, and that for £350 he would stop this nameless person's mouth. Quite the old Sheridan trick! This £350 evidently for himself; but how could he have the face to say that such a sum would settle everything![1]

These difficulties made Moore hesitate. He looked through the two large bags of Sheridan papers Wilkie brought him, but did not open another couple of parcels of them, because he did not want 'to lose any more time with this work, till there is some prospect of our being able to publish'.[2]

In the midst of this confusion John Murray brought out another list of 'Works in the Press'. This one was dated 'January, 1819', and indicated that the Sheridan undertaking was (in Murray's eyes, at least) much more ambitious than it had been:

The Life of the Right Hon. R. B. Sheridan, from a variety of interesting Documents, and original Communications. By Thomas Moore, Esq., Author of Lalla Rookh. 4to.
The Works of the Right Hon. R. B. Sheridan, now first collected, comprising many hitherto unpublished Writings, and printed from authentic and original Copies. The whole arranged and edited, with an Essay on the Life and Genius of the Author, by Thomas Moore, Esq. 6 vols. 8vo.[3]

The reality behind these public announcements may be glimpsed when Wilkie wrote to Moore on 24 February 1819, begging him 'to send up some of the MS. to go to press immediately'; and Moore commented, 'Poor little man! if he gets it within the year he may be very well satisfied.'[4] He was rather less frank when he replied to Wilkie on 4 March, pointing out that while he desired to receive 'so many hundreds as I am to have for this book'[5] as soon as possible, he must make full inquiries so as to produce a finished piece of work. He also referred to the new proposal for a biography in place of the prefatory essay by adding that he had to take into account 'the more enlarged scale and more serious responsibility which our new plan of a Quarto has brought with it'.[6]

In the next six months his enthusiasm fluctuated, partly because of his uncertainty about his position and partly because of his own money troubles. On 8 March he recorded:

In the evening looked over some of Sheridan's papers. Various copies, both rough and correct, of the 'School for Scandal'. Strange that 'The Rivals' should be the only one of his pieces of which there appears to be no trace among his papers. Resolved to resume my Sheridan task, and be industrious about it.[7]

[1] Ibid. 221.
[2] Ibid. 243–4.
[3] Bound with a copy of Richard Sheil's *Evadne; or, The Statue* (1819), owned by the present editor.
[4] Moore, *Journal*, ii. 271.
[5] Or 'work'.
[6] Add. MS. 29764, f. 32: printed by Dowden, ii. 472.
[7] Moore, *Journal*, ii. 275.

In this mood he set about comparing the Dublin edition of 1799 of *The School for Scandal* with the manuscript version in Sheridan's own hand;[1] but by June he had decided to ask Murray to give him 'a guarantee against the claims of Sheridan's creditors' on the papers that Charles Sheridan had placed in his hands with a view to publication. Murray put off a decision, and Moore went on with his task until the end of August.[2] By that time his financial position had become unbearable, and he took refuge abroad. He joined Lord John Russell on 4 September 1819 on a visit to Paris, and was out of England at various places on the Continent until 25 September 1821.[3]

During that period the publishers were naturally anxious to make progress with the Sheridan materials, so Wilkie asked Moore to provide some 'prefatory remarks' for an edition of *The Rivals* that he and Murray now intended bringing out separately. Moore objected to the idea in a letter to Murray of 14 April 1820, and added that he thought the scheme for a full-length biography should be abandoned and that they should return to 'no more than was originally intended—an Essay'.[4]

In October 1820 he made out a case for suspending his work on Sheridan until he returned to England, but the publishers asked him 'at least, to give them a few pages of preface for the collection of Sheridan's works which they are about to publish'.[5] He agreed to do so, and on 23 November copied out his preface 'or, as I prefer calling it, advertisement'.[6] Its twelve pages made up the sum of his contribution to *The Works of the late Right Honourable Richard Brinsley Sheridan*, as published in two volumes in 1821, by Murray, Ridgway, and Wilkie, and is really an explanation for the delay in completing the biography. One passage may have misled readers: 'After all, however, let the biographer do his duty as he may, it is in the volumes which are here presented to the world . . . that the most durable memorials of Mr. Sheridan's name exist.'[7] He did not make clear that he had not edited the plays, and people seem to have concluded from the fact that his name was appended to the preface that he had been responsible for supervising the text.

Moore was abroad and all the evidence confirms that he was not involved in this work, beyond the twelve-page preface. Who was responsible for an edition so different from that originally envisaged? It is not easy to name the culprit, but, fortunately, a previously unpublished letter by Charles Sheridan reviews the whole transaction and clarifies much of its obscurity. He too had been abroad, and on his return

[1] Moore, *Journal*, ii. 296, 331. Cf. Dowden, ii. 476.
[2] Ibid. 319, 331, 355.
[3] Ibid. iii. 5, 279–80.
[4] Dowden, ii. 483.
[5] Moore, *Journal*, iii. 153, 166.
[6] Ibid. 171. Cf. p. 188 (4 Jan. 1821).
[7] *Works*, i. xii.

home was indignant to find that this edition had been foisted on the public:

. . . In 1818 I made an agreement with Messrs. Wilkie and Murray (a copy of which I will shew you) to give up to them all my Father's MSS, for them to publish his entire works according to a Programme drawn up by himself, with a life prefix'd, in composing which the Biographer should have the use of his papers. Messrs. Wilkie and Murray agreed to print three thousand copies, of the entire works, and to pay for the use of my Brother's[1] family a guinea for each copy actually sold, and to have the power of printing as many more copies as they chose on similarly paying fifteen Shillings a copy, till the whole sum so paid amounted to £8400. This agreement was not made a legal instrument of because, a Mr .Burgess impress'd on Messrs. Murray and Wilkie the fear that some Creditor of my Father would take out administration, and afterwards oblige them to account in Chancery for the profits of the publication, when they would be found to have paid Monies to Mrs. Thomas Sheridan in their own wrong. At the same time without my authority, but on the strength of having been my Brother's Attorney, he publish'd an advertisement desiring all claims on my Father to be sent in to *him*. Messrs. Wilkie's and Murray's fear of being committed was natural tho' I believe unfounded, as I apprehend Burgess to have alarm'd them for the purpose of forcing me to fall into a proposal of his, which was for him to get an Administrator at his command to pay my Father's debts, nominally more than £8000 with £3000, which he had formerly told me and still contended was the fair amount of what ought to be paid. Were I not afraid of making this letter too long, I would tell you my reasons for Supposing that his object was the plunder to be got by my entrusting him with the £3000, the chief of which is his having since swindled me out of £350, which he persuaded me to lend him by a scheme for recovering £1400 for my Brother's Children, from a Man who had owed that Sum to my Father, but to whom the Burgess owed £350, the larger Sum having no more been recover'd than the smaller was ever repaid. I left England in the beginning of February 1819 the papers having all being given up, the faith of the agreement subsisting, but its Form not having been legalized, as it was impossible to secure the Publisher against the claims of an administering creditor, tho' in the belief that as no Creditor had administer'd none would, I expected the guineas on no claim being made would be paid to Mrs. Thomas Sheridan. In two years I return'd in February 1821 and found advertized the Works of R. B. Sheridan from Copies and MSS supplied by the Family. No Claim having been, after some time, made to the profits, as, after Burgess's motive for exciting such had ceased by my reluctance to trust him with Money: I asked Mr. Murray what he proposed allowing on these copies of the partial works, as of course I could not expect any thing like a Guinea on a £1 8s. work; His Answer was that this was what any Body might have printed that he had abandon'd the original plan of the work from fear of the Creditors, and that he consider'd nothing due. I asked why then had it been advertized as printed from Autographs supplied by the family; and he answer'd 'it had been so advertized *by mistake*'.[2] It

[1] MS. 'Brothers''.

[2] Rhodes was wrong when he claimed that the *Works* 'had the authority of Sheridan's executors' (*The Library*, 4th ser., ix (1928–9), 234).

required the very high opinion I entertain'd of Mr. Murray, founded on the assurances of several respected Friends, and which I did not finally abandon till this morning[1] to make me remain satisfied with such an answer. . . .[2]

Murray's attitude, as reported here, seems disingenuous. If the advertisement that an edition of the works would be drawn from 'many hitherto unpublish'd writings' and printed 'from authentic and original Copies', was a mistake, nevertheless he had benefited from it and had a moral (though no legal) obligation to Tom Sheridan's dependants. He appears to have been quite truthful, however, when he said that he knew nothing about Sheridan's papers, because they had passed through the hands of Wilkie to Moore.

This is confirmed in an unpublished letter[3] from Moore to Charles Sheridan, written on 31 December 1823:

. . . I confess to you that I was not aware of the existence of any agreement between you and Murray, under which you meant to claim a share in the profits of the Life—I had heard of the first terms suggested, but thought that these had been long since abandoned on both sides, and Murray has always spoken to me as if he had nothing whatever to do with the papers, but considered them as entrusted solely to me. Wilkie, indeed, I remember, used, on the contrary to take great pains to inculcate on me that the papers were given to *him*, not to me, and that when I had finished my task it was to him they were to be returned. So far was Murray, however, from taking this responsibility upon himself, that at the time when the Creditors seemed likely to interfere, not only he but others alarmed me with the suggestion, that it was to me, as the person to whom the materials had been given by the family, they would look for the profits resulting from the sale. Your letter has thrown a new colour over the whole transaction, and, if you consider yourself as having any legal hold over Murray for a share of the profits, I think it would be, perhaps, [?] injustice both to yourself and your father's family, not to enforce it, though I own I am not so sanguine about the success of the Work as to expect that any share you may acquire in the proceeds will be of much service to the persons you so amiably intend it for.—With respect to myself, I will tell you fairly my present position in the business. When Murray had advanced me (or rather Murray and Wilkie between them)

1 Charles Sheridan's letter was not written until 20 Dec. 1823, and his change of attitude was caused by Murray's note to him of 17 Dec. 1823, assuring him, 'I *know nothing* of the nature or contents of your Father's papers, except that a *mass* was sent to Mr. Wilkie, I *think*, and by him deliver'd to Mr. Moore—for the purpose, *as I understood*, of assisting him in writing the Life of Mr. Sheridan. For this life I have engaged to pay £1000 of which Sum Mr. Moore has already received £500. This is all I have to do with the papers—and I shall instantly resign this Contract with Mr. Moore if you think you could make any arrangement for the benefit of the family' (Yale MS. Copy in Charles Sheridan's hand. For the original letter, see Sotheby's Catalogue, 28 Feb. 1955, lot 422). Moore stated to Murray that he 'was not aware . . . that there was any claim meant to be brought forward for a share in the profits of the Life . . .' (*Journal*, ii. 319, and Dowden, ii. 521).

2 Yale MS. Copy in the hand of Charles Sheridan.

3 Owned by Professor F. W. Hilles, who has kindly made it available.

near £500 on account of the Work, I deposited with the former, under my seal, a copy of all I had then written of it, which included all the early part of your father's life, till about the appearance of the Rivals, and certainly contained the cream of what the Papers furnished, for, after that period, there is little left in them that a biographer can turn to account. Since then, I have paid back to Murray £200, which leaves my debt to him on this score only 300—The MS. still remains in his hands, and I saw it the last time I was in town, with the seal unbroken. Neither he nor any one else, except myself, has ever had access to the papers, and the announcement you mention prefixed to the Works (which, by the bye, I do not remember having ever seen) was as unfounded as it was improper. I resumed my operations on the Life this last summer, and, with the exception of a Pamphlet about Ireland which I wrote on my return from thence, it has been the chief object of my attention—so that I fully expected to be able to take it up to town in May or June next, in such a state as to enable me to consult with greater effect those persons to whose information I trust for filling up the lacunae that must naturally occur in the narrative. Notwithstanding all this, you need not (I assure you most sincerely) feel the slightest hesitation in either interrupting or, if necessary, putting an end to my task altogether—for, from a variety of circumstances, some of which I once ventured to hint to you, I consider it so beset with difficulties and delicacies that I shall not be disposed to feel *very* great regret at any decision of yours which may, without affecting in the least degree the friendship that exists between us, occasion the transfer of the task into other hands.[1] So judge for yourself, my dear Sheridan, without any restraint or reserve whatever, and let me know the result.

Murray had certainly been culpable about the announcement that the *Works* would be based on family manuscripts, but if he had not seen these papers presumably he had gained a false impression from Thomas Wilkie, who seems to have taken a much more active part in these transactions than has been acknowledged. Moore states plainly that his advance came from Murray and Wilkie. Murray's records have revealed that Wilkie and Moore were paid 'for their labour with regard to preparing Sheridan's plays for the press'.[2] Since Moore was responsible only for the preface, we must assume that Wilkie assembled the edition from wherever he could find texts, but not from the Sheridan papers. He could always justify himself by referring to the agreement he had made with Sheridan in 1809: if the playwright did not supply corrected copies, Wilkie was authorized 'to print and publish the said Works from such Copies as he may be enabled to obtain'.[3] So he produced some reasonably acceptable texts of *The Rivals*, *The Duenna*, *The Critic*, and *Pizarro*. Those of *A Trip to Scarborough* and *The School for Scandal* are less useful because they contain variants of very doubtful authority. *St. Patrick's Day* and

[1] Moore decided to ask Lord Lansdowne's advice on this: see his letter to Murray of 26 Dec. 1823, printed by Dowden, ii. 520–1.

[2] Rae, p. xiv.

[3] Cf. p. 7 above.

The Camp are taken from Dublin piracies. The edition was a commercial undertaking designed to satisfy immediate public demand and, as far as it went, it was highly successful. It was well printed, and for many years enjoyed an authority that was drawn from Moore's preface and the announcement that the edition was based on Sheridan's papers. Wilkie's share in the profits of the edition amounted to three hundred pounds.[1]

Yet the edition did not realize, in any sense, the original intentions of the Sheridan family or even of the publishers, for nobody could really claim that it contained 'his entire works according to a Programme drawn up by himself'.

He certainly wrote more than is printed in the 1821 edition. When it comes to deciding just what his 'Programme' was, the evidence is not quite so straightforward. I am inclined to accept the unnoticed list to be found in the British Museum on a sheet bound up with Thomas Wilkie's letters[2] as an authentic copy. Its watermark is dated '1809' (the year of the agreement with Wilkie), and the document reads:

Volm 1st
Mr Sheridans Works
Dedication.
Preface by the Author and Editor
The Rivals
St Patrick's Day or the Scheeming Lieutenant.
Prelude on Opening Covent Garden next Season[3]
The Duenna
Two or three prologues and Epilogues within that Year

Volm 2nd
Preface and introduction
Trip to Scarborough
School for Scandal
Two or three prologues and Epilogues

Volm 3d
Monody on the Death of Garrick
Richard Coeur de Lion[4]
Critic or a Tragedy Rehearsed

[1] Rhodes, i, p. xvi. Apart from Murray himself, Ridgway (owner of the copyright of *The School for Scandal* and of *Pizarro*), also drew a share.
[2] Add. MS. 29764, f. 72: hand unknown. Cf. Sichel, i. 480 n.
[3] This has never before been attributed to Sheridan.
[4] For the discussion of Sheridan's authorship of this play, see pp. 815–16.

The Camp[1]
The Stranger[2]
The Storming of Fort Omoor[3]
Several prologues and Epilogues

Volm 4th
Pizzarro
A Dramatic Proverb[4]
and
A New Play[5]

There are several reasons for thinking that the list was copied from a 'programme' written in Sheridan's hand. The spelling of *Pizarro* is his. Besides, who else would have claimed at that date that he was the author of *Richard Coeur de Lion*, *The Stranger*,[6] and even the prologue for the opening of Covent Garden Theatre in 1775? Who else remembered the 'dramatic proverb'? And who but Sheridan would have shown such optimism as to promise 'a new play'? There is, of course, no certainty in the attribution, but some degree of probability.

The list does not include juvenilia like *Ixion/Jupiter* or the sketch based on *The Vicar of Wakefield*, nor does it note extracts from manuscripts of plays that were never completed, like 'The Foresters' or 'Affectation'. Possibly Sheridan did not wish to recall them, though if that is really the case it is strange that his son made them available to Wilkie and Moore. Here, again, we can only ponder on possibilities.

Moore duly printed extracts from them. His disagreements with Charles Sheridan were resolved in 1824, and though he went on grumbling about the 'millstone'[7] and the 'troublesome task . . . far beyond that I at first anticipated',[8] he completed it so that it came out as *Memoirs of the Life of the Right Honourable Richard Brinsley Sheridan*, in the autumn of 1825. Charles Sheridan was delighted with it, and Moore recorded that he was full of 'the warmest admiration and gratitude'.[9] Others were more critical, but the book remains a good account.

Even from the textual point of view, Moore has much to offer the reader. For example, it is noticeable that his very brief extracts from

[1] See pp. 705–50.
[2] See pp. 788–90.
[3] See pp. 782–4.
[4] See p. 816.
[5] See p. 816.
[6] Though Samuel Rogers told Moore that Sheridan 'said to him *twice* that every sentence in the "Stranger", as it is acted, was written by him' (Moore, *Journal*, iv. 222).
[7] Dowden, ii. 534.
[8] Sotheby's Catalogue, 4 Nov. 1969, lot 308.
[9] Moore, *Journal*, iv. 322; cf. Dowden, ii. 538–9.

St. Patrick's Day were not taken from the Dublin pirated version that was reproduced in the Murray edition of 1821, but from a source (either Sheridan's original or, as is more likely, an early prompt copy) that is much closer to the text sent to the Lord Chamberlain. In the case of *The Duenna*, too, he printed Sheridan's letters on the early stages of composition, and compared early manuscript copies with later printed versions, illustrating his remarks with some eighty-four lines of dialogue and eighty-six of verse.[1]

Moore also printed a humorous, satirical essay by Richard Tickell[2] that recognized, while laughing at, Sheridan's astonishing ability to meet some challenge or urgent demand. One quotation may make the point:

> His confidence in the resources of his own genius and his aversion to any sort of labour were so great that he could not be prevailed upon to learn either to read or write. He was, for a short time, Manager of one of the play-houses, and conceived the extraordinary and almost incredible project of composing a play extempore, which he was to recite in the Green-room to the actors, who were immediately to come on the stage and perform it. The players refusing to undertake their parts at so short a notice, and with so little preparation, he threw up the management in disgust.[3]

Moore contrasted this well-known facility with the hard labour and skilful revision that went into the making of *The School for Scandal.* He printed extracts from the early drafts, noting that 'the greater part of the dialogue is evidently experimental'.[4] He added, 'There is not a page of these manuscripts that does not bear testimony to the fastidious care with which he selected, arranged, and moulded his language. . . . His chief objects in correcting were to condense and simplify.'[5] Moore printed, though inaccurately, the famous 'doxology' from the last page of the late draft in Sheridan's own hand, a page that was soon to be 'lost' for over a century and one which showed the strain under which Sheridan and his copyist, Hopkins, worked.[6]

Moore's *Memoirs of . . . Sheridan* may have suffered from his timidity in omitting facts concerning Sheridan's life that were discreditable, but his approach to the plays was sound. In fact, his intelligent handling of the manuscripts in his possession makes one regret that he did not edit the *Works* in 1821.

Editions of Sheridan's plays were printed over and over again in the nineteenth century, but most of them repeated the Murray text. In that

[1] Moore, i. 157–80.

[2] 1751–93. He was Sheridan's brother-in-law, and a man of letters himself.

[3] Moore, ii. 228. [4] Ibid. i. 210–34. [5] Ibid. 236.

[6] Ibid. i. 242. See also C. Price, 'Sheridan's "Doxology" ', *T.L.S.*, 4 May 1962, and the present edition, pp. 288–300, 333–7, for the early and late drafts of the manuscript of *The School for Scandal.*

period the really important contributions to Sheridan studies were made not so much by editors as by descendants of the playwright: they preserved the early manuscripts and encouraged scholarly examination of them.

Sheridan's grandson, Brinsley Sheridan,[1] married an heiress and devoted himself at Frampton Court, Dorset, to his namesake's memory. His sister, Caroline Norton, wrote an article on 'Sheridan and his Biographers', and announced in it[2] that she hoped to produce a history of Sheridan from the family papers at Frampton, only 'a portion of which papers were in the hands of Tom Moore'. She never carried out this plan, though her brother said she had 'fully intended to have written the lives of the Sheridans and often mentioned this intention to me and to her friends. She had even collected opinions and ideas from strangers as well as friends.'[3] Her nephew, the first Marquis of Dufferin and Ava, was another enthusiastic admirer of Sheridan.

When Lord Dufferin was Governor-General of Canada he received from Brander Matthews a copy of an article on *The School for Scandal* (printed in *Appleton's Magazine*),[4] and wrote to the American scholar expressing appreciation of its 'delicate criticism'.[5] He also introduced Matthews to Brinsley Sheridan, who said, '[I] am most willing that you should look over the original MS. of the School for Scandal, the same of portions of the Critic, Duenna, the Trip to Scarborough, and other M.S.S. not used by earlier biographers'.[6] Matthews spent a day (6 July 1883) at Frampton Court looking at them,[7] and on 5 October Brinsley Sheridan wrote to him again to say that he had found

> amongst the papers of my sister, better known as Mrs. Norton (which I have only lately received) three full-sized copy books, in which I am inclined to think is the *first* sketch of the School for Scandal, and not that as thought to be the first sketch by Mr. Moore at p. 210, Vol. I, of the 8vo ed. I am now in possession of both sketches.[8]

On 9 June 1884 he expressed the hope that Matthews would pay him another visit 'and not in the same hurried way'.[9]

In his preface to *Sheridan's Comedies* (Boston, 1885) Matthews thanked Brinsley Sheridan for allowing him to examine the manuscripts,[10] but

[1] His full name was Richard Brinsley Sheridan, and he married Marcia Grant of Frampton Court in 1835.

[2] *MacMillan's Magazine*, iii (1860–1), 178.

[3] To Torrens, Sept. 1877 (Osborn MS.).

[4] Vol. xvii, pp. 556–62.

[5] 25 May 1877. The letter is bound in an extra-illustrated copy of Matthews's *Sheridan's Comedies* (824 Sh5 M3), in the Butler Library of Columbia University.

[6] To Matthews, 14 June 1883 (bound in Butler Library 824 Sh5 M3).

[7] From Matthews's diary entry. Location: as note 6.

[8] 5 Oct. 1883 (bound in Butler Library 824 Sh5 M3).

[9] Location: as note 8.

[10] p. 6. Sichel, i. 565 n. jumps to the conclusion that Matthews's edition of *The School for Scandal* was 'taken from the Frampton Court manuscript'.

honestly declared that his text followed the Murray versions of 1821. He noted, however, that his long biographical introduction was 'the result of original research'. Brinsley Sheridan thanked him for his 'careful editing',[1] but had already made quite clear that he had encouraged Matthews because the American was 'disposed to view his [R. B. Sheridan's] life and character more favourably than many other biographers have done. His temptations and difficulties have never been fairly considered, and justice has been withheld.'[2] In other words, Brinsley Sheridan sought just what Hester Sheridan had so ardently desired for her husband's memory: 'honor, glory, and *truth*', a difficult combination.

The same outlook[3] was apparent in Lord Dufferin's encouraging W. Fraser Rae to write a biography, for he deplored 'the unfortunate treatment'[4] of Sheridan by earlier writers. Under his auspices, too, Rae set about preparing an edition of the plays, drawn from the original manuscripts at Frampton Court. Rae noted that he could find no trace of the manuscript of *The Rivals* there, and had to be satisfied with the printed text of the first edition. The manuscript of *St. Patrick's Day* was defective, containing only the third and fourth scenes of the second act, and of these lines a quarter were in the hand of Sheridan's first wife. For *The Duenna* and *The Critic* the manuscript versions were much fuller. For *The School for Scandal* he used the late draft in Sheridan's hand[5] and was criticized for not taking his text from a version revised for performance. This is not, perhaps, a great error in a book called *Sheridan's Plays Now Printed as He Wrote Them* (1902). A much more serious fault is that his transcriptions are not always to be trusted. For example, he was responsible for the very plausible (but inaccurate) reading, 'a pair of white cobs' in place of 'a pair of white cats'.[6] Worse still, he filled up gaps in his text from 'current versions', without specifying what they were. So, while he performed a useful service in making his selected manuscripts available in print, he might have rendered an invaluable one had he taken full advantage of his opportunities.

Sheridan's descendants continued to guard the manuscripts at Frampton Court for many years, but in January 1929 one of the treasures was sold in America. Brinsley Sheridan's son, Algernon,[7] had entrusted the

[1] To Matthews, 26 June 1885. He added, 'All you have already written in Magazines has invariably been so favourable.'

[2] 11 July 1883. Location: as note 8, p. 21.

[3] Dufferin phrased it carefully: 'Accuracy and impartiality were all that they [Sheridan's connections] bargained for, tempered by that benevolence of treatment of which the most blameless stand in need' (Preface to Rae, *Sheridan* (1896), i. xiii). Certainly, Percy Fitzgerald's attack on Rae in *Sheridan Whitewashed* (1896) was too savage.

[4] Rae, *Sheridan*, i, p. vii.

[5] See p. 334 below.

[6] *The School for Scandal*, II. i.

[7] Algernon Thomas Brinsley Sheridan (1845–1931). Brinsley Sheridan had died in May 1888.

original manuscripts of *The School for Scandal* to 'a confidential representative'[1] for disposal privately, in spite of the fact that his action conflicted with the terms of his father's will. Prices for books and manuscripts were very high—the sale of Jerome Kern's library was taking place—and there was every prospect that a good sum would be realized for the Sheridan manuscripts even outside the auction rooms. It so happened, then, that Barton Currie, editor of *World's Work* and a keen collector, walked into the New York office of the bookdealer Gabriel Wells and was astonished to find these manuscripts available for purchase. He paid over a large sum of money quickly, but within twenty-four hours Wells asked him to cancel the transaction. The Sheridan family, with the exception of Algernon, was angry at the loss of the heirloom, but Currie refused to return it and would not be intimidated. He was threatened with a lawsuit if he attempted to dispose of the manuscripts, but, two years later, the family gave its reluctant consent to the sale.[2]

Other items from Frampton Court were offered for sale at Sotheby's on 2 July 1930. They included the manuscripts of *St. Patrick's Day*, *The Duenna*, *The Critic*, and *Pizarro*.[3] According to the record, these plays were sold to one Kahn, but this appears to have been a polite fiction to cover the fact that the family had bought them in. As they formed part of an entailed estate, they were held for another Richard Brinsley Sheridan,[4] then a minor.

He and his mother (Clare Sheridan) and sister moved to Biskra, Algeria, and took these manuscripts with them. Pursuing some whim of his own, he later put them on a boat he owned, with the idea of sailing back to England. The boat was wrecked off the Algerian coast, and the manuscript volumes in their heavy cases sank to the bottom of the Mediterranean and were lost.[5]

Some original manuscripts of the plays were more successfully preserved by another member of the family. Sophie was the younger daughter of Algernon Sheridan, and she married the wealthy brewer, William Hall Walker, afterwards first Baron Wavertree. Her excellent Sheridan collection contained the holograph draft of the Teazle sketch and of 'The

[1] *New York Times*, 4 Feb. 1929.

[2] Barton Currie, *Fishers of Books* (Boston, 1931), pp. 323–31. Cf. David A. Randall, *Dukedom Large Enough* (New York, 1969), pp. 77–8. The present owner, Mr. Robert H. Taylor, purchased them from the Currie collection on 7 Sept. 1956.

[3] Lots 634 and 635. They are described in the Frampton Catalogue, p. 137, as 'Detached portions of the original Manuscripts of the Plays, The Duenna, St. Patrick's Day and The Critic, or A Tragedy Rehearsed, 1 vol. small 4to. *red mor.* illustrated with portraits. *Frampton* 1880.' For *Pizarro* see p. 625, below.

[4] 1915–36. He was the grandson of Algernon T. B. Sheridan, and son of Wilfred and Clare Sheridan. See Clare Sheridan, *Without End* (1939), p. 3.

[5] Clare Sheridan, *To the Four Winds* (1957), p. 304; Mary Motley, *Morning Glory* (1961), pp. 272–4.

Foresters', as well as the prompt copy of *The Critic* presented by R. B. Sheridan to Mrs. Crewe.[1]

All three are part of the splendid Sheridan holdings at Yale, and it is typical of our century that they should have moved out of the hands of the family to find new owners in the United States. In fact, nearly all the most important manuscripts of Sheridan's plays are now to be found in American institutions. Georgetown University owns the manuscript of *The School for Scandal* presented by Sheridan to Mrs. Crewe; Harvard has the draft of *Pizarro*; Princeton holds on deposit Mr. Robert H. Taylor's magnificent collection.

THE TEXT

The usual aim of an editor is to present to the reader texts that can be said to be as close as possible to the author's final intentions. In studying the work of Sheridan, we have to face his rather daunting statement that, apart from *Pizarro*, *The Critic* was the only play he put his name to. I have already interpreted this as meaning that it was the only one that met, finally, with his approval. The implication is that the remainder were left in a more or less unpolished state.

In trying to discover how Sheridan would have prepared them for a correct edition, we can look at some manuscripts of *The Critic* as well as a prompt copy of it, and compare their texts with the printed version. This exercise should reveal the principles on which Sheridan worked in the choice of readings that he made. Two years passed between the first acting of the burlesque in 1779 and the first edition of 1781, and the corrections that he made during that period indicated that he was more concerned to put out a text that read well than one that represented exactly the lines spoken in the most recent of stage performances.

Mr. F. W. Bateson considered this problem in connection with a Harvard prompt-book (1782) of the burlesque, and came to the conclusion that 'the accepted text of *The Critic*, which was authorized by Sheridan himself, was not in use on the stage at any time in his lifetime'.[2] He also said that 'Sheridan was capable of drawing a distinction between the acting and the reading versions of his plays'.

The truth of this statement may be shown in its simplest and most obvious form in a comparison of one passage in the Larpent and Crewe manuscripts with the corresponding one in the printed version. In Act II, Puff criticizes Tilburina's reaction to Whiskerandos's cry, 'Where is my love—my—', and Tilburina replies, 'Well, we'll try again.' In the

[1] All three were among the manuscripts sold, after Lady Wavertree's death, at Sotheby's on 25 May 1954, as lots 269, 266, 270.

[2] F. W. Bateson, 'Notes on the Text of Two Sheridan Plays', *R.E.S.*, xvi (1940), 316–17. For the prompt-book's call number, see p. 489 below.

manuscript copies the four lines are given once again, but they are not repeated in the printed text. The reader would take it for granted that Tilburina and Whiskerandos tried again; the prompter had to make sure that the players spoke the lines a second time.

The differences between acting and printed versions can also be seen from another prompt copy going back, at least, to 1811, and from reports of performances. It is clear that actors introduced topical jests into the text, and were given freedom to do so. This is not at all surprising since *The Critic* followed in the tradition of *The Rehearsal*, in which Bayes had always been expected to make pungent comments on some matter of current interest. So, when Sheridan was elected to Parliament as member for Stafford, the *Morning Chronicle*[1] reported 'two or three new strokes, that were highly relished' at a performance of *The Critic* in Drury Lane:

The first that occurred was in the scene between Dangle, Sir Fretfull Plagiary, and Sneer. When Sir Fretfull tells Sneer, 'he will never carry another piece to Drury Lane house, because the manager *writes himself*,' Parsons [Sir Fretful] added, 'besides, he is now turned *politician*, and writes nothing but *franks*.' The next novelty came from the mouth of Puff—who in looking over his papers and memorandums, previous to his *exit*, said, '*To take Paul Jones*—damn it, I've been trying to take him these two years, without success, I'll therefore give over that project.'—'Ah, what have we here?—oh, aye, to endeavour to bring about a general insurrection in South America,—for the *Morning Spy*—to reinforce Rodney, in tomorrow's *Publick Advertiser*; and to *shoot Charles Fox*, in the *Morning Post*.'

The last addition made, appeared to be an impromptu of Mr. Bannister, senior, who performed the character of Wiskerandos, instead of his son, who is ill. When Puff in the last scene desired Don Ferrolo, to get up and die again, Bannister answered, 'Damn it, Sir, I'd better apply at once to Mr. King, and ask him to engage me as a *Tumbler* at Sadler's Wells, if I am expected to stay *tumbling* on this carpet all night.'

Five years later, Mary Tickell wrote to her sister, Sheridan's wife, to say that Richard Tickell, her husband, had been asked by Thomas King to supply some topicalities for the Drury Lane performances:

The Critic went off with very great Applause but it certainly wants a judicious prunning Knife very much. King beg'd T—— to give him some new Strokes for the end of the first Act—but as he did not send up to him till near the end of the Play he had not much time to think of anything—however the following Hits were receiv'd with amazing Applause—

'Let me see—Oh! I find I must revive the irish Propositions in the Morning Post—and overflow an Austrian Army in the G[eneral] Advertiser, I shall then metamorphose the Minister to a Shark at Brighthelmstone and conclude the Day with a *Merry* Attack on the Commissioner at Guildhall, and write down the Shop Tax with their own *ink*.'[2]

[1] 6 Oct. 1780. [2] Folger MS. Y.d. 35, f. 146.

In 1794, too, 'the *ad libitums* of Puff were highly relished'.[1] As late as 2 September 1807 Andrew Cherry played the part when he became manager of the Swansea Theatre, and introduced a jest that pleased his Welsh audience: 'There is no expressing the indignation of the great Bonaparte in finding it impossible to land his myrmidons on the Cambrian coast; it has quite defeated his purposes of aggrandisement to his followers, as he purposed creating a Grand Duke of Oystermouth Castle and a Supreme Elector of the Mumbles.'[2] These 'novelties' obviously delighted playgoers, and we have only to look at a prompt copy of *The Critic*, once used at Drury Lane Theatre, to find further proof that the habit of interpolation went on for over thirty years. It contains the following statement:

N.B. All the Political Part of the Piece must be carefully attended to—and has always been alter'd to suit the Times. J. Stokes[3]

Stokes is named in a Drury Lane account book[4] on 10 June 1793 as 'Prompter's Assistant', and in its *Journal, 1812–13*,[5] as 'copyist'. As far as prompt-books and theatre manuscripts are concerned, any statement he makes has authority.

His prompt-book is an interleaved copy of the printed edition of 1781, into which he has written certain emendations. One of them, in Act I, Sc. i, is of particular interest. Sheridan printed the following lines:

SNEER. From sickness and misfortunes!—You practised as a Doctor and an Attorney at once?
PUFF. No egad, both maladies and miseries were my own.
SNEER. Hey!—what the plague!
DANGLE. 'Tis true, efaith.[6]

Stokes revised this to read:

PUFF. But before I begin, Mr. Sneer, let me premise that 'tis not my wish to deaden your feelings or lessen your humanity; but I think putting people on their guard against imposition, and leading them into an enquiry after proper objects for the distribution of their benevolence may be considered as doing a very essential Service to the cause of true Charity.

The source of this correction is to be found in the second performance of the play. The *Morning Chronicle* describes the occasion:

The whole piece was received with the greatest applause, excepting only that part of Puff's advertisement of himself, in which he ridicules in the lump, those

[1] *The Times*, 13 Dec. 1794.
[2] C. Price, *The English Theatre in Wales in the Eighteenth and Early Nineteenth Centuries* (Cardiff, 1948), p. 96.
[3] Folger MS. Prompt C 53.
[4] Folger MS. W. b. 295.
[5] Folger MS. W. b. 315.
[6] They also appeared in the Larpent MS., the text sent to the Lord Chamberlain for licensing.

addresses to the humane and benevolent which occasionally appear in the daily prints,—to this a great part of the audience opposed a long and virtuous hiss; their displeasure however was converted into expressions of approbation, when Mr. King seized a lucky moment to 'promise to tell Mr. Sneer, that he did not mean to deaden his feelings, or lessen his humanity; that he intended merely to awaken his prudence, and instruct him in future to make a proper enquiry into the truth of the cases stated in such advertisements before he parted with his money for the relief of the parties from whom the advertisements came.'[1]

Although Sheridan is said to have provided King, in advance, with these lines,[2] he obviously preferred his original thoughts when he came to print the work. King had to deal with current sensibility and turn play-house hisses into applause, but Sheridan could please himself in the seclusion of his own study.

One other addition of more than a few words is to be found in Stokes's version, though its authorship is not clear. When the Earl of Leicester begins his prayer, 'O mighty Mars', Puff cries, 'Stop, my dear Sir, you do not expect to find Mars there. No, Sir, whenever you address the Gods always look into the upper gallery.'[3] Generally, however, cuts were more necessary than additional lines. *The Critic* was very long for an afterpiece that had to follow a tragedy. Some cutting was made before the second performance, which with the normal increase in speed of presentation when a play is repeated meant that the first act took twenty minutes less than before. '*The Tragedy Rehearsed* had also had the author's pruning knife applied to it, as well as that of the comedians.'[4] In spite of these excisions, the *Morning Chronicle* of 6 October 1780 renewed its objection to *The Critic*'s 'immoderate length, and the great space of time its performance occupies. Last night it was full two hours in representation. If Mr. Sheridan be determined to continue it, as it was given yesterday evening, it would be but civil in him to announce that night-caps, pillows, and pallet-beds, are prepared for the audience whenever *The Critick* is to be represented.' No concession is made to these complaints in the printed version of 1781, but the theatre had to take heed of them, and it is not surprising that Stokes's version was at least 225 lines shorter than the first edition. This amounts to about one-tenth of the printed dialogue.

It is easy to understand why certain passages were deleted from the acting text. Some were no longer topical: for instance, Mrs. Dangle's third speech was not altogether appropriate in the changed circumstances: 'No, no; you never will read any thing that's worth listening to:—you hate to hear about your country; there are letters every day with

[1] 2 Nov. 1779.

[2] Boaden, *Kemble*, i. 64: without giving his authority.

[3] Not in the Larpent MS. or any other prompt copy that I have seen.

[4] See p. 480 below.

Roman signatures, demonstrating the certainty of an invasion, and proving that the nation is utterly undone.—But you never will read any thing to entertain one.' The use of 'Roman signatures' fell out of fashion; light-hearted references to invasion would have angered audiences once Napoleon threatened to land on the English coast.

Some speeches were indelicate, and even alluded to 'the artificial bashfulness of a courtesan'.[1] Others were too figurative, like the one referring to 'a presiding Mercury, the god of traffic and fiction'.[2] Descriptive passages were sometimes too detailed: Mrs. Dangle's sixth speech, on her drawing-room's being 'an absolute register-office for candidate actors', is delightful to read but holds up the development of the plot: it was eliminated.

The Critic has long been enjoyed as a satirical demonstration of the natural conflict between actors and dramatists, but its irony has an even sharper edge once we realize that this play too has been subjected to the performers' merciless attentions. Sheridan could well declare with Puff: 'The pruning-knife—zounds the axe! why, here has been such a lopping and topping, I shan't have the bare trunk of my play left presently. —Very well, Sir—the performers must do as they please, but upon my soul, I'll print it every word.' This is what he did himself in practice.

There is evidence, also, to suggest that this reluctance to give up passages he had written was not confined to *The Critic*, but was a normal part of his attitude to creative work. At some date between 1776 and 1779, he discussed with Hannah Cowley the merits of her tragedy *Albina*, and made some minor criticism. She described what was said: 'On my attempting a timorous defence, he added, "Don't alter this, or any other passage, unless it strikes you as It does me; *you* ought to be tenacious: *every original Writer must give up passages with difficulty: it is only Translators, and Borrowers, who are so ready to comply with every hint that is proposed.*" '[3] He may have been flattering Mrs. Cowley, but he was also expressing something he felt genuinely and strongly. There are a number of examples in his manuscripts of words and phrases that he himself had discarded, being accommodated later in another context. He was economical in this, if in nothing else.

Manuscripts also reveal points of general interest concerning Sheridan's practice as an editor of his own work. I have already mentioned[4] that a new phrase, inserted in one of the later transcripts of *The School for Scandal*, is not certain to appear in another. This habit of minor correction, suggested in Sheridan's telling Ridgway that he had not satisfied his taste in *The School for Scandal*,[5] is also to be found to a lesser degree

[1] I. i. [2] I. ii.
[3] H. Cowley, *Albina* (1779), p. iv.
[4] See p. 5 above.
[5] See p. 6 above.

in *The Critic*. A couple of examples in a manuscript copy[1] of Sir Fretful's lines and cues may make the point. When Sir Fretful rejects the idea that his play sinks in the fifth act, he cries, 'No, no, it don't fall off.' Sheridan substitutes in his own hand a more emphatic and punning denial: 'I'll be damn'd if it falls off.' A few lines later, when Sir Fretful is pleased by Mrs. Dangle's compliment and remarks, 'Upon my soul, the women are the best judges after all', Sheridan adds a stage direction: 'to Mrs. D. and offer her snuff.' Neither of the changes is in the printed text.

Most of these new ideas are expressed in brief phrases, but occasionally they are more developed, as is the case in a set of stage directions to be found in the Crewe MS. of *The Critic*. At the beginning of the second act, the Larpent MS. and first edition read:

The THEATRE

Enter DANGLE, PUFF, and SNEER, *as before the Curtain.*

Puff. No, no, Sir; what Shakespeare. . . .

The Crewe MS. makes the situation much clearer:

Before the Curtain

Enter Under Prompter, who speaks to the Band, while they are playing.

Under Prompter. Gentlemen—Gentlemen—As I suppose you are only Practising an Overture for your own Diversion,—I must beg the favour of you to stop, As The Author is come and we are Just going to begin the Rehearsal. *Exit Under Prompter*

Enter Dangle, Puff and Sneer

(Band stops)

Puff. Sir I say what Shakespear. . . .

In many ways it is a pity that this does not appear in the printed version.

The collation of prompt copy and manuscripts of *The Critic* also helps us to reach other conclusions. The Larpent MS. may be regarded as the text of the dress rehearsal, to be amended in the second and subsequent performances. The first edition has a literary finish, but does not include some amusing ideas that occurred to Sheridan on reflection; it ignores the topicalities and cuts introduced by the actors. Stokes's version is, by comparison, very bare.

It will be necessary to consider these conclusions afresh in the case of any of Sheridan's plays that present special problems. Accordingly, a full discussion of them will be found in the textual sections that precede the plays themselves. One general point, however, may be dealt with here. It may be argued that *The Critic*, as a burlesque, belonged to a special category in which lines were commonly added to, or cut from, the text to suit the mood of the moment. Sheridan seems to have given his own

[1] New York Public Library MS.

answer to this problem by printing 'the political part' in 1781, as it had been spoken in 1779, and not bringing allusions up to date. Whatever the actors liked to do with *The Critic*, he was content to see that the printed version was full of the spirit of the late summer of 1779. It follows that he would have retained the allusions to the 'd——d register' and the Annuity Bill in *The School for Scandal*. Whether or not he would have retained the 'High-roomians and Low-roomians' in *The Rivals* is more controversial, because the jest is local rather than national. No one can accuse Sheridan of always being consistent, but he possessed certain habits of mind. An editor must assume that these habits will normally be at work when an author makes decisions about his final text.

Some comment must be made on the accidentals. Five hands[1] were at work in the transcription of the Larpent MS., and presumably the scribes had Sheridan's manuscript or the prompter's copy in front of them. They differ in their practices, and appear to alter punctuation and particularly capitalization to suit their fancies. There is no evidence to show that Sheridan corrected their work in any way, and he contented himself with scrawling at the conclusion of this text of *The Critic*:

Battle and Procession
End.

Other manuscripts reveal that he occasionally corrected wording where a copyist had been very careless. He himself was inconsistent in capitalization and sometimes inaccurate in spelling, and it is likely that, in the main, he left such finicking matters to professional copyists and compositors. They sometimes treated his peculiarities with reverence; more frequently, not.

When we turn to *The School for Scandal*, we have the advantage of examining a text that, for the most part, is written in Sheridan's own hand. It reveals some of the traits already mentioned but in greater quantity. His use of the dash is particularly interesting. He employs it, at times, to give emphasis to the word or phrase following it:

. . . professes the noblest—Sentiments. . . . (p. 386).
. . . Harry diets himself—for Gaming. . . . (p. 397).

Hesitation and doubt can easily be suggested in the timing:

. . . to my—Friend Joseph . . . . (p. 391).

Sometimes the insistent use of the dash gives a jerkiness or vehemence to the lines, as in Sir Peter's greeting Sir Oliver: 'Hah! Sir Oliver—my Old Friend:—welcome to England—a thousand Times' (II. iii). Uneasy rhythms are marked in this way in Sir Peter's conversation with Joseph

[1] It was very laborious for one man. When copying a prelude for Mrs. Wells, E. C. Everard noted, 'I had to write it over again for the license—again for the prompter—to write again all the parts' (*Memoirs of an Unfortunate Son of Thespis* (Edinburgh, 1818), p. 151).

early in the Screen Scene: 'Well now we are alone—there *is* a Subject—my dear—Friend—on which I wish to unburthen my Mind to you—a Point of the greatest moment to my Peace—in short—my good Friend—Lady Teazle's Couduct of late has made me extremely unhappy.' It is not at all surprising that Sheridan should have taken such care to indicate just what he had in mind. His father had spent the best part of his life considering the most effective ways of delivering lines, and Richard Brinsley Sheridan was to show how much he had learned when he came to make some of his most famous orations. Besides, he attentively supervised rehearsals, and we might reasonably assume that he used his manuscript copy as a conductor reads a score. He was undoubtedly fastidious about the way in which his lines were delivered. Look at his behaviour at a performance of *Pizarro*, as recounted by Daniel Stuart:

About the third night of *Pizarro*, I went up into Sheridan's private box, or rather, the box he was privately in with Richardson. The box was on the Prince's side, up one flight of stairs, making a sharp angle towards the stage; one window looking obliquely towards the audience, the other behind upon the stage. My business was politics, but Sheridan was so deeply interested with what was going on, (*Pizarro*) that I could not speak to him for a length of time. He repeated every syllable after each performer, counting poetically the measure upon his fingers, and sounding with his voice like a music-master, with a degree of earnestness beyond my power to describe. He was in the utmost ill-humour, shocked, almost stamping with anger at every thing Mrs. Jordan said. With every thing Kemble uttered he was invariably delighted; clapping his hands with pleasure, like a child. With some passages, by Mrs. Siddons, he was charmed; at others he was shocked, frequently stating to Richardson and me that 'THIS was the way the passage *should* be spoken,' and then repeating it in his *own* way. Upon his sometimes referring to Mrs. Siddons, Richardson said to him, with his Newcastle *burr*, 'Well, well, Sheridan, you should not be so impatient! You know, Kemble told you, that after some time she would fall into it.'[1]

The comparision with a music-master is interesting because it reminds us of the stress, earlier in the century, on modulation of voice. John Hill refers to it in *The Actor* (1755, p. 241): 'Of old the delivery of speeches in tragedy was regulated by certain musical notes.'

With such positive views Sheridan might have been expected to demand that the theatre scribes should also obey his wishes by copying his manuscripts with absolute fidelity. Possibly he did so, but the copies available show that they followed their own conventions and largely ignored his devices for conveying a particular meaning.

In general, the compositors showed more respect, but there is an example at hand showing a publisher himself presenting simultaneously texts that differ in accidentals. John Wilkie, who brought out the first

[1] James Boaden, *The Life of Mrs. Jordan* (1831), ii. 16–17.

edition of *The Rivals*, gave an extract 'from the printed Play just published' in his newspaper, the *London Chronicle*, 11–14 February 1775. The differences are minor but worth looking at, and one reads:

First ed. . . . shall roll like the Bull's in Coxe's musaeum.
Lond. Chron. bull's in Cox's museum.

More important changes are to be found in Wilkie's printing of the prologue in the *London Chronicle*, 4–7 February 1775:

First ed. Come, courage, Sir, we did *amend* our *Plea.*
Lond. Chron. we *will amend* our plea.

and

First ed. Then heark'ee, Dibble, did you *mend* your *Pleadings.*
Lond. Chron. hearken, Dibble, we must *mend* our pleadings.

The printers may have been working from different copies[1] or may have made errors. Whatever the cause, little attempt seems to have been made to ensure that the printed versions were identical. If Sheridan was dissatisfied, no note of grievance is now extant. He probably felt that haste and improvisation are characteristic of journalism and the theatre, and only a pedant would expect uniformity.

I have usually accepted authorized first editions as copy text, but when they are not available have fallen back on the author's manuscript or the theatre copy prepared for the Lord Chamberlain's examination. Reasons for every decision in the choice of text are given in the preface to each play. The author's revisions (or what are accepted as such) will be substituted in the copy text for earlier readings, and will include changes in punctuation that alter meaning. Forms of spelling that were not incorrect then, even if they were uncommon, are preserved. Neologisms, too, have been accepted: 'insiduous' (*The Critic*, p. 502) may really have been a printer's error but is taken as Sheridan's way of effectively combining 'insidious' and 'assiduous'. Throughout I have expanded the ampersand, brought the £ sign before the figures, and lowered superior letters to the line.

In the textual notes, I have not printed variants of the following: 'it's', 'it is', ''tis'; 'it was', 'it were', ''twas', ''twere'; 'Ha! ha! ha!', 'Ha! ha!'; 'them', ''em'; 'are not', 'aren't', 'an't'; 'will not', 'won't'; 'in it', 'in't'; 'madam', 'ma'am'; 'thou hast', 'thou'st'; 'I am', 'I'm', 'I'am'; 'for it', 'for't'; 'you would', 'you'd'; 'through', 'thro''; 'faith', 'ifaith', 'efaith', 'efacks'; 'cannot', 'can't'; chuse, choose; d——d, damned; Psha!, Pshaw!

[1] Some manuscripts of Sheridan's plays appear to have been copied from dictation. In *The School for Scandal*, for example, this is suggested by his spellings of foreign words. 'Table d'hote at Spa' (II. i) is an example. Sheridan's own version was 'Table Dot at Spaw', and there are others favoured by the copyists: 'Table, a Hote at Spaw', 'Table Dole at Spaw', 'Table d'Note at Spa', 'Table Coté at Spa'.

'Yours' and 'your's' are printed as they stand in the copy text, but 'its' and 'it's' are distinguished according to present usage to avoid confusion. Variants of '-ed' (i.e. '-d' and '-'d') have not been recorded.

I have not tried to convey the curves and flourishes of engraved title pages, but have recorded the titles in roman and italic.

Some apology may be required for printing long extracts from newspaper reports of the reception of the plays. They are important because they often give us information about cuts and changes in the text, and an indication of the manner in which the plays were staged. They also indicate that Sheridan made alterations in response to newspaper comment. In fact he was praised for doing so by the *Morning Chronicle*, 23 Nov. 1775: 'Although youthful merit and vanity are generally inseparable, Mr. Sheridan is not like some other writers, deaf to instruction; he has very prudently adopted such hints for the alteration of the DUENNA as the several critics of yesterday suggested; this is a clear proof of his good sense.' Some of the criticism was clearly judicious; some full of malice. The newspaper had become the arbiter of public taste, and Sheridan was quick to show in both *The School for Scandal* and *The Critic* that its judgements could be personal and vindictive. Yet the variety of tone and manner sets the plays in a suitable background and helps us to understand them better.

The revisals, printed at the end of the present volumes, show the author (as he told his wife)[1] breaking through his indolence and earning his brown bread. They prove that Rhodes was wrong when he wrote, 'After his entry into Parliament, Sheridan did not even write prologues and epilogues, or use his pen in any way for the assistance of his theatrical property.'[2] There is increasing evidence to indicate that he touched up the dialogue of a number of plays, credited to other writers. He sensibly looked on this activity as journeyman's work that helped to improve the takings at his theatre. *Pizarro* alone among these later works, appeared under his name.

[1] *Letters*, ii. 208.
[2] *Harlequin Sheridan* (Oxford, 1933), p. x.

THE RIVALS

THE RIVALS

COMPOSITION

On 17 November 1774 Sheridan wrote to his father-in-law to say that a comedy he had written would be rehearsed at Covent Garden in a few days. He added, 'I had not written a line of it two months ago, except a scene or two, which I believe you have seen in an odd act of a little farce.'[1] Just what this 'little farce' was about can barely be surmised.

Sheridan clearly picked up some ideas for the fully developed play from his mother's unfinished comedy, *A Journey to Bath*. Mrs. Tryfort (like Mrs. Malaprop) is 'the vainest poor creature, and the fondest of hard words, which without *miscalling*, she always takes care to misapply'.[2] She describes Lord Stewkly as 'a progeny! a perfect progeny', and says, 'Oh if you were to hear him describe contagious countries as I have done, it would astonish you.'[3] She rebukes Edward Bull with the words, 'Sir you are a little pert let me tell you, and so much taciturnity doesn't become a young man.'[4]

Another snatch of dialogue reminds us of *The Rivals*:

SIR JEREMY. If I had your ladyship at Bull-hall, I cou'd shew you a line of ancestry, that wou'd convince you we are not a people of yesterday.
EDWARD. Pray Uncle how came it, you never shewd them to me?
SIR JEREMY. Why the land and the Mansion house has slipp'd thro' our fingers boy; but thank heaven the family pictures are still extant.[5]

Sheridan paraphrases this in Sir Lucius O'Trigger's speech:

I could shew you a range of ancestry, in the O'Trigger line, that would furnish the new room; every one of whom has killed his man!—For though the mansion-house and dirty acres have slipt through my fingers, I thank Heav'n our honour and the family-pictures, are as fresh as ever.[6]

Sheridan's sister stated that her 'mother's sketch of a comedy, unfinished, was put into my brother Richard's hands by my father at Bath',[7] and the resemblances prove that Sheridan had read it with care.

There is, however, little to justify Rhodes's guess that Sheridan, 'in attempting a revision of his mother's *A Trip to Bath* as *A Journey to Bath*, added these lines himself, and out of them grew the characters of Mrs. Malaprop and Sir Lucius O'Trigger, whom he transferred to

[1] *Letters*, i. 85.
[2] Rae, p. 273.
[3] Ibid., pp. 282, 299.
[4] Ibid., p. 284.
[5] Ibid., pp. 311–12. The last clause takes one on to *The School for Scandal*.
[6] *The Rivals*, III. iv: p. 116 below.
[7] *Lady* [Sydney] *Morgan's Memoirs* (1862), ii. 61.

his own comedy. He was his own plagiary.'[1] Because Thomas Sheridan mentioned, in August 1766, that his wife had been working on 'a comedy called *A Trip to Bath*', Rhodes assumes that this is different from *A Journey to Bath*; but a manuscript of the latter is extant in the British Museum[2] and is in Frances Sheridan's handwriting. The two titles appear to refer to the same play. Sheridan quite clearly borrowed some ideas from it, but there is no evidence to prove that he rewrote it in any way.

If we are looking for recurring ideas, we may discover an interesting one in an extract from a brief dramatic sketch drafted by Sheridan in late adolescence and based on Goldsmith's *The Vicar of Wakefield*.[3] In Scene II, we find Moses Primrose saying

> Why no Mother you are always gibing me because I was six months at the university, it would be better if you would take a little care of my sister and not let her be filling her head [with] noveles. I never knew any good come of such stuf[f], they get their hands so plaguey[4] full of purling streams and dying swain that w[h]ere they cant find an Oroondates they'll pack off with Thomas.—[5]

Part of this appears in the Larpent text of *The Rivals*, when Sir Anthony denounces circulating libraries:

> Oh, our London Nunneries are more obliged to them than to all the Recruiting Officers in the Kingdom,—The vicious Trash they send forth, not only disturbs the Imagination of our Girls, but sets their Passions afloat—And then, rely on it, Mrs. Malaprop, if they cannot find an Oroondates they will take up with Thomas—A circulating Library in a Town, is as an Ever green Tree of Diabolical Knowledge. . . .[6]

All but the last sentence was cut in the first printed edition of the play, but the phrase 'purling streams' was given to Jack Absolute for his description of Julia's singing.[7]

Satire at the expense of a young miss who had taken too seriously the romantic notions in popular novels was best remembered in Sheridan's day for its expression in George Colman's piece, *Polly Honeycombe*. This had been acted at Drury Lane from 1760 onwards, and it is possible that Sheridan saw a performance when it was revived on 10 February 1773,[8]

[1] Rhodes, *Harlequin Sheridan*, p. 57.

[2] Add. MS. 25975.

[3] Moore, i. 304–7, prints extracts from the manuscript, and suggests that the drafts were made when Sheridan was in his seventeenth year. He could have been a couple of years older.

[4] MS. 'pluagy'.

[5] See p. 803 below, and Purdy, p. 119.

[6] Purdy, p. 17.

[7] II. i.

[8] *The London Stage*, p. 1694. Another play he was said to be indebted to (Cibber's *The Double Gallant*) was presented on 18 Feb. He could have seen yet another that influenced him, Congreve's *The Old Batchelor*, at the Haymarket on 8 Sept. 1772.

for he remarked in a letter dated 24 February 1773 that he 'was obliged to go to London the other day'.[1] If he saw *Polly Honeycombe* or even read it, he may have been reminded of the sentiments he had already put into the mouth of Moses Primrose. Besides, there is other evidence to support the idea that Sheridan wrote 'a little farce' at this period: manuscript notes made by one of his friends stated that he did so,[2] and he himself recalled writing *The Rivals* when he was 'just past twenty one'.[3]

Whatever the truth of this may be, there can be no doubt that *The Rivals* was composed mainly in the six weeks before 17 November 1774. On that day Sheridan wrote to his father-in-law in some excitement:

> . . . There will be a *Comedy* of mine in rehearsal at Covent-Garden within a few days. I did not set to work on it till within a few days of my setting out for *Crome*, so you may think I have not, for these last six weeks, been very idle. I have done it at Mr. Harris's (the manager's) own request; it is now complete in his hands, and preparing for the stage. He, and some of his friends who have heard it, assure me in the most flattering terms that there is no doubt of its success. It will be very well played, and Harris tells me the least shilling I shall get (if it succeeds) will be six hundred pounds. . . .[4]

Croome Park was the seat of Lord Coventry, and Sheridan and his wife had stayed there in September 1773 when, at the Worcester music-meeting of the Three Choirs, she had given her last public performance.[5] The couple were at Croome again a year later,[6] and Sheridan obviously spent the weeks after his return home working at full pressure on his comedy.

He took the completed drafts to Harris when the theatrical season was well under way but though the piece was 'at least double the length of any acting comedy', Harris was impressed by it and advised Sheridan on how to improve it for performance.[7] In the last days of the year, the *London Chronicle* noted that 'the comedy of *The Rivals* is expected to be brought out at this house [Covent Garden] in the course of a fortnight'.[8] It seems to have been talked about with interest, and on 13 January 1775 David Garrick wrote to a friend to say, 'Sheridan's Comedy has rais'd great Expectation in the Publick.'[9] Just before it was acted, it was 'deemed the *ne plus ultra* of Comedy' in the Covent Garden green room.[10]

[1] *Letters*, i. 78.
[2] R. C. Rhodes, 'The Text of Sheridan', *T.L.S.*, 19 Dec. 1929, p. 1082.
[3] *Letters*, ii. 251.
[4] Ibid. i. 85.
[5] *Worcester Journal*, 19 Aug., 16 Sept. 1773; Add. MS. 35118, f. 13.
[6] 'During the summer of 1774, they passed some time at Mr. Canning's and Lord Coventry's' (Moore, i. 121).
[7] See p. 70 below.
[8] 29–31 Dec. 1774.
[9] *Garrick Letters*, iii. 985.
[10] *Morning Chronicle*, 19 Jan. 1775; cf. Rae, p. xx.

Joyful anticipation of success suddenly gave way to uneasy feelings. On 17 January, the day of the first production, *The Gazetteer* stated: 'It having been reported, that the story of the new comedy of The Rivals was not a fictitious one, we have authority to assert, that such a report is entirely void of foundation, and that there is not the slightest local or personal allusion whatever throughout the piece.' *The Town and Country Magazine* explained this rather fully:

It was believed by the friends of the author that it would meet with opposition from a certain quarter, as it was thought by many to have a close connexion with a certain affair at Bath, in which the celebrated Miss Linley (now Mrs. Sheridan) was the subject of rivalship; but in this respect they appear to have been mistaken, as no comedy that we recollect has met with fairer play. After a pretty warm contest towards the end of the last act, it was suffered to be given out for the ensuing night.[1]

Sheridan and his friends do not appear to have been entirely mistaken, however, for 'Mr. B——d' was rebuked by 'A Librarian' in the *Morning Post*[2] for his attempt to 'create a prejudice against the performance, by every mode that malevolence could suggest'. 'B——d' was probably William Barnett (also called 'Barnard'), who had been Thomas Mathews's second in the duel with Sheridan in July 1772 and the compiler of an 'exact narrative' of what had occurred.[3] Possibly he and his Bath associates feared ridicule, and Sheridan may have been referring to them when he wrote that 'some part of the attack on the Piece was begun too early to pass for the sentence of *Judgment*',[4] though hissing may also have come from jealous authors like the one who complained that this literary cadet had had the luck to get promoted over the heads of veteran officers, who had 'done the state some service'.[5]

Whatever dissatisfaction the cliques may have stirred up, Sheridan recognized that there was some justice in the general disapproval of certain elements in the comedy. He wrote: 'If I felt any emotion of surprise at the disapprobation, it was not that they were disapproved of, but that I had not before perceived that they deserved it.'[6] The play was much too long and unwieldy. It contained many bad puns and indelicate allusions.[7] The characterization of Sir Lucius offended Irishmen, and that of Mrs. Malaprop irritated members of the audience who wished to study 'faithful copies from nature'. Lee, as Sir Lucius, was badly miscast, and Shuter, as Sir Anthony, was far from word-perfect.[8]

[1] vii (1775), 42.

[2] 20 Jan. 1775.

[3] See *Letters*, i. 30, 34, 73–6.

[4] See p. 70.

[5] *The London Review*, Feb. 1775, p. 141 n.

[6] See p. 70 below.

[7] 'Salivation', for instance (in p. 135, l. 36), is changed to 'simulation' later, probably because of its connection with the mercury cure of venereal disease.

[8] See Purdy, pp. xiv–xviii.

Sheridan claimed afterwards that he knew the comedy was too long, but hoped to revise it after seeing the first performance.[1] If this were deliberate policy (for it undoubtedly described his later attitude to his plays), he really gambled on his future. Yet he admitted that the withdrawing of a piece to remove imperfections had not happened before.[2] His good fortune was shown in the words of Sir Joshua Reynolds's nephew: 'it is a play that has but just escap'd [damning], tho' some people admire it'.[3] What was important was that Harris admired it and was eager to encourage the young dramatist. The play that had read so well in the green room must be made more suitable for the stage.

In the next ten days Sheridan revised it, indicating that he had taken the many criticisms to heart. He tidied up the plot, made Sir Anthony a testy not lascivious old man, and turned Sir Lucius into an Irish man of honour.[4] He removed the *doubles entendres* and some of Mrs. Malaprop's more outrageous blunders. He cut the play considerably, and when it was put on again on 28 January, the *London Chronicle* remarked (with one minor qualification) that 'the cuttings have been everywhere judicious'. Clinch took Lee's place as Sir Lucius, and Shuter gave an inimitable performance as Sir Anthony. *The Rivals* took a place in the theatre's repertoire.

RECEPTION

The Comedy of THE RIVALS, performed last night for the first time on Covent-Garden stage, sufficiently speaks itself the production of a young author, who never attempted the drama. It is by no means destitute of merit, but that merit is greatly obscured by a number of disadvantageous circumstances which attend it, and which are evidently occasioned by the author's want of knowledge of the stage, and the artifices which are not only allowable but necessary in the construction of an acting play. The fable of THE RIVALS is ill-conducted and intricate; the sentiments are in many places too refined, and the humour occasionally borders upon ribaldry. The characters are not only larger than life, but are rather aukwardly placed. The diction is an odd mixture of the elegant and the absurd. Some of the scenes are written in a very masterly stile; others in a low, farcical kind of dialogue, more fit for a Bartholomew-fair droll than a comedy. THE RIVALS certainly has many faults; it nevertheless affords room for expectation, that when the author's judgment is matured, the town may see a good play of his writing. The Prologue, like that to the PLATONIC WIFE, of Mrs. Griffith, is two-part, and comes from two

[1] See p. 70 below.

[2] See p. 69 below.

[3] *Sir Joshua's Nephew* (ed. S. M. Radcliffe, 1930), p. 61.

[4] Who now has 'too much pride and delicacy to sacrifice the feelings of a gentleman to the necessities of his fortune' (I. ii: p. 88 below).

limbs of the law; but is neither so witty nor so laughable. The Epilogue is poetical and pertinent. The performers, for the most part, did THE RIVALS, strict justice. Mrs. Bulkeley (to use a Green-room hyperbole) spoke the Epilogue *like an Angel*! (*The London Packet*, 16–18 Jan. 1775.)

This Comedy was acted so imperfectly, either from the Timidity of the Actors on a first Night's Performance, or from an improper Distribution of the Parts, that it was generally disapproved: however, we do not pretend to say that the original Merit of the Piece was so great, that nothing but the bad Performance of it could possibly hurt it. The Author has by an Advertisement promised some necessary Alterations, which implies that he would [be] glad the Town would suspend their Judgement till a farther Hearing. We think it would be illiberal on this Submission and Address to the Public, to make any severe Remarks on the Fable or conduct of the Rivals.

We would recommend it to Mr. Lee to give up most Characters of Humour and Pleasantry that he may possibly be fond of, for he can very seldom make People laugh with him; and I should be very sorry to see him so much laughed at, as he was in this new Play. What the Devil Business can he have with the Part of a mere Irishman? (*St. James's Chronicle*, 17–19 Jan. 1775.)

The prologue delivered by Messrs. Lee and Quick, in the characters of a Serjeant at Law and an Attorney's Clerk, pleads in favour of the author, that he is a novice in the drama, and has never before been tried at the awful bar of the public. In consideration of that plea, and in tenderness to a young bard, who betrays not, as is sometimes the case, any unbecoming forwardness, but rather discovers an ingenuous diffidence of his abilities,—in respect to such a situation, we should rather wish to abate the edge of public censure, than to animadvert with severity on the lapses of an inexperienced writer, in the midst of whose very imperfections we may trace the man of genius, the gentleman and the scholar. His fable indeed is not happily chosen, nor skillfully conducted; nor are his characters faithfully copied from nature; but many parts of the dialogue, the graver scenes especially, are chaste and elegant; and the defects of the other parts of the drama do not appear to be the offspring of dullness or ignorance. A very little more acquaintance with the business of the stage would have instructed the author to curtail some of the scenes, which were last night insufferably tedious; and some of that stage art, much of which Cibber derived from his connection with the theatre, would have taught our juvenile poet to give more *effect* to the part of *Jack Absolute*, who is, in some sort, a second *Atall*, or *Double Gallant*. The romantic vein of *Lydia Languish* is not so well imagined, or so ably sustained as Steele's Lady (we forget her name) in the *Accomplished*

Fools; and the characters of Falkland and Julia are even beyond the pitch of *sentimental* comedy, and may be not improperly stiled *metaphysical*. We would wish however, to make a particular exception to the scene between them in the beginning of the fifth act, in which we are at a loss to determine whether the author or the actress (Mrs. Bulkeley) were most to be commended. What evil spirit could influence the writer and the managers to assign the part of *Sir Lucius O'Trigger* to *Mr. Lee* or Mr. Lee himself to receive it? One would imagine they had intended, in Mr. Lee's person, to realize the unjust satire of Sir Charles Hanbury Williams on the whole Irish nation:

> '*But nature, who denied them* sense,
> *Has giv'n them legs and impudence,*
> *Which beats all* understanding.'[1]

This representation of Sir Lucius is indeed an affront to the common sense of an audience, and is so far from giving the manners of our brave and worthy neighbours, that it scarce equals the picture of a *respectable* Hotentot; gabbling in an uncouth dialect, neither Welch, English, nor Irish. Shuter was pleasant, but, as usual, shamefully imperfect. Woodward has often appeared to more advantage. Mr. Lewis struggled with a very difficult character, and acquitted himself creditably. Quick's character betrayed him into farce; and Lee-Lewes, and Dunstall, exhibited their accustomed pert valet and country bumpkin. The ladies, Mrs. Bulkeley especially, did great justice to their parts and we want words to express the satisfaction the last-mentioned lady gave by her just and elegant manner of speaking one of the most excellent and poetical Epilogues we ever remember to have heard. The scenes and dresses were many of them new, but we think we remember a better view of the North Parade at Bath in a play of Dr. Kenrick's exhibition some years ago at Drury Lane Theatre. (*Morning Chronicle*, 18 Jan. 1775.)

By the Prologue, our curiosity respecting the author of this piece is happily satisfied; for we are told 'that he is a STUDENT, who finding Coke, Littleton, Plowden, Blackstone, and other law writers, afford but dull amusement, hath commenced Poet, to grace his brow with a sprig of bay from Mount Parnassus'.

Whatever of candour there may be in this declaration, it favours but little of judgment. The Author of a new Play should industriously conceal himself until the success of his Piece be known; a precipitate disclosure may bespeak our pity, but neither can [n]or ought to spare the Writer from the animadversions of Criticism.

The 'Rivals', as a Comedy, requires much castigation, and the pruning

[1] 'Nature, indeed, denies them sense | But gives them legs and impudence | That beats all understanding.' (Sir Charles Hanbury Williams, *Works* (1822), i. 93.)

hand of judgment, before it ever can pass on the Town as even a tolerable Piece. In language it is defective to an extreme, in Plot outré, and one of the Characters is an absolute exotic in the wilds of nature.

The author seems to have considered puns, witticisms, similes and metaphors, as admirable substitutes for polished diction; hence they abound in every sentence; and hence it is that instead of the 'METAMORPHOSIS' of Ovid, one of the characters is made to talk of Ovid's 'MEAT-FOR-HOPES'; a Lady is called the 'PINE APPLE of beauty'; the Gentleman in return 'an ORANGE of perfection'. A Lover describes the sudden change of disposition in his mistress by saying, that 'she flies off in a TANGENT born down by the CURRENT of disdain;' and a second Tony Lumpkin, to describe how fast he rode, compares himself to a 'COMET with a TAIL of DUST at his heels'.

These are shameful absurdities in language, which can suit no character how widely soever it may depart from common life and common manners.

Whilst thus censure is freely passed, not to say that there are various sentiments in the Piece which demonstrate the Author's soul no stranger to the finer feelings, would be shameful partiality.

Time will not permit a thorough investigation of this Comedy; but if the 'RIVALS' rests its claim to public favour, solely on the basis of merit, the hisses of the auditors on the first night of representation, give reason to suspect a most fatal disappointment. However, that it may be SUFFERED to have the usual nine nights run, is what, on the Author's account, we most sincerely wish; but this we can assure him, that if the dulness of Law-writers have made him YAWN, the dulness of the 'RIVALS' lulled several of the middle gallery spectators into a profound SLEEP.

The Prologue was delivered by Mr. Lee in the character of a Serjeant at Law who received the Author's brief to plead his cause before the Jury of Spectators.

The Epilogue was spoken by Mrs. Bulkeley.

Many of the parts were improperly cast. Mr. Lee is a most execrable Irishman, Miss Barsanti is calculated only for a Mimic; she has that archness of look and manner, that shrug of the shoulders, which must for ever unqualify her for genteel Comedy; and when she is represented as a girl of thirty thousand pounds fortune, we curse the blind Goddess for bestowing her favours so absurdly; then she has the agreeable LISP of THOMAS HULL, and cannot be expected to articulate her words so as to be understood, unless her tongue first undergoes a cutting. (*Public Ledger*, 18 Jan. 1775.)

This Comedy, said to be written by Mr. *Sherridan*, Jun. seems to be the hasty composition of a young man of more genius than present knowledge of the English drama; hence those defects in the main pillars, which are the only supports of a dramatic composition.

The fable is not the most natural or intelligible, nor have the characters any great claim to novelty.—Sir *Lucius O'Trigger* and Sir *Anthony Absolute*, indifferent as they are, were most barbarously handled by the inattention of the performers, neither of the two being perfect in one sentence of their parts: Shameful! that the fame of an author should thus be sported with by persons, to whom he is under the necessity of intrusting it; for to their conduct we attribute a part of the bad reception which attended the representation.

The dialogue, in many scenes, was natural and pleasing; in one or two, far superior to that of the modern race of comic writers; the situation between Capt. *Absolute* and Mrs. *Malaprop*, was well conceived and wrought up. We think the writer has here and there mistaken ribaldry for humour, at which the audience seemed displeased.—All the performers, the two already excepted, exerted themselves to the utmost.—A prologue by Mr. Lee, in the character of a Serjeant at Law, and Mr. Quick, as an Attorney, who brings the former a fee to plead for the bard, tho' novel, was not much relished. The epilogue, however, made amends; for it struck us, as one of the most harmonious, pretty pieces of the kind we have heard for some time. There were three new scenes upon the occasion, one of which, a perspective view through the south parade at Bath, to the late Mr. Allen's delightful villa, was universally admired. ('Scorpion'[1] in the *Morning Post*, 18 Jan. 1775.)

The Comedy of the RIVALS, at *Covent Garden*, is withdrawn for the present, to undergo some severe prunings, trimmings, and patchings, before its second performance: The Author, we are informed, seeing the general disapprobation with which it was received, was very desirous of withdrawing it entirely, but the managers would not consent to it, determined to stand the event of a second embarkation, let the consequences be what they may.

Two Gentlemen conversing on Tuesday evening together in the boxes, on the subject of the new Comedy at Covent-garden Theatre, the one remarked that he supposed they meant to cut it deeply, the other, a literary wag, immediately replied, they may *cut* I allow, but I'll be d——d if ever it *comes again*! (*Morning Post*, 19 Jan. 1775.)

If we examine this comedy by the rules of criticism, many objections may be made to it. Few of the characters are new, and scarce any well supported: those of Falkland and Miss Melville are the most *outré* sentimental ones that ever appeared upon the stage: the acts are long, in many parts uninteresting, and of course tedious. But the most reprehensible part is in many low quibbles and barbarous puns that

[1] Identified as Henry Bate, by Charles Harold Gray in *Theatrical Criticism in London to 1795* (New York, 1931), pp. 231–2.

disgrace the very name of comedy. Nevertheless there are some scenes lively, spirited, and entertaining; and if it were properly pruned by a competent judge of what is called *Jeu de théatre*, it might probably go down with less opposition. (*The Town and Country Magazine*, vii (1775), 43.)

There is certainly some evil genius attends the proceedings of Covent Garden Theatre. Our expectations have been some time raised with the hope that they were at last to produce us a truly good comedy; the hour of proof arrives, and we are presented with a piece got up with such flagrant inattention, that half the performers appear to know nothing of their parts, and the play itself is a *full hour* longer in the representation than any piece on the stage.—This last circumstance is an error of such a nature as shows either great obstinacy in the author, or excessive ignorance in the managers; but the casting Mr. Lee for the part of *Sir Lucius O'Trigger*, is a blunder of the first brogue, which Mr. Lee plainly shewed us he was not *Irishman* enough to have committed for himself. If there had been no one in the theatre fit for the part, it should have been taken out of the piece, which is full exuberant enough to spare it. As I find the further representation of it is put off for the present, I suppose this will be the case; for to attempt to continue him in the character will inevitably damn the play. There seemed to be a little malice from one corner of the gallery, which shewed itself too early to produce any effect; but it was absolutely impossible for the author's warmest well wishers to over-rule the disapprobation that was shewn to Lee's horrid medley of discordant brogues. The character of Faulkland[1] is touched with a delicate and masterly hand, yet Lewis was perfect enough to be at home in it: it is just such a part as Mr. Garrick twenty years ago would have marked among his first performances. There is as much true humour in *Acres* and *David* as in any character on the stage whatever. What the characters of *Sir Anthony* and *Sir Lucius* ought to have appeared I cannot take upon me to say, but Shuter, from being imperfect, appeared to ruin some scenes, which, from the situations, seemed to promise noble effects from his *Vis Comica*. The versification of the Prologue was sadly marred in the delivery, for we cannot suppose it to have been written by the Author of the Epilogue; which, after a vein of elegant humour, runs to the conclusion in some as beautiful lines as ever did credit to our language. ('A Friend to Comedy' in the *Morning Chronicle*, 20 Jan. 1775.)

[1] For the source of the character in Tamper (in Colman's *The Deuce is in Him*), Beverley (in Murphy's *All in the Wrong*), and Malvil (in Fielding's *Love in Several Masques*), see M. Gabriel and P. Mueschke, 'Two Contemporary Sources of Sheridan's *The Rivals*', *P.M.L.A.* xliii (1928), 237–50; and T. Bloch, 'The Antecedents of Sheridan's Faulkland', *P.Q.* xlix (1970), 266–7.

Mr. Editor, I am the last man in the world who would step forth to upbraid a degraded poet, but when I find a performer is execrated by the wretched puffs of the author's friends, in order to throw the principal part of the odium from his own shoulders on those of the player, I own I cannot help taking fire. I shall be acknowledged no partizan, either of Mr. *Lee* or Mr. *Shuter*, when I confess their performance was in every way reprehensible, nay shocking—but at the same time I will aver, that neither of them were invested with anything like a *character*: *Sir Lucius O'Trigger* was so ungenerous an attack upon a nation, that must justify any severity with which the piece will hereafter be treated: it is the first time I ever remember to have seen so villainous a portrait of an Irish Gentleman, permitted so openly to insult the country upon the boards of an English theatre. For the rest of the piece, the author has my pity; but for this unjustifiable attack, my warmest resentment. ('A Briton' in the *Morning Post*, 21 Jan. 1775.)

Covent-garden Theatre. The new comedy of The Rivals has been delayed, in order to give time for another performer to study the character, which was undertaken by Mr. Lee, at the particular request of the Author: the play will be performed, for the second time, on Saturday next, with alterations. (*The Gazetteer*, 24 Jan. 1775.)

. . . Character itself is now almost extinct among us; a frivolous French sameness infects our manners; can we blame an author for drawing us as we are, when the least stretch of his fancy is called caricature? Sir Antony Absolute is a very amusing one, if justly represented; and almost every genteel family now presents us a Lydia Languish. Falkland is a great proof of heart-felt delicacy; he is a beautiful exotic, and tho' not found in every garden, we cannot deny it may in some; the exquisite refinement in his disposition, opposed to the noble simplicity, tenderness, and candor of Julia's, give rise to some of the most affecting sentimental scenes I ever remember to have met with. The general applause of the audience was proof enough of the merit of those scenes. . . .

The story opens with ease and clearness, the first and second acts pass with spirit, but the third and fourth grow somewhat complicated, and appear heavy, because uncommonly long; some of the incidents are scarcely within the bounds of probability, but when I remember how many of our best poets have been guilty of the same fault, it appears very pardonable in the first attempt of so young a man. In a word, with some faults it has many beauties and is in my mind very preferable to that dull mediocrity which so often escapes censure, and sometimes obtains praise; nor do I doubt, when properly abbreviated, but it will give the same pleasure to many auditors it did to me.

I cannot conclude without making a few observations about the actors, of whom I must in general say they did their utmost, excepting one whose name I from motives of tenderness forbear to mention; but he has so often offended us by the abuse of his talents, that I am amazed an author dares trust a part of any consequence to him; and, whenever utterly deficient in the words, he has a custom as odious as improper, of filling up the chasm with numberless *oaths*: he ought to be cautious; the English are not sudden, but strong in their resentments, and if he persists in such scandalous negligence of his duty, he may one day experience it. Mr. Sheridan's power of persuasion will surely be very serviceable to him at the bar, when it could prevail on two actors of experience to trifle with their reputations in accepting improper parts; Mr. Woodward is certainly a very confined actor, and altho' he acquitted himself with ease in Absolute, he neither looked the young, gay, handsome Officer, likely to captivate a romantic girl, nor could assume that enthusiasm in his flights of conversation with her absolutely necessary to deceive her; and Lydia, if not very dull, would be apt to think he was ridiculing her. Mr. Lee was wrong too, but did not meet with the same allowance, though perhaps more excusable, as he looked the Irish Baronet very well; but he should have known, though we can pardon Irish tragedians for throwing, when disconcerted, into their parts a touch of *their* natural dialect, gentlemen of that nation would not excuse his giving them a touch of *his* natural dialect, although in the same situation. Mr. Lewis was gentlemanlike, animated and easy: the evident attention this young performer pays to every part, entitles him to more commendation than he generally meets with, and his character was so difficult and delicate, that, to do it tolerably the first night, required judgment and talents; he may hereafter appear more advantageously, if with Julia he is less precipitate and more tender—Mrs. Green was in his situation, and has the same claim to distinction; she supported her character with as much ease and spirit as if familiarised to it; in that very well-conceived and executed scene where she talks of Captain Absolute to himself under the name of Beverley, she was so excellent in both her laughter and speaking, that I almost forgot she was acting. Miss Barsanti was easy and agreeable, but rather cold in her quarrel with her lover and descriptions to her friend; a young actress claims great indulgence on a first night, and I only mean by this observation to advise her against the next representation of the comedy. Mrs. Bulkeley deserved, and met with, applause in the theatre, and praise out of it; yet there is a certain stiffness in her air, and formality in her pronunciation, which appears studied, and lessens, particularly in the character of Julia, that amiable frankness which renders it so engaging; if she speaks the part as easily as the epilogue, she will always find me among the warmest admirers.—Of that epilogue I shall only say it might have saved even a wretched piece; the versification was as soft and elegant as the thoughts were poetical,—it mingled the simplicity of nature with the utmost refinement of fancy and taste; as the happy description of an universal passion, it suits all times and degrees, and will be repeated with pleasure as a poem, when those composed on local or temporary subjects are as much forgotten as most of our past ones. ('One of the Pit' in the *Morning Chronicle*, 27 Jan. 1775.)

On Saturday evening last, Mr. Sheridan's comedy of *The Rivals* was performed, for the second time with additions and alterations, at the theatre-royal, Covent-Garden. Its present state is widely different from that in which we found it on the first night's representation. Sir *Lucius O'Trigger* being retouched, has now the appearance of a character; and his assigning Beverley's reflection on his country as the grounds for his desire to quarrel with him is a reasonable pretence, and wipes off the former stigma undeservedly thrown on the sister kingdom:—it is due to the merit of Mr. *Clinch* to say, he did the strictest justice to the part, and from his ease in this character we soon expect to see him fill more capital walks in genteel comedy with credit to himself, and pleasure to his audience. . . .

An alteration of a principal incident, gave a very favourable turn to the fable and the whole piece, viz. that where young *Acres* now delivers his challenge to his friend *Absolute*, begging him to carry it to his rival *Beverly*, not knowing the two characters composed but one man; its being at first given to Sir *Lucius*, the person who indited it, was highly inconsistent.—The cuttings have been everywhere judicious, except where they have deprived *Lydia* of that comic and picturesque description of her lover, standing like a *dripping-statue* in the garden etc.—The hiss that occasioned this cut, was that of party or ignorance, not of judgment.—We think the play still too long, and would recommend the total deprivation of the scene, where J. *Absolute* meets his father upon the parade, as he goes out to fight; it being an evident obstruction to the business, and that to answer no purpose whatever.

The performers were very attentive to the discharge of their duty; and though honest *Ned Shuter* was unfortunately reprehensible the first night, he has now wiped off the odium, and charmed as much as he had before displeased.—Mrs. Bulkley, though struggling with a violent cold, was excellent in the character of *Julia*. Upon the whole, if we could once bring ourselves to be reconciled to the extraordinary circumstance of Ensign *Beverley's* loosing the affections of a woman who doated upon him, merely because she found him a Captain and a man of family and fortune, we should be induced from many evident traits of literary genius to pronounce the *Rivals*, a good comedy. ('S*******' [?'Scorpion'] in the *Morning Post*, 30 Jan. 1775.)

We heartily wish it was the general custom for authors to withdraw their pieces after a first performance, in order to remove the objectionable passages, heighten the favourite characters, and generally amend the play. The author of THE RIVALS has made good use of his time; his comedy is altered much for the better since it was first acted. The cast of it is improved, and all the performers are now perfect, and better acquainted with their several parts. It comes within a reasonable compass as to the time taken up in representation, and the sentiments thrown into the mouth of Sir Lucius O'Trigger produce a good effect, at the same time that they take away every possible idea of the character's being designed as an insult on our neighbours on the other side of St. George's channel. In the room of the objectionable and heavy scenes which are cut out, two new ones of a very different turn are introduced, and we remarked more than one judicious alteration in the prologue. THE RIVALS will now stand its ground; and although we cannot pronounce it, with all its amendments, a comic *chef d'œuvre*, it certainly encourages us to hope for a very capital play from the same writer at a future season; he therefore, from motives of candour and encouragement, is entitled to the patronage and favour of a generous public. (*Morning Chronicle*, 30 Jan. 1775.)

Mr. Garrick was at the play of the *Rivals* last Saturday, and was very attentive; he told a gentleman who sat next to him, and a friend to the author, 'I see this play will creep;' the gentleman made no answer but at the end of the play (after repeated peals of approbation) he told him, 'I see this play will run.' (*Morning Post*, 31 Jan. 1775.)

The just ideas of Comedy, which *The Rivals* impressed me with the first night of its performance, notwithstanding the extraordinary *length* of some of the scenes, and the *short* memories of some of the actors, induced me last Saturday to see it once more in its amended state. This second exhibition has convinced me of two circumstances which I much insisted on the first night, which was, that the author had talents which a greater maturation would make very useful on the stage, and that the part of Sir *Lucius O'Trigger* (which to make use of a bad pun, *missed fire* in the hands of Mr. Lee) was far from being an ill written character. I had many critical opponents to both these opinions, but the applause which this comedy met with last Saturday, confirmed me I was right in both. *The Rivals*, as it is now played, possesses, in general, much characteristical dialogue, and no inconsiderable share of the *Vis Comica*. Mr. Lee (who in another line is a very respectable actor) was on the first night so obviously embarrassed in the part of Sir Lucius O'Trigger, that it was rather difficult to define the character. Mr. Clinch has very fortunately brought it more to sight, and by a very gentlemanly brogue, and naiveté of manner, made Sir Lucius so agreeable to the audience, that the part is likely to be as fortunate to him as that of Major O'Flaherty was to Mr. Moody. The performers in general did great justice to their parts, and seemed to join with the audience in exerting themselves in the interest of a young author, who has shewn abilities as a writer, and a very becoming deference to the public.[1] ('Impartial' in the *London Evening Post*, 31 Jan.–2 Feb. 1775.)

The literary plunderers, and sentimental blockheads, so much admired by the gaping multitude of our century, were not a little disappointed at the success of Mr. Sheridan. The first night of performing his Comedy, they took particular care to station the serpents of envy in every corner of the house, in order to nip the young adventurer in the bud; but Mr. Sheridan, Hercules-like, even *in the cradle of genius*, tore the serpents asunder by the vigour of his mind, and baulked the cankered malice of his foes. (*Morning Post*, 31 Jan. 1775.)

. . . We have been to see the new comedy of young Sheridan, 'The Rivals'. It was very unfavourably received the first night, and he had the prudence to prevent a total defeat, by withdrawing it, and making great and various improvements; the event has been successful, for it is now *better* though not *very* much liked. For my own part, I think he ought to be treated with great indulgence: much is to be forgiven in an author of three and twenty, whose genius is likely to be his principal inheritance. I love him for the sake of his amiable and ingenious mother. On the whole I was tolerably entertained. (Hannah More to Mrs. Gwatkin, *c.* 31 Jan. 1775, in W. Roberts, *Memoirs and Correspondence of Hannah More* (2nd ed., 1834), i. 38–9.)

Mr. Cholmondeley presents his Compliments to Mr. Sheridan and is much obliged to him for the play he was so good as to send him yesterday.

The voice of so inconsiderable a critic can at no time be of much consequence, but when it concerns a work so universally esteemed as The Rivals must be totally lost in the general clamour of applause. He is conscious how little his praise can add to Mr. Sheridan's satisfaction, yet the great entertainment he received from reading his play forces him to trouble Mr. Sheridan with this assurance of his approbation. Begs his best respects to Mrs. Sheridan. (Harvard MS.)[2]

[1] Cf. '*Aristarchus*' in the *Morning Chronicle*, 2 Feb. 1775: reprinted in *Letters*, iii. 292–3, with the suggestion, that 'Aristarchus' may have been Sheridan himself. He, too, praises his 'acquiescence to the taste of the public'.

[2] Addressed to 'Sheridan Esqre/Orchard Street/Portman Square': Sheridan lived there from Feb. 1774 to Oct. 1776. Possibly the letter belongs to Feb. 1775, soon after the publication of the first edition of *The Rivals*, but it could refer to the third edition, published later.

The Comedy of the *Rivals* was performed at this[1] theatre for the first time last night, and, what is rarely the case, was in general far better represented than at the other house, where it was brought out.—The part of Sir *Anthony Absolute* is calculated for Mr. King, and therefore it was no wonder it sat so easily upon him.—Mr. Palmer played Capt. *Absolute* with great spirit and propriety.—Mr. Reddish never appeared to more advantage in comedy than in the character of *Faulkland*, particularly in the second act with Captain *Absolute* and *Acres*; the last of which was represented by Mr. Dodd, who would have done more justice to the part and himself, had he not been quite so vociferous:—his frock had buttons upon it as large as common sized saucers, the droll appearance of which threw the house into repeated bursts of clapping and laughter that lasted several minutes. Mr. Moody *O'Flahertized*[2] Sir *Lucius O'Trigger* very laughably.—Mrs. Hopkins and Mrs. Baddeley were very decent in Mrs. *Malaprop* and *Julia*, and Mrs. Abington easy and elegant in *Lydia Languish*, especially in the last act.

There were no material alterations in the piece, except the restoration of a good scene between Sir *Anthony* and his son, upon the discovery of the sword in the last act, which tho' generally left out at Covent-garden theatre, was here introduced last night with very good effect. The beautiful epilogue was well spoken by Mrs. Abington, and highly relished by a very numerous and brilliant audience. If we may judge from the great applause it met with last night, the *Rivals* will rise in the list of modern comedies now upon the stage. (*Morning Post*, 17 Jan. 1777.)

This play is the first effort of the acting manager's Muse; it was originally brought out at Covent-Garden two seasons ago; where, though some of the characters were exceedingly well played, others were as feebly, and *one* in particular miserably represented. It is to this then we are to account for its not having a greater run on that theatre, as it certainly has a considerable share of merit; and though not the *best first piece that ever was produced* (whilst the *Old Bachelor*, and some others, are upon the list of our stock plays) yet it possesses a sufficient share of merit to announce the *poetical manhood* of its *parent*.

The attention which was shewn in the disposition of the parts, answered every expectation. Mr. King's Sir Anthony Absolute was much in his walk; as were those characters played by Messrs. Parsons, Baddeley, Reddish, Palmer, and Moody.—Mr. Dodd's dress might be *literally* said to have *emblazoned* his part; he appeared in a brown maccaroni coat, set off (to use a phrase of Sir Lucius O'Trigger)[3] with a *full side-board of plate buttons*, which exhibiting a very *pointed*, though *silent* critique on the ridiculous rage for *large buttons*, brought on universal

[1] Drury Lane. [2] O'Flaherty is in Cumberland's *The West Indian* (1771).
[3] This was presumably an improvisation at the Drury Lane performance.

and repeated bursts of applause. The Ladies were equally respectable in their several characters. Mrs. Hopkins, though inferior to so celebrated an actress as Mrs. Green, was a very natural Mrs. Malaprop, and shewed *more* than endeavours to please, in the laughing scene with Capt. Absolute. Mrs. Baddeley, in Julia, was tender and affecting; whilst the visionary, romantic Lydia Languish (although little more than a dramatic sketch) received every embellishment from Mrs. Abington's comic powers. (*London Evening Post*, 16–18 Jan. 1777.)

The *Rivals* has had the least success and yet it is the most original of all his pieces. It was nearly damned on the first night, and Mr. Sheridan—profiting by the experience with which its reception furnished him—withdrew it with this remark, 'I have now got the *last*, and it shall be my fault if I don't make the shoe to fit next time.' His labour however being only cobler's work, it required too much of method for his volatile genius to buckle to, and we may venture to pronounce, without any great outrage on probability, that had not Mr. Sheridan so much influence in the *theatre*, *The Rivals* would never have made its appearance a *second season*. It is a neat, well written piece, but has that sort of cold correctness which will not go to the galleries. The incident, from *The Nut-brown Maid*, though written with great sweetness and delicacy, is no more proper for the *theatre* than the fine strokes of a miniature painter would be in the finishing of flats and wings. (*The Musical Tour of Mr. Dibdin* (Sheffield, 1778), p. 259.)

The fine written and delightful Play of the Rivals, has been translated for the CZARINA. (*The World*, 28 Apr. 1790.)

This favourite Play can want but few words to be said about it—every body knows the successful skill of the Dialogue and chief Characters; both of them charming with surprises equal, if it can be, to the SCHOOL FOR SCANDAL!—beyond that, praise cannot go. (*The World*, 4 May 1790.)

The plot of this play is busy, and the author has managed it with great dexterity to the very denou[e]ment of the piece; but the characters are injudiciously drawn; for the contradictions in that of Fa[u]lkland are beyond nature; and though every allowance may be made for the opposite effects of love and jealousy, still the colouring is too high, and consequently the lover's part rendered paradoxical.—Lydia Languish is equally imperfect—she is unnaturally romantic.—Mrs. Malaprop the same—it is not to be supposed that a woman who could make use of such language as she does, could misapply her words.—The most finished characters are Acres and Sir Anthony Absolute.—The first part of the last act is borrowed from Prior's Henry and Emma. Upon the whole, we think this piece contains more of the *broad farce* than the *genteel comedy*; and were it curtail'd, would doubtless answer the purpose of the former. (*The Thespian Magazine and Literary Repository*, i (1792), 16).

[On the first night] the play was so intolerably long, and so decidedly opposed in its composition to the taste of the day, as to draw down a degree of censure, which convinced me, on quitting the house, that it would never succeed. It must be remembered that this was the English 'age of sentiment', and that Hugh Kelly and Cumberland had flooded the Stage with moral poems under the title of Comedies, which took their views of life from the drawing-room exclusively, and coloured their characters with a nauseous French affectation. 'The Rivals', in my opinion, was a decided attempt to overthrow this taste, and to follow up the blow which Goldsmith had given in 'She Stoops to Conquer'. My recollection of the manner in which the former was received, bears me out in the supposition. The audience on this occasion were composed of two parties—those who supported the prevailing taste, and those who were indifferent to it and liked nature. On the first night of a new play, it was very natural that the former should predominate;—and what was the consequence? why that Faulkland and Julia (which Sheridan had obviously introduced to conciliate the sentimentalists, but which in the present day are considered heavy incumbrances,) were the characters which were most favourably received; whilst Sir Anthony, Acres and Lydia, those faithful and diversified pictures of life, were barely tolerated; and Mrs. Malaprop (as she deserved to be) was singled out for peculiar vengeance. To this character alone must be attributed the partial failure of the play.—Sheridan intended it perhaps as a burlesque upon the life which Faulkland and Julia represented—but he did it so grossly, as to defeat the end proposed. His want of judgment, in this respect, was remarkable as his want of policy. That was a time in which there was not a greater straining for the proprieties of language, than the proprieties of character—the error of that taste was the considering the Stage an arena only for the exhibition of high and refined characters. But Mrs. Malaprop was denounced as a rank offence against all probability (which in dramatic life is possibility)—as a thing without parallel in society—a monstrous absurdity which had originated with the author. Thus Sheridan's weapon was effectually turned against himself. The critics desired no better hand than he afforded them: and in my humble opinion, their censure was highly judicious. . . .

Again, nothing can be more unfounded than the reason which is commonly assigned for the first night's failure of the play; namely, the acting of a Mr. Lee in Sir Lucius O'Trigger. I remember his acting very well; it was very indifferent, particularly to the audience, who cared as little about Sir Lucius as did Lydia; it was his juxta-position with Mrs.

Malaprop that brought him into notice—her disease was infectious, and contaminated all that came into her society. The other characters were better drawn than his, and had the advantage of being supported by established favourites; but under any other circumstances, I will be bold to say, Mr. Lee's acting would have passed muster. It was therefore not less false than ungenerous in Sheridan (who originated this excuse) to transfer to the back of an unfortunate actor, a fault which was inherent to his own composition.

On the acting of the night (seen under so much disadvantage), that which made the greatest impression on me was Shuter's in 'Sir Anthony',—the character fitted him like his clothes; all the others I have seen better performed since. Lewis was not at home in Faulkland; a serious sentiment was never upon friendly terms with his lips. Woodward would have played Acres better than the Captain, though not better than Quick; John Bannister's has been the best of any; but Shuter was inimitable in the full and racy humour which so peculiarly characterised the acting of the 'Old School'. . . . (John Bernard, *Retrospections of the Stage* (1830), i. 142–6.)

CHOICE OF TEXT

Sheridan did not leave behind him a finally corrected version of *The Rivals*. He was reported, in 1788, to be going to alter the play 'in some of the Scenes' for the private theatricals at Richmond House but, as usual, put off doing so.[1] Then it was proposed that the play should be revived at Drury Lane Theatre so that Mrs. Jordan could make her first appearance there in the part of Lydia Languish. Mrs. Sheridan commented on the matter in a letter to her husband: 'I am very glad the Rivals is to be got up at D. Lane, I dare say it will bring very good Houses especially if we alter Lydia Languish for Mrs. Jordan—is that to be done, or how? —but I can't bear you sh[oul]d be wasting your time, and your pretty thoughts, on foolish Epilogues for them, when, if you are to write, you ought to write something that w[oul]d be of real Service to yourself.'[2] Her words indicate the usual problem of getting Sheridan to concentrate on work of this kind when he was so much more willing to give his 'pretty thoughts' to oratory or occasional verse. Yet when the play was given at Drury Lane on 14 April 1790, it met with such a splendid reception as to deceive onlookers into thinking it had been revised again. *The World* declared: 'Some scenes appeared with such increased magic, that they must have been retouched. The improved effect could not have been from

[1] 'The alteration coming from Mr. Sheridan—is not yet come' (*The World*, 14 Feb. 1788). Fifteen days later, the same newspaper noted: 'Mr. Sheridan's alteration of the Rivals, will scarcely come in time for the present year.'

[2] W.T. But Rae, *Sheridan*, ii. 130, prints '. . . if you alter. . . .'

long absence only.'[1] Three days later it printed a correction: '*The Rivals*, we find, has not been altered. The improved effect of this very clever and delightful play, is merely from the improved manner of representing it.'[2]

He watched the comedy at the Marquess of Abercorn's house party at Christmas, 1805, when it was acted in such a way as 'even to satisfy Mr. Sheridan who was forced to laugh at all his own jokes and applaud all his own sentiments'.[3] He was also reported to have grown ashamed of it: he 'always said the "Rivals" was one of the worst plays in the language, and he would give anything he had not written it'.[4] Perhaps this feeling belonged to his later years, when his dislike of the farcical and of punning was so marked.

He omitted *The Rivals* from the plays 'he had put his name to' and we may find good reason for his doing so. It happens to be literally true of the first and second editions, where the author's name does not appear on the title page. The third edition bears the words 'By Richard Brinsley Sheridan, Esquire', phrasing that is surely the work of someone else. Probably too he felt that the comedy was still in need of revision. On his deathbed he told Chateauneuf that he had spent three years correcting it.[5] The actual sentence is given in French: 'J'ai moi-même employé trois années à la corriger.' French is less subtle than English in its use of this tense, and it is difficult to know whether the translation is 'I spent' or 'I have spent'. It may be argued that were the first intended, Sheridan would have been referring to the early years of composition between 1773 and 1775. If the sense was 'I have spent', then presumably the allusion is to the period 1814–16, when he may have tinkered a little with the plays. Whatever the truth of this is, no late corrections in Sheridan's hand have been found in a copy of *The Rivals*. Any discussion concerning his final intentions must turn upon the first and third editions, because they are the only ones that seem to possess authority.[6]

It has been interestingly argued that some abbreviated acting versions, from Mrs. Inchbald's onwards, show Sheridan at work as editor.[7] For

[1] *The World*, 19 Apr. 1790. It had not been performed at Drury Lane since 2 May 1781, but it was, of course, a Covent Garden play.

[2] No fewer than seven leading performers acted the following parts for the first time in London: Mrs. Jordan as Lydia, Miss Farren (Julia), J. P. Kemble (Faulkland), Wroughton (Jack), Bannister, junior (Sir Anthony), Moody (Sir Lucius), and Dodd (Acres). After this date, it was given each season at Drury Lane.

[3] *Hary-O* (ed. Sir. G. Leveson Gower and Iris Palmer, 1940), p. 140. Cf. *Letters*, ii. 250–1.

[4] Moore, *Journal*, ii. 335: Lady Cork to Moore, 4 July 1819.

[5] A. Chateauneuf, *Infidélité conjugale ou École de Médisance* (Paris, 1834), p. [5]. Cf. *Letters*, iii. 248.

[6] The Larpent MS. must be regarded only as an interesting earlier version.

[7] F. W. Bateson, 'The Text of Sheridan', *T.L.S.*, 28 Nov. 1929, p. 998. Mr. Bateson refers to Mrs. Inchbald's edition (1808), Thomas Dibdin's in *The London Theatre* (1814), Oxberry's in *The New English Drama* (1818), Dolby's in *British Theatre* (1823):

several reasons, I doubt this. An unnoticed receipt in the records of Longman, the bookseller, is from George Wilkie and is dated 4 January 1809: it acknowledges payment of twenty-one pounds and the gift of a fine paper copy of Mrs. Inchbald's *British Theatre* (twenty-five volumes in quires) in return for 'the right of printing the Comedy of the Rivals in the said work'.[1] Publishers and editors are named, but there is no mention of any part played by Sheridan in the transaction, nor do the cuts and corrections seem to me to be typical of his methods. The thirteen lines omitted from the Fag/Thomas conversation (I. i), and the shortening of Faulkland's speeches could be dictated by theatrical considerations[2] only, and made by the prompter. The deletion of swearing and of Jack Absolute's more cynical remarks may represent the new propriety in general or Mrs. Inchbald's religious scruples.[3] I accept R. L. Purdy's case for believing that Sheridan 'had very little part in these later stage versions', and that no text now available prints *The Rivals* as Sheridan intended it to be acted.[4] J. P. Kemble's note on Julia's lines ('No, Lydia, he is too proud, too noble to be jealous. . . .')[5] seems quite as significant as Purdy suggests it is: 'The Ladies cut this Speech very often in a very improper Manner as it is necessary for the explanation of Faulkland's Character. The Speech so cut fell by accident into the Author's hands who wrote under it "The only Speech in the Play that cannot be admitted!—The Pruning Knife! Damme, the Axe, the Hatchet!" '[6] Sheridan's laughing contempt for the intelligence of his actresses is plain, and so too is the fact that he had to put up with the hacking of his text because he made no later effort to prepare stage versions himself. His 'pretty thoughts' were often available to readers only.

Let us now examine the texts that possess authority:

I. OF THE PROLOGUES

The original prologue, in Sheridan's hand, is in the Amelia Edwards collection at Somerville College, Oxford. It has been printed elsewhere in full and with comment.[7]

'. . . there are a few differences between these editions; but the differences are explicable and do not affect the certainty that they must all derive from a single well-defined text. The proposition I am advancing is that this text represents Sheridan's third and final revision of *The Rivals*, and should in future take the place of the edition of 1776 as the *textus receptus*.'

[1] Information given to me by Cyprian Blagden, in a letter dated 24 Feb. 1960.

[2] Like the omission of the eighteen lines on the songs Julia may have sung (II. i). The titles had long lost any topicality by Mrs. Inchbald's day.

[3] Suggested in the deletion of Jack Absolute's thirteen lines (III. iii) on the theme, 'Love shall be our idol.'

[4] Purdy, p. li.

[5] I. ii.

[6] Purdy, p. li, quoting from a Garrick Club MS. Another prompt copy, once owned by J. P. Kemble, is in the Huntington Library (298350): see p. 58 n. 5.

[7] C. Price, 'The First Prologue to *The Rivals*', *R.E.S.*, N.S. XX (1969), 192–5.

A revised version, spoken on the second night (28 Jan.), is not available in holograph manuscript, but was printed in the first edition (1775) of the play.

The 'Prologue by the Author. Spoken on the Tenth Night'[1] (i.e. 15 Feb. 1775) is not extant in the author's manuscript, but was printed in the third edition (1776) of the comedy.

2. OF THE EPILOGUE

No holograph version is available. The epilogue was recited at the first performance on 17 January, was much admired,[2] and was printed in the first edition (1775) of the play.

3. OF THE PLAY

When Thomas Moore worked through Sheridan's manuscripts, he found no trace of the play,[3] and no holograph version has yet come to light. In default of an original manuscript, the following texts assume great importance:

(i) *The Lord Chamberlain's Copy*

In a letter dated 9 January 1775, Thomas Harris applied for permission to present the play, and enclosed a copy of the text for examination. It is now Larpent MS. 383 in the Huntington Library,[4] and is in the neat hand of a Covent Garden Theatre copyist. For a collation, see Purdy, p. xxvi. Purdy prints the text in parallel columns with that of the first edition, and provides a valuable introduction.

(ii) *First Edition*[5]

John Wilkie, the bookseller, bought the copyright of the play. An unnoted remark by Wilkie's son, made many years later, is of much

[1] See R. C. Rhodes, *Harlequin Sheridan* (Oxford, 1933), p. 64, for the suggestion that the first performance was regarded as a *dies non*, and the author's nights (usually the third, sixth, and ninth) were the fourth, seventh, and tenth. These were the occasions when he took the night's receipts, minus a fixed charge for playhouse expenses.

[2] See pp. 43, 45, 49 above.

[3] J. Q. Adams, Jr., 'The Text of Sheridan's *The Rivals*', *M.L.N.* xxv (1910), 172, remarks: 'I have furthermore, a definite statement from the Sheridan family that no manuscript of the play is at Frampton Court; nor, indeed, is one known by them to exist anywhere.' For Moore's statement, see p. 13 above.

[4] MacMillan, p. 66.

[5] Sichel, i. viii–ix, and ii. 526, refers to a 'copy annotated apparently by Mrs. Sheridan herself', and at Frampton Court. He gives no details other than a note (i. 496) showing that the whole play took three hours to perform (the first act, 28 minutes), and a suggestion (i. 489) that it shows that Sheridan was forced to cut down some high-flown apostrophes in Faulkland's part. Adams, however, wonders if the annotations are in the hand of Tickell, as described by Moore, i. 144. I have not found the copy Moore mentions, but the Frampton Court one is now in the Huntington Library (298350). It has notes and cuts in J. P. Kemble's writing, but nothing in the hands of R. B. or E. A. Sheridan.

interest in this connection: 'It may not be amiss for me to add that the Copy-Right of Mr. Sheridan's first Comedy "The Rivals" has always been in our Family:—My Father having purchased that Comedy from Mr. S. previous to its representation at Covent Garden Theatre.'[1] If we accept this literally, we must also believe that John Wilkie bought it before 17 January when, as Garrick said,[2] public expectation concerning it was very high. Wilkie must have thought that he was purchasing a very valuable property, for the *London Review* of February 1775 declared that he had been 'booby enough to give almost twice as much for the copy, as ever was before given for the best comedy exhibited on the English stage'.[3] The amount was disclosed by the disreputable John Williams in 1791: 'the late Mr. *Wilkie*, of St. Paul's Church-yard, gave Mr. Sheridan £200 for the copy right of the *Rivals*, though he afterwards confessed to me, that he was a considerable loser by the purchase'.[4]

Even if Wilkie bought the copyright before 17 January, it seems unlikely that Sheridan made over a text by that date. The first edition clearly shows that Sheridan learned much from the play's reception on its first night, and this is, in fact, stressed by the *Critical Review*[5] in its notice of the edition:

> This comedy affords a singular proof of the ingenuity of the writer, and the candour of an English audience. Some parts of it were much disliked on the first representation: the author therefore instantly withdrew his performance, altered a great part of it, and *in a few days* produced, as it were, a new play; which was immediately brought on the stage, and received with applause.

It is reasonably certain that the text Wilkie received was one revised after 17 January but before 28 January.[6]

[1] Thomas Wilkie to Sheridan's second wife, 5 Aug. 1816 (W.T.). Proof of their ownership was found by the late Cyprian Blagden in Longman's records and kindly communicated to me. It takes the form of a receipt from George Wilkie to Longman, dated 4 Jan. 1809; and is for twenty-one pounds and a fine paper copy of Inchbald's *British Theatre*, 25 volumes in quires, 'for the right of printing the comedy of *The Rivals* in the said work'.

[2] See p. 39 above.

[3] p. 140 n. Quoted by Purdy, p. xlviii.

[4] 'Anthony Pasquin', *The Eccentricities of John Edwin* [1791], ii. 344. Rhodes, *Harlequin Sheridan*, p. 65, guesses that the sum was made up of £100 for the first edition, and £100 for the third.

[5] xxxix (1775), 161.

[6] From her close study of Add. MS. 48801 Professor Patricia Hernlund has concluded that 'the first edition was revised lightly by the author after he had received the first corrected proofs from the "house" proof-reader. One correction involved revision to the extent of "reprinting" half a sheet from standing type ("recomposition" would be charged if the revision of that half sheet was more than half of the sheet). In addition, the author made very light corrections elsewhere and he asked for speed of production (or his bookseller did). There wasn't much over-time work. . . . Without knowing the history of the text, I can judge only from experience with other ledger entries in saying that the price per sheet for the first edition is high and would indicate bad copy (such as might be caused by interlinear changes by the author on the manuscript).' These valuable comments were conveyed to me in a private letter. Cf. p. 64 n.

Wilkie's newspaper, the *London Chronicle*, 28–31 January 1775, contained the announcement, 'In a few Days will be published, Price 1s. 6d., THE RIVALS. . . .' The same newspaper, in its issue of 9–11 February 1775, gave further details:

This Day was published, Price 1s. 6d
THE RIVALS, a Comedy: As it is now
performing, with universal applause, at the
Theatre Royal in Covent Garden.
Printed for J. Wilkie, No. 71, St. Paul's Church-
yard; and J. Walter, at Charing-cross.

No copies with Walter's name on them have come to hand. Strahan's register shows that three thousand copies were printed for Wilkie, and that an extra charge was made for a 'Half Sheet reprinted, and Corrections, and Night-work'.[1]

For the title-page see p. 67.

Collation: 8vo in half-sheets: π^4 a^4 B–E^4 (–F^2; +*F^2) G–N^4 O^2.

Contents: pp. [xvi]+100.

[i] Half-title, 'THE | RIVALS, | A | COMEDY. | [Price one Shilling and Sixpence.]'; [ii] blank; [iii] title; [iv] blank; [v]–x, Preface; [xi–xii] Prologue. By the Author; [xiii–xiv] Epilogue. By the Author; [xv] Errata; [xvi] Dramatis Personæ; 1–100, text.

Comment:

*F^2 is a cancel, with forty-two lines to the page instead of the normal forty. The extra two lines are occupied by a sentence spoken by Sir Lucius: '—However, when affection guides the pen, Lucy, he must be a brute who finds fault with the style.' This is not in the Larpent MS. or the third and later editions by Wilkie, but reappears in the *British Theatre* text, edited by Mrs. Inchbald.[2] If the reprinting of the two pages was caused merely by Sheridan's desire to insert these lines, it would indicate once again his stubborn resolve to publish his 'pretty thoughts' at all costs.

There is evidence to support the idea that the text of the first edition was set from a manuscript in Sheridan's hand. Look at the following readings:

1st edn.	*Larpent MS., 3rd edn., and 4th edn.*
(p. 99, l. 2) weakness	meekness
(p. 110, l. 31) save if	sure if
(p. 141, l. 4) clear	clean

In all three cases the first edition is at fault, but the errors are ones that could be made quite easily by anyone attempting to read Sheridan's scrawl. The repetition of an exclamation mark is also typical of Sheridan,

[1] Add. MS. 48801, f. 63. [2] Vol. xix (1808), 34.

though not peculiar to him: the holograph version of the first prologue of *The Rivals* shows him writing 'Oh! No!', and the manuscript of *The School for Scandal*, in his own hand, contains 'Odds! Life!' Similarly, the first edition of *The Rivals* prints 'Ah! Madam!',[1] where the third reads 'Ah, Madam!' These are all minor points but, taken together, they indicate that the first edition possesses a certain authority.

Finding presentation copies of it is not easy.[2] One was described in an auction catalogue of 1903 as 'morocco extra, 1775, uncut. A presentation copy, with inscription in Sheridan's autograph "From the Author". On the last leaf (which has been mended), containing the mis-printed catchword "Epi-", Sheridan has written the word "Finis" and crossed out the catchword.[3] Inserted is the original playbill of the performance at Covent Garden on February 27, 1775. An uncut presentation copy is extremely rare.'[4] It went to America, being among the books of William H. Buckler of Baltimore in 1907, when it was described with new detail: 'Full crimson crushed levant morocco gilt, inside gilt borders, gilt tops, other edges entirely uncut, by Rivière. An uncut presentation copy of the highest interest, with inscription in Sheridan's hand on the half-title—"from the Author".'[5] It became the property of G. D. Smith, a book-dealer, but re-appeared at an American Art Association auction on 6 April 1915 as lot 901, and was bought (or bought in) by Smith. I have been unable to trace its present location. Unlike many of Smith's purchases it is not in the Huntington Library.

Although I have not seen a presentation copy, I am satisfied that there is sufficient evidence to prove that one was in existence not long ago, and that the inscription suggests that Sheridan was reasonably proud of *The Rivals* when it was first published.[6]

(iii) *Second Edition*

The 'second edition' is the same as the first, except in two particulars: the title-page has been reset to include the words 'THE SECOND EDITION.';

[1] p. 11, l. 7.

[2] The copy received by Cholmondeley could be of the first or the third edition. See p. 51 n. above.

[3] The first edition contains in its very last line the catchword 'EPI-', but the epilogue is usually printed on pp. [xiii–xiv]. However, the Bemens copy in the Huntington Library (106604) contains neither 'EPI-' nor the press figure '3', in the last line of p. 100, but prints 'FINIS.' in their place. The same is true of the Wheeler copy in the Lilly Library, University of Indiana.

[4] Sotheby's Catalogue, 16–21 Mar. 1903, lot 1017. It was sold to Rylett for £41.

[5] Anderson Auction Co. Catalogue, New York, 3 Dec. 1907, lot 351.

[6] For other bibliographical points, see Williams, p. 212, and Wise, v. 152. The ten copies with the half-title that I have examined, all print the numeral on p. 79, but Wise records a copy without it. He also records 'Buckley' for 'Bulkley' on p. 13 of his copy.

and 'FINIS.' has been substituted at the foot of p. 100 for press figure 3 and 'EPI-'. This 'second edition' is, as Adams said,[1] 'nothing but a later issue of the first edition, from the same setting of type'. F² is a cancel in both; III. 4 and IV. 3 are misnumbered III. 5 and IV. 4; and the epilogue appears before the text of the play.

The second edition mentioned in Strahan's register is certainly not this one, but the next item below.

(iv) *Third Edition*

Strahan's register of printing[2] undertaken contains a note that reads:

Octr. The Rivals, 2d. Edit. 8½ Sheets, No. 1000 @ £1: 2: 0   9 7 0
Extra Corrections in Do.   12 0

This is to be found with the entries for 1775, but the earliest reference to its publication that I have been able to locate occurs in the *Public Advertiser*, 10 May 1776. It is at the foot of an advertisement of an issue of the songs in *The Duenna*: 'Also, by the same Author, a new Edition (being the third) of, The Rivals, a Comedy.' The *London Chronicle*, 8–10 October 1776, gives further details:

> *This Day was published*, Price 1. 6d.
> The Third Edition, corrected by the Author,
> THE RIVALS: A COMEDY As it is
> acted at the Theatre Royal in Covent Garden.
> Written by RICHARD BRINSLEY SHERIDAN
> Esquire.
> Printed for John Wilkie, No. 71, St. Paul's
> Church-yard.

Hitherto, the earliest advertisement quoted has been one from the *London Chronicle*, 14–16 January 1777, and it has been thought that the edition was prepared to coincide with the first performance of the play on 16 January at Drury Lane. Obviously this cannot now be sustained.

The title-page reads:

> THE | RIVALS, | A | COMEDY. | As it is ACTED at the | Theatre-Royal in Covent-Garden. | WRITTEN BY | RICHARD BRINSLEY SHERIDAN, ESQ. | THE THIRD EDITION CORRECTED. | [double rule] | LONDON: | Printed for JOHN WILKIE, No. 71, St. Paul's Church-Yard. | MDCCLXXVI.

Collation: 8vo: π^3 a^4 B–Q^4 R^2.

Contents: pp. [xiv]+123, [1].

> [i] half-title, 'THE | RIVALS. | A | COMEDY. | [Price One Shilling and Sixpence.]'; [ii] blank; [iii] engraved title on heavier paper; [iv] blank; [v] title; [vi] blank; [vii–viii] Prologue. By the Author. [ix–x] Prologue. By the Author. Spoken on the Tenth Night, by Mrs. Bulkley; [xi–xiii] Epilogue. By the Author; [xiv] Dramatis Personæ; [1]–123, text; [124] blank.

[1] J. Q. Adams, Jr., op. cit., p. 171.   [2] Add. MS. 48801, f. 63.

Comment:

The collation shows that Strahan's 'second' edition is Wilkie's third.

A copy of this edition in the Dyce collection at the Victoria and Albert Museum contains a presentation inscription in Sheridan's hand: 'David Garrick Esqr. From the Author.'[1]

J. Q. Adams argued that the third edition was the stage version of the play as it was then acted: 'It contains the old Serjeant-at-Law prologue in a slightly modified form; prints for the first time the "Prologue Spoken on the Tenth Night"; makes a few verbal changes in the text; and . . . omits a large number of passages. These omissions, doubtless, represent actual cuts made by the actors. As such they may have had the sanction of Sheridan, though in matters of this kind he was notoriously careless.'[2] It is difficult to be certain on this subject, particularly about the cuts made by actors, yet there is clear evidence to show that Sheridan retained in the third edition a whole scene that was frequently omitted in representation. This is v. ii, which holds up the climax but is very entertaining. When Sheridan became manager of Drury Lane Theatre, and presented *The Rivals* for the first time there, the *Morning Post* commented favourably on 'the restoration of a good scene between *Sir Anthony* and his son, upon the discovery of the sword in the last act . . . generally left out at Covent-garden'.[3] Sheridan preserved his material for print whenever he could and, as far as his readers were concerned, seems to have paid little attention to actors' cuts.[4]

It is likely, however, that Sheridan himself left out the preface apologizing for failure on the first night, modified the Serjeant-at-Law's prologue, and supplied the text of the prologue given on the tenth night. Wilkie advertised that this edition was corrected by the author and even if we think of this as a device to sell a new edition, we must also recollect that Sheridan was sufficiently proud of it to give Garrick a signed copy. From this we tend to assume that he was responsible for some other changes.

It is worth looking at a few of them to see what they reveal. There are eight brief passages printed in the first edition but not in the Larpent MS.[5] or the third edition.[6] Two of them mar the character relationships

[1] Pressmark D6 M25. It appeared in the Saunders Catalogue of Garrick's library, 23 Apr. 1823, lot 2196, and was sold to Thorpe. Possibly Sheridan had made the gift to Garrick between Jan. and May 1776.

[2] Op. cit., p. 171.

[3] *Morning Post*, 17 Jan. 1777.

[4] Purdy, p. l, makes the point that, to decide whether or not the third edition was based on the stage version of 28 Jan., we need to see the prompt-book of the day. It has not come to light, though there are a number available for early nineteenth-century performances. See also Folger MS. Prompt Temp 9.

[5] For a careful examination of the differences between the Larpent MS. and the first edition, see Purdy, pp. xxvi–xlviii.

[6] Purdy, p. xlix, mentions that they make up almost one half of the excisions, and sees them as vestiges of Sheridan's earliest version of the play.

in the play, and that is probably the reason why they were taken out. In IV. ii, Lydia cries, 'No, Sir, you could not think that such paltry artifices could please me, when the mask was thrown off!—But I suppose since your tricks have made you secure of my *fortune*, you are little solicitous about my *affections*.' Her exaggerated reproach cheapens them both. In V. i, Julia talks of 'A trick of such a nature, as to shew me plainly, that when I thought you lov'd me best, you even then regarded me as a mean dissembler; an artful, prudent hypocrite.' The accusation is far more justified, but is a little shrill and spoils the comic tone. Some other speeches are omitted[1] for the sake of a faster response in the theatre, or even in reading. The deletion of the 'High-roomians and low-roomians' of Bath was probably caused by the very local nature of the allusion. The topical references in *The Critic* were at least of national interest.

The fact that many of the alterations are of a minor nature accords with his practice in correcting *The School for Scandal* and *The Critic*, and on the whole, I suppose, the balance of probability suggests that Sheridan himself cut out the passages I have mentioned. Yet it is not really characteristic of him to delete phrases and speeches invented for the occasion or retrieved from early drafts.[2]

A very minor correction provides a puzzle. It has been accepted that Lucy's 'I transferr'd' (I. ii) was changed by Sheridan in the third edition to 'I travers'd'. There is good reason for the alteration, since one Mrs. Malaprop is enough in any play, but is this really Sheridan's doing? He was sensitive to the connection between vocabulary and social standing, and was hardly likely to allow a maidservant who did not know the meaning of 'sal volatile' to use so literary a word as 'travers'd'. I guess that this was the compositor's misreading of Sheridan's scribbled insertion of the much commoner word 'traips'd'.

Purdy puts forward the acceptable suggestion that the third edition 'reproduces typographical idiosyncrasies of the first edition too closely to have been set from a new MS.—Sheridan must rather have made his alterations in a copy of the first edition.'[3] This is true, but what we must also bear in mind when assessing his share in the alterations is the fact that he was not always methodical in revision once a play had achieved success. Judging from his other work, I think it probable that he made the corrections mentioned,[4] then tired and left the more mechanical part to

[1] For example, pp. 81, after line 2, 85, line 30, and 90, line 22, below.

[2] Or to use Purdy's phrase (p. xlviii), 'excrescences . . . reintroduced into their old settings by an admiring author'. Sheridan did not willingly give them up.

[3] p. xlix. This is confirmed by Professor Hernlund's acute examination of the entries in the Strahan registers: 'the price per sheet for the . . . second [i.e. Wilkie third] edition is about average and would indicate to me that the compositors worked from a copy of the first edition, with changes or without.' (Communicated privately.)

[4] And those caused by attraction. It seems probable, however, that the printer was responsible for the omission on p. 105, lines 28–32, below.

the printer. The accidentals of the first edition are, in that case, likely to be closer to what he originally wrote than those of the third edition.

(v) *Fourth Edition*

Rhodes tentatively dated this '1785' from the general style and appearance of the only copy he had seen.[1] The book is not quite so rare nowadays: there are copies in the Library of Congress, the Bodleian, Folger, and Pennsylvania State University libraries, as well as in the present editor's own collection.

The last advertisement of the third edition that I have been able to find, appeared in the *Public Advertiser*, 30 Oct.–1 Nov. 1781, under an advertisement of the first edition of *A Trip to Scarborough*, 'Printed for G. Wilkie'. A number of other books and pamphlets came out under George Wilkie's name until May 1784, when he joined with his brother Thomas in publishing ventures. They remained at 71 St. Paul's Church Yard until September 1790, when 'G. and T. Wilkie, No. 57 Paternoster row' became their designation. From all this I think we may reasonably conclude that the fourth edition of *The Rivals* was printed at some time between 1782 and May 1784. Yet in referring to this edition in the lists of variants, I propose to retain '1785', since it has been commonly used for a long time and is more quickly recognised.

The title-page reads:

> THE | RIVALS, | A | COMEDY. | As it is Perform'd at the | THEATRE–ROYAL | IN | *COVENT–GARDEN.* | [rule] | The FOURTH EDITION. | [double rule] | *LONDON:* | Printed for G. WILKIE, No. 71, St. Pauls | Church Yard.

Collation: 8vo: π^2 a^4 B–N^4 O^2.

Contents: pp. [xii]+100.

> [i] half-title, 'THE | RIVALS, | A| COMEDY, | [Price One Shilling and Sixpence.]'; [ii] blank; [iii] title-page; [iv] blank; [v–vi] Prologue. By the Author; [vii–viii] Prologue. By the Author. Spoken on the Tenth Night, by Mrs. Bulkley; [ix–xi] Epilogue. By the Author; [xii] Dramatis Personæ; [1]–99, text; [100], blank.

Comment:

This reprints the third edition, making some changes in accidentals and introducing three substantives.

Other reprints were the fifth edition ('. . . for G. & T. WILKIE, No. 57, Paternoster-row. / MDCCXCI.') and sixth edition ('. . . for G. WILKIE,

[1] Rhodes, i. 132. He notes that a 'Fourth Edition' dated 1776 is also recorded, but without other particulars, by Sichel and Allardyce Nicoll. The Bodleian Library owns a 91-page edition ('Shuttleworth 37') that has been tentatively placed in 1785.

No. 57, Paternoster-row. / 1798.'). There is no reason to believe that Sheridan had a hand in any edition after the third.

Conclusion

I propose to use the first edition as copy-text, and to admit into the edited text new readings from the third edition and, where they correct errors, from the fourth edition. Since the first edition appears to preserve Sheridan's accidentals more closely than the third, this seems, marginally, to be the safer course to take.

I have recorded the variants from the Larpent MS. only when they were useful for comparison with the readings in the first and third editions. For full collations of the Larpent MS., see Purdy, and *English Plays, 1660–1820* (ed. A. E. Morgan (1935), pp. 993–1049).

The following abbreviations are used in the textual notes of this play:

L The Lord Chamberlain's copy, Larpent MS. 383.
75 The first edition (1775).
76 The third edition corrected (1776).
85 The fourth edition (99 pp.)

In the notes on the prologue, 'S' stands for the text in the Somerville College MS.

The preface appears in Wilkie's first and second editions, but is afterwards omitted. The prologue spoken on the tenth night is printed in Wilkie's third and later editions.

THE

RIVALS,

A

COMEDY.

As it is ACTED at the

Theatre-Royal in Covent-Garden.

LONDON:
Printed for JOHN WILKIE, No. 71, St. Paul's Church-Yard.
MDCCLXXV.

The title-page of the first edition of *The Rivals*

PREFACE

A PREFACE to a Play seems generally to be considered as a kind of Closet-prologue, in which—if his Piece has been successful—the Author solicits that indulgence from the Reader which he had before experienced from the Audience: But as the scope and immediate object of a Play is to please a mixed assembly in *Representation* (whose judgment in the Theatre at least is decisive) its degree of reputation is usually as determined as public, before it can be prepared for the cooler tribunal of the Study. Thus any farther solicitude on the part of the Writer becomes unnecessary at least, if not an intrusion: and if the Piece has been condemned in the Performance, I fear an Address to the Closet, like an Appeal to Posterity, is constantly regarded as the procrastination of a suit, from a consciousness of the weakness of the cause. From these considerations, the following Comedy would certainly have been submitted to the Reader, without any further introduction than what it had in the Representation, but that its success has probably been founded on a circumstance which the Author is informed has not before attended a theatrical trial, and which consequently ought not to pass unnoticed.

I need scarcely add, that the circumstance alluded to, was the withdrawing of the Piece, to remove those imperfections in the first Representation which were too obvious to escape reprehension, and too numerous to admit of a hasty correction. There are few writers, I believe, who, even in the fullest consciousness of error, do not wish to palliate the faults which they acknowledge; and, however trifling the performance, to second their confession of its deficiencies, by whatever plea seems least disgraceful to their ability. In the present instance, it cannot be said to amount either to candour or modesty in me, to acknowledge an extreme inexperience and want of judgment on matters, in which, without guidance from practice, or spur from success, a young man should scarcely boast of being an adept. If it be said, that under such disadvantages no one should attempt to write a play—I must beg leave to dissent from the position, while the first point of experience that I have gained on the subject is, a knowledge of the candour and judgment with which an impartial Public distinguishes between the errors of inexperience and incapacity, and the indulgence which it shews even to a disposition to remedy the defects of either.

It were unnecessary to enter into any farther extenuation of what was thought exceptionable in this Play, but that it has been said, that the Managers should have prevented some of the defects before its appearance to the Public—and in particular the uncommon length of the piece as represented the first night.—It were an ill return for the most liberal and gentlemanly conduct on their side, to suffer any censure to rest where none was deserved. Hurry in writing has long been exploded as an excuse for an Author;—however, in the dramatic line, it may happen, that both an Author and a Manager may wish to fill a chasm in the entertainment of the Public with a hastiness not altogether culpable. The season was advanced when I first put the play into Mr. Harris's hands:—it was at that time at least double the length of any acting comedy.—I profited by his judgment and experience in the curtailing of it—'till, I believe, his feeling for the vanity of a young Author got the better of his desire for correctness, and he left many excrescences remaining, because he had assisted in pruning so many more. Hence, though I was not uninformed that the Acts were still too long, I flatter'd myself that, after the first trial, I might with safer judgment proceed to remove what should appear to have been most dissatisfactory.—Many other errors there were, which might in part have arisen from my being by no means conversant with plays in general, either in reading or at the theatre.—Yet I own that, in one respect, I did not regret my ignorance: for as my first wish in attempting a Play, was to avoid every appearance of plagiary, I thought I should stand a better chance of effecting this from being in a walk which I had not frequented, and where consequently the progress of invention was less likely to be interrupted by starts of recollection: for on subjects on which the mind has been much informed, invention is slow of exerting itself.—Faded ideas float in the fancy like half-forgotten dreams; and the imagination in its fullest enjoyments becomes suspicious of its offspring, and doubts whether it has created or adopted.

With regard to some particular passages which on the First Night's Representation seemed generally disliked, I confess, that if I felt any emotion of surprise at the disapprobation, it was not that they were disapproved of, but that I had not before perceived that they deserved it. As some part of the attack on the Piece was begun too early to pass for the sentence of *Judgment*, which is ever tardy in condemning, it has been suggested to me, that much of the disapprobation must have arisen from virulence of Malice, rather than severity of Criticism: But as I was more apprehensive of there being just grounds to excite the latter, than conscious of having deserved the former, I continue not to believe that probable, which I am sure must have been unprovoked. However, if it was so, and I could even mark the quarter from whence it came, it would be ungenerous to retort; for no passion suffers more than malice from disappointment. For my own part, I see no reason why the Author of a Play should not regard a First Night's Audience, as a candid and judicious friend attending, in behalf of the Public, at his last Rehearsal. If he can dispense with flattery, he is sure at least of sincerity, and even though the annotation be rude, he may rely upon the justness of the comment. Considered in this light, that Audience, whose *fiat* is essential to the Poet's claim, whether his object be Fame or Profit, has surely a right to expect some deference to its opinion, from principles of Politeness at least, if not from Gratitude.

As for the little puny Critics, who scatter their peevish strictures in private circles, and scribble at every Author who has the eminence of being unconnected with them, as they are usually spleen-swoln from a vain idea of increasing their consequence, there will always be found a petulance and illiberality in their remarks, which should place them as far beneath the notice of a Gentleman, as their original dulness had sunk them from the level of the most unsuccessful Author.

It is not without pleasure that I catch at an opportunity of justifying myself from the charge of intending any national reflection in the character of Sir *Lucius O'Trigger*. If any Gentlemen opposed the Piece from that idea, I thank them sincerely for their opposition; and if the condemnation of this Comedy (however misconceived the provocation,) could have added one spark to the decaying flame of national attachment to the country supposed to be reflected on, I should have been happy in its fate; and might with truth have boasted, that it had done more real service in its failure, than the successful morality of a thousand stage-novels will ever effect.

It is usual, I believe, to thank the Performers in a new Play, for the exertion of their several abilities. But where (as in this instance) their merit has been so striking and uncontroverted, as to call for the warmest and truest applause from a number of judicious Audiences, the Poet's after-praise comes like the feeble acclamation of a child to close the shouts of a multitude. The conduct, however, of the Principals in a Theatre cannot be so apparent to the Public.—I think it therefore but justice to declare, that from this Theatre (the only one I can speak of from experience,) those Writers who wish to try the Dramatic Line, will meet with that candour and liberal attention, which are generally allowed to be better calculated to lead genius into excellence, than either the precepts of judgment, or the guidance of experience.

THE AUTHOR

PROLOGUE

BY THE AUTHOR

Spoken by Mr. WOODWARD and
Mr. QUICK

Enter SERJEANT AT LAW, *and* ATTORNEY *following, and giving a Paper.*

SERJ. What's here—a vile cramp hand! I cannot see
Without my spectacles. ATT. He means his fee.
Nay, Mr. Serjeant, good Sir, try again. [*Gives Money.*
SERJ. The scrawl improves [*more*] O come, 'tis pretty plain.
Hey! how's this?—*Dibble*!—sure it cannot be!
A Poet's Brief! A Poet and a Fee!
ATT. Yea Sir!—tho' *you* without Reward, I know,
Would gladly plead the muses cause—[SERJ.] So—So!
And if the Fee offends—your wrath should fall
On me—[SERJ.] Dear *Dibble* no offence at all—
ATT. Some Sons of Phœbus—in the Courts we meet,
SERJ. And fifty Sons of Phœbus in the Fleet!
ATT. Nor pleads he worse, who with a decent sprig
Of Bays—adorns his legal waste of wig.
SERJ. Full-bottom'd Heroes thus, on signs, unfurl
A leaf of laurel—in a grove of curl!
Yet tell your Client, that, in adverse days,
This Wig is warmer than a bush of Bays.

1–4 PROLOGUE . . . QUICK] *75*, *76*, *85*; *om. S* 5 *Enter* . . . ATTORNEY] *75*, *76*, *85*; *om. S* 5–6 *following* . . . *Paper*] *76*, *85*; *om* *75*, *S* 7–9 What's . . . *Money*] *75*, *76*, *85*; *om. S* 10 The . . . plain] *75*, *76*, *85*; They'll either clear the Sight—or Serve as Blinkers *S* 11 Hey! . . . be] *76*, *85*; How's this! The Poet's Brief *again*! O ho! *75*; How's this?—a *Poet's* Brief!—(ATT.) Aye even so *S* 12 A . . . Fee] *76*, *85*; Cast, I suppose? ATT. O pardon me—No—No—*75*; The Deuce!—A *Poet* and a *Fee*!—O Ho!—*S* 13 Yea . . . know] *76*, *85*; We found the Court, o'er-looking stricter laws *75*;—Some noble writer I suppose?—(ATT.) 'Oh! No!' *S* 14 Would . . . So—So!] *76*, *85*; *Indulgent* to the *merits* of the Cause *75* A Student erring from the Temple's Bounds *S* 15 And . . . fall] *76*, *85*; By *Judges* mild, unus'd to harsh denial *75*; Pleads to a Trespass on the Muses Grounds.' *S* 16 On . . . all] *76*, *85*; *Serj.* Ill fare the Truant who with giddy Haste | Forsakes an *Orchard* for a barren *Waste S*; A Rule was granted for *another trial.* | *Serj.* Then heark'ee, *Dibble*, did you *mend* your *Pleadings*, | *Errors*, no few; we've found in our *Proceedings.* | *Att.* Come, courage, Sir, we did *amend* our *Plea*, | Hence your *new Brief*, and this *refreshing Fee. 75* 17–18 Some . . . Fleet!] *75*, *76*, *85*; *om. S*

ATT. Do you then, Sir, my Client's place supply,
Profuse of robe, and prodigal of tye—
Do you, with all those blushing pow'rs of face,
And wonted bashful hesitating grace,
Rise in the Court, and flourish on the Case.
[*Exit.*

SERJ. For practice then suppose—this Brief will shew it,——
Me, Serjeant *Woodward*,—Counsel for the Poet.
Us'd to the ground—I know 'tis hard to deal
With this dread *Court*, from whence there's *no appeal*;
No *Tricking* here, to blunt the edge of *Law*,
Or, damn'd in *Equity*—escape by *Flaw*:
But *Judgment* given—*your Sentence* must remain;
—No *Writ of Error* lies—to *Drury-lane*!
Yet when so kind you seem—'tis past dispute
We gain some favour, if not *Costs of Suit*.
No spleen is here! I see no hoarded fury;
—I think I never fac'd a milder Jury!
Sad else our plight!—where frowns are transportation,
A hiss the gallows,—and a groan, damnation!
But such the public candour, without fear
My Client waves all *right of challenge* here.
No Newsman from *our* Session is dismiss'd,
Nor Wit nor Critic *we* scratch off the list;
His faults can never hurt another's ease,
His crime at worst—a *bad attempt* to please:
Thus, all respecting, he appeals to all,
And by the general voice will *stand* or *fall*.

Before 1, S inserts 'And tell him too—how hard it is to deal', *adding ll. 10–14 from this page, but reading* 'that' *for* 'this' *in line 10.* 1 my Client's] *75*, *76*, *85*; our Student's *S* 8 *Woodward*] *75*, *76*, *85*; *Lewis S* 9 Us'd . . . deal] *75*, *76*, *85*; But first —lest partial Spleen our words pervert—*S* 10–16 With . . . *Suit*] *75*, *76*, *85*;—My Client's *Right of Challenge* I'll exert. | —Above—Below—In Jackets Silk—or flannel— | *Hissers* of all kind I—strike off the Pannel.—(*looking round*) *S* 17 No . . . fury] *75*, *76*, *85*; No!—No such Thing!—No Spite!—No hoarded Fury! *S* 21–8 such . . . *fall*] *75*, *76*, *85*; from so mild a Court—'tis past Dispute | *He*'ll gain **some Favour** —if not *Costs of Suit*. | There's One thing only I shall mention more—(going) |—This Culprit—ne'er was at your Bar before: | Of all Intruders should He prove the worst, | Forgive the Trespass—since it is the FIRST. *S*

PROLOGUE

BY THE AUTHOR

Spoken on the Tenth Night, by Mrs.
BULKLEY

Granted our Cause, our suit and trial o'er,
The worthy Serjeant need appear no more:
In pleasing I a different Client chuse,
He serv'd the Poet,—I would serve the Muse:
Like him, I'll try to merit your applause,
A female counsel in a female's cause.
  Look on this form,[1]—where Humour quaint and fly,
Dimples the cheek, and points the beaming eye;
Where gay Invention seems to boast its wiles
In amorous hint, and half-triumphant smiles;
While her light masks or[2] covers Satire's strokes,
All hides the conscious blush, her wit provokes.
—Look on her well—does she seem form'd to teach?
Shou'd you *expect* to hear this lady—preach?
Is grey experience suited to her youth?
Do solemn sentiments become that mouth?
Bid her be grave, those lips should rebel prove
To every theme that slanders mirth or love.
  Yet thus adorn'd with every graceful art
To charm the fancy and yet reach the heart——
Must we displace her? And instead advance
The Goddess of the woeful countenance—
The sentimental Muse!—Her emblems view
The Pilgrim's progress, and a sprig of rue!
View her—too chaste to look like flesh and blood—
Primly portray'd on emblematic wood!
There fix'd in usurpation shou'd she stand,
She'll snatch the dagger from her sister's hand:
And having made her votaries *weep a flood*
Good Heav'n! she'll end her Comedies in blood—

[1] 'Pointing to the Figure of Comedy.' It was shown on one side of the stage and Tragedy appeared on the other.

[2] O'er?

Bid *Harry Woodward* break poor *Dunstall*'s crown!
Imprison *Quick*—and knock *Ned Shuter* down;
While sad *Barsanti*—weeping o'er the scene,
Shall stab herself—or poison Mrs. *Green*.——
  Such dire encroachments to prevent in time,
Demands the Critic's voice—the Poet's rhyme.
Can our light scenes add strength to holy laws!
Such puny patronage but hurts the cause:
Fair Virtue scorns our feeble aid to ask;
And moral Truth disdains the trickster's mask.
For here their fav'rite stands,[1] whose brow—severe
And sad—claims Youth's respect, and Pity's tear;
Who—when oppress'd by foes her worth creates—
Can point a poignard at the Guilt she hates.

[1] 'Pointing to Tragedy.'

DRAMATIS PERSONÆ

MEN

SIR ANTHONY ABSOLUTE	Mr. Shuter
CAPT. ABSOLUTE	Mr. Woodward
FAULKLAND	Mr. Lewes
ACRES	Mr. Quick
SIR LUCIUS O'TRIGGER	Mr. Clinch
FAG	Mr. Lee-Lewes
DAVID	Mr. Dunstal[l]
COACHMAN	Mr. Fearon

WOMEN

MRS. MALAPROP	Mrs. Green
LYDIA LANGUISH	Miss Barsanti
JULIA	Mrs. Bulkley
LUCY	Mrs. Lessingham

MAID, BOY, SERVANTS, &c.

SCENE, *Bath*

Time of Action, *within One Day*

9 Lee-Lewes] *76*, *85*; Lee-Lewis *75*   18 *within One Day*] *76*, *85*: Five Hours *75*

THE RIVALS

ACT I

SCENE I[1]

A STREET *in* Bath

COACHMAN *crosses the stage.—Enter* FAG, *looking after him.*

FAG. What!—Thomas!—Sure 'tis he?—What!—Thomas!—Thomas!

COACH. Hay!—Odd's life!—Mr. Fag!—give us your hand, my old fellow-servant.

FAG. Excuse my glove, Thomas:—I'm dev'lish glad to see you, my lad: why, my prince of charioteers, you look as hearty!—but who the deuce thought of seeing you in Bath!

COACH. Sure, Master, Madam Julia, Harry, Mrs. Kate, and the postillion be all come!

FAG. Indeed!

COACH. Aye! Master thought another fit of the gout was coming to make him a visit:—so he'd a mind to gi't the slip, and whip we were all off at an hour's warning.

FAG. Aye, aye! hasty in every thing, or it would not be Sir Anthony Absolute!

COACH. But tell us, Mr. Fag, how does young Master? Odd! Sir Anthony will stare to see the Captain here!

FAG. I do not serve Capt. Absolute now.—

COACH. Why sure!

FAG. At present I am employ'd by Ensign Beverley.

COACH. I doubt, Mr. Fag, you ha'n't changed for the better.

FAG. I have not changed, Thomas.

COACH. No! why didn't you say you had left young Master?

FAG. No——Well, honest Thomas, I must puzzle you no farther:—briefly then—Capt. Absolute and Ensign Beverley are one and the same person.

COACH. The devil they are!

FAG. So it is indeed, Thomas; and the *Ensign* half of my master being on guard at present—the *Captain* has nothing to do with me.

7 Hay!] *L*, *75*; Hey! *76*, *85*

---

[1] An interleaved, early nineteenth-century prompt copy of *The Rivals* (. . . Dublin, Printed for R. Moncrieffe, 1775), now in the Bodleian Library, as Vet A. 5 e. 1849, contains a note, opposite p. 17 and reading, 'This Scene is generally left out.'

COACH. So, so!—what, this is some freak, I warrant!—Do, tell us, Mr. Fag, the meaning o't—you know I ha' trusted you.

FAG. You'll be secret, Thomas.

COACH. As a coach-horse.

FAG. Why then the cause of all this is—LOVE,—Love, Thomas, who (as you may get read to you) has been a masquerader ever since the days of Jupiter.[1]

COACH. Aye, aye;—I guessed there was a lady in the case:—but pray, why does your Master pass only for *Ensign*?—now if he had shamm'd *General* indeed——

FAG. Ah! Thomas, there lies the mystery o' the matter.—Hark'ee, Thomas, my Master is in love with a lady of a very singular taste: a lady who likes him better as a *half-pay Ensign* than if she knew he was son and heir to Sir Anthony Absolute, a baronet with three thousand a-year!

COACH. That is an odd taste indeed!—but has she got the stuff, Mr. Fag; is she rich, hey?

FAG. Rich!—why, I believe she owns half the stocks!—Z——ds! Thomas, she could pay the national debt as easy as I could my washer-woman!—She has a lap-dog that eats out of gold,—she feeds her parrot with small pearls,—and all her thread-papers are made of bank-notes!

COACH. Bravo!—faith!——Odd! I warrant she has a set of thousands at least:—but does she draw kindly with the Captain?

FAG. As fond as pigeons.

COACH. May one hear her name?

FAG. Miss Lydia Languish—But there is an old tough aunt in the way;—though by the bye—she has never seen my Master—for he got acquainted with Miss while on a visit in Gloucestershire.

COACH. Well—I wish they were once harness'd together in matrimony.—But pray, Mr. Fag, what kind of a place is this Bath?—I ha' heard a deal of it—here's a mort o'merry-making—hey?

FAG. Pretty well, Thomas, pretty well—'tis a good lounge; in the morning we go to the pump-room (though neither my Master nor I drink the waters); after breakfast we saunter on the parades or play a game at billiards; at night we dance: but d—n the place, I'm tired of it: their

11 Ah] *75*, *76*, *85*; Oh *L* there] *L*, *75*, *85*; their *76* 14 with] *L*, *75*; of *76*, *85* 19 easy] *L*, *75*; easily *76*, *85* 32 lounge; in] *L*, *76*, *85*; lounge. Though at present we are, like other great assemblies, divided into parties—High-roomians and Low-roomians; however, for my part, I have resolved to stand neuter; and so I told Bob Brush at our last committee.

Coach. But what do the folks do here?

Fag. Oh! there are little amusements enough—in *75*

---

[1] See pp. 793–6, for *Ixion*, the play by Halhed that Sheridan revised. In it, Jupiter came down to earth to woo Major Amphitryon's wife.

regular hours stupify me—not a fiddle nor a card after eleven!—however Mr. Faulkland's gentleman and I keep it up a little in private parties; —I'll introduce you there, Thomas—you'll like him much.

COACH. Sure I know Mr. Du-Peigne—you know his Master is to marry Madam Julia.

FAG. I had forgot.—But Thomas, you must polish a little—indeed you must:—here now—this wig!—what the devil do you do with a *wig*, Thomas?—none of the London whips of any degree of Ton wear *wigs* now.

COACH. More's the pity! more's the pity, I say.—Odd's life! when I heard how the lawyers and doctors had took to their own hair,[1] I thought how 'twould go next:—Odd rabbit it! when the fashion had got foot on the Bar, I guess'd 'twould mount to the Box!—but 'tis all out of character, believe me, Mr. Fag: and look'ee, I'll never gi' up mine—the lawyers and doctors may do as they will.

FAG. Well, Thomas, we'll not quarrel about that.

COACH. Why, bless you, the gentlemen of they professions ben't all of a mind—for in our village now tho'ff[2] *Jack Gauge* the *exciseman*, has ta'en to his carrots, there's little Dick the farrier swears he'll never forsake his *bob*, tho' all the college should appear with their own heads!

FAG. Indeed! well said Dick! but hold—mark! mark! Thomas.

COACH. Zooks! 'tis the Captain—Is that the lady with him?

FAG. No! no! that is Madam Lucy—my Master's mistress's maid.—They lodge at that house—but I must after him to tell him the news.

COACH. Odd! he's giving her money!—well, Mr. Fag——

FAG. Good bye, Thomas.—I have an appointment in Gyde's Porch[3] this evening at eight; meet me there, and we'll make a little party.

[*Exeunt severally.*

SCENE II

A Dressing-room in Mrs. MALAPROP'*s lodgings*
LYDIA *sitting on a sopha with a book in her hand.*—
LUCY,[4] *as just returned from a message.*

LUCY. Indeed, Ma'am, I transferr'd half the town in search of it:—I don't believe there's a circulating library[5] in Bath I ha'n't been at.

4 Peigne] *L*, *75*; Peign *76*, *85* 26 Gyde's] *L*, *76*, *85*; Gydes' *75* 33 transferr'd] *L*, *75*; travers'd *76*, *85*: *see p. 64 above.*

[1] Cf. the prologue to *A Trip to Scarborough*, p. 570, lines 21–4.

[2] This appears to suggest a vulgar pronunciation. Cf. Win Jenkins's 'thof' in Smollett's *Humphry Clinker* (ed. L. M. Knapp, 1966), pp. 42, 107, 220, 338, 352.

[3] Gyde kept the old (or lower) assembly rooms on the Lower Walks.

[4] Lucy is also the maid in Congreve's *The Old Batchelor*.

[5] 'Where we read novels, plays, pamphlets, and news-papers, for so small a subscription as a crown a quarter' (Smollett, *Humphry Clinker*, ed. cit., p. 40).

LYD. And could not you get '*The Reward of Constancy*?'[1]

LUCY. No, indeed, Ma'am.

LYD. Nor '*The Fatal Connection*?'[2]

LUCY. No, indeed, Ma'am.

LYD. Nor '*The Mistakes of the Heart*'?[3]

LUCY. Ma'am, as ill-luck would have it, Mr. Bull[4] said Miss Sukey Saunter had just fetch'd it away.

LYD. Heigh-ho!—Did you inquire for '*The Delicate Distress*'?[5]——

LUCY. ——Or '*The Memoirs of Lady Woodford*?'[6] Yes indeed, Ma'am.—I ask'd every where for it; and I might have brought it from Mr. Frederick's,[7] but Lady Slattern Lounger, who had just sent it home, had so soiled and dog's-ear'd it, it wa'n't fit for a christian to read.

LYD. Heigh-ho![8]—Yes, I always know when Lady Slattern has been before me.—She has a most observing thumb; and I believe cherishes her nails for the convenience of making marginal notes.—Well, child, what *have* you brought me?

LUCY. Oh! here Ma'am.

[*Taking books from under her cloke, and from her pockets.*]

This is '*The Gordian Knot*,'—and this '*Peregrine Pickle*.' Here are '*The Tears of Sensibility*'[9] and '*Humphry Clinker*.' This is '*The Memoirs of a Lady of Quality, written by herself*,'—and here the second volume of '*The Sentimental Journey*.'

LYD. Heigh-ho!—What are those books by the glass?

LUCY. The great one is only '*The whole Duty of Man*'[10]—where I press a few blonds, Ma'am.

LYD. Very well—give me the *sal volatile*.[11]

LUCY. Is it in a blue cover, Ma'am?

1 Possibly *The Happy Pair, or, Virtue and Constancy Rewarded* (1771).

2 A novel by Mrs. Fogerty in two volumes (1773).

3 A novel in French, dedicated to Rousseau and probably by Pierre Treyssac de Vergy. It appeared in English in three volumes in 1769, with the subsidiary title of 'Memoirs of Lady Caroline Pelham and Lady Victoria Nevil. In a Series of Letters'.

4 Lewis Bull, bookseller at Bath.

5 *The Delicate Distress and The Gordian Knot* (1769–70). The first was by Elizabeth Griffith (d. 1793), and the second by her husband, Richard Griffith (d. 1788).

6 Anonymous (1771).

7 William Frederick, Bath bookseller. In the *Bath Journal*, 24 Sept. 1770, he announced that he was giving up his circulating library.

8 'When I say Heigho! it means yes.' (Biddy, in *Miss in her Teens*, I. ii.)

9 Baculard D'Arnaud's *Les Épreuves du Sentiment*, translated into English by J. Murdoch, as *The Tears of Sensibility* (2 vols., 1773).

10 *The Whole Duty of Man* (1659), by Richard Allestree (1618–91). Possibly Lucy meant the folio *Works of the learned and pious Author of The Whole Duty of Man*, published in 1704 and 1723.

11 Cf. Mrs. Tryfort, in Frances Sheridan's *A Journey to Bath*, II, ii: 'I am so low every morning, ha, ha, ha, I protest I use almost an ounce of sal volatile constantly in my tea.'

LYD. My smelling-bottle, you simpleton!

LUCY. O, the drops![1]—here Ma'am.

LYD. Hold!—here's some one coming—quick, see who it is.——

[*Exit* LUCY.

Surely I heard my cousin Julia's voice! [*Re-enter* LUCY.

LUCY. Lud! Ma'am, here is Miss Melville.

LYD. Is it possible!——

Enter JULIA.

LYD. My dearest Julia, how delighted am I!—[*Embrace*] How unexpected was this happiness!

JUL. True, Lydia—and our pleasure is the greater;—but what has been the matter?—you were denied to me at first!

LYD. Ah! Julia, I have a thousand things to tell you!—but first inform me, what has conjur'd you to Bath?—Is Sir Anthony here?

JUL. He is—we are arrived within this hour—and I suppose he will be here to wait on Mrs. Malaprop as soon as he is dress'd.

LYD. Then before we are interrupted, let me impart to you some of my distress!—I know your gentle nature will sympathize with me, tho' your prudence may condemn me!—My letters have inform'd you of my whole connexion with Beverley;—but I have lost him, Julia!—my aunt has discover'd our intercourse by a note she intercepted, and has confin'd me ever since!——Yet, would you believe it? she has fallen absolutely in love with a tall Irish baronet she met one night since we have been here, at Lady Macshuffle's rout.

JUL. You jest, Lydia!

LYD. No, upon my word.—She really carries on a kind of correspondence with him, under a feigned name though, till she chuses to be known to him;——but it is a *Delia* or a *Celia*, I assure you.

JUL. Then, surely, she is now more indulgent to her niece.

LYD. Quite the contrary. Since she has discovered her own frailty, she is become more suspicious of mine. Then I must inform you of another plague!—That odious Acres is to be in Bath to-day; so that I protest I shall be teased out of all spirits!

After l. 2, insert:
Lyd. No note, Lucy?
Lucy. No indeed, Ma'am—but I have seen a certain person——
Lyd. What, my Beverley!—well Lucy?
Lucy. O Ma'am! he looks so desponding and melancholic! *75*

3 Hold!] *76*, *85*; Hold Lucy! *L*, *75* 26 really] *76*, *85*; absolutely *L*, *75*

[1] *Lady Rusport*. Give me the drops; I'm all in a flutter.
Major. Hark'e sweetheart, what are those same drops? . . .
Lucy. Oh! Sir, they are called the cordial restorative elixir, or the nervous golden drops; they are only for ladies cases.
(R. Cumberland, *The West Indian* (1771), II. xi.)

JUL. Come, come, Lydia, hope the best.—Sir Anthony shall use his interest with Mrs. Malaprop.

LYD. But you have not heard the worst. Unfortunately I had quarrell'd with my poor Beverley, just before my aunt made the discovery, and I have not seen him since, to make it up.

JUL. What was his offence?

LYD. Nothing at all!—But, I don't know how it was, as often as we had been together, we had never had a quarrel!—And, somehow I was afraid he would never give me an opportunity.—So, last Thursday, I wrote a letter to myself, to inform myself that Beverley was at that time paying his addresses to another woman.—I sign'd it *your Friend unknown*, shew'd it to Beverley, charg'd him with his falsehood, put myself in a violent passion, and vow'd I'd never see him more.

JUL. And you let him depart so, and have not seen him since?

LYD. 'Twas the next day my aunt found the matter out. I intended only to have teased him three days and a half, and now I've lost him for ever.

JUL. If he is as deserving and sincere as you have represented him to me, he will never give you up so. Yet consider, Lydia, you tell me he is but an ensign, and you have thirty thousand pounds!

LYD. But you know I lose most of my fortune, if I marry without my aunt's consent, till of age; and that is what I have determin'd to do, ever since I knew the penalty.—Nor could I love the man, who would wish to wait a day for the alternative.

JUL. Nay, this is caprice!

LYD. What, does Julia tax me with caprice?—I thought her lover Faulkland had enured her to it.

JUL. I do not love even *his* faults.

LYD. But a-propos—you have sent to him, I suppose?

JUL. Not yet, upon my word—nor has he the least idea of my being in Bath.—Sir Anthony's resolution was so sudden, I could not inform him of it.

LYD. Well, Julia, you are your own mistress, (though under the protection of Sir Anthony) yet have you, for this long year, been a slave to the caprice, the whim, the jealousy of this ungrateful Faulkland,[1] who will ever delay assuming the right of a husband, while you suffer him to be equally imperious as a lover.

JUL. Nay, you are wrong entirely.—We were contracted before my father's death.—*That*, and some consequent embarrassments, have delay'd what I know to be my Faulkland's most ardent wish.—He is too generous to trifle on such a point.—And for his character, you wrong

1 hope] *L*, *75*, *76*; hope for *85* 33 a] *76*, *85*; the *L*, *75*

[1] 'His [Faulkland's] ideas of love, honour, generosity, and gratitude, are so refined, that no hero in romance ever went beyond him' (Frances Sheridan, *Memoirs of Miss Sidney Bidulph*, 1761, p. 23).

him there too.—No, Lydia, he is too proud, too noble to be jealous; if he is captious, 'tis without dissembling; if fretful, without rudeness. —Unus'd to the fopperies of love, he is negligent of the little duties expected from a lover—but being unhackney'd in the passion, his affection is ardent and sincere; and as it engrosses his whole soul, he expects every thought and emotion of his mistress to move in unison with his.—Yet, though his pride calls for this full return—his humility makes him undervalue those qualities in him, which would entitle him to it; and not feeling why he should be lov'd to the degree he wishes, he still suspects that he is not lov'd enough:—This temper, I must own, has cost me many unhappy hours; but I have learn'd to think myself his debtor, for those imperfections which arise from the ardour of his attachment.

LYD. Well, I cannot blame you for defending him.—But tell me candidly, Julia, had he never sav'd your life, do you think you should have been attach'd to him as you are?—Believe me, the rude blast that overset your boat was a prosperous gale of love to him.

JUL. Gratitude may have strengthened my attachment to Mr. Faulkland, but I lov'd him before he had preserv'd me; yet surely that alone were an obligation sufficient.

LYD. Obligation!—Why a water-spaniel would have done as much.—Well, I should never think of giving my heart to a man because he could swim!

JUL. Come, Lydia, you are too inconsiderate.

LYD. Nay, I do but jest.——What's here?

Enter LUCY *in a hurry.*

LUCY. O Ma'am, here is Sir Anthony Absolute just come home with your aunt.

LYD. They'll not come here.—Lucy do you watch. [*Exit* LUCY.

JUL. Yet I must go.—Sir Anthony does not know I am here, and if we meet, he'll detain me, to shew me the town.—I'll take another opportunity of paying my respects to Mrs. Malaprop, when she shall treat me, as long as she chooses, with her select words so ingeniously *misapplied*, without being *mispronounced*.[1]

Re-enter LUCY.

LUCY. O Lud! Ma'am, they are both coming up stairs.

LYD. Well, I'll not detain you Coz.—Adieu, my dear Julia, I'm sure you are in haste to send to Faulkland.——There—through my room you'll find another stair-case.

3 fopperies] *76*, *85*; foppery *L*, *75* 5 affection] *76*, *85*; love, *L*, *75* 8 would] *76*, *85*; should *L*, *75* 12 attachment] *76*, *85*; love *L*, *75*

[1] Cf. Lady Filmot's description of Mrs. Tryfort in Frances Sheridan's *A Journey to Bath*, I. v, quoted on p. 37 above.

JUL. Adieu.—[*Embrace.*] [*Exit* JULIA.

LYD. Here, my dear Lucy, hide these books.—Quick, quick.—Fling *Peregrine Pickle* under the toilet—throw *Roderick Random* into the closet—put *the Innocent Adultery*[1] into *The Whole Duty of Man*—thrust *Lord Aimworth*[2] under the sopha—cram *Ovid* behind the bolster—there—put *the Man of Feeling*[3] into your pocket—so, so, now lay *Mrs. Chapone*[4] in sight, and leave *Fordyce's Sermons*[5] open on the table.

LUCY. O burn it, Ma'am, the hair-dresser has torn away as far as *Proper Pride*.

LYD. Never mind—open at *Sobriety*.—Fling me *Lord Chesterfield's Letters*.——Now for 'em.

Enter Mrs. MALAPROP *and Sir* ANTHONY ABSOLUTE.

MRS. MAL. There, Sir Anthony, there sits the deliberate Simpleton, who wants to disgrace her family, and lavish herself on a fellow not worth a shilling!

LYD. Madam, I thought you once——

MRS. MAL. You thought, Miss!—I don't know any business you have to think at all—thought does not become a young woman. But the point we would request of you is, that you will promise to forget this fellow—to illiterate him, I say, quite from your memory.

LYD. Ah! Madam! our memories are independent of our wills.—It is not so easy to forget.

MRS. MAL. But I say it is, Miss; there is nothing on earth so easy as to *forget*, if a person chooses to set about it.—I'm sure I have as much forgot your poor dear uncle as if he had never existed—and I thought it my duty so to do; and let me tell you, Lydia, these violent memories don't become a young woman.

SIR ANTH. Why sure she won't pretend to remember what she's order'd not!—aye, this comes of her reading!

LYD. What crime, Madam, have I committed to be treated thus?

MRS. MAL. Now don't attempt to extirpate yourself from the matter; you know I have proof controvertible of it.—But tell me, will you pro-

18 woman. But the] *76*, *85*; woman; the *75*

[1] Paul Scarron's *L'Adultère innocente*, translated by Samuel Croxall, in 1722. In Congreve's *The Old Batchelor*, IV. ii, Bellmour remarks, 'I have out-fac'd Suspicion, and even dar'd Discovery—This Cloak my Sanctity, and trusty *Scarron's* Novels my Prayer-Book.'

[2] *The History of Lord Aimsworth, and the Honourable Charles Hartford, Esq., in a Series of Letters*. By the author of *Dorinda Catsby*, and *Ermina, or the Fair Recluse*, 3 vols. (1773).

[3] Henry Mackenzie, *The Man of Feeling* (1771).

[4] *Letters on the Improvement of the Mind. Addressed to a Young Lady* (1773).

[5] *Sermons to Young Women* (1765; 7th edn., 1771), by James Fordyce (1720–96).

mise to do as you're bid?—Will you take a husband of your friend's choosing?

LYD. Madam, I must tell you plainly, that had I no preference for any one else, the choice you have made would be my aversion.

MRS. MAL. What business have you, Miss, with *preference* and *aversion*? They don't become a young woman; and you ought to know, that as both always wear off, 'tis safest in matrimony to begin with a little *aversion*. I am sure I hated your poor dear uncle before marriage as if he'd been a black-a-moor—and yet, Miss, you are sensible what a wife I made!—and when it pleas'd Heav'n to release me from him, 'tis unknown what tears I shed!—But suppose we were going to give you another choice, will you promise us to give up this Beverley?

LYD. Could I belie my thoughts so far, as to give that promise, my actions would certainly as far belie my words.

MRS. MAL. Take yourself to your room.—You are fit company for nothing but your own ill-humours.

LYD. Willingly, Ma'am—I cannot change for the worse. [*Exit* LYDIA.

MRS. MAL. There's a little intricate hussy for you!

SIR ANTH. It is not to be wonder'd at, Ma'am—all this is the natural consequence of teaching girls to read.—Had I a thousand daughters, by Heaven! I'd as soon have them taught the black-art as their alphabet!

MRS. MAL. Nay, nay, Sir Anthony, you are an absolute misanthropy.

SIR ANTH. In my way hither, Mrs. Malaprop, I observed your niece's maid coming forth from a circulating library!—She had a book in each hand—they were half-bound volumes, with marble covers!—From that moment I guess'd how full of duty I should see her mistress!

MRS. MAL. Those are vile places, indeed!

SIR ANTH. Madam, a circulating library in a town is, as an ever-green tree, of diabolical knowledge!—It blossoms through the year!—And depend on it, Mrs. Malaprop, that they who are so fond of handling the leaves, will long for the fruit at last.

MRS. MAL. Fie, fie, Sir Anthony, you surely speak laconically!

SIR ANTH. Why, Mrs. Malaprop, in moderation, now, what would you have a woman know?

3 friend's] *L*, *76*, *85*; friends *75* 23 Heaven] *76*, *85*; Heavens *L*, *75* 28 marble] *76*, *85*; marbled *L*, *75* *After line 30 insert*:

Mrs. Mal. Well, but Sir Anthony, your wife, Lady Absolute, was fond of books.

Sir Anth. Aye—and injury sufficient they were to her, Madam.—But were I to chuse another helpmate, the extent of her erudition should consist in her knowing her simple letters, without their mischievous combinations;—and the summit of her science be—her ability to count as far as twenty.—The first, Mrs. Malaprop, would enable her to work *A.A.* upon my linen;—and the latter would be quite sufficient to prevent her giving me a shirt, No. 1. and a stock, No. 2.

MRS. MAL. Observe me, Sir Anthony.—I would by no means wish a daughter of mine to be a progeny[1] of learning; I don't think so much learning becomes a young woman; for instance—I would never let her meddle with Greek, or Hebrew, or Algebra, or Simony, or Fluxions, or Paradoxes,[2] or such inflammatory branches of learning—neither would it be necessary for her to handle any of your mathematical, astronomical, diabolical instruments;—But, Sir Anthony, I would send her, at nine years old, to a boarding-school, in order to learn a little ingenuity and artifice.—Then, Sir, she should have a supercilious knowledge in accounts;—and as she grew up, I would have her instructed in geometry, that she might know something of the contagious[3] countries;—but above all, Sir Anthony, she should be mistress of orthodoxy, that she might not mis-spell, and mis-pronounce words so shamefully as girls usually do; and likewise that she might reprehend the true meaning of what she is saying.—This, Sir Anthony, is what I would have a woman know;—and I don't think there is a superstitious article in it.

SIR ANTH. Well, well, Mrs. Malaprop, I will dispute the point no further with you; though I must confess, that you are a truly moderate and polite arguer, for almost every third word you say is on my side of the question.—But, Mrs. Malaprop, to the more important point in debate,—you say, you have no objection to my proposal.

MRS. MAL. None, I assure you.—I am under no positive engagement with Mr. Acres, and as Lydia is so obstinate against him, perhaps your son may have better success.

SIR ANTH. Well, Madam, I will write for the boy directly.—He knows not a syllable of this yet, though I have for some time had the proposal in my head. He is at present with his regiment.

MRS. MAL. We have never seen your son, Sir Anthony; but I hope no objection on his side.

SIR ANTH. Objection!—let him object if he dare!—No, no, Mrs. Malaprop, Jack knows that the least demur puts me in a frenzy directly.—My process was always very simple—in their younger days, 'twas 'Jack, do this;'—if he demur'd—I knock'd him down—and if he grumbled at that—I always sent him out of the room.

MRS. MAL. Aye, and the properest way, o' my conscience!—nothing is so conciliating to young people as severity.—Well, Sir Anthony, I shall give Mr. Acres his discharge, and prepare Lydia to receive your son's invocations;—and I hope you will represent *her* to the Captain as an object not altogether illegible.

SIR ANTH. Madam, I will handle the subject prudently.—Well, I must leave you—and let me beg you, Mrs. Malaprop, to enforce this matter

[1] See p. 37. [2] Cyclometry, or fluxions, or parallax?
[3] See p. 37.

roundly to the girl;—take my advice—keep a tight hand—if she rejects this proposal—clap her under lock and key:—and if you were just to let the servants forget to bring her dinner for three or four days, you can't conceive how she'd come about! [*Exit Sir* ANTH.

MRS. MAL. Well, at any rate I shall be glad to get her from under my intuition.—She has somehow discovered my partiality for Sir Lucius O'Trigger—sure, Lucy can't have betray'd me!—No, the girl is such a simpleton, I should have made her confess it.—Lucy!—Lucy!—[*calls*] Had she been one of your artificial ones, I should never have trusted her.

Enter LUCY.

LUCY. Did you call, Ma'am?

MRS. MAL. Yes, girl—Did you see Sir Lucius while you was out?

LUCY. No, indeed, Ma'am, not a glimpse of him.

MRS. MAL. You are sure, Lucy, that you never mention'd——

LUCY. O Gemini! I'd sooner cut my tongue out.

MRS. MAL. Well, don't let your simplicity be impos'd on.

LUCY. No. Ma'am.

MRS. MAL. So, come to me presently, and I'll give you another letter to Sir Lucius;—but mind Lucy—if ever you betray what you are entrusted with—(unless it be other people's secrets to me) you forfeit my malevolence for ever:—and your being a simpleton shall be no excuse for your locality. [*Exit Mrs.* MALAPROP.

LUCY. Ha! ha! ha!—So, my dear *simplicity*, let me give you a little respite—[*altering her manner*]—let girls in my station be as fond as they please of appearing expert, and knowing in their trusts;—commend me to a mask of *silliness*, and a pair of sharp eyes for my own interest under it!—Let me see to what account I have turn'd my *simplicity* lately— [*looks at a paper*]
For *abetting Miss Lydia Languish in a design of running away with an Ensign!—in money—sundry times—twelve pound twelve—gowns, five —hats, ruffles, caps,* etc. etc.—*numberless!—From the said Ensign, within this last month, six guineas and a half.*—About a quarter's pay!—Item, *from Mrs. Malaprop, for betraying the young people to her*—when I found matters were likely to be discovered—*two guineas, and a black paduasoy.*—Item, *from Mr. Acres, for carrying divers letters*—which I never deliver'd—*two guineas, and a pair of buckles.*—Item, *from Sir Lucius O'Trigger—three crowns—two gold pocket-pieces*[1]*—and a silver*

28 I have] *L*, *75*; have I *76*, *85*   36 *paduasoy*] *L*, *75*; padusoy *76*, *85*

[1] Coins carried as lucky charms, or medallions: cf. S. Foote, *The Maid of Bath* (1771), II. i:

Flint. Here is a Porto-Bello pocket piece of Admiral Varnon, with his image on one side, and six men of war only, all in full sail, on the other—

L. Cath. That's a curious medallion!

snuff-box!——Well done, *simplicity*!—yet I was forced to make my Hibernian believe, that he was corresponding, not with the *Aunt*, but with the *Niece*: for, though not over rich, I found he had too much pride and delicacy to sacrifice the feelings of a gentleman to the necessities of his fortune. [*Exit.*

END OF THE FIRST ACT

ACT II

SCENE I

Captain ABSOLUTE'*s Lodgings*

Captain ABSOLUTE *and* FAG

FAG. Sir, while I was there, Sir Anthony came in: I told him, you had sent me to inquire after his health, and to know if he was at leisure to see you.

ABS. And what did he say, on hearing I was at Bath?

FAG. Sir, in my life I never saw an elderly gentleman more astonished! He started back two or three paces, rapt out a dozen interjectoral oaths,[1] and asked, what the devil had brought you here!

ABS. Well, Sir, and what did you say?

FAG. O, I lied, Sir—I forget the precise lie, but you may depend on't; he got no truth from me. Yet, with submission, for fear of blunders in future, I should be glad to fix what *has* brought us to Bath: in order that we may lie a little consistently.—Sir Anthony's servants were curious, Sir, very curious indeed.

ABS. You have said nothing to them——?

FAG. O, not a word, Sir—not a word.—Mr. Thomas, indeed, the coachman (whom I take to be the discreetest of whips)—

ABS. S'death!—you rascal! you have not trusted him!

FAG. O, *no*, Sir—no—no—not a syllable, upon my veracity!—He was, indeed, a little inquisitive; but I was sly, Sir—devilish sly!—My Master (said I) honest Thomas (you know, Sir, one says *honest* to one's inferiors) is come to Bath to *recruit*—Yes, Sir—I said, *to recruit*—and whether for men, money, or constitution, you know, Sir, is nothing to him, nor any one else.

6 END . . . ACT] *L*, *75*; *om* *76*, *85*   19 forget] *76*, *85*; forgot *L*, *75*

[1] Cf. L. Sterne, *Tristram Shandy*, Bk. 3, ch. 11: 'Dr. Slop . . . was just beginning to return my Uncle *Toby* the compliment of his Whu-u-u or interjectional whistle.'

ABS. Well—*recruit* will do—let it be so—

FAG. O, Sir, recruit will do surprisingly—indeed, to give the thing an air, I told Thomas, that your Honour had already inlisted, five disbanded chairmen, seven minority waiters,[1] and thirteen billiard markers.

ABS. You blockhead, never say more than is necessary.

FAG. I beg pardon, Sir—I beg pardon—But with submission, a lie is nothing unless one supports it.—Sir, whenever I draw on my invention for a good current lie, I always forge *indorsements*, as well as the bill.

ABS. Well, take care you don't hurt your credit, by offering too much security.—Is Mr. Faulkland returned?

FAG. He is above, Sir, changing his dress.

ABS. Can you tell whether he has been informed of Sir Anthony's and Miss Melville's arrival?

FAG. I fancy not, Sir; he has seen no one since he came in, but his gentleman, who was with him at Bristol.—I think, Sir, I hear Mr. Faulkland coming down—

ABS. Go, tell him I am here.

FAG. Yes, Sir—[*going*] I beg pardon, Sir, but should Sir Anthony call, you will do me the favour to remember, that we are *recruiting*, if you please.

ABS. Well, well.

FAG. And in tenderness to my character, if your Honour could bring in the chairmen and waiters, I shall esteem it as an obligation;—for though I never scruple a lie to serve my Master, yet it *hurts* one's conscience, to be found out. [*Exit.*

ABS. Now for my whimsical friend—if he does not know that his mistress is here, I'll tease him a little before I tell him——

Enter FAULKLAND.

Faulkland, you're welcome to Bath again; you are punctual in your return.

FAULK. Yes; I had nothing to detain me, when I had finished the business I went on. Well, what news since I left you? How stand matters between you and Lydia?

ABS. Faith, much as they were; I have not seen her since our quarrel, however I expect to be recalled every hour.

FAULK. Why don't you persuade her to go off with you at once?

ABS. What, and lose two thirds of her fortune? You forget that my friend. —No, no, I could have brought her to that long ago.

23 chairmen] *85*; chairman *75*, *76*; *om. L* 29 you're] *L*, *75*, *85*; your're *76*

[1] Young waiters? Philip B. Daghlian suggests, in *Modern Language Quarterly*, vi (1945), 421–2, that it bears some reference to Robert Mackreth (?1725–1819), once a waiter but M.P. for Castle Rising from 1774.

FAULK. Nay then, you trifle too long—if you are sure of *her*, propose to the aunt *in your own character*, and write to Sir Anthony for his consent.

ABS. Softly, softly, for though I am convinced my little Lydia would elope with me as Ensign Beverley, yet am I by no means certain that she would take me with the impediment of our friend's consent, a regular humdrum wedding, and the reversion of a good fortune on my side; no, no, I must prepare her gradually for the discovery, and make myself necessary to her, before I risk it.—Well, but Faulkland, you'll dine with us to-day at the Hotel?

FAULK. Indeed I cannot: I am not in spirits to be of such a party.

ABS. By Heavens! I shall forswear your company. You are the most teasing, captious, incorrigible lover!—Do love like a man.

FAULK. I own I am unfit for company.

ABS. Am not *I* a lover; aye, and a romantic one too? Yet do I carry every where with me such a confounded farago of doubts, fears, hopes, wishes, and all the flimsy furniture of a country Miss's brain!

FAULK. Ah! Jack, your heart and soul are not, like mine, fixed immutably on one only object.—You throw for a large stake, but losing—you could stake, and throw again:—but I have set my sum of happiness on this cast, and not to succeed, were to be stript of all.

ABS. But for Heaven's sake! what grounds for apprehension can your whimsical brain conjure up at present?

FAULK. What grounds for apprehension did you say? Heavens! are there not a thousand! I fear for her spirits—her health—her life.—My absence may fret her; her anxiety for my return, her fears for me, may oppress her gentle temper. And for her health—does not every hour bring me cause to be alarmed? If it rains, some shower may even then have chilled her delicate frame!—If the wind be keen, some rude blast may have affected her! The heat of noon, the dews of the evening, may endanger the life of her, for whom only I value mine. O! Jack, when delicate and feeling souls are separated, there is not a feature in the sky, not a movement of the elements; not an aspiration of the breeze, but hints some cause for a lover's apprehension!

ABS. Aye, but we may choose whether we will take the hint or not.—So then, Faulkland, if you were convinced that Julia were well and in spirits, you would be entirely content.

FAULK. I should be happy beyond measure—I am anxious only for that.

22 *After* '*at present?*', *insert*:

Has Julia miss'd writing this last post? or was her last too tender, or too cool; or too grave, or too gay; or——

Faulk. Nay, nay, Jack.

Abs. Why, her love—her honour—her prudence, you cannot doubt.

Faulk. O! upon my soul, I never have;—but . . . *75*

33 for a] *L*, *75*, *85*; a for *76*

34–5 not.—So] *76*, *85*; no.—Well *75*

35 were well] *76*, *85*; was well *L*, *75*

37 I am] *85*; I'm *L*, *75*; I'am *76*

ABS. Then to cure your anxiety at once—Miss Melville is in perfect health, and is at this moment in Bath.

FAULK. Nay Jack—don't trifle with me.

ABS. She is arrived here with my father within this hour.

FAULK. Can you be serious?

ABS. I thought you knew Sir Anthony better than to be surprised at a sudden whim of this kind.—Seriously then, it is as I tell you—upon my honour.

FAULK. My dear friend!—Hollo, Du-Peigne! my hat—my dear Jack—*now nothing on earth can give me a moment's uneasiness.*

Enter FAG.

FAG. Sir, Mr. Acres just arrived is below.

ABS. Stay, Faulkland, this Acres lives within a mile of Sir Anthony, and he shall tell you how your mistress has been ever since you left her.—Fag, shew the gentleman up. [*Exit* FAG.

FAULK. What, is he much acquainted in the family?

ABS. O, very intimate: I insist on your not going: besides, his character will divert you.

FAULK. Well, I should like to ask him a few questions.

ABS. He is likewise a rival of mine—that is of my *other self's*, for he does not think his friend Capt. Absolute ever saw the lady in question;—and it is ridiculous enough to hear him complain to me of *one Beverley*, a concealed sculking rival, who——

FAULK. Hush!—He's here.

Enter ACRES.

ACRES. Hah! my dear friend, noble captain, and honest Jack, how do'st thou? just arrived faith, as you see.—Sir, your humble servant. Warm work on the roads Jack—Odds whips and wheels, I've travelled like a Comet, with a tail of dust all the way as long as the Mall.

ABS. Ah! Bob, you are indeed an excentric Planet, but we know your attraction hither—give me leave to introduce Mr. Faulkland to you; Mr. Faulkland, Mr. Acres.

ACRES. Sir, I am most heartily glad to see you: Sir, I solicit your connections.—Hey Jack—what this is Mr. Faulkland, who——

ABS. Aye, Bob, Miss Melville's Mr. Faulkland.

ACRES. Od'so! she and your father can be but just arrived before me—I suppose you have seen them.——Ah! Mr. Faulkland, you are indeed a happy man.

FAULK. I have not seen Miss Melville yet, Sir—I hope she enjoyed full health and spirits in Devonshire?

ACRES. Never knew her better in my life, Sir,—never better.—Odd's Blushes and Blooms! she has been as healthy as the German Spa.

40 Devonshire?] *76, 85*; Devonshire. *L, 75*

FAULK. Indeed!—I did hear that she had been a little indisposed.

ACRES. False, false, Sir—only said to vex you: quite the reverse I assure you.

FAULK. There, Jack, you see she has the advantage of me; I had almost fretted myself ill.

ABS. Now are you angry with your mistress for not having been sick.

FAULK. No, no, you misunderstand me:—yet surely a little trifling indisposition is not an unnatural consequence of absence from those we love.—Now confess—isn't there something unkind in this violent, robust, unfeeling health?

ABS. O, it was very unkind of her to be well in your absence to be sure!

ACRES. Good apartments, Jack.

FAULK. Well, Sir, but you were saying that Miss Melville has been so *exceedingly* well—what then she has been merry and gay I suppose?—Always in spirits—hey?

ACRES. Merry, Odds Crickets! she has been the bell and spirit of the company wherever she has been—so lively and entertaining! so full of wit and humour!

FAULK. There, Jack, there.—O, by my soul! there is an innate levity in woman, that nothing can overcome.—What! happy and I away!

ABS. Have done: how foolish this is! just now you were only apprehensive for your mistress's *spirits*.

FAULK. Why, Jack, have I been the joy and spirit of the company?

ABS. No, indeed, you have not.

FAULK. Have I been lively and entertaining?

ABS. O, upon my word, I acquit you.

FAULK. Have I been full of wit and humour?

ABS. No, faith, to do you justice, you have been confoundedly stupid indeed.

ACRES. What's the matter with the gentleman?

ABS. He is only expressing his great satisfaction at hearing that Julia has been so well and happy—that's all—hey, Faulkland?

FAULK. Oh! I am rejoiced to hear it—yes, yes, she has a *happy* disposition!

ACRES. That she has indeed—then she is so accomplished—so sweet a voice—so expert at her Harpsichord—such a mistress of flat and sharp, squallante, rumblante, and quiverante!—there was this time month—Odds Minnums and Crotchets! how she did chir[r]up at Mrs. Piano's Concert.

FAULK. There again, what say you to this? you see she has been all mirth and song—not a thought of me!

ABS. Pho! man, is not music the food of love?[1]

28 confoundedly] *76*, *85*; confounded *L*, *75*

[1] *Twelfth Night*, I. i. 'If music be the food of love, play on.'

FAULK. Well, well, it may be so.—Pray Mr. —— what's his d—d name? —Do you remember what songs Miss Melville sung?

ACRES. Not I, indeed.

ABS. Stay now, they were some pretty, melancholy, purling stream airs, I warrant; perhaps you may recollect:—did she sing—'*When absent from my soul's delight*?'[1]

ACRES. No, that wa'n't it.

ABS. Or—'*Go, gentle Gales*!'[2]——'*Go, gentle Gales*!' [sings]

ACRES. O no! nothing like it.—Odds! now I recollect one of them—'*My heart's my own, my will is free*.'[3] [sings]

FAULK. Fool! fool that I am! to fix all my happiness on such a trifler! S'death! to make herself the pipe and ballad-monger of a circle! to sooth her light heart with catches and glees!—What can you say to this, Sir?

ABS. Why, that I should be glad to hear my mistress had been so merry, *Sir*.

9 Odds!] *76*, *85*; Odds slips? *L*, *75*

---

[1] The sixth of *Twelve Songs set to Music by William Jackson of Exeter: Opera Quarta*. (n.d.), pp. 14–19. The first of the three stanzas reads:

When absent from my Soul's Delight,
What terrors fill my troubled Breast,
Once more return'd to thy lov'd sight,
Hope too returns, my Fears have rest.

[2] The fifth of the same set of songs by Jackson, pp. 10–14. The words are from Pope, 'Autumn: the third Pastoral', ll. 17–22. The first two stanzas (of four) read:

Go, gentle Gales, go gentle Gales
And bear my sighs away
To Delia's Ear, to Delia's Ear,
The tender Notes convey.

As some sad Turtle his long lost Love deplores
And with deep Murmurs fills the sounding Shores,
Thus far from Delia to the Wood I mourn,
Alike unheard, unpitied, and forlorn.

[3] From Isaac Bickerstaff's *Love in a Village* (1762), Act I:

My heart's my own, my will is free,
And so shall be my voice;
No mortal man shall wed with me,
Till first he's made my choice.

Let parents rule, cry nature's laws;
And children still obey;
And is there then no saving clause
Against tyrannic sway.

'Charles', writing in *The Gazetteer*, 21 Sept. 1771, remarks that the 'ill-effects, which romance and novel-reading, has upon the minds of the fair sex has been often and justly exposed; but there is another part of their study, which, is in my opinion, of a similar nature . . . I mean the fashionable songs and airs which young ladies are taught from their childhood to sing, and get by heart.' He mentions 'My heart's my own' as among the fifteen that seem to him to be 'extravagant' and 'inflammatory'.

FAULK. Nay, nay, nay—I am not sorry that she has been happy—no, no, I am glad of that—I would not have had her sad or sick—yet surely a sympathetic heart would have shewn itself even in the choice of a song—she might have been temperately healthy, and somehow, plaintively gay;—but she has been dancing too, I doubt not!

ACRES. What does the gentleman say about dancing?

ABS. He says the lady we speak of dances as well as she sings.

ACRES. Aye truly, does she—there was at our last race-ball———

FAULK. Hell and the devil!—There! there!I— told you so! I told you so! Oh! she thrives in my absence!—Dancing!—but her whole feelings have been in opposition with mine!—I have been anxious, silent, pensive, sedentary—my days have been hours of care, my nights of watchfulness.—She has been all Health! Spirit! Laugh! Song! Dance! —Oh! d—n'd, d—n'd levity!

ABS. For Heaven's sake! Faulkland, don't expose yourself so.—Suppose she has danced, what then?—does not the ceremony of society often oblige——

FAULK. Well, well, I'll contain myself—perhaps, as you say—for form sake.—What, Mr. Acres, you were praising Miss Melville's manner of dancing a *minuet*—hey?

ACRES. O I dare insure her for that—but what I was going to speak of was her *country dancing*:—Odds swimmings! she has such an air with her!—

FAULK. Now disappointment on her!—defend this, Absolute, why don't you defend this?—Country-dances! jiggs, and reels! am I to blame now? A Minuet I could have forgiven—I should not have minded that—I say I should not have regarded a Minuet—but *Country-dances*! Z——ds! had she made one in a *Cotillon*—I believe I could have forgiven even that—but to be monkey-led for a night!—to run the gauntlet thro' a string of amorous palming puppies!—to shew paces like a managed[1] filly!—O Jack, there never can be but *one* man in the world, whom a truly modest and delicate woman ought to pair with in a *Country-dance*; and even then, the rest of the couples should be her great uncles and aunts!

ABS. Aye, to be sure!—grand-fathers and grand-mothers!

FAULK. If there be but one vicious mind in the Set, 'twill spread like a contagion—the action of their pulse beats to the lascivious movement of the jigg—their quivering, warm-breath'd sighs impregnate the very air—the atmosphere becomes electrical to love, and each amorous spark[2] darts thro' every link of the chain!—I must leave you—I own

[1] Taught the 'manège', stepping and moving according to the strict practice of the riding school.

[2] 'These exhalations, or subtle effluvia, constitute electricity . . . They seem to adhere to the extremities of the bodies which they surround, and from which they recede, in the form of sparks' (*A New and Complete Dictionary of Arts and Sciences* (2nd edn., 1763), p. 1050).

I am somewhat flurried—and that confounded looby has perceived it. [*Going*.

ABS. Nay, but stay Faulkland, and thank Mr. Acres for his good news.

FAULK. D—n his news! [*Exit* FAULKLAND.

ABS. Ha! ha! ha! poor Faulkland five minutes since—'nothing on earth could give him a moment's uneasiness!'

ACRES. The gentleman wa'n't angry at my praising his mistress, was he?

ABS. A little jealous, I believe, Bob.

ACRES. You don't say so? Ha! ha! jealous of me—that's a good joke.

ABS. There's nothing strange in that, Bob: let me tell you, that sprightly grace and insinuating manner of your's will do some mischief among the girls here.

ACRES. Ah! you joke—ha! ha! mischief—ha! ha! but you know I am not my own property, my dear Lydia, has forestalled me.——She could never abide me in the country, because I used to dress so badly—but odds frogs and tambours! I shan't take matters so here—now ancient Madam has no voice in it—I'll make my old clothes know who's master—I shall straitway cashier the hunting-frock—and render my leather breeches incapable—My hair has been in training some time.

ABS. Indeed!

ACRES. Aye—and tho'ff[1] the side-curls are a little restive, my hind-part takes to it very kindly.

ABS. O, you'll polish, I doubt not.

ACRES. Absolutely I propose so—then if I can find out this Ensign Beverley, odds triggers and flints! I'll make him know the difference o't.

ABS. Spoke like a man——but pray, Bob, I observe you have got an odd kind of a new method of swearing——

ACRES. Ha! ha! you've taken notice of it—'tis genteel, isn't *it*?—I didn't invent it myself though; but a commander in our militia—a great scholar, I assure you—says that there is no meaning in the common oaths, and that nothing but their antiquity makes them respectable;—because, he says, the ancients would never stick to an oath or two, but would say By Jove! or by Bacchus! or by Mars! or by Venus! or by Pallas! according to the sentiment—so that to swear with propriety, says my little Major, the 'oath should be an echo to the sense;'[2] and

2 *After* '*Going*', *insert*:
Abs. Aye, aye, you are in a hurry to throw yourself at Julia's feet.
Faulk. I'm not in a humour to be trifled with—I shall see her only to upbraid her. [*Going*. *75*

13 ACRES.] *L*, *76*, *85*; *Abs*. *75*; 28 isn't *it*] *L*, *76*, *85*; isn't *75*

[1] See p. 79 n. 2.

[2] A. Pope, *An Essay in Criticism* (1711), ll. 364–5:
'Tis not enough no harshness gives offence,
The sound must seem an echo to the sense.

this we call the *oath referential*, or *sentimental swearing*[1]—ha! ha! ha! 'tis genteel, isn't it?

ABS. Very genteel, and very new indeed—and I dare say will supplant all other figures of imprecation.

ACRES. Aye, aye, the best terms will grow obsolete——D—ns have had their day.

Enter FAG.

FAG. Sir, there is a gentleman below, desires to see you—shall I shew him into the parlour?

ABS. Aye—you may.

ACRES. Well, I must be gone——

ABS. Stay; who is it, Fag?

FAG. Your father, Sir.

ABS. You puppy, why didn't you shew him up directly? [*Exit* FAG.

ACRES. You have business with Sir Anthony.—I expect a message from Mrs. Malaprop at my lodgings—I have sent also to my dear friend Sir Lucius O'Trigger.—Adieu, Jack, we must meet at night, when you shall give me a dozen bumpers to little Lydia.

ABS. That I will with all my heart. [*Exit* ACRES.
Now for a parental lecture—I hope he has heard nothing of the business that has brought me here.—I wish the gout had held him fast in Devonshire, with all my soul!

Enter Sir ANTHONY.

ABS. Sir, I am delighted to see you here; and looking so well!—your sudden arrival at Bath made me apprehensive for your health.

SIR ANTH. Very apprehensive, I dare say, Jack.—What, you are recruiting here, hey?

ABS. Yes, Sir, I am on duty.

SIR ANTH. Well, Jack, I am glad to see you, tho' I did not expect it, for I was going to write to you on a little matter of business.—Jack, I have been considering that I grow old and infirm, and shall probably not trouble you long.

ABS. Pardon me, Sir, I never saw you look more strong and hearty; and I pray frequently that you may continue so.

SIR ANTH. I hope your prayers may be heard with all my heart. Well then, Jack, I have been considering that I am so strong and hearty, I may continue to plague you a long time.—Now, Jack, I am sensible that the income of your commission, and what I have hitherto allowed you, is but a small pittance for a lad of your spirit.

17 night, when] *76*, *85*; night—Odds bottles and glasses! *75*

[1] Cf. L. Sterne, *Tristam Shandy*, 3. 12: 'I declare I object only to a connoisseur in swearing.'

ABS. Sir, you are very good.

SIR ANTH. And it is my wish, while yet I live, to have my Boy make some figure in the world.—I have resolved, therefore, to fix you at once in a noble independence.

ABS. Sir, your kindness overpowers me—such generosity makes the gratitude of reason more lively than the sensations even of filial affection.

SIR ANTH. I am glad you are so sensible of my attention—and you shall be master of a large estate in a few weeks.

ABS. Let my future life, Sir, speak my gratitude: I cannot express the sense I have of your munificence.——Yet, Sir, I presume you would not wish me to quit the army?

SIR ANTH. O, that shall be as your wife chooses.

ABS. My wife, Sir!

SIR ANTH. Aye, aye, settle that between you—settle that between you.

ABS. A *wife*, Sir, did you say?

SIR ANTH. Aye, a wife—why; did not I mention her before?

ABS. Not a word of her, Sir.

SIR ANTH. Odd so!—I mustn't forget *her* tho'.—Yes, Jack, the independence I was talking of is by a marriage—the fortune is saddled with a wife—but I suppose that makes no difference.

ABS. Sir! Sir!—you amaze me!

SIR ANTH. Why, what the d——l's the matter with the fool? Just now you were all gratitude and duty.

ABS. I was, Sir,—you talked to me of independence and a fortune, but not a word of a wife.

SIR ANTH. Why—what difference does that make? Odd's life, Sir! if you have the estate, you must take it with the live stock on it, as it stands.

ABS. If my happiness is to be the price, I must beg leave to decline the purchase.——Pray, Sir, who is the lady?

SIR ANTH. What's that to you, Sir?—Come, give me your promise to love, and to marry her directly.

ABS. Sure, Sir, this is not very reasonable, to summon my affections for a lady I know nothing of!

SIR ANTH. I am sure, Sir, 'tis more unreasonable in you to *object* to a lady you know nothing of.

ABS. Then, Sir, I must tell you plainly, that my inclinations are fix'd on another—my heart is engaged to an Angel.

SIR ANTH. Then pray let it send an excuse.——It is very sorry—but *business* prevents its waiting on her.

17 her] *76*, *85*; it *L*, *75*

37 *After* '*another*', *insert*:

Sir Anth. They are, are they? well, that's lucky—because you will have more merit in your obedience to me.

Abs. Sir, *75*

ABS. But my vows are pledged to her.

SIR ANTH. Let her foreclose, Jack; let her foreclose; they are not worth redeeming: besides, you have the Angel's vows in exchange, I suppose; so there can be no loss there.

ABS. You must excuse me, Sir, if I tell you, once for all, that in this point I cannot obey you.

SIR ANTH. Hark'ee Jack;—I have heard you for some time with patience —I have been cool,—quite cool;—but take care—you know I am compliance itself—when I am not thwarted;—no one more easily led—when I have my own way;—but don't put me in a phrenzy.

ABS. Sir, I must repeat it—in this I cannot obey you.

SIR ANTH. Now, d—n me! if ever I call you *Jack* again while I live!

ABS. Nay, Sir, but hear me.

SIR ANTH. Sir, I won't hear a word—not a word! not one word! so give me your promise by a nod—and I'll tell you what, Jack—I mean, you Dog—if you don't, by——

ABS. What, Sir, promise to link myself to some mass of ugliness! to——

SIR ANTH. Z——ds! sirrah! the lady shall be as ugly as I choose: she shall have a hump on each shoulder; she shall be as crooked as the Crescent; her one eye shall roll like the Bull's in Cox's musæum[1]—she shall have a skin like a mummy, and the beard of a Jew—she shall be all this, sirrah!—yet I'll make you ogle her all day, and sit up all night to write sonnets on her beauty.

ABS. This is reason and moderation indeed!

SIR ANTH. None of your sneering, puppy! no grinning, jackanapes!

ABS. Indeed, Sir, I never was in a worse humour for mirth in my life.

SIR ANTH. 'Tis false, Sir! I know you are laughing in your sleeve: I know you'll grin when I am gone, sirrah!

ABS. Sir, I hope I know my duty better.

SIR ANTH. None of your passion, Sir! none of your violence! if you please.—It won't do with me, I promise you.

ABS. Indeed, Sir, I never was cooler in my life.

SIR ANTH. 'Tis a confounded lie!—I know you are in a passion in your heart; I know you are, you hypocritical young dog! but it won't do.

ABS. Nay, Sir, upon my word.

SIR ANTH. So you will fly out! can't you be cool, like me? What the devil good can *Passion* do!—*Passion* is of no service, you impudent, insolent, over-bearing Reprobate!—There you sneer again!—don't

20 Cox's] *L*, *76*, *85*; Coxe's *75*

[1] James Cox exhibited mechanical 'toys'—singing birds, chronoscopes, costly and jewelled ornaments—in Spring Gardens. One of them was described as 'a curious bull', and another was 'a pedestal of four bulls'. See the *Hibernian Magazine*, Feb. 1772, pp. 205–10.

provoke me!—but you rely upon the mildness of my temper—you do, you Dog! you play upon the meekness of my disposition! Yet take care —the patience of a saint may be overcome at last!—but mark! I give you six hours and a half to consider of this: if you then agree, without any condition, to do every thing on earth that I choose, why—confound you! I may in time forgive you——If not, z——ds! don't enter the same hemisphere with me! don't dare to breathe the same air, or use the same light with me; but get an atmosphere and a sun of your own! I'll strip you of your commission; I'll lodge a five-and-threepence in the hands of trustees, and you shall live on the interest.—I'll disown you, I'll disinherit you, I'll unget you![1] and—d—n me, if ever I call you Jack again! [*Exit* SIR ANTHONY.

ABSOLUTE, *solus*.

ABS. Mild, gentle, considerate father—I kiss your hands.—What a tender method of giving his opinion in these matters Sir Anthony has! I dare not trust him with the truth.—I wonder what old, wealthy Hag it is that he wants to bestow on me!—yet he married himself for love! and was in his youth a bold Intriguer, and a gay Companion!

Enter FAG.

FAG. Assuredly, Sir, our Father is wrath to a degree; he comes down stairs eight or ten steps at a time—muttering, growling, and thumping the bannisters all the way: I, and the Cook's dog, stand bowing at the door—rap! he gives me a stroke on the head with his cane; bids me carry that to my master, then kicking the poor Turnspit into the area, d—ns us all, for a puppy triumvirate!——Upon my credit, Sir, were I in your place, and found my father such very bad company, I should certainly drop his acquaintance.

ABS. Cease your impertinence, Sir, at present.—Did you come in for nothing more?——Stand out of the way!

[*Pushes him aside, and Exit.*

FAG, *solus*.

FAG. Soh! Sir Anthony trims my Master; He is afraid to reply to his Father—then vents his spleen on poor Fag!——When one is vexed by one person, to revenge one's self on another, who happens to come in the way—is the vilest injustice! Ah! it shews the worst temper—the basest——

2 meekness] *L*, *76*, *85*; weakness *75* 7 breathe] *76*, *85*; breath *75*; *om. L*
8 a sun] *76*, *85*; sun *75*; *om. L*

[1] Cf. Sir Sampson (Congreve, *Love for Love*, II. i): 'Are you not my Slave? Did I not beget you? And might I not have chosen whether I would have begot you or no?'

Enter ERRAND-BOY.

BOY. Mr. Fag! Mr. Fag! your Master calls you.

FAG. Well, you little, dirty puppy, you need not baul so!——The meanest disposition! the——

BOY. Quick, quick, Mr. Fag.

FAG. *Quick, quick*, you impudent Jackanapes! am I to be commanded by you too? you little, impertinent, insolent, kitchen-bred——

[*Exit, kicking and beating him.*

SCENE II

The North Parade

Enter LUCY.

LUCY. So—I shall have another Rival to add to my mistress's list—Captain Absolute.——However, I shall not enter his name till my purse has received notice in form. Poor Acres is dismissed!—Well, I have done him a last friendly office, in letting him know that Beverley was here before him.—Sir Lucius is generally more punctual, when he expects to hear from his *dear Dalia*,[1] as he calls her: —I wonder he's not here!—I have a little scruple of conscience from this deceit; tho' I should not be paid so well, if my hero knew that *Delia* was near fifty, and her own mistress.

Enter SIR LUCIUS O'TRIGGER.

SIR LUC. Hah! my little embassadress—upon my conscience I have been looking for you; I have been on the South Parade this half-hour.

LUCY. (*Speaking simply*) O gemini! and I have been waiting for your worship here on the North.

SIR LUC. Faith!—may be, that was the reason we did not meet; and it is very comical too, how you could go out and I not see you—for I was only taking a nap at the Parade-Coffee-house, and I chose the *window* on purpose that I might not miss you.

19 *After* 'own mistress', *insert*:—I could not have thought he would have been so nice, when there's a golden egg in case, as to care whether he has it from a pullet or an old hen! *75*

---

[1] Cf. 'The Bath Toast', a glee for three voices, by Henry Harrington (1727–1816):

To Delia fill the sprightly wine,
The health's engaging and divine;
O'er ev'ry heart this toast shall reign,
Whose eyes out-sparkle bright Champaign.
Let purest odours scent the air,
And wreaths of roses bind our hair,
In her chaste lips these blushing lie,
And those her gentle sighs supply.

[J. Bowen], *A Selection of Favourite Catches, Glees, &c., as sung at the Meetings of the Harmonic Society in the City of Bath* (Bath, 1798), pp. 33–4.

LUCY. My stars! Now I'd wager a six-pence I went by while you were asleep.

SIR LUC. Sure enough it must have been so——and I never dreamt it was so late, till I waked. Well, but my little girl, have you got nothing for me?

LUCY. Yes, but I have:——I've got a letter for you in my pocket.

SIR LUC. O faith! I guessed you weren't come empty-handed—well—let me see what the dear creature says.

LUCY. There, Sir Lucius. [*Gives him a letter.*

SIR LUC. (Reads) '*Sir—there is often a sudden incentive impulse in love, that has a greater induction than years of domestic combination: such was the commotion I felt at the first superfluous view of Sir Lucius O'Trigger.*' Very pretty, upon my word. '*Female punctuation forbids me to say more; yet let me add, that it will give me joy infallible to find Sir Lucius worthy the last criterion of my affections.*——DELIA.' Upon my conscience! Lucy, your lady is a great mistress of language.—Faith, she's quite the queen of the dictionary!—for the devil a word dare refuse coming at her call—tho' one would think it was quite out of hearing.

LUCY. Aye, Sir, a lady of her experience.

SIR LUC. Experience! what, at seventeen?

LUCY. O true, Sir—but then she reads so——my stars! how she will read off-hand!

SIR LUC. Faith, she must be very deep read to write this way—tho' she is rather an arbitrary writer too—for here are a great many poor words pressed into the service of this note, that would get their *habeas corpus* from any court in Christendom.

LUCY. Ah! Sir Lucius, if you were to hear how she talks of you!

SIR LUC. O tell her, I'll make her the best husband in the world, and Lady O'Trigger into the bargain!—But we must get the old gentlewoman's consent—and do every thing fairly.

LUCY. Nay, Sir Lucius, I thought you wa'n't rich enough to be so nice!

SIR LUC. Upon my word, young woman, you have hit it:—I am so poor that I can't afford to do a dirty action.—If I did not want money I'd steal your mistress and her fortune with a great deal of pleasure.—However, my pretty girl, (*gives her money*) here's a little something to buy you a ribband; and meet me in the evening, and I'll give you an answer to this. So, hussy, take a kiss before-hand, to put you in mind. [*Kisses her.*

LUCY. O lud! Sir Lucius—I never seed such a gemman! My lady won't like you if you're so impudent.

12 *After* '*my word*', *insert*: '*As my motive is interested, you may be assured my love shall never be miscellaneous*' Very well. *75* 14 *affections*] *75*, *76*, *85*; affection *L* *After* '*affections*', *insert*: '*Yours, while meretricious.*' *L*, *75* 25 *After* '*Christendom*', *insert*:—However, when affection guides the pen, Lucy, he must be a brute who finds fault with the style. *75*

SIR LUC. Faith she will, Lucy——that same——pho! what's the name of it?——*Modesty*!——is a quality in a lover more praised by the women than liked; so, if your mistress asks you whether Sir Lucius ever gave you a kiss, tell her *fifty*—my dear.

LUCY. What, would you have me tell her a lie?

SIR LUC. Ah then, you baggage! I'll make it a truth presently.

LUCY. For shame now; here is some one coming.

SIR LUC. O faith, I'll quiet your conscience!

[*Sees* FAG.—*Exit*, *humming a Tune*.

Enter FAG.

FAG. So, so, Ma'am. I humbly beg pardon.

LUCY. O lud!—now, Mr. Fag—you flurry one so.

FAG. Come, come, Lucy, here's no one bye—so a little less simplicity, with a grain or two more sincerity, if you please.——You play false with us, Madam.——I saw you give the Baronet a letter.——My Master shall know this—and if he don't call him out—I will.

LUCY. Ha! ha! ha! you gentlemen's gentlemen are so hasty.——That letter was from Mrs. Malaprop, simpleton.——She is taken with Sir Lucius's address.

FAG. How! what tastes some people have!——Why I suppose I have walked by her window an hundred times.——But what says our young lady? Any message to my master?

LUCY. Sad news! Mr. Fag.—A worse Rival than Acres!—Sir Anthony Absolute has proposed his son.

FAG. What, Captain Absolute?

LUCY. Even so.—I overheard it all.

FAG. Ha! ha! ha!—very good, faith.—Goodbye, Lucy, I must away with this news.

LUCY. Well—you may laugh—but it is true, I assure you. [*Going*.] But —Mr. Fag—tell your master not to be cast down by this.

FAG. O, he'll be so disconsolate!

LUCY. And charge him not to think of quarrelling with young Absolute.

FAG. Never fear!—never fear!

LUCY. Be sure—bid him keep up his spirits.

FAG. We will—we will. [*Exeunt severally*.

END OF THE SECOND ACT

20 How! what] *76*, *85*; What *75* 36 END . . . ACT] *L*, *75*; *om*. *76*, *85*

ACT III

SCENE I

The North Parade

Enter ABSOLUTE.

'Tis just as Fag told me, indeed.—Whimsical enough, faith! My Father wants to *force* me to marry the very girl I am plotting to run away with!——He must not know of my connection with her yet a-while.——He has too summary a method of proceeding in these matters.——However, I'll read my recantation instantly.——My conversion is something sudden, indeed—but I can assure him it is very *sincere*.——So, so—here he comes.—He looks plaguy gruff.

[*Steps aside*.

Enter Sir ANTHONY.

SIR ANTH. No—I'll die sooner than forgive him.—*Die*, did I say? I'll live these fifty years to plague him.——At our last meeting, his impudence had almost put me out of temper.—An obstinate, passionate, self-willed boy!—Who can he take after? This is my return for getting him before all his brothers and sisters!—for putting him, at twelve years old, into a marching regiment, and allowing him fifty pounds a year, beside his pay ever since!—But I have done with him;—he's any body's son for me.——I never will see him more,—never—never—never—never.[1]

ABS. Now for a penitential face.

SIR ANTH. Fellow, get out of my way.

ABS. Sir, you see a penitent before you.

SIR ANTH. I see an impudent scoundrel before me.

ABS. A sincere penitent.——I am come, Sir, to acknowledge my error, and to submit entirely to your will.

SIR ANTH. What's that?

ABS. I have been revolving, and reflecting, and considering on your past goodness, and kindness, and condescension to me.

SIR ANTH. Well, Sir?

ABS. I have been likewise weighing and balancing what you were pleased to mention concerning duty, and obedience, and authority.

SIR ANTH. Well, Puppy?

ABS. Why then, Sir, the result of my reflections is—a resolution to sacrifice every inclination of my own to your satisfaction.

9 *After* '*matters*', *insert*:—and Lydia shall not yet lose her hopes of an elopement. *75*

[1] Cf. *King Lear*, v. iii:

Thou'lt come no more
Never, never, never, never, never.

SIR ANTH. Why now, you talk sense—absolute sense—I never heard any thing more sensible in my life.———Confound you; you shall be *Jack* again.

ABS. I am happy in the appellation.

SIR ANTH. Why, then, Jack, my dear Jack, I will now inform you—who the lady really is.——Nothing but your passion and violence, you silly fellow, prevented my telling you at first. Prepare, Jack, for wonder and rapture—prepare.——What think you of Miss Lydia Languish?

ABS. Languish! What, the Languishes of Worcestershire?

SIR ANTH. Worcestershire! No. Did you never meet Mrs. Malaprop and her Niece, Miss Languish, who came into our country just before you were last ordered to your regiment?

ABS. Malaprop! Languish! I don't remember ever to have heard the names before. Yet, stay—I think I do recollect something.——*Languish! Languish!* She squints, don't she?——A little, red-haired girl?

SIR ANTH. Squints?——A red-haired girl!——Z——ds, no.

ABS. Then I must have forgot; it can't be the same person.

SIR ANTH. Jack! Jack! what think you of blooming, love-breathing seventeen?

ABS. As to that, Sir, I am quite indifferent.—If I can please you in the matter, 'tis all I desire.

SIR ANTH. Nay, but Jack, such eyes! such eyes! so innocently wild! so bashfully irresolute! Not a glance but speaks and kindles some thought of love! Then, Jack, her cheeks! her cheeks, Jack! so deeply blushing at the insinuations of her tell-tale eyes! Then, Jack, her lips! —O Jack, lips smiling at their own discretion; and if not smiling, more sweetly pouting; more lovely in sullenness!

ABS. That's she indeed.—Well done, old gentleman!

SIR ANTH. Then, Jack, her neck.——O Jack! Jack!

ABS. And which is to be mine, Sir, the Niece or the Aunt?

SIR ANTH. Why, you unfeeling, insensible Puppy, I despise you. When I was of your age, such a description would have made me fly like a rocket! The *Aunt*, indeed!—Odds life! when I ran away with your mother, I would not have touched any thing old or ugly to gain an empire.

ABS. Not to please your father, Sir?

SIR ANTH. To please my father!——Z——ds! not to please——O my father!——Oddso!——yes—yes! if my father indeed had desired——that's quite another matter.——Tho' he wa'n't the indulgent father that I am, Jack.

ABS. I dare say not, Sir.

SIR ANTH. But, Jack, you are not sorry to find your mistress is so beautiful.

ABS. Sir, I repeat it; if I please you in this affair, 'tis all I desire. Not that I think a woman the worse for being handsome; but, Sir, if you please to recollect, you before hinted something about a hump or two, one eye, and a few more graces of that kind—now, without being very nice, I own I should rather chuse a wife of mine to have the usual number of limbs, and a limited quantity of back: and tho' *one* eye may be very agreeable, yet as the prejudice has always run in favour of *two*, I would not wish to affect a singularity in that article.

SIR ANTH. What a phlegmatic sot it is! Why, sirrah, you're an anchorite! —a vile insensible stock.—You a soldier!—you're a walking block, fit only to dust the company's regimentals on!——Odds life! I've a great mind to marry the girl myself!

ABS. I am entirely at your disposal, Sir; if you should think of addressing Miss Languish yourself, I suppose you would have me marry the *Aunt*; or if you should change your mind, and take the old lady—'tis the same to me—I'll marry the *Niece*.

SIR ANTH. Upon my word, Jack, thou'rt either a very great hypocrite, or——but, come, I know your indifference on such a subject must be all a lie—I'm sure it must—come, now—d—n your demure face!—come, confess, Jack—you have been lying—ha'n't you? You have been playing the hypocrite, hey—I'll never forgive you, if you ha'n't been lying and playing the hypocrite.

ABS. I'm sorry, Sir, that the respect and duty which I bear to you should be so mistaken.

SIR ANTH. Hang your respect and duty! But, come along with me, I'll write a note to Mrs. Malaprop, and you shall visit the lady directly.

ABS. Where does she lodge, Sir?

SIR ANTH. What a dull question!—only on the Grove here.

ABS. O! then I can call on her in my way to the coffee-house.

SIR ANTH. In your way to the coffee-house! You'll set your heart down in your way to the coffee-house, hey? Ah! you leaden-nerv'd, wooden-hearted dolt! But come along, you shall see her directly; her eyes shall be the Promethian torch to you—come along, I'll never forgive you, if you don't come back, stark mad with rapture and impatience—if you don't, egad, I'll marry the girl myself! [*Exeunt*.

1 ABS.] *L*, *76*, *85*; *Sir Anth. 75* 11 regimentals] *76*, *85*; regiment *75* [corrected in 'Errata'] 14 Languish], *L*, *76*, *85*; Anguish *75* [corrected in 'Errata'] 15 your] *L*, *76*, *85*; you're *75* 20 *After 'ha'n't you?'*, *insert*: You have been lying, hey? I'll never forgive you, if you ha'n't:—so now, own, my dear Jack, *75* 27–8 Where . . . on the] *L*, *75*; *om. 76*, *85* 28 Grove here] *75*; North Parade, here *L*; *om. 76*, *85* 29–30 O! . . . coffee-house] *L*, *75*; *om. 76*, *85* 30–1 You'll set . . . hey?] *75*; *om. L*, *76*, *85* 31 Ah!] *75*; Oh! *L*; *om. 75*, *85* 31–2 you leaden . . . directly] *L*, *75*; *om. 76*, *85* 34–5 if . . . myself!] *75*, *76*, *85*; 'Who boasts he feels not Beautie's Fire, | To be a Man—must be a Lyar.' *L*

SCENE II

JULIA's *Dressing-room*

FAULKLAND, *solus.*

FAULK. They told me Julia would return directly; I wonder she is not yet come!—How mean does this captious, unsatisfied temper of mine appear to my cooler judgment! Yet I know not that I indulge it in any other point:—but on this one subject, and to this one subject, whom I think I love beyond my life, I am ever ungenerously fretful, and madly capricious!—I am conscious of it—yet I cannot correct myself! What tender, honest joy sparkled in her eyes when we met!—How delicate was the warmth of her expressions!——I was ashamed to appear less happy—though I had come resolved to wear a face of coolness and upbraiding. Sir Anthony's presence prevented my proposed expostulations:—yet I must be satisfied that she has not been so *very* happy in my absence.—She is coming!—Yes!—I know the nimbleness of her tread, when she thinks her impatient Faulkland counts the moments of her stay.

Enter JULIA.

JUL. I had not hop'd to see you again so soon.

FAULK. Could I, Julia, be contented with my first welcome—restrained as we were by the presence of a third person?

JUL. O Faulkland, when your kindness can make me thus happy, let me not think that I discovered something of coldness in your first salutation.

FAULK. 'Twas but your fancy, Julia.—I *was* rejoiced to see you—to see you in such health—Sure I had no cause for coldness?

JUL. Nay then, I see you have taken something ill.—You must not conceal from me what it is.

FAULK. Well then—shall I own to you that my joy at hearing of your health and arrival here, by your neighbour Acres, was somewhat damped, by his dwelling much on the high spirits you had enjoyed in Devonshire—on your mirth—your singing—dancing, and I know not what!—For such is my temper, Julia, that I should regard every mirthful moment in your absence as a treason to constancy:—The mutual tear that steals down the cheek of parting lovers is a compact, that no smile shall live there till they meet again.

4 I wonder] *L*, *76*, *85*; wonder *75*   7 subject, whom] *76*, *85*; object, whom *75*; *om. L*   23 something of coldness] *76*, *85*; more coolness *L*, *75*   24 *After* '*salutation*', *insert*: than my long-hoarded joy could have presaged *L*, *75*   29 *After* '*to you*', *insert*:—but you will despise me, Julia—nay, I despise myself for it.—Yet I *will* own, *75*   30 somewhat] *76*, *85*; something *L*, *75*

JUL. Must I never cease to tax my Faulkland with this teasing minute caprice?—Can the idle reports of a silly boor weigh in your breast against my tried affection?

FAULK. They have no weight with me, Julia: no, no—I am happy if you have been so—yet only say, that you did not sing with *mirth*—say that you *thought* of Faulkland in the dance.

JUL. I never can be happy, in your absence.——If I wear a countenance of content, it is to shew that my mind holds no doubt of my Faulkland's truth.——If I seem'd sad—it were to make malice triumph; and say, that I had fixed my heart on one, who left me to lament his roving, and my own credulity.——Believe me, Faulkland, I mean not to upbraid you, when I say, that I have often dressed sorrow in smiles, lest my friends should guess whose unkindness had caused my tears.

FAULK. You were ever all goodness to me.—O, I am a brute, when I but admit a doubt of your true constancy!

JUL. If ever, without such cause from you, as I will not suppose possible, you find my affections veering but a point, may I become a proverbial scoff for levity, and base ingratitude.

FAULK. Ah! Julia, that *last* word is grating to me. I would I had no title to your *gratitude*! Search your heart, Julia; perhaps what you have mistaken for Love, is but the warm effusion of a too thankful heart!

JUL. For what quality must I love you?

FAULK. For no quality! To regard me for any quality of mind or understanding, were only to *esteem* me. And for person—I have often wish'd myself deformed, to be convinced that I owed no obligation *there* for any part of your affection.

JUL. Where Nature has bestowed a shew of nice attention in the features of a man, he should laugh at it, as misplaced. I have seen men, who in *this* vain article perhaps might rank above you; but my heart has never asked my eyes if it were so or not.

FAULK. Now this is not well from *you*, Julia—I despise person in a man——Yet if you lov'd me as I wish, though I were an Æthiop, you'd think none so fair.

JUL. I see you are determined to be unkind.—The *contract* which my poor father bound us in gives you more than a lover's privilege.

FAULK. Again, Julia, you raise ideas that feed and justify my doubts.——I would not have been more free—no—I am proud of my restraint.——Yet—yet—perhaps your high respect alone for this solemn compact has fettered your inclinations, which else had made a worthier choice.—How shall I be sure, had you remained unbound in thought and promise, that I should still have been the object of your persevering love?

41 a worthier] *76*, *85*; worthier *L*, *75*

JUL. Then try me now.—Let us be free as strangers as to what is past:—*my* heart will not feel more liberty!

FAULK. There now! so hasty, Julia! so anxious to be free!—If your love for me were fixed and ardent, you would not loose your hold, even tho' I wish'd it!

JUL. O, you torture me to the heart!—I cannot bear it.

FAULK. I do not mean to distress you.—If I lov'd you less, I should never give you an uneasy moment.—But hear me.—All my fretful doubts arise from this—Women are not used to weigh, and separate the motives of their affections:—the cold dictates of prudence, gratitude, or filial duty, may sometimes be mistaken for the pleadings of the heart. ——I would not boast—yet let me say, that I have neither age, person, or character, to found dislike on;—my fortune such as few ladies could be charged with *indiscretion* in the match.—O Julia! when *Love* receives such countenance from *Prudence*, nice minds will be suspicious of its *birth*.

JUL. I know not whither your insinuations would tend:—But as they seem pressing to insult me—I will spare you the regret of having done so.—I have given you no cause for this! [*Exit in Tears.*

FAULK. In Tears! stay, Julia: stay but for a moment.——The door is fastened!—Julia!—my soul—but for one moment:—I hear her sobbing!—'Sdeath! what a brute am I to use her thus! Yet stay.—Aye—she is coming now:—how little resolution there is in woman!—how a few soft words can turn them!——No, faith!—she is *not* coming either.——Why, Julia—my love—say but that you forgive me—come but to tell me that—now, this is being *too* resentful:—stay! she *is* coming too—I thought she would—no *steadiness* in any thing! her going away must have been a mere trick then—she sha'n't see that I was hurt by it.—I'll affect indifference——[*hums a tune: then listens*]——No—Z—ds! she's *not* coming!—nor don't intend it, I suppose.—This is not *steadiness*, but *obstinacy*! Yet I deserve it.—What, after so long an absence, to quarrel with her tenderness!—'twas barbarous and unmanly!——I should be ashamed to see her now.—I'll wait till her just resentment is abated—and when I distress her so again, may I lose her for ever! and be linked instead to some antique virago, whose knawing passions, and long-hoarded spleen, shall make me curse my folly half the day, and all the night! [*Exit.*

4 loose] *L*, *75*; lose *76*, *85* 17 But] *76*, *85*; *om. L*, *75*

SCENE III

Mrs. MALAPROP'*s Lodgings*

Mrs. MALAPROP, *with a letter in her hand, and Captain* ABSOLUTE.

MRS. MAL. Your being Sir Anthony's son, Captain, would itself be a sufficient accommodation;—but from the ingenuity of your appearance, I am convinced you deserve the character here given of you.

ABS. Permit me to say, Madam, that as I never yet have had the pleasure of seeing Miss Languish, my principal inducement in this affair at present, is the honour of being allied to Mrs. Malaprop; of whose intellectual accomplishments, elegant manners, and unaffected learning, no tongue is silent.

MRS. MAL. Sir, you do me infinite honour!—I beg, Captain, you'll be seated.—(*Sit*)—Ah! few gentlemen, now a days, know how to value the ineffectual qualities in a woman! few think how a little knowledge becomes a gentlewoman! Men have no sense now but for the worthless flower of beauty!

ABS. It is but too true indeed, Ma'am;—yet I fear our ladies should share the blame—they think our admiration of *beauty* so great, that *knowledge* in *them* would be superfluous. Thus, like garden-trees, they seldom shew fruit, till time has robb'd them of the more specious blossom.—Few, like Mrs. Malaprop and the Orange-tree, are rich in both at once!

MRS. MAL. Sir—you overpower me with good-breeding.—He is the very Pine-apple of politeness! You are not ignorant, Captain, that this giddy girl has somehow contrived to fix her affections on a beggarly, strolling, eves-dropping Ensign, whom none of us have seen, and nobody knows any thing of.

ABS. O, I have heard the silly affair before.—I'm not at all prejudiced against her on *that* account.

MRS. MAL. You are very good, and very considerate, Captain.—I am sure I have done every thing in my power since I exploded the affair! long ago I laid my positive conjunctions on her never to think on the fellow again;—I have since laid Sir Anthony's preposition before her; —but I'm sorry to say she seems resolved to decline every particle that I enjoin her.

ABS. It must be very distressing indeed, Ma'am.

MRS. MAL. Oh! it gives me the hydrostatics to such a degree!—I thought she had persisted from corresponding with him; but behold this very

3 *with . . . hand*] *76*, *85*; *om.* *L*, *75* 16 becomes] *L*, *76*, *85*; become *75* 17 flower of beauty] *76*, *85*; flower, beauty *L*, *75* 21 fruit] *76*, *85*; fruits *75*; the fruit *L* 32 conjunctions] *L*, *76*, *85*; conjunction *75* 37 Oh!] *76*, *85*; *om.* *L*, *75*

day, I have interceded another letter from the fellow! I believe I have it in my pocket.

ABS. O the devil! my last note. [*Aside.*

MRS. MAL. Aye, here it is.

ABS. Aye, my note indeed! O the little traitress Lucy. [*Aside.*

MRS. MAL. There, perhaps you may know the writing.

[*Gives him the letter.*

ABS. I think I have seen the hand before—yes, I *certainly must* have seen this hand before:——

MRS. MAL. Nay, but read it, Captain.

ABS. [*Reads*] '*My soul's idol, my ador'd Lydia!*'—Very tender indeed!

MRS. MAL. Tender! aye, and prophane too, o' my conscience!

ABS. '*I am excessively alarmed at the intelligence you send me, the more so as my new rival*'——

MRS. MAL. That's *you*, Sir.

ABS. '*has universally the character of being an accomplished gentleman, and a man of honour.*'——Well, that's handsome enough.

MRS. MAL. O, the fellow has some design in writing so——

ABS. That he had, I'll answer for him, Ma'am.

MRS. MAL. But go on, Sir—you'll see presently.

ABS. '*As for the old weather-beaten she-dragon who guards you,*'—Who can he mean by that?

MRS. MAL. *Me*, Sir—*me*—he means *me* there—what do you think now?—but go on a little further.

ABS. Impudent scoundrel!—'*it shall go hard but I will elude her vigilance, as I am told that the same ridiculous vanity, which makes her dress up her coarse features, and deck her dull chat with hard words which she don't understand*'——

MRS. MAL. There, Sir! an attack upon my language! what do you think of that?—an aspersion upon my parts of speech! was ever such a brute! Sure if I reprehend any thing in this world, it is the use of my oracular tongue, and a nice derangement of epitaphs!

ABS. He deserves to be hang'd and quartered! let me see—'*same ridiculous vanity*'——

MRS. MAL. You need not read it again, Sir.

ABS. I beg pardon, Ma'am '*does also lay her open to the grossest deceptions from flattery and pretended admiration*'—an impudent coxcomb! '*so that I have a scheme to see you shortly with the old Harridan's consent, and even to make her a go between in our interviews.*'——Was ever such assurance.

MRS. MAL. Did you ever hear any thing like it?—he'll elude my vigilance, will he?—yes, yes! ha! ha! he's very likely to enter these doors!—we'll try who can plot best!

16 ABS.] *L*, *76*, *85*; *om.* *75* 18 has] *L*, *76*, *85*; had *75* 31 Sure] *L*, *76*, *85*; save *75* 41 doors] *L*, *76*, *85*; floors *75*

ABS. So we will Ma'am—so we will.—Ha! ha! ha! a conceited puppy, ha! ha! ha!——Well, but Mrs. Malaprop, as the girl seems so infatuated by this fellow, suppose you were to wink at her corresponding with him for a little time—let her even plot an elopement with him—then do you connive at her escape—while *I*, just in the nick, will have the fellow laid by the heels, and fairly contrive to carry her off in his stead.

MRS. MAL. I am delighted with the scheme, never was any thing better perpetrated!

ABS. But, pray, could not I see the lady for a few minutes now?—I should like to try her temper a little.

MRS. MAL. Why, I don't know——I doubt she is not prepared for a visit of this kind.——There is a decorum in these matters.

ABS. O Lord! she won't mind *me*—only tell her Beverley——

MRS. MAL. Sir!——

ABS. Gently, good tongue. [*Aside.*

MRS. MAL. What did you say of Beverley?

ABS. O, I was going to propose that you should tell her, by way of jest, that it was Beverley who was below—she'd come down fast enough then—ha! ha! ha!

MRS. MAL. 'Twould be a trick she well-deserves—besides you know the fellow tells her he'll get my consent to see her—ha! ha!—Let him if he can, I say again.—Lydia, come down here! [*Calling.* —He'll make me a *go-between in their interviews*!—ha! ha! ha! Come down, I say, Lydia!—I don't wonder at your laughing, ha! ha! ha! his impudence is truly ridiculous.

ABS. 'Tis very ridiculous, upon my soul, Ma'am, ha! ha! ha!

MRS. MAL. The little hussy won't hear.—Well, I'll go and tell her at once who it is—she shall know that Capt. Absolute is come to wait on her.—And I'll make her behave as becomes a young woman.

ABS. As you please, Ma'am.

MRS. MAL. For the present, Captain, your servant—Ah! you've not done laughing yet, I see—*elude my vigilance*! yes, yes, ha! ha! ha! [*Exit.*

ABS. Ha! ha! ha! one would think now that I might throw off all disguise at once, and seize my prize with security—but such is Lydia's caprice, that to undeceive were probably to lose her.—I'll see whether she knows me.

[*Walks aside, and seems engaged in looking at the pictures.*

Enter LYDIA.

LYD. What a scene am I now to go thro'! surely nothing can be more dreadful than to be obliged to listen to the loathsome addresses of a stranger to one's heart.—I have heard of girls persecuted as I am, who

1 So we . . . will.—] *76*, *85*; *om. L*, *75*   12 visit] *76*, *85*; first visit *L*, *75*

have appealed in behalf of their favoured lover to the generosity of his rival: suppose I were to try it—there stands the hated rival—an officer too!—but O how unlike my Beverley!—I wonder he don't begin—truly he seems a very negligent wooer!—quite at his ease, upon my word! I'll speak first—Mr. Absolute.

ABS. Madam. [*Turns round.*

LYD. O Heav'ns! Beverley!

ABS. Hush!—hush, my life!—softly! be not surprised!

LYD. I am so astonished! and so terrified! and so overjoy'd!—for Heav'n's sake! how came you here?

ABS. Briefly—I have deceived your Aunt—I was informed that my new rival was to visit here this evening, and contriving to have him kept away, have passed myself on *her* for Capt. Absolute.

LYD. O, charming!—And she really takes you for young Absolute?

ABS. O, she's convinced of it.

LYD. Ha! ha! ha! I can't forbear laughing to think how her sagacity is over-reached!

ABS. But we trifle with our precious moments—such another opportunity may not occur—then let me now conjure my kind, my condescending angel, to fix the time when I may rescue her from undeserved persecution, and with a licensed warmth plead for my reward.

LYD. Will you then, Beverley, consent to forfeit that portion of my paltry wealth?—that burthen on the wings of love?

ABS. O come to me—rich only thus—in loveliness—Bring no portion to me but thy love—'twill be generous in you, Lydia—for well you know, it is the only dower your poor Beverley can repay.

LYD. How persuasive are his words!—how charming will poverty be with him!

ABS. Ah! my soul, what a life will we then live? Love shall be our idol and support! we will worship him with a monastic strictness; abjuring all worldly toys, to center every thought and action there.—Proud of calamity, we will enjoy the wreck of wealth; while the surrounding gloom of adversity shall make the flame of our pure love show doubly bright.—By Heav'ns! I would fling all goods of fortune from me with a prodigal hand to enjoy the scene where I might clasp my Lydia to my bosom, and say, the world affords no smile to me—but here——

[*Embracing her.*

If she holds out now the devil is in it! [*Aside.*

LYD. Now could I fly with him to the Antipodes! but my persecution is not yet come to a crisis.

Enter Mrs. MALAPROP, *listening.*

MRS. MAL. I'm impatient to know how the little huzzy deports herself.

[*Aside.*

ABS. So pensive, Lydia!—is then your warmth abated?

MRS. MAL. *Warmth abated*!—so!—she has been in a passion, I suppose.

LYD. No—nor ever can while I have life.

MRS. MAL. An ill-temper'd little devil!—She'll be *in a passion all her life*—will she?

LYD. Think not the idle threats of my ridiculous aunt can ever have any weight with me.

MRS. MAL. Very dutiful, upon my word!

LYD. Let her choice be *Capt. Absolute*, but Beverley is mine.

MRS MAL. I am astonished at her assurance!—*to his face—this is to his face!*

ABS. Thus then let me enforce my suit. [*Kneeling.*

MRS. MAL. Aye—poor young man!—down on his knees entreating for pity!—I can contain no longer.——Why, thou vixen!—I have overheard you.

ABS. O confound her vigilance! [*Aside.*

MRS. MAL. Capt. Absolute—I know not how to apologize for her shocking rudeness.

ABS. So—all's safe, I find. [*Aside.*
I have hopes, Madam, that time will bring the young lady——

MRS. MAL. O, there's nothing to be hoped for from her! she's as headstrong as an allegory on the banks of Nile.

LYD. Nay, Madam, what do you charge me with now?

MRS. MAL. Why, thou unblushing rebel—didn't you tell this gentleman to his face that you loved another better?—didn't you say you never would be his?

LYD. No, Madam—I did not.

MRS. MAL. Good Heav'ns! what assurance!—Lydia, Lydia, you ought to know that lying don't become a young woman!—Didn't you boast that Beverley—that stroller Beverley, possessed your heart?—Tell me that, I say.

LYD. 'Tis true, Ma'am, and none but Beverley—

MRS. MAL. Hold;—hold Assurance!—you shall not be so rude.

ABS. Nay, pray Mrs. Malaprop, don't stop the young lady's speech:—she's very welcome to talk thus—it does not hurt *me* in the least, I assure you.

MRS. MAL. You are *too* good, Captain—*too* amiably patient—but come with me, Miss—let us see you again soon, Captain—remember what we have fixed.

ABS. I shall, Ma'am.

MRS. MAL. Come, take a graceful leave of the gentleman.

LYD. May every blessing wait on my Beverley, my lov'd Bev——

11 *this is*] *76, 85*; this *L, 75*   15 thou vixen!] *76, 85*; huzzy! huzzy! *L, 75*

MRS. MAL. Huzzy! I'll choak the word in your throat!—come along—come along. [*Exeunt severally.*

[BEVERLEY *kissing his hand to* LYDIA—*Mrs.* MALAPROP *stopping her from speaking.*

SCENE IV. ACRES'*s lodgings*

ACRES *and* DAVID

ACRES *as just dress'd.*

ACRES. Indeed, David—do you think I become it so?

DAVID. You are quite another creature, believe me Master, by the Mass! an' we've any luck we shall see the Devon monkeyrony[1] in all the print-shops in Bath!

ACRES. Dress *does* make a difference, David.

DAVID. 'Tis all in all, I think—difference! why, an' you were to go now to Clod-Hall, I am certain the old lady wouldn't know you: Master Butler wouldn't believe his own eyes, and Mrs. Pickle would cry, 'Lard presarve me!' our dairy-maid would come giggling to the door, and I warrant Dolly Tester, your Honour's favourite, would blush like my waistcoat.—Oons! I'll hold a gallon, there an't a dog in the house but would bark, and I question whether *Phillis* would wag a hair of her tail!

ACRES. Aye, David, there's nothing like *polishing*.

DAVID. So I says of your Honour's boots; but the boy never heeds me!

ACRES. But, David, has Mr. De-la-Grace been here? I must rub up my balancing, and chasing, and boring.

DAVID. I'll call again, Sir.

ACRES. Do—and see if there are any letters for me at the post-office.

DAVID. I will.——By the Mass, I can't help looking at your head!—if I hadn't been by at the cooking, I wish I may die if I should have known the dish again myself! [*Exit.*

[ACRES *comes forward, practising a dancing step.*

ACRES. Sink, slide—coupee—Confound the first inventors of cotillons! say I—they are as bad as algebra to us country gentlemen—I can walk a Minuet easy enough when I'm forced!—and I have been accounted a good stick in a Country-dance.—Odd's jigs and tabors!—I never

5 SCENE IV] *76, 85*; SCENE V *L, 75*

---

[1] A macaroni, between 1772 and 1775, was a fop affecting Italian fashions. John Quick, who created the part of Acres, gave 'A Dissertation on Macaronies' at his benefit night in Bristol: see *Felix Farley's Bristol Journal*, 2 Sept. 1775, 'Monkey' was used more generally for a fop. Cf. 'A slim beast made for shew | Which the men call a monkey, but ladies a beau!' (Anthony Pasquin, *A Postscript to the New Bath Guide* (1790), p. 62.)

valued your cross-over to couple—figure in—right and left—and I'd foot it with e'er a captain in the county!—but these outlandish heathen Allemandes and Cotillons are quite beyond me!—I shall never prosper at 'em, that's sure—mine are true-born English legs—they don't understand their curst French lingo!—their *Pas* this, and *Pas* that, and *Pas* t'other!—d—n me, my feet don't like to be called Paws! no, 'tis certain I have most Antigallican Toes!

Enter SERVANT.

SERV. Here is Sir Lucius O'Trigger to wait on you, Sir.

ACRES. Shew him in.

Enter Sir LUCIUS.

SIR LUC. Mr. Acres, I am delighted to embrace you.

ACRES. My dear Sir Lucius, I kiss your hands.

SIR LUC. Pray, my friend, what has brought you so suddenly to Bath?

ACRES. Faith! I have followed Cupid's Jack-a-Lantern, and find myself in a quagmire at last.—In short, I have been very ill-used, Sir Lucius. —I don't choose to mention names, but look on me as a very ill-used gentleman.

SIR LUC. Pray, what is the case?—I ask no names.

ACRES. Mark me, Sir Lucius, I fall as deep as need be in love with a young lady——her friends take my part—I follow her to Bath—send word of my arrival; and receive answer, that the lady is to be otherwise disposed of.—This, Sir Lucius, I call being ill-used.

SIR LUC. Very ill, upon my conscience—Pray, can you divine the cause of it?

ACRES. Why, there's the matter: she has another lover, *one* Beverley, who, I am told, is now in Bath.—Odds slanders and lies! he must be at the bottom of it.

SIR LUC. A rival in the case, is there?—and you think he has supplanted you unfairly.

ACRES. *Unfairly*!—to be sure he has.—He never could have done it fairly.

SIR LUC. Then sure you know what is to be done!

ACRES. Not I, upon my soul!

SIR LUC. We wear no swords here,[1] but you understand me.

ACRES. What! fight him!

SIR LUC. Aye, to be sure: what can I mean else?

1 to] *76*, *85*; two *L*, *75*   20 fall] *76*, *85*; falls *L*, *75*   26 *one* Beverley] *75*; one *Beverley* *76*, *85*

[1] Beau Nash, Master of Ceremonies at Bath, forbade the wearing of swords 'as they often tore the ladies' clothes'.

ACRES. But he has given me no provocation.

SIR LUC. Now, I think he has given you the greatest provocation in the world.——Can a man commit a more heinous offence against another than to fall in love with the same woman? O, by my soul, it is the most unpardonable breach of friendship!

ACRES. Breach of *friendship*! Aye, aye; but I have no acquaintance with this man. I never saw him in my life.

SIR LUC. That's no argument at all—he has the less right then to take such a liberty.

ACRES. 'Gad that's true—I grow full of anger, Sir Lucius!—I fire apace! Odds hilts and blades![1] I find a man may have a deal of valour in him, and not know it! But couldn't I contrive to have a little right of my side?

SIR LUC. What the d——l signifies *right*, when your *honour* is concerned? Do you think *Achilles*, or my little *Alexander the Great* ever inquired where the right lay? No, by my soul, they drew their broad-swords, and left the lazy sons of peace to settle the justice of it.

ACRES. Your words are a grenadier's[2] march to my heart! I believe courage must be catching!—I certainly do feel a kind of valour rising as it were——a kind of courage, as I may say——Odds flints, pans, and triggers! I'll challenge him directly.

SIR LUC. Ah, my little friend! if we had *Blunderbuss-Hall* here[3]—I could shew you a range of ancestry, in the O'Trigger line, that would furnish the new room;[4] every one of whom had killed his man!——For though the mansion-house and dirty acres have slipt through my fingers, I thank Heav'n our honour, and the family-pictures, are as fresh as ever.

ACRES. O Sir Lucius! I have had ancestors too! every man of 'em colonel or captain in the militia!——Odds balls and barrels! say no more—I'm brac'd for it—The thunder of your words has soured the milk of human kindness in my breast![5]——Z—ds! as the man in the play says, 'I could do such deeds!'[6]

26 Heav'n] *76*, *85*; God *L*, *75* 29 militia!] *L*, *91*; militia? *75*, *76*, *85* 30 *After 'for it', insert*: my nerves are become catgut! my sinews wire! and my heart Pinchbeck! *L*, *75*

[1] Cf. Sir Joseph Wittol's oath in Congreve's *The Old Batchelor* (1693), II. i: 'Gads-Daggers-Belts-Blades-and Scabbards'.

[2] Acres connects Achilles and Alexander with the first line of 'The British Grenadiers': 'Some talk of Alexander, and some of Achilles'. For recent research on the wording of the song, see *The Times*, 22 Jan. 1969.

[3] See Sir Jeremy's lines on p. 37.

[4] The Upper Assembly rooms at Bath, built by John Wood (d. 1782), and opened in 1771.

[5] *Macbeth*, I. v.

[6] Possibly misquoting Lear's 'I will do such things' (II. iv).

SIR LUC. Come, come, there must be no passion at all in the case—these things should always be done civilly.

ACRES. I must be in a passion, Sir Lucius——I must be in a rage——Dear Sir Lucius let me be in a rage, if you love me.——Come, here's pen and paper. [*Sits down to write*] I would the ink were red!——Indite, I say, indite!—How shall I begin? Odds bullets and blades! I'll write a good *bold hand*, however.

SIR LUC. Pray compose yourself.

ACRES. Come—now shall I begin with an oath? Do, Sir Lucius, let me begin with a damme.

SIR LUC. Pho! pho! do the thing *decently* and like a Christian. Begin now,——'*Sir*'——

ACRES. That's too civil by half.

SIR LUC. '*To prevent the confusion that might arise.*'

ACRES. Well——

SIR LUC. '*From our both addressing the same lady.*'

ACRES. Aye—there's the reason—'*same lady*'—Well——

SIR LUC. '*I shall expect the honour of your company*'——

ACRES. Z——ds! I'm not asking him to dinner.

SIR LUC. Pray be easy.

ACRES. Well then, 'honour of your company'

SIR LUC. '*To settle our pretensions.*'

ACRES. Well.

SIR LUC. Let me see, aye, *King's Mead-fields* will do.——'*In King's Mead fields.*'

ACRES. So that's done.——Well, I'll fold it up presently; my own crest—a hand and dagger shall be the seal.

SIR LUC. You see now this little explanation will put a stop at once to all confusion or misunderstanding that might arise between you.

ACRES. Aye, we fight to prevent any misunderstanding.

SIR LUC. Now, I'll leave you to fix your own time.—take my advice, and you'll decide it this evening if you can; then let the worst come of it, 'twill be off your mind to-morrow.

ACRES. Very true.

SIR LUC. So I shall see nothing more of you, unless it be by letter, till the evening.——I would do myself the honour to carry your message; but, to tell you a secret, I believe I shall have just such another affair on my own hands. There is a gay captain here, who put a jest on me lately, at the expence of my country, and I only want to fall in with the gentleman, to call him out.

ACRES. By my valour, I should like to see you fight first! Odds life! I should like to see you kill him, if it was only to get a little lesson.

SIR LUC. I shall be very proud of instructing you.——Well for the present——but remember now, when you meet your antagonist, do every thing in a mild and agreeable manner.——Let your courage be as keen, but at the same time as polished as your sword. [*Exeunt severally.*

END OF THE THIRD ACT

ACT IV

SCENE I

ACRES'*s Lodgings*

ACRES *and* DAVID.

DAVID. Then, by the Mass, Sir! I would do no such thing—ne'er a Sir Lucius O'Trigger in the kingdom should make me fight, when I wa'n't so minded. Oons! what will the old lady say, when she hears o't!

ACRES. Ah! David, if you had heard Sir Lucius!—Odds sparks and flames! he would have rous'd your valour.

DAVID. Not he, indeed. I hates such bloodthirsty cormorants. Look'ee, Master, if you'd wanted a bout at boxing, quarter-staff, or short-staff, I should never be the man to bid you cry off: But for your curst sharps[1] and snaps,[2] I never knew any good come of 'em.

ACRES. But my *honour*, David, my *honour*! I must be very careful of my honour.

DAVID. Aye, by the Mass! and I would be very careful of it; and I think in return my *honour* couldn't do less than to be very careful of *me*.

ACRES. Odds blades! David, no gentleman will ever risk the loss of his honour!

DAVID. I say then, it would be but civil in *honour* never to risk the loss of a *gentleman*.——Lookee, Master, this *honour* seems to me to be a marvellous false friend; aye, truly, a very courtier-like servant.——Put the case, I was a gentleman (which, thank God, no one can say of me); well—my honour makes me quarrel with another gentleman of my acquaintance.—So—we fight. (Pleasant enough that) Boh!—I kill him—(the more's my luck.) Now, pray who gets the profit of it?—Why, my *honour*.——But put the case that he kills me!——by the Mass! I go to the worms, and my honour whips over to my enemy!

ACRES. No, David—in that case!—Odds crowns and laurels! your honour follows you to the grave.

3 END . . . ACT] *L*, *75*; *om. 76*, *85*   24 a *gentleman*] *L*, *76*, *85*; the *gentleman 75*

[1] Swords. Cf. Farquhar, *The Recruiting Officer*, v. vi: *Brazen*: Look'e, my dear, I do not care for pistols. Pray oblige me and let us have a bout at sharps.

[2] Pistols.

DAVID. Now, that's just the place where I could make a shift to do without it.

ACRES. Z——ds, David! you're a coward!—It doesn't become my valour to listen to you.——What, shall I disgrace my ancestors?—Think of that, David—think what it would be to disgrace my ancestors!

DAVID. Under favour, the surest way of not disgracing them, is to keep as long as you can out of their company. Look'ee now, Master, to go to them in such haste—with an ounce of lead in your brains—I should think might as well be let alone. Our ancestors are very good kind of folks; but they are the last people I should choose to have a visiting acquaintance with.

ACRES. But David, now, you don't think there is such very, very, *very* great danger, hey?——Odds life! people often fight without any mischief done!

DAVID. By the Mass, I think 'tis ten to one against you!——Oons! here to meet some lion-headed fellow, I warrant, with his d——n'd double-barrell'd swords, and cut and thrust pistols! Lord bless us! it makes me tremble to think o't!——Those be such desperate bloody-minded weapons! Well, I never could abide 'em!—from a child I never could fancy 'em!—I suppose there a'n't so merciless a beast in the world as your loaded pistol!

ACRES. Z——ds! I *won't* be afraid—Odds fire and fury! you shan't make me afraid.——Here is the challenge, and I have sent for my dear friend Jack Absolute to carry it for me.

DAVID. Aye, I'the name of mischief, let *him* be the messenger.—For my part, I wouldn't lend a hand to it for the best horse in your stable. By the Mass! it don't look like another letter!—It is, as I may say, a designing and malicious-looking letter!—and I warrant smells of gun-powder like a soldier's pouch!—Oons! I wouldn't swear it mayn't go off!

ACRES. Out, you poltroon!—you ha'n't the valour of a grass-hopper.

DAVID. Well, I say no more—'twill be sad news, to be sure, at Clod-Hall!—but I ha'done.—How Phyllis will howl when she hears of it!—Aye, poor bitch, she little thinks what shooting her Master's going after!—And I warrant old Crop, who has carried your honour, field and road, these ten years, will curse the hour he was born. [*Whimpering.*]

ACRES. It won't do, David—I am determined to fight—so get along, you Coward, while I'm in the mind.

Enter SERVANT.

SERV. Captain Absolute, Sir.

ACRES. O! shew him up. [*Exit* SERVANT.

DAVID. Well, Heaven send we be all alive this time to-morrow.

ACRES. What's that!—Don't provoke me, David!

DAVID. Good bye, Master. [*Whimpering.*]

ACRES. Get along, you cowardly, dastardly, croaking raven. [*Exit* DAVID.

Enter ABSOLUTE.

ABS. What's the matter, Bob?

ACRES. A vile, sheep-hearted blockhead!—If I hadn't the valour of St. George and the dragon to boot——

ABS. But what did you want with me, Bob?

ACRES. O!—There— [*Gives him the challenge.*]

ABS. '*To Ensign Beverley.*' So—what's going on now! [*Aside.* Well, what's this?

ACRES. A challenge!

ABS. Indeed!—Why, you won't fight him; will you Bob?

ACRES. 'Egad but I will, Jack.—Sir Lucius has wrought me to it. He has left me full of rage—and I'll fight this evening, that so much good passion mayn't be wasted.

ABS. But what have I to do with this?

ACRES. Why, as I think you know something of this fellow, I want you to find him out for me, and give him this mortal *defiance.*

ABS. Well, give it to me, and trust me he gets it.

ACRES. Thank you, my dear friend, my dear Jack; but it is giving you a great deal of trouble.

ABS. Not in the least—I beg you won't mention it.—No trouble in the world, I assure you.

ACRES. You are very kind.——What it is to have a friend!——You couldn't be my second—could you, Jack?

ABS. Why no, Bob—not in *this* affair—it would not be quite so proper.

ACRES. Well then I must get my friend Sir Lucius. I shall have your good wishes, however, Jack.

ABS. Whenever he meets you, believe me.

Enter SERVANT.

SERV. Sir Anthony Absolute is below, inquiring for the Captain.

ABS. I'll come instantly.——Well, my little hero, success attend you. [*Going.*

ACRES. Stay—stay, Jack.——If Beverley should ask you what kind of a man your friend Acres is, do tell him I am a devil of a fellow—will you, Jack?

ABS. To be sure I shall.——I'll say you are a determined dog—hey, Bob!

ACRES. Aye, do, do—and if that frightens him, 'egad perhaps he mayn't come. So tell him I generally kill a man a week; will you, Jack!

ABS. I will, I will; I'll say you are call'd in the country '*Fighting Bob*!'

29 get] *76*, *85*; fix on *75*; *om. L*

ACRES. Right, right—'tis all to prevent mischief; for I don't want to take his life if I clear my honour.

ABS. No!—that's very kind of you.

ACRES. Why, you don't wish me to kill him—do you, Jack?

ABS. No, upon my soul, I do not.—But a devil of a fellow, hey? [*Going.*

ACRES. True, true—but stay—stay, Jack—you may add that you never saw me in such a rage before—a most devouring rage!

ABS. I will, I will.

ACRES. Remember, Jack——a determined dog!

ABS. Aye, aye, '*Fighting Bob*!' [*Exeunt severally.*

SCENE II

Mrs. MALAPROP'*s Lodgings*

Mrs. MALAPROP *and* LYDIA.

MRS. MAL. Why, thou perverse one!—tell me what you can object to him?——Isn't he a handsome man?—tell me that.—A genteel man? a pretty figure of a man?

LYD. She little thinks whom she is praising! [*aside*]—So is Beverley, Ma'am.

MRS. MAL. No caparisons, Miss, if you please!—Caparisons don't become a young woman.—No! Captain Absolute is indeed a fine gentleman!

LYD. Aye, the Captain Absolute *you* have seen. [*Aside.*

MRS. MAL. Then he's *so* well bred;—*so* full of alacrity, and adulation!—and has *so much* to say for himself:—in such good language too!—His physiognomy so grammatical!—Then his presence is so noble!—I protest, when I saw him, I thought of what Hamlet says in the Play:—'Hesperian curls!—the front of *Job* himself!—an eye, like *March*, to threaten at command!—a Station, like Harry Mercury, new—' Something about kissing—on a hill—however, the similitude struck me directly.[1]

LYD. How enraged she'll be presently when she discovers her mistake! [*Aside.*

Enter SERVANT.

SERV. Sir Anthony, and Captain Absolute are below Ma'am.

MRS. MAL. Shew them up here. [*Exit* SERV.
Now, Lydia, I insist on you behaving as becomes a young woman.—Shew your good breeding at least, though you have forgot your duty.

[1] From *Hamlet*, III. iv:

Hyperion's curls; the front of Jove himself;
An eye like Mars to threaten and command;
A station like the herald Mercury
New-lighted on a heaven-kissing hill.

LYD. Madam, I have told you my resolution;—I shall not only give him no encouragement, but I won't even speak to, or look at him.

[*Flings herself into a chair, with her face from the door.*

Enter SIR ANTHONY *and* ABSOLUTE.

SIR ANTH. Here we are, Mrs. Malaprop; come to mitigate the frowns of unrelenting beauty—and difficulty enough I had to bring this fellow.—I don't know what's the matter; but if I hadn't held him by force, he'd have given me the slip.

MRS. MAL. You have infinite trouble, Sir Anthony, in the affair.—I am ashamed for the cause! Lydia, Lydia, rise I beseech you!—pay your respects! [*Aside to her.*

SIR ANTH. I hope, Madam, that Miss Languish has reflected on the worth of this gentleman, and the regard due to her Aunt's choice, and *my* alliance.—Now, Jack, speak to her! [*Aside to him.*

ABS. What the d—l shall I do!—[*Aside*]—You see, Sir, she won't even look at me, whilst you are here.—I knew she wouldn't!—I told you so—Let me intreat you, Sir, to leave us together!

[ABSOLUTE *seems to expostulate with his Father.*

LYD. [*aside.*] I wonder I ha'n't heard my Aunt exclaim yet! sure she can't have look'd at him!—perhaps their regimentals are alike, and she is something blind.

SIR ANTH. I say, Sir, I won't stir a foot yet.

MRS. MAL. I am sorry to say, Sir Anthony, that my affluence over my Niece is very small.—Turn round Lydia, I blush for you!

[*Aside to her.*

SIR ANTH. May I not flatter myself that Miss Languish will assign what cause of dislike she can have to my son!—Why don't you begin, Jack?—Speak, you puppy—speak! [*Aside to him.*

MRS. MAL. It is impossible, Sir Anthony, she can have any.—She will not *say* she has.——Answer, hussy! why don't you answer? [*Aside to her.*

SIR ANTH. Then, Madam, I trust that a childish and hasty predilection will be no bar to Jack's happiness.—Z—ds! sirrah! why don't you speak? [*Aside to him.*

LYD. [*aside*] I think my lover seems as little inclined to conversation as myself.—How strangely blind my Aunt must be!

ABS. Hem! hem!—Madam—hem! [Absolute *attempts to speak, then returns to Sir* Anthony]—Faith! Sir, I am so confounded!—and so—so—confused!—I told you I should be so, Sir,—I knew it.—The—the—tremor of my passion, entirely takes away my presence of mind.

SIR ANTH. But it don't take away your voice, fool, does it?—Go up, and speak to her directly! [ABS. *makes signs to Mrs.* MAL. *to leave them together.*]

35 must be] *76*, *85*; is *L*, *75*

MRS. MAL. Sir Anthony, shall we leave them together?—Ah! you stubborn, little vixen! [*Aside to her.*

SIR ANTH. Not yet, Ma'am, not yet!—what the d—l are you at? unlock your jaws, sirrah, or— [*Aside to him.*

[ABSOLUTE *draws near* LYDIA.]

ABS. Now Heav'n send she may be too sullen to look round!—I must disguise my voice—[*Aside*]— [*Speaks in a low hoarse tone.* —Will not Miss Languish lend an ear to the mild accents of true love? —Will not——

SIR ANTH. What the d—l ails the fellow?—Why don't you speak out? —not stand croaking like a frog in a quinsey!

ABS. The—the—excess of my awe, and my—my—my modesty, quite choak me!

SIR ANTH. Ah! your *modesty* again!—I'll tell you what, Jack; if you don't speak out directly, and glibly too, I shall be in such a rage!—Mrs. Malaprop, I wish the lady would favour us with something more than a side-front!

[*Mrs.* MALAPROP *seems to chide* LYDIA.

ABS. So!—all will out I see!

[*Goes up to* LYDIA, *speaks softly.*

Be not surprised, my Lydia, suppress all surprise at present.

LYD. [*Aside*] Heav'ns! 'tis Beverley's voice!—Sure he can't have impos'd on Sir Anthony too!— [*Looks round by degrees, then starts up.* Is this possible!—my Beverley!—how can this be?—my Beverley?

ABS. Ah! 'tis all over. [*Aside.*

SIR ANTH. Beverley!—the devil—Beverley!——What can the girl mean? —This is my son, Jack Absolute!

MRS. MAL. For shame, hussy! for shame!—your head runs so on that fellow, that you have him always in your eyes!—beg Captain Absolute's pardon directly.

LYD. I see no Captain Absolute, but my lov'd Beverley!

SIR ANTH. Z—ds! the girl's mad!—her brain's turn'd by reading!

MRS. MAL. O' my conscience, I believe so!—what do you mean by Beverley, hussy?—You saw Captain Absolute before to-day; there he is —your husband that shall be.

LYD. With all my soul, Ma'am—when I refuse my Beverley——

SIR ANTH. O! she's as mad as Bedlam!—or has this fellow been playing us a rogue's trick!—Come here, sirrah! who the d—l are you?

ABS. Faith, Sir, I am not quite clear myself; but I'll endeavour to recollect.

SIR ANTH. Are you my son, or not?—answer for your mother, you dog, if you won't for me.

MRS. MAL. Aye, Sir, who are you? O mercy! I begin to suspect!—

ABS. Ye Powers of Impudence befriend me! [*aside*] Sir Anthony, most assuredly I am your wife's son; and that I sincerely believe myself to be *your's* also, I hope my duty has always shewn.—Mrs. Malaprop, I am your most respectful admirer—and shall be proud to add *affectionate nephew*.—I need not tell my Lydia, that she sees her faithful Beverley, who, knowing the singular generosity of her temper, assum'd that name, and a station, which has proved a test of the most disinterested love, which he now hopes to enjoy in a more elevated character.

LYD. So!—there will be no elopement after all! [*sullenly*.]

SIR ANTH. Upon my soul, Jack, thou art a very impudent fellow![1] to do you justice, I think I never saw a piece of more consummate assurance!

ABS. O, you flatter me, Sir—you compliment—'tis my *modesty* you know, Sir—my *modesty* that has stood in my way.

SIR ANTH. Well, I am glad you are not the dull, insensible varlet you pretended to be, however!—I'm glad you have made a fool of your father, you dog—I am.——So this was your *penitence*, your *duty*, and *obedience*!—I thought it was d—n'd sudden!—You *never heard their names before*, not you!—*What, Languishes of Worcestershire*, hey?—*if you could please me in the affair*, *'twas all you desired*!—Ah! you dissembling villain!—What! (*pointing to* Lydia) *she squints, don't she?—a little red-hair'd girl*!—hey?—Why, you hypocritical young rascal—I wonder you a'n't asham'd to hold up your head!

ABS. 'Tis with difficulty, Sir—I *am* confus'd—very much confus'd, as you must perceive.

MRS. MAL. O Lud! Sir Anthony!—a new light breaks in upon me!—hey! how! what! Captain, did *you* write the letters then?—What!—am I to thank *you* for the elegant compilation of '*an old weather-beaten she-dragon*'—hey?—O mercy!—was it *you* that reflected on my parts of speech?

ABS. Dear Sir! my modesty will be overpower'd at last, if you don't assist me.—I shall certainly not be able to stand it!

SIR ANTH. Come, come, Mrs. Malaprop, we must forget and forgive; —odds' life! matters have taken so clever a turn all of a sudden, that I could find in my heart, to be so good-humour'd! and so gallant!—hey! Mrs. Malaprop!

MRS. MAL. Well, Sir Anthony, since *you* desire it, we will not anticipate the past;—so mind young people—our retrospection will now be all to the future.

19 *Languishes*] *75*; Languishes *L*; The LANGUISHES *76*, *85* 27–8 am I] *76*, *85*; I am *L*, *75*

---

1 Cf. Lord Foppington's line in Vanbrugh's *The Relapse*, IV. vi: 'Strike me dumb, Tam, thou art a very impudent fellow.'

SIR ANTH. Come, we must leave them together; Mrs. Malaprop, they long to fly into each other's arms, I warrant!—Jack—is'n't the *cheek* as I said, hey?—and the eye, you rogue!—and the lip—hey? Come, Mrs. Malaprop, we'll not disturb their tenderness—their's is the time of life for happiness!——'*Youth's the season made for joy*'[1]—[sings]—hey!—Odds'life! I'm in such spirits,—I don't know what I couldn't do!—Permit me, Ma'am—[*gives his hand to Mrs.* Mal.] [*sings*] Tol-de-rol—'gad I should like a little fooling myself—Tol-de-rol! de-rol!

[*Exit singing, and handing Mrs.* MAL.

[LYDIA *sits sullenly in her chair.*]

ABS. So much thought bodes me no good [*aside*]—So grave, Lydia!

LYD. Sir!

ABS. So!—egad! I thought as much!—that d—n'd monosyllable has froze me! [*aside*]—What, Lydia, now that we are as happy in our *friends consent*, as in our *mutual vows*——

LYD. *Friends consent*, indeed! [*peevishly*]

ABS. Come, come, we must lay aside some of our romance—a little *wealth* and *comfort* may be endur'd after all. And for your fortune, the lawyers shall make such settlements as——

LYD. *Lawyers*! I *hate* lawyers!

ABS. Nay then, we will not wait for their lingering forms, but instantly procure the licence, and—

LYD. The *licence*!—I *hate* licence!

ABS. O my Love! *be* not so unkind!—thus let me intreat——

[*Kneeling.*

LYD. Pshaw!—what signifies kneeling, when you know I *must* have you?

ABS. [*rising*] Nay, Madam, there shall be no constraint upon your inclinations, I promise you.—If I have lost your *heart*,—I resign the rest.—'Gad, I must try what a little *spirit* will do. [*Aside.*

3 rogue] *76*, *85*; dog *L*, *75*

---

[1] J. Gay, *The Beggar's Opera* (1728), II. iv:

Youth's the season made for joys,
Love is then our duty;
She alone who that employs,
Well deserves her beauty.
  Let's be gay,
  While we may,
Beauty's a flower, despised in decay.

Let us drink and sport today,
Ours is not tomorrow.
Love with youth flies swift away,
Age is nought but sorrow,
  Dance and sing,
  Time's on the wing,
Life never knows the return of spring.

LYD. [*rising*] Then, Sir, let me tell you, the interest you had there was acquired by a mean, unmanly imposition, and deserves the punishment of fraud.—What, you have been treating *me* like a *child*!—humouring my romance! and laughing, I suppose, at your success!

ABS. You wrong me, Lydia, you wrong me—only hear——

LYD. So, while *I* fondly imagined we were deceiving my relations, and flatter'd myself that I should outwit and incense them *all*—behold! my hopes are to be crush'd at once, by my Aunt's consent and approbation!—and *I* am *myself*, the only dupe at last!

[*Walking about in heat.*

—But here, Sir, here is the picture—Beverley's picture! [*taking a miniature from her bosom*] which I have worn, night and day, in spite of threats and entreaties!—There, Sir, [*flings it to him*] and be assured I throw the original from my heart as easily!

ABS. Nay, nay, Ma'am, we will not differ as to that.—Here, [*taking out a picture*] *here* is Miss Lydia Languish.—What a difference!—aye, *there* is the heav'nly assenting smile, that first gave soul and spirit to my hopes!—those are the lips which seal'd a vow, as yet scarce dry in Cupid's calendar!—and *there* the *half* resentful blush, that *would* have check'd the ardour of my thanks—Well, all that's past!—all over indeed! —There, Madam—in *beauty*, that copy is not equal to you, but in my mind its merit over the original, in being still the same, is such—that —I cannot find in my heart to *part with* it. [*Puts it up again.*

LYD. [*Softening*] 'Tis *your own* doing, Sir—I, I, I suppose you are perfectly satisfied.

ABS. O, most certainly—sure now this is much better than being in love! —ha! ha! ha!—there's some spirit in *this!*—What signifies breaking some scores of solemn promises:—all that's of no consequence you know.—To be sure people will say, that Miss didn't know her own mind—but never mind that:—or perhaps they may be ill-natured enough to hint, that the gentleman grew tired of the lady and forsook her—but don't let that fret you.

LYD. There's no bearing his insolence. [*Bursts into tears.*

Enter Mrs. MALAPROP *and Sir* ANTHONY.

MRS. MAL. [*Entering*] Come, we must interrupt your billing and cooing a while.

10 *After* ['*in heat*'.], *insert*:
Abs. Nay, but hear me—
Lyd. No, Sir, you could not think that such paltry artifices could please me, when the mask was thrown off!—But I suppose since your tricks have made you secure of my *fortune*, you are little solicitous about my *affections*. *75*

28 *After* '*promises*,' *insert*: half an hundred vows, under one's hand, with the marks of a dozen or two angels to witness. *L*, *75*

LYD. *This* is *worse* than your treachery and deceit, you base ingrate! [*Sobbing.*

SIR ANTH. What the devil's the matter now!—Z—ds! Mrs. Malaprop, this is the *oddest billing* and *cooing* I ever heard!—but what the deuce is the meaning of it?—I'm quite astonish'd!

ABS. Ask the lady, Sir.

MRS. MAL. O mercy!—I'm quite analys'd for my part!—why, Lydia, what is the reason of this?

LYD. Ask the *gentleman*, Ma'am.

SIR ANTH. Z—ds! I shall be in a phrenzy!—why Jack, you are not come out to be any one else, are you?

MRS. MAL. Aye, Sir, there's no more *trick*, is there?—you are not like Cerberus, *three* Gentlemen[1] at once, are you?

ABS. You'll not let me speak—I say the *lady* can account for *this* much better than I can.

LYD. Ma'am, you once commanded me never to think of Beverley again —*there* is the man—I now obey you:—for, from this moment, I renounce him for ever. [*Exit* LYDIA.

MRS. MAL. O mercy! and miracles! what a turn here is—why sure, Captain, you haven't behaved disrespectfully to my Niece.

SIR ANTH. Ha! ha! ha!—ha! ha! ha!—now I see it—Ha! ha! ha!—now I see it—you have been too lively, Jack.

ABS. Nay, Sir, upon my word——

SIR ANTH. Come, no lying, Jack—I'm sure '*twas* so.

MRS. MAL. O Lud! Sir Anthony!——O fie, Captain!

ABS. Upon my soul, Ma'am——

SIR ANTH. Come, no excuses, Jack;—why, your father, you rogue, was so before you:—the blood of the Absolutes was always impatient.—Ha! ha! ha! poor little Lydia!—why, you've frighten'd her, you Dog, you have.

ABS. By all that's good, Sir——

SIR ANTH. Z—ds! say no more, I tell you.—Mrs. Malaprop shall make your peace.—You must make his peace, Mrs. Malaprop; —you must tell her 'tis Jack's way—tell her 'tis all our ways—it runs in the blood of our family!—Come, get on, Jack—ha! ha! ha! Mrs. Malaprop—a young villain! [*Pushes him out.*

MRS. MAL. O! Sir Anthony!—O fie, Captain! [*Exeunt severally.*

10 Jack] *76*, *85*; Jack, you scoundrel *L*, *75* 34 get on] *L*, *75*; away *76*, *85*
35 *Pushes*] *76*, *85*; *Pushing L*, *75*

[1] In Garrick's *A Peep behind the Curtain* (1767), pp. 15–17, Glib claims that a stroke of genius to fill the boxes for a month, is the use of Cerberus to guard the entrance to Hades. 'Author' then remarks, 'You know, I suppose, that Cerberus is a dog and has three heads? . . . I make the three heads sing a *trio*.'

SCENE III[1]

The North-Parade

Enter SIR LUCIUS O'TRIGGER.

SIR LUC. I wonder where this Capt. Absolute hides himself.—Upon my conscience!—these officers are always in one's way in love-affairs:—I remember I might have married Lady Dorothy Carmine, if it had not been for a little rogue of a Major, who ran away with her before she could get a sight of me!—And I wonder too what it is the ladies can see in them to be so fond of them—unless it be a touch of the old serpent in 'em, that makes the little creatures be caught, like vipers with a bit of red cloth.—Hah!—isn't this the Captain coming?—faith it is!—There is a probability of succeeding about that fellow, that is mighty provoking!—Who the devil is he talking to? [*Steps aside.*

Enter CAPT. ABSOLUTE.

ABS. To what fine purpose I have been plotting! a noble reward for all my schemes, upon my soul!—a little gypsey!—I did not think her romance could have made her so d—nd absurd either—S'death, I never was in a worse humour in my life—I could cut my own throat, or any other person's, with the greatest pleasure in the world!

SIR LUC. O, faith! I'm in the luck of it—I never could have found him in a sweeter temper for my purpose—to be sure I'm just come in the nick! now to enter into conversation with him, and so quarrel genteelly. [SIR LUCIUS *goes up to* ABSOLUTE.]——With regard to that matter, Captain, I must beg leave to differ in opinion with you.

ABS. Upon my word then, you must be a very subtle disputant:—because, Sir, I happen'd just then to be giving no opinion at all.

SIR LUC. That's no reason.—For give me leave to tell you, a man may *think* an untruth as well as *speak* one.

ABS. Very true, Sir, but if the man never utters his thoughts,[2] I should think they *might* stand a *chance* of escaping controversy.

SIR LUC. Then, Sir, you differ in opinion with me, which amounts to the same thing.

ABS. Hark'ee, Sir Lucius,—if I had not before known you to be a gentleman, upon my soul, I should not have discovered it at this interview:—for what you can drive at, unless you mean to quarrel with me, I cannot conceive!

[1] This is mistakenly numbered 'IV' in all early editions from the Larpent MS. onwards.

[2] Cf. Buckingham's *The Rehearsal* (1671), II. iv:

Smith: That's very complaisant, I swear, Mr. Bayes, to be of another man's opinion, before he knows what it is.

SIR LUC. I humbly thank you, Sir, for the quickness of your apprehension, [*Bowing.* —you have nam'd the very thing I would be at.

ABS. Very well, Sir—I shall certainly not baulk your inclinations:——but I should be glad you would please to explain your motives.

SIR LUC. Pray, Sir, be easy—the quarrel is a very pretty quarrel as it stands—we should only spoil it, by trying to explain it.—However, your memory is very short—or you could not have forgot an affront pass'd you on me within this week.—So no more, but name your time and place.

ABS. Well, Sir, since you are so bent on it, the sooner the better;—let it be this evening—here, by the Spring Gardens.[1]—We shall scarcely be interrupted.

SIR LUC. Faith! that same interruption in affairs of this nature, shews very great ill-breeding.——I don't know what's the reason, but in England, if a thing of this kind gets wind, people make such a pother, that a gentleman can never fight in peace and quietness.—However, if it's the same to you, Captain, I should take it as a particular kindness, if you'd let us meet in King's-Mead-Fields,[2] as a little business will call me there about six o'clock, and I may dispatch both matters at once.

ABS. 'Tis the same to me exactly.—A little after six, then we will discuss this matter more seriously.

SIR LUC. If you please, Sir, there will be very pretty small-sword light, tho' it won't do for a long shot.—So that matter's settled! and my mind's at ease. [*Exit* SIR LUCIUS.

Enter FAULKLAND, *meeting* ABSOLUTE.

ABS. Well met.—I was going to look for you.—O, Faulkland! all the Dæmons of spite and disappointment have conspired against me! I'm so vex'd, that if I had not the prospect of a resource in being knock'd o'the head by and bye, I should scarce have spirits to tell you the cause.

FAULK. What can you mean?——Has Lydia chang'd her mind?—I should have thought her duty and inclination would now have pointed to the same object.

ABS. Aye, just as the eyes do of a person who squints[3]:—when her *love eye* was fix'd on *me*——t'other—her *eye* of *duty*, was finely obliqued:—but when duty bid her point *that* the same way—off t'other turn'd on a swivel, and secured its retreat with a frown!

[1] A summer meeting-place for public breakfasts, teas, concerts, and fireworks. It lay on the Bathwick side of the Pulteney Bridge.

[2] Sheridan himself had lived in Kingsmead Street. Open fields lay beyond it.

[3] Was the comparison prompted by the following exchange in Wycherley's *The Plain Dealer* (1676), II. i?

Olivia. First, can any one be call'd beautiful that squints?
Lord Plausible. Her eyes languish a little, I own.
Novel. Languish! ha, ha.

FAULK. But what's the resource you——

ABS. O, to wind up the whole, a good natured Irishman here has (*mimicking* SIR LUCIUS) beg'd leave to have the pleasure of cutting my throat—and I mean to indulge him—that's all.

FAULK. Prithee, be serious.

ABS. 'Tis fact, upon my soul.——Sir Lucius O'Trigger—you know him by sight—for some affront, which I am sure I never intended, has obliged me to meet him this evening at six o'clock:—'tis on that account I wish'd to see you—you must go with me.

FAULK. Nay, there must be some mistake, sure.—Sir Lucius shall explain himself—and I dare say matters may be accommodated:—but this evening, did you say?—I wish it had been any other time.

ABS. Why?—there will be light enough:——there will (as Sir Lucius says) 'be very pretty small-sword light, tho' it won't do for a long shot.'—Confound his long shots!

FAULK. But I am myself a good deal ruffled, by a difference I have had with Julia—my vile tormenting temper has made me treat her so cruelly, that I shall not be myself till we are reconciled.

ABS. By Heav'ns, Faulkland, you don't deserve her.

Enter SERVANT, *gives* FAULKLAND *a letter.*

FAULK. O Jack! this is from Julia—I dread to open it—I fear it may be to take a last leave—perhaps to bid me return her letters—and restore ——O! how I suffer for my folly!

ABS. Here—let me see. [*Takes the letter and opens it.*
Aye, a final sentence indeed!—'tis all over with you, faith!

FAULK. Nay, Jack—don't keep me in suspence.

ABS. Hear then.—'*As I am convinced that my dear* Faulkland's *own reflections have already upbraided him for his last unkindness to me, I will not add a word on the subject.—I wish to speak with you as soon as possible.—Your's ever and truly*, Julia.'—There's stubborness and resentment for you! [*Gives him the letter.*
Why, man, you don't seem one whit the happier at this.

FAULK. O, yes, I am—but—but——

ABS. Confound your *buts.*—You never hear any thing that would make another man bless himself, but you immediately d—n it with a *but.*

FAULK. Now, Jack, as you are my friend, own honestly—don't you think there is something forward—something indelicate in this haste to forgive?—Women should never sue for reconciliation:—*that* should *always* come from us.—*They* should retain their coldness till *woo'd* to kindness—and their *pardon*, like their *love*, should 'not unsought be won.'[1]

[1] From *Paradise Lost*, viii. 502–3:

Her virtue, and the conscience of her worth,
That would be wooed, and not unsought be won.

ABS. I have not patience to listen to you:—thou'rt incorrigible!—so say no more on the subject.—I must go to settle a few matters—let me see you before six—remember—at my lodgings.——A poor industrious devil like me, who have toil'd, and drudg'd, and plotted to gain my ends, and am at last disappointed by other people's folly—may in pity be allowed to swear and grumble a little;—but a captious sceptic in love,—a slave to fretfulness and whim—who has no difficulties but of *his own* creating—is a subject more fit for ridicule than compassion!

[*Exit* ABSOLUTE.

FAULK. I feel his reproaches!—yet I would not change this too exquisite nicety, for the gross content with which *he* tramples on the thorns of love.—His engaging me in this duel, has started an idea in my head, which I will instantly pursue.—I'll use it as the touch-stone of Julia's sincerity and disinterestedness—if her love prove pure and sterling ore—my name will rest on it with honour!—and once I've stamp'd it there, I lay aside my doubts for ever:—but if the dross of selfishness, the allay of pride predominate—'twill be best to leave her as a toy for some less cautious Fool to sigh for. [*Exit* FAULKLAND.

END OF THE FOURTH ACT

ACT V

SCENE I

JULIA'*s Dressing-Room*

JULIA, *sola.*

How this message has alarmed me! what dreadful accident can he mean! why such charge to be alone?——O Faulkland!—how many unhappy moments!—how many tears have you cost me!

Enter FAULKLAND, *muffled up in a Riding-coat.*

JUL. What means this?——why this caution, Faulkland?

FAULK. Alas! Julia, I am come to take a long farewell.

JUL. Heav'ns! what do you mean?

FAULK. You see before you a wretch, whose life is forfeited.—Nay, start not!—the infirmity of my temper has drawn all this misery on me.—

19 END ... ACT] *L, 75; om. 76, 85*   27 muffled up in a Riding-] *L, 75; om. 76, 85*
coat] *75*; cloak *L*; *om. 76, 85*

I left you fretful and passionate—an untoward accident drew me into a quarrel—the event is, that I must fly this kingdom instantly.—O Julia, had I been so fortunate as to have call'd you mine intirely, before this mischance had fallen on me, I should not so deeply dread my banishment!——

JUL. My soul is oppress'd with sorrow at the *nature* of your misfortune: had these adverse circumstances arisen from a less fatal cause, I should have felt strong comfort in the thought that I could *now* chase from your bosom every doubt of the warm sincerity of my love.——My heart has long known no other guardian—I now entrust my person to your honour—we will fly together.—When safe from pursuit, my Father's will may be fulfilled—and I receive a legal claim to be the partner of your sorrows, and tenderest comforter. Then on the bosom of your wedded Julia, you may lull your keen regret to slumbering; while virtuous love, with a Cherub's hand, shall smooth the brow of upbraiding thought, and pluck the thorn from compunction.

FAULK. O Julia! I am bankrupt in gratitude! but the time is so pressing, it calls on you for so hasty a resolution.—Would you not wish some hours to weigh the advantages you forego, and what little compensation poor Faulkland can make you beside his solitary love?

JUL. I ask not a moment.—No, Faulkland, I have lov'd you for yourself: and if I now, more than ever, prize the solemn engagement which so long has pledged us to each other, it is because it leaves no room for hard aspersions on my fame, and puts the seal of duty to an act of love.—But let us not linger.—Perhaps this delay——

FAULK. 'Twill be better I should not venture out again till dark.—Yet am I griev'd to think what numberless distresses will press heavy on your gentle disposition!

JUL. Perhaps your fortune may be forfeited by this unhappy act.—I know not whether 'tis so—but sure that alone can never make us unhappy.—The little I have will be sufficient to *support* us; and *exile* never should be splendid.

FAULK. Aye, but in such an abject state of life, my wounded pride perhaps may increase the natural fretfulness of my temper, till I become a rude, morose companion, beyond your patience to endure. Perhaps the recollection of a deed, my conscience cannot justify, may haunt me in such gloomy and unsocial fits, that I shall hate the tenderness that would relieve me, break from your arms, and quarrel with your fondness!

JUL. If your thoughts should assume so unhappy a bent, you will the more want some mild and affectionate spirit to watch over and

5 *After* '*banishment*!', *insert*:—But no more of that—your heart and promise were given to one happy in friends, character, and station! they are not bound to wait upon a solitary, guilty exile. *L*, 75

console you:—One who, by bearing *your* infirmities with gentleness and resignation, may teach you *so* to bear the evils of your fortune.

FAULK. Julia, I have proved you to the quick! and with this useless device I throw away all my doubts. How shall I plead to be forgiven this last unworthy effect of my restless, unsatisfied disposition?

JUL. Has no such disaster happened as you related?

FAULK. I am ashamed to own that it was all pretended; yet in pity, Julia, do not kill me with resenting a fault which never can be repeated: But sealing, this once, my pardon, let me to-morrow, in the face of Heaven, receive my future guide and monitress, and expiate my past folly, by years of tender adoration.

JUL. Hold, Faulkland!—that you are free from a crime, which I before fear'd to name, Heaven knows how sincerely I rejoice!—These are tears of thankfulness for that! But that your cruel doubts should have urged you to an imposition that has wrung my heart, gives me now a pang, more keen than I can express!

FAULK. By Heav'ns! Julia——

JUL. Yet hear me.——My Father lov'd you, Faulkland! and you preserv'd the life that tender parent gave me; in his presence I pledged my hand—*joyfully* pledged it—where before I had given my heart. When, soon after, I lost that parent, it seem'd to me that Providence had, in Faulkland, shewn me whither to transfer, without a pause, my grateful duty, as well as my affection: Hence I have been content to bear from you what pride and delicacy would have forbid me from another.—I will not upbraid you, by repeating how you have trifled with my sincerity.——

FAULK. I confess it all! yet hear——

JUL. After such a year of trial—I might have flattered myself that I should not have been insulted with a new probation of my sincerity, as cruel as unnecessary! I now see it is not in your nature to be content, or confident in love. With this conviction—I never will be yours. While I had hopes that my persevering attention, and unreproaching kindness might in time reform your temper, I should have been happy to have gain'd a dearer influence over you; but I will not furnish you with a licensed power to keep alive an incorrigible fault, at the expence of one who never would contend with you.

FAULK. Nay, but Julia, by my soul and honour, if after this——

JUL. But one word more.—As my faith has once been given to you, I

4 Julia] *76*, *85*; O Julia *L*, *75*   11 expiate] *L*, *75*, *85*; expatiate *76*   31 *After 'unnecessary!', insert*: A trick of such a nature, as to shew me plainly, that when I thought you lov'd me best, you even then regarded me as a mean dissembler; an artful, prudent hypocrite.

FAULK. Never! Never! *75*

never will barter it with another.—I shall pray for your happiness with the truest sincerity; and the dearest blessing I can ask of Heaven to send you, will be to charm you from that unhappy temper, which alone has prevented the performance of our solemn engagement.—All I request of *you* is, that you will yourself reflect upon this infirmity, and when you number up the many true delights it has deprived you of—let it not be your *least* regret, that it lost you the love of one—who would have follow'd you in beggary through the world! [*Exit.*

FAULK. She's gone!—for ever!—There was an awful resolution in her manner, that rivetted me to my place.——O Fool!—Dolt!—Barbarian! —Curst as I am, with more imperfections than my fellow-wretches, kind Fortune sent a heaven-gifted cherub to my aid, and, like a ruffian, I have driven her from my side!—I must now haste to my appointment.—Well my mind is tuned for such a scene.—I shall wish only to become a principal in it, and reverse the tale my cursed folly put me upon forging here.——O Love!—Tormentor!—Fiend!—whose influence, like the Moon's, acting on men of dull souls, makes idiots of them, but meeting subtler spirits, betrays their course, and urges sensibility to madness! [*Exit.*

Enter MAID *and* LYDIA.

MAID. My Mistress, Ma'am, I know, was here just now—perhaps she is only in the next room. [*Exit* MAID.

LYD. Heigh ho!—Though he has used me so, this fellow runs strangely in my head. I believe one lecture from my grave Cousin will make me recall him.

Enter JULIA.

LYD. O Julia, I am come to you with such an appetite for consolation. —Lud! Child, what's the matter with you?—You have been crying! —I'll be hanged, if that Faulkland has not been tormenting you!

JUL. You mistake the cause of my uneasiness.—Something *has* flurried me a little.—Nothing that you can guess at.——I would not accuse Faulkland to a Sister! [*Aside.*

LYD. Ah! whatever vexations you may have, I can assure you mine surpass them.——You know who Beverley proves to be?

JUL. I will now own to you, Lydia, that Mr. Faulkland had before inform'd me of the whole affair. Had young Absolute been the person you took him for, I should not have accepted your confidence on the subject, without a serious endeavour to counteract your caprice.

9 awful] *L*, *75*; aweful *76*, *85*

LYD. So, then, I see I have been deceived by every one!—but I don't care—I'll never have him.

JUL. Nay, Lydia——

LYD. Why, is it not provoking; when I thought we were coming to the prettiest distress imaginable, to find myself made a mere Smithfield bargain[1] of at last——There had I projected one of the most sentimental elopements!—so becoming a disguise!—so amiable a ladder of Ropes!—Conscious Moon—four horses—Scotch parson—with such surprise to Mrs. Malaprop—and such paragraphs in the News-papers!——O, I shall die with disappointment.

JUL. I don't wonder at it!

LYD. Now—sad reverse!—what have I to expect, but, after a deal of flimsy preparation with a bishop's licence, and my Aunt's blessing, to go simpering up to the Altar; or perhaps be cried three times in a country-church, and have an unmannerly fat clerk ask the consent of every butcher in the parish to join John Absolute and Lydia Languish, *Spinster*! O, that I should live to hear myself called Spinster!

JUL. Melancholy, indeed!

LYD. How mortifying, to remember the dear delicious shifts I used to be put to, to gain half a minute's conversation with this fellow!——How often have I stole forth, in the coldest night in January, and found him in the garden, stuck like a dripping statue!—There would he kneel to me in the snow, and sneeze and cough so pathetically! he shivering with cold, and I with apprehension! and while the freezing blast numb'd our joints, how warmly would he press me to pity his flame, and glow with mutual ardour!——Ah, Julia! that was something like being in love.

JUL. If I were in spirits, Lydia, I should chide you only by laughing heartily at you: but it suits more the situation of my mind, at present, earnestly to entreat you, not to let a man, who loves you with sincerity, suffer that unhappiness from your *caprice*, which I know too well caprice can inflict.

LYD. O Lud! what has brought my Aunt here!

Enter MRS. MALAPROP, FAG, *and* DAVID.

MRS. MAL. So! so! here's fine work!—here's fine suicide, paracide, and simulation going on in the fields! and Sir Anthony not to be found to prevent the antistrophe!

JUL. For Heaven's sake, Madam, what's the meaning of this?

MRS. MAL. That gentleman can tell you—'twas he enveloped the affair to me.

36 simulation] *76*, *85*; salivation *L*, *75*

[1] A marriage of interest, in which money is the chief consideration (*O.E.D.*).

LYD. Do, Sir, will you inform us. [*To* FAG.

FAG. Ma'am, I should hold myself very deficient in every requisite that forms the man of breeding, if I delay'd a moment to give all the information in my power to a lady so deeply interested in the affair as you are.

LYD. But quick! quick, Sir!

FAG. True, Ma'am, as you say, one should be quick in divulging matters of this nature; for should we be tedious, perhaps while we are flourishing on the subject, two or three lives may be lost!

LYD. O patience!—Do, Ma'am, for Heaven's sake! tell us what is the matter?

MRS. MAL. Why, murder's the matter! slaughter's the matter! killing's the matter!—but he can tell you the perpendiculars.

LYD. Then, prythee, Sir, be brief.

FAG. Why then, Ma'am—as to murder—I cannot take upon me to say —and as to slaughter, or man-slaughter, that will be as the jury finds it.

LYD. But who, Sir—who are engaged in this?

FAG. Faith, Ma'am, one is a young gentleman whom I should be very sorry any thing was to happen to—a very pretty behaved gentleman!—We have lived much together, and always on terms.

LYD. But who is this? who! who! who!

FAG. My Master, Ma'am—my Master—I speak of my Master.

LYD. Heavens! What, Captain Absolute!

MRS. MAL. O, to be sure, you are frightened now!

JUL. But who are with him, Sir?

FAG. As to the rest, Ma'am, this gentleman can inform you better than I.

JUL. Do speak, friend. [*To* DAVID.

DAVID. Look'ee, my Lady——by the Mass! there's mischief going on. ——Folks don't use to meet for amusement with fire-arms, firelocks, fire-engines, fire-screens, fire-office,[1] and the devil knows what other crackers besides!——This, my Lady, I say, has an angry favour.

JUL. But who is there beside Captain Absolute, friend?

DAVID. My poor Master—under favour, for mentioning him first.—You know me, my Lady—I am David—and my Master of course is, or *was*, Squire Acres.—Then comes Squire Faulkland.

JUL. Do, Ma'am, let us instantly endeavour to prevent mischief.

MRS. MAL. O fie—it would be very inelegant in us:—we should only participate things.

DAVID. Ah! do, Mrs. Aunt, save a few lives—they are desperately given, believe me.—Above all, there is that blood-thirsty Philistine, Sir Lucius O'Trigger.

25 this] *L*, *76*, *85*; his *75* 30 besides] *75*; beside *L*, *76*, *85* 36 inelegant] *L*, *75*; enelegant *76*, *85*

[1] Office of an insurance company dealing with fires.

MRS. MAL. Sir Lucius O'Trigger!—O mercy! have they drawn poor little dear Sir Lucius into the scrape?—why, how, how you stand, girl! you have no more feeling than one of the Derbyshire Putrefactions![1]

LYD. What are we to do, Madam?

MRS. MAL. Why, fly with the utmost felicity to be sure, to prevent mischief:—here, friend—you can shew us the place?

FAG. If you please, Ma'am, I will conduct you.—David, do you look for Sir Anthony. [*Exit* DAVID.

MRS. MAL. Come, girls!—this gentleman will exhort us.—Come, Sir, you're our envoy—lead the way, and we'll precede.

FAG. Not a step before the ladies for the world!

MRS. MAL. You're sure you know the spot.

FAG. I think I can find it, Ma'am; and one good thing is, we shall hear the report of the pistols as we draw near, so we can't well miss them; never fear, Ma'am, never fear. [*Exeunt, he talking.*

SCENE II

South-Parade

Enter ABSOLUTE, *putting his sword under his greatcoat.*

ABS. A sword seen in the streets of Bath[2] would raise as great an alarm as a mad-dog.—How provoking this is in Faulkland!—never punctual! I shall be obliged to go without him at last.—O, the devil! here's Sir Anthony!——how shall I escape him? [*Muffles up his, face, and* [*takes a circle to go off.*

Enter SIR ANTHONY.

SIR ANTH. How one may be deceived at a little distance! only that I see he don't know me, I could have sworn that was Jack!—Hey!—'Gad's life; it is.—Why, Jack,—what are you afraid of?—hey! sure I'm right. —Why, Jack—Jack Absolute! [*Goes up to him.*

ABS. Really, Sir, you have the advantage of me:—I don't remember ever to have had the honour——my name is Saunderson, at your service.

SIR ANTH. Sir, I beg your pardon—I took you—hey!—why, z—ds! it is——Stay—— [*Looks up to his face.*

15 *Exeunt, he talking*] 75; *Exit, he talking 76, 85*; *Exeunt L* 27 Jack] *76, 85*; Jack, you Dog! *L, 75*

[1] The 'wonders of the Peak' were often described, and R. Brookes's *General Gazetteer* (10th edn., 1797) says of Pool's Hole, near Buxton, that it 'contains many stalactitious concretions, and several curious representations both of art and nature, produced by the petrifying water continually dropping from the rock'.

[2] Beau Nash had both parties arrested whenever he heard of a challenge to a duel at Bath.

So, so—your humble servant, Mr. Saunderson!—Why, you scoundrel, what tricks are you after now?

ABS. O! a joke, Sir, a joke!—I came here on purpose to look for you, Sir.

SIR ANTH. You did! well, I am glad you were so lucky:—but what are you muffled up so for?—what's this for?—hey?

ABS. 'Tis cool, Sir; isn't it?—rather chilly somehow:—but I shall be late—I have a particular engagement.

SIR ANTH. Stay.—why, I thought you were looking for me?—Pray, Jack, where is't you are going?

ABS. Going, Sir!

SIR ANTH. Aye—where are you going?

ABS. Where am I going?

SIR ANTH. You unmannerly puppy!

ABS. I was going, Sir, to—to—to—to Lydia—Sir to Lydia—to make matters up if I could;—and I was looking for you, Sir, to—to——

SIR ANTH. To go with you, I suppose—Well, come along.

ABS. O! z—ds! no, Sir, not for the world!—I wish'd to meet with you, Sir, to—to—to—— You find it cool, I'm sure, Sir—you'd better not stay out.

SIR ANTH. Cool!—not at all—Well, Jack—and what will you say to Lydia?

ABS. O, Sir, beg her pardon, humour her—promise and vow:—but I detain you, Sir—consider the cold air on your gout.

SIR ANTH. O, not at all!—not at all!—I'm in no hurry.—Ah! Jack, you youngsters when once you are wounded here.

[*Putting his hand to* ABSOLUTE'*s breast.*

Hey! what the deuce have you got here?

ABS. Nothing, Sir—nothing.

SIR ANTH. What's this?—here's something d—d hard!

ABS. O, trinkets, Sir! trinkets—a bauble for Lydia!

SIR ANTH. Nay, let me see your taste.

[*Pulls his coat open, the sword falls.*

Trinkets!—a bauble for Lydia!—z—ds! sirrah, you are not going to cut her throat, are you?

ABS. Ha! ha! ha!—I thought it would divert you, Sir, tho' I didn't mean to tell you till afterwards.

SIR ANTH. You didn't?—Yes, this is a very diverting trinket, truly.

ABS. Sir, I'll explain to you.—You know, Sir, Lydia is romantic—dev'lish romantic, and very absurd of course:—now, Sir, I intend, if she refuses to forgive me—to unsheath this sword—and swear—I'll fall upon its point, and expire at her feet!

SIR ANTH. Fall upon a fiddle-stick's end!—why, I suppose it is the very thing that would please her—Get along, you Fool.—

42 a fiddle-stick's] *L*, *76*, *85*; fiddle-sticks *75*

ABS. Well, Sir, you shall hear of my success—you shall hear.—'O, Lydia!—forgive me, or this pointed steel'—says I.

SIR ANTH. 'O, Booby! stab away, and welcome'—says she—Get along! —and d—n your trinkets! [*Exit* ABSOLUTE.

Enter DAVID, *running.*

DAVID. Stop him! stop him! Murder! Thief! Fire!—Stop fire! Stop fire! —O! Sir Anthony—call! call! bid 'em stop! Murder! Fire!

SIR ANTH. Fire! Murder! where?

DAVID. Oons! he's out of sight! and I'm out of breath, for my part! O, Sir Anthony, why didn't you stop him? why didn't you stop him?

SIR ANTH. Z—ds! the fellow's mad!—Stop whom? stop Jack?

DAVID. Aye, the Captain, Sir!—there's murder and slaughter——

SIR ANTH. Murder!

DAVID. Aye, please you, Sir Anthony, there's all kinds of murder, all sorts of slaughter to be seen in the fields: there's fighting going on, Sir—bloody sword-and-gun fighting!

SIR ANTH. Who are going to fight, Dunce?

DAVID. Every body that I know of, Sir Anthony:—every body is going to fight, my poor Master, Sir Lucius O'Trigger, your son, the Captain——

SIR ANTH. O, the Dog!—I see his tricks:—do you know the place?

DAVID. King's-Mead-Fields.

SIR ANTH. You know the way?

DAVID. Not an inch;—but I'll call the Mayor—Aldermen—Constables—Church-wardens—and Beadles—we can't be too many to part them.

SIR ANTH. Come along—give me your shoulder! we'll get assistance as we go—the lying villain!—Well, I shall be in such a phrenzy—So—this was the history of his d—d trinkets! I'll bauble him! [*Exeunt.*

SCENE III

King's-Mead-Fields

SIR LUCIUS *and* ACRES, *with pistols.*

ACRES. By my valour! then, Sir Lucius, forty yards is a good distance—Odds levels and aims!—I say it is a good distance.

SIR LUC. Is it for muskets or small field-pieces? upon my conscience, Mr. Acres, you must leave those things to me.—Stay now—I'll shew you. [*Measures paces along the stage.* there now, that is a very pretty distance—a pretty gentleman's distance.

ACRES. Z—ds! we might as well fight in a sentry-box!—I tell you, Sir Lucius, the farther he is off, the cooler I shall take my aim.

SIR LUC. Faith! then I suppose you would aim at him best of all if he was out of site!

27 d—d] *L, 75; om. 76, 85*

ACRES. No, Sir Lucius—but I should think forty or eight and thirty yards——

SIR LUC. Pho! pho! nonsense! three or four feet between the mouths of your pistols is as good as a mile.

ACRES. Odds bullets, no!—by my valour! there is no merit in killing him so near:—no, my dear Sir Lucius, let me bring him down at a long shot:—a long shot, Sir Lucius, if you love me!

SIR LUC. Well—the gentleman's friend and I must settle that.—But tell me now, Mr. Acres, in case of an accident, is there any little will or commission I could execute for you?

ACRES. I am much obliged to you, Sir Lucius—but I don't understand——

SIR LUC. Why, you may think there's no being shot at without a little risk—and if an unlucky bullet should carry a *Quietus* with it—I say it will be no time then to be bothering you about family matters.

ACRES. A *Quietus*!

SIR LUC. For instance, now—if that should be the case—would you chuse to be pickled and sent home?—or would it be the same to you to lie here in the Abbey?—I'm told there is very snug lying in the Abbey.

ACRES. Pickled!—Snug lying in the Abbey!—Odds tremors! Sir Lucius, don't talk so!

SIR LUC. I suppose, Mr. Acres, you never were engaged in an affair of this kind before?

ACRES. No, Sir Lucius, never before.

SIR LUC. Ah! that's a pity!—there's nothing like being used to a thing.—Pray now, how would you receive the gentleman's shot?

ACRES. Odds files![1]—I've practised that—there, Sir Lucius—there [*Puts himself in an attitude.* ——a side-front, hey?—Odd! I'll make myself small enough:—I'll stand edge-ways.

SIR LUC. Now—you're quite out—for if you stand so when I take my aim—— [*Levelling at him.*

ACRES. Z—ds! Sir Lucius—are you sure it is not cock'd?

SIR LUC. Never fear.

ACRES. But—but—you don't know—it may go off of its own head!

SIR LUC. Pho! be easy—Well, now if I hit you in the body, my bullet has a double chance—for if it misses a vital part on your right side—'twill be very hard if it don't succeed on the left!

ACRES. A vital part!

41 part!] *L*, *76*, *85*; part! O, my poor vitals! *75*

[1] A file was a sword used in fencing.

SIR LUC. But, there—fix yourself so— [*Placing him.* let him see the broad side of your full front—there—now a ball or two may pass clean thro' your body, and never do any harm at all.

ACRES. Clean thro' me!—a ball or two clean thro' me!

SIR LUC. Aye—may they—and it is much the genteelest attitude into the bargain.

ACRES. Look'ee! Sir Lucius—I'd just as leive be shot in an aukward posture as a genteel one—so, by my valour! I will stand edge-ways.

SIR LUC. [*Looking at his watch.*] Sure they don't mean to disappoint us. —Hah?—no faith—I think I see them coming.

ACRES. Hey!—what!—coming!——

SIR LUC. Aye—Who are those yonder getting over the stile?

ACRES. There are two of them, indeed!—well—let them come—hey, Sir Lucius!—we—we—we—we—won't run—

SIR LUC. Run!

ACRES. No—I say—we *won't* run, by my valour!

SIR LUC. What the devil's the matter with you?

ACRES. Nothing—nothing—my dear friend——my dear Sir Lucius—but—I—I—I don't feel quite so bold, somehow—as I did.

SIR LUC. O fie!—consider your honour.

ACRES. Aye—true—my honour——Do, Sir Lucius, edge in a word or two every now and then about my honour.

SIR LUC. Well, here they're coming. [*Looking.*

ACRES. Sir Lucius—if I wa'n't with you, I should almost think I was afraid—if my valour should leave me!—Valour will come and go.

SIR LUC. Then, pray keep it fast, while you have it.

ACRES. Sir Lucius—I doubt it is going—yes—my valour is certainly going!—it is sneaking off!—I feel it oozing out as it were at the palms of my hands!

SIR LUC. Your honour—your honour——Here they are.

ACRES. O mercy!—now—that I were safe at *Clod-hall!* or could be shot before I was aware!

Enter FAULKLAND *and* ABSOLUTE.

SIR LUC. Gentlemen, your most obedient—hah!—what Captain Absolute!—So, I suppose, Sir, you are come here, just like myself—to do a kind office, first for your friend—then to proceed to business on your own account.

ACRES. What, Jack!—my dear Jack!—my dear friend!

ABS. Heark'ee, Bob, Beverley's at hand.

SIR LUC. Well, Mr. Acres—I don't blame your saluting the gentleman civilly.—So, Mr. Beverley, [*to* FAULKLAND] if you'll chuse your weapons, the Captain and I will measure the ground.

3 clean] *76*, *85*; clear *L*, *75* 21 edge] *76*, *85*; hedge *L*, *75*

FAULK. *My* weapons, Sir.

ACRES. Odds life! Sir Lucius, I'm not going to fight Mr. Faulkland; these are my particular friends.

SIR LUC. What, Sir, did not you come here to fight Mr. Acres?

FAULK. Not I, upon my word, Sir.

SIR LUC. Well, now, that's mighty provoking! But I hope, Mr. Faulkland, as there are three of us come on purpose for the game—you won't be so cantanckerous as to spoil the party by sitting out.

ABS. O pray, Faulkland, fight to oblige Sir Lucius.

FAULK. Nay, if Mr. Acres is so bent on the matter.

ACRES. No, no, Mr. Faulkland—I'll bear my disappointment like a Christian—Look'ee, Sir Lucius, there's no occasion at all for me to fight; and if it is the same to you, I'd as lieve let it alone.

SIR LUC. Observe me, Mr. Acres—I must not be trifled with. You have certainly challenged somebody—and you came here to fight him—Now, if that gentleman is willing to represent him—I can't see, for my soul, why it isn't just the same thing.

ACRES. Why no—Sir Lucius—I tell you, 'tis one Beverley I've challenged—a fellow, you see, that dare not shew his face! If *he* were here, I'd make him give up his pretensions directly!——

ABS. Hold, Bob—let me set you right—there is no such man as Beverley in the case.—The person who assumed that name is before you; and as his pretensions are the same in both characters, he is ready to support them in whatever way you please.

SIR LUC. Well, this is lucky—Now you have an opportunity—

ACRES. What, quarrel with my dear friend Jack Absolute—not if he were fifty Beverleys! Z—ds! Sir Lucius, you would not have me be so unnatural.

SIR LUC. Upon my conscience, Mr. Acres, your valour has *oozed* away with a vengeance!

ACRES. Not in the least! Odds Backs[1] and Abettors! I'll be your second with all my heart—and if you should get a *Quietus*, you may command me entirely. I'll get you a *snug lying* in the *Abbey here*; or *pickle* you, and send you over to Blunderbuss-hall, or any thing of the kind with the greatest pleasure.

SIR LUC. Pho! pho! you are little better than a coward.

ACRES. Mind, gentlemen, he calls me a *Coward*; Coward was the word, by my valour!

SIR LUC. Well, Sir?

ACRES. Look'ee, Sir Lucius, 'tisn't that I mind the word Coward—

18 Why no—] *76*, *85*; Zounds *L*; Z—ds, *75*   34 any thing] *L*, *76*, *85*; any *75*

[1] Cf. Congreve, *The Old Batchelor*, II. i: 'Ah my Hector of *Troy*, welcome my Bully, my Back.'

Coward may be said in joke.—But if you had call'd me a *Poltroon*, Odds Daggers and Balls!

SIR LUC. Well, Sir?

ACRES. ——I should have thought you a very ill-bred man.

SIR LUC. Pho! you are beneath my notice.

ABS. Nay, Sir Lucius, you can't have a better second than my friend, Acres—He is a most *determined dog*—call'd in the country, *Fighting Bob.*—He generally *kills a man a week*; don't you, Bob?

ACRES. Aye—at home!

SIR LUC. Well then, Captain, 'tis we must begin—so come out, my little counsellor, [*draws his sword.* and ask the gentleman, whether he will resign the lady, without forcing you to proceed against him?

ABS. Come on then, Sir; (*draws*) since you won't let it be an amicable suit, here's *my reply.*

Enter Sir ANTHONY, DAVID, *and the* WOMEN.

DAVID. Knock 'em all down, sweet Sir Anthony, knock down my Master in particular—and bind his hands over to their good behaviour!

SIR ANTH. Put up, Jack, put up, or I shall be in a frenzy—how came you in a duel, Sir?

ABS. Faith, Sir, that gentleman can tell you better than I; 'twas he call'd on me, and you know, Sir, I serve his Majesty.

SIR ANTH. Here's a pretty fellow; I catch him going to cut a man's throat, and he tells me, he serves his Majesty!——Zounds! sirrah, then how durst you draw the King's sword against one of his subjects?

ABS. Sir, I tell you! That gentleman call'd me out, without explaining his reasons.

SIR ANTH. Gad! Sir, how came you to call my son out, without explaining your reasons?

SIR LUC. Your son, Sir, insulted me in a manner which my honour could not brook.

SIR ANTH. Zounds! Jack, how durst you insult the gentleman in a manner which his honour could not brook?

MRS. MAL. Come, come, let's have no Honour before ladies—Captain Absolute, come here—How could you intimidate us so?—Here's Lydia has been terrified to death for you.

ABS. For fear I should be kill'd, or escape, Ma'am?

MRS. MAL. Nay, no delusions to the past—Lydia is convinc'd; speak child.

SIR LUC. With your leave, Ma'am, I must put in a word here—I believe I could interpret the young lady's silence—Now mark—

LYD. What is it you mean, Sir?

SIR LUC. Come, come, Delia, we must be serious now—this is no time for trifling.

LYD. 'Tis true, Sir; and your reproof bids me offer this gentleman my hand, and solicit the return of his affections.

ABS. O! my little angel, say you so?—Sir Lucius—I perceive there must be some mistake here—with regard to the affront, which you affirm I have given you—I can only say, that it could not have been intentional. —And as you must be convinced, that I should not fear to support a real injury—you shall now see that I am not ashamed to atone for an inadvertency—I ask your pardon.—But for this lady, while honour'd with her approbation, I will support my claim against any man whatever.

SIR ANTH. Well said, Jack, and I'll stand by you, my Boy.

ACRES. Mind, I give up all my claim—I make no pretensions to any thing in the world—and if I can't get a wife, without fighting for her, by my Valour! I'll live a bachelor.

SIR LUC. Captain, give me your hand—an affront handsomely acknowledged becomes an obligation—and as for the Lady—if she chuses to deny her own hand writing here— [*Takes out letters.*

MRS. MAL. O, he will dissolve my mystery!—Sir Lucius, perhaps there's some mistake—perhaps, I can illuminate—

SIR LUC. Pray, old gentlewoman, don't interfere, where you have no business.—Miss Languish, are you my Delia, or not?

LYD. Indeed, Sir Lucius, I am not.

[LYDIA *and* ABSOLUTE *walk aside.*

MRS MAL. Sir Lucius O'Trigger—ungrateful as you are—I own the soft impeachment—pardon my blushes, I am Delia.

SIR LUC. You Delia—pho! pho! be easy.[1]

MRS. MAL. Why, thou barbarous Vandyke—those letters are mine—When you are more sensible of my benignity—perhaps I may be brought to encourage your addresses.

SIR LUC. Mrs. Malaprop ,I am extremely sensible of your condescension; and whether you or Lucy have put this trick upon me, I am equally beholden to you.—And to shew you I'm not ungrateful, Captain Absolute! since you have taken that lady from me, I'll give you my Delia into the bargain.

ABS. I am much obliged to you, Sir Lucius; but here's our friend, fighting Bob, unprovided for.

SIR LUC. Hah! little Valour—here, will you make your fortune?

20 *Takes out letters*] *76*, *85*; *Taking out letters 75*; *om. L* 21 dissolve] *85*; disolve *76*; desolve *75*; *om. L*

[1] Don't be sought after: a sense still used on the Stock Exchange.

ACRES. Odds Wrinkles! No.—But give me your hand, Sir Lucius, forget and forgive; but if ever I give you a chance of *pickling* me again, say Bob Acres is a Dunce, that's all.

SIR ANTH. Come, Mrs. Malaprop, don't be cast down—you are in your bloom yet.

MRS. MAL. O Sir Anthony!—men are all barbarians—

[*All retire but* JULIA *and* FAULKLAND.

JUL. He seems dejected and unhappy—not sullen—there was some foundation, however, for the tale he told me—O woman! how true should be your judgment, when your resolution is so weak!

FAULK. Julia!—how can I sue for what I so little deserve? I dare not presume—yet Hope is the child of Penitence.

JUL. Oh! Faulkland, you have not been more faulty in your unkind treatment of me, than I am now in wanting inclination to resent it. As my heart honestly bids me place my weakness to the account of love, I should be ungenerous not to admit the same plea for your's.

FAULK. Now I shall be blest indeed! [SIR ANTHONY *comes forward.*

SIR ANTH. What's going on here?—So you have been quarrelling too, I warrant.——Come, Julia, I never interfered before; but let me have a hand in the matter at last.—All the faults I have ever seen in my friend Faulkland, seemed to proceed from what he calls the *delicacy* and *warmth* of his affection for you——There, marry him directly, Julia, you'll find he'll mend surprisingly! [*The rest come forward.*

SIR LUC. Come now, I hope there is no dissatisfied person, but what is content; for as I have been disappointed myself, it will be very hard if I have not the satisfaction of seeing other people succeed better—

ACRES. You are right, Sir Lucius.—So, Jack, I wish you joy—Mr. Faulkland the same.—Ladies,—come now, to shew you I'm neither vex'd nor angry, Odds Tabors and Pipes! I'll order the fiddles in half an hour, to the New Rooms[1]—and I insist on your all meeting me there.

SIR ANTH. Gad! Sir, I like your spirit; and at night we single lads will drink a health to the young couples, and a husband to Mrs. Malaprop.

FAULK. Our partners are stolen from us, Jack—I hope to be congratulated by each other—yours for having checked in time, the errors of an ill-directed Imagination, which might have betray'd an innocent heart; and mine, for having, by her gentleness and candour, reformed the unhappy temper of one, who by it made wretched whom he loved most, and tortured the heart he ought to have ador'd.

ABS. Well, Faulkland, we have both tasted the Bitters, as well as the Sweets of Love—with this difference only, that *you* always prepared the bitter cup for yourself, while *I*——

1 me] *76*, *85*; us *75*; *om. L*   30 your] *L*, *76*, *85*; you *75*   39 Faulkland] *L*; Jack *75*, *76*, *85*

[1] Built by John Wood the younger, and opened in 1771.

LYD. Was always obliged to *me* for it, hey! Mr. Modesty?——But come, no more of that—our happiness is now as unallay'd as general.

JUL. Then let us study to preserve it so: and while Hope pictures to us a flattering scene of future Bliss, let us deny its pencil those colours which are too bright to be lasting.—When Hearts deserving Happiness would unite their fortunes, Virtue would crown them with an unfading garland of modest, hurtless flowers; but ill-judging Passion will force the gaudier Rose into the wreath, whose thorn offends them, when its Leaves are dropt!

Finis

6 fortunes] *L*, *76*, *85*; fortune *75* 10 Finis] *L*, *76*, *85*; *om.* *75*

EPILOGUE

BY THE AUTHOR

Spoken by Mrs. BULKLEY

Ladies for *You*—I heard our Poet say—
He'd try to coax some *Moral* from his Play:
'One moral's plain'—cried I—'without more fuss;
Man's social happiness all rests on Us—
Thro' all the Drama—whether damn'd or not—
Love gilds the *Scene*, and *Women* guide the *plot*.
From ev'ry rank—obedience is our due—
D'ye doubt?—The world's great stage shall prove it true.'

The Cit—well skill'd to shun domestic strife—
Will sup abroad;—but first—he'll ask his *wife*:
John Trot, his friend for once, will do the same,
But then—he'll just *step home to tell his dame*.—

The *surly* '*Squire*—at noon resolves to rule,
And half the day—Zounds! Madam is a fool!
Convinc'd at night—the vanquish'd Victor[1] says,
Ah! Kate! *you women have such coaxing ways*!——

The *jolly Toper* chides each tardy blade,—
Till reeling Bacchus calls on Love for aid:
Then with each Toast, he sees fair bumpers swim,
And kisses Chloe on the sparkling Brim!

Nay, I have heard that Statesmen—great and wise—
Will *sometimes* counsel with a Lady's eyes;
The servile suitors—watch her various face,
She smiles preferment—or she frowns disgrace,
Curtsies a pension here—there nods a place.

15 *his*] *85*; my *75*, *76*

[1] Dryden, 'Alexander's Feast', 114–15:

At length, with Love and Wine at once oppress'd,
The vanquish'd Victor sunk upon her Breast.

Nor with less awe, in scenes of humbler life,
Is *view'd* the *mistress*, or is *heard* the *wife*.
The poorest Peasant of the poorest soil,
The child of Poverty, and heir to Toil—
Early from radiant Love's impartial light,
Steals one small spark, to cheer his world of night:
Dear spark!—that oft thro' winter's chilling woes,
Is all the warmth his little cottage knows!

The wand'ring *Tar*—who, not for *years*, has press'd
The widow'd partner of his *day* of rest—
On the cold deck—far from her arms remov'd—
Still hums the ditty[1] which his Susan lov'd:
And while around the cadence rude is blown,
The Boatswain whistles in a softer tone.

The *Soldier*, fairly proud of wounds and toil,
Pants for the *triumph* of his Nancy's smile;
But ere the battle, should he list' her cries,
The Lover trembles—and the Hero dies!
That heart, by war and honour steel'd to fear,
Droops on a sigh, and sickens at a tear!

But Ye more cautious—ye nice judging few,
Who give to Beauty only Beauty's due,
Tho' friends to Love—*Ye* view with deep regret
Our conquests marr'd—and triumphs incomplete,
'Till polish'd Wit more lasting charms disclose,
And Judgment fix the darts which Beauty throws!
—In female breasts did Sense and Merit rule,
The Lover's mind would ask no other school;
Sham'd into sense—the Scholars of our eyes,
Our Beaux from *Gallantry* would soon be wise;
Would gladly light, their homage to improve,
The Lamp of Knowledge at the Torch of Love!

24 and] *76*, *85*; our *75*

[1] Gay's ballad, 'Sweet William's Farewell to Black-eyed Susan'. Stanza six runs:

If to far India's coast we sail,
  Thy eyes are seen in di'monds bright,
Thy breath is Africk's spicy gale,
  Thy skin is ivory, so white.
Thus ev'ry beauteous object that I view,
Wakes in my soul some charm of lovely Sue.

ST. PATRICK'S DAY

OR

THE SCHEMING LIEUTENANT

A Farce

ST. PATRICK'S DAY,

OR,

THE SCHEMING LIEUTENANT.

COMPOSITION

WILLIAM LINLEY, Sheridan's brother-in-law, told Thomas Moore that Sheridan wrote *St. Patrick's Day* 'for a poor man who was in distress'.[1] In other words, Sheridan paid off a debt of gratitude to Lawrence Clinch, whose performance as Sir Lucius O'Trigger had greatly contributed to the success of the revised version of *The Rivals*.[2] Another report claimed that the farce was written in forty-eight hours.[3] No other information is extant about its composition.

On 24 April 1775 Thomas Harris wrote to the Examiner of Plays at the Lord Chamberlain's office, seeking a licence for it: 'This Farce is intended to be perform'd at The Theatre Royal in Covent Garden with the Permission of The Rt. Honble. Lord Hertford.'[4] Presumably rehearsals went on; possibly additions and corrections to the manuscript were made. Just before the first night (2 May), the *Morning Chronicle* remarked:

> We are this evening to be presented at Covent-Garden Theatre with a new farce. . . . The title promises much, and by the modest appellation of *farce* being prefixed to it, we are led to expect some of that strong humour which has of late been banished the stage, to make room for crying comedies, and tedious trifling tragedies. Farce is of true English growth; may it thrive again in its native soil, and exotic refinement no longer prevail.

RECEPTION[5]

As this piece was . . . declared in the Prologue to be a hasty production, designed merely to assist a Performer at his Benefit, it would be illiberal and unfair to judge it with rigid severity. . . . We ought to be contented if we meet with broad humour, homely jests, and extravagant caricature. *St. Patrick's Day* is replete with all three; Dosy and Credulous are very

[1] Moore, *Journal*, ii. 174.

[2] Kelly, ii. 322, says that Clinch was an intimate friend of Sheridan's father.

[3] Rhodes, i. 139, quoting *Public Characters* for 1799.

[4] Huntington MS. LA 388.

[5] Rhodes, i. 141, declared that *St. Patrick's Day* 'was generally ignored by the periodical press'; but the passage he quotes from the *Whitehall Evening Post*, 6 May 1775, had appeared two days earlier in a long summary of the plot in the *Morning Chronicle*. Had Rhodes made a greater search, he would have found a number of references in the leading journals. I quote only a few significant passages from them.

laughable instances of the extravagant in dramatic portrait painting. The Doctor talks in the technical terms of his profession with great pleasantry, while the Justice presents us with a truly farcical father. The language in general shews the author a man of humour and observation; the situations are whimsical, and produce that mirth which the audience in the Prologue were invited to partake of. Upon the whole, we think the piece before us, (considered as mere *Farce*), by no means destitute of merit; at the same time we cannot so far acquit the author, as to pronounce him entirely undeserving of censure. His jests are occasionally too low and vulgar, and his scene too extravagantly absurd; indeed he more than once reminded us of a Bartholomew-fair droll, and he three several times hazarded such in[n]uendoes as challenged decency and morality to the blush; what heightened this fault, his gross allusions were put into the mouths of his female characters. . . .

St. Patrick's Day was better acted than Benefit Novelities usually are; Mr. Quick, Miss Brown, and Mr. Lee-Lewes deserved particular praise; the latter the most, as he strove against a character much out of his customary line of performance—by the by, when he next personates an old man, we advise him to spare his Indian Ink; the lines on his face were last night so ridiculously strong, that he appeared to wear a mask, cut out of the hide of the Queen's Zebra. (*Morning Chronicle*, 3 May 1775.)

Last night was performed for the first time, at Covent Garden Theatre, a new farce of two acts, called St. Patrick's Day, or the Scheming Lieutenant; said to be written by Mr. Sheridan, Junior.

If this is not the most regular well finished afterpiece upon the stage, we will venture to say it is by no means the worst. It contains some truly farcical situations, and though the humour is here and there extravagant, it is not too strong for what is called farce. It occasioned much laughter, and was well received throughout by a candid audience. The piece was ushered in by a tolerable good prologue. (*Morning Post*, 3 May 1775.)

As the new Farce, called *St. Patrick's Day*; *or the Scheming Lieutenant*, was on Tuesday evening received with universal applause; Mr. Lee-Lewes thought it would be more agreeable to his friends than a Pantomime, he therefore applied to the Author and the Managers, to indulge him with it tomorrow-evening, who kindly complied with his request. (*Morning Post*, 5 May 1775.)

St. Patrick's Day, or The Scheming Lieutenant, was on Saturday evening presented to the town with a few alterations. This Farce certainly has more humour, satire and observation in it than most of the afterpieces lately produced; it is therefore no wonder that it was highly applauded. (*Morning Chronicle*, 8 May 1775.)

Whatever pieces are presented on a benefit night, are in no degree fair objects of public criticism, from being intended chiefly for the entertainment of the actor or actress's particular friends.—It is perhaps well for the author of *St. Patrick's Day* that such is the public idea; for his canvas is certainly filled with the likeness of no one human creature in existence. —The prologue promises a high feast to the sons and daughters of *fun*, and it cannot be denied that the writer of the farce has contrived to keep his word with them: though it is not altogether so clear as might be wished, whether the laugh his scenes excite, is a laugh of applause or ridicule. (*London Magazine*, xliv (1775), 242.)

CHOICE OF TEXT

After its first two performances (2 and 6 May), the farce went into the repertory at Covent Garden Theatre and was acted twelve times in twelve months.

At the beginning of the following season (Sept. 1776), Sheridan became manager of Drury Lane Theatre but, as far as I can discover, *St. Patrick's Day* was not performed there during the thirty-two years of his connection with that playhouse. It was not uncommon for farces to be given only at the theatre in which they were first performed, but it is also certain that Sheridan was not proud of having written farce. Three years passed before he publicly admitted that he was the author of *St. Patrick's Day*.[1] In later life he even tried to stop his son Tom from presenting some that he (Tom) had written. 'Monk' Lewis gives a reason for Sheridan's attitude: 'Tom Sheridan has written great part of a Farce; but He says, it is not to come out, because His Father has given his opinion, that though the piece is very laughable, yet writing farce is *infra dignitatem*.'[2] Yet a writer in *Blackwood's Magazine* (Feb. 1826, p. 122), stated that Sheridan was 'deep read in the whole catalogue of forgotten farces'.

The following texts are of interest:

I. OF THE PROLOGUE

The prologue has not previously been located, but can now be identified from a description in the *London Evening Post*, 2–4 May 1775: 'The main drift of the Prologue was to tell the audience that a fine spring impeded the theatrical harvest; and that at this season, the benefits of nature were the greatest enemies to the performers' benefits.' This tallies with the content of some verse printed by Moore as an epilogue. He writes, 'The Epilogue, which I am about to give, though apparently finished,

[1] In an article on Sheridan in the *London Magazine*, xliii (1778), 483–4, one 'T.M.' refers to the very entertaining new farce, *St. Patrick's Day*, 'which has lately been owned by Mr. Sheridan'.

[2] Add. MS. 51641, f. 142: M. G. Lewis to Lady Holland, 19 April 1803. Cf. the Earl of Ilchester, *The Home of the Hollands, 1805–1820* (1937), p. 160.

has not, as far as I can learn, yet appeared in print, nor am I at all aware for what occasion it was intended.'[1] No epilogue to *St. Patrick's Day* was ever mentioned in the newspaper reports, and it seems certain that the passage Moore quoted was the missing prologue. The original manuscript in Sheridan's hand is in Yale University Library, and is the source of the present text.

Moore says that the passage was 'apparently unfinished', and this would appear to be true. The *Morning Chronicle*, 3 May 1775, noted that in the prologue delivered on the first night, the author excused the farce 'as a hasty production, designed merely to assist a Performer at his Benefit'. No sign of an excuse is to be found in the prologue as we have it at present, either in the Yale version or as printed by Moore. Nor is there any promise of 'a high feast for the sons and daughters of fun'.[2]

2. OF THE PLAY

Part of the holograph manuscript of the farce was in the Frampton Court collection and, as already mentioned,[3] was lost at sea. When it appeared at Sotheby's sale-room on 2 July 1930, as part of lot 634, it was listed as 'St. Patrick's Day, A Farce, Auto. Manuscript of portions of scenes III and IV, 21 pp. 4to.'

(i) *Rae's Copy of the Frampton Court MS.*

Rae says that the sheets of manuscript begin with 'Scene 3d.—The Walk', and end in Scene 4th[4] with 'Finis'. The only indication that portions of the manuscript are not in Sheridan's hand is the note that the last few sheets from 'Enter Lauretta' (p. 95) to the conclusion are in Mrs. Sheridan's handwriting. But if we accept Sotheby's description literally, then only a portion of Scene iii will be in Sheridan's hand.

Since the manuscript sheets are not now available, I have accepted Rae's transcription of these scenes for the purpose of collation. I have ignored his version of the remainder of the farce because it is a reprint of the Murray text of 1821.

(ii) *The Lord Chamberlain's Copy*

This is a manuscript copy prepared by the Covent Garden scribe who wrote out the first version of *The Rivals*. It is in the same neat hand throughout, and in default of a full rendering in Sheridan's hand, presents the best available text of the farce.[5] It is Larpent MS. 388 in the Huntington Library.

[1] Moore, i. 337–8.
[2] See p. 153 above.
[3] See p. 23 above.
[4] II. iii and iv.
[5] For an argument in its favour, see C. Price, 'The Larpent MS. of *St. Patrick's Day*', *The Huntington Library Quarterly*, xxix (1966), 183–9.

(iii) *Text—'with a few alterations'—given on 6 May 1775*

If this were found, it would probably prove to be the authoritative text but, as far as I know, it is not extant. No other manuscript copies of this year are available, though it is abundantly clear that some demand for them was soon made. For example, W. T. Lewis[1] wrote to Sheridan begging a transcript or, better still, a revised copy:

Mr. Lewis's Compliments wait on Mr. Sheridan takes the liberty of reminding him of his obliging promise. If he has not yet began the Address for Ranger,[2] or finds it difficult wou'd he write him anything Introductory it wou'd serve him equally.—the Idea 'that if improv'd I shou'd in Duty employ it for their Enter[tainmen]t who first patroniz'd any dawn of merit they saw etc'

If he has not yet made the purpos'd alteration to St. Patrick's Day he wou'd entreat it in its present form (if Mr. Sheridan has no objection) as it wou'd materially serve Lewis and he will take care Mr. S. shall lose no reputation in the representation.

He wou'd not have been thus importunate but he leaves Town on Tuesday noon.

C[oven]t Garden Saturd[a]y Morn[ing][3]—

His destination was Dublin, as is clear from the *Hibernian Journal*, 5–8 May 1775. It records that 'Mr. Spranger Barry intends to open the Summer Campaign with a select Company, whom he has engaged to follow his Fortunes on this Side the Water; beside others of lesser note, are Mr. William Lewis. . . .' It was from Dublin, then, that Lewis wrote to Sheridan on 10 June:

Sir

As I was not favour'd with any Answer to the last I troubled you with I fear it did not reach you in time to comply with the Contents. Yet, tho' I have lost the flattering Circumstance of being introduc'd to the Irish Theatre as I cou'd wish, I cannot therefore give up the expectation of your Assistance while in it.

The Use of your Farce for my Night wou'd, beside serving me, add to the high opinion they entertain of your Dramatic Productions. If you have no Objection (and when I first made the request to you you seem'd to have none) and it is necessary to apply to Mr. Harris, I will entreat to know it.

I hope Sir you will excuse the freedom of this address, as it is occasion'd by the great opinion conceived of your good nature by, Sir, Your most Humble Servant

Wm. Thos. Lewis[4]

If you will be so obliging as to leave a line directed for me a Gentleman will call for it.

I have been unable to discover if this favour was granted.

[1] (1748?–1811). He played Faulkland in *The Rivals*.
[2] In Benjamin Hoadly's *The Suspicious Husband* (1747).
[3] Harvard MS.
[4] Pierpont Morgan Library MS.

Performances in the provinces show that copies of the text were made available on occasion later in the year. A number of members of the Covent Garden company acted at Liverpool and gave the farce 'by permission of the Author . . . as it was acted last season at the Theatre Royal, Covent Garden, with universal applause'. Clinch, Lee Lewes, Mrs. Pitt, and Miss Brown took their London parts.[1] The *Bath Journal*, 30 October 1775, advertised a production at the Bath Theatre of 'a farce never performed here by Richard Sheridan Esq. called St. Patrick's Day'. It would be reasonable to assume from this that Sheridan allowed copies to be used sparingly and as a great favour.

The farce, by its very title, was naturally of greater interest in Ireland, and a number of performances are recorded there in the next few years.[2]

(iv) *The First Irish Edition, and First Edition Generally*

This text seems to be drawn from a theatre copy made after the Larpent MS. had been completed. We may reach this conclusion after reading the long summary of the plot of the farce printed by the *Morning Chronicle*, 4 May 1775, and comparing it with the Dublin first edition. Three phrases are identical, and are different from those in the Larpent MS. Since some unspecified alterations were made for the performance at Covent Garden on 6 May 1775, it is also possible that the Dublin first edition incorporates other changes authorized by Sheridan. For these reasons, it deserves study.

Many of the changes, however, are clearly corruptions accumulating over the years. Mr. F. W. Bateson has noted[3] an actor's gag in I. ii:

ROSY. We must all die.
LIEUT. Doctor.
ROSY. Kings, lords, and common whores——

He indicates that the last phrase is drawn from Colley Cibber's *She Wou'd and She Wou'd Not*, v. i: 'we must all Dye when we have done our Best, Sooner or Later, Old or Young, Prince or Peasant, High or Low, Kings, Lords and——Common Whores must dye.' Actors, too, seem responsible for the Justice's very obvious pun in reply to the Lieutenant's 'Curum bono fullum':

What, does he say I must row in a boat to Fulham?

This would seem to appeal more to a London audience than a Dublin one.

These 'improvements' make the first edition unreliable, and they mar what might well have been in origin an authentic version provided for W. T. Lewis or some other favoured performer. The copying, too, is sometimes unintelligent: we find 'galen a-bridge' (for 'Galen abridg'd'),

[1] *Williamson's Liverpool Advertiser*, 25 Aug. 1775.

[2] *Freeman's Journal*, 10–13 May 1777; W. S. Clark, *The Irish Stage in the County Towns* (Oxford, 1965), p. 334.

[3] In a letter to the editor.

'Amosen' (for 'Amazon'), and 'circumvaluation' (for 'circumvallation'). 'Credilous' and 'O'Conner' are usual.

The title-page reads:

St PATRICK's DAY; | OR, THE | SCHEMING LIEUTENANT. | A | COMIC OPERA: | AS IT IS ACTED | AT THE | *THEATRE-ROYAL*, | SMOKE-ALLEY. | [Short rule] | PRINTED FOR THE BOOKSELLERS. | [Short rule] | M,DCC, LXXXVIII.

Collation: 12mo in half-sheets: [A]^3 B^6 C^5.

Contents: pp. 28.

[1] title; [2] Dramatis Personæ; [3] and 4–27, text; [28] blank.

Comment:

The Rothschild Library (Cambridge, 1954), ii. 503, gives the collation as 2E4^r–3C5^r, listing it as bound with five other plays. It adds, 'these plays were probably printed together with the intention of separating them for sale; certainly at some stage the copy of *St. Patrick's Day* recorded by I. A. Williams had become separated and he described the first three leaves (in fact [E4], [E5], [E6]) as "[A] three leaves" '.

For other bibliographical points, see Williams, p. 229; Wise, v. 155.

The first edition was only lightly edited for inclusion as the text of the farce printed in *The Works of . . . Sheridan* (1821),[1] and is also largely followed in Cumberland's edition (*c.* 1831).

(v) *The Dublin Edition of 1789*

This text is interesting because it is sometimes closer than the first edition to the readings in the Larpent MS. and the transcription by Rae. It prints 'King William' (p. 165, l. 23), 'Boston' (p. 170, l. 13), and the colloquial 'old Mag' (p. 172, l. 7). However, it also has its share of oddities: 'circumlocution' (p. 166, l. 21), 'Cammel' (p. 177, l. 2), and 'look for you' (p. 163, l. 20). Like the first edition, it prints 'What does he say, I must row in a boat to Fulham?' (p. 189, l. 22).

The title-page reads:

St. PATRICK's DAY: | OR, THE | SCHEMING LIEUTENANT. | [short swelled rule] | By Mr. Sheridan. | [short double rule] | DUBLIN: | Printed by P. BYRNE, (108) Grafton-street. | [short swelled rule] | M,DCC,LXXXIX.

Collation: 12mo: A–D^6.

Contents: pp. 48.

[1] title; [2] blank; [3] Dramatis Personæ; [4] blank; [5] and 6–48, text.

[1] It makes a few grammatical corrections, and prints 'Credulous' and 'O'Connor', 'circumvallation' and 'Amazon'. But it repeats 'Oh, hang fortune', 'skurry villains', and the gibberish generally.

Comment:

Two copies of this edition are in Trinity College Library, Dublin: press marks Gall 6 t. 16 (9), and 190 s. 92 (5).

Rhodes, i. 172, lists an edition similar to this one but said to be printed by 'Byrne, 93 Grafton Street, Dublin', and with the last speech beginning, 'Come, I insist upon one day without quarreling.' This was thought to be in Trinity College Library, Dublin, but has not been located there or elsewhere.

Conclusion

It seems unlikely that Sheridan had any hand in the farce after the 'few alterations' made for the performance on 6 May 1775.

I propose to use the Larpent MS. as copy-text, and to admit into the edited text a few readings from Rae and the Dublin editions of 1788 and 1789, where they correct errors, seem more plausible, or are given support elsewhere. 'O Connor' and 'O Conner' are printed as 'O'Connor', and 'Bridgett' as 'Bridget'.[1]

The following abbreviations are used in the textual notes of this play:

L The Lord Chamberlain's copy, Larpent MS. 388.
Rae Rae, pp. 89–96.
88 The first edition, unauthorized, Dublin 1788.[2]
89 The Dublin edition, unauthorized, of 1789.

In the notes on the prologue, 'Yale' stands for the manuscript in Yale University Library (the copy-text), and 'Moore' for *Memoirs of . . . Sheridan* (2nd edn., 1825), i. 337–8.

[1] No edition gives the text of Lauretta's song at the beginning of Act II, Sc. 2. Since Sheridan referred in *The Rivals* to two songs by Jackson of Exeter, I wonder if he had in mind for performance here, yet another from Jackson's *Opera Quarta*. Song X would be suitable in theme:

Ah! what avails this sweetly solemn Bow'r,
That silent Stream where dimpling Eddies play.
Yon' thymy Bank bedeckt with many a Flow'r,
Where branching Trees exclude the Beam of Day.
Far from my Love Ah! how can these delight
Tho' lavish Spring her smiles around has cast.
Despair alas that whelms the Soul in Night,
Dims the sad Eye and deadens ev'ry Taste.

[2] T. J. Wise, in *The Ashley Library* (1924), v. 155, claims that signatures A1 and C6 were blanks in this edition. Ashley 1685 (in the British Museum) does not conform to this description, nor have I found any copy that does.

DRAMATIS PERSONÆ[1]

JUSTICE CREDULOUS	Mr. Lee Lewes
LIEUTENANT O'CONNOR	Mr. Clinch
DOCTOR ROSY	Mr. Quick
SERJEANT TROUNCE	Mr. Dunstall
CORPORAL FLINT	Mr. Fox
SOLDIERS, AND COUNTRYMEN	
BRIDGET	Mrs. Pitt
LAURETTA	Miss Brown

[1] The names of the actors and actresses are taken from the *Morning Chronicle*, 3 May 1775. It mentions that Davies, Wewitzer, and Chaplin performed the parts of soldiers. *The London Stage*, p. 1889, lists a further five names: Fearon (probably the blacksmith: cf. p. 1913), Thompson, Cushing, Bates, and Hollingsworth. When the farce was given at Bristol Theatre on 17 Apr. 1779 the cast included 'Steward—Mr. Brookes': see *Felix Farley's Bristol Journal*, 17 Apr. 1779.

PROLOGUE

In this gay Month when thro' the sultry Hour
The vernal Sun denies the wonted Shower
When youthful Spring usurps maturer sway—
And pal[l]id April Steals the Blush of May
How joys the rustic Tribe to view display'd
The Lib'ral Blossom and the early Shade!
—But Ah! far other Air our Soil delights!
—Here 'Charming Weather' is the worst of Blights!
No genial Beams rejoice our rustic Train
Their Harvest's still the better for the Rain!
To Summer Suns our Groves no tribute owe
They thrive in Frost, and flourish best in Snow!
When other Woods resound the feather'd throng
Our Groves, our Woods, are destitute of Song.
The Thrush—the Lark—all leave our mimic Vale
—No more we boast the Christmas Nightingale—
Poor Ros[s]ignol[1]—The Wonder of his Day—
Sung thro the Winter—but is mute in May.
Then boastful Spring that gilds fair Nature's Scene
O'ercasts our Lawns—and deadens ev'ry Green
Obscures our Sky, embrowns the wooden Shade
And dries the Channel of each tin Cascade!
O hapless We whom such ill fate Betides!
Hurt by the Beam, which chears the World besides!
Who love the ling'ring Frost, nice, chilling Showers
While Nature's BENEFIT—is Death to ours
Who, Witch-like, best in noxious Mists perform,
Thrive in the Tempest and enjoy the Storm.
O hapless We—unless your generous care
Bids us no more lament that Spring is fair,
But plenteous glean from the dramatic Soil,
The Vernal Harvest of our Winter's Toil.

20 boastful] *Yale*; bashful *Moore*

[1] Signor Rossignol, bird-imitator, gave his last performance of the season at Covent Garden Theatre on 16 Mar. 1775. A contemporary was impressed by his 'most amazing imitations of singing Birds, which He does to that perfection that it is impossible to distinguish them from the finest notes of the Nightingale, Canary Bird, Goldfinch, Linnet, etc., for all appearance of the human voice is entirely lost' (*Sir Joshua's Nephew*, ed. S. M. Radcliffe, 1930, p. 83).

For April Suns to us no pleasure bring
Your Presence here is all we feel of Spring
May's Riper Beauties here no Bloom display
Your fostering Smile alone to Us is May.

4 to Us is] *Yale*; proclaims it *Moore*

ST. PATRICK'S DAY

OR

THE SCHEMING LIEUTENANT

Act 1st—Scene 1st

A walk near the JUSTICE'*s house*

Enter SERJEANT TROUNCE, CORPORAL FLINT,—*and several Soldiers,—Some with Shambrogues*[1] *in their Hats.*

1ST SOLDIER. I say you're wrong—We should all speak together—each for himself—and all at once—that we may be heard the better.

2ND SOLDIER. Right, Jack, we'll argue in Platoons.

3RD SOLDIER. Aye, aye, let him have our Grievances in a Volley:—or if we be to have a Spokesman,—there's our Corporal is the Lieutenant's Countryman, and knows his humour.

CORPORAL. Let me alone for that—I sarv'd three years within a little bit, under his Honour in the Royal Inniskillins; and I never will see a sweeter timper'd officer, nor one more free with his Purse—I put a great Shambrogue in his hat this Morning, and I'll be bound for him he'll wear it, if it was as big as Stephen's Green.

4TH SOLDIER. I say again then, ye talk like Youngsters—like Militia Striplings.—There is a Discipline—lookee, in all things—whereof the Serjeant must be our Man.—Besides, he is a Gentleman of Words. —He understands your foreign Lingo—your Figures—and such Auxiliaries in scoring—confess now, for a reckoning—whether in Chalk or writing,—ben't he your only Interpreter?

5 *A walk . . . house*] *L*, *89*; *om. 88* 6–7 *Enter . . . Hats*] *L*; Enter TROUNCE, FLINT, and FOUR SOLDIERS *88*; *Enter three* Soldiers *and the* Corporal *89* 11 or] *L*, *89*; and *88* 12 our] *L*, *89*; the *88* 14 little] *L*, *89*; *om. 88* 15 Inniskillins] *L*, *89*; Inniskillions *88* 16 timper'd officer] *L*; temper'd officer *89*; tempered gentleman *88* 17 Shambrogue] *L*; shamrogue *88*; Shambruck *89* 18 if it was] *L*, *89*; was it *88* Stephen's] *89*; Steven's *88*; Stevens' *L* 19 again] *L*, *88*; *om. 89* ye] *L*; you *88*, *89* 20 lookee] *L*, *88*; look for you *89* 21 Man.—Besides,] *L*, *89*; guide *88* 22 Lingo] *L*, *88*; lingo's *89* such] *L*, *89*; such like *88* 24 Chalk] *L*, *88*; cloth *89* your . . . Interpreter] *L*; your only man *88*; the only man *89*

[1] Cf. Samuel Whyte, *The Shamrock* (1772), p. vii: 'The old *Milesians* contend for original orthography, and write *Shambrogue*, *Shamrogue*, or *Shamrog*; *Spenser* and Dr. *S. Johnson* authorize our spelling, conformably to the established idiom of pronunciation, the rational way of writing all words. . . .'

CORPORAL. Why the Serjeant is a Scholar, to be sure, and has the Gift of Reading.

SERJEANT. Good Soldiers, and fellow Gentlemen, if ye will make me your Spokesman—So—ye will shew the more Judgment: and let me alone for the Argument, I'll be as loud as a Drum—and point blank from the Purpose.

ALL SOLDIERS. Agreed! agreed!

CORPORAL. O faith, here comes the Lieutenant—Now, Serjeant.

SERJEANT. So then—to order—look out your mutiny looks—let every man grumble a little to himself—and some of you hum the Deserter's march.[1]

Enter LIEUTENANT O'CONNOR.

LIEUT. Well, honest Lads, what is it ye have to complain of?

SERJEANT. Ahem!—hem!—hem!

4TH SOLDIER. There—damme!—did you ever hear a better hem! to begin with?—The Lieutenant's stagger'd already.

SERJEANT. So please your Honour,—the Grievance of the matter is this—Ever since your Honour has differ'd with Justice Credulous, here, our Inn-keepers use us most scurvily—by my Halbert, their treatment is such, that if our Spirit was willing to put up with it, Flesh and Blood would by no means agree—So we humbly petition, that your Honour would make an end of the matter, by running away with the Justice's Daughter at once, or else get us fresh Quarters—hem!—hem!

LIEUT. Indeed! pray which of the Houses use you ill?

1ST SOLDIER. There's the red Lion ha'n't half the civility as the old red Lion had.

1 the Serjeant . . . sure] *L, 88*; to be sure, the serjeant is a scholar *89* 3 ye will] *L*; you *88, 89* 7 ALL . . . agreed!] *L, 88*; *om. 89* 8 O faith] *L*; O Fait *88*; Arrah faith *89* 9 look out . . . looks—let every] *L, 89*; Put on your mutiny looks, every *88* 10 a little to himself] *L, 88*; to himself a little *89* Deserter's] *L, 88*; Doctor's *89* 12 O'CONNOR] *L*; *om. 88, 89* 13 ye] *L*; you *88, 89* 14 Ahem!—hem!—hem!] *L*; Ahem! hem! *88*; Hem! hem! hem! *89* 15–16 There . . . with] *L, 89*; *om. 88* 16 The Lieutenant's] *L*; *om. 88*; the Lieutenant *89* stagger'd already] *L*; staggers already *89*; *om. 88* 17 Grievance] *L*; very grievance *88*; grievances *89* 18 has differ'd] *L, 89*; differed *88* 19 here] *L, 89*; *om. 88* Inn-keepers] *L*; Inkeepers *88*; Inn-keeper *89* 20 our Spirit was] *L*; your *spirit* was *88*; our spirits were *89* 21 would] *L, 89*; could *88* 22–3 by . . . Daughter at once] *L, 89*; at once, by . . . daughter *88* 26 There's] *L, 88*; Here's *89* half] *L, 88*; howf *89* 26–7 as the old red Lion had] *L, 89*; of the old Red Lion *88*

[1] *Le Déserteur*, with music by P. A. Monsigny and text by J. M. Sédaine, was presented in Paris on 6 Mar. 1769, and proved very popular. It was adapted for production at Drury Lane Theatre on 2 Nov. 1773, by Charles Dibdin. The British Museum Music Catalogue lists a single sheet folio, *c.* 1775, as 'March in the Desertore' and describes it as 'from the Overture to *Le Déserteur*'.

2ND SOLDIER. Aye, and there's the White horse, if he wa'n't case hardened, ought to be asham'd to shew his face.

LIEUT. Very well, the Horse and Lion shall answer for it at the Quarter Sessions.

SERJEANT. The two Magpies are civil enough, but the Angel uses us like devils,[1] and the rising Sun refuses us light to go to bed by.

LIEUT. Indeed! then upon my word I'll have the rising Sun put down, and the Angel shall give Security for his good behavior—but are you sure you do nothing to quit Scores with them?

CORPORAL. Nothing at all, your Honour, unless now and then we happen to fling a Cartridge into the Kitchen fire, or put a Spatterdash or so into the Soup—and sometimes Ned drums a little up and down Stairs of a night.

LIEUT. Oh that's all fair—Well, harkee, Lads, I must have no grumbling on St. Patrick's day so, here, take this, and divide it amongst you. But observe me now, Shew yourselves Men of Spirit, and don't spend a Sixpence of it in Drink.

SERJEANT. Nay, hang it, Soldiers shouldn't bear Malice—We must drink St. Patrick, and your Honour's health.

ALL SOLDIERS. Oh! damn Malice! St. Patrick and his Honour, by all means.

CORPORAL. Come away then, Lads—And first we'll parade round the Market Cross, for the honour of King William.

ALL SOLDIERS. Thank your Honour—Come along—His honour, St. Patrick, and strong beer for ever. [*Exeunt all but* LIEUTENANT.

LIEUT. Get along ye thoughtless Vagabonds—Yet, upon my Conscience, 'tis very hard, that these poor Fellows should scarcely have bread from the Soil they would die to defend.

1 Aye, and] *L*, *89*; *om. 88* 3 Lion] *L*, *89*; the Lion *88* 6 devils] *88*, *89*; Pick-pockets *L* bed by] *L*, *88*; bed with *89* 7 Indeed!] *L*; *om. 88*, *89* 12–13 a little up and down Stairs] *L*; up and down stairs *89*; up and down stairs a little *88* 13 of a night] *L*, *88*; *om. 89* 14 that's all fair] *L*, *89*; all that's fair *88* Well, harkee] *L*; but harkee *88*; but *89* 17 a Sixpence] *L*, *89*; six pence *88* 18 Soldiers shouldn't] *L*, *89*; your honour, soldiers should never *88* 19 St. Patrick] *L*; St. Patrick's *88*, *89* 20 St. Patrick] *L*; St. Patrick's *88*, *89* his Honour] *L*, *88*; your honour's *89* 23 King William] *L*, *89*; King George *88* 24–5 His honour . . . ever] *L*, *89*; St. Patrick's, his honour, and strong beer for ever *88* 25 *Exeunt* . . . LIEUTENANT] *L*; Exit Soldiers *88*; Exeunt Soldiers *89* 26 ye . . . Vagabonds] *L*; you thoughtless vagabonds *88*, *89* 27 that these] *L*, *89*; these *88* have] *L*, *88*; get *89* 28 Soil] *L*, *88*; very soil *89*

---

[1] The plot summary in the *Morning Chronicle*, 4 May 1775, records that the Serjeant 'says they are very ill-treated at their several quarters; that at the Angel they are used *devilish* bad. . . .'

Enter DR. ROSY.

Ah! my little Doctor Rosy, my Galen abridg'd, what's the News?

DOCTOR. All things are as they were, my Alexander,—the Justice is as violent as ever.—I felt his Pulse on the matter again, and thinking his Rage began to intermit, I wanted to throw in the Bark[1] of good Advice—but it would not do—he says, you and your Cut throats have a Plot upon his Life, and swears he had rather see his Daughter in a scarlet Fever, than in the arms of a Soldier.

LIEUT. Upon my word, the Army is very much obliged to him—Well then I must marry the Girl first, and ask his Consent afterwards.

DOCTOR. So then the case of her Fortune is desperate, that's given over, hey?

LIEUT. O hang the Fortune, let that take its chance—There is a beauty in Lauretta's Manner, so pure a bloom upon her Charms,—something so interesting in her Simplicity.—

DOCTOR. So there is—So there is—I understand you—You are for Loveliness as Nature made her, hey?—No artificial Graces—no Cosmetic Varnish—no Beauty in Grain, hey, Lieutenant?

LIEUT. Upon my word, Doctor, you're right—The London Ladies were always too handsome for me—Then they are so defended—Such a Circumvallation of Hoop—with a breast work of whalebone, that would turn a Pistol bullet—much less Cupid's Arrows—. Then Turret on Turret on top, with store of conceal'd weapons, under pretence of black pins—and above all, a Standard of Feathers, that would do Honour to a Knight of the Bath![2]—Upon my Conscience, I could as soon embrace an Amazon, arm'd at all Points.

DOCTOR. Right, right, my Alexander—my Taste to a tittle.

2 Ah!] *L*, *88*; Oh, *89* Galen abridg'd] *L*, *89*; galen a-bridge *88* what's] *L*, *88*; why what's *89* 7 had] *L*, *88*; wou'd *89* 9–10 Well then] *L*, *88*; well *89* 11 that's given over] *L*, *89*; *om.* *88* 13 the Fortune] *L*; fortune *88*; her fortune *89* that] *L*, *88*; it *89* 14 Manner [correcting 'Simplicity']] *L*; simplicity *88*, *89* 14–15 something . . . her] *L*, *89*; *om.* *88* 15 Simplicity] *L*; manner *89*; *om.* *88* 16 I understand you] *L*; *om.* *88*, *89* 17 Loveliness] *L*; beauty *88*, *89* her] *L*, *88*; it *89* 18 hey, Lieutenant] *L*; hey? *88*; hey, my Alexander! *89* 19 word] *L*, *88*; honour *89* 21 Circumvallation] *L*; circumvaluation *88*; circumlocution *89* 22 would] *88*, *89*; could *L* bullet *88*; ball *L*, *89* less] *L*, *88*; more *89* 23 top] *L*, *88*; the top *89* store] *L*, *89*; stores *88* 24 pretence] *L*, *88*; the pretence *89* 25 a Knight of the Bath!—Upon] *88*; the Knights of the Bath!—O! *L*; the Knight of the Bath. Upon *89* 26 could] *88*, *L*; wou'd *89* Amazon] *L*, *89*; Amosen *88*

---

[1] Peruvian bark or quinine, used for reducing fever.

[2] 'The town ladies . . . are surrounded by a circumvallation of hoop, six feet in circumference; a breast work of whalebone, which would turn a pistol bullet; a plume of feathers, large enough for the cap of a Knight of the Bath. . . .' (*Morning Chronicle*, 4 May 1775.)

LIEUT. Then, Doctor, tho' I admire Modesty in Women,—yet I like to see their faces—I'm for the changeable Rose—but with one of these Quality Amazons,—if their Midnight Dissipations had left them blood enough, to raise a blush—they haven't room on their Cheeks to shew it.—To be sure, Bashfullness is a very pretty thing,—but in my mind, there is nothing on Earth so impudent as an everlasting blush.[1]

DOCTOR. My taste, my taste, Lieutenant!—Well, Lauretta is none of these—Ah! I never see her, but she reminds me of my poor dear Wife.

LIEUT. Aye!—Faith, and in my Opinion, she can't do a worse thing—Now he's going to bother me about an old fat Hag, who has been dead these six years—[*aside*]

DOCTOR. Ah! poor Dolly!—I never shall see her like again!—such an arm for a Bandage—Veins that seem'd to invite the Lancet—then her Skin—smooth and white as a Gallypot—her Mouth round, and not larger than the mouth of a penny Phial!—Her lips!—Conserve of Roses!—then her Teeth!—none of your sturdy Fixtures—ach[e], as they would—'twas but a Pull, and out they came—I beleive I've drawn half a score of her poor dear Pearls—[*weeps*]—but what avails her Beauty,—Death has no Consideration—one must die as well as another.

LIEUT. O! if he begins to moralize—[*takes out his snuff box*]

DOCTOR. Fair or ugly—Crooked or straight—Rich or Poor—Flesh is Grass[2]—Flowers fade.

LIEUT. Here, Doctor, take a Pinch, and keep up your Spirits.

DOCTOR. True—true, my Friend—Grief can't mend the matter—All's for the best—but such a Woman was a great loss, Lieutenant.

LIEUT. To be sure, for doubtless she had mental Accomplishments equal to her Beauty.

DOCTOR. Mental Accomplishments!—She should have stuff'd an Alligator,—or pickled a Lizard, with any Apothecary's wife in the Kingdom!—Why, she could decypher a prescription, and invent the

1 Women] *L*, *88*; woman *89* yet] *L*, *89*; *om. 88* 3 Dissipations] *L*, *88*; dissipation *89* 4 room on] *L*; room enough in *88*; room enough on *89* 5 a . . . thing] *L*, *88*; a mighty pretty thing *89* 7 Lieutenant!] *L*, *89*; *om. 88* 8 Ah!] *L*, *88*; *om. 89* reminds me of] *L*, *89*; puts me in mind of *88* Wife] *L*, *88*; wife Dolly *89* 9 Faith . . . Opinion] *L*; faith, in my opinion *88*; Then in my mind I think *89* 10 he's going] *L*; is he going *88*, *89* old . . . who] *L*; old hag that *88*, *89* 12 Ah!] *L*, *89*; Oh! *88* never shall] *L*, *88*; shall never *89* 14 Mouth] *L*, *89*; mouth as *88* 16 then] *L*, *89*; and then *88* 17 Pull] *L*, *89*; small pull *88* 19 one must die] *L*, *88*; we must all die; one *89* 20 *takes . . . box*]] *L*, *88*; (*aside*) *89* 21 is] *L*; as *88*; or *89* 23 Pinch, and] *L*, *88*; pinch of snuff—(*offers snuff*) *89* 28 should] *L*; would *88*, *89*

[1] Sichel, i. 565 n., shows that a similar thought appeared in a very early draft sheet of dialogue called 'The Slanderers—A *Pump-Room* Scene': 'The most intrepid Blush;—I've known her complexion stand fire for an hour together.' Cf. Moore, i. 211.

[2] Isaiah 40: 6.

Ingredients[1] almost as well as myself—Then she was such a hand at making foreign waters—for Seltzer[2]—Pyrmont[3]—Islington[4]—or Chalybeate, she had not her equal—And her Bath and Bristol Springs[5] exceeded the Originals.—King Bladud[6] never dipt his toe in better—Ah! poor Dolly!—She fell a Martyr to her Discoveries.

LIEUT. How so pray?

DOCTOR. Poor Soul, her Illness was all occasioned by her zeal in trying an improvement on her Spaw water, by an infusion of Rum and Acid.

LIEUT. Aye, aye, Spirits never agree with Water Drinkers.

DOCTOR. No!—no—you mistake—The Rum agreed with her well enough—'twas the water that kill'd the dear Creature—for she died of a Dropsy—Well! She's gone!—Never to return!—and has left no Pledge of our Loves behind—No little Baby, to hang like a labell round Papa's neck—well—we're all mortal—sooner or later—Flesh is Grass—Flowers fade!—

LIEUT. O! the Devil! again—

DOCTOR. Life's a Shadow![7]—The World's a Stage![8]—we strut our hour.

LIEUT. Here, Doctor. [*gives snuff*.

DOCTOR. True, true, my Friend—well—Grief can't mend it—All's for the best—hey, my Alexander!

1 almost] *L*, *88*; *om.* *89* 2 Seltzer] *L*, *89*; Setzer *88* or] *L*, *88*; *om.* *89* 3 had not] *L*, *89*; never had *88* 4 King . . . dipt] *L*, *89*; *om.* *88* his] *L*; *om.* *88*, *89* toe in better] *L*, *89*; *om.* *88* 5 Discoveries] *L*, *89*; own discoveries *88* 7 was all] *L*; was *88*, *89* 8 her Spaw water] *L*; the Spa water *88*; her spa waters *89* 10–11 The Rum . . . that] *L*, *89*; Rum . . . it was not the rum that *88* 13 Loves] *L*, *88*; love *89* Baby] *L*, *89*; babe *88* 14 well] *L*, *89*; well, well *88* 17 World's] *L*, *89*; world *88* our] *L*, *89*; an *88* 18 *gives*] *L*; (*offers*) *88*; take a pinch (*gives*) *89* 19 Grief can't mend] *L*; high grief can't cure *88*; high grief can't mend *89* 20 my] *L*, *89*; my little *88*

---

[1] 'She could spread a plaister, prepare a bolus, compound a draught, aye, and *invent ingredients*, as well as ever an apothecary's wife in the country.' (*Morning Chronicle*, 4 May 1775.)

[2] 'Seltzer Nieder . . . 10 miles from Francfort on the Maine; celebrated for a spring of mineral water, which is exported, in great quantities, to other countries.' (R. Brookes, *The General Gazetteer*, 10th edn., 1797.)

[3] 'Pyrmont, a town of Westphalia. . . . Near it are mineral waters, well known to all Europe, and often frequented by persons of the highest rank.' (R. Brookes, op. cit.)

[4] 'Islington, a large village, N of London, to which it is now contiguous. The New River is received at the SW end of it, into a large reservoir, called the New River Head, whence its water is conveyed, in pipes, to all parts of the metropolis. Near this, is a famous spring of Chalybeate water. . . .' (R. Brookes, op. cit.)

[5] Of Clifton Wells.

[6] The mythical discoverer of the mineral springs at Bath.

[7] 'Life's but a walking shadow.' (*Macbeth*, v. v.)

[8] 'All the world's a stage.' (*As You Like It*, II. vii.)

LIEUT. Right! right!—An apothecary should never be out of Spirits,—But, come,—Faith 'tis time honest Humphry, should wait on the Justice—that must be out first Scheme.

DOCTOR. True—true—you should be ready—The Clothes are at my House—and I have given you such a Character, that he is impatient to have you—He swears you shall be his Body Guard—Well, I honour the Army—or I should never do so much to serve you.

LIEUT. Indeed I'm bound to you for ever, Doctor, and when once I'm possessed of my Dear Lauretta, I'll endeavour to make work for you as fast as possible.

DOCTOR. Now you put me in mind of my poor wife again.

LIEUT. Ah! pray forget her a little,—faith, we shall be too late.

DOCTOR. Poor Dolly!

LIEUT. 'Tis past twelve.

DOCTOR. Inhuman Dropsy!

LIEUT. The Justice will wait.

DOCTOR. Cropt in her Prime.

LIEUT. For Heaven's sake, come.

DOCTOR. Well, Flesh is Grass.

LIEUT. Oh, the Deuce!—come, come along.

DOCTOR. Flowers fade! [*Exeunt, the* LIEUTENANT *hawls him out.*

Scene 2nd

A Room in the JUSTICE*'s house*

Enter LAURETTA *and* BRIDGET.

LAUR. I repeat it again, Mama,—officers are the prettiest men in the World—and Lieutenant O'Connor, the prettiest Officer I ever saw.

BRID. For shame, Laury, how can you talk so,—or if you must have a Military Man—there's Lieutenant Plough—or Captain Haycock—or Major Dray, the Brewer—Are all your Admirers—and tho' they are

1 Right! right!] *L*, *88*; True, true *89* 4 are] *L*, *88*; are all *89* 5 you] *L*, *88*; him *89* 8 Doctor] *L*, *88*; *om. 89* 8–9 I'm possessed] *L*, *88*; I am in possession *89* 10 as possible] *L*, *88*; as I can *89* 12 Ah! pray] *L*, *88*; Oh! *89* faith] *L*; *om. 88*, *89* 20 Deuce!] *L*, *89*; devil *88* come, come along] *L*; come along *89*; *om. 88*

21 DOCTOR . . . *out*] *L*; *Doctor.* We must all die.
Lieut. Doctor.
Doctor. Kings, Lords and common Whores—[*Forces him off. 88*
Doct. Flowers fade.
Lieut. Come along I say.
Doct. Time will tell all. [*All this time the Lieutenant is endeavouring to pull the Doctor off the stage. Exeunt. 89*

23 *A . . . house*] *L*; *Chamber. Justice's House. 89*; *om. 88* 24 BRIDGET] *L*, *88*; Mrs. Bridget *89* 26 the] *L*; is the *88*, *89* Officer] *L*, *88*; man *89* 27 Laury] *L*; Laura *88*, *89* 29 Are] *L*, *88*; *om. 89*

peaceable, good kind of Men, they have as large Cockades, and become Scarlet, as well as the fighting Folks.

LAUR. Psha! Mama! you know I hate the Militia—officers indeed!—a set of Dunghill cocks with spurs on—Heroes scratch'd off a church door—Clowns in Military masquerade—wearing the Dress without supporting the Character—No, give me the bold, upright, noble Youth, —who makes love one day, and has his head shot off the next—Dear!—to think how the sweet Fellows sleep on the Ground, and fight in silk Stockings and lac'd Ruffles.

BRID. O barbarous! to want a husband, who may wed you in the morning, and be sent the Lord knows where, before Night.—Then in a Twelve month, perhaps, to have him come home like a Colossus, with one leg at Boston, and the other in Chelsea Hospital.

LAUR. Then I would be his Crutch, Mama.

BRID. No, give me a husband who knows where his limbs are—tho' he hasn't the use of 'em;—or, if he should take you with him, Child, —what a Scene!—to sleep in a Baggage Cart—and stroll about the Camp like a Gypsey, with a Knapsack, and two Children at your back—then by way of Entertainment in the Evening, to make a Party with the Serjeant's wife, to drink Bohea Tea, and play at all fours[1] on a Drum top,—O! 'tis a precious life, to be sure.

LAUR. Nay, Mama, you should not be against my Lieutenant,—for I heard him say you were the best natur'd, and best looking woman that cou'd be.

BRID. Why, Child, I never said but that Lieutenant O'Connor was a very well bred discerning young man—'Tis your Papa is so violent against him.

LAUR. Why, Mama, Cousin Sophy married an Officer.

BRID. Ay, Laury, an Officer in the Militia.

LAUR. No, indeed, Mama, he was in a Marching regiment.

1 peaceable] *L*, *88*; quiet, peaceable *89* 3 Psha! . . . know] *L*; Psha! you know mama *88*; Officer! Mama, you know *89* the . . . indeed!] *L*, *89*; militia officers *88* 6 noble] *L*; *om.* *88*, *89* 7 one day . . . next] *L*, *89*; today and his head shot off to-morrow *88* 8 Dear!] *L*, *88*; O dear *89* Fellows sleep . . . fight] *L*, *88*; fellow sleeps . . . fights *89* 9 lac'd] *L*; lace *88*, *89* 10 who] *L*, *89*; that *88* in the morning] *L*, *89*; to-day *88* 11 Then] *L*, *88*; And then *89* 12 home] *L*, *89*; *om.* *88* one] *L*, *88*; a *89* 13 Boston] *L*, *89*; New York *88* in] *L*; at *88*, *89* 14 I would] *L*, *89*; I'll *88* 15 who] *L*; that *88*, *89* are] *L*, *88*; are to be found *89* 16 hasn't] *L*, *89*; want *88* or] *L*; and *88*; Oh! *89* Child] *L*; *om.* *88*, *89* 17 what a Scene] *L*, *89*; *om.* *88* 21 Drum top,—O!] *L*, *89*; drumhead *88* 22 Mama] *L*, *88*; madam *89* 23–4 that could be] *L*, *89*; in the world *88* 25 that] *L*, *88*; *om.* *89* 26 bred] *L*, *89*; bred and *88* 28 Mama] *L*, *89*; *om.* *88* 29 Laury] *L*, *88*; Laura *89* 30 he was in] *L*, *89*; *om.* *88*

[1] A card game, described in C. Cotton, *The Compleat Gamester* (1709), p. 81, as 'very much played in Kent'.

BRID. No, Child, I tell you he was a Major of Militia.

LAUR. Indeed, Mama, he wa'n't.

Enter JUSTICE CREDULOUS.

JUS. Bridget, my lovee, I've had a message.

LAUR. It was Cousin Sophy, Mama, told me so.

JUS. I have had a message, my Love.

BRID. Pho, Child, she could say no such thing.

JUS. A message, I say—

LAUR. How could he be in the Militia, when he was order'd abroad?

JUS. Why, Laury—

BRID. Aye, Girl, hold your Tongue—Well, my Dear?

JUS. I have had a message I say, from Doctor Rosy.

BRID. He wasn't order'd abroad, Miss, he went for his health.

JUS. Why, Bridget—

BRID. Well, Dearee,—now hold your tongue, miss.

JUS. A message I say from Doctor Rosy, and Doctor Rosy says—

LAUR. I am sure, Mama, his Regimentals—

JUS. Damn his Regimentals, why don't you listen hussy.

BRID. Aye, Girl, how durst you interrupt your Papa?

LAUR. Well, Papa.

JUS. Doctor Rosy says that he will bring—

LAUR. Were blue turn'd up with red, Mama.

JUS. Laury!—says that he will bring the young man—

BRID. Red and yellow, if you please.

JUS. Bridget!—the young man to be hired.

BRID. Besides, Miss, it is very unbecoming of you to want to have the last word with your Mama—you ought to know—

JUS. Why, zounds! will you hear me, or no?

BRID. I'm listening, my love—I'm listening—but what signifies my silence,—what good is my not speaking a word, if this Girl will interrupt, and let her tongue run, and try for the last word—and let nobody speak but herself—I don't wonder, my Life, at your impatience—your poor dear lips quiver to speak,—but I suppose she'll

1 of] *L*, *88*; in the *89* 2 he wa'n't] *L*, *89*; it wasn't *88* 3 *Enter* . . . CREDULOUS] *L*; *Enter* Justice *88*, *89* 4 lovee] *L*; love *88*, *89* 5 Mama] *L*; madam *89*; *om.* *88* 6 my] *L*, *89*; *om.* *88* 7 Pho] *L*; No *88*, *89* 8 A message] *L*, *88*; I've had a message *89* 10 Why, Laury] *L*, *89*; *om.* *88* 11 Aye, Girl] *L*, *88*; Oh! child *89* 12 I say] *L*; *om.* *88*, *89* 13 He wasn't] *L*; He *88*; *om.* *89* Miss, he went] *L*, *89*; He went abroad *88* 15 now] *L*, *88*; *om.* *89* 16 I say] *L*; *om.* *88*, *89* 18 hussy] *L*; *om.* *88*, *89* 21 that] *L*; *om.* *88*, *89* 22 Mama] *L*, *88*; *om.* *89* 23 that] *L*; *om.* *88*, *89* 24 Red . . . please] *L*, *89*; Red! yellow if you please, miss *88* 25 to] *L*, *89*; that is to *88* 26 of] *L*, *89*; in *88* 27 ought to know] *L*; should know *88*; ought to know better *89* 29 love] *L*, *88*; dear *89* 30 is] *L*, *88*; does *89* 31 and let . . . last word] *L*; *om.* *88*, *89* 32 I] *L*, *89*; Ay, I *88* 33 poor] *L*, *88*; *om.* *89*

run on, and not let you put in a word—Aye, Lovee, you may well be angry, there is nothing to be sure so provoking, as a chattering talking—

LAUR. Nay, Mama, I'm sure 'tis you won't let Papa speak now.

BRID. Why you little provoking Minx—

JUS. Get out of the Room directly, both of ye get out.

BRID. Ay, go, Girl.

JUS. Go, Bridget, you're worse than she, you old Mag[1]—and I wish you were both up to your necks in the Canal—to argue there, 'till I took you out.

Enter a SERVANT.

SER. Doctor Rosy, Sir.

JUS. Shew him up. [*Exit* SERVANT.

LAUR. Then, Mama, you own he was in a marching Regiment.

BRID. You're an obstinate Fool—for, if that had been the case—

JUS. You won't go?

BRID. We're going, Mr. Surly—if that had been the Case, I say, how could—

LAUR. Nay, Mama, one Proof—

BRID. How could Major—

LAUR. And a full proof— [*Exit* BRIDGET *and* LAURETTA—*arguing.*

JUS. There they go, ding dong, in for the Day—Good lack! a fluent tongue is the only thing a mother don't like her Daughter to resemble her in.

Enter DOCTOR ROSY.

Well, Doctor, where's the Lad!—where's Trusty?

DOCTOR. At hand—He'll be here in a minute—I'll answer for't, he's such a one as you ha'n't met with—brave as a Lion, and at the same time as gentle as a saline Draught.

1 Aye, Lovee] *L*; *om. 88, 89* well] *L*, *89*; very well *88* 2 to be] *L*; *om. 88, 89* chattering talking] *L*, *88*; talking, chattering, prating *89* 3 Mama, I'm sure] *L*, *89*; I'm sure mama *88* Papa speak now] *L*, *88*, *om. 89* 5 directly . . . ye] *L*; directly both of you *88*; both of you *89* 7 Mag—and I] *L*, *89*; hag I *88* 8 your necks] *L*; the neck *88*, *89* 10 *a*] *L*; *om. 88, 89* 13 Mama, you own he was in] *L*, *89*; you own mama, it was *88* 14 Fool] *L*, *89*; fool, I tell you *88* for . . . case] *L*, *88*; for if—*89* 16 Surly] *L*, *88*; Surly—now Miss *89* 16–17 been . . . could] *L*, *88*; *om. 89* 20 *Exit . . . arguing*] *L*; [*Justice drives them off*] *88*;

Bridg. When you know your cousin—

Laur. Is, that papa has a letter

Bridg. Order'd the taylor. [*All this time the* JUSTICE *is very impatient, and by degrees pushes them off. 89*

22 to] *L*, *89*; should *88* 27–8 and . . . as gentle] *L*; gentle *88*, *89*

[1] Scold or magpie.

JUS. Ah! he comes in the place of a Rogue! a Dog! that was corrupted by the Lieutenant.—But this is a sturdy fellow, is he?

DOCTOR. A very Hercules—and the best back sword[1] in the County—he'll make the red coats keep their distance.

JUS. Ah! the Villain!—this is St. Patrick's day,—and the Rascals have been parading round my house, all the morning—I know they have a design on me—but I have taken all precautions,—I have Magazines of Arms—and if this Fellow proves faithful, I shall be more at ease.

DOCTOR. Doubtless, he'll be a Comfort to you.

Enter a SERVANT.

SER. There is a Man below, Sir, enquiring for Doctor Rosy.

DOCTOR. Shew him up here.

JUS. Hold—hold—a little caution.—How does he look?

SER. A Country looking Fellow, your Worship.

JUS. O well—well—for Doctor, the Rascals try all ways to get in here.

SER. Aye, please your Worship, there was one here this morning, would ha' spoke to you, who said A's name was Corporal Break-bones.

JUS. Corporal Break-bones—there, you see.—

SER. And there was Drummer Crack-skull come again.

DOCTOR. Drummer Crack-skull!

JUS. Aye! did you ever hear of such a damn'd confounded Crew? well bring the lad here. [*Exit* SERVANT.

DOCTOR. Aye! he'll be your Porter, he'll give such Rogues their answer.

Re-enter the SERVANT, *introducing the* LIEUTENANT *in a Countryman's dress.*

JUS. So—a tall fellow—i'faith!—what, has he lost an eye?

1 Ah!] *L, 88*; Ay *89* 2 he?] *L, 89*; he, Doctor? *88* 3 A very] *L*; As *88*; A *89* back sword] *L, 88*; back sword player *89* 3–4 County—he'll] *L*; country, he'll *89*; country. Egad he'll *88* 5 Ah! the Villain!] *L*; O the villains! *88, 89* Rascals] *L, 88*; dogs *89* 6 round] *L*; about *89*; *om. 88* the] *L, 88*; this *89* 7 on] *L*; upon *88, 89* 8 proves] *L, 89*; does but prove *88* 11 Sir] *L, 88*; *om. 89* enquiring] *L, 89*; enquires *88* 12 here] *L*; *om. 88, 89* 13 Hold—hold] *L, 89*; Hold *88* 15 O] *L, 88*; *om. 89* Doctor, the] *L, 89*; Doctor Rosy, these *88* 16 Aye] *L, 89*; Yes *88* 16–17 would ha' spoke] *L*; wanted to speak *88*; *om. 89* 17 who said A's] *L*; he said his *88*; said his *89* 18 there . . . see] *L*; *om. 88, 89* 19 there was . . . come] *L, 89*; Drummer Crackskull came *88* 20 Drummer Crack-skull!] *L, 89*; *om. 88* 21 Aye!] *L, 88*; Drummer Crackskull! aye *89* 22 bring . . . here] *L*; shew the lad in here *88*; bring the lad up here *89* 23 such Rogues their] *L, 89*; the rogues an *88* 24–5 *Re-enter . . . dress*] *L*; *Enter* Lieutenant *disguised as* Humphrey *88*; *Enter* Lieutenant *in a Countryman's dress, and a patch on one Eye 89* 26 tall . . . lost] *L*; tall Efacks, what! has lost *88*; good stout fellow faith—what he has lost *89*

[1] Best at single-stick: a contest with staves, in which victory usually went to the player who made his opponent's head bleed first. But see, too, the *Sporting Magazine*, xliv (1814), 129: 'The Hampshire man saved his head, but received so much beating on his arm, that he could not raise his stick, which obliged him to quit the stage.'

DOCTOR. Only a bruise he got one day in taking seven or eight Highwaymen.

JUS. Hey!—but he has a damn'd wicked leer somehow with t'other.

DOCTOR. Oh! no! he's bashful—a sheepish look.

JUS. Well, my lad, what's your name?

LIEUT. Humphry[1] Hum.

JUS. Humphry Hum!—I don't like Hum![2]

LIEUT. But I be mostly call'd Honest Humphry.

DOCTOR. There, I told you so—of noted Honesty.

JUS. Honest Humphry—well—the Doctor has told you my terms,—you're willing to serve? hey?

LIEUT. An't please your Worship, I shall be well content.

JUS. Well then, hearkee, honest Humphry, you're sure now you'll never be a Rogue—never be brib'd?—hey, honest Humphry?

LIEUT. Brib'd! what's that?

JUS. A very ignorant Fellow indeed.

DOCTOR. His Worship hopes you will never part with your honesty for money, Humphry?

LIEUT. O Noa!—noa![3]—

JUS. Well, honest Humphry,—my chief business for you is to watch the motions of a Rake helly fellow here, one Lieutenant O'Connor.

DOCTOR. Aye!—you don't value the Soldiers, do you, Humphry?

LIEUT. Not I—they are but Swaggerers—and you'll see they will be as much afraid of me, as they would of their Captain.

JUS. And, i'faith, Humphry, you have a pretty Cudgel there.

LIEUT. Aye—the Switch is better than nothing, but I should be glad of a Stouter—ha' ye got such a thing in the house as an old Coach pole, or a spare Bed post?

JUS. Ouns! what a Dragon it is!—Well, Humphry, come with me, I'll

1 one day] *L*, *89*; *om. 88* 3 Hey!—but] *L*, *89*; *om. 88* somehow] *L*, *88*; *om. 89* 6 Humphrey Hum] *L*, *88*; *Lieut.* Humphrey—
Just. Humphrey's a good name—Humphrey what?
Lieut. Humphrey Hum. *89*
7 Humphrey Hum!] *L*; Hum *88*, *89* 10 Honest . . . well] *L*, *89*; Well, honest Humphrey *88* 11 you're] *L*; and you are *88*, *89* hey?] *L*, *88*; hey—Honest Humphrey? *89* 13 now] *L*, *88*; *om. 89* 13–14 never . . . Rogue] *L*, *88*; *om. 89* 14 be brib'd] *L*; take a bribe *88*, *89* 15 Brib'd] *L*; a bribe *88*, *89* 19 O] *L*; *om. 88*, *89* 20 Well, honest Humphry . . . for] *L*; Well said Humphrey my chief business with *88*, *89* 21 here] *L*, *88*; there *89* 23 Swaggerers] *L*, *89*; zwaggerers *88* will] *L*, *88*; *om. 89* 25 have] *L*, 88; have got *89* 26 Switch] *L*, *89*; zwitch *88* nothing . . . should] *L*, *88*; nothing, but I shall *89* 27 ye] *L*, *89*; you *88*

---

[1] 'Humphry' was suitable for 'awkward country clowns': Lady Willit describes one of that name in this phrase in Gay's *The Distress'd Wife*, IV.

[2] A hoax.

[3] Twelve lines have been struck out of the Larpent MS. after 'noa!'.

just shew him to Bridget, Doctor, and then we'll agree—Come, honest Humphry. [*Exit.*

LIEUT. My dear Doctor—now remember to bring the Justice presently to the walk—I've a Scheme to get into his Confidence at once.

DOCTOR. I will, I will.

Re-enter JUSTICE CREDULOUS.

JUS. Why, Humphry, Humphry—what the devil are you at?

DOCTOR. I was just giving him a little advice.—Well, I must go for the present—good morning to your Worship—you need not fear the Lieutenant, while he's in your house.

JUS. Well—get on, Humphry—good-bye, Doctor—Come along, Humphry—Now I think I'm a match for the Lieutenant. Ha! ha! ha!— [*Exeunt.*

END OF THE FIRST ACT

Act 2d. Scene 1st

Enter SERJEANT, *some* SOLDIERS, *and a* DRUMMER.

SERJ. Come, silence your Drum, There is no valour stirring today,—I had hoped St. Patrick would have given us a Recruit or two.

1ST SOLDIER. Mark, Serjeant!—

Enter a BLACKSMITH,[1] *and an* IRISHMAN, *drunk.*

SERJ. Hah! my fine fellows—Come, now for the honour of St. Patrick,—will ye be after serving his Majesty?—and instead of drowsy[2] beer, have Seas of Punch, and Shambrogue Islands, all your lives after.

1 then we'll agree] *L*; then agree *89*; we'll agree *88* Come] *L*; come along *88*, *89* 3 presently] *L*, *88*; *om.* *89* 6 *Re-enter* . . . CREDULOUS] *L*; (*Shakes hands,* Justice *enters and sees them*) *88*; *Re-enter* Justice *89* 7 Humphry, Humphry] *L*; honest Humphrey, hey! *88*, *89* 8 a little] *L*, *88*; some *89* 10 he's] *L*, *88*; honest Humphrey is *89* house] *L*, *88*; house. (*Exit Doctor*) *89* 11 Well . . . Doctor] *L*; Well, get in Humphry—good morning to you Doctor. (*Exit Doctor.*) *88*; Good morning to you, Doctor—well, get in, Humphrey.—(*Exit* Lieutenant.) *89* 11–12 Come along, Humphry] *L*, *88*; *om.* *89* 12 Now I] *L*, *88*;—'Faith he's a strapper—now I *89* Lieutenant. Ha! ha! ha!] *L*; Lieutenant and all his gang. *88*, *89* 13 *Exeunt*] *L*; *Exit* *88*, *89* 14 END . . . ACT] *L*, *89*; *om.* *88* 16 *Enter* . . . DRUMMER] *L*; *Enter* TROUNCE, DRUMMER *and* SOLDIERS *88*; *Enter* Serjeant, Drummer, *and* Soldiers *89* 18 had hoped] *L*; thought *88*, *89* two] *L*, *89*; two, to-day *88* 19 1ST . . . Serjeant!] *L*, *88*; *om.* *89* 20–3 *Enter* . . . after] *L*; *om.* *88*, *89*

[1] Farquhar's *The Recruiting Officer*, IV. ii, introduces a smith who is recruited.

[2] Possibly warm beer, described in the *Weekly Journal*, 22 Feb. 1724: 'beer, so qualified, is far more wholesome than that which is drank cold'. See *The Poetical Works of Richard Savage*, ed. C. Tracy (Cambridge, 1962), p. 70.

IRISH. Come, Neighbour, what say you? shall we make a Friend of his Majesty? I feel as if I could handle a Musket.

2ND MAN. Taddy,[1] you're drunk—but I who am sober, know better—sometimes when I'm merry, I thinks how I could make a Soldier, but when I'm sober, I knows that I am fit for nothing but a civil employment.

IRISH. Aye! Neighbour, but I feel bould at all times.

2ND MAN. Taddy, you're a Fool, I tell ye, You're brave only when you are drunk; and if you were a General, 'twould cost his Majesty five Shillings a day to keep you in Courage, so, come along—Good liquor and a whole Skin to put it in for ever—

[*Exeunt* IRISHMAN *and* BLACKSMITH.

SERJ. Poltroons, by my halbert.

Enter 2 Countrymen.

Oh! here are the Lads I was looking for, these have the looks of gentlemen—A'n't you single, my Lads?

1ST CLOWN. Yes, an't please you, I be quite single,—Thank God, my Relations be all dead, more or less; I have but one poor Mother left in the world, and She's a helpless Woman.

SERJ. Indeed. A very extraordinary Case; quite your own Master then—the fitter to serve his Majesty—Can you read?

1ST CLOWN. Noa—I was always too lively to take to my Larning.

SERJ. A good Quality in a Soldier;—look for Preferment.

1ST CLOWN. But Jan here is main Clever at it.

SERJ. So,—what you are a Scholar, friend?

2ND CLOWN. I was born so, Master—Fayther taught Grammar School.

SERJ. Lucky man!—In a Campaign or two, put yourself down Chaplain to the Regiment—and I warrant you have read of Warriors, and Hero's.

2ND CLOWN. Yes, that I have—I ha' read of Jack the Giant killer, and

1–13 IRISH . . . halbert] *L*; *om.* *88*, *89*   15 here] *L*, *89*; these *88*   I was] *L*, *88*; you have been *89*   these] *L*; they *88*, *89*   16 A'n't] *L*, *88*; Are you *89*   17 1ST CLOWN] *L*; 1st Coun. *88*; 1st Count. *89*   an't] *L*; an *88*, *89*   17–18 Thank . . . dead] *L*; my relations be all dead, thank heavens *88*; my relations, thank heav'n, be all dead *89*   19 a] *L*; an *88*, *89*   21 Can you read?] *L*, *88*; *om.* *89*   22 to my Larning] *L*; to learning *88*; to take in learning *89*   23 SERJ . . . Preferment] *L*; *om.* *88*, *89*   24 Jan] *L*; John *88*, *89*   main] *L*, *88*; very *89*   26 Master . . . taught] *L*; measter— Feyther kept *88*, *89*   28–9 Warriors . . . Hero's] *L*, *88*; heroes and warriors *89*

[1] The late J. O. Bartley suggested that this meant 'Thady', not 'Paddy'. Cf. Teady Shagnessy in Thomas Sheridan's *The Brave Irishman* (1737).

the Dragon of Wantley[1]—and the—Noa—I believe that's all in the Hero way—except once a little about a Comet.[2]

SERJ. Wonderful Knowledge!—Well, my Warriors, I'll write word to the King directly of your good Intentions, and meet me in half an hour at the two Magpies.

BOTH. We wull, your honour, we wull.

SERJ. But stay—for fear I shou'dn't know ye again in the Croud, clap these little bits of Ribband into your Hats.

1ST CLOWN. Our hats are none of the best.

SERJ. Well, stay at the Magpies, and I'll fetch ye money to buy new ones.

BOTH. Bless your Honour.

[1ST CLOWN.] Come, Jan, [*Exeunt* CLOWNS.

SERJ. Jack! [*to the Soldiers, who go off after the Clowns*]. Soh!—here comes one would make a Grenadier.

Enter LIEUTENANT.

Stop, Friend, will ye list?

LIEUT. Who shall I serve under?

SERJ. Under me to be sure.

LIEUT. Isn't Lieutenant O'Connor, your Officer?

SERJ. He is, and I am Commander over him.

LIEUT. What be you Serjeants greater than Captains?

SERJ. To be sure we are—'Tis our business to keep them in Order—For instance—The General writes to me—Dear Serjeant—or Dear Trounce—or Dear Serjeant Trounce (according to his hurry) if your Lieutenant does not demean himself accordingly, let me know—Yours to Command—General Deluge.

LIEUT. And do you complain of him often?

2 a little . . . Comet] *L*; about a Comet *88*; about a Cammel *89* 3 Warriors] *L*; heroes *88*, *89* 4 directly] *L*; *om. 88*, *89* in . . . hour] *L*; half an hour hence *88*, *89* 6 wull] *L*; will *88*, *89* 7 know ye] *L*; know you *89*; see you *88* 8 Ribband] *L*; ribbon *88*; ribbands *89* into your Hats] *L*, *88*; in your hat *89* 10 stay at] *L*; meet me at *88*; We'll meet at *89* fetch ye] *L*; give you *88*, *89* 11 Honour] *L*; honour, thank your honour. (Exit) *88*; honour, thank your honour. (*Exeunt*) *89* 12 Come . . . CLOWNS] *L*; *om. 88*, *89* 13 Jack . . . *Clowns*] *L*; (*Winking at* Sol.) Jack. (*Exit* Soldiers.) *88*; (*winking at the soldiers*) Jack—(*Exit after* Countrymen) *89* 15 *Enter* LIEUTENANT] *L*, *88*; *Enter* Lieutenant *as* Humphrey Hum *89* 16 ye] *L*; you *88*, *89* 21 you] *L*; your *88*, *89* than] *L*; than your *88*, *89* Captains?] *L*; your officers? *89*; your Captains? *88* 25–6 Yours to command] *L*, *89*; Yours *88* 27 him] *L*, *88*; them *89*

---

[1] The monster, killed by More of More Hall, is the centre of a favourite chap-book story. Henry Carey's musical burlesque of this theme, *The Dragon of Wantly*, was first performed at the Haymarket on 16 May 1737, and was revived in 1774.

[2] We can read in the article on comets in E. Chambers, *Cyclopaedia* (5th edn., 1741), of the 'popular division of comets into three kinds, viz. *bearded*, *tailed*, and *hairy*'.

SERJ. Why, know, the lad is good natur'd at bottom,—so I pass over small things—but hearkee, between ourselves—he is confoundedly given to wenching.[1]

Enter CORPORAL.

CORP. Please your Honour, the Doctor is coming with his worship, we are all ready, and have our Cues.

LIEUT. Then, my dear Serjeant—or dear Trounce—or dear Serjeant Trounce—take yourself away.

SERJ. Ouns! 'tis the Lieutenant!—I smell the black hole[2] already.

CORP. Come away—Quick— [*Exeunt* SERJEANT *and* CORPORAL.

LIEUT. [*walks about, whistling*]

Enter the JUSTICE *and* DOCTOR.

JUST. I thought I saw some of the Cut throats.

DOCTOR. I fancy not—there's no one but honest Humphry—Ha! Odds-life! here are some of them—We'll stay by these Trees, and let them pass.

JUST. Oh the bloody looking dogs. [*Stands aside*

Enter CORPORAL, *and 2* SOLDIERS.

CORP. Hollo, Friend, do you serve Justice Credulous?

LIEUT. I do.

CORP. Are you rich?

LIEUT. No.

CORP. Nor ever will be with that old stingy Booby—look here take it.—[*Shews a Purse*]

LIEUT. What must I do for this?

CORP. Mark me—Our Lieutenant is in love with the old Rogue's Daughter—help us to break his Worship's bones—and carry off the Girl, and you are a made man.

1 Why, know] *L*; No, hang him *88*, *89* bottom] *L*, *88*; the bottom *89* 2 things] *L*, *88*; faults *89* confoundedly] *L*; most confoundedly *88*, *89* 4 *Enter* CORPORAL] *L*, *88*; *Enter* Corporal, *and whispers 89* 5 coming] *L*; going *89*; coming this way *88* 7 Serjeant . . . Trounce—or] *L*, *89*; Trounce, or my dear Serjeant, or my *88* 9 Ouns! 'tis] *L*; Zounds! *88*, *89* smell] *L*, *89*; smell of *88* 10 Come away—Quick] *L*, *89*; *om. 88* *Exeunt* . . . CORPORAL] *L*, *89*; (*Exit.*) *88* 11 *whistling*] *L*; (*listening.*) *89*; *om. 88* 12 *the*] *L*, *88*; *om. 89* 14–15 Odds-life!] *L*, *88*; odds my life *89* 15 are] *L*; comes *88*; come *89* stay by] *L*, *88*; step behind *89* 17 JUST.] *L*, *88*; DOCTOR. *89* *Stands aside*] *L*; (*Walks aside*) *88*, *89* 19 Hollo] *L*; Hark'ee *89*; Holloa *88* 22 No] *L*; Noa *88*, *89* 23 be] *L*; *om. 88*, *89* old] *L*, *88*; *om. 89* 24 *Shews*] *L*, *89*; (*Gives him*) *88* 25 must] *L*, *88*; mun *89* 27 Worship's] *L*, *88*; lordship's *89*

[1] 'Their Lieutenant is an arrant whore-master.' (*Morning Chronicle*, 4 May 1775.)

[2] Cell. Cf. the *Public Advertiser*, 6 July 1779: five 'impressed men . . . confined in Covent Garden Watch-house, having forced their way up from the Black Hole, in which they had been thrown' pelted glass at the constables.

LIEUT. I'll see you hang'd first ye pack of scurvy Villains—[*flings down the purse*]

CORP. What, Sirrah!—mutinous—lay hold of him.

LIEUT. Nay then—I'll try your Armour for you. [*beats them*

SOLDIERS. Oh!—oh!—Quarter! Quarter! [*Lieutenant beats them off*]

[JUSTICE *and* DOCTOR *come forward.*

JUST. Trim 'em!—trounce 'em, Humphry—break me all their bones, honest Humphry—what a Spirit he has, Doctor.

DOCTOR. Aqua fortis.

LIEUT. Betray my Master, indeed!—

DOCTOR. What a Miracle of fidelity.

JUST. Ay, and it sha'n't go unrewarded—I'll give him Sixpence on the Spot—here, honest Humphry—there's for yourself. As for this base Bribe, such trash is best in the hands of Justice[1]—[*picks up the purse*]—Now then, Doctor, I think I may trust him to guard the Women—While he is with them, I may go out with Safety.

DOCTOR. Doubtless, you may—I'll answer for the Lieutenant's good behavior, while honest Humphry is with your Daughter.

JUST. Aye,—aye—She shall go nowhere without him—Come follow, honest Humphry—how rare it is to meet with such a Servant.—

[*Exeunt, the* DOCTOR *and* LIEUTENANT *making signs to each other.*

Scene 2nd. The Garden. A Summer house near

LAURETTA—*Sitting with a Guittar*[2]

Song[3]

Enter JUSTICE *and* LIEUTENANT.

JUST. Why, you little Truant, how durst you leave the House without

1 ye] *L*; you *88, 89* scurvy] *L, 89*; skurry *88* 1–2 *flings down*] *L*; (*Throws away*) *88*; (*throws down the purse, and lays hold of him.*) *89* 3 mutinous] *L*; do you mutiny? *88*; mutiny *89* 5 Oh!—oh!] *L, 88*; *om. 89* *Lieutenant . . . off*] *L*; (*Exit*) *88*; (*runs off*) *89* 6 *Justice . . . forward*] *L*; *Enter* Justice *and* Doctor *89*; *om. 88* 7 Humphry . . . bones] *L*; break their bones, honest Humphrey *88, 89* 8 Doctor] *L, 89*; *om. 88* 10 Betray . . . indeed] *L, 89*; Betray my master *88* 12 Ay] *L, 88*; Hey *89* 13 base] *L*; *om. 88, 89* 14 trash] *L, 88*; trash as this *89* *picks*] *L*; *takes 88, 89* 16 I may go] *L, 88*; I think I may go *89* with] *L, 88*; in *89* 17 good] *L, 89*; *om. 88* 19 follow] *L*; along *88, 89* 21 *Exeunt*] *L*; *89*; (*Exit*) *88* *the . . . Lieutenant*] *L*; *Lieutenant and Doctor 89*; *om. 88* *making*] *L*, *make 89*; *om. 88* signs . . . other] *L, 89*; *om. 88* 22 *The Garden . . . near*] *L*; A Garden *88, 89* 23 LAURETTA . . . *Guittar*] *L, 89*; LAURETTA DISCOVERED *88* 24 *Song*] *L*; *om. 88, 89* 26 leave] *L*; wander so far from *88, 89*

[1] 'Such bribes are safest in the hands of justice.' (*Morning Chronicle*, 4 May 1775.)

[2] 'His daughter . . . is discovered seated in a garden and singing.' (ibid.)

[3] The text is missing: see p. 158 above. Mr. F. W. Bateson tells me that though the song was a regular item in the playbills until 1783, he has not been able to find a copy.

my leave?—Do you want to invite that Scoundrel Lieutenant to scale the walls, and carry you off?

LAUR. Lud Papa, you are so apprehensive about nothing—

JUST. What, Hussy!

LAUR. Well then, I can't bear to be shut up so all day long, like a Nun!—I'm sure 'tis enough to make one wish to be run away with—and I wish I was run away with,—I do—and I wish the Lieutenant knew it.

JUST. You do—do you, Hussy?—well, I think I'll take pretty good care to prevent that—Here, Humphry—I leave this Lady in care to you—Now you may walk about the Garden, Miss Pert—but Humphry shall go with you where ever you go—So mind honest Humphry—I am obliged to go abroad for a little while—Let no one but yourself come near her—Don't be shame fac'd you Booby—but keep close to her.—And now, Miss, let your Lieutenant, or any of his Crew come near you, if they can. [*Exit* JUSTICE.

LAUR. How the Looby gapes after him— [*sits down, and Sings*

LIEUT. Lauretta!

LAUR. Not so free, Fellow—[*sings*]

LIEUT. Lauretta, look on me.

LAUR. Don't interrupt me, Booby, [*sings*]

LIEUT. No recollection!

LAUR. Honest Humphry, be quiet. [*sings*]

LIEUT. Have you forgot your faithful Soldier?

LAUR. Oh! preserve me!

LIEUT. 'Tis I—my Soul—your truest Slave—passing in this disguise—

LAUR. Well—now I declare this is charming—You are so disguised, my dear Lieutenant,—and you do look so delightfully ugly—I'm sure no one will find you out—Ha! ha! ha!—You know I'm under your Protection—ha! ha! ha!—Papa charg'd you to keep close to me.

LIEUT. True, my angel,—and thus let me fulfil—

LAUR. O pray now—Dear Humphry—

3 about] *L*; for *88*, *89* 4 What] *L*; Why *88*, *89* 5 so . . . Nun] *L*; all day so like a nun *88*; shut up like a Nun all day *89* 10 to prevent that] *L*, *89*; of you *88* Here, Humphry] *L*, *88*; honest Humphrey *89* in care to you] *L*; in your care *88*, *89* 11 Now you] *L*, *88*; and you *89* Miss Pert] *L*, *88*; Miss Flirt *89* 12 with] *L*, *88*; along with *89* 15–16 Crew . . . can] *L*, *88*; crew, came if they dare (*Exit*) *89* 17 the Looby gapes] *L*; this booby stares *88*; the booby stares *89* 19 *sings*] *L*, *88*; *om.* *89* 20 LIEUT. . . . me] *L*, *88*; *om.* *89* 21 LAUR. . . . Booby] *L*; *om.* *89*; Not so free fellow *88* *sings*] *L*; *om.* *88*, *89* 23 *sings*] *L*; *om.* *88*, *89* 24 Soldier?] *L*, *88*; soldier? (*sings*) *89* 25 Oh! . . . me] *L*; Ah: O preserve me *88*; Ah! save me, preserve me! (*frighted*) *89* 26 I] *L*, *89*; *om.* *88* Soul . . . truest] *L*, *88*; love . . . honest *89* in] *L*; on your father in *88*, *89* 28 you do look] *L*, *88*; you look *89* 29 will] *L*, *88*; wou'd *89* 30 ha! ha! ha!] *L*; *om.* *88*, *89* 33 O pray] *L*, *88*; I pray *89*

LIEUT. Nay, 'tis but what old Mittimus[1] commanded [*strug*[*g*]*ling to kiss her*].

Enter the JUSTICE.

JUST. Stay, Laury—my—Hey! what the Devil's here?

LAUR. Well now, one kiss, and be quiet—O Mercy!

JUST. Your humble Servant, honest Humphry—don't mind me—pray don't let me interrupt you.

LAUR. Lud, Papa—now that's so good-natur'd—indeed there's no harm—you didn't mean any rudeness, did you, Humphry?

LIEUT. No, indeed, Miss—His Worship knows it isn't in me.

JUST. I know that you are a lying, canting Hypocritical Scoundrel—and if you don't take yourself out of my Sight—

LAUR. Indeed, Papa, now I'll tell you how it was—I was somehow taken with a sudden Giddyness—and Humphry seeing me begin to totter, ran to my assistance—quite frighted poor Fellow—and got me in his Arms.

JUST. O, poor Fellow, was that all—nothing but a little giddyness, hey?

LIEUT. That's all, indeed your Worship—for seeing Miss change colour—I ran up instantly.

JUST. O! 'twas very kind in you.

LIEUT. And luckily recover'd her.

JUST. And who made you a Doctor, you impudent Scoundrel, hey?—Get out, I say, this instant—or by all the Statutes—

LAUR. O now, Papa, you frighten me, and I'm giddy again—oh! help!—

LIEUT. O dear Lady—she'll fall!— [*catches her in his arms*

JUST. Zounds! what, before my face!—why, thou mirrour of Impudence!— [*lays hold of his hair, his wig comes off, and discovers him*] Mercy on me! who have we here?—Murder! Robbery—Fire—Rape—John,—Susan—Bridget—

2 *strugling . . . her*] *L*, *89* (*Offers to kiss her*) *88* 3 *Enter . . .* JUSTICE] *L*; *Enter Justice 88*, *89* 4 Stay] *L*; *om. 88*, *89* Laury] *L*, *88*; Laura *89* my] *L*, *88*; my love *89* 5 now, one kiss] *L*, *88*; one kiss now *89* O Mercy] *L*; *om. 88*, *89* 6 humble] *L*; very humble *88*, *89* mind] *L*, *89*; *om. 88* pray] *L*, *88*; *om. 89* 8 there's] *L*, *88*; *om. 89* 9 any rudeness] *L*, *88*; me any harm *89* 11 that] *L*, *89*; that that *88* lying . . . Scoundrel] *L*, *88*; canting, lying, hypocritical scoundrel *89* 12 yourself] *L*, *88*; yourself away *89* 13 somehow] *L*; sometime *88*; *om. 89* 15 quite . . . Fellow] *L*; quite frighten'd poor fellow *88*; poor fellow, quite frighted *89* got] *L*; took *88*, *89* 16 poor Fellow] *L*; *om. 88*, *89* 18 up] *L*, *88*; *om. 89* 19 O!] *L*, *88*; *om. 89* 21 Scoundrel] *L*; rascal *88*, *89* 22 out] *L*, *89*; out of my sight *88* instant] *L*, *88*; minute *89* 23 frighten me] *L*, *88*; fright me *89* oh! help!] *L*, *88*; help! help *89* 24 O dear] *L*, *88*; Dear *89* *Catches . . . in*] *L*; (*Takes her into*) *88*; (*takes her in*) *89* 25 thou mirrour] *L*; then thou miracle *88*; thou miracle *89* 26 *his hair . . . off*] *L*; him *88*; his hair, comes off *89* 27–8 Rape—John] *L*; Rape—Gun-powder—Soldiers—John *88*; gunpowder, soldiers *89*

[1] A magistrate's warrant, but used here to denote the magistrate himself.

LIEUT. Good sir, don't be so alarm'd, I intend you no harm.

JUST. Thieves—Robbers—Soldiers—

LIEUT. You know my Love for your Daughter—

JUST. Fire—Cut throats—

LIEUT. And that alone—

JUST. Treason—Gun Powder.

Enter SERVANTS *with Arms.*

The JUSTICE *takes a Blunderbuss.*

Now, you Scoundrel, let her go this Instant.

LAUR. Oh! Papa, you'll kill me.

JUST. Honest Humphry, be advis'd—aye, miss, this way, if you please.

LIEUT. Nay, Sir, but hear me—

JUST. I'll shoot.

LIEUT. And you'll be convinc'd—

JUST. I'll shoot.

LIEUT. How very injurious—

JUST. I'll shoot—take her along [*to a* SERVANT]. And so, your humble Servant, honest Humphry Hum. [*Exeunt severally.*

Scene 3d. The Walk

Enter Dr. ROSY.

DOCTOR. Well, I think my Friend is now in a fair way of succeeding—. Ah!—I warrant he's full of hope—and doubt,—and fear—and Anxiety—Truly he has the fever of Love strong upon him—Faint—Peevish—Languishing all day—with burning restless Nights.—Ah! just my Case—when first I pined for my poor Dear Dolly—when she used to have daily Cholics, that her little Doctor might be sent for—then would I interpret the language of the Pulse—declare my own sufferings in my Recipes for hers—Send her a pearl necklace in a Pill

1 Good] *L*, *88*; Lord *89* so] *L*; *om. 88*, *89* intend] *L*; mean *88*, *89* 6 Gun Powder *L*, *88*; gunpowder, bring me a blunderbuss *89* 7 SERVANTS . . . *Arms*] *L*; Servant *with a Blunderbuss 88*, *89* 8 *The . . . Blunderbuss*] *L*; *om. 88*, *89* 9 you] *L*; *om. 88*, *89* 11 aye, miss] *L*, *88*; ay *89* you please] *L*, *88*; you you please. (*Exit Lauretta*) *89* 16 very] *L*, *89*; *om. 88* 17 take him along] *L*; *om. 88*, *89* shoot . . . SERVANT] *L*; shoot *88*; shoot—(*Exit* Lieut.—Justice *drives him off*) *89* humble] *L*; very humble *88*, *89* 18 honest] *L*, *88*; *om. 89* *Exeunt severally*] *L*; *Exit separately 88*; *Exeunt 89* 19 *The Walk*] *L*, *Rae*; *A Walk 88*; a Street or Walk *89* 20 *Enter Dr.* ROSY] *L*, *88*; Dr. Rosy *Rae*; Enter Doctor *89* 22 Ah!] *L*, *Rae*, *88*; and *89* doubt,—and fear] *L*, *Rae*, *89*; fear, doubt *88* 24 restless] *L*, *Rae*, *88*; love, restless *89* 25 first] *L*, *Rae*; *om. 88*, *89* 26 daily] *L*, *Rae*; her daily *88*, *89* that] *L*, *88*, *89*; and *Rae* might] *L*, *89*; *om. Rae*, *88* 27 the pulse] *L*; her pulse *Rae*, *88*, *89* 28 sufferings] *L*, *88*, *89*; suffering *Rae* Recipes] *L*, *Rae*, *89*; receipt *88* for hers] *Rae*; for her *L*, *88*, *89*

box, or a Cordial Draught with an acrostic on the Labell! well those days are over,—No happiness lasting! all's Vanity! now Sunshine! now Clouded!—we are as we were made—King and Peasant! then what avails—

Enter LIEUTENANT.

LIEUT. O Doctor! ruined and undone!

DOCTOR. The Pride of Beauty—

LIEUT. I'm discovered, and—

DOCTOR. The gaudy Palace—

LIEUT. The Justice is—

DOCTOR. The pompous wig—

LIEUT. More enrag'd than ever.

DOCTOR. The gilded Cane[1]—

LIEUT. Why, Doctor.

DOCTOR. Hey!

LIEUT. Confound your morals! I tell you I'm discovered! discomfited! disappointed! ruined!

DOCTOR. Indeed! Good lack! to think of the Instability of human Affairs!—nothing certain in this world! most deceiv'd when most confident!—Fools of Fortune all!—

LIEUT. My dear Doctor, I want at present a little practical Wisdom!—I am resolved this instant, to try the Scheme we were going to put into Execution last week—The present event will give probability to the Plan—I have the Letter ready written, and only want your assistance to recover my Ground.

DOCTOR. With all my heart, I warrant I'll bear my part in it—but how the deuce were you discovered?

LIEUT. I'll tell you as we go—there's not a moment to be lost.

DOCTOR. Heaven send we succeed better at present—but there's no knowing.

LIEUT. Very true.

1 those] *L*, *88*; these *89*   3 Clouded!] *L*; cloud *Rae*; cloudy *88*, *89*   we were made] *L*, *Rae*; we are *89*; it were *88*   King and Peasant] *L*, *Rae*; king and beggar *88*; kings and beggars *89*   5 *Enter* LIEUTENANT] *L*, *Rae*, *88*; *Enter* Lieutenant, *not disguised 89*   12 More] *L*, *Rae*, *89*; Is more *88*   14 Doctor] *L*; Doctor! (*loud*) *Rae*; Doctor! (*slapping him on the shoulder*) *88*; Doctor—(*slapping him*) *89*   15 Hey!] *L*, *88*, *Rae*; Hey! (*starts*) *89*   18 Good lack] *L*, *Rae*; good lack, good lack *88*, *89*   21 My] *L*, *Rae*, *88*; *om.* *89*   22 to try] *L*, *Rae*, *88*; to put in practice *89*   going to put] *L*, *Rae*, *88*; talking of *89*   22–3 into Execution] *L*, *Rae*; in execution *88*; *om.* *89*   23–4 The present . . . Plan] *L*, *Rae*; *om.* *88*, *89*   24 ready written] *L*, *Rae*; ready *88*; wrote *89*   26 I warrant] *L*, *Rae*, *89*; I'll warrant you *88*   my part] *L*, *Rae*; a part *88*, *89*   29 at present] *L*, *Rae*; *om.* *88*, *89*   but] *L*, *Rae*, *88*; *om.* *89*

[1] The cane of John Radcliffe (1650–1741), the symbol of a successful physician.

DOCTOR. We may, and we may not.

LIEUT. Right.

DOCTOR. Time must shew.

LIEUT. Certainly.

DOCTOR. We are but blind Guessers.

LIEUT. Nothing more.

DOCTOR. Thick sighted mortals.

LIEUT. Remarkably.

DOCTOR. Wand'ring in error.

LIEUT. Even so.

DOCTOR. Futurity is dark.

LIEUT. As a Cellar.

DOCTOR. Men are Moles— [*Exeunt*; *the* DOCTOR *pondering.*

Scene 4th. The JUSTICE'S *house*

Enter the JUSTICE *and* BRIDGET.

JUST. Addslife, Bridget, you are enough to make one mad,—I tell you he would have deceived a Chief Justice—The dog seem'd as ignorant as my Clerk—and talk'd of Honesty as if he had been a Church Warden.

BRID. Pho! Nonsense! Honesty indeed! what had you to do, pray with Honesty!—a fine business indeed, you have made of it, with your Humphry Hum, truly.—And Miss too, she must have been privy to it—Lauretta!—aye, you would have her called so—but for my part, I never knew any good come of giving Girls these Heathen Christian Names. If you had call'd her Deborah—or Tabitha—or Ruth—or Rebecca—nothing of this would have happened—but I always knew Lauretta was a run away name.

JUST. Pshaw! you're a fool.

12 As a Cellar] *L*, *Rae*, *88*; *Lieut*. As a cellar.
Doct. The world's a stage
Lieut. Right
Doct. Flesh is grass
Lieut. Very true
Doct. Flowers fade
Lieut. I can't deny it. *89*

13 *Exeunt . . . pondering*] *L*; *Exeunt* DR. *moralizing Rae*; (Lieut. *forcing him out*) *88*; (*Exeunt Doctor and Lieutenant*) *89* 14 *The . . . house*] *L*, *Rae*; JUSTICE'S HOUSE *88*; *a Chamber 89* 15 *Enter . . .* BRIDGET] *L*; JUSTICE *and* BRIDGET *Rae*; *Enter* JUSTICE *and* BRIDGETT *88*, *89* 16 Addslife] *L*; Odds life *Rae*, *88*, *89* one] *L*, *Rae*, *88*; a man *89* 19 Pho] *L*, *Rae*; Po *88*; Pshaw *89* to do, pray] *L*, *Rae*, *88*; pray to do *89* 20 indeed] *L*, *Rae*; *om. 88*, *89* have] *L*, *Rae*, *88*; must have *89* of it] *L*, *Rae*, *88*; on't *89* 21 truly] *L*, *89*; *om. Rae*, *88* 22 Lauretta] *L*, *88*, *89*; Lauretta! indeed *Rae* these] *L*, *88*, *Rae*; those *89* 24 or Tabitha] *L*, *Rae*, *88*; Tabitha *89* 25 Rebecca] *L*, *Rae*, *89*; Rebecca, or Joan *88* would have] *L*, *Rae*, *89*; have ever *88*

BRID. No, Mr. Credulous, 'tis you are the fool, and no one but such a Simpleton, would have been so imposed on.

JUST. Why zounds, Madam, how durst you talk so? If you have no respect for your Husband—I should think Unus Quorum[1] might command a little Deference.

BRID. Don't tell me—Unus Fiddlestick!—you ought to be asham'd to shew your Face at the Sessions—You'll be the laughing stock of the Bench, and a bye word with all the Pigtail'd Lawyers and Bobwig Attornies.

JUST. Is this Language to his Majesty's Representative? By the Statutes 'tis High Treason, and Petty Treason both at once.

Enter a SERVANT.

SERV. A Letter for your Worship.

JUST. Who brought it?

SERV. A Soldier, your Worship. [*Exit.*

JUST. Take it away—and bury it—Combustible Stuff, I warrant it—a threatening letter—Put ten pounds under a Stone—with damn'd inflammatory Spelling—and the bloody hands of a dozen rogues at bottom.

BRID. Stay now—you're in such a hurry—'tis some canting Scrawl from the Lieutenant, I suppose—here—let me see.—Aye, 'tis signed Lieutenant O'Connor—[*taking the letter*]

JUST. Well, come read it out.

BRID. [*Reads*] 'Revenge is sweet.'[2]

JUST. It begins so, does it?—I'm glad of that—and I'll let the dog know I'm of his Opinion.

BRID. [*reads*] 'And tho' disappointed in my Designs on your Daughter, I have still the Satisfaction of knowing that I am reveng'd on her

1 are the] *L*; who are a *Rae*, *88*; are a *89* no one] *L*, *Rae*, *88*; none *89* 2 have been] *L*, *Rae*, *89*; be *88* 3 durst] *L*, *Rae*, *88*; dare *89* 4 and 6 Unus] *L*, *Rae*, *88*; Unis *89* Quorum] *L*, *Rae*, *88*; Coram *89* 5 Deference] *L*, *Rae*, *88*; difference *89* 6 ought to] *L*, *Rae*, *88*; might *89* 7 be the] *L*, *Rae*; be a *88*, *89* 7–8 of the Bench] *L*, *Rae*; to the whole Bench *88*; *om.* *89* 8 Bobwig] *L*, *Rae*; bag-wig'd *88*; bag-wig *89* 9 Attornies] *L*, *Rae*, *89*; attornies about town *88* 10 to] *L*, *Rae*, *89*; for *88* 12 *Enter a* SERVANT] *L*; Enter Servant *Rae*, *88*; *Enter a* Servant *with a letter* *89* 13 for] *L*, *Rae*, *88*; *om.* *89* 15 your Worship *Exit*] *L*; *om.* *88*, *89*; your Worship *Rae* 16–19 Combustible . . . bottom] *L*, *Rae*; *om.* *88*, *89* 21 here] *L*, *Rae*; *om.* *88*, *89* see] *L*, *Rae*, *88*; see it *89* 22 Lieutenant] *L*, *Rae*, *89*; *om.* *88* [*taking . . . letter*] *L*; *om.* *88*; (*takes the letter*) *Rae*; *Exit* Servant. *89* 23 Well, come] *L*, *Rae*, *88*; *om.* *89* 24 *Reads*] *L*; (reads) Sir, *Rae*; *om.* *88*; (*reading*) *89* 26 his] *L*, *Rae*, *88*; the same *89* 27 *reads*] *L*; *om.* *Rae*, *88*; (*reading*) *89* in] *L*, *89*; of *Rae*, *88* on] *L*; upon *Rae*, *88*, *89* 28 that] *L*, *89*; *om.* *Rae*, *88* on] *L*, *Rae*, *88*; of *89*

[1] One of the justices constituting a bench.

[2] Cf. Jonson, *The Silent Woman*, IV. v: 'O revenge, how sweet art thou'.

unnatural Father—for this morning, in your Chocolate, I had the pleasure of Administ[e]ring to you a Dose of Poison.'—Mercy on us.

JUST. No Tricks, Bridget, come now you know 'tis not so—you know 'tis a lie.

BRID. Read it yourself—[*crying*]

JUST. [*Reads*] 'Pleasure of administering a dose of Poison.'—O horrible!—Cut throat Villain!—Bridget—

BRID. Lovee!—stay here's a Postscript—'N.B. 'tis not in the power of Medicine to save you!'—Oh! oh!

JUST. Odds life, Bridget, why don't you call for help?—I've lost my Voice—my Brain's giddy—I shall burst—and no assistance—John! Laury! John!

BRID. Oh! oh!—you see, my Lovee, what you have brought on yourself.

Enter JOHN.

JOHN. Your Worship!

JUST. Stay, John!—did you perceive any thing in my Chocolate cup, this morning?

JOHN. Nothing your Worship, unless it was a little Grounds.

JUST. Aye, Arsenick—Arsenick!—'tis plain enough—why don't you run for Doctor Rosy, you Rascal.

JOHN. Now, your Worship?

BRID. Oh! Lovee! you may be sure 'tis in vain—Let him go for the Lawyer, to witness your will, my Life.

JUST. Zounds! go for the Doctor, you Scoundrel—you are all confederate murderers.

JOHN. O! here he is, your Worship!

JUST. Now Bridget—hold your tongue—let me see if my horrid situation is apparent.

1 Father] *L*, *Rae*, *88*; parents *89* in . . . Chocolate] *L*, *Rae*, *88*; *om. 89* 2 of administ[e]ring] *L*, *Rae*, *89*; to administer *88* Dose] *L*, *Rae*, *89*; doze *88* us] *L*, *Rae*, *88*; me *89* 3 now] *L*, *Rae*, *89*; *om. 88* you . . . so] *L*, *Rae*, *88*; *om. 89* 5 *crying*] *L*, *Rae*; *om. 88*, *89* 6 *Reads*] *L*, *89*; *om. Rae*, *88* of administering] *L*, *Rae*, *89*; *to administer 88* 7 Cut . . . Villain] *L*, *Rae*, *88*; cutthroats, villains *89* 8 Lovee!] *L*, *Rae*, *88*; Lovee—(takes the letter) *89* Postscript] *L*, *Rae*; postscript (*reads*) *88*, *89* 9 save] *L*, *Rae*, *88*; cure *89* Oh! oh!] *L*, *Rae*, *89*; *om. 88* 10 Odds life] *L*, *Rae*, *89*; Odds my life *88* 11–12 John . . . John] *L*, *Rae*, *88*; John, Laury, Susan—John *89* 12 Oh! oh!—you see] *L*; Oh! you see *Rae*; you see *88*, *89* my Lovee] *L*, *Rae*; lovee *88*; my love *89* 14 JOHN] *L*, *Rae*; Servant *88*, *89* 16 cup] *L*, *Rae*, *88*; *om. 89* 18 *After* 'Grounds', *insert another two lines*: *Just.* What colour were they? | *Ser.* Blackish, your worship *88* 19 Aye] *L*, *Rae*, *88*; *om. 89* Arsenick . . . enough] *L*, *Rae*, *89*; arsenac, black arsenac *88* 21 your Worship] *L*, *Rae*, *89*; sir *88* *After* 'Worship', *add another line*: *Just.* Ay, now, you rascal *89* 22 go] *L*, *Rae*, *89*; run *88* 24–5 confederate murderers] *L*, *88*, *Rae*; confederates, murderers *89* 24 you Scoundrel] *L*, *Rae*, *88*; *om. 89* 26 O . . . is] *L*, *Rae*, *88*; Here comes the Doctor *89* Worship!] *L*, *Rae*, *89*; Worship! (*exit*) *88* 27–8 JUST. Now . . . apparent] *L*, *Rae*; Now Bridget, hold your tongue, and let me see if my horrid situation be apparent *88*; *om. 89*

Enter DOCTOR ROSY.

DOCTOR. I have but just call'd in to inform—hey!—bless me, what's the matter with your Worship?

JUST. There—he sees it already—Poison in my face in Capitals—Yes, yes, I am a sure job for the Undertakers indeed!

BRID. Oh! oh!—alas, Doctor!

JUST. Peace, Bridget—why Doctor—my dear old Friend—do you really—see any change in me—hey?

DOCTOR. Change?—Never was man so alter'd—how came those black Spots on your nose?

JUST. Spots on my nose.

DOCTOR. And that wild stare in your right eye?

JUST. In my right eye?

DOCTOR. Aye—and—O! lack! O! lack! how you're swell'd.

JUST. Swell'd!

DOCTOR. Aye—don't you think he is Madam?

BRID. Oh! 'tis in vain to conceal it—indeed, Lovee, you are as big again as you were in the morning.

JUST. Yes—I feel it now—I'm poison'd, Doctor—help me for the love of Justice—give me life to see my murderer hang'd.

DOCTOR. What?

JUST. I'm poison'd, I say.

DOCTOR. Speak out.

JUST. What, can't you hear me?

DOCTOR. Your voice—is so low and hollow, as it were, I can't hear a word you say.

JUST. I am gone then—Hic Jacet—many years one of His Majesty's Justices.

BRID. Read that, Doctor.—Ah!—Lovee, the Will—Consider, my life, how soon you'll be dead.

JUST. No, Bridget, I shall die by inches—

BRID. Well, Lovee, and at twelve inches a day, and that's good slow dying—you'll be gone in five days and a half.

JUST. 'Tis false, Cockatrice!—I'm five foot eight.

1 *Enter* . . . ROSY] *L*; *Enter* Doctor *Rae*, *88*, *89* 2 inform] *L*, *Rae*, *88*; inform you *89* 5 Undertakers indeed!] *L*, *Rae*, *88*; undertakers, indeed, Bridget *89* 6 Oh! . . . Doctor] *L*, *Rae*, *88*; *om. 89* 7 Peace, Bridget] *L*, *Rae*, *88*; *om. 89* dear] *L*, *Rae*, *88*; good *89* 8 hey] *L*, *Rae*; *om. 88*, *89* 13 eye?] *L*, *88*, *89*; eye? O look!—*Rae* 14 Aye—and—O! lack!] *L*; ay, and alack, efack! *Rae*; Aye, and alack, alack *88*; And oh! lack! *89* 17 Lovee] *L*, *Rae*, *88*; love *89* 18 were in the] *L*, *Rae*; was this *88*; were this *89* 20 murderer] *L*, *Rae*, *88*; murderers *89* 24 can't] *L*, *Rae*, *88*; don't *89* 25 hollow] *L*, *Rae*; hallow *88*; so hollow *89* I] *L*, *Rae*, *88*; that I *89* 27 Jacet] *L*, *Rae*, *88*; jacet Robartis Credulous, Esq. *89* Majesty's] *Rae*, *88*, *89*; Majesties *L* 28 that] *L*, *Rae*, *89*; *om. 88* Ah!] *L*, *Rae*, *88*; (*gives a letter*) oh! *89* 28–9 consider . . . how] *L*, *Rae*, *88*; consider the will, consider how *89* 31–3 BRID. Well . . . eight] *L*, *Rae*; *om. 88*, *89*

DOCTOR. I never heard of such a monstrous Iniquity—Ah! you are gone indeed, my Friend—The mortgage of your little bit of clay is up—and the Sexton has nothing to do but foreclose—we must all go—Sooner or later—High or Low—Death's a Debt—his Mandamus[1] binds all alike—no Bail—no Demurrer—

JUST. Silence, Doctor Croaker[2]—will you cure me, or will you not?

DOCTOR. Alas, my Friend—it isn't in my power—but I'll certainly see justice done on your Murderer.

JUST. I thank you, my dear Friend—but I had rather see it myself.

DOCTOR. Aye, but if you recover, the Villain will escape.

BRID. Will he?—then indeed Lovee, 'twould be a pity you should recover—I'm so enraged against the Villain, that I can't bear the thought of his escaping the halter.

JUST. That's very kind, my Dear—but if it is the same to you, I had as lieve recover, notwithstanding.—Doctor, no assistance?

DOCTOR. Efacks—I can do nothing—but here is the German Quack, whom you wanted to send from the Town,—I met him at the next door,—I know that he has Antidotes for all Poisons.

JUST. Fetch him, my dear Friend, fetch him—I'll get him a Diploma if he cures me.

DOCTOR. Well, there's no time to be lost—you continue to swell immensely. [*Exit*.

BRID. What, my Dear, will you submit to be cur'd by a Quack? a Nostrum-monger?—For my part, as much as I love you, I had rather follow you to the Grave, than see you owe your life to any one but a regular bred Physician.

JUST. I'm sensible of your affection, Dearest—and believe me nothing consoles me in my present melancholy situation, so much as the thought of leaving you behind, my Angel.

1 of] *L*, *89*; *om. Rae*, *88* such a] *L*; such *Rae*, *88*, *89* Ah!] *L*, *Rae*; Oh! *88*, *89* 2 up] *L*, *Rae*, *89*; out *88* 3 foreclose] *L*, *Rae*, *89*; to close *88* 4 or] *L*, *Rae*, *89*; and *88* Low—Death's] *L*, *Rae*, *88*; low—rich and poor—death's *89* 5 no Bail] *L*, *88*, *89*; to bail *Rae* 7 Friend—it isn't] *L*, *Rae*, *89*; dear friend, it is not *88* 9 had] *L*, *Rae*, *88*; wou'd *89* 11 Lovee] *L*, *Rae*; *om. 88*, *89* 13 thought] *L*, *Rae*, *88*; thoughts *89* 14 kind] *L*, *Rae*; kind of you *89*; kind in you *88* same] *L*; same thing *Rae*, *88*, *89* you] *L*, *Rae*; you my dear *88*, *89* 15 lieve] *L*, *Rae*; soon *88*, *89* Doctor] *L*, *Rae*; What, doctor *88*, *89* 16 Efacks] *Rae*, *88*; Efecks *L*; *om. 89* here is] *L*, *Rae*, *89*; there's *89* 17 the Town] *L*, *Rae*, *89*; town *88* 18 I] *L*, *Rae*, *89*; and I *88* that he] *L*, *89*; he *Rae*, *88* 19 Friend] *L*, *88*, *Rae*; Doctor *89* 21 lost—you] *L*, *Rae*, *88*; lost. (*going—returns*) You *89* 22 *Exit*] *L*, *88*, *89*; *Exit* Doctor *Rae* 23–4 Quack? a Nostrum-monger] *L*, *Rae*, *89*; Quack Nostrum-monger *88* *After* '*Nostrum monger*', *insert*: there's something creditable in being kill'd in a regular way *Rae* 26 believe] *L*, *Rae*, *89*; be assured *88* 27 me] *L*, *Rae*, *89*; me more *88* present melancholy] *L*, *Rae*; melancholy *88*; present *89* thought] *L*, *Rae*; thoughts *88*, *89* 28 my Angel] *L*, *Rae*, *89*; me *88*

---

[1] Command from a superior court to an inferior one.

[2] Croaker in Goldsmith's *The Good Natur'd Man* (1768) thinks all life is vanity but Sheridan is probably using the name more generally to suggest utter despair.

Enter DOCTOR ROSY, *and the* LIEUTENANT.

The LIEUTENANT *dress'd in a wig and Cloak, as a Physician.*

DOCTOR. Great luck—I met him passing by the door— [*they salute*

LIEUT. Metto—dowsci pulseum.

DOCTOR. He desires to feel your pulse.

JUST. Can't he speak English.

DOCTOR. Not a word.

LIEUT. Palio-vivem-mortem-soonem.[1]

DOCTOR. He says you have not six hours to live.

JUST. O mercy! does he know my Distemper?

DOCTOR. I beleive not.

JUST. Tell him 'tis Arsenick they have given me.

DOCTOR. Geneabant illi Arseneca.[2]

LIEUT. Poisonatus.

JUST. What does he say?

DOCTOR. He says then, that you are poison'd!

JUST. We know that—but what will be the Effect?

DOCTOR. Quid Effectum?

LIEUT. Diabet toutalar.[3]

DOCTOR. He says you'll die presently.

JUST. O Horrible! what no Antidote?

LIEUT. Curum—Benakere—bono—Fullum.

DOCTOR. He says he'll undertake to cure you for three thousand pounds.[4]

1–2 *Enter . . . Physician*] *L*, *Rae*; *Enter* Doctor *and* Lieutenant *disguised 88*; *Enter* Lieutenant, *as* Doctor *89* 3 Great luck—I] *L*, *Rae*; Great luck, met *88*; Great luck, great luck, I *89* passing] *L*, *Rae*, *88*; as passing *89* 4 Metto . . . pulseum] *L*; Metto dowsin Pulseum *Rae*; Metto dowsei pulsum *88*; Multo, dowscie pulsum *89* 8 Palio . . . soonem] *L*, *Rae*, *88*; Palis, vivam, mortam, snoram *89* 11 I] *L*, *Rae*, *88*; No, I *89* 12 Arsenick] *L*, *Rae*; black arsenick *88*, *89* 13 Geneabant . . . Arseneca] *L*; Geneable illi arsnecca *Rae*, *88*; Geneabant—illi—arsenica—poisonatas *89* 14 Poisonatus] *L*, *Rae*; poisonatas *89*; Pisonatus *88* 16 says] *Rae*, *88*, *89*; says then *L* that] *L*, *Rae*, *88*; *om. 89* 18 Effectum] *L*, *Rae*, *88*; effectam *89* 19 Diabet toutalar] *L*; Diable tutellum *Rae*; Diable tutellem *88*; Diabel toutalar *89*; Diabit Tantalum *Sichel*, i. 504, *reading Frampton Court MS.* 20 you'll] *L*, *Rae*, *89*; you *88* 21 what no] *L*, *Rae*, *88*; no *89* 22 Curum . . . Fullum] *L*, *Rae*, *88*; Curam, bonakree, bona, fullam *89* *After 'Fullum', insert another line*: *Just.* What does he say, I must row in a boat to Fulham? *88*, *89* 23 He] *L*, *Rae*, *88*; No, he *89* three thousand] *L*, *Rae*, *88*; 30,000 l. *89*

[1] 'At length Dosy returns, introducing the Lieutenant disguised as Doctor; the latter talks gibberish on first seeing Credulous, which Dosy interprets, declaring that the German Doctor, after having felt his pulse, is of opinion that he'll be a dead man in less than an hour.' (*Morning Chronicle*, 4 May 1775.)

[2] Mr. F. W. Bateson has suggested that 'the sentence must originally have run "Giveabant illi Arsenica", i.e. they gave him arsenic.'

[3] Mr. Bateson suggests 'Diabit toutalar', i.e. he will die presently (*tout à l'heure*).

[4] 'He'll cure him for 3000 guineas.' (*Morning Chronicle*, 4 May 1775.)

BRID. Three thousand halters—No, Lovee, you shall never submit to such an imposition.—Die at once my Life, and be a Customer to none of them.

JUST. I will not die, Bridget—I do not like death.

BRID. Pshaw! there's nothing in it—a moment and it is over.

JUST. Ay, but it leaves a numbness behind, that lasts for a plaguy long time.

Enter LAURETTA.

LAUR. O! my Father! what is it I hear?

LIEUT. Quiddum seeo miram Deos tollam Rosum.

DOCTOR. The Doctor is astonished at the sight of your Daughter.

JUST. How so?

LIEUT. Damsellum—Luvum—even—vislebani—

DOCTOR. He says, that he has long lost his heart to her—and that if you will give him leave to pay his Addresses to the young Lady, and promise your consent to their union, if he should gain her affections, he will, on those Conditions, cure you instantly without Fee, or Reward.

JUST. The devil! did he say all that in so few words? what a fine Language it is!—well, I agree—if he can prevail on the girl—and that I am sure he never will— [*aside*

DOCTOR. Greeat.

LIEUT. Writum Bothum.

DOCTOR. He says you must give this under your hand, while he writes you a miraculous Recipe.— [*Both write at the Table*

LAUR. Do, Mama, tell me the meaning of all this.

1 Three . . . halters] *L, Rae;* £. 3000! 3000 halters *88*; 30,000 l.—thirty thousand halters first *89* 2 an imposition] *L, Rae, 89*; impositions *88* my Life] *L, Rae*; *om. 88, 89* 4 Pshaw! . . . it] *L, Rae*; Psha! there is nothing in it *88*; Pshaw! I don't like death *89* it is] *L, Rae, 88*; all is *89* 6 time] *L, Rae, 88*; while *89* *After 'time', insert another line*: *Bri.* O my dear, pray do consider the will. *88* *Bridget.* Oh! my dear—do consider—the will. *89* 8 my] *L, Rae, 88*; my dear *89* I hear] *L, Rae, 88*; I have heard *89* 9 Quiddum . . . Deos] *L*; Quiddam seomriam deos *Rae, 88*; Quiddum, seomenicum, deus *89* tollam] *Rae, 88, 89*; tollan *L* Rosum] *L*; rosam *Rae 88, 89* 10 Daughter] *L, Rae, 89*; fair daughter *88* 11 How] *L, Rae, 88*; Why *89* *After 'so', insert another line*: *Doct.* Thorico, pausada, Pulaviro, *89* 12 Damsellum . . . vislebani] *L*; Damsellum livivum suvum rislibani *Rae, 88*; Damsellam, luvam evam vislibane *89*; Damsellam luvum cum videbam *Sichel*, i. 504, *reading Frampton Court MS.* 13 that . . . her] *L*; that he has lost his heart to her *Rae, 88*; she has robb'd him of his heart *89* 14 the young Lady] *L, Rae, 88*; her *89* 15 their] *L, 89*; the *Rae, 88* 15–16 he . . . Conditions] *L, Rae, 88*; on those conditions, he will *89* 16 instantly] *L, Rae, 88*; *om. 89* 20 Greeat] *L*; Great *Rae*; Greal *88*; Settlum, greatum? *89* 21 Writum Bothum] *L*; Writhum Bothum *Rae, 88*; Lieutenant—writum, boltum *89* 23 Recipe . . . *table*] *L, Rae*; receipt. (*Both sit down to write*) *88*; recipe. (*both sit and write at the table*) *89* 24 all this] *L, Rae*; this *88*; all this; wou'd he have me to marry a man that speaks as if he had a doctor's shop in his mouth *89*

BRID. Don't speak to me, Girl, unnatural Parasite.

JUST. There, Doctor, that's what he requires.

DOCTOR. And here's your Recipe, read it yourself.

JUST. Hey!—what's here? plain English?

DOCTOR. Read it out—a wondrous Nostrum, I'll answer for't. [*While the Justice reads, the Lieutenant throws off his disguise, and kneels with Lauretta.*]

JUST. [*Reads*] 'On reading this, you are Cured by your affectionate Son in law, O'Connor.'

JUST. What the deuce is the meaning of all this?

BRID. Oh! monstrous imposition.

JUST. In the name of Belzebub, who have we here?

LIEUT. Lieutenant O'Connor, at your Service, and your faithful Servant, honest Humphry.

BRID. So, so, another Trick.

JUST. Out of my Sight, Varlet. I'll be off the bargain, I'll be poison'd again—and you shall be hang'd.

DOCTOR. Come, come, my Dear Friend, don't put yourself in a Passion—a man just escap'd from the Jaws of Death shou'dn't be so violent—Come, make a merit of Necessity, and let your Blessing join those, whom nothing on Earth can keep asunder.

JUST. I'll not do it—I'd sooner die, and leave my Fortune to Bridget.

BRID. To be sure—O' my Conscience, I'd rather you should die, and leave me ten Estates, than consent to such a thing.

JUST. You had, had you.—Harkee, Bridget, you behaved so affectionately

1 Parasite] *Rae*; parent *88*; Parasyte *L*; Parricide *89* 2 that's] *L*, *Rae*; there's *88*; is *89* 3 here's] *L*, *Rae*, *88*; there's *89* yourself] *L*, *Rae*, *88*; aloud *89* 4 Hey!—what's here] *L*, *Rae*, *88*; What's this *89* 5 out] *L*, *Rae*, *88*; read it *89* 5–7 *While . . . Lauretta*] *L*, *Rae*; *om. 88*, *89* 8 *Reads*] *L*, *Rae*; (*reading*) *89*; *om. 88* On] *L*, *Rae*, *89*; In *88* Cured] *L*, *Rae*, *88*; effectually cur'd *89* 9 O'Connor] *L*, *89*; O'Connor.—Who in the name of Beelzebub, sirrah, who are you? *Rae*, *88* 10 What] *L*, *Rae*, *89*; *om. 88* the deuce] *L*, *Rae*; *om. 88*, *89* is this] *L*, *Rae*; *om. 88*; is the meaning of all this (*Lieutenant throws off his disguise*) 11 Oh . . . imposition] *L*, *Rae*; Monstrous imposition *89*; *om. 88* 13–14 Lieutenant . . . Humphry] *L*, *Rae*; Your affectionate son-in-law, O'Connor, and your very humble servant, Humphrey Hum *88*; Lieut. O'Connor, at your service *89* 15 So . . . Trick] *L*, *Rae*; *om. 88*; Your humble servant Humphrey Hum. So another trick. *89* 16–17 Out . . . hang'd] *L*, *Rae*; 'Tis false you dog, you are not my son-in-law, for I'll be poison'd again, and you shall be hang'd—I'll die sirrah, and leave Bridgett my Estate *88*; 'Tis false, you are not my son in law—I'll be poison'd again, and leave Bridget my estate, but he shall be hang'd *89* 18–19 Come . . . violent] *L*, *Rae*, *89*; *om. 88* 20 Come] *L*, *Rae*; come, my old friend *89*; *om. 88* 20–1 make . . . asunder] *L*, *Rae*, *89*; *om. 88* 22 I'll . . . Bridget] *L*, *Rae*; *om. 88*, *89* 23–4 To . . . thing] *L*, *Rae*; Ay, Pray do my dear, leave me your Estate, I'm sure he deserves to be hang'd *88*; Ay, pray do, my dear, be poison'd again, for I'm sure he deserves to be hang'd *89* 25 You had, had you] *L*, *Rae*; He does, you say *88*, *89* Harkee] *L*, *Rae*, *88*; Look'ee *89* 25–line 1, page 192 behaved . . . that] *L*, *Rae*; shew'd such a tender concern for me, when you thought me poison'd, that *88*, *89*

just now, that I'll never follow your advice again, while I live—so, Mr. Lieutenant—

LIEUT. Sir!

JUST. You're an Irishman, and an officer, ar'n't you?

LIEUT. I am, and proud of both.

JUST. The two things in the world I hate most—So mark me—Forswear your Country, and quit the Army—and I'll receive you as my Son in law.

LIEUT. You, Mr. Justice, if you were not the father of your Daughter there, I'd pull your nose for mentioning the first, and break your bones for proposing the latter.[1]

DOCTOR. You're right, Lieutenant.

JUST. Is he?—why then I must be wrong—here, Lauretta, you're a sly tricking little Baggage, and I believe no one so fit to manage you, as my honest friend here, who is the most impudent dog, I ever saw.

LIEUT. With such a Gift, every word is a Compliment.

BRID. Come, then, since everything's settled, I give my Consent, and this day's Adventure, Lovee, will be a good scolding Subject for you and me these ten years.

JUST. So it will, my Dear—tho' we are never much at a loss.

DOCTOR. Come, I insist on one day without wrangling—The Captain

1 I'll . . . live] *L*, *Rae*; for the future I am resolv'd never to take your advice again in any thing *88*; for . . . in any one thing *89* 1–2 so . . . Lieutenant] *L*, *Rae*; So, do you hear sir, *88*, *89* 3 Sir!] *L*, *Rae*; *om.* *88*, *89* 4 and . . . you?] *L*, *Rae*; and a soldier, ar'n't you? *88*; you say, and a soldier, you say—*89* 5 am] *L*, *Rae*; am, Sir *88*, *89* 6 in . . . most] *L*, *Rae*; on earth I most hate *88*, *89* So . . . me] *L*, *Rae*; so I'll tell you what *88*; Now I'll tell you what *89* Forswear] *L*, *Rae*; renounce *88*, *89* 7 and . . . Army] *L*, *Rae*; and sell your commission *88*; sell your commission *89* 7–8 receive . . . law] *L*, *Rae*; forgive you *88*, *89* 9 You, Mr.] *L*, *Rae*; Hark'ee, Mr. *88*, *89* 9–10 your . . . there] *L*, *Rae*; my dear Lauretta *89*; my Lauretta *88* 10 mentioning] *L*, *Rae*; asking *88*, *89* 11 proposing the latter] *L*, *Rae*; desiring the latter *89*; desiring the second *88* 12 You're] *L*, *Rae*, *89*; Aye, aye, you're *88* 13 why then] *L*, *Rae*; then I'm sure *88*, *89* 13–15 Lauretta . . . is] *L*, *Rae*; Sir, I give you my daughter; but you are *89*; sir, I give my daughter to you, who are *88* 15 saw] *L*, *Rae*; saw in my life *88*; saw in my life. (*aside*) *89* 16 With . . . Compliment] *L*, *Rae*; O sir, say what you please, with such a gift as Lauretta, every word is a compliment *88*; With such a gift, every word is a compliment, from the father of my dear Lauretta *89* 17 Come . . . settled] *L*, *Rae*; Come then, since every thing is settled between you *89*; *om.* *88* 17–19 I give . . . years] *L*, *Rae*; Well my lovee, I think this will be a good subject for us to quarrel about the rest of our lives *88*; this day's adventure, lovee, will be a subject for you and me these ten years *89* 20 So . . . loss] *L*, *Rae*; So it will, my dear, though we are seldom at a loss for any thing to quarrel about *89*; Why truly, my dear, I think so, tho' we are seldom at a loss for that *88* 21–line 2, page 193 Come . . . o'clock] *L*, *Rae*, *89*; This is all as it should be. My Alexander, I give you joy *88*

---

[1] 'Mentioning the first . . . proposing the second.' (*Morning Chronicle*, 4 May 1775.)

shall give us a Dinner at the two Magpies, and your Worship shall put every man in the Stocks, who is sober at Eight o'clock—So, joy to you, my little Favourite [*to Lauretta*]—And I wish you may make just such a Wife, as my poor Dear Dolly—

FINIS[1]

2–3 So . . . Favourite] *L*, *Rae*, *89*; and you my little god-daughter *88* 3 *to Lauretta*] *L*, *Rae*; *om.* *88*, *89* And] *L*, *88*, *89*; *om.* *Rae* 3–4 I . . . Wife] *L*, *Rae*; and now my sincere wish is, that you may make just such a wife *88*; and I wish you may prove just as good a wife *89*

---

[1] Sichel, i. 503 n., notes that in the Frampton Court MS. 'the whole is signed "S" with a flourish, and a triumphant "Finis" afterwards'. Rae, p. 96, says that the manuscript ends '&c. &c.' and 'Finis', and that 'an L. is written between "&c." and "Finis" '. Rhodes, i. 170 n., interpreted this 'as meaning that "L." (Lauretta or Lieutenant) spoke a final tag, possibly in rhyme'. I think it is just possible that Lauretta recited a verse, but there is no mention of an epilogue in the newspaper reports.

THE DUENNA

COMPOSITION

It is often difficult to discover the original ideas on which a dramatist founds a play. In default of real evidence, the critic may be inclined to look for characters and situations that seem to possess more imaginative life than the others or, at the opposite extreme, to be rather forcibly dragged in. If he hazards the guess that these are the true bases, he does so because he thinks the one has matured in the author's imagination over a period, while the other retains its place in the play merely because it was a part, possibly adventitious, of the original conception. In *The Duenna*, these clues would lead to an emphasis on the scene between the duenna and Isaac and, by contrast (because of its seeming irrelevance), to that of the drinking friars. Besides, in any consideration of the characters, the lively Isaac is a complete contrast to the makeweight Carlos.

The earliest draft of any part of the play to survive[1] appears to be the scene where Isaac introduces his friend Moses to the duenna:

ISAAC. Moses, sweet coz, I thrive, I prosper.

MOSES. Where is your mistress?

ISAAC. There, you booby, there she stands.

MOSES. Why, she's damn'd ugly.

ISAAC. Hush! (*stops his mouth.*)

DUENNA. What is your friend saying, Don?

ISAAC. Oh, ma'am, he's expressing his raptures at such charms as he never saw before.

MOSES. Aye, such as I never saw before indeed (*aside*).

DUENNA. You are very obliging, gentlemen; but, I dare say, sir, your friend is no stranger to the influence of beauty. I doubt not but he is a lover himself.

MOSES. Alas! madam, there is now but one woman living, whom I have any love, and truly, ma'am, you resemble her wonderfully.

DUENNA. Well, sir, I wish she may give you her hand as speedily as I shall mine to your friend.

MOSES. Me her hand!—O Lord, ma'am—she is the last woman in the world I could think of marrying.

DUENNA. What then, sir, are you comparing me to some wanton—some courtezan?

ISAAC. Zounds! he durstn't.

MOSES. O not I, upon my soul.

DUENNA. Yes, he meant some young harlot—some—

MOSES. Oh, dear madam, no—it was my mother I meant, as I hope to be saved.

[1] Moore, i. 170–1.

ISAAC. Oh the blundering villain! (*aside*)

DUENNA. How, sir—am I so like your mother?

ISAAC. Stay, dear madam—my friend meant—that you put him in mind of what his mother was when a girl—didn't you, Moses?

MOSES. O yes, madam, my mother was formerly a great beauty, a great beauty, a great toast, I assure you;—and when she married my father about thirty years ago, as you may perhaps remember, ma'am—

DUENNA. I, sir! I remember thirty years ago!

ISAAC. Oh, to be sure not, ma'am—thirty years! no, no—it was thirty months he said, ma'am—wasn't it, Moses?

MOSES. Yes, yes, ma'am—thirty months ago, on her marriage with my father, she was, as I was saying a great beauty;—but catching cold, the year afterwards, in child-bed of your humble servant—

DUENNA. Of you, sir!—and married within these thirty months!

ISAAC. Oh the devil! he has made himself out but a year old!—Come, Moses, hold your tongue.—You must excuse him, ma'am—he means to be civil—but he is a poor, simple fellow—an't you, Moses?

MOSES. 'Tis true, indeed, ma'am &c. &c. &c.

At some time in the process of rewriting, Sheridan transferred many of the lines from Moses to Isaac, yet only twenty-six of them in the above passage appear (in slightly altered form) in Act II, Sc. ii, of W. Fraser Rae's transcript of Sheridan's later manuscript of the play. In the edition of 1794, only ten of the lines remain. Possibly Sheridan felt that the lines he omitted put a strain upon credibility. Isaac's character was sufficiently developed without them, and there was a good reason for not giving them to Carlos, the character who replaced Moses. It lay in Leoni, the singer who took the part:

Moore found in Sheridan's papers that the part intended for Isaac's friend, first called Moses, contained much more dialogue than was given to Don Carlos, for which he cannot well account. I can assist him. Leoni could sing English but could not speak it . . . could barely pronounce [it] so as to be intelligible . . . music of his voice made ample amends for deficiencies of articulation. Sheridan showed much ingenuity in contriving to give him much to sing and little to say.[1]

The same writer described Leoni's voice as 'a fine oboe', and it certainly contributed greatly to the opera's success. His particular skill in 'a plaintive or pastoral style' is described by Sheridan in a letter probably written in October 1775,[2] but since the *Morning Chronicle* later declared that 'his character [i.e. Carlos] was introduced into this opera after it was written', we may perhaps come to the conclusion that Sheridan had completed the dramatic framework before he wrote his letter and that he then added

[1] 'Senex' in *Blackwood's Magazine*, July 1826, p. 25.

[2] See p. 202. Leoni's appearance as Arbuces in *Artaxerxes* on 18 Oct. 1775, was only his second on that stage: see *The London Stage*, pp. 1886, 1919–20. 'For sweetness of tone, few even of the soprani, ever surpassed Leoni.' (*The Oracle*, 15 Feb. 1797.)

songs and a few lines to make up Leoni's part. At one point this leads to a decided irony, for the song that Carlos has studied at the end of Act II, Sc. ii, has a sweetness of sentiment that contrasts comically with the pair of lovers it celebrates:

> The youth excelling so in mien,
> The maid in ev'ry grace of feature.

Possibly it was so beautifully sung that it even dignified the proposed liaison between Isaac and the duenna.

Because it was so perfectly suited to Leoni, the part was not easy to cast in later companies. It had to be taken by Mrs. Kennedy in a performance at Covent Garden on 22 September 1779. At Liverpool in the same year, Leoni's songs were sung by Webster in the role of Ferdinand, while another actor took what must have been merely the walk-on part of Carlos.[1] The American cast list[2] omits Carlos, but his songs and lines are retained and may have been transferred to another character. The difficulty of finding singers like Leoni was considerable, but when Charles Incledon gave an admirable performance as Carlos in November 1801, the *Theatrical Repertory*[3] commented: 'we blush to recollect that Jews and Italians, with falsettas, have been engaged, at the most extravagant salaries, to feminize the part'.

When Moses became Carlos he moved to the periphery of the plot, but Isaac, taking over some of his function, came even closer to the centre. He is the best-drawn character in the opera, and a further example of Sheridan's desire to make good use of the talent available. The part was played by John Quick, who had been the original Tony Lumpkin and Bob Acres, and was now to give a remarkable performance as the trickster who was 'the dupe of his own art'. Yet there is something innocent about Isaac. His vanity and self-satisfaction make him appear naïve rather than vicious, and he is presented in so comical a way that we overlook the meanness of his aims. Like Acres, he is an egotist and spirited talker, something of a coward and a fop. Quick, like Mrs. Green who created the roles of Mrs. Hardcastle, Mrs. Malaprop, and the duenna, took full advantage of the opportunities presented to him by Sheridan. One is bound to wonder if the sketch I have transcribed from Moore was not the original centre of the play, and if Sheridan, there, had not very much in mind the character relationships that had been so successful in Goldsmith's *She Stoops to Conquer* and his own *The Rivals*. The first performance of the latter certainly taught him one lesson he was never to forget: the importance of fitting out parts to suit the particular abilities of the players who were to take them.

[1] *Morning Chronicle*, 23 Sept. 1779; Williamson's *Liverpool Advertiser*, 16 July 1779.
[2] Published by Longworth in New York, 1808. See p. 222, below.
[3] 13 Nov., p. 141.

The scene with the drinking friars is certainly not central to the action, and it was criticized as irrelevant and, in its thinking, out of date.[1] Yet it has a definite place in Sheridan's satirical outlook, as shown both in *The Duenna* and *The School for Scandal*. Look at the lines in Act III, Sc. iii, of *The Duenna*:

ANTONIO. Come, then—there is a friar of a neighbouring convent is my friend; you have already been diverted by the manners of a nunnery—let us see, whether there is less hypocrisy among the holy fathers.

LOUISA. I'm afraid not, Antonio—for in religion, as in friendship, they who profess most are the least sincere.

Satire upon hypocrites was commonplace enough during the eighteenth century, and Sheridan is quite clearly following an accepted convention. Here the satire was incidental; in his next play, it was to be all important.

Some resemblance has been noted between *The Duenna* and Dryden's *The Spanish Fryar*, that goes beyond their subsidiary titles (*The Double Elopement* and *The Double Discovery*) to a comparison of Sheridan's Father Paul with Dryden's Father Dominick and Gomez.[2] No reason has been found why Sheridan should have picked on this particular play for emulation. Possibly the connection was accidental. Dryden's play was in the news on 29 August 1775, when the *Morning Chronicle* reported:

We hear that the Ambassadors from the Roman Catholic powers now residing at our Court, have received instructions to apply to the Lord Chamberlain, and prevent the performance of the Spanish Fryar. This excellent piece of Dryden's has ever been obnoxious to the advocates of popery; the manner of his conducting the fable happily ridicules monkish hypocrisy and humorously exposes the vice concealed under a sanctified appearance; the great Lord Bolingbroke declared that the Spanish Fryar had done more service to the Protestant religion, than the writings of our ablest divines.

The play was given at the Haymarket on 4 and 12 September, without hindrance. Sheridan may have seen one of the performances, or he may merely have recollected its satirical theme when he was working out his ideas for *The Duenna*. It seems pretty certain that, at this period, *The Spanish Fryar* was at the back of his mind.

Several other plays are also said to have influenced him. Felix and Violante in Mrs. Centlivre's *The Wonder: A Woman keeps a Secret*, have something in common with Ferdinand and Clara, while Col. Briton and Isabella are like Antonio and Louisa.[3] Charles Dibdin, a hostile witness,

[1] See p. 211.

[2] See Rhodes, i. 181; and *More Kotzebue* (1799), p. 13.

[3] Cf. J. W. Bowyer, *The Celebrated Mrs. Centlivre* (Durham, N.C., 1952), p. 171; and on this and the Molière reference, J. Dulck, *Les Comédies de Sheridan* (Paris, 1962), pp. 153–4.

thought that the idea of turning a daughter out of doors and the passing of maid for mistress came from Molière's *Le Sicilien* and Goldoni's *Il Filosofo di Campagna*, and Father Paul's drinking burgundy while praising the wholesome crystal stream from Marmontel's *Philosophe soi disant.*[1] Both *The Wonder* and *Il Filosofo di Campagna* (in Dibdin's own version called *The Wedding Ring*) were acted frequently in London and it is certainly possible that Sheridan saw them and took hints from them. The fairest conclusion, however, seems to be that of J. W. Calcraft:[2] 'it may be so, but it requires a very minute comparison to detect the relationship'. Sheridan had mentioned 'starts of recollection'[3] in the Preface to *The Rivals*: they were to recur, but are of little significance when, as in *The Duenna*, he is able to bring them into new patterns and give them imaginative force.

The first direct mention of an opera for which Sheridan was writing the libretto[4] is to be found in a letter written by his father-in-law to John Hoadly, poet and dramatist, on 22 September 1775. It reads:

> . . . I have engaged to assist my son-in-law Sheridan in composing an opera, which he is to bring out at Covent Garden this winter. I am a good deal distressed that, from some misunderstanding between him and Mr. Garrick, he is not connected with Drury-lane house; for though I believe they are now on very good terms, yet Sheridan thinks he has been so honourably treated by Mr. Harris, that he ought not to keep any thing he has hitherto written from him. However, I hope Mr. Garrick will not take any thing amiss in my assisting him on this occasion; for it is a matter of absolute necessity that he should endeavour to get money by this means, as he will not be prevailed upon to let his wife sing. . . .[5]

In an earlier letter, Linley had asked Hoadly to be kind enough to send him two verse pieces, 'Love's Artifice' and 'The Song of Moses'. Since

[1] *The Musical Tour of Mr. Dibdin* (Sheffield, 1788), p. 260. Sheridan could have seen *The Wonder* and *The Wedding Ring* during his Waltham Abbey period: they were presented at Drury Lane Theatre on 15 Dec. 1772 and 1 Feb. 1773. For comment on both plays, see Garland Forbes Taylor's 'Richard Brinsley Sheridan's *The Duenna*' (Yale University Ph.D. thesis, 1940), pp. 29–32.

[2] *Dublin University Magazine*, xlvi (1855), 41.

[3] Mrs. Inchbald saw borrowings from Wycherley's *The Country Wife*, but a more unusual suggestion came from Professor Dulck (op. cit., pp. 152–3), who drew attention to Sheridan's use of certain situations in his mother's novel, *Eugenia and Adelaide*. The play and novel, however, are very different in tone and treatment, even if there are the following superficial resemblances in the intrigue: Louisa escapes in the duenna's clothes just as Faustina runs away disguised as her cousin, Adelaide. Both fathers want their daughters to marry elderly misers. The Duenna marries Mendoza just as Faustina weds the Chevalier de Ponces. In both stories, the convent is a common retreat when affairs of the heart become difficult.

[4] John Graham jotted down some of Sheridan's statements shortly before he died, and one of them was that *The Duenna* had been written at Waltham Abbey before his marriage: see Rhodes, *Harlequin Sheridan* (Oxford, 1933), p. 58. Rhodes then assumes that it took the form of a farce.

[5] *Garrick Corr.*, ii. 99–101.

Garrick had both in his possession, Hoadly then requested him to send them on to Linley at Bath, and when Garrick complied, sent him the above 'ingenious and good letter from Mr. Linley, to which I think you have a good right, as he speaks so handsomely of you, and with real concern for his own situation, which your liberal mind will make allowances for'.[1] However, Linley thought it essential to make his own apologies, and did so on 28 September in a letter (from Bath) to Garrick:[2]

. . There is a Circumstance, which because relative to myself in the good Opinion I wish you should preserve of me, that I must mention, otherwise, I know not if I ought; it is, that as often as I am called upon, I have promissed to assist Sheridan in, compiling, I believe is the properest Term, an Opera, which I understand from him, he has engaged to produce at Covent Garden this winter. I have already sett some Airs which he has given me, and he intends writing new Words to some other Tunes of mine. My Son has likewise written some Tunes for him, and I understand, he is to have others from Mr. Jackson of Exeter. This is a Mode of proceeding in regard to his Composition I do not by any Means approve of, I think he ought first to have finish'd his Opera with the Songs he intends to introduce in it and have got it entirely new set: no Musician can set a Song properly unless he understands the Character and knows the Performer who is to exhibit it. For my Part I shall be very unwilling for either my own Name, or my Son's, to appear in this Business, and it is my present Resolution to forbid it, for I have great Reason to be diffident of my own Abilities and Genius, and my Son has not had Experience in Theatrical compositions, though I think well of his Invention and musical Skill. I would not have been concerned in this Business at all, but that I know there is an absolute necessity for him [Sheridan] to endeavour to get some Money by this Means, as he will not be prevailed upon to let his Wife sing, and indeed at present she is incapable, and Nature will not permit me to be indifferent to his Success. You are deservedly at that Point of Fame, which few of the great Genius's the world has produced ever arrived at, above the reach of Envy, and are the Protector of dramatic Merit in what Shape, or Place soever you find it, and I look up to you, as the Patron and Director of both Theatres, Virtual[l]y, if not officially. I hope Sheridan has done nothing to forfeit the Protection you have hitherto shewn him. . . .

The two letters make it abundantly clear that Linley was anxious not to offend Garrick, who had approached him earlier with a view to his joining Drury Lane Theatre, and that he found it necessary to excuse his son-in-law's allegiance to Harris. We may even read into the first communication the suggestion that only what Sheridan had 'hitherto written' would be performed at Covent Garden, and that the time had come for him to take his new plays to Drury Lane. We know that, before long, negotiations were to begin that would lead (within four months) to the purchase of Garrick's share in the Drury Lane patent by Linley, Sheridan, and Ford,

[1] *Garrick Corr.*, ii. 99.
[2] Garrick Correspondence, Victoria and Albert Museum, vol. 22, ff. 12–13.

and we may see in Linley's careful phrasing the knowledge that he had reached a crucial stage in his own and his son-in-law's career. But if this is true, it seems odd that, in a later letter, Linley should stress Sheridan's improvidence. Here I think we must recall that Linley had to give some good reason for not setting Hoadly's poems as he had contemplated doing, and he found the best one he could: the demands made on him by Sheridan at a time when Linley was already busy preparing concerts for the new Bath season. He also alluded to the fact that Mrs. Sheridan was seven months gone in her pregnancy, and that her husband's need for money was greater than ever. Her family must rally to their assistance.

Linley made clear that he did not like Sheridan's methods of composition, and that a librettist ought to finish his work completely before turning it over to a musician. In this particular grumble he seems to indicate that whatever Sheridan had 'hitherto written' could only have been a draft version, and that it was not only unfinished but that the author cheerfully looked forward to completing it while the composers and company were working on it, too. This is of particular interest because we find that Sheridan completed *The School for Scandal* and *The Critic* in a similar way. Some outside pressure was always necessary before he could summon up all his powers and bring his work into a triumphant unity.

As Sheridan made progress with the work, he found it more and more necessary to consult his father-in-law about the music. His wife, Betsy, gave him considerable help, but had to appeal to her father for advice. Linley seems to have responded not only with the musical settings expected of him, but with suggestions for enlivening the words, too. Sheridan therefore wrote[1] to him to say:

We received your songs to-day, with which we are exceedingly pleased. I shall profit by your proposed alterations; but I'd have you to know that we are much too chaste in London to admit such strains as your Bath spring inspires. We dare not propose a peep beyond the ancle on any account; for the critics in the pit at a new play are much greater prudes than the ladies in the boxes. Betsey intended to have troubled you with some music for correction and I with some stanzas, but an interview with Harris to-day has put me from the thoughts of it, and bent me upon a much more important petition. You may easily suppose it is nothing else than what I said I would not ask in my last. But, in short, unless you can give us three days in town, I fear our opera will stand a chance to be ruined. Harris is extravagantly sanguine of its success as to plot and dialogue, which is to be rehearsed next Wednesday at the theatre. They will exert themselves to the utmost in the scenery, etc., but I never saw any one so disconcerted as he was at the idea of there being no one to put them in the right way as to music. . . . As to the state of the music, I want but three more airs, but there are some glees and quintets in the last act, that will be inevitably ruined, if we have no one to set the performers at least in the right way. Harris

[1] *Letters*, i. 86–7.

has set his heart so much on my succeeding in this application, that he still flatters himself we may have a rehearsal of the music in Orchard Street to-morrow se'nnight. Every hour's delay is a material injury both to the opera and the theatre, so that if you can come and relieve us from this perplexity, the return of the post must only forerun your arrival; or (what will make us much happier) might it not bring *you*?

Linley does not appear to have made the journey from Bath to London, so in his next letter[1] Sheridan justified the request, then sought more help by post:

Mr. Harris wishes so much for us to get you to town, that I could not at first convince him that your proposal of not coming till the music was in rehearsal, was certainly the best, as you could stay but so short a time. The truth is, that what you mention of my getting a *master* to teach the performers is the very point where the matter sticks, there being no such person as a master among them. Harris is sensible there ought to be such a person; however, at present, every body sings there according to their own ideas, or what chance instruction they can come at. We are, however, to follow your plan in the matter; but can at no rate relinquish the hopes of seeing you in eight or ten days from the date of this; when the music (by the specimen of expedition you have given me) will be advanced as far as you mention. The parts are all writ out and doubled, etc. as we go on, as I have assistance from the theatre with me.

He went on to ask Linley's assistance with the curtain duet, solo, and trio, for Act I, and in adapting a tune Linley himself had composed to Sheridan's verses beginning 'O the days when I was young':

My intention was to have closed the first act with a song, but I find it is not thought so well. Hence I trust you with one of the inclosed papers; and, at the same time, you must excuse my impertinence in adding an idea of the cast I would wish the music to have; as I think I have heard you say you never heard Leoni, and I cannot briefly explain to you the character and situation of the persons on the stage with him. The first (a dialogue between Quick and Mrs. Mattocks),[2] I would wish to be a pert, sprightly air; for, though some of the words mayn't seem suited to it, I should mention that they are neither of them in earnest in what they say. Leoni takes it up seriously, and I want him to show himself advantageously in the six lines, beginning 'Gentle maid.'[3] I should tell you, that he sings nothing well but in a plaintive or pastoral style; and his voice is such as appears to me always to be hurt by much accompaniment. I have observed, too, that he never gets so much applause as when he makes a cadence. Therefore my idea is, that he should make a flourish at 'Shall I grieve thee?' and return to 'Gentle maid,' and so sing that part of the tune again. After that, the two lines, sung by the three, with the persons only varied,

[1] *Letters*, i. 88–90.
[2] Duet for baritone and soprano (Isaac and Donna Louisa) at the end of Act I.
[3] Don Carlos's air 'Gentle maid, ah! why suspect me?' at the end of Act I.

may get them off with as much spirit as possible.[1] The second act ends with a *slow* glee,[2] therefore I should think the two last lines in question had better be brisk, especially as Quick and Mrs. Mattocks are concerned in it.

The other is a song of Wilson's in the third act. I have written it to your tune, which you put some words to, beginning 'Prithee, prithee pretty man!' I think it will do vastly well for the words: Don Jerome sings them when he is in particular spirits; therefore the tune is not too light, though it might seem so by the last stanza—but he does not mean to be grave there, and I like particularly the returning to 'O the days when I was young!' We have mislaid the notes, but Tom remembers it. If you don't like it for words, will you give us one? but it must go back to 'O the days,' and be *funny*. I have not done troubling you yet, but must wait till Monday.

Sheridan knew little about music, but he was one of the most observant of men. He had noticed exactly how Leoni could best please an audience, and he had no difficulty in instructing Linley in what effects were needed.

When the first musical rehearsal of the opera took place, Linley was not present and the score was still not finished. From Sheridan's next letter to his father-in-law,[3] we can see him at work as a librettist, putting new words to well-known tunes or parodying the old ones; but what is even more apparent is that of the eight songs now mentioned, two were removed and others substituted for them before the first performance:

Sunday evening next is fixed for our first musical rehearsal, and I was in great hopes we might have completed the score. The songs you have sent up of 'Banna's Banks',[4] and 'Deil take the Wars',[5] I had made words for before they arrived, which answer excessively well; and this was my reason for wishing for the next in the same manner, as it saves so much time. They are to sing 'Wind, gentle evergreen' just as you sing it (only with other words), and I wanted only such support from the instruments, or such joining in, as you should think would help to set off and assist the effort. I inclose the words I

[1] The trio at the end of Act I, on the two lines:

Never mayst thou happy be
If in aught thou'rt false to me.

[2] 'Soft pity never leaves the gentle breast', sung by Don Carlos, Antonio, and Louisa.

[3] *Letters*, i. 90–2.

[4] 'Grammachree Molly' [*Morning Post*, 5 July 1780]

As down on Banna's Banks I stray'd, one evening in May,
The little birds, in blithest notes made vocal every spray;
They sung their little tales of love; they sung them o'er and o'er,
Ah Grammachree, ma Calleenouge, ma Molly Astore.

'Had I a heart for falsehood fram'd' was fitted to this tune.

[5] A glee for four voices by Corfe. The first four lines read:

De'il tak the wars that hurri'd Willy fra me,
Wha to loo me just had sworn,
They made him Captain sure to undo me,
Wae is me! he'll ne'er return.

See Rhodes, *Harlequin Sheridan*, pp. 61–2, for Sheridan's use of these lines.

had made for 'Wind, gentle evergreen,' which will be sung, as a catch,[1] by Mrs. Mattocks, Dubellamy, and Leoni. I don't mind the words not fitting the notes so well as the original ones. 'How merrily we live,' and 'Let's drink and let's sing,' are to be sung by a company of *friars* over their wine.[2] The words will be parodied, and the chief effect I expect from them must arise from their being *known*; for the joke will be much less for these jolly fathers to sing anything new, than to give what the audience are used to annex the idea of jollity to. For the other things Betsy mentioned, I only wish to have them with such accompaniments as you would put to their *present* words, and I shall have got words to my liking for them by the time they reach me.

My immediate wish at present is to give the performers their parts in the music (which they expect on Sunday night), and for any assistance the orchestra can give to help the effect of the glees, etc., that may be judged of and added at a rehearsal, or, as you say, on enquiring how they have been done; though I don't think it follows that what Dr. Arne's method is must be the best. If it were possible for Saturday and Sunday's post to bring us what we asked for in our last letters, and what I now enclose, we should still go through it on Sunday, and the performers should have their parts complete by Monday night. We have had our rehearsal of the speaking part, and are to have another on Saturday. I want Dr. Harrington's catch,[3] but, as the sense must be the same, I am at a loss how to put other words. Can't the under part ('A smoky house,' etc.) be sung by one person and the other two change? The situation is—Quick and Dubellamy, two lovers, carrying away Father Paul (Reinold) in great raptures, to marry them:—the Friar has before warned them of the ills of a married life, and they break out into this. The catch is particularly calculated for a stage effect; but I don't like to take another person's words, and I don't see how I can put others, keeping the same idea ('of seven squalling brats,' etc.) in which the whole affair lies. However, I shall be glad of the notes, with Reinold's part, if it is possible, as I mentioned....

[1] For three voices, and by Hayes:

Winde gentle Evergreens to form a shade
Around the tomb where Sophocles is laid;
Sweet Ivy winde thy boughs, and intertwine
With blushing roses and the clust'ring vine:
Thus with thy lasting leaves, with beauties hung,
Prove grateful emblems of the lays he sung.

(from *A Selection of Favourite Catches, Glees, &c. as sung at the Meetings of the Harmonic Society in the City of Bath* (Bath, 1798), p. 67.)

[2] For III. v; Moore, i. 163, notes: 'For these was afterwards substituted Mr. Linley's lively glee, "This bottle's the sun of our table." '

[3] Henry Harrington (1727–1816), physician and composer, lived at Bath. His catch reads:

Give me the sweet delights of Love,
Let not anxious Care destroy them:
Oh! how divine, still to enjoy them!
Pure are the blessings Love bestowing,
Peace and Harmony ever flowing,
A smoaky house, a failing trade,
Six squalling brats, and a scolding jade.

(*A Selection of Favourite Catches*, . . ., p. 53.)

The inclosed are the words for 'Wind, gentle evergreen;' a passionate song for Mattocks, and another for Miss Brown, which solicit to be clothed with melody by you, and are all I want. Mattocks's I could wish to be a broken, passionate affair, and the first two lines may be recitative, or what you please, uncommon. Miss Brown sings hers in a joyful mood: we want her to show in it as much execution as she is capable of, which is pretty well;[1] and, for variety, we want Mr. Simpson's[2] hautboy to cut a figure, with replying passages, etc., in the way of Fisher's '*M'ami, il bel idol mio*,'[3] to abet which I have lugged in 'Echo', who is always allowed to play her part. I have not a moment more.

On 2 November, Sheridan wrote again[4] to his father-in-law to report progress:

Our music is now all finished and rehearsing, but we are greatly impatient to see *you*. We hold your coming to be *necessary* beyond conception. You say you are at our service after Tuesday next; then 'I conjure you by that you do possess,' in which I include all the powers that preside over harmony, to come next Thursday night (this day se'nnight) and we will fix a rehearsal for Friday morning. From what I see of their rehearsing at present, I am become still more anxious to see you.

We have received all your songs, and are vastly pleased with them. You misunderstood me as to the hautboy song; I had not the least intention to fix on 'Bel idol mio.' However, I think it is particularly well adapted, and, I doubt not, will have a great effect. . . .

A little later, Thomas Linley had occasion to write to Garrick,[5] and it is interesting to note his views on Sheridan's constant procrastination:

My business in Town is to attend two or three Rehearsals of Sheridan's Opera this is exceedingly inconvenient to me, but he has drove off the Business in such a manner, and his musical Part of it is in such confussion that he has made me believe there is an absolute necessity for me to come, in order to render it practicable, for my Part I tremble for him: but did I not firmly believe the Exigence he is drove to, I would not stir a Foot, for I think his neglect and Extravagance are unpardonable, but I will this once try if I can be of any use to him. . . .

These letters are very revealing, and it is a pity that there are not more of them to indicate how *The Duenna* was completed in the fortnight before its first performance on Tuesday, 21 November. The Frampton Court MS., however, suggested that four of the songs were added after the main body of the work had been written up. They were 'What bard, O Time, discover', 'When a tender maid', 'When sable Night', and 'If a Daughter

[1] Moore, i. 165 n., suggests that the song is 'Adieu, thou dreary pile' (III. iv).
[2] Redmond Simpson, principal oboist at Covent Garden.
[3] See G. F. Taylor's thesis, pp. 76–7, for full details.
[4] *Letters*, i. 92–3.
[5] Garrick Correspondence, Victoria and Albert Museum, vol. 22, ff. 14–15.

you have, she's the plague of your life'. The last three of these seem to have been written on separate sheets. It was also noted that 'I ne'er could any lustre see' was at first erased.[1] Unfortunately the Frampton Court MS. was not complete when it was examined, so it did not disclose as much as it might have done.

RECEPTION

[*The Duenna*] might very aptly . . . be stiled a COMEDY *interspersed with an* OPERA.

The story of it greatly resembles the story of a Spanish Play, to be met with in a collection of French translations of Theatrical Pieces, entitled *Le Théâtre Espagnol*. . . .

The Duenna abstracted from any claim on the score of musical merit, is a very well-contrived, humorous comedy. . . . The situations are truly comic and happily introduced, and the dialogue is in general easy, natural, and pointed. In some places indeed we find a few coarsenesses, and aims at St. Giles's wit, which we hope the author will expunge.—Among these we particularly advise the taking out the allusion to the print of Bajazet in a cage;—the threatening to send home Margaret's property in a frank;—the story Isaac tells of his mother;—and some of the repetitions of the description of Margaret's ordinary face. The first is neither a correct nor a comic allusion; the second is vulgar, stale and improbable; the third too low and farcical; and the fourth both unnecessary and disgusting. These are not the only alterations necessary; as the piece now stands, it is longer in performance than it ought to be, and from the redundancy of songs, and the dull music of some of them, it is rendered heavy and serious where the business of the scene should evidently be sprightly and laughable. The necessary alterations, however, may be easily made, and if they are judiciously done, we shall not scruple to pronounce the *Duenna*, the best comic opera that has been produced since the time of Gay. It is said to be written by Mr. Sheridan, author of the Rivals; if that gentleman continues to improve as much as he has done in the course of the last year, he will shortly be one of the best comic writers for the stage in existence—he has by this opera given proof that he possesses those grand and essential requisites for dramatic authorship—a fertile imagination, great ability, and real genius.

The music was partly compos'd and partly compiled: The Overture afforded a sample of solemn, and a sample of airy movements; the selected airs gave universal satisfaction, though it was thought that some of them were rather ill-adapted to the words they accompanied. Those that were composed did not please so much, and not for want of innate merit, but on account of their being more serious than the subject seemed to require.

[1] Sichel, i. 507.

Many of the songs were admirably written; indeed some of them were beautifully poetical, as one of the following specimens will evince:

Friendship is the bond of reason

. . . . .

The performers in general deserve praise for their exertion of yesterday evening; Mrs. Green in particular;—that lady strongly shewed her good sense in accepting her character, which some actresses, with more caprice and less ability, would have scrupled to perform. Mr. Quick was remarkably in Isaac, and Mr. Wilson in some of the scenes of Don Jerome, so near in his imitation of Shuter, that were it not for his unfortunate eyes, the counterfeit could scarcely have been discovered. Mr. Leoni was evidently introduced merely to strengthen the piece, with which his character had no immediate and necessary connection. It was not only a fair advantage taken of the town, but the managers deserve thanks for giving them such a feast as his singing afforded. . . .

The Dance was unpleasing;[1] as it tended to lengthen time, too long stretched for a more essential purpose, it had better be omitted. (*Morning Chronicle*, 22 Nov. 1775.)

The new Opera of THE DUENNA is more like a comedy than any piece exhibited in either theatre since Mess[rs]. Garrick and Colman clubbed their wits to produce that excellent play THE CLANDESTINE MARRIAGE. Mr. Sheridan is the declared author of this Opera, and he deserves great praise for having revived the honour of the drama, by boldly rescuing the stage from that state of lethargy, and melancholy madness, into which Cumberland and his sentimental compeers had lulled it. The contrast to dramatic sermonizing is glaring in THE DUENNA; the spectator, whose risible muscles are not put in motion by the pleasantry of its situations, and the humour of its characters, must be a Stoic indeed. If the author has committed any error, it is that of having so far distanced his dialogue from the insipid, proverb-strung phraseology of *La Comédie larmoyante*, that he sometimes sinks into absolute farce; this however is not only a fault on the right side, but it is also the fault of a young writer, which experience will correct. The words of the airs of this opera differ much from those of most other operas. They are not mere vehicles to sound. They contain meaning, sense, and poetry. Would we could add that the music deserved equal praise; but alas, instead of expressing the hilarity and merriment which should be heard at a birth, it is for the most part as solemn and slow as a dirge at a funeral.[2] (*The London Packet*, 20–22 Nov. 1775.)

[1] 'End of Act II—A new Spanish Dance by Signor and Signora Zucelli, Mr. Dagueville, Signora Vidini, etc.' (*The Gazetteer*, 21 Nov. 1775.)

[2] The painter, James Barry (1741–1806), said that *The Duenna* would not succeed because there was too much 'church music' in it: 'by which singular expression he meant the slow and solemn airs, "Oft does Hymen", "O had my love", "Gentle Maid",

. . . The third Act, bating its extreme length, is far superior to the other two; the Scene of the Friars revelling in the Convent, and the disposition they make of the donations given to the fraternity, has great merit, and shews the genius of the Writer in a very favourable light. . . . (*Lloyd's Evening Post*, 22–24 Nov. 1775.)

[*The Duenna*] as a dramatic performance has in general more merit, than any other comic opera we remember to have seen on the English stage; it has an interesting plot, a pleasing variety of incidents, and a smartness of dialogue which few of them can boast: the operatical part is in some places exceptionable, particularly as it more than once destroys the natural progression of the drama:—the first scene is rendered tedious, by an unnecessary number of airs: as are some others, where Mr. Leoni sings two or three long Scotch airs in *Don Carlos*, an exotic kind of character, artificially created, in order to introduce his excellent pipe, to the violation of all propriety, and the stagnation of the business of the piece: and indeed the plot is a little forced, with the oaths of *Don Jerome* and *Louisa*, to keep it within the pale of probability: however there are numberless excellencies to compensate for this trifling defect.—We would recommend the reflection on the legitimacy of our Nobility, to be omitted in future.—As to the music, the compiled part has the only claim to merit; —we know not the composer of the rest, but we think he has not done justice to the words, some of which are beautiful little poems. . . . (*Morning Post*, 22 Nov. 1775.)

We cannot do justice to this piece by speaking of it as an opera only, for there is more character and plot in it, than in most comedies. Nothing can be more humorous than the scene in the second act, between Isaac and the Duenna. His astonishment at finding her so old and so ugly; and Don Jerome's positiveness confirming him in his error, afford as comic situations as any on the stage. The character of Isaac is an admirable one, and not before on the stage, though frequent in real life. A man piquing himself on cunning—content to accomplish nothing, but by tricking; yet for ever the dupe of his own art. . . . (*London Chronicle*, 21–23 Nov. 1775.)

The Duenna seems to bid fair for a run equal to that of the Beggar's Opera; but it can never be performed on a *Friday*, on account of Leoni's engagement with the Synagogue.—The Jews Sabbath commences at six on the Friday evening, and terminates at the same hour on Saturday.

A musical correspondent observes, that many people were deceived in their division of the new and old airs in the comic opera of the Duenna: for those who thought they were acquainted with Mr. Linley's style, conjectured most of the serious airs and glees to be his, and the lighter

"What Bard, O Time", and others.' (A. Lefanu, *Memoirs of the Life and Writings of Mrs. Frances Sheridan* . . . (1824), pp. 403–4.)

ones to be compiled; when, in fact, the case is the reverse, as the songs of humour (as, 'Give Isaac the nymph'—'I ne'er could [any] Lustre see' —'O the Days!' etc.) are mostly new, and the glees etc. are selected. (*Morning Chronicle*, 25 Nov. 1775.)

Among the various instances of national inconstancy that occur almost every hour in this strange metropolis, none has surprised me more than the sudden partiality of the Town to Covent-Garden Theatre, and their ungrateful desertion of poor old Drury-lane: Mr. Garrick, with a spirit undiminished by age, has beautified and adorned his playhouse, and made it the prettiest Assembly-room in the whole Town. He himself performs his best parts three or four times a week; and yet this new sing song thing, the Duenna, brings crowded houses to Covent-Garden, and leaves Roscius almost in utter solitude.—I know the general taste for musick may be alledged as an explanation of this phaenomenon. But surely the wit of Shakespear, and the incomparable humour of Ben Johnson, should still retain the admiration of every sensible Englishman. Benedick, and Abel Drugger, have a natural claim to our constant attention.—I do not, however, mean to depreciate Mr. Sheridan's Opera; I allow it all its merit; perhaps it would deserve more approbation, if it was freed from its musical appendage, and performed as a comedy. The spirited dialogue of that piece is interrupted by the songs, and the comic muse is driven off the stage by her childish musical sister.

I cannot, however, doubt, that when Mr. Garrick appears in some of his best tragedy parts,[1] he will meet with the usual reception an admiring nation has ever bestowed on his unparalleled abilities. In a few years, perhaps months, this bright luminary of the stage must yield to the common lott of mortality.—Let us suspend our love of Operas, till that melancholy period. I really think it will be mentioned as among the many instances of our degeneracy, that we lose the favourable moment of beholding Garrick's Macbeth, Hamlet, and Lear, to listen to a little Spanish Opera, and indulge an unaccountable partiality for music.

Why does not Mr. Sheridan produce a more sublime work? A Tragedy of his, under Mr. Garrick's direction, would secure a greater degree of fame, than even the Beggar's Opera, or the Duenna can obtain. Braganza's laurels should provoke his emulation—Let him snatch that glorious wreath from Mr. Jephson, and he will secure the admiration of every impartial lover of taste and genius. ('Adelphos' in the *Morning Chronicle*, 27 Nov. 1775.)

. . . To find fault with an opera, because an opera is waste of words, and the recommendation of tragedy to the pen of Mr. Sheridan, jun. when his

[1] Garrick wrote to Rackett on 2 Dec. to say 'the Devil of a Duenna has laid hold upon the Town, and nothing but your old Friend can get her a little out of her clutches' (Garrick, *Letters*, p. 1051). Consequently, between 25 Nov. and 23 Dec., he performed six of his most famous parts.

talent so plainly and creditably leans to the opposite, is the *ne plus ultra* of finesse; so that I think Adelphos concludes with a pitiful veil of affected good nature, loosely thrown over a spiteful intention, and leaves conjecture to suppose his whole letter, the ebullition of a disappointed author. ('Verax' in the *Morning Chronicle*, 29 Nov. 1775.)

Extempore.

To Mr. SHERIDAN, *on the merited success of his Opera called*

The Duenna

Hail to the bard who writes with grace and ease,
And plainly, by the plainest rules, can please!
The rules of nature, wide and unconfin'd,
As free as air, or as the free-born mind;
No musty plot throughout thy piece prevails,
Stale, aukward, and uncouth, from twice-told tales,
But witty, lively, interesting, new;
Such thy *Duenna*, Sheridan, we view;
No envious critic from thy scene withdraws,
But with the generous many joins applause.
While crowded theatres extol thy fame,
See Royal George himself confirms the same.

('T.S.' in the *Morning Chronicle*, 30 Nov. 1775.)

The alterations in the finale of the new opera of the Duenna, performed for the first time last night before their Majesties, seemed to give universal satisfaction. (*The Gazeteer*, 30 Nov. 1775.)

We hear the Author of the Duenna is determined not to sell the Copy-right of his Opera for less than five hundred Pounds. It is thought that the Purchasers will re-imburse themselves, should they give that Price, in fourteen Years. (*St. James's Chronicle*, 28–30 Nov. 1775.)

I have heard a great deal said of the words of the songs in the Duenna. Now, tho' I admire the music extremely, I own I cannot say as much for the poetry. If I am not a very bad judge, the first object of a song should always be a *simile*: in short a song without a simile is like a play without a plot; the animating principle is wanting, and no graces of thought or language can make it entertaining. Now, throughout the poetry of the *Duenna*, I can find but one simile, and that is a very pretty one about a wreck and a storm in the last song Carlos sings. Yet shall the name of Gay be brought up on this occasion? Gay, who, in his admirable Opera, has scarcely suffered one of his sixty-nine songs to escape without a simile expressed or implied? . . . ('Simon Simile' in the *Morning Chronicle*, 4 Dec. 1775.)

No dramatic piece ever received greater countenance from Royalty than the *Duenna* has. Her Majesty after the first time of seeing it, ordered a copy of the music with the harpsichord part, to be made out for her by Mr. Simpson,[1] and the instance of their commanding it twice successively is unprecedented. (*Morning Chronicle*, 16 Dec. 1775.)

. . . The last Act, however, convinces me that even this Piece has its Faults, and is big with some Absurdities; I mean the Scene and Dress of the Friars in the last Act. Any one the least conversant in Ecclesiastical Reading, or that has ever landed on the Continent, must be sensible that the Jacobins, or Friars, are never dressed in blue; the former wearing a black Habit mixed with white on the fore Part, and the latter either a brown one, as in France, or a black one, as in Italy, or other hot Climates. I not only never heard of Drinking being a Vice the Spaniards, whether Clerical or Secular were addicted to, much less of their ever Toasting, a Ceremony almost banished this Country, I believe, at present, after an uninterrupted Reign of many years. As to the Joke of taking Money to pay for the Dead, I shall not enter into the Merits of the Cause, or examine how far the Custom is founded on Scripture or Tradition; but shall only remark that it is no more worthy of Reprehension in that Country than a Clergyman would be in this, who would take Fees for Christenings, Burials, Marriages. . . . ('Spectator' in *St. James's Chronicle*, 12–14 Dec. 1775.)

The success of this opera as a musical entertainment, would have been very doubtful; but for the very uncommon and distinguished support it received from the richness of the plot, the strong and natural connection and succession of incident, the drollery and contrast of situation, and the humour of the dialogue. Several of the airs are Scotch or Irish; and some of them would have had a much happier effect, if they had been sung in their native stile.

To judge of the Duenna by the rigid rules of criticism, as a regular dramatic composition, would not be acting candidly. The author, by making choice of this species of writing, has given no slender proof of his knowledge of the taste of the town, and of the *dearth* of good comic players; as well as the advantages he must derive, by uniting the lovers of comedy and musick in his favour. By this means the *Duenna* has escaped the censures it might have been liable to on either hand. To the former it presents plot, humour and character; to the latter, many pleasing airs, tender scenes, and amorous *embarras*. Were old Dennis[2] to again revisit the pit of Covent-Garden play-house, he would forgive the improbable incident of the change of clothes between the Duenna and Louisa, which is the point on which the whole business of the opera depends; and join in the laugh, in spite of Aristotle and Bossu; or in the last scene, though

[1] See p. 205 n. [2] John Dennis (1657–1734).

Handel might think very little of the composer, he would postpone the enjoyments of the table, and wait for half an hour to see little Isaac, taunted with a repetition of his boasting expressions of his own superior art and cunning, by his intended father in law, and his very amiable spouse.

. . . we repeat again that we do not wish to try it by the laws and ordinances issued by that great legislator the stagyrite; but this does not preclude us from pronouncing judgment on errors of a lesser nature, which the author *might* by very little industry and attention have avoided. To swear *ore rotundo* on the parade, the St. James's coffee house, at Arthur's, Almack's, or the *scavoir vivre*, may be very graceful during a run of ill-luck, but it does not sound so well on the stage. A little *double entendre* is pretty enough, but gross allusions savour too strongly of the hot-beds in the neighbourhood of the piazza. . . .

These hints are merely suggested to the author, that he may avoid such wanton violations of propriety, when he shall next think proper to write for the stage; his expressions might besides be frequently better chosen, and the humour, though generally arising from character and situation, has not much novelty to recommend it; neither can we see what purpose the bacchanal vespers of the order of St. Anthony can possibly answer; we will venture to say, they are not founded in fact, nor supported by probability. . . . Such a scene might have a very proper effect towards the latter end of King Charles, or during the reign of James the Second, but at present, we think this *pious fraud* totally unnecessary. (*London Magazine*, xlv (1776), 47–8.)

The Managers of the Theatre Royal in Edinburgh, have also advertised their intention of exhibiting some scenes *selected* from the *Duenna*, for the benefit of Mr. Wilkinson, now playing there . . . for a few nights. (*Morning Chronicle*, 1 Mar. 1777.)

The Irish counsel, when the managers of Covent-Garden sued the managers of Dublin, advanced that your *Duenna* was no *piece*, but a collection of *pieces* patched together, which they compared to a *hotch potch* in law; called you a *literary* Taylor, who had formed a Merry Andrew's coat from the shreds and clippings of other men's garments. . . . Nay, one fellow insolently asserted, that your *Duenna* is only a revised and altered piece, originally drawn by a student of Dublin University, and that *he* stole the most striking incidents from an old Irish pantomime. (*Coalition, A Farce*, 1779, p. 3.)

We have more than once seen a dramatic piece from frequency of repetition sink into a state of careless representation, almost beneath contempt; the *Duenna* in particular we recollect to have observed in that condition, even while the whole of the *dramatis personæ* was sustained by those comedians, who originally excited great applause in the respective characters. (*Morning Chronicle*, 16 Oct. 1780.)

The astonishing success of his Duenna led the way to a false taste in our theatres, which was not much improved by the moral of the School for Scandal, pleasing as both those pieces undoubtedly are. (*The British Magazine*, iii (1782–3), 173.)

He produced *The Duenna*—where there is not a single new situation from beginning to end. The whole plot of turning the daughter out of doors, and passing the maid for the mistress, is conjointly the *Sicilienne* of Molière and *Il Filosofo di Campagna*—where every circumstance is to be found, from the serenade at the beginning to the marriage at the end. The other plot is *The Wonder*—which, the moment it is told, must be obvious to every body—because every body knows both pieces. Not even a single subordinate circumstance is original. *Father Paul* is Marmontel's *Philosophe soi disant*—who, as he eats delicacies, talks of the roots of the earth—and, as he drinks burgundy, praises the wholesome chrystal stream. The dialogue is by no means brilliant, but Mr. Sheridan was determined it should penetrate every where, and in particular the *aside* speeches of *Isaac*—shewing beforehand how clearly he shall himself be taken in by his different attempts to deceive others, is the most artful species of anticipation that ever was practised, and shews a judgment of theatrical effect powerful, new, and extraordinary. (*The Musical Tour of Mr. Dibdin* (Sheffield, 1788), p. 260.)

The Duenna: an Opera in Three Acts, is justly an admired and esteemed piece—The language of the songs, is both lofty and energetic: the characters well finished, particularly that of the Jew, which is highly drawn—The scene between him and the Duenna is truly comic. The fault in this piece is, the mistake is discovered too soon; and the under plot is not sufficient to keep curiosity alive, when the old man turns his daughter out of doors: It is, however, an excellent piece, though inferior to *Lionel and Clarissa*; yet far beyond the generality of operas, which are continually performing. (*The Thespian Magazine and Literary Repository*, i (1792), 16.)

I believe few have seen the Duenna, when well acted, without pleasure; and I believe as few have read it with pleasure. A good actor may make something both of the incidents and the dialogue; but in the closet, 'little Isaac' is almost as dull as the unaccountable appendage Don Carlos. As a vehicle for songs, however, it may be so so, as times go: but alas! is it from the author of the School for Scandal that we ought to expect *more vehicles*. ([Lady Ann Hatton?], *The Epics of the Ton*, 2nd edn., 1807, p. 195, n.)

The Duenna is unrivalled among modern operas, for the elegance of its language and the natural and simple succession of the plot. The songs are not forced upon the parts; and the fortunate thought of selecting popular tunes, which no one then or since, ever heard without true musical delight, furnished the excellence of a production which was conceived and produced in the happiest moment of genius. (*The Times*, 21 Sept. 1811.)

The Duenna is a perfect work of art. It has the utmost sweetness and point. The plot, the characters, the dialogue, are all complete in themselves, and they are all his own; and the songs are the best that ever were written, except those in the Beggar's Opera. They have a joyous spirit of intoxication in them, and a strain of the most melting tenderness. Compare the softness of that beginning,

'Had I a heart for falsehood framed,'

with the spirited defiance to Fortune in the lines,

'Half thy malice youth could bear,
And the rest a bumper drown.'

(W. Hazlitt, *Lectures on the English Comic Writers* (1819), pp. 336–7.)

When I first began life, the world was thinking and talking of nothing but the Duenna and the School for Scandal. With what enjoyment, with what glistening eyes and eagerness of delight, did I listen at the theatre of Liverpool, to Quick in the character of little Isaac, the tones of his voice, that were so irresistibly comic, conveying in the most perfect manner all the wit and humour of his sarcasms on the antiquated Duenna. ([W. Smyth], *Memoir of Mr. Sheridan*, Leeds (1840), p. 6.)

CHOICE OF TEXT

The Duenna was one of the most successful theatrical entertainments of the century, and naturally attracted the attention of music sellers and actors who wanted to make use of the text. This is best indicated in an unnoted passage from Parke:

Musical copyright at that time not being so well defined as it is now, an adventurer opened a shop in Long Acre[1] for the sale of the pirated edition of the songs in 'The Duenna', executed on a cheap plan. These were sold at so low a price as fourpence each; and the demand for them was so great, that I have seen the door besieged by a crowd of purchasers from morning till night; and what with the rapidity of the sale and the law's delay, the pirate had gained a considerable sum before he could be restrained.[2]

This is confirmed in the *Daily Advertiser*, 7 March 1776, where a printer named Robert Falkener of Peterborough Court, offered eight of the songs at a penny a page. Sheridan had already entered *The Duenna* in the Stationers' Register on 2 March, and now, with Thompson, the authorized music seller, brought a case against Falkener, stating that the overture and eleven songs had been published by the pirate. Falkener replied that

[1] Bland's, no. 114.

[2] W. T. Parke, *Musical Memoirs* (1830), ii. 138.

some of the music had been printed twenty-eight years earlier, and that his profits were 'trifling and inconsiderable'.[1] What happened after this is not clear from the available evidence, but it is likely that Sheridan and Thompson were able to protect their own interests.[2]

It was more difficult to protect the rest of the text. Sheridan sold it to Harris,[3] who took very good care of it but was unable to stop clandestine performances and printings. In Dublin, different managers, Ryder and Vandermere, put on versions of the opera, and called them *The Governess* in the one case and *The Duenna* in the other. Both were corrupt texts, badly put together, but Vandermere's *The Duenna* seemed more of an affront than Ryder's *The Governess*. The managers of Covent Garden Theatre, therefore, took action against Vandermere to secure an injunction to prevent him giving further performances. It was refused on the ground that any man might repeat what was already made public, but the Lord Chancellor made clear that his words bore only on the matter of acting. After that decision, pirated versions were performed and published in Ireland without much challenge.[4]

What is more extraordinary is that a pirated version was in use in one of the London theatres.[5] The reason is to be found in the fact that the authorized text was very closely guarded at Covent Garden, and only acted elsewhere as a considerable favour. The advertisement of a performance at Bristol Theatre on 13 July noted that it had never been performed there before, and would now be given for one night only for the benefit of Quick. When it was repeated in August,[6] the advertisement stated that it was given 'by permission of the Proprietors of the Piece'.

[1] See Howard P. Vincent, 'An Attempted Piracy of *The Duenna*', *M.L.N.* lxii (1947), 268–70, and his quotations from the Bill of Complaint (C 12/1355/14) of 18 Apr. 1776, in the Public Record Office.

[2] Though provincial printers could probably escape their vigilance. For example, *Chester Chronicle*, 31 Oct. 1777, printed the following advertisement: 'Books of the songs of *The Duenna*, to be had of J. Monk, Printer . . . and at the doors of the Theatre, at two-pence each.'

[3] 'The comic opera of the Duenna is not to be published; the managers of Covent-garden house having bought the literary property of it, to prevent its exhibition at any other Theatre' (*General Evening Post*, 5–7 Dec. 1775). Cf. p. 210, above.

[4] Yesterday se'nnight the great question concerning literary property, received a final decision in the Court of Chancery in Ireland. The matter in debate was the favourite opera called the Duenna, which the Managers of Covent-garden alledged they had purchased from Richard Brinsley Sheridan, Esq; the author, for a certain stipulated sum. . . . [They] complained against John Byron Vandermere and his partners, adventurers in the new theatre in Fishamble-street, Dublin, for having exhibited on their stage the said piece . . . and prayed that they might be restrained and injoined from printing, publishing, or acting said piece. . . . The Lord Chancellor delivered his sentiments on the whole, viz. that the injunction sought by the plaintiffs to restrain the acting or exhibiting the piece ought not to be granted. . . .' (*The Gazetteer*, 3 May 1777).

[5] See p. 4, above.

[6] Felix Farley's *Bristol Journal*, 11 July, 22 Aug. 1778.

Tate Wilkinson, manager of the York Theatre, made up the deficiency by manufacturing a text in his own peculiar way:

The fashion of not publishing is quite modern, and the favourite pieces not being printed, but kept under lock and key, is of infinite prejudice to us poor devils in the country theatres, as we really cannot afford to pay[1] for the purchase of MSS.—The only time I ever exercised my pen on such an occasion was on a trial of necessity. Mr. Harris bought that excellent comic opera of the Duenna from Mr. Sheridan. I saw it several times, and finding it impossible to move Mr. Harris's tenderness, I locked myself up in my room, set[2] down first the jokes I remembered, then I laid the book of the songs before me, and with magazines kept the regulation of the scenes, and by the help of a numerous collection of obsolete Spanish plays I produced an excellent opera; I may say *excellent*—and an unprecedented compilement; for whenever Mr. Younger,[3] or any other country manager wanted a copy of the Duenna, Mr. Harris told them they might play Mr. Wilkinson's: hundreds have seen it in every town in Great-Britain and Ireland.[4]

It is impossible to tell how far Wilkinson's version was the basis of *The Governess* and Vandermere's *Duenna*, but if Wilkinson is to be believed it was very popular and widely enjoyed. The outcome, then, of Harris's policy of restriction was that he preserved the authentic version at Covent Garden until 1794, but that the comic opera was known to most people outside London through seeing Wilkinson's feeble version or reading the equally poor adaptations, Ryder's *The Governess* and Vandermere's *The Duenna*.[5]

The following versions may be considered as being worth study:

I. OF THE SONGS

On 21 November 1775, the very day of the first performance of *The Duenna*, the *Public Advertiser* printed the following:

This Afternoon, at Five, will be published, Price Sixpence, THE Airs, Duets, Trios, and Chorusses in the new Comic Opera of the DUENNA; or, The Double Elopement, to be performed This Evening, for the first Time, at the Theatre Royal, Covent Garden.

Printed for J. Wilkie, No. 71, St. Paul's Church-yard; and T. Evans, No. 50, in the Strand.

[1] Cf. the entry in the Covent Garden account books for 2 Feb. 1789, of £30 from the Norwich theatre manager for permission to act *The Highland Reel*, quoted by C. B. Hogan, *The London Stage, 1776–1800. A Critical Introduction* (Carbondale and London, 1968), p. clxxxi.

[2] Printed as 'sat'.

[3] Manager of Birmingham, Liverpool, and Manchester theatres.

[4] *Memoirs of His Own Life* (York, 1790), ii. 230. Cf. p. 212 above.

[5] For editions of *The Governess*, published in 1777, 1788, 1793, and the pirated *Duenna* of 1783, 1785, and 1786, see Rhodes, i. 272–3. G. F. Taylor's Ph.D. thesis, pp. 202–15, includes some other editions, also.

The title-page of this first edition reads:

> SONGS, DUETS, | TRIOS, &c. | IN THE | DUENNA; | OR, THE | DOUBLE ELOPEMENT. | AS PERFORMED AT THE | THEATRE-ROYAL | IN | COVENT-GARDEN. | [Double rule] | LONDON: | Printed for J. WILKIE in St. Paul's Church-Yard, and | T. EVANS in the Strand. | M,DCC,LXXV. | [Price Six-Pence.]

Collation: 8vo. in half-sheets: $[A]^2$ $B–C^4$ D^2.

Contents: pp. [iv]+20.

[i] title; [ii] blank; [iii] Dramatis Personæ; [iv] blank; 1–20, text.

Only the words were printed. Less than a year later, the *London Chronicle* advertised the publication of the eighteenth edition.[1]

2. OF THE MUSIC

The musical accompaniments to the songs were partly original and partly adapted. Thomas Linley, senior and junior, Jackson of Exeter, Michael Arne, Rauzzini, and William Hayes, were among the contributors.[2]

Charles and Samuel Thompson, the London music publishers, bought the music copyright from Sheridan for £150, with a further fifty if the comic opera ran for thirty nights, and another thirty if it ran for sixty. Sheridan's receipt for £200 is extant.[3]

An advertisement of the publication that day appeared in the *Public Advertiser*, 23 December 1775. On 31 December, Sheridan wrote to his father-in-law, Thomas Linley, saying: 'I have had some books of the music these many days to send you down. I wanted to put Tom's name in the new music, and begged Mrs. L. to ask you, and let me have a line on

[1] 8–10 Oct. 1776. *The Daily Advertiser*, 4 May 1776, advertised the fifteenth edition, a quarto, 'embellished with a Frontispiece, designed by G. B. Cipriani, engraved by F. Bartolozzi'.

[2] See J. S. Gaudry's transcriptions in Egerton MS. 2493, ff. 58–88; C. Black, *The Linleys of Bath* (new edn., 1926), p. 110; G. F. Taylor's Ph.D. thesis, pp. 63–79; Roger Fiske, 'A Score for *The Duenna*', *Music and Letters*, xlii (1961), 132–41; Gwilym Beechey, 'Thomas Linley, Junior, 1756–1778', *The Musical Quarterly*, liv (1968), 74–82.

[3] The Puttick and Simpson sale catalogue, 20 July 1846, lot 342, contains a 'receipt dated 1776 for £200 for the songs and music in the Duenna'. One in A. Edward Newton's possession was transcribed as: 'Recd 25 March 1776 of Mess C and S Thompson fifty Pounds, which together with One Hundred and fifty pounds *Paid before* makes the sum of two Hundred pounds and is in full of all Demands for the Songs and Musick in the Comic Op. of the Duenna. Richard Brinsley Sheridan.' See Parke-Bernet sale catalogue (New York), 29–30 October 1941, lot 264. The amount named is considerably smaller than that described by Thomas Wilkie in 1818: 'Sheridan had agreed for the music with (I forget the name of the music seller) at £30 for every three successive nights, and made a good deal of money by it' (Moore, *Journal*, ii. 160).

her arrival, for which purpose I kept back the index of the songs. If you or he have no objection, pray, let me know.—I'll send the music to-morrow.'[1] But Linley had resolved from the start that their names should not appear.[2]

The title-page of the first edition reads:

> *THE* | DUENNA | *or* | *Double Elopement*, | a | *COMIC-OPERA* | *As performed at the Theatre Royal in Covent Garden* | for the | VOICE, HARPSICHORD, or VIOLIN. | Price 10^{s}-6. | *London, Printed for C. and S. THOMPSON, N°. 75, S^{t}. Paul's Church Yard.*

Oblong folio. Both title-page and music are engraved.

Contents:

> [i] title; [ii] blank; [iii] 'A Table of the Songs in the Comic Opera of the Duenna'; [iv] blank; [1] blank, 2–58, music and words.

3. OF THE COMIC OPERA

(i) *The 'Rough Copy'*

The earliest draft appears to be that mentioned by Moore: 'It does not appear, from the rough copy in my possession, that any material change was made in the plan of the work, as it proceeded. Carlos was originally meant to be a Jew, and is called "Cousin Moses" by Isaac, in the first sketch of the dialogue; but, possibly, from the consideration that this would apply too personally to Leoni, who was to perform the character, its designation was altered.'[3] Moore's extract from this 'rough copy' has already been quoted. From the fact that he ends with 'etc., etc., etc.', we may reasonably conclude that he might have printed much more. Unfortunately, these manuscripts have not been seen (or, at any rate, described) since he published his brief description of them in 1825.

(ii) *The Frampton Court MS.*

Rae transcribed the version at Frampton Court,[4] warning his readers that 'the manuscript is incomplete, and I have had to fill up gaps from the current versions'.[5] It is a pity that he was not more specific since we depend so much on him for our knowledge of this early text. Nevertheless, he gave us some guidance in a few footnotes. When he came to Louisa's air, 'Thou canst not boast of fortune's store', he added: ' "Song" was written here and the pen was drawn through it. The words were not added; these now given are taken from a printed version.'[6] He points out that 'several sheets of the manuscript' from II. i onwards, are in Mrs. Sheridan's handwriting, but also notes that the song 'When a tender maid' had been copied out by Sheridan himself.[7] The passage about Moses making himself out to be

[1] *Letters*, i. 95.
[2] *Garrick Corr.*, ii. 101.
[3] Moore, i. 169–70.
[4] Rae, pp. 97–146.
[5] Ibid., p. xxxv.
[6] Ibid., p. 103.
[7] Ibid., pp. 113, 118.

only a year old,[1] was now revised and given to Isaac. The joke was to be excised from the printed texts, and the lines about Isaac's mother were severely cut. Rae went on to observe that in II. iv, 'the handwriting is Sheridan's and the ink is red',[2] and that several sheets of the manuscript were missing from the beginning of Act III to the duet at the end of Scene vi.[3] From that last point onwards, he appears to be transcribing from the manuscript.

Collation suggests that Rae supplied missing lines from the Inchbald text.

When Walter Sichel saw the Frampton Court MS. some years later, there was less of it to read. He described it as 'contained in a copybook, on the back of which is a rough sketch of a sea-battle. The third act is missing. The first act is in Sheridan's hand, the second in his wife's. The manuscript ends with his song of "A bumper of good liquor".'[4] This tallies in part with the description in Sotheby's Catalogue, 2 July 1930, of lot 634: '... Autograph MS., comprising a part of Act I, and consisting of 52 pp., 4to.; Act II, consisting of 39 pp. in the hand of Mrs. Sheridan, with numerous additions and corrections by the author.' It appears to have been bought in at the sale, and, as already mentioned, was later lost at sea.[5]

The Sotheby catalogue includes a photograph of the first page of the lost manuscript. It reveals that Sheridan carefully indicated the setting of the first scene: 'A Piaza before Don Jerome's House—The morning breaking—Clock strikes 3. Enter MANUEL from the House with a Dark Lantern in his Hand.' This and the rest of the page are accurately transcribed by Rae (p. 97). The twelve lines on 'haughty damsels' are also printed by him, as well as by Moore, i. 172–3.

(iii) *The Lord Chamberlain's Copy*

A copy of the play would have been required by law for submission to the Lord Chamberlain's examiner, but the manuscript has never been located.

(iv) *The Text of the First Performance*

This, too, has not been found. I have argued[6] that it was closer to Rae's transcription than to the text of 1794, and based this idea on some newspaper criticisms of 'a few coarsenesses': '... the threatening to send home Margaret's property in a frank; the story Isaac tells of his mother; and some of the repetitions of the description of Margaret's ordinary face.' The *Morning Post* recommended that 'the reflection on the legitimacy of our nobility' be omitted.[7] These references are all to lines that are in Rae, but not in other versions.

[1] See p. 196, above. [2] Rae, p. 124. [3] Ibid., p. 129.

[4] Sichel, i. 506, n. Clearly II. iv, the last part of III. vi, and the whole of III. vii, had been lost recently. [5] See p. 23.

[6] 'The text of the first performance of *The Duenna*', *P.B.S.A.* iii (1960), 268–70.

[7] See p. 208, and p. 258, lines 10–11.

(v) *Folger MS. D. a.* 48

The Folger text is close to Rae's transcription, though it is also frequently corrupt. It is copied out in a small, neat hand in a volume of prompt copies of the following plays: G. S. Carey's *Old Women Weatherwise*, Foote's *Piety in Pattens*, Garrick's *Harlequin's Invasion*, Macklin's *Love à la Mode*, and, lastly (pp. 125–71), *The Duenna*. The fly-leaf bears the inscription, 'Isabella Downman[1] presented by Mr. Rietti 1812', but it is not in the handwriting of the copyist of the manuscript. It may be of interest to note that one Rietti was concerned with James Lacy of Drury Lane Theatre, in the purchase of Ranelagh in 1733.[2] The manuscript may have belonged to a descendant of his.

(vi) *Printed at Kingston, Jamaica*

The Duenna was performed at Kingston on 27 November 1779, by Hallam's company. Two days later the *Jamaica Mercury* advertised that the comic opera would be published 'and sold at the New Printing Office in Harbour-Street and at the shop of W. Aikman in King Street (Price 3s. 9d.)'.[3] It added:

> The very extraordinary merit of this Opera (which was acted 74 nights successively the first season, and repeated every winter since oftener than any piece that ever appeared on the stage) induced the proprietors to decline printing it, in order to increase the avidity of the Public for its frequent representation, and the copy now offered for sale is the only edition in print, except a very incorrect one that crept into the world in Dublin, under the title of 'The Governess', mangled, hackt and alter'd, in order to avoid the penalty of the acts of parliament for securing literary property.[4]

The text is said to have been published on 4 December,[4] but I have not been able to trace a copy. From the rather self-righteous tone of the statement, I assume, perhaps mistakenly, that this was the authentic version, but how it was obtained I cannot tell.

(vii) *The First Authorized Edition*

For the title-page, see p. 227 below.

Collation: 8vo. in half-sheets: [A][2] B–K4.

Contents: [iv]+9–78.

[5] title; [6] blank; [7] 'Dramatis Personæ'; [8] blank; [9] and 10–78, text; [79 and 80] blank.

[1] John Downman, A.R.A., had a daughter Isabella (1797–1840), who married Richard Benjamin of Wrexham and is buried there.

[2] Cf. Mollie Sands, *Ranelagh* (1946), p. 16.

[3] Quoted by Richardson Wright, *Revels in Jamaica* (New York, 1937), p. 99.

[4] Ibid., p. 100.

There are only four pages of preliminaries, though the page numbers allow for eight.[1]

There is another issue of this edition in which the title-page is a cancel, omitting the price and inserting 'Printed by G. Woodfall Paternoster-Row' before 'for T. N. Longman'. The texts are from the same setting of type.

The edition appears to have been printed from the Covent Garden prompt-book. It is unlikely that Sheridan revised the text in 1794.

(viii) *Mrs. Inchbald's Edition*

Messrs. Longman's records show that *The Duenna* and a miscellaneous collection of twenty-five other plays were bought from Thomas Harris by Longman in 1800 for £420.[2]

Possibly they were used as the basis of *The British Theatre*, which Longman published under Mrs. Inchbald's editorship from 1806 onwards. *The Duenna* appeared in the nineteenth volume (1808). It is a good acting edition, carefully prepared and reprinted.

Its title-page reads:

> THE DUENNA; | A COMIC OPERA, | IN THREE ACTS; | BY RICHARD BRINSLEY SHERIDAN, ESQ. | AS PERFORMED AT THE THEATRES ROYAL, | DRURY LANE AND COVENT GARDEN. | PRINTED UNDER THE AUTHORITY OF THE MANAGERS | FROM THE PROMPT BOOK. | WITH REMARKS | BY MRS. INCHBALD. | [Short rule] | LONDON: | PRINTED FOR LONGMAN, HURST, REES, AND ORME, | PATERNOSTER ROW.

Collation: 12mo.: [A] B–G^6 H.

> The inserted frontispiece is an engraving by Stewart and Burnet after a painting by Singleton, illustrating Ferdinand's confusion in III, vi; or may be one by Heath after Cobould's drawing of Father Paul in III. v.

Contents: pp. 74.

> [1] title-page; [2] 'William Savage, Printer, London.'; [3]–5, 'Remarks'; 6, 'Dramatis Personæ'; 7–74, text.

The text is usually very close to that of 1794,[3] but departs from it in making corrections inspired either by the copy purchased in 1800 or by commonsense. It also omits 'What bard, O time discover', printed in 1794; and prints another song, 'How oft, Louisa', omitted in 1794.

(ix) *Printed by Longworth, New York, 1808*

This, too, is close to the first edition of 1794 in most of its readings, but also shows occasional affinity with the Rae and Folger texts, as in p. 234, l. 15; p. 244, l. 33; p. 260, l. 14; and p. 276, l. 32 below.

[1] For the bibliographical points, see Williams, p. 230; Wise, v. 155.
[2] I am indebted to the late Cyprian Blagden for this piece of information.
[3] Even omitting 'think' on p. 241, l. 14 below.

It also includes the text of three songs not printed in 1794, the most notable being 'Shall not my soul'.[1]

The title-page reads:

> THE | DUENNA. | A | Comic Opera. | *IN THREE ACTS.* | [short orn. rule] | *BY R. B. SHERIDAN, ESQ.* | [short orn. rule] | *As performed at* | THE THEATRES COVENT-GARDEN AND NEW-YORK. | *SECOND EDITION.* | [Between rules] *From the original prompt book—by permission.* | NEW-YORK: | PUBLISHED BY DAVID LONGWORTH, | At the Dramatic Repository, | *Shakspeare Gallery* [short swelled rule] | 1808.

Collation: 8vo.: [A]^4 B–C^6 D–E^8 [F]^4.

Contents: pp. 72.

> [1] half-title, 'The Duenna. Price 25 Cents.'; [2] blank; [3] title; [4] 'Dramatis Personæ.'; [5] and 6–72, text.

Conclusion

As far as accidentals go, it is likely that the Frampton Court MS. was closer to Sheridan's practices than any other available text, but the manuscript is not now extant and there are good reasons for rejecting Rae's transcription as copy-text. We cannot assess from it the 'numerous additions and corrections' of the original, and the portion copied from Sheridan's handwriting is a comparatively small part of the whole.

The edition of 1794 is the first of the authentic version and I propose to use it as copy-text, and to admit into it readings from Rae, Inchbald, Longworth, or the Folger edition, where they appear to correct errors or even to make better sense. I have introduced missing songs into the text, not because they were all presented on the first night, but because I assume that Sheridan would have included them in any final edition.

While printing most variants, I have omitted some that I now mention. Sheridan seems to have written 'Anthonio' in the Frampton Court MS., and the same spelling is to be found in *Songs, Duets*. In Rae's transcript, too, titles are more frequently used than elsewhere, but I have omitted 'Don', 'Donna', and 'Father' unless they are repeated in other versions. Sheridan appears, from Rae, to have been occasionally confused about Clara and Luisa. In six places (pp. 232, l. 21, 23; 234, l. 10, 13, 15, 23, below), Luisa in Rae, is Clara in the other texts. In two lines (pp. 234, l. 18, and 241, l. 11), Clara in Rae is Louisa in the others. The change from 'Gusman' in Rae to 'Pedro' (p. 232, l. 211), like 'd'Ercilla' becoming 'd'Arcilla' (p. 267, l. 15) in the Folger manuscript, has no particular significance. I have omitted the prompt copy markings in the Folger manuscript, and stage directions like 'thro' the Doors' (p. 237, l. 41) and 'Enter thro' Flatt' (p. 260, l. 30).

[1] It also reads 'Porter' for 'Lay-Brother' in III. v, and it is significant that the *London Chronicle*, 21–23 Nov. 1775, gives him as 'Porter' in the cast-list. Clearly some of this text's variants come from a very early source.

The following spellings in the 1794 edition have been silently corrected: 'T'll' (p. 234, l. 4), 'tyrannaical' (p. 239, l. 9), 'persume' (p. 239, l. 20), may'nt (p. 247, l. 12), 'you' (p. 254, l. 21), 'inofrmation' (p. 272, l. 7), 'know h r' (p. 272, l. 13).

The following abbreviations are used in the textual notes:

Rae	Rae, pp. 97–146.
F	Folger MS. D.a.48.
94	The first edition (London, 1794).
I	Mrs. Inchbald's edition in *The British Theatre*, xix.
NY	Longworth's second edition (New York, 1808).
Songs	*Songs, Duets, Trios, etc. in The Duenna* (1775).
Th	*The Duenna . . . for the Voice, Harpsichord, or Violin . . . Printed for C. and S. Thompson. . . .*
G	J. S. Gaudry's transcription in Egerton MS. 2493, ff. 58–88.

THE DUENNA

THE

DUENNA:

A COMIC OPERA.

IN THREE ACTS.

AS PERFORMED AT THE

THEATRE ROYAL,

COVENT GARDEN:

WITH UNIVERSAL APPLAUSE.

By R. B. SHERIDAN, Esq

LONDON.

Printed for T. N. LONGMAN, No. 39, Pater Noster Row.

[PRICE EIGHTEEN-PENCE]

1794.

DRAMATIS PERSONÆ

ORIGINAL CAST OF CHARACTERS, 1775[1]

DON JEROME	Mr. Wilson
FERDINAND	Mr. Mattocks
ANTONIO	Mr. Du Bellamy
CARLOS	Mr. Leoni
ISAAC MENDOZA	Mr. Quick
FATHER PAUL	Mr. Mahon
LOPEZ	Mr. Wewitzer
LEWIS	Mr. Castevens
LOUISA	Mrs. Mattocks
CLARA	Miss Brown
MARGARET (*the Duenna*)	Mrs. Green

[1] To this list of performers at the first representation at Covent Garden Theatre on 21 Nov. 1775, we may add 'Augustin', Mr. Baker; 'Francis', Mr. Fox; 'Porter', Mr. Besford; as well as 'Friars, Servants, Masks'. Folger MS. D.a. 48 describes the extra characters as Francis and Augustine, fathers of the Convent of St. Catherine, Lay Brother, four other fathers, a nun, a maid servant to Louisa, 1st and 2nd Masks, and other Masks.

THE DUENNA:

AN OPERA

ACT I

SCENE I—A STREET

Enter LOPEZ, *with a dark Lanthorn.*

LOPEZ. Past three o'clock! soh! a notable hour for one of my regular disposition to be strolling like a bravo thro' the streets of Seville; well, of all services, to serve a young lover is the hardest—not that I am an enemy to love; but my love and my master's differ strangely—Don Ferdinand is much too gallant to eat, drink or sleep—now, my love gives me an appetite—then I am fond of dreaming of my mistress, and I love dearly to toast her—This cannot be done without good sleep, and good liquor, hence my partiality to a feather bed, and a bottle—what a pity now, that I have not further time for reflections; but thy master expects thee, honest Lopez, to secure his retreat from Donna Clara's window, as I guess [*Music without*] hey! sure I heard music! so! so! who have we here? Oh, Don Antonio, my master's friend, come from the Masquerade to serenade my young mistress, Donna Louisa, I suppose! soh! we shall have the old gentleman up presently—lest he shou'd miss his son, I had best lose no time in getting to my post.
[*Exit.*

Enter ANTONIO, *with Masks and Music.*

ANTONIO.—SONG.—[*Soft Sym.*]

Tell me, my lute, can thy fond strain
So gently speak thy master's pain;
So softly sing, so humbly sigh,
That tho' my sleeping love shall know

4 I—A STREET] *94*, *I*, *NY*; *1st:—| A Piazza: Jerome's House. Clock strikes 3 F*; *for Rae*, *see* p. 219 above. 5 *Enter . . . Lanthorn*] *94*, *I*, *NY*; *Enter Lopez F*; *for Rae*, see p. 219. 8 hardest] *94*, *I*, *NY*; hardest—truly a prudent Domestick would do well to make a Clause in favour of double Wages when his Master shall think proper to fall in Love. *Rae*, *F* 9 but] *94*, *I*, *NY*; but then *F*; *om. Rae* 10 my] *94*, *I*, *NY*, *F*; for my part *Rae* 14 further . . . reflections] *Rae*, *94*, *I*, *NY*; time for further reflections *F* thy *F*, *NY*; my *94*, *Rae*, *I* 16 *without*] *94*, *I*, *NY*; *om. Rae*, *F* 19 lest] *Rae*, *F*, *I*; least *NY*, *94* 22 *with . . . Music*] *94*, *NY*, *I*; and Masks with Music *Rae*; & Masks *F* 24 fond] *Rae*, *F*, *Songs*, *Th*; soft *94*, *G*, *I*, *NY* 25 speak] *Rae*, *F*, *Songs*, *94*, *I*, *NY*, *Th*; tell *G* 26 softly] *Rae*, *F*, *Songs*, *94*, *I*, *NY*; sweetly *G*, *Th*

Who sings—who sighs below.
Her rosy slumbers shall not fly?
Thus may some vision whisper more
Than ever I dare speak before.

IST MASK. Antonio, your mistress will never wake while you sing so dolefully; love, like a cradled infant, is lull'd by a sad melody.

ANTONIO. I do not wish to disturb her rest.

IST MASK. The reason is, because you know she does not regard you enough, to appear if you waked her.

ANTONIO. Nay, then I'll convince you.

SINGS

The breath of morn bids hence the night,
Unveil those beauteous eyes, my fair,
For till the dawn of love is there,
I feel no day, I own no light.

LOUISA *replies from a Window.*

Waking I heard thy numbers chide,
Waking, the dawn did bless my sight,
'Tis Phœbus sure that woos, I cried,
Who speaks in song, who moves in light.

DON JEROME *from a Window.*

What vagabonds are these I hear
Fid[d]ling, fluting, rhyming, ranting,
Piping, scraping, whining, canting,
Fly, scurvy minstrels, fly.

TRIO

LOUISA. Nay, prythee, father, why so rough,
ANT. An humble lover I,
JER. How durst you daughter lend an ear
To such deceitful stuff?
Quick from the window fly.

6 by a] *Rae*, *94*, *I*, *NY*; by *F* 9 waked] *Rae*, *94*, *NY*; should wake *F*; awaked *I* 12 breath of morn] *F*, *Songs*, *NY*, *I*; breadth of morn *94*; crimson Dawn *Rae*; crimson morn *Th* 14 For] *F*, *Rae*, *Songs*, *I*; Nor *94*, *NY* dawn] *F*, *Songs*, *94*, *I*, *NY*; morn *Rae* 16 *from a*] *94*, *I*, *NY*; from the *Rae*, *F* 21 *from a*] *94*, *I*, *NY*; appears at another, *Rae*, *F* 25 Fly] *F*, *94*, *I*, *Songs*, *NY*, *Th*; Hence *Rae* 27 Nay,] *F*, *94*, *Songs*, *I*, *NY*.; *om. Rae* 29 How . . . daughter] *F*, *94*, *Songs*, *I*, *NY*, *Th*; Daughter how durst *Rae* 31 Quick . . . fly] *94*, *I*, *NY*, *Rae*, *Th*; Quick . . . fly. (*disappears*) *F*

LOUISA. Adieu, Antonio!
ANT. Must you go?
LOUISA.} We soon perhaps, may meet again
ANT.} For tho' hard fortune is our foe,
The god of love will fight for us.
JER. Reach me the Blunderbuss.
ANT. & LOU. The god of love, who knows our pain,
JER. Hence, or these slugs are thro' your brain. [*Exeunt severally.*

SCENE II.—*A* PIAZZA

Enter FERDINAND *and* LOPEZ.

LOPEZ. Truly, sir, I think that a little sleep once in a week or so.

FERD. Peace fool, don't mention sleep to me.

LOPEZ. No, no, sir, I don't mention your low-bred, vulgar, sound sleep; but I can't help thinking that a genteel slumber, or half an hour's dozing, if it were only for the novelty of the thing.

FERD. Peace, booby, I say. O Clara, dear, cruel disturber of my rest.

LOPEZ. And of mine too.

FERD. S'death! to trifle with me at such a juncture as this—now to stand on punctilios—love me! I don't believe she ever did.

LOPEZ. Nor I either.

FERD. Or is it that her sex never know their desires for an hour together.

LOPEZ. Ah, they know them oftner than they'll own them.

FERD. Is there in the world so inconsistent a creature as Clara?

LOPEZ. I cou'd name one.

FERD. Yes; the tame fool who submits to her caprice.

LOPEZ. I thought he coudn't miss it.

FERD. Is she not capricious, teizing, tyrannical, obstinate, perverse, absurd, ay, a wilderness of faults and follies, her looks are scorn, and her very smiles—s'death! I wish I hadn't mention'd her smiles; for she does smile such beaming loveliness, and fascinating brightness—O death and madness, I shall die if I lose her.

LOPEZ. O those damn'd smiles have undone all.

6 Reach] *F*, *94*, *Songs*, *NY*, *Th*, *I*; Get *Rae* 8 are thro'] *Rae*, *F*, *94*, *I*, *NY*, *Songs*; in *Th* 8 *Exeunt severally*] *94*, *I*, *NY*; *Exe. Anth. and Masks and Don Jer. and Clara from the window Rae*; *Ext Anto: &c F* 9 II.—*A* PIAZZA] *94*, *I*, *NY*; 2d A Street *Rae*; *2d Piazza F* 10 *Enter . . .* LOPEZ] *F*, *94*, *I*, *NY*; Enter Ferdinand and Manuel *Rae* 13 mention] *94*, *I*, *NY*, *F*; recommend *Rae* 14 genteel] *Rae*, *F*; gentle *94*, *I*, *NY* 21 is it] *94*, *I*, *NY*; else *F*; is *Rae* know] *Rae*, *94*, *I*, *NY*; knew *F* 23 inconsistent] *Rae*, *F*; inconstant *94*, *I*, *NY* 26 it.] *94*, *F*, *I*, *NY*; it. | *Ferd.* By my Life now it were justice to renounce her for ever! | *Man.* I was always of that opinion *Rae* 28 absurd] *94*, *I*, *NY*; absurd | *Lop.* Yes, very. *F*; absurd | *Man.* Yes—yes—a very wilderness of Faults and Follies *Rae* 29 for] *94*, *I*, *NY*; for when *Rae*, *F* 30 and] *Rae*, *F*; such *94*, *I*, *NY* 31 and] *94*, *F*, *I*, *NY*; *om. Rae* 32 O] *94*, *F*, *I*, *NY*; Ah! *Rae*

AIR

FERDINAND.

Could I her faults remember,
  Forgetting ev'ry charm,
Soon would impartial reason
  The tyrant love disarm.
But when enraged I number
  Each failing of her mind,
Love still suggests her beauty,
  And sees—while reason's blind.

LOPEZ. Here comes Don Antonio, sir.

FERD. Well, go you home—I shall be there presently.

LOPEZ. Ah those curst smiles. [*Exit.*

Enter ANTONIO.

FERD. Antonio, Lopez tells me he left you chaunting before our door—was my father wak'd?

ANT. Yes, yes; he has a singular affection for music, so I left him roaring at his barr'd window like the print of Bajazet in the cage. And what brings you out so early?

FERD. I believe I told you that to-morrow was the day fix'd by Don Pedro and Clara's unnatural step-mother, for her to enter a Convent, in order that her brat might possess her fortune, made desperate by this, I procur'd a key to the door, and brib'd Clara's maid to leave it unbolted; at two this morning I entered, unperceived, and stole to her chamber—I found her waking and weeping.

ANT. Happy Ferdinand!

FERD. S'death, hear the conclusion—I was rated as the most confident ruffian, for daring to approach her room at that hour of night.

ANT. Ay, ay, this was at first.

FERD. No such thing! she wou'd not hear a word from me, but threat'ned to raise her father if I did not instantly leave her.

3 her faults] *Rae, 94, F, I, NY, Songs*; each fault *G, Th* 8 Each failing] *Rae, 94, F, NY, I, Songs*; the failings *G, Th* 9 her] *Rae, F, Songs, Th, G*; each *94, I, NY* 10 while] *Rae, F, NY, 94, I, Songs*; whilst *G* 13 Ah] *Rae, 94, I, NY*; Oh *F* *Two speeches are added in Rae after line 14*: *Anth:* Ferdinand—! Soh! another troubled spirit come from hovering round the walls that entomb his mistress and sculking from Daybreak—| *Ferd.* A troubled spirit indeed of one inhumanly murder'd by—a barbarous Disappointment!—but Manuel tells 18 window] *94, I, NY, F*; *om. Rae* And] *94, I, NY*; but *Rae, F* 19 brings . . . early] *94, F, I, NY*; no festal Disappointment I hope: | *Ferd.* Worse than ever was outlived by a Lover before—I am just returned from Luisa's bedchamber—| *Anth.* What then 'tis *she* that's Disappointed—*Rae* 26 Happy Ferdinand!] *94, F, I, NY*; *om. Rae* 27–8 S'death . . . night] *F, 94, I, NY*; *om. Rae* 30 thing . . . but] *F, 94, I, NY*; thing I tell you—she call'd her maid—who Slep'd in the next room—I urged every argument—to persuade her to elope with me, but all in vain! She vow'd to die in a convent sooner—and *Rae* 31 father] *Rae, F*; mother *94, I, NY*

ANT. Well; but at last?—

FERD. At last! why, I was forced to leave the house as I came in.

ANT. And did you do nothing to offend her?

FERD. Nothing, as I hope to be saved—I believe I might snatch a dozen or two kisses.

ANT. Was that all? well, I think I never heard of such assurance.

FERD. Zounds! I tell you I behaved with the utmost respect.

ANT. O lord! I dont mean you, but in her—but, hark'y, Ferdinand, did you leave your key with them?

FERD. Yes; the maid who saw me out took it from the door.

ANT. Then my life for it, her mistress elopes after you.

FERD. Ay, to bless some rival perhaps—I am in a humour to suspect everybody—you lov'd her once, and thought her an angel, as I do now.

ANT. Yes, I loved her till I found she wou'dn't love me, and then I discovered that she hadn't a good feature in her face.

AIR

I ne'er could any lustre see[1]
In eyes that wou'd not look on me:
I ne'er saw nectar on a lip,
But where my own did hope to sip.
Has the maid who seeks my heart
Cheeks of rose untouch'd by art?
I will own the colour true,
When yielding blushes aid their hue.

2 leave] *Rae*, *94*, *I*, *NY*; quit *F* 5 kisses] *Rae*; of kisses *F*, *94*, *I*, *NY* 6 all] *F*, *94*, *I*, *NY*; all—and you were really forced to decamp? | *Ferd.* Aye—and treated like a Dog—*Rae* 7 Zounds! . . . respect] *F*, *94*, *I*, *NY*; *om. Rae* 8 O] *F*, *94*, *I*, *NY*; *om. Rae* her] *F*, *94*, *I*, *NY*; her— | *Ferd.* Aye—did you ever hear anything equal to it? | *Anth.* Never! Well the confidence of some women is amazing—! and the curst maid too—what business had she to hear—? | *Ferd.* Aye a treacherous confounded Huzzy that came with my Ducats clinking in her Pocket—*Rae* hark'y] *94*, *I*, *NY*, *F*; hearken *Rae* 12 some] *Rae*, *F*; my *94*, *I*, *NY* 13 you] *94*, *I*, *NY*; you, Antonio *Rae*, *F* 15 that] *94*, *I*, *NY*, *Rae*; *om. F* 17 I . . . see] *Rae*, *F*, *94*, *Songs*, *I*, *NY*; I cou'd never Lustre see *Th* 19 a] *Rae*, *94*, *I*, *Songs*, *NY*, *Th*; her *F* 21 maid] *F*, *94*, *I*, *NY*, *Th*, *Songs*; Nymph *Rae*

---

[1] A comic poem originally. Two stanzas in a Yale MS. in Sheridan's hand, read:

I ne'er could any Lustre see
In Eyes that would not look on me—
And when a Glance aversion hints
I always think the Lady squints—

I ne'er saw Nectar on a Lip
But where my own did hope to sip.
No pearly Teeth rejoice my view
Unless a Yes displays their hue.

Is her hand so soft and pure?
I must press it to be sure:
Nor can I be certain then
Till it grateful press again:
Must I with attentive eye
Watch her heaving bosom sigh?
I will do so when I see
That heaving bosom sigh for me.

Besides, Ferdinand, you have full security in my love for your sister, help me there, and I can never disturb you with Clara.

FERD. As far as I can consistently with the honor of our family, you know I will; but there must be no eloping.

ANT. And yet now, you wou'd carry off Clara.

FERD. Ay, that's a different case—we never mean that others shou'd act to our sisters and wives as we do to theirs—But to-morrow Clara is to be forc'd into a convent.

ANT. Well: and am not I as unfortunately circumstanc'd? To-morrow your father forces Louisa to marry Isaac, the Portugueze—but come with me, and we'll devise something, I warrant.

FERD. I must go home.

ANT. Well, adieu.

FERD. But, Antonio, if you did not love my sister, you have too much honor and friendship to think of supplanting me with Clara.

AIR

ANTONIO.

Friendship is the bond of reason,
  But if beauty disapprove,
Heaven absolves all other treason
  In the heart that's true to love.

The faith which to my friend I swore
  As a civil oath I view,
But to the charms which I adore,
  'Tis religion to be true.

3 can I] *94*, *I*, *NY*, *Th*; can I e'en *F*, *Rae*, *Songs* 7 I see] *94*, *I*, *NY*, *F*; see *Rae* 10 can never] *Rae*, *94*, *I*, *NY*; never can *F* 11 consistently] *Rae*, *94*, *I*, *NY*; consistent *F* 15 theirs] *Rae*, *NY*; others *94*, *F*, *I* 17 and] *94*, *I*, *NY*; *om.* *F*, *Rae* as] *Rae*, *F*; so *94*, *I*; too so *NY* 20 home] *F*, *94*, *I*, *NY*; home first *Rae* 21 Well, adieu] *F*, *94*, *I*, *NY*; And I to lay aside these trappings, adieu—let us meet presently *Rae* 23 honor and friendship] *94*, *I*, *NY*; honour—Friendship and Honour *Rae*; friendship and honor *F* think of supplanting] *Rae*, *F*; supplant *94*, *I*, *NY* 28 absolves] *Rae*, *F*, *G*, *Th*, *Songs*; dissolves *94*, *I*, *NY*

Then if to one I false must be;
  Can I doubt which to prefer—
A breach of social faith with thee,
  Or sacrilege to love and her. [*Exit* ANTONIO.

FERD. There is always a levity in Antonio's manner of replying to me on this subject, that is very alarming—S'death, if Clara shou'd love him after all.

AIR

Tho' cause for suspicion appears,
  Yet proofs of her love too are strong;
I'm a wretch if I'm right in my fears,
  And unworthy of bliss if I'm wrong.
What heart-breaking torments from jealousy flow,
Ah, none but the jealous, the jealous can know.

When blest with the smiles of my fair,
  I know not how much I adore;
Those smiles let another but share,
  And I wonder I priz'd them no more.
Then whence can I hope a relief from my woe,
When the falser she seems still the fonder I grow. [*Exit.*

SCENE III. *A Room in Don Jerome's house*

Enter LOUISA *and* DUENNA.

LOUISA. But my dear Margaret, my charming Duenna, do you think we shall succeed?

DUENNA. I tell you again I have no doubt on't; but it must be instantly put to the trial—Every thing is prepared in your room, and for the rest we must trust to fortune.

LOUISA. My father's oath was never to see me till I had consented to—

DUENNA. 'Twas thus I overheard him say to his friend, Don Guzman, 'I will demand of her to-morrow, once for all, whether she will consent to marry Isaac Mendoza—If she hesitates, I will make a solemn oath never to see or speak to her till she returns to her duty'—these were his very words.

1–4 Then . . . her] *Rae, F, G, Th, Songs*; *om. 94, I, NY*   1 Then] *F, Songs, G, Th*; And *Rae*   be] *Rae, F, Songs, Th*; prove *G*   3 with] *Rae, F, Songs*; to *G, Th*   22 *Enter*] *94, I, NY, F*; *om. Rae*   25 be instantly] *94, I, Rae, F*; instantly be *NY*   29 friend] *94, F, I, NY*; confident *Rae*   30 tomorrow] *94, I, NY*; tomorrow morning *F, Rae*   31 Mendoza] *94, F, I, NY*; *om. Rae*   32 her] *94, I, NY, F*; her from that hour *Rae*   these] *94, F, I, NY*; those *Rae*   33 very] *Rae, F*; *om. 94, I, NY*

LOUISA. And on his known obstinate adherence to what he has once said, you have form'd this plan for my escape—But have you secured my maid in our interest.

DUENNA. She is a party in the whole—but remember, if we succeed, you resign all right and title in little Isaac the Jew, over to me.

LOUISA. That I do with all my soul, get him if you can, and I shall wish you joy most heartily. He is twenty times as rich as my poor Antonio.

AIR

Thou cans't not boast of fortune's store,
My love, while me they wealthy call,
But I was glad to find thee poor,
For with my heart I'd give thee all.
And then the grateful youth shall own,
I lov'd him for himself alone.

But when his worth my hand shall gain,
No word or look of mine shall shew,
That I, the smallest thought retain
Of what my bounty did bestow.
Yet still his grateful heart shall own,
I lov'd him for himself alone.

DUENNA. I hear Don Jerome coming—Quick, give me the last letter I brought you from Antonio—you know that is to be the ground of my dismission—I must slip out to seal it up as undelivered. [*Exit*.

Enter DON JEROME *and* FERDINAND.

JEROME. What, I suppose you have been serenading too! Eh, disturbing some peaceable neighbourhood with villainous catgut and lascivious piping, out on't! you set your sister here a vile example—but I come to tell you, madam, that I'll suffer no more of these midnight incantations, these amorous orgies that steal the senses in the hearing, as they say Egyptian Embalmers serve mummies, extracting the brain thro' the ears; however, there's an end of your frolics—Isaac Mendoza will be here presently, and to-morrow you shall marry him.

3 interest] *94, F, I, NY*; interests *Rae* 5 title] *94, F, I, NY*; tittle *Rae* little . . . Jew] *94, I, NY*; this little Jew *Rae*; the little Jew *F* 7 He . . . Antonio] *94, F, I, NY*; *om. Rae* 12 I'd] *94, I, NY, Songs, Rae, F*; I'll *Th* 13 grateful] *Rae, 94, I, NY, Th*; graceful *F, Songs* 18 shall] *94, I, NY, Songs, Rae*; will *Th* did] *Rae, 94, I, Songs, Th, NY*; shall *F* 25 Eh] *94, I, NY*; *om. Rae, F* 27 I come] *F, 94, I, NY*; I'm come *Rae* 31 the] *94, I, NY*; their *Rae, F* 31–2 however . . . him] *F, 94, I, NY*; *Luisa*. If young men will divert themselves at my window can I help it? and if the music is pleasing my ears have a will of their own, and yield Attention in spite of Duty! | *Don Jer*. No—nor you can't help rising and opening the window and replying to the Rakes I suppose? What, I warrant your legs and your Tongue have a will of their own too? *Rae*

LOUISA. Never while I have life.

FERD. Indeed, Sir, I wonder how you can think of such a man for a son-in-law.

JEROME. Sir, you are very kind to favour me with your sentiments—and pray, what is your objection to him.

FERD. He is a Portugueze in the first place.

JEROME. No such thing, boy, he has forsworn his country.

LOUISA. He is a Jew.

JEROME. Another mistake: he has been a christian these six weeks.

FERD. Ay, he left his old religion for an estate, and has not had time to get a new one.

LOUISA. But stands like a dead wall between church and synagogue, or like the blank leaves between the Old and New Testament.

JEROME. Any thing more?

FERD. But the most remarkable part of his character, is his passion for deceit, and tricks of cunning.

LOUISA. Tho' at the same time, the fool predominates so much over the knave, that I am told he is generally the dupe of his own art.

FERD. True, like an unskilful gunner, he usually misses his aim, and is hurt by the recoil of his own piece.

JEROME. Any thing more?

LOUISA. To sum up all, he has the worst fault a husband can have—he's not my choice.

JEROME. But you are his; and choice on one side is sufficient—two lovers shou'd never meet in marriage—be you sour as you please, he is sweet temper'd, and for your good fruit, there's nothing like ingrafting on a crab.

LOUISA. I detest him as a lover, and shall ten times more as a husband.

JEROME. I don't know that—marriage generally makes a great change—but to cut the matter short, will you have him or not?

LOUISA. There is nothing else I could disobey you in.

JEROME. Do you value your father's peace?

LOUISA. So much, that I will not fasten on him the regret of making an only daughter wretched.

JEROME. Very well, ma'am, then mark me—never more will I see or converse with you till you return to your duty—no reply—this and your chamber shall be your appartments, I never will stir out without leaving you under lock and key, and when I'm at home no creature can approach you but thro' my library—we'll try who can be most obstinate—out of my sight—There remain till you know your duty.

[*Pushes her out.*

21 more?] *Rae*, *94*, *I*, *NY*; more? | *Lou.* I am sure such a man can never make a good husband. | *Jer.* No, but he may make very good settlements. Any thing more? *F*
40 There] *Rae*, *94*, *I*, *NY*; There, there *F*

FERD. Surely, Sir, my sister's inclinations should be consulted in a matter of this kind, and some regard paid to Don Antonio, being my particular friend.

JEROME. That, doubtless, is a very great recommendation—I certainly have not paid sufficient respect to it.

FERD. There is not a man living I wou'd sooner chuse for a brother-in-law.

JEROME. Very possible; and if you happen to have e'er a sister, who is not at the same time a daughter of mine, I'm sure I shall have no objection to the relationship—but at present, if you please, we'll drop the subject.

FERD. Nay, sir, 'tis only my regard for my sister makes me speak.

JEROME. Then, pray, sir, in future, let your regard for your father make you hold your tongue.

FERD. I have done, sir—I shall only add a wish that you wou'd reflect what at our age you wou'd have felt, had you been crost in your affection for the mother of her you are so severe to.

JEROME. Why I must confess I had a great affection for your mother's ducats, but that was all, boy—I married her for her fortune, and she took me in obedience to her father, and a very happy couple we were —we never expected any love from one another, and so we were never disappointed—If we grumbled a little now and then, it was soon over, for we were never fond enough to quarrel, and when the good woman died, why, why—I had as lieve she had lived, and I wish every widower in Seville cou'd say the same—I shall now go and get the key of this dressing room—So, good son, if you have any lecture in support of disobedience to give your sister, it must be brief; so make the best of your time d'ye hear. [*Exit* JEROME.

FERD. I fear indeed, my friend Antonio, has little to hope for—however Louisa has firmness, and my father's anger will probably only increase her affection—In our intercourse with the world, it is natural for us to dislike those who are innocently the cause of our distress; but in the heart's attachment, a woman never likes a man with ardor till she has suffer'd for his sake [*Noise.*] soh! what bustle is here! between my father and the Duenna too—I'll e'en get out of the way. [*Exit.*

Enter DON JEROME (*with a Letter*) *pulling in the* DUENNA.

JEROME. I'm astonished! I'm thunder struck! here's treachery and conspiracy with a vengeance! you, Antonio's creature, and chief

8 happen . . . e'er] *Rae*, *F*, *94*, *I*; ever happen to have *NY* 13 sir, in] *Rae*, *94*, *I*, *NY*; for the *F* 17 her you] *Rae*, *94*, *I*, *NY*; her whom you *F* 30 anger] *Rae*, *94*, *I*, *NY*; rigour *F* 33 attachment] *Rae*, *94*, *I*, *NY*; attachments *F* likes] *Rae*, *94*, *I*, *NY*; loves *F* 36 *Enter*] *94*, *I*, *NY*, *F*; Re-enter *Rae* *pulling*] *Rae*, *I*; *pushing NY*; *putting F*, *94* 37–8 and conspiracy] *F*, *94*, *I*, *NY*; *om. Rae*

manager of this plot for my daughter's eloping! you that I placed here as a scare-crow.

DUENNA. What?

JEROME. A scare-crow—To prove a decoy duck—what have you to say for yourself?

DUENNA. Well, sir, since you have forced that letter from me, and discover'd my real sentiments, I scorn to renounce 'em—I am Antonio's friend, and it was my intention that your daughter shou'd have serv'd you as all such old tyrannical sots shou'd be serv'd—I delight in the tender passions, and would befriend all under their influence.

JEROME. The tender passions! yes, they wou'd become those impenetrable features—why, thou deceitful hag! I plac'd thee as a guard to the rich blos[s]oms of my daughter's beauty—I thought that dragon's front of thine wou'd cry aloof to the sons of gallantry—steel traps and spring guns seem'd writ in every wrinkle of it—but you shall quit my house this instant—the tender passions, indeed! go thou wanton sybil, thou amorous woman of Endor,[1] go!

DUENNA. You base, scurrilous, old—but I wont demean myself by naming what you are—yes, Savage, I'll leave your den, but I suppose you don't mean to detain my apparel—I may have my things I presume.

JEROME. I took you, mistress, with your wardrobe on—what have you pilfer'd, heh?

DUENNA. Sir, I must take leave of my mistress, she has valuables of mine, besides, my cardinal and veil are in her room.

JEROME. Your veil for sooth! what do you dread being gazed at? or are you afraid of your complexion? well, go take your leave, and get your veil and cardinal! soh! you quit the house within these five minutes—In—in—quick. [*Exit* DUENNA.

Here was a precious plot of mischief—! these are the comforts daughters bring us.

AIR

If a daughter you have, she's the plague of your life,
No peace shall you know, tho' you've buried your wife,
At twenty she mocks at the duty you taught her,
O, what a plague is an obstinate daughter.
Sighing and whining,
Dying and pining,
O what a plague is an obstinate daughter.
When scarce in their teens, they have wit to perplex us,

3–4 What? . . . scare-crow] *Rae, 94, I, NY*; *om. F* 13 dragon's] *94, Rae, I, NY*; Dragon *F* 27 these] *94, Rae, I, NY*; this *F* 30 us] *94, Rae, I, NY*; on us *F*

---

[1] The witch consulted by Saul before the battle of Gilboa: see 1 Samuel 28: 7.

With letters and lovers for ever they vex us,
While each still rejects the fair suitor you've brought her,
O what a plague is an obstinate daughter.
Wrangling and jangling,
Flouting and pouting,
O what a plague is an obstinate daughter.

Enter LOUISA, *dress'd as the* DUENNA, *with Cardinal and Veil, seeming to cry.*

JEROME. This way, mistress, this way—what, I warrant, a tender parting soh! tears of turpentine down those deal cheeks—Aye, you may well hide your head—yes, whine till your heart breaks, but I'll not hear one word of excuse—so you are right to be dumb, this way—this way. [*Exeunt.*

Enter DUENNA.

DUENNA. So speed you well, sagacious Don Jerome! O, rare effects of passion and obstinacy—now shall I try whether I can't play the fine lady as well as my mistress, and if I succeed, I may be a fine lady for the rest of my life—I'll lose no time to equip myself. [*Exit.*

SCENE IV. *The Court before* DON JEROME'*s house*

Enter DON JEROME *and* LOUISA.

JEROME. Come, mistress, there is your way—The world lies before you, so troop, thou antiquated Eve, thou original sin—hold, yonder is some fellow skulking, perhaps it is Antonio—go to him, d'ye hear, and tell him to make you amends, and as he has got you turn'd away, tell him I say it is but just he shou'd take you himself, go. [*Exit* LOUISA. Soh! I am rid of her, thank heaven! and now I shall be able to keep my oath, and confine my daughter with better security. [*Exit.*

SCENE V.—*The* PIAZZA

Enter CLARA, *and her Maid.*

MAID. But where madam, is it you intend to go?

CLARA. Any where to avoid the selfish violence of my mother-in-law, and Ferdinand's insolent importunity.

4 Wrangling and jangling] *94, I, NY, F*; jangling and wrangling *Th* 7–8 *Enter . . . cry*] *94, I, NY*; Re enter DUENNA—her veil on seeming to cry *Rae, Enter Louisa dress'd as the Duenna, thro', with Veil seeming to cry F* 13 *Exeunt*] *94, NY, I, Rae*; *Exit F* 16 obstinacy . . . now] *94, F, I, NY*; Obstinacy! The first will blind him to the cheat—and the second will continue him in his Delusion—now *Rae* 19 SCENE IV. *The Court*] *94, I, NY*; *Scene, Court F*; SCENE IV. *The Court Yard Rae* 20 *and* LOUISA] *94, I, NY, F*; and DUENNA. | He unlocks the Gate *Rae* 21 is] *94, F, I, NY*; lies *Rae* 24 amends] *94, I, NY*; amends d'ye hear *F, Rae* and] *94, F, I, NY*; *om. Rae* 27 *Exit*] *94, I, NY, F*; (Re enters the House) *Rae*

MAID. Indeed, ma'am, since we have profited by Don Ferdinand's key in making our escape, I think we had best find him, if it were only to thank him.

CLARA. No—he has offended me exceedingly. [*Retire.*

Enter LOUISA.

LOUISA. So, I have succeeded in being turn'd out of doors—but how shall I find Antonio? I dare not enquire for him for fear of being discovered; I would send to my friend Clara, but that I doubt her prudery wou'd condemn me.

MAID. Then suppose, ma'am, you were to try if your friend Donna Louisa would not receive you.

CLARA. No, her notions of filial duty are so severe, she would certainly betray me.

LOUISA. Clara is of a cold temper, and would think this step of mine highly forward.

CLARA. Louisa's respect for her father is so great, she would not credit the unkindness of mine. [LOUISA *turns, and sees* CLARA *and* MAID.

LOUISA. Ha! who are those? sure one is Clara—if it be, I'll trust her—Clara! [*Advances.*

CLARA. Louisa! and in Masquerade too!

LOUISA. You will be more surprized when I tell you that I have run away from my father.

CLARA. Surprized indeed! and I should certainly chide you most horridly, only that I have just run away from mine.

LOUISA. My dear Clara! [*Embrace.*

CLARA. Dear sister truant! and whither are you going?

LOUISA. To find the man I love to be sure—And I presume you wou'd have no aversion to meet with my brother.

CLARA. Indeed I should—he has behaved so ill to me, I don't believe I shall ever forgive him.

AIR

CLARA.

When sable night, each drooping plant restoring,
  Wept o'er the flowers her breath did cheer,
As some sad widow o'er her babe deploring,
  Wakes its beauty with a tear;

2 find him] *94, I, NY, Rae*; find him out *F* 4 *Retire*] *94, I, NY, F*; retires *Rae* 12–15 *Spoken by Louisa in Rae* 14 think] *Rae, F, NY*; *om. 94, I* 16–17 *Spoken by Louisa in Rae*, 'Her respect. . .' 17 *turns, and sees*] *94, Rae, I, NY*; *turning and seeing F* 19 *Advances*] *Rae, 94, I, NY*; *om. F* 22 my] *Rae, 94, I, F*; my own *NY* 24 horridly] *94, Rae, I, NY*; horribly *F* 29 I don't] *94, Rae, I, NY*; that I don't *F* 36 beauty] *94, Rae, I, NY, F, Songs*; beauties *Th*

When all did sleep, whose weary hearts did borrow
One hour from love and care to rest,
Lo! as I prest my couch in silent sorrow,
My lover caught me to his breast;
He vowed he came to save me
From those who would enslave me!
Then kneeling,
Kisses stealing
Endless faith he swore,
But soon I chid him thence,
For had his fond pretence,
Obtain'd one favour then,
And he had press'd again
I fear'd my treacherous heart might grant him more.

LOUISA. Well, for all this, I would have sent him to plead his pardon, but that I would not yet awhile have him know of my flight. And where do you hope to find protection?

CLARA. The lady Abbess of the convent of St. Catherine is a relation and kind friend of mine—I shall be secure with her, and you had best go thither with me.

LOUISA. No; I am determined to find Antonio first, and as I live, here comes the very man I will employ to seek him for me.

CLARA. Who is he? he's a strange figure!

LOUISA. Yes, that sweet creature is the man whom my father has fixed on for my husband.

CLARA. And will you speak to him? are you mad?

LOUISA. He is the fittest man in the world for my purpose—for, tho' I was to have married him to-morrow, he is the only man in Seville, who I am sure never saw me in his life.

CLARA. And how do you know him?

LOUISA. He arrived but yesterday, and he was shewn me from the window as he visited my father.

CLARA. Well, I'll be gone.

LOUISA. Hold, my dear Clara—a thought has struck me, will you give me leave to borrow your name as I see occasion.

CLARA. It will but disgrace you—but use it as you please—I dare not stay [*going*] but, Louisa, if you shou'd see your brother, be sure you don't inform him that I have taken refuge with the Dame Prior of the convent of St. Catherine, on the left hand side of the Piazza which leads to the church of St. Anthony.

1 did borrow] *94*, *Rae*, *I*, *NY*; cou'd borrow *Th*, *F*, *Songs* 12 Obtain'd one favour then] *94*, *Rae*, *I*, *NY*, *F*, *Songs*; Found favour then *Th* 14 my . . . might] *94*, *Rae*, *I*, *NY*, *F*, *Songs*; in my heart I might *Th* 15 his] *94*, *Rae*, *I*, *NY*; for his *F* 34 has] *Rae*, *94*, *I*, *F*; has just *NY* 39 Catherine] *94*, *Rae*, *I*, *NY*; Catharine's *F*

LOUISA. Ha, ha, ha! I'll be very particular in my directions where he may not find you. [*Exeunt* CLARA *and* MAID. So! my swain yonder has done admiring himself and draws nearer. [*Retires.*

Enter ISAAC *and* CARLOS, ISAAC *with a pocket glass.*

ISAAC. [*Looking in the glass.*] I tell you, friend Carlos, I will please myself in the habit of my chin.

CARLOS. But, my dear friend, how can you think to please a lady with such a face.

ISAAC. Why, what's the matter with the face? I think it is a very engaging face; and I am sure a lady must have very little taste, who could dislike my beard [*Sees* LOUISA.] See now—I'll die if here is not a little damsel struck with it already.

LOUISA. Signor, are you disposed to oblige a lady who greatly wants your assistance. [*Unveils.*

ISAAC. Egad, a very pretty black-eyed girl; she has certainly taken a fancy to me, Carlos—first ma'am, I must beg the favour of your name.

LOUISA. Soh! it's well I am provided. [*Aside*] My name, sir, is Donna Clara D'Almanza.

ISAAC. What!—Don Guzman's daughter? I'faith, I just now heard she was missing.

LOUISA. But, sure sir, you have too much gallantry and honor to betray me, whose fault is love.

ISAAC. So! a passion for me! poor girl! why, ma'am, as for betraying you, I don't see how I cou'd get any thing by it; so you may rely on my honour; but as for your love, I am sorry your case is so desperate.

LOUISA. Why so Signor?

ISAAC. Because I'm positively engaged to another—an't I Carlos?

LOUISA. Nay, but hear me.

ISAAC. No, no; what should I hear for? It is impossible for me to court you in an honourable way; and for any thing else, if I were to comply now, I suppose you have some ungrateful brother, or cousin, who would want to cut my throat for my civility—so, truly you had best go home again.

LOUISA. Odious wretch! [*aside*] But, good Signor, it is Antonio d'Ercilla, on whose account I have eloped.

ISAAC. How! what! it is not with me then, that you are in love?

LOUISA. No indeed it is not.

ISAAC. Then you are a forward, impertinent simpleton! and I shall certainly acquaint your father.

1 I'll] *94, Rae, I, NY*; to be sure—I'll *F* 5 *with . . . glass*] *94, I, NY*; a pocket Glass Isaac *F*; *om. Rae* 6 *Looking . . . glass*] *94, I, NY*; (*Looking in a pocket-glass*) *Rae*; *om. F* 10 is] *Rae, 94, I, F*; *om. NY* 12 here] *94, Rae, I, NY*; there *F* 20 now] *Rae, 94, I, NY*; *om. F* 25 on] *94, Rae, I, NY*; upon *F*

LOUISA. Is this your gallantry.

ISAAC. Yet hold—Antonio d'Ercilla did you say? egad, I may make something of this—Antonio d'Ercilla?

LOUISA. Yes, and if ever you hope to prosper in love, you will bring me to him.

ISAAC. By St. Iago, and I will too—Carlos, this Antonio is one who rivals me (as I have heard) with Louisa—now, if I could hamper him with this girl, I should have the field to myself, hey, Carlos! A lucky thought, isn't it?—

CARLOS. Yes, very good—very good—

ISAAC. Ah! this little brain is never at a loss—cunning Isaac! cunning rogue! Donna Clara, will you trust yourself a while to my friend's direction.

LOUISA. May I rely on you good Signor?

CARLOS. Lady, it is impossible I should deceive you.

AIR

Had I a heart for falsehood framed,
  I ne'er could injure you;
For tho' your tongue no promise claimed,
  Your charms wou'd make me true.
To you no soul shall bear deceit,
  No stranger offer wrong,
But friends in all the aged you'll meet;
  And lovers in the young.

But when they learn that you have blest
  Another with your heart,
They'll bid aspiring passion rest,
  And act a brother's part;
Then, lady, dread not here deceit,
  Nor fear to suffer wrong;
For friends in all the aged you'll meet,
  And brothers in the young.

ISAAC. Conduct the lady to my lodgings, Carlos; I must haste to Don Jerome—perhaps you know Louisa, ma'am. She is divinely handsome—isn't she?

LOUISA. You must excuse me not joining with you.

ISAAC. Why, I have heard it on all hands.

3 this—Antonio d'Ercilla] *94*, *Rae*, *I*, *NY*; this (*aside*) *F* 4–5 me to him] *94*, *Rae*, *F*, *I*; him to me *NY* 8 A lucky] *94*, *Rae*, *I*, *NY*; lucky *F* 13 direction] *94*, *Rae*, *I*, *NY*; protection *F* 18 ne'er] *Rae*, *F*, *I*, *Th*, *NY*, *Songs*; near *94* 27 passion] *Rae*, *F*, *Songs*, *Th*; passions *94*, *I*, *NY* 32 brothers] *Rae*, *F*, *Songs*, *Th*; lovers *94*, *I*, *NY* 33 Conduct] *Rae*, *F*, *NY*; I'll conduct *94*, *I* 36 me] *Rae*, *94*, *I*, *NY*; my *F*

LOUISA. Her father is uncommonly partial to her, but I believe you will find she has rather a matronly air.

ISAAC. Carlos, this is all envy—you pretty girls never speak well of one another—[*To Don Carlos*] hark'y, find out Antonio, and I'll saddle him with this scrape, I warrant! oh, 'twas the luckiest thought—Donna Clara, your very obedient—Carlos, to your post.

DUETT

ISAAC. My mistress expects me, and I must go to her,
Or how can I hope for a smile?

LOUISA. Soon may you return a prosperous wooer,
But think what I suffer the while:
Alone and away from the man whom I love,
In strangers I'm forced to confide,

ISAAC. Dear lady, my friend you may trust, and he'll prove,
Your servant, protector, and guide.

AIR

CARLOS.

Gentle maid, ah! why suspect me?
Let me serve thee—then reject me,
Can'st thou trust, and I deceive thee?
Art thou sad, and shall I grieve thee?
Gentle maid, Ah! why suspect me?
Let me serve thee—then reject me.

TRIO

LOUISA. Never may'st thou happy be,
If in ought thou'rt false to me.

ISAAC. Never may he happy be,
If in ought he's false to thee.

CARLOS. Never may I happy be,
If in ought I'm false to thee.

LOUISA. Never may'st thou &c.

ISAAC. Never may he &c.

CARLOS. Never may I &c.

[*Exeunt.*

END OF ACT I

4 *To . . . Carlos*] *Rae*; *om.* *94*, *I*, *NY*, *F* 15 servant] *94*, *Rae*, *F*, *I*, *NY*, *Songs*; guardian *G*, *Th* 25 Never . . . thou] *94*, *Rae*, *F*, *I*, *NY*, *Songs*; May'st thou never *G*, *Th* 27 Never . . . he] *94*, *Rae*, *I*, *NY*, *F*, *Songs*; May he never *Th*, *G* 29 Never . . . I] *94*, *Rae*, *I*, *NY*, *F*, *Songs*; May I never *Th*, *G*

ACT II

SCENE I.—*A Library in* JEROME'*s House*

Enter DON JEROME *and* ISAAC.

JEROME. Ha, ha, ha! run away from her father, has she? given him the slip! Ha, ha, ha! poor Don Guzman!

ISAAC. Ay; and I am to conduct her to Antonio; by which means you see I shall hamper him so that he can give me no disturbance with your daughter—this is a trap, isn't it? a nice stroke of cunning, heh!

JEROME. Excellent! Excellent! yes, yes, carry her to him, hamper him by all means, ha, ha, ha! poor Don Guzman! an old fool! imposed on by a girl!

ISAAC. Nay, they have the cunning of serpents, that's the truth on't.

JEROME. Psha! they are cunning only when they have fools to deal with—why don't my girl play me such a trick—let her cunning over-reach my caution, I say—heh little Isaac!

ISAAC. True, true; or let me see any of the sex make a fool of me—No, no, egad, little Solomon, (as my aunt used to call me) understands tricking a little too well.

JEROME. Ay, but such a driveller as Don Guzman.

ISAAC. And such a dupe as Antonio.

JEROME. True; sure never were seen such a couple of credulous simpletons, but come, 'tis time you should see my daughter—you must carry on the siege by yourself, friend Isaac,

ISAAC. Sure, you'll introduce me—

JEROME. No—I have sworn a solemn oath not to see or speak to her till she renounces her disobedience; win her to that, and she gains a father and a husband at once.

ISAAC. Gad, I shall never be able to deal with her alone; nothing keeps me in such awe as perfect beauty—now there is something consoling and encouraging in ugliness.

SONG

Give Isaac the nymph who no beauty can boast;
But health and good humour to make her his toast,
If strait, I dont mind whether slender or fat,
And six feet or four—we'll ne'er quarrel for that.

2 *in . . . House*] *94*, *I*, *NY*, *Rae*; *om. F* 4 father . . . she?] *Rae*, *F*; father! has she *94*, *I*, *NY* 5 slip] *94*, *I*, *NY*; slip, hey? *Rae*, *F* 8 a] *Rae*; *om. 94*, *I*, *F*, *NY* 10 ha, ha, ha!] *Rae*, *94*, *I*, *NY*; *om. F* 24 Sure] *Rae*; Sir *94*, *I*, *NY*, *F* me] *Rae*, *F*; *om. 94*, *I*, *NY* 25 speak] *94*, *I*, *NY*, *F*; to speak *Rae* 33 his] *94*, *I*, *NY*, *F*, *Th*, *Songs*; my *Rae* 35 A . . . feet] *94*, *I*, *NY*, *F*, *Songs*; Or six foot *Th* we'll] *94*, *I*, *NY*, *Th*, *F*, *Songs*; I'll *Rae*

Whate'er her complexion, I vow I don't care,
If brown it is lasting, more pleasing if fair;
And tho' in her cheeks I no dimples shou'd see,
Let her smile, and each dell is a dimple to me.

Let her locks be the reddest that ever were seen,
And her eyes may be e'en any colour but green,
For in eyes, tho' so various in lustre and hue,
I swear I've no choice, only let her have two.

'Tis true I'd dispense with a throne on her back,
And white teeth I own, are genteeler than black,
A little round chin too's a beauty I've heard,
But I only desire she mayn't have a beard.

JEROME. You will change your note, my friend, when you've seen Louisa.

ISAAC. O Don Jerome, the honour of your alliance—

JEROME. Aye, but her beauty will affect you—she is, tho' I say it, who am her father, a very prodigy—there you will see Features with an eye like mine—yes I'faith, there is a kind of wicked sparkling—something of a roguish brightness that shews her to be my own.

ISAAC. Pretty rogue!

JEROME. Then, when she smiles, you'll see a little dimple in one cheek only; a beauty it is certainly, yet you shall not say which is prettiest, the cheek with the dimple, or the cheek without.

ISAAC. Pretty rogue!

JEROME. Then the roses on those cheeks are shaded with a sort of velvet down, that gives a delicacy to the glow of health.

ISAAC. Pretty rogue!

JEROME. Her skin pure dimity, yet more fair, being spangled here and there with a golden freckle.

ISAAC. Charming pretty rogue!

3 cheeks] *Rae, F, Songs, Th*; face *94, I, NY*   6 e'en] *Rae, F, Songs, 94, I, NY*; faith *Th*   7 For . . . various] *Rae, F, Songs, Th*; Be they light, grey or black *94, I, NY*   in] *Rae, F*; the *Songs, Th*; their *94, I, NY*   12 *F. After* 'beard', *two stanzas are added in Rae:*

To one thus accomplish'd I durst speak my Mind
And flattery doubtless would soon make her kind
For the Man who should praise her she needs must adore
Who ne'er in her Life received praises before.

But the frowns of a Beauty in hopes to remove
Should I prate of her Charms and tell of my Love
No thanks wait the praise which she knows to be true
Nor smiles for the Homage she takes as her due.

21 prettiest] *94, Rae, I, NY*; the prettiest *F*

DUET

JEROME. Dominion was given
To Beauty from Heav'n
Pleasing Bondage to the Mind!—
Will *you* then alone
Its Worship disown?—
ISAAC. Never!—could I favour find
But when for my Pain
I meet with Disdain
JEROME. Coax her, kiss her, till she's kind.

JEROME. Come courage man—you must not be dismay'd if you find Louisa a little haughty at first.

ISAAC. Pray how is the tone of her voice?

JEROME. Remarkably pleasing—but if you cou'd prevail on her to sing you would be enchanted—she is a nightingale—a Virginia nightingale[1] —but come, come, her maid shall conduct you to her Antichamber.

ISAAC. Well, egad, I'll pluck up resolution and meet her frowns intrepidly.

JEROME. Aye! woo her briskly—win her and give me a proof of your address, my little Solomon.

ISAAC. But hold—I expect my friend Carlos to call on me here—If he comes will you send him to me?

JEROME. I will—Lauretta, come—she'll shew you to the room—what! do you droop? here's a mournful face to make love with.

SONG

When the maid whom we love
No entreaties can move,
Who'd lead a life of pining?
If her charms will excuse
The fond rashness we use,
—Away with idle whining!

Never stand like a fool
With looks sheepish and cool—
Such bashful love is tiezing:

1–12 *DUET* | Dominion . . . first] *Rae. Cf. Sichel*, i. 507; *om. 94, I, Th, Songs, NY, F*
22 I will] *94, I, NY*; I will, I will *Rae, F* Lauretta] *94, I, NY, F*; Lisetta *Rae*
24–line 9, page 249 *SONG* | When . . . boldness] *Rae, Songs, Th, NY, F*; *om. 94, I*
29 we] *Rae*; you *F, NY, Th, Songs* 32 looks] *Rae, F, Songs, Th*; look *NY*

---

[1] The cardinal. Cf. Christopher Smart's 'Ode to a Virginia Nightingale' (1754):
O let us fellow warblers join,
Our patroness to crown.

But with spirit address
And you're sure of success
—For honest warmth is pleasing.

Nay tho' wedlock's your view,
Like a rake if you'll woo,
Girls sooner quit their coldness:
They know beauty inspires
Less respect than desires
—Hence love is prov'd by boldness. [*Exeunt.*

SCENE II.—LOUISA'*s Dressing Room*

Enter MAID *and* ISAAC.

MAID. Sir, my mistress will wait on you presently [*Goes to the door.*

ISAAC. When she's at leisure—don't hurry her. [*Exit* MAID. I wish I had ever practised a love-scene—I doubt I shall make a poor figure—I cou'd'nt be more afraid if I was going before the Inquisition[1] —so! the door opens—yes, she's coming—the very rustling of her silks has a disdainful sound.

Enter DUENNA (*drest as* LOUISA.)

Now dar'n't I look round for the soul of me—her beauty will certainly strike me dumb if I do. I wish she'd speak first.

DUENNA. Sir, I attend your pleasure.

ISAAC. So! the ice is broke, and a pretty civil beginning too! [*aside*] hem! madam—Miss—I'm all attention.

DUENNA. Nay, Sir, 'tis I who shou'd listen, and you propose.

ISAAC. Egad, this is'nt so disdainful neither—I believe I may venture to look—No—I dar'n't—one glance of those roguish sparklers wou'd fix me again.

DUENNA. You seem thoughtful, Sir—let me persuade you to sit down.

ISAAC. So, so; she mol[l]ifies apace—she's struck with my figure, this attitude has had its effect. [*aside.*

DUENNA. Come, Sir, here's a chair.

4 Nay] *Rae, F, Songs*; And *Th, NY* 5 you'll] *Rae, F, Songs*; you *Th, NY* 6 coldness] *Rae, F, Songs, NY*; coyness *Th* 11 *Enter* MAID *and* ISAAC] *94, F, I*; *enter* LAURETTA *and* ISAAC *NY*; *Maid crosses the Stage and goes to the Door in the back Scene Rae* 13 MAID] *Rae, 94, I, F*; Lauretta *NY* 16 silks] *Rae, F*; silk *94, I, NY* 18 *drest*] *Rae, 94, I, NY*; *om. F* 22 *aside*] *NY*; *om. Rae, F, 94, I* 23 I'm] *Rae, 94, I, NY*; Madam, I am *F* 26 sparklers] *Rae, F, 94, I*; sparkles *NY* 30 *aside*] *NY*; *om. Rae, F, 94, I*

[1] It lasted in Spain from the Middle Ages to 1835.

ISAAC. Madam, the greatness of your goodness overpowers me—that a lady so lovely shou'd deign to turn her beauteous eyes on one so. [*She takes his hand, he turns and sees her.*

DUENNA. You seem surpriz'd at my condescension.

ISAAC. Why, yes, madam, I am a little surprized at—at—zounds! this can never be Louisa—she's as old as my mother. [*aside.*

DUENNA. But former prepossessions give way to my father's commands.

ISAAC. [*aside*,] Her father! Yes, 'tis she then—Lord, lord; how blind some parents are!

DUENNA. Signor Isaac.

ISAAC. Truely, the little damsel was right—she has rather a matronly air indeed! ah! 'tis well my affections are fixed on her fortune and not her person.

DUENNA. Signor Isaac, wont you sit? [*she sits.*

ISAAC. Pardon me, madam, I have scarce recover'd my astonishment at —your condescension, madam—she has the devil's own dimples to be sure. [*aside.*

DUENNA. Nay, you shall not stand [*he sits*] I do not wonder, Sir, that you are su[r]priz'd at my affability—I own Signor, that I was vastly prepossessed against you, and being teiz'd by my father, I did give some encouragement to Antonio, But then, Sir, you were described to me as a quite different person.

ISAAC. Aye, and so you were to me upon my soul, madam.

DUENNA. But when I saw you, I was never more struck in my life.

ISAAC. That was just my case too, madam; I was struck all of a heap for my part.

DUENNA. Well, Sir, I see our misapprehension has been mutual—you expected to find me haughty and averse, and I was taught to believe you a little black snub-nosed fellow, without person, manners or address.

ISAAC. Egad, I wish she had answer'd her picture as well. [*aside.*

DUENNA. But, Sir, your air is noble—something so liberal in your carriage, with so penetrating an eye, and so bewitching a smile.

ISAAC. Efaith, now I look at her again, I dont think she is so ugly. [*aside.*

DUENNA. So little like a jew, and so much like a gentleman.

ISAAC. Well, there certainly *is* something pleasing in the tone of her voice.

2 one] *Rae*, *F*; me *94*, *I*, *NY* 5 at—at—] *Rae*, *F*; at it *94*, *I*, *NY* 7 commands] *Rae*, *94*, *I*, *F*; command *NY* 8 Yes] *Rae*, *94*, *I*, *NY*; Yes, yes *F* 14 Isaac] *Rae*, *F*; *om.* *94*, *I*, *NY* 17 sure] *94*, *I*, *NY*, *F*; sure. | *Duenna.* Signor Mendoza! | *Isaac.* Yes Madam her Roguish sparklers too! by St. Jago I believe she has but one eye. (*Aside*) *Rae* 18 Nay . . . *sits*] *94*, *F*, *NY*; Nay, you shall stand (Both sit.) *Rae*; *om.* *I* 21 were] *Rae*, *94*, *I*, *NY*; was *F* 22 a quite] *Rae*, *94*, *I*, *NY*; quite a *F* 23 you were] *Rae*; you was *94*, *I*, *NY*; were you *F* 25 of] *Rae*; on *94*, *F*, *NY*, *I* 30 *aside*] *F*, *NY*; *om.* *Rae*, *94*, *I* 33 Efaith] *Rae*; Egad *94*, *I*, *NY*, *F* *aside*] *NY*; *om.* *F*, *Rae*, *94*, *I* 35 there . . *is*] *Rae*; certainly there is *94*, *I*, *NY*; there is certainly *F*

DUENNA. You will pardon this breach of decorum in my praising you thus, but my joy at being so agreeably deceiv'd has given me such a flow of spirits.

ISAAC. O dear lady, may I thank those sweet lips for this goodness [*kisses her*] why, she has a pretty sort of velvet down, that's the truth on't. [*aside.*

DUENNA. O Sir, you have the most insinuating manner, but indeed you shou'd get rid of that odious beard—one might as well kiss a hedge-hog.

ISAAC. Yes ma'am—the razor wou'd'nt be amiss for either of us [*aside*]. Could you favour me with a song?

DUENNA. Willingly, Sir, tho' I am rather hoarse—Ahem! [*Begins to sing.*

ISAAC. Very like a Virginia nightingale—ma'am, I perceive you're hoarse —I beg you will not distress—

DUENNA. O not in the least distressed;—now, Sir.

SONG

When a tender maid
Is first essayed,
By some admiring swain.
How her blushes rise,
If she meets his eyes,
While he unfolds his pain;
If he takes her hand, she trembles quite,
Touch her lips, and she swoons outright,
While a pit a pat, &c.
Her heart avows her fright.

But in time appear,
Fewer signs of fear,
The youth she boldly views,
If her hand he grasp,
Or her bosom clasp,
No mantling blush ensues.
Then to church well pleas'd the lovers move,
While her smiles her contentment prove,
And a pit a pat, &c.
Her heart avows her love.

1 my] *Rae*, *F*; *om.* *94*, *I*, *NY* 4 sweet] *Rae*, *F*; dear *94*, *I*, *NY* 5 *kisses her*] *Rae*, *94*, *I*, *NY*; (*kisses*) *F* velvet] *Rae*, *94*, *I*, *NY*; a velvet *F* 8 a] *Rae*, *F*; an *94*, *I*, *NY* 13 hoarse] *Rae*, *94*, *I*, *NY*; a little hoarse *F* 15 in . . . distressed] *94*, *I*, *NY*; in the least Distress *Rae*; the least distress'd *F* 18 essayed] *94*, *I*, *NY*, *F*, *Songs*, *Th*; assay'd *Rae* 22 While . . . pain] *94*, *Rae*, *I*, *F*, *Songs*, *Th*; *om.* *NY* 24 lips] *94*, *I*, *NY*, *F*, *Songs*, *Th*; lip *Rae* 29 The] *F*, *Rae*, *Songs*, *I*; Tho' *94*, *NY* 30 grasp] *Rae*, *F*, *Songs*, *Th*; grasps *94*, *I*, *NY* 31 bosom] *Rae*, *F*, *NY*, *I*, *Songs*, *Th*; bosoms *94* clasp] *Rae*, *F*, *Songs*, *Th*; clasps *94*, *I*, *NY*

ISAAC. Charming, ma'am! Enchanting! and truely your notes put me in mind of one that's very dear to me, a lady indeed, whom you greatly resemble.

DUENNA. How! is there then another so dear to you?

ISAAC. O, no, ma'am, you mistake me—

DUENNA. No—no you offer me your hand—then another has your Heart—

ISAAC. Oh Lud! no ma'am—'twas my Mother I meant as I hop'd to be saved.

DUENNA. What—Sir—am I like your Mother?

ISAAC. Stay, dear ma'am, I meant that you put me in mind of what my mother was when a Girl!—Yes—yes—ma'am my Mother was formerly a great Beauty I assure you—and when she married my Father about thirty years ago—as you may perhaps remember Ma'am—

DUENNA. I Sir—I remember thirty years ago?

ISAAC. O good lack—no ma'am—thirty years! No—no Ma'am it was thirty months I said—yes—yes Ma'am thirty months ago on her marriage with my Father who was as I was saying a great Beauty—but catching cold the year afterwards in Child Bed of your humble Servant.

DUENNA. Of *you* Sir—and married within these thirty months?

ISAAC. O the Devil I've made myself out but a year old!

DUENNA. Come, Sir, I see you are amazed and confounded at my condescension and know not what to say.

ISAAC. It is very true indeed, ma'am—but it is a judgment, I look on it as a judgment on me for delaying to urge the time when you'll permit me to compleat my happiness, by acquainting Don Jerome with your condescension.

DUENNA. Sir, I must frankly own to you that I can never be yours with my father's consent.

ISAAC. Good lack! how so?

DUENNA. When my father in his passion swore he would not see me again 'till I acquiesced in his will—I also made a vow that I would never take a husband from his hand—nothing shall make me break that oath—but if you have spirit and contrivance enough to carry me off without his knowledge, I'm yours.

ISAAC. Hum!

DUENNA. Nay, Sir, if you hesitate—

ISAAC. I'faith no bad whim this—if I take her at her word, I shall secure her fortune, and avoid making any settlement in return; thus I shall not

5 O, no] *94*, *I*, *NY*, *F*; No *Rae* me] *Rae*, *F*; it was my mother I meant *94*, *I*, *NY* 6 No . . . hand] *Rae*, *F*; *om.* *94*, *I*, *NY* then] *Rae*; when *F*; *om.* *94*, *I*, *NY* 6–10 another . . . am I] *Rae*, *F*; *om.* *94*, *I*, *NY* 10 like . . . mother?] *Rae*; so like your mother? *F*; *om.* *94*, *I*, *NY* 11 Stay, dear ma'am] *Rae*, *F*; *om.* *94*, *I*, *NY* 11–21 I meant . . . old] *Rae*; *om.* *94*, *I*, *NY*, *F* 24 it is a judgment] *94*, *I*, *NY*, *F*; *om.* *Rae* 31 not] *Rae*, *F*; never *94*, *I*, *NY*

only cheat the lover but the father too, Oh! cunning rogue, Isaac! Ay, ay, let this little brain alone—Egad, I'll take her in the mind. [*aside.*

DUENNA. Well, Sir, what's your determination?

ISAAC. Madam, I was dumb only from rapture—I applaud your spirit, and joyfully close with your proposal; for which, thus let me on this lilly hand express my gratitude. [*Kisses her hand.*

DUENNA. Well, Sir, you must get my father's consent to walk with me in the garden. But by no means inform him of my kindness to you.

ISAAC. No, to be sure—that wou'd spoil all—But trust me when tricking is the word—let me alone for a piece of cunning; this very day you shall be out of his power.

DUENNA. Well, I leave the management of it all to you, I perceive plainly, Sir, that you are not one that can be easily outwitted.

ISAAC. Egad, you're right, madam—you're right I'faith.

ENTER MAID. Here's a gentleman at the door, who begs permission to speak with Signor Isaac.

ISAAC. O, a friend of mine ma'am, and a trusty friend—Let him come in. [*Exit* MAID.
He is one to be depended on, ma'am.

ENTER CARLOS. So, coz. [*aside.*

CARLOS. I have left Donna Clara safe at your lodgings; but can no where find Antonio.

ISAAC. Well I will search him out myself anon—Carlos, you rogue, I thrive, I prosper.

CARLOS. Where is your mistress?

ISAAC. There, you booby, there she stands.

CARLOS. Why she's dam'd ugly.

ISAAC. Hush! [*Stops his mouth.*

DUENNA. What is your friend saying, Signor?

ISAAC. O ma'am, he is expressing his raptures at such charms as he never saw before, hey Carlos?

CARLOS. Aye, such as I never saw before, indeed.

DUENNA. You are a very obliging Gentleman—well, Signor Isaac, I believe we had better part for the present. Remember our plan.

ISAAC. O, ma'am, it is written in my heart, fixed as the image of those divine beauties—adieu, Idol of my soul—yet, once more permit me.— [*kisses her.*

DUENNA. Sweet, courteous Sir, adieu.

ISAAC. Your slave eternally—come Carlos, say something civil at taking leave.

2 *aside*] *NY*; *om.* *94*, *Rae*, *F*, *I* 6 (*Kisses her hand*)] *Rae*; *om.* *94*, *I*, *NY*, *F* 9 No] *Rae*, *94*, *I*, *NY*; No, no *F* 12 plainly] *Rae*, *F*; plain *94*, *I*, *NY* 15 and 18 MAID] *94*, *Rae*, *I*, *F*; LAURETTA *NY* 17 O] *Rae*, *F*; *om.* *94*, *I*, *NY* 20 *aside*] *94*, *I*, *NY*, *F*; Aside to him *Rae* 21 safe] *Rae*, *F*; *om.* *94*, *NY*, *I* 23 anon] *Rae*, *F*; *om.* *94*, *NY*, *I* 39 say] *Rae*, *94*, *I*, *NY*; now say *F*

CARLOS. I'faith, Isaac, she is the hardest woman to compliment I ever saw, however, I'll try something I had studied for the occasion.

SONG

Ah! sure a pair was never seen,
So justly form'd to meet by nature.
The youth excelling so in mien,
The maid in ev'ry grace of feature.
O how happy are such lovers,
When kindred beauties each discovers.
For surely she
Was made for thee,
And thou to bless this lovely creature.

So mild your looks, your children thence,
Will early learn the task of duty,
The boys with all their father's sense,
The girls with all their mother's beauty.
Oh! how charming to inherit,
At once such graces and such spirit.
Thus while you live
May fortune give,
Each blessing equal to your merit.

[*Exeunt* ISAAC, CARLOS, *and* DUENNA.

SCENE III—*A Library*

JEROME *and* FERDINAND *discovered.*

JEROME. Object to Antonio? I have said it! his poverty, can you acquit him of that?

FERD. Sir, I own he is not over rich—but he is of as antient and as reputable a family as any in the kingdom.

JEROME. Yes, I know the beggars are a very ancient family in most kingdoms; but never in any great repute, boy.

FERD. Antonio, Sir, has many amiable qualities.

JEROME. But he is poor, can you clear him of that, I say—is he not a gay, dissipated rake, who has squander'd his patrimony?

FERD. Sir, he inherited but little; and that his generosity, more than his profuseness, has stript him of—but he has never sullied his honor, which, with his title, has outlived his means.

7 grace of] *94*, *Rae*, *I*, *NY*, *Songs*, *F*; gracefull *Th* 12 lovely] *94*, *Rae*, *I*, *NY*, *Songs*, *F*; charming *Th* 17 charming] *Rae*, *Th*; happy *94*, *I*, *NY*, *Songs*, *F* 18 graces] *Rae*, *94*, *I*, *Songs*, *Th*, *F*; grace *NY* 21 your] *Rae*, *I*, *Songs*, *Th*, *F*, *NY*; you *94* 27 as reputable] *Rae*; reputable *F*; honourable *94*, *I*, *NY* 30 any] *Rae*; *om.* *94*, *I*, *NY*, *F* 33 who] *94*, *I*, *NY*; that *Rae*, *F* 34 little] *Rae*, *F*, *94*, *I*; a little *NY*

JEROME. Psha! you talk like a blockhead! nobility without an estate is as ridiculous as gold-lace on a frize-coat.

FERD. This language, Sir, wou'd better become a Dutch or English trader, than a Spaniard.

JEROME. Yes; and those Dutch and English traders, as you call them, are the wiser people. Why, booby, in England they were formerly as nice as to birth and family as we are—but they have long discover'd what a wonderful purifier gold is—and now no one there regards pedigree in any thing but a horse.

FERD. True Sir, and the consequence is, that a nobleman is surer of the breed of his poney than the legitimacy of his heir.

JEROME. Ferdinand—I insist on it that this subject be dropt once for all.—O, here comes Isaac! I hope he has prosper'd in his suit.

FERD. Doubtless, that agreeable figure of his must have help'd his cause surprizingly.

JEROME. How now? [FERD. *walks aside.*

Enter ISAAC.

Well, my friend, have you soften'd her?

ISAAC. O yes; I have soften'd her.

JEROME. What, does she come to?

ISAAC. Why, truely, she was kinder than I expected to find her.

JEROME. And the dear pretty little Angel was civil, hey!

ISAAC. Yes, the pretty little Angel was very civil.

JEROME. I'm transported to hear it, well, and you were astonished at her beauty, hey?

ISAAC. I was astonished indeed! pray, how old is miss?

JEROME. How old? let me see—eight and twelve—she is just twenty.

ISAAC. Twenty?

JEROME. Aye, to a month.

ISAAC. Then, upon my soul, she is the oldest looking girl of her age in Christendom.

JEROME. Do you think so? but I believe you will not see a prettier girl.

ISAAC. Here and there one.

JEROME. Louisa has the family face.

ISAAC. Yes, egad, I shou'd have taken it for a family face, and one that has been in the family some time too. [*half aside.*

JEROME. She has her father's eyes.

ISAAC. Truely I shou'd have guess'd them to have been so—and if she had her mother's spectacles I believe she would not see the worse. [*aside.*

Before line 1, *Rae*, p. 121, prints nine lines on property and poverty. Cf. Moore, i. 173. 10–13 True . . . all] *Rae*; *om.* *94, I, NY, F* 14 cause] *Rae*; suit *94, I, NY, F* 22 pretty] *Rae*; *om.* *94, I, NY, F* 24 were] *Rae, 94, I, NY*; was *F* 26 pray] *Rae, 94, I, NY*; pray now *F* 27 just] *Rae, F*; *om.* *94, I, NY* 36 *half aside*] *Rae, F*; *aside* *94, I, NY* 38 and if] *Rae, F*; if *94, I, NY*

JEROME. Her aunt Ursula's nose, and her grandmother's forehead to a hair.

ISAAC. Ay, faith, and her grandfather's chin to a hair. [*aside*.

JEROME. Well, if she was but as dutiful as she's handsome—and harky, friend Isaac, she is none of your made up beauties—her charms are of the lasting kind.

ISAAC. I'faith, so they shou'd—for if she be but twenty now, she may double her age, before her years will overtake her face.

JEROME. Why, zounds, master Isaac, you are not sneering, are you?

ISAAC. Why, now seriously, Don Jerome, do you think your daughter handsome?

JEROME. By this light, she's as handsome a girl as any in Seville.

ISAAC. Then, by these eyes, I think her as plain a woman as ever I beheld.

JEROME. By St. Iago you must be blind.

ISAAC. No, no; 'tis you are partial.

JEROME. How! have I neither sense nor taste? If a fair skin, fine eyes, teeth of ivory, with a lovely bloom, and a delicate shape—if these, with a heavenly voice, and a world of grace, are not charms, I know not what you call beautiful.

ISAAC. Good lack, with what eyes a father sees! As I have life, she is the very reverse of all this, as for the dimity skin you told me of, I swear 'tis a thorough nankeen as ever I saw; for her eyes, their utmost merit is in not squinting—for her teeth, where there is one of ivory, its neighbour is pure ebony, black and white alternately, just like the keys of an harpsicord. Then as to her singing, and heavenly voice—by this hand, she has a shrill crack'd pipe, that sounds for all the world like a child's trumpet.

JEROME. Why, you little Hebrew scoundrel, do you mean to insult me? out of my house, out, I say.

FERD. Dear Sir, what's the matter?

JEROME. Why, this Israelite here, has the impudence to say your sister's ugly.

FERD. He must be either blind or insolent.

ISAAC. So, I find they are all in a story. Egad, I believe I have gone too far. [*aside*.

FERD. Sure, Sir, there must be some mistake—It can't be my sister whom he has seen.

JEROME. S'death! you are as great a fool as he, what mistake can there be? did not I lock up Louisa myself, and hav'n't I the key in my own

1 to a hair] *Rae*, *F*, *I*; *om*. *94*, *NY* 2 grandfather's] *Rae*, *F*, *I*; grandmother's *94*, *NY* hair] *94*, *I*, *NY*; hair, I think *Rae*, *F* 15 nor] *94*, *I*, *NY*, *F*; or *Rae* 17 grace] *Rae*, *94*, *I*, *F*; graces *NY* 20 this] *94*, *I*, *NY*, *Rae*; these F me] *94*, *I*, *NY*, *F*; one *Rae* 28 out, I] *Rae*, *F*; I *94*, *I*, *NY* 34 *aside*] *NY*; *om*. *Rae*, *F*, *94*, *I* 35 Sure] *94*, *I*, *NY*, *F*; Or sure *Rae* 38 myself] *Rae*, *F*; *om*. *94*, *I*, *NY*

pocket? And didn't her maid shew him into the dressing room? and yet you talk of a mistake, no, the Portugueze meant to insult me—and, but that this roof protects him, old as I am, this sword shou'd do me justice.

ISAAC. I must get off as well as I can—her fortune is not the less handsome. [*aside.*

DUET

ISAAC. Believe me, good Sir, I ne'er meant to offend,
My mistress I love, and I value my friend:
To win her, and wed her, is still my request,
For better, for worse, and I swear I don't jest.
JEROME. Zounds! you'd best not provoke me, my rage is so high.
ISAAC. Hold him fast, I beseech you, his rage is so high,
Good Sir, you're too hot and this place I must fly.
JEROME. You're a knave and a sot, and this place you'd best fly.

ISAAC. Don Jerome, come now, let us lay aside all joking and be serious.

JEROME. How?

ISAAC. Ha, ha, ha! I'll be hang'd if you hav'n't taken my abuse of your daughter seriously.

JEROME. You meant it so, did not you?

ISAAC. O mercy, no! a joke—just to try how angry it wou'd make you.

JEROME. Was that all I'faith! I did'n't know you had been such a wag; ha, ha, ha! By St. Iago, you made me very angry tho', well, and you do think Louisa handsome?

ISAAC. Handsome! Venus de Medicis was a sybil to her.

JEROME. Give me your hand, you little jocose rogue—Egad, I thought we had been all off.

FERD. So! I was in hopes this would have been a quarrel; but I find the Jew is too cunning.

JEROME. Aye, this gust of passion has made me dry—I am but seldom ruffled; order some wine in the next room—let us drink the girl's health—poor Louisa! ugly, heh! Ha, ha, ha! 'Twas a very good joke indeed.

ISAAC. And a very true one for all that. [*aside.*

JEROME. And, Ferdinand, I insist upon your drinking success to my friend.

1 maid] *Rae, 94, I, NY*; own maid *F* 6 *aside*] *NY, Rae*; *om. F, 94, I* 11 and] *94, I, NY, F, Songs, Th, G*; *om. Rae* 15 You're . . . and] *94, I, NY, Songs, Rae, F*; Good Knave, You're a sot, from *G, Th* you'd best] *94, I, NY, Rae, F, Songs*; you must *Th* *After line 16, Rae prints*: *Jer.* Joking! | *Isaac.* Aye—why sure you did not think I was in earnest? 21 a joke] *94, I, NY, F*; a joke, a joke *Rae* 28 was in hopes] *94, I, NY, F*; did hope *Rae* 30 Aye, this] *94, I, NY, F*; As I live—that little *Rae* but] *Rae, F*; *om. 94, I, NY* 31 order] *94, I, NY, F*; Boy, bring *Rae* girl's] *Rae, F*; poor girl's *94, I, NY* 34 *aside*] *Rae, F, NY*; *om. 94, I* 35 And] *94, I, NY, F*; And here *Rae* upon] *Rae, 94, I, NY*; on *F*

FERD. Sir, I will drink success to my friend with all my heart.

JEROME. Come, little Solomon, if any sparks of anger had remain'd, this would be the only way to quench them.

TRIO

A bumper of good liquor,
Will end a contest quicker,
Than justice, judge or vicar.
So fill a cheerful glass,
And let good humour pass.

But if more deep the quarrel,
Why, sooner drain the barrel,
Than be the hateful fellow,
That's crabbed when he is mellow.
A bumper, &c. [*Exeunt.*

SCENE IV—ISAAC'*s Lodgings*

Enter LOUISA.

LOUISA. Was ever truant daughter so whimsically circumstanced as I am! I have sent my intended husband to look after my lover—the man of my father's choice is gone to bring me the man of my own, but how dispiriting is this interval of expectation?

SONG

What bard, O time discover,
With wings first made thee move;
Ah! sure he was some lover,
Who ne'er had left his love.

For who that once did prove,
The pangs which absence brings,
Tho' but one day,
He were away,
Could picture thee with wings.

Enter CARLOS.

So, friend, is Antonio found?

CARLOS. I could not meet with him, lady; but I doubt not my friend Isaac will be here with him presently.

8 a] *Rae, 94, I, NY, Songs*; each *F, Th* 9 *Th. omits the line* 17 ever] *Rae, 94, I, NY*; ever a *F* 18 look after] *Rae, 94, I, NY*; in search of *F* 22–30 What . . . wings] *Rae, 94, NY, F, Songs*; *om. I* 33 my friend] *94, I, NY, F*; *om. Rae*

LOUISA. O shame! you have used no diligence—Is this your courtesy to a lady who has trusted herself to your protection?

CARLOS. Indeed, madam, I have not been remiss.

LOUISA. Well, well; but if either of you had known how each moment of delay weighs upon the heart of her who loves, and waits the object of her love, O, ye wou'd not then have trifled thus.

CARLOS. Alas! I know it well.

LOUISA. Were you ever in love then?

CARLOS. I was, lady: but while I have life will never be again.

LOUISA. Was your mistress so cruel?

CARLOS. If she had always been so, I shou'd have been happier.

SONG

O had my love ne'er smil'd on me,
  I ne'er had known such anguish;
But think how false, how cruel she,
  To bid me cease to languish.
To bid me hope her hand to gain,
  Breathe on a flame half perish'd,
And then with cold and fix'd disdain,
  To kill the hope she cherish'd.

Not worse his fate, who on a wreck,
  That drove as winds did blow it,
Silent had left the shatter'd deck,
  To find a grave below it.
Then land was cried—no more resign'd,
  He glow'd with joy to hear it,
Not worse his fate, his woe to find,
  The wreck must sink ere near it.

LOUISA. As I live, here is your friend coming with Antonio—I'll retire for a moment to surprize him. [*Exit.*

Enter ISAAC *and* ANTONIO.

ANTONIO. Indeed, my friend Isaac, you must be mistaken. Clara D'Almanza in love with me, and employ you to bring me to meet her! It is impossible!

ISAAC. That you shall see in an instant—Carlos, where is the lady? [CARLOS *points to the doors*] In the next room is she?

1 you] *94, I, NY, F*; ye *Rae* 6 not then] *94, I, NY, Rae*; not *F* 11 shou'd have] *Rae, 94, I, NY*; had *F* 28 ere] *Rae, I*; e're *NY*; e'er *94, F, Songs, Th* 32 friend Isaac] *Rae, F*; good friend *94, I, NY* 34 It is] *Rae, 94, I, NY*; *om. F* 35–6 lady? . . . *doors*] *94, I*; lady? (*Carlos points to the door*) *NY*; Lady?—[DON CARLOS *points to the closet*) *Rae*; lady? *F*

ANTONIO. Nay, if that lady is really here, she certainly wants me to conduct her to a dear friend of mine, who has long been her lover.

ISAAC. Psha! I tell you 'tis no such thing—you are the man she wants, and nobody but you. Here's, ado to persuade you to take a pretty girl that's dying for you.

ANTONIO. But I have no affection for this lady.

ISAAC. And you have for Louisa, hey? but take my word for it, Antonio, you have no chance there—so you may as well secure the good that offers itself to you.

ANTONIO. And could you reconcile it to your conscience, to supplant your friend?

ISAAC. Pish! Conscience has no more to do with gallantry than it has with politicks—why, you are no honest fellow, if love can't make a rogue of you—so come,—do go in and speak to her at least.

ANTONIO. Well, I have no objection to that,

ISAAC. [*opens the door*]. There—there she is—yonder by the window—get in, do [*pushes him in, and half shuts the door*] now, Carlos, now I shall hamper him I warrant—stay—I'll peep how they go on—egad, he looks confoundedly posed—now she's coaxing him—see, Carlos, he begins to come to—aye, aye, he'll soon forget his conscience.

CARLOS. Look! now they are both laughing.

ISAAC. Aye! so they are both laughing—yes, yes, they are laughing at that dear friend he talked of—aye poor devil, they have outwitted him.

CARLOS. Now he's kissing her hand.

ISAAC. Yes, yes, faith, they're agreed—he's caught, he's entangled—my dear Carlos, we have brought it about. O, this little cunning head! I'm a Machiavel, a very Machieval.

CARLOS. I hear somebody enquiring for you—I'll see who it is.

[*Exit* CARLOS.

Enter ANTONIO *and* LOUISA.

ANTONIO. Well, my good friend, this lady has so entirely convinc'd me of the certainty of your success at Don Jerome's, that I now resign my pretensions there.

ISAAC. You never did a wiser thing, believe me—and as for deceiving your friend, that's nothing at all—tricking is all fair in love, isn't it, ma'am?

LOUISA. Certainly, Sir, and I am particularly glad to find you are of that opinion.

ISAAC. O lud, yes, ma'am—let any one outwit me that can, I say—but here let me join your hands—there you lucky rogue, I wish you happily married from the bottom of my soul.

4 ado] *94, I, NY, F*; ado indeed *Rae* 6 this] *Rae, 94, I, F*; the *NY* 12 Pish!] *94, I, NY, Rae*; *om. F* 14 least] *Rae, F, NY*; last *94, I* 16 *opens . . . door*] *Rae, 94, I, NY*; *Isaac opens the door in Flatt F* 22 both laughing] *Rae, F*; *om. 94, I, NY* 25 they're] *Rae, 94, NY, I*; they've *F* 40 soul] *Rae, 94 ,I, NY*; heart *F*

LOUISA. And I am sure, if you wish it, no one else shou'd prevent it.

ISAAC. Now, Antonio, we are rivals no more, so let us be friends, will you.

ANTONIO. With all my heart, Isaac.

ISAAC. It is not every man, let me tell you, that wou'd have taken such pains, or been so generous to a rival.

ANTONIO. No, faith, I don't believe there's another beside yourself in Spain.

ISAAC. Well, but you resign all pretensions to the other lady?

ANTONIO. That I do most sincerely.

ISAAC. I doubt you have a little hankering there still.

ANTONIO. None in the least, upon my soul.

ISAAC. I mean after her fortune?

ANTONIO. No, believe me. You are heartily welcome to every thing she has.

ISAAC. Well, I'faith, you have the best of the bargain as to beauty, twenty to one—now I'll tell you a secret—I am to carry off Louisa this very evening.

LOUISA. Indeed!

ISAAC. Yes, she has sworn not to take a husband from her father's hand—so, I've persuaded him to trust her to walk with me in the garden, and then we shall give him the slip.

LOUISA. And is Don Jerome to know nothing of this?

ISAAC. O lud no: there lies the jest! Don't you see that, by this step, I over-reach him, I shall be intitled to the girl's fortune without settling a ducat on her, ha, ha, ha! I'm a cunning dog, a'n't I? A sly little villain, heh?

ANTONIO. Ha, ha, ha! you are indeed!

ISAAC. Roguish you'll say—but keen hey?—devilish keen!

ANTONIO. So you are indeed—keen—very keen.

ISAAC. And what a laugh we shall have at Don Jerome's, when the truth comes out, hey?

LOUISA. Yes, I'll answer for't, we shall have a good laugh when the truth comes out, ha, ha, ha!

Enter CARLOS.

CARLOS. Here are the dancers come to practice the fandango you intended to have honor'd Donna Louisa with.

ISAAC. O, I sha'n't want them, but as I must pay them, I'll see a caper for my money—will you excuse me?

LOUISA. Willingly.

2 so] *Rae*, *94*, *I*, *NY*; so do *F* 8 Spain] *Rae*, *F*; all Spain *94*, *I*, *NY* 17 now] *94*, *I*, *NY*, *F*; but now *Rae* 21 walk . . . garden] *94*, *Rae*, *I*, *NY*; walk in the garden with me *F* 33 Yes] *94*, *I*, *NY*, *F*; Yes-Yes *Rae* 39 me] *Rae*, *94*, *I*, *NY*; my leaving you *F*

ISAAC. Here's my friend, whom you may command for any services, Madam, your most obedient—Antonio, I wish you all happiness. O the easy blockhead! what a fool I have made of him?—This was a master-piece. [*Exit* ISAAC.

LOUISA. Carlos, will you be my guard again, and conduct me to the Convent of St. Catherine?

ANTONIO. Why, Louisa, why shou'd you go thither?

LOUISA. I have my reasons, and you must not be seen to go with me, I shall write from thence to my father, perhaps, when he finds what he has driven me to, he may relent.

ANTONIO. I have no hope from him—O Louisa, in these arms should be your sanctuary.

LOUISA. Be patient but for a little while—my father cannot force me thence. But let me see you there before evening, and I will explain myself.

ANTONIO. I shall obey.

LOUISA. Come friend—Antonio, Carlos has been a lover himself.

ANTONIO. Then he knows the value of his trust.

CARLOS. You shall not find me unfaithful.

TRIO

Soft pity never leaves the gentle breast,
Where love has been received a welcome guest,
As wand'ring saints poor huts have sacred made,
He hallows ev'ry heart he once has sway'd;
And when his presence we no longer share,
Still leaves compassion as a relic there.

[*Exeunt* CARLOS, LOUISA, *and* ANTONIO.

END OF ACT II

ACT III

SCENE I.—*A Library*

Enter JEROME, *and* SERVANT.

JEROME. Why, I never was so amazed in my life! Louisa gone off with Isaac Mendoza! what, steal away with the very man whom I

3 fool] *Rae*, *F*; tool *94*, *I*, *NY* 5 conduct] *Rae*, *F*; convey *94*, *I*, *NY* 7 thither] *Rae*, *F*; there *94*, *I*, *NY* 13 thence] *Rae*, *F*; from thence *94*, *I*, *NY* 24 And . . . share] *F*, *Songs*, *94*, *I*, *NY*; And when obliged to quit the kind Abode *Rae*, *Th* 25 Still . . . there] *F*, *Songs*, *94*, *I*, *NY*; Still leaves a Relick that bespeaks the God *Rae*, *Th* 29 *Library*] *94*, *I*, *NY*, *F*; *Library in* DON JEROME's *House Rae* 32 whom] *94*, *I*, *NY*, *Rae*; *om. F*

wanted her to marry—elope with her own husband as it were—it is impossible.

SERVANT. Her maid says, Sir, they had your leave to walk in the garden while you was abroad: The door by the shrubbery was found open, and they have not been heard of since. [*Exit.*

JEROME. Well, it is the most unaccountable affair! s'death, there is certainly some infernal mystery in it, I can't comprehend.

Enter 2D SERVANT, *with a Letter.*

SERVANT. Here is a letter, Sir, from Signor Isaac. [*Exit.*

JEROME. So, so, this will explain—ay, 'Isaac Mendoza,' let me see. [*Reads*] 'Dearest Sir, you must, doubtless, be much surprized at my flight with your daughter'—Yes, faith and well I may. 'I had the happiness to gain her heart at our first interview'—The devil you had! 'But she having unfortunately made a vow not to receive a husband from your hands, I was obliged to comply with her whim' So, so! 'We shall shortly throw ourselves at your feet, and I hope you will have a blessing ready for one who will then be

Your son-in-law,
ISAAC MENDOZA.'

A whim, heigh? Why, the devil's in the girl, I think—This morning she wou'd die sooner than have him, and before evening she runs away with him. Well, well, my will's accomplished—let the motive be what it will—and the Portugueze, sure, will never deny to fulfill the rest of the article.

Re-enter SERVANT *with another letter.*

SERVANT. Sir, here's a man below who says he brought this from my young lady, Donna Louisa, [*Exit.*

JEROME. How! yes, it is my daughter's hand indeed! lord, there was no occasion for them both to write; well, let's see what she says: [*reads*] 'My dearest father, how shall I intreat your pardon for the rash step I have taken, how confess the motive?' Pish! hasn't Isaac just told me the motive—one would think they weren't together, when they wrote. 'If I have a spirit too resentful of ill usage, I have also a heart as easily affected by kindness'—So, so, here the whole matter comes out, her resentment for Antonio's ill usage, has made her sensible of Isaac's

5 *Exit*] *Rae, I, NY*; *om. F, 94* 8 *Letter*] *Rae, I, NY, 94*; LETTER WRIT *F* 9 *Exit*] *Rae, I, NY*; *om. 94, F* 22 him. Well] *Rae, 94, I, NY*; him—Hold, hold, now I see it—as sure as can be, she has heard that her false swain Antonio has seduc'd away Don Guzman's daughter; aye, it must be so & she marries Isaac in revenge—well *F* 24 article] *Rae, 94, I, NY*; article. What's here? *L* 25 *Re-enter*] *Rae*; *enter 94, I, NY, F* *letter*] *Rae, I, 94, NY*; LETTER, WRIT *F* 26 a] *Rae, 94, I, NY*; another *F* 27 *Exit*] *Rae, I, NY*; *om. 94, F* 28 yes] *Rae, 94, I, NY*; yet *F* 33 wrote] *Rae, 94, I, NY*; wrote—well, confess the motive *F*

kindness—yes, yes, it is all plain enough—well 'I am not married yet, tho' with a man I am convinced adores me'—Yes, yes, I dare say Isaac is very fond of her—'but I shall anxiously expect your answer, in which, should I be so fortunate as to receive your consent, you will make compleatly happy,

Your ever affectionate daughter,
LOUISA.'

My consent! to be sure she shall have it; egad, I was never better pleased—I have fulfilled my resolution—I knew I should—O there's nothing like obstinacy—Lewis! [*Calls.*

Enter SERVANT.

Let the man who brought the last letter wait, and get me a pen and ink below. (*Exit* SERVANT) I am impatient to set poor Louisa's heart at rest, holloa! Lewis! Sancho!

Enter SERVANTS.

See that there be a noble supper provided in the Saloon to-night—serve up my best wines, and let me have music, d'ye hear?

SERVANTS. Yes, sir. [*Exeunt.*

JEROME. And order all my doors to be thrown open—admit all guests with masks or without masks—I'faith, we'll have a night of it—And I'll let 'em see how merry an old man can be.

SONG

O the days when I was young,
  When I laugh't in fortune's spight,
Talk'd of love the whole day long,
  And with nectar crown'd the night,
Then it was old father Care,
  Little reck'd I of thy frown,
Half thy malice youth could bear,
  And the rest a bumper drown.

Truth they say lies in a well,
  Why I vow I ne'er could see,
Let the water-drinkers tell,
  There it always lay for me.
For when sparkling wine went round,

3 very] *Rae*, *94*, *I*, *NY*; *om. F*   I] *Rae*, *94*, *I*, *NY*; *om. F*   4 fortunate] *Rae*, *94*, *I*, *NY*; happy *F*   8 to] *Rae*, *94*, *I*, *NY*; Why, to *F*   was never] *Rae*, *94*, *I*, *NY*; never was *F*   10 (*Calls*)] *Rae*; *om. 94*, *I*, *NY*, *F*   11 *Enter*] *94*, *I*, *NY*; *Re-enter Rae*; ENTER A *F*   12 who . . . letter] *Rae*, *94*, *I*, *NY*; that brought this letter *F*   a pen] *Rae*, *94*, *I*, *NY*; pen *F*   13 (*Exit* SERVANT)] *NY Rae*; *om. 94*, *I*, *F*   16 See . . . there] *Rae*, *94*, *I*; See there *F*, *NY*

Never saw I falsehood's mask,
But still honest truth I found,
In the bottom of each flask.

True, at length my vigour's flown,
I have years to bring decay;
Few the locks that now I own,
And the few I have, are grey.
Yet, old Jerome, thou may'st boast,
While thy spirits do not tire,
Still beneath thy age's frost;
Glows a spark of youthful fire. [*Exit.*

SCENE II.—*The New Piazza*

Enter FERDINAND, *and* LOPEZ.

FERD. What, cou'd you gather no tidings of her? Nor guess where she was gone? O Clara! Clara!

LOPEZ. In truth, Sir, I could not—that she was run away from her father, was in every body's mouth,—and that Don Guzman was in pursuit of her, was also a very common report—where she was gone, or what was become of her, no one could take upon 'em to say.

FERD. S'death and fury, you blockhead, she cant be out of Seville.

LOPEZ. So I said to myself, Sir! S'death and fury, you blockhead, says I, she can't be out of Seville—then some said, she had hang'd herself for love, and others have it, Don Antonio had carried her off.

FERD. 'Tis false, scoundrel! no one said that.

LOPEZ. Then I misunderstood 'em, Sir.

FERD. Go, fool, get home, and never let me see you again, till you bring me news of her. [*Exit* LOPEZ.
O! how my fondness for this ungrateful girl, has hurt my disposition!

SONG

Ah, cruel maid, how hast thou changed
The temper of my mind?
My heart by thee from mirth estrang'd
Becomes, like thee, unkind.

14 where] *Rae*, *94*, *I*, *NY*; whither *F* 19 could] *Rae*, *94*, *I*, *NY*; would *F* 20 you] *Rae*, *94*, *I*, *NY*; ye *F* 21 myself] *Rae*, *NY*, *I*, *94*; many *F* 23 have] *Rae*, *94*, *I*, *NY*; would have *F* her] *Rae*, *94*, *I*, *NY*; *om.* *F* 27 her] *Rae*, *94*, *I*, *NY*; her—Begone! *F* 30–3 Ah . . . unkind] *F*, *94*, *NY*, *Songs*, *Th*; *om.* *Rae*, *I*

By fortune favour'd, clear in fame
  I once ambitious was;
And friends I had, that fann'd the flame,
  And gave my youth applause.

But now my weakness all abuse,
  Yet vain their taunts on me,
Friends, fortune, fame itself I'd lose;
  To gain one smile from thee.
Yet, only thou shouldst not despise
  My folly, or my woe;
If I am mad in others eyes,
  'Tis thou hast made me so.

But days like these, with doubting curst
  I will not long endure;
Am I despised, I know the worst,
  And also know my cure.
If false, her vows she dare renounce,
  She instant ends my pain,
For, Oh, that heart must break at once;
  Which cannot hate again.

Enter ISAAC.

ISAAC. So, I have her safe—and have only to find a priest to marry us, Antonio now may marry Clara, or not, if he pleases.

FERD. What? what was that you said of Clara?

ISAAC. O Ferdinand! my brother-in-law that shall be, who thought of meeting you.

FERD. But what of Clara?

ISAAC. I'faith, you shall hear.—This morning as I was coming down, I met a pretty damsel, who told me her name was Clara d'Almanza, and begg'd my protection.

FERD. How?

ISAAC. She said she had eloped from her father, Don Guzman, but that love for a young gentleman in Seville, was the cause.

FERD. O heavens! did she confess it?

ISAAC. O yes, she confess'd at once—but then, says she, my lover is not inform'd of my flight, nor suspects my intention.

FERD. Dear creature! no more I did indeed! O, I am the happiest fellow—well, Isaac! [*aside*.

1–20 By . . . again] *F*, *94*, *NY*, *Songs*; *om. Rae*, *I* 8 from] *F*, *94*, *NY*, *Songs*; of *Th* 22 marry] *94*, *Rae*, *I*, *NY*; join *F* 23 if] *94*, *Rae*, *I*, *NY*; as *F* 24 that] *Rae*, *94*, *I*, *NY*; it *F* 35 at] *Rae*, *94*, *I*, *NY*; it at *F*

ISAAC. Why, then she intreated me to find him out for her, and bring him to her.

FERD. Good heavens, how lucky! well, come along, lets lose no time, [*pulling him.*

ISAAC. Zooks! where are we to go?

FERD. Why, did any thing more pass?

ISAAC. Any thing more!—yes, the end on't was, that I was moved by her speeches, and complied with her desires.

FERD. Well, and where is she?

ISAAC. Where is she? why, dont I tell you I complied with her request, and left her safe in the arms of her lover.

FERD. S'death! you trifle with me—I have never seen her.

ISAAC. You! O lud, no! How the devil shou'd you? 'Twas Antonio she wanted, and with Antonio I left her.

FERD. Hell and madness [*aside*] what Antonio d'Ercilla?

ISAAC. Aye, aye, the very man; and the best part of it was, he was shy of taking her at first—He talk'd a good deal about honor and conscience, and deceiving some dear friend; but, lord, we soon over ruled that.

FERD. You did?

ISAAC. O yes, presently—such deceit, says he—Pish! says the lady, tricking is all fair in love—but then, my friend, says he—Psha! damn your friend, says I—so, poor wretch, he has no chance—no, no—he may hang himself as soon as he pleases.

FERD. I must go, or I shall betray myself. [*aside.*

ISAAC. But stay, Ferdinand, you han't heard the best of the joke.

FERD. Curse on your joke.

ISAAC. Goodlack! what's the matter now? I thought to have diverted you.

FERD. Be rack'd, tortur'd, damn'd—

ISAAC. Why, sure you're not the poor devil of a lover are you? I'faith, as sure as can be, he is—this is a better joke than t'other, ha, ha, ha!

FERD. What do you laugh, you vile, mischievous varlet [*collars him*] but that you're beneath my anger, I'd tear your heart out. [*Throws him from him.*

ISAAC. O mercy! here's usage for a brother-in-law!

FERD. But, harky, rascal! tell me directly where these false friends are gone, or by my soul [*draws.*]

ISAAC. For heavens sake, now, my dear Brother-in-law don't be in a rage—I'll recollect as well as I can.

FERD. Be quick then!

7 by] *F*; with *Rae, 94, I, NY* 24 *aside*] *Rae, NY*; *om. F, 94, I* 32 do you] *Rae, 94, I, NY*; you do *F* 33–4 out . . . *him*] *Rae, 94, I, NY*; out, reptile I would *F* 38 dear] *Rae, 94, I, NY*; sweet *F*

ISAAC. I will, I will—but people's memories differ—some have a treacherous memory—now mine is a cowardly memory—it takes to its heels at sight of a drawn sword, it does I'faith—and I could as soon fight as recollect.

FERD. Zounds, tell me the truth, and I won't hurt you.

ISAAC. No, no; I know you won't, my dear brother-in-law—but that ill looking thing there.

FERD. What, then, you won't tell me?

ISAAC. Yes, yes, I will—I'll tell you all upon my soul, but why need you listen sword in hand.

FERD. Well, there [*puts up*] now.

ISAAC. Why then, I believe they are gone to—that is my friend, Carlos, told me he had left Donna Clara—dear Ferdinand keep your hand off—at the Convent of St. Catherine.

FERD. St. Catherine!

ISAAC. Yes; and that Antonio was to come to her there.

FERD. Is this the truth?

ISAAC. It is indeed; and all I know, as I hope for life.

FERD. Well, coward, take your life—'tis that false, dishonourable Antonio, who shall feel my vengeance.

ISAAC. Ay, ay, kill him—cut his throat and welcome.

FERD. But for Clara—infamy on her—she is not worth my resentment.

ISAAC. No more she is, my dear brother-in-law, I'faith I would not be angry about her—she is not worth it indeed.

FERD. 'Tis false—she is worth the enmity of princes.

ISAAC. True, true; so she is, and I pity you exceedingly for having lost her.

FERD. S'death, you rascal! how durst you talk of pitying me.

ISAAC. O dear brother-in-law, I beg pardon—I don't pity you in the least, upon my soul.

FERD. Get hence, fool, and provoke me no further—Nothing but your insignificance saves you.

ISAAC. (*Aside*) I'faith, then my insignificance is the best friend I have—I'm going, dear Ferdinand—What a curst, hot-headed bully it is! [*Exit.*

3 at] *Rae*, *94*, *I*, *NY*; at the *F* 11 Well] *F*; Why *Rae*, *94*, *I*, *NY* 13 keep] *Rae*, *94*, *I*, *NY*; now keep *F* hand] *F*; hands *Rae*, *94*, *I*, *NY* 33 (*Aside*)] *Rae*; *om.* *94*, *I*, *NY*, *F* 34 (*Exit*)] *F*; (*apart & exeunt*) *NY*; (*Exeunt severally*) *Rae*; (*Exeunt*) *94*, *I*. *After line 20*, *NY prints*:

AIR—FERDINAND

Shall not my soul to vengeance now be moved?
By him I trusted, robb'd of her I loved.
Sharp is the woe that wounds the jealous mind,
When treach'ry two fond hearts would rend;
But o, how keener far the pang to find
That traitor in your bosom friend.

FERD. From this hour, I disclaim all trust in man, or love for woman, but does Antonio think to triumph with impunity, when he has left me no hope of joy on earth, but in revenge.

SONG

Sharp is the woe, that wounds the jealous mind,
When treachery two fond hearts would rend,
But oh, how keener far, the pang to find
That traitor is our bosom friend. [*Exit.*

SCENE III.—*The Garden of the Convent*

Enter LOUISA *and* CLARA.

LOUISA. And you really wish my brother may not find you out.

CLARA. Why else, have I conceal'd myself under this disguise?

LOUISA. Why, perhaps, because the dress becomes you, for you certainly don't intend to be a nun for life.

CLARA. If, indeed, Ferdinand had not offended me so, last night.

LOUISA. Come, come, it was his fear of losing you, made him so rash.

CLARA. Well, you may think me cruel—but I swear if he were here this instant, I believe I shou'd forgive him.

SONG

CLARA

By him we love offended,
How soon our anger flies,
One day apart, 'tis ended,
Behold him and it dies,

Last night, your roving brother,
Enrag'd I bade depart,
And sure his rude presumption,
Deserv'd to lose my heart.

Yet, were he now before me,
In spite of injured pride,
I fear my eyes wou'd pardon,
Before my tongue cou'd chide.

1–8 From . . . *Exit*] *F*; *om.* *94*, *Rae*, *I*; *for the version and location in NY*, *see preceding page* 5 Sharp] *F*, *Songs*; Shall not my Soul to Vengeance now be mov'd | By him I trusted robb'd of her I lov'd | Sharp *Th*, *G* 7 the pang] *F*, *Songs*, *Th*; his pangs *G* 8 is our] *F*; in our *Songs*, *Th*; in a *G* 12 disguise] *94*, *I*, *NY*, *Rae*; habit *F* 17 here] *94*, *I*, *NY*, *Rae*; here at *F* 32 cou'd] *94*, *I*, *Rae*, *NY*, *Songs*, *Th*; wou'd *F*

With truth, the bold deceiver,
  To me thus oft has said,
'In vain wou'd Clara slight me,
  In vain wou'd she upbraid;
No scorn those lips discover,
  Where dimples laugh the while,
No frowns appear resentful,
  Where Heaven has stampt a smile.

LOUISA. I protest Clara, I shall begin to think you are seriously resolved to enter on your probation.

CLARA. And, seriously, I very much doubt whether the character of a nun wou'd not become me best.

LOUISA. Why, to be sure, the character of a nun is a very becoming one—at a masquerade—but no pretty woman in her senses ever thought of taking the veil for above a night.

CLARA. Yonder I see your Antonio is returned—I shall only interrupt you; ah, Louisa, with what happy eagerness you turn to look for him! [*Exit.*

Enter ANTONIO.

ANTONIO. Well, my Louisa, any news since I left you?

LOUISA. None—The messenger is not returned from my father.

ANTONIO. Well, I confess, I do not perceive what we are to expect from him.

LOUISA. I shall be easier however, in having made the trial, I do not doubt your sincerity, Antonio: but there is a chilling air around poverty that often kills affection, that was not nurs'd in it—If we would make love our household god, we had best secure him a comfortable roof.

SONG

How oft Louisa hast thou said
  (Nor wilt thou the fond boast disown)
Thou wouldst not lose Antonio's love
  To reign the partner of a throne.

1–8 With . . . smile] *F*, *94*, *NY*, *Songs*, *Th*; *om. Rae*, *I* 4 wou'd she] *94*, *NY*, *Th*; she wou'd *F*, *Songs* 24–8 I do not doubt . . . comfortable roof] *94*, *Rae*, *I*, *NY*; besides, Antonio, are you not rash impressing me to be yours, so long before I am intitled to my fortune? How shall we live, if my father should dispute my right then? I could not endure to contend with him: *F The lines*, '*I do . . . roof*', *are printed in F after line 12 on* p. 271 25 around] *Rae*, *I*; round *94*, *F*, *NY* 30–line 12, p. 271 How . . . thine] *F*, *Rae*, *I*, *Songs*; *om. 94*; *NY prints the song after line 23*, p. 271 30 said] *F*, *Songs*, *NY*, *Th*; told *Rae*, *I* 31 the] *Rae*, *F*, *NY*, *I*, *Th*; thy *Songs*

And by those lips that spoke so kind,
  And by this hand, I press'd to mine;
To be the lord of wealth and power,
  I swear, I would not part with thine.

Then how, my soul, can we be poor
  Who own what kingdoms could not buy?
Of this true heart, thou shalt be queen,
  And serving thee, a monarch I.

Thus uncontroul'd in mutual bliss,
  And rich in love's exhaustless mine;
Do thou snatch treasures from my lips,
  And I'll take kingdoms back from thine.

[*Enter* MAID, *with a letter to* LOUISA *and Exit.*

My father's answer I suppose.

ANTONIO. My dearest Louisa, you may be assured that it contains nothing but threats and reproaches.

LOUISA. Let us see however [*reads*] 'Dearest daughter, make your lover happy, you have my full consent to marry as your whim has chosen, but be sure come home to sup with your affectionate father'.

ANTONIO. You jest, Louisa.

LOUISA. [*Gives him the Letter*] Read—read.

ANTONIO. 'Tis so, by heavens! sure there must be some mistake; but that's none of our business—now, Louisa, you have no excuse for delay.

LOUISA. Shall we not then return and thank my father?

ANTONIO. But first let the priest put it out of his power to recall his word.—I'll fly to procure one.

LOUISA. Nay, if you part with me again, perhaps you may lose me.

ANTONIO. Come then—there is a friar of a neighbouring convent is my friend; you have already been diverted by the manners of a nunnery—let us see, whether there is less hypocrisy among the holy fathers.

LOUISA. I'm afraid not, Antonio—for in religion, as in friendship, they who profess most are ever the least sincere. [*Exeunt.*

Enter CLARA.

CLARA. So, yonder they go, as happy as a mutual and confess'd affection can make them; while I am left in solitude. Heigho! love may perhaps

2 this] *F*, *Songs*, *NY*, *Th*; that *Rae*, *I*   I press'd] *F*, *Songs*; I press *NY*; I've press'd *Rae*, *I*   3 To . . . power] *Rae*, *NY*, *I*, *Th*; To gain a subject nation's love *F*, *Songs*   4 I swear] *F*, *Songs*, *NY*, *Th*; By Heav'ns *Rae*, *I*   6 could] *Rae*, *I*, *NY*, *Songs*; would *F*   8 And] *F*, *Songs*, *NY*; In *Rae*, *I*   13 *to . . . Exit*] *F*; *om.* *94*, *I*, *NY*, *Rae*   15 that] *94*, *Rae*, *I*, *NY*; *om.* *F*   16 reproaches] *94*, *Rae*, *I*, *NY*; upbraidings *F*   21 *him the*] *Rae*, *94*, *I*, *NY*; *om.* *F*

excuse the rashness of an elopement from one's friend; but I am sure; nothing but the presence of the man we love can support it—Ha! what do I see; Ferdinand as I live, how cou'd he gain admission—by potent gold I suppose, as Antonio did—how eager and disturbed he seems—he shall not know me as yet. [*Lets down her veil.*]

Enter FERDINAND.

FERD. Yes, those were certainly they—my information was right. [*going.*

CLARA. [*Stops him*] Pray, Signor, what is your business here.

FERD. No matter—no matter—Oh, they stop—[*looks out*] yes, that is the perfidious Clara indeed.

CLARA. So, a jealous error—I'm glad to see him so mov'd. [*aside.*

FERD. Her disguise can't conceal her—No, no, I know her too well.

CLARA. Wonderful discernment! but Signor—

FERD. Be quiet, good nun, don't teize me—by heavens she leans upon his arm, hangs fondly on it! O woman! woman!

CLARA. But, Signor, who is it you want?

FERD. Not you, not you, so, prythee don't torment me. Yet pray stay—gentle nun, was it not Donna Clara d'Almanza just parted from you?

CLARA. Clara d'Almanza, Signor, is not yet out of the garden.

FERD. Aye, aye, I knew I was right—and pray, is not that gentleman now at the porch with her, Antonio d'Ercilla?

CLARA. It is indeed, Signor.

FERD. So, so, now but one question more—can you inform me for what purpose they have gone away?

CLARA. They are gone to be married, I believe.

FERD. Very well—enough—now if I don't marr their wedding. [*Exit.*

CLARA. [*unveils*] I thought jealousy had made lovers quick-sighted, but it has made mine blind—Louisa's story accounts to me for this error, and I am glad to find I have power enough over him to make him so unhappy—but why should not I be present at his surprize when undeceived? When he's thro' the porch I'll follow him, and, perhaps, Louisa shall not singly be a bride.

SONG

Adieu, thou dreary pile, where never dies,
The sullen echo of repentant sighs:

5 *Lets . . . veil*] *Rae*, *94*, *I*, *NY*; *om. F* 10 *looks out*] *Rae*, *94*, *I*, *NY*; *om. F* 15 heavens] *Rae*, *94*, *I*, *NY*; heav'n *F* 18 torment] *F*; tease *Rae*, *94*, *I*, *NY* 21 I was] *Rae*, *94*, *I*, *NY*; he was *F* 28 *unveils*] *Rae*, *I*, *94*, *NY*; unveiling *F* lovers] *Rae*, *I*, *94*, *NY*; a lover *F* 35 where] *Rae*, *I*, *F*, *94*, *NY*, *Songs*; where sadness *Th* 36 The . . . repentant] *Rae*, *F*, *I*, *94*, *NY*, *Songs*; where echo still repeats the mourners plaintive *Th* echo] *Rae*, *F*, *I*, *94*, *Songs*, *Th*; echoes *NY*

Ye sister mourners of each lonely cell,
Inured to hymns and sorrow, fare ye well;
For happier scenes I fly this darksome grove,
To saints a prison, but a tomb to love. [*Exit.*

SCENE IV—*A Court before the Priory*

Enter ISAAC, *crossing the Stage.*

Enter ANTONIO.

ANTONIO. What, my friend Isaac:

ISAAC. What, Antonio! wish me joy! I have Louisa safe.

ANTONIO. Have you? I wish you joy with all my soul.

ISAAC. Yes, I am come here to procure a priest to marry us.

ANTONIO. So, then we are both on the same errand, I am come to look for father Paul.

ISAAC. Hah! I am glad on't—but I'faith he must tack me first, my love is waiting.

ANTONIO. So is mine—I left her in the porch.

ISAAC. Aye, but I am in haste to get back to Don Jerome.

ANTONIO. And so am I too.

ISAAC. Well, perhaps he'll save time and marry us both together—or I'll be your father and you shall be mine—Come along—but you're oblig'd to me for all this.

ANTONIO. Yes, yes. [*Exeunt.*

SCENE V.[1]—*A Room in the Priory*

Friars at a Table drinking

GLEE and CHORUS

This bottle's the sun of our Table,
  His beams are rosy wine;
We, Planets that are not able,
  Without his help to shine,

1–2 Ye . . . well] *Rae, F, I, 94, Songs, NY*; *om. Th* 3 darksome] *Rae, F, I, 94, Songs, NY*; hateful *Th* 4 To . . . love] *Rae, F, I, 94, Songs, NY*; To ev'ry joy a foe; a grave to hapless love *Th* 9 joy] *Rae, I, 94, NY*; joy, rogue *F* 11 Yes] *Rae, I, 94, NY*; Yes, yes *F* 18 too] *Rae, 94, I, NY*; too (*aside*) *F* 20 along] *94, I, NY, F*; alone *Rae* 24 *Friars . . . drinking*] *94, I, NY, F*; FATHER PAUL, FATHER FRANCIS, FATHER AUGUSTINE, *and other* FRIARS, *discovered at a table drinking. Rae* a] *Rae, F*; the *94, I, NY* 27 His] *Rae, F, 94, I, NY, Songs*; Whose *Th*

[1] Rhodes, ii. 265–7, prints this scene as it appeared in the *European Magazine*, iii (1783), 335–6, and suggests that the version is a reconstruction from memory.

Let mirth and glee abound,
You'll soon grow bright,
With borrow'd light;
And shine as he goes round.

PAUL. Brother Francis, toss the bottle about, and give me your toast.

FRANCIS. Have we drank the abbess of St. Ursuline?

AUG. Yes, yes; she was the last.

FRANCIS. Then I'll give you the blue-ey'd nun of St. Catherine's.

PAUL. With all my heart [*drinks*]. Pray brother, Augustine, were there any benefactions left in my absence?

FRANCIS. Don Juan Corduba has left an hundred ducats to remember him in our masses.

PAUL. Has he! let them be paid to our wine merchant, and we'll remember him in our cups, which will do just as well. Any thing more?

AUG. Yes, Baptista, the rich miser, who died last week, has bequeath'd us a thousand Pistoles, and the silver lamp he used in his own chamber, to burn before the image of St. Anthony.

PAUL. 'Twas well meant; but we'll employ his money better—Baptista's bounty shall light the living, not the dead—St. Anthony is not afraid to be left in the dark, tho' he was—see who's there.

[*A knocking*, FRANCIS *goes to the door*, *and opens it.*

Enter PORTER.

PORTER. Here's one without in pressing haste to speak with father Paul.

AUG. Brother Paul!

[PAUL *comes from behind a curtain with a glass of wine, and in his hand a piece of cake.*

PAUL. Here! how durst you, fellow, thus abruptly break in upon our devotions?

PORTER. I thought they were finished.

PAUL. No they were not—were they brother Francis?

1–4 *Th omits the second quatrain, and substitutes*
Put it round
Let mirth and glee abound.
5 toss] *Rae*, *I*, *94*, *NY*; pass *F* 8 the] *Rae*, *I*, *94*, *NY*; the little *F* 9 Augustine] *Rae*, *94*, *F*; Francis *NY*, *I* 14 cups] *94*, *I*, *Rae*, *NY*; glasses *F* 19 not the] *Rae*, *94*, *NY*, *I*; and not the *F* 20 see . . . there] *94*, *I*, *Rae*, *NY*; Who's here? *F* 21 *A*] *94*, *I*, *NY*; *om. Rae*, *F* FRANCIS . . . *it*] *94*, *I*, *Rae*, *NY*; (*Move Table behind Curtain.*) *F* 22 *Enter* PORTER] *94*, *I*, *Rae*, *NY*; *Enter Lay-Brother F* 23 without] *94*, *I*, *Rae*, *NY*; within *F* 25 Brother] *94*, *I*, *Rae*, *NY*; Father *F* 26–7 PAUL . . . *cake*] *94*, *I*, *Rae*, *NY*; *Peeps thro the Curtain. Comes forward with a large Rummer of Wine, and a Piece of Plumb-cake F* 30 were] *94*, *I*, *Rae*, *NY*; had been *F*

AUG. Not by a bottle each.

PAUL. But neither you nor your fellows mark how the hours go—no, you mind nothing but the gratifying of your appetites; ye eat and swill, and sleep, and gormandize, and thrive while we are wasting in mortification.

PORTER. We ask no more than nature craves.

PAUL. 'Tis false, ye have more appetites than hairs, and your flush'd, sleek, and pampered appearance is the disgrace of our order—out on't—if you are hungry, can't you be content with the wholesome roots of the earth, and if you are dry, isn't there the crystal spring [*drinks*]? Put this away [*gives a glass*] and shew me where I'm wanted. [PORTER *drains the glass*—PAUL *going, turns*]—so, you wou'd have drunk it, if there had been any left. Ah, glutton! glutton! [*Exeunt.*

SCENE VI. *The Court before the Priory*

Enter ISAAC *and* ANTONIO.

ISAAC. A plaguy while coming this same father Paul—He's detain'd at vespers I suppose, poor fellow.

ANTONIO. No, here he comes.
Good father Paul, [*Enter* PAUL] I crave your blessing.

ISAAC. Yes good father Paul, we are come to beg a favour.

PAUL. What is it pray?

ISAAC. To marry us, good father Paul; and in truth, thou do'st look the very priest of Hymen.

PAUL. In short I may be called so; for I deal in repentance and mortification.

ISAAC. No, no, thou seem'st an officer of Hymen, because thy presence speaks content and good humour.

PAUL. Alas! my appearance is deceitful. Bloated I am, indeed, for fasting is a windy recreation, and it hath swoln me like a bladder.[1]

ANTONIO. But thou hast a good fresh colour in thy face father, rosy I'faith.

PAUL. Yes, I have blush'd for mankind, till the hue of my shame is as fixed as their vices.

ISAAC. Good man!

1 each] *Rae*, *94*, *F*, *I*; each. (*aside*) *NY* 6–7 flush'd, sleek] *Rae*, *94*, *I*, *NY*; flush cheek *F* 8 roots] *Rae*, *94*, *I*, *NY*; herbs *F* 9 earth] *Rae*, *94*, *I*, *NY*; earth? (*Eating*) *F* *drinks*] *Rae*, *94*, *I*, *NY*; *drinks it off F* 10 *gives a*] *94*, *I*, *NY*; Gives the *Rae*; *give F* 10–11 PORTER . . . *turns*] *Rae*, *94*, *I*, *NY*; *Going turns and sees Lay-brother with the Rummer at his mouth F* 11 drunk] *Rae*; drank *F*, *94*, *I*, *NY* 12 if there had] *Rae*, *94*, *I*, *NY*; had there *F* Ah] *Rae*, *94*, *I*, *NY*; Oh *F* *Exeunt*] *Rae*, *94*, *I*, *NY*; *Exit. Lay-brother after him F* 13 *the Priory*] *Rae*, *94*, *I*, *NY*; *Monast*[*e*]*ry F* 22 very priest] *94*, *I*, *NY*; priest *Rae*; very high priest *F* 23 short] *94*, *Rae*, *I*, *NY*; some sort *F* 29 rosy] *Rae*, *94*, *I*, *NY*; pretty rosy *F* 30 my] *94*, *I*, *NY*, *Rae*; their *F*

[1] Gomez in Dryden's *Spanish Friar* is carbuncled and bloated, 'which he attributes to abstinence and fasting.... Paul says almost the same'. (*More Kotzebue* (1799), p. 13 n.)

PAUL. And I have labour'd too—but to what purpose, they continue to sin under my very nose.

ISAAC. Efecks, father, I shou'd have guess'd as much, for your nose seems to be put to the blush more than any other part of your face.

PAUL. Go, you're a wag.

ANTONIO. But to the purpose, father—will you officiate for us?

PAUL. To join young people thus clandestinely is not safe, and indeed, I have in my heart many weighty reasons against it.

ANTONIO. And I have in my hand many weighty reasons for it—Isaac, hav'n't you an argument or two in our favour about you?

ISAAC. Yes, yes; here is a most unanswerable purse.

PAUL. For shame, you make me angry; you forget that I am a Jacobin,[1] and when importunate people have forced their trash—aye, into this pocket here—or into this—why, then the sin was theirs [*they put money into his pockets*] fie! now you distress me!—I wou'd return it, but that I must touch it that way, and so wrong my oath.

ANTONIO. Now then, come with us.

ISAAC. Aye, now give us our title to joy and rapture.

FRIAR. Well, when your hour of repentance comes, don't blame me.

ANTONIO. No bad caution to my friend Isaac [*aside*]. Well, well, father, do you do your part and I'll abide the consequence.

ISAAC. Aye, and so will I [*they are going.*]

Enter LOUISA [*running.*]

LOUISA. O, Antonio, Ferdinand is at the porch and enquiring for us.

ISAAC. Who? Don Ferdinand! he's not enquiring for me I hope.

ANTONIO. Fear not, my love, I'll soon pacify him.

ISAAC. Egad, you won't—Antonio, take my advice and run away; this Ferdinand is the most unmerciful dog! and has the cursedest long sword! and upon my soul he comes on purpose to cut your throat.

ANTONIO. Never fear, never fear.

ISAAC. Well, you may stay if you will—but I'll get some body else to marry me, for by St. Iago, he shall never meet me again, while I am master of a pair of heels. [*Runs out*—DONNA LOUISA *lets down her veil.*

1 continue] *94, I, NY, Rae*; come *F* 3 your nose] *94, I, NY, Rae*; yours *F* 7 safe] *Rae, 94, I, NY*; safe with us *F* 9 And] *94, I, NY, Rae*; Aye, and *F* 12 that . . . Jacobin] *94, NY, F*; who I am *Rae, I* 13 trash] *94, I, NY, Rae*; trash—into this *F* 14 then] *94, I, NY, Rae*; *om. F* 14–15 *they . . . pockets*] *94, I, NY, Rae*; *Put money in F* 15 now] *F*; now, how *94, I, NY, Rae* 16 that I] *94, I, NY, Rae*; I, *F* 18 our] *F, Rae*; your *94, I, NY* 21 consequence] *94, I, NY, Rae*; consequences *F* 22 *they . . . going*] *94, I, NY*; *om. F, Rae* 31 some body else] *F*; some one *94, I, NY, Rae* 32 meet] *Rae, NY*; examine *F*; marry *94, I* 34 *Runs . . . veil*] *Rae*; *Runs out 94, I, NY*; *Exit Isaac F*

[1] See p. 211, above.

Enter FERDINAND.

FERD. So, Sir, I have met with you at last.

ANTONIO. Well, Sir?

FERD. Base treacherous man! whence can a false, deceitful soul like yours borrow confidence to look so steadily on the man you've injured?

ANTONIO. Ferdinand, you are too warm—'tis true you find me on the point of wedding one I love beyond my life, but no argument of mine prevail'd on her to elope—I scorn deceit as much as you—by heav'n, I knew not she had left her father's till I saw her.

FERD. What a mean excuse! you have wrong'd your friend then, for one, whose wanton forwardness anticipated your treachery—of this indeed, your Jew pander inform'd me; but let your conduct be consistent, and since you have dar'd to do a wrong, follow me, and shew you have spirit to avow it.

LOUISA. Antonio, I perceive his mistake—leave him to me.

PAUL. Friend, you are rude to interrupt the union of two willing hearts.

FERD. No, meddling priest, the hand he seeks is mine.

PAUL. If so, I'll proceed no further—lady, did you ever promise this youth your hand? [*To* LOUISA, *who shakes her head.*]

FERD. Clara, I thank you for your silence—I would not have heard your tongue avow such falsity—be't your punishment to remember I have not reproached you.

Enter CLARA

CLARA. What mockery is this?

FERD. Antonio, you are protected now, but we shall meet.

[*Going*, CLARA *holds one arm and* LOUISA *the other.*]

DUET

LOUISA. Turn thee round I pray thee,
Calm awhile thy rage,
CLARA. I must help to stay thee,
And thy wrath assuage.

1 FERDINAND] *Rae*, *NY*, *I*, *F*; FERDINAND *and* LOUISA *94* 5 you've] *94*, *I*, *NY*, *Rae*; you've so much *F* 8 prevail'd on] *94*, *I*, *NY*, *Rae*; seduc'd *F* 8 heav'n] *94*, *I*, *NY*, *Rae*; heav'ns *F* 9 father's] *94*, *I*, *NY*, *Rae*; father *F* 12 pander] *94*, *I*, *NY*, *Rae*; pedlar *F* conduct] *94*, *I*, *NY*, *Rae*; confidence *F* 13 do] *94*, *I*, *Rae*; do *F*; *om. NY* 15 me] *Rae*, *I*, *NY*, *94*; me. (*Aside to Antonio*) *F* 17 mine] *I*, *Rae*; mine. | *Enter Clara F*; mine. | *Enter* CLARA, *behind 94*, *NY* 18 further] *94*, *NY*, *Rae*, *I*; farther *F* 19 *To . . . who*] *94*, *NY*, *I*; *To* DONNA LOUISA *Rae*; *om. F* *head*] *94*, *I*, *NY*, *Rae*; (*head*) Did you ever think of making him your husband? (*shakes her head*). There, you see *F* 23 *Enter* CLARA] *I*; *Enter* DONNA CLARA, *veiled Rae*; *om. 94*, *NY*, *F* 24 What . . . this?] *I*, *Rae*; *om. 94*, *NY*; *spoken by Ferdinand in F*, *after line 26*. 26 *Going . . . other*] *I*, *Rae*, *94*, *NY*; (*Going they take hold of his arms*) *F*

LOUISA. Could'st thou not discover
One so dear to thee?
CLARA. Can'st thou be a lover,
And thus fly from me? [*both unveil.*

FERD. How's this! my sister! Clara too—I'm confounded.

LOUISA. 'Tis even so, good brother.

PAUL. How! what impiety! Did the man want to marry his own sister?

LOUISA. And arn't you asham'd of yourself not to know your own sister?

CLARA. To drive away your own mistress—

LOUISA. Don't you see how jealousy blinds people?

CLARA. Aye, and will you ever be jealous again?

FERD. Never—never—you, sister, I know will forgive me—but how, Clara, shall I presume——

CLARA. No, no, just now you told me not to tieze you 'Who do you want, good Signor?' 'not you, not you.' O you blind wretch! but swear never to be jealous again, and I'll forgive you.

FERD. By all—

CLARA. There, that will do—you'll keep the oath just as well. [*gives her hand.*

LOUISA. But, brother, here is one, to whom some apology is due.

FERD. Antonio, I am asham'd to think—

ANTONIO. Not a word of excuse, Ferdinand—I have not been in love myself, without learning that a lover's anger shou'd never be resented—but come—let us retire with this good father, and we'll explain to you the cause of your error.

GLEE and CHORUS

Oft' does Hymen smile to hear,
Wordy vows of feign'd regard;
Well he knows when they're sincere.
Never slow to give reward:
For his glory is to prove,
Kind to those who wed for love. [*Exeunt.*

1 Could'st] *94, I, NY, Rae, F, Songs, Th*; Canst *G* 2 dear] *94, I, NY, Rae*; near *F, Songs, G, Th* 4 thus] *94, I, NY, F, Rae, Songs*; yet *Th* *both unveil*] *Rae, 94, I, NY*; *om. F* 9 yourself] *94, I, NY, F*; yourself to have come hither and behaved so rashly. | CLARA. And arn't you ashamed of your own sagacity? *Rae* 11 To drive] *94, I, NY, F*; And to turn *Rae* 14 how] *Rae, F, I*; now *94, NY* 20 There] *Rae, 94, I, NY*; There, there *F* 21 *gives*] *94, I, NY, Rae*; *Kisses F* 22 to . . . due] *94, I, NY, F*; whom some apology is due to. *Rae* 25 a lover's] *94, I, NY, Rae*; lovers *F* 27 your] *Rae, F*; this *94, I, NY* 30 Wordy] *Rae, Songs, 94, I, NY, F*; Words and *Th* 34 who] *Rae, 94, I, NY, F*; that *Th*

SCENE VII.—*and Last. A Grand Saloon*

Enter DON JEROME, LOPEZ, *and* SERVANTS.

JEROME. Be sure now let every thing be in the best order—let all my Servants have on their merriest faces—but tell 'em to get as little drunk as possible till after supper. So, Lopez, where's your master? sha'n't we have him at supper.

LOPEZ. Indeed, I believe not, Sir—he's mad, I doubt; I'm sure he has frighted me from him.

JEROME. Aye, aye, he's after some wench, I suppose, a young rake! Well, well, we'll be merry without him.

Enter a SERVANT.

SERVANT. Sir, here is Signor Isaac.

Enter ISAAC.

JEROME. So, my dear son-in-law—there, take my blessing and forgiveness, but where's my daughter? where's Louisa?

ISAAC. She's without impatient for a blessing, but almost afraid to enter.

JEROME. O fly and bring her in. [*Exit* ISAAC.
Poor girl, I long to see her pretty face.

ISAAC. [*without*] Come, my charmer! my trembling Angel!

Enter ISAAC *and* DUENNA, DON JEROME *runs to meet them* [*she kneels.*]

JEROME. Come to my arms, my—[*starts back*] why who the devil have we here?

ISAAC. Nay, Don Jerome, you promised her forgiveness; see how the dear creature droops.

JEROME. Droops indeed! Why, gad take me, this is old Margaret—but where's my daughter, where's Louisa?

ISAAC. Why here, before your eyes—nay, don't be abashed, my sweet wife!

JEROME. Wife with a vengeance! Why, zounds you have not married the Duenna!

MARGARET. [*kneeling*] O dear papa! you'll not disown me sure!

JEROME. Papa! dear papa! Why, zounds, your impudence is as great as your ugliness.

ISAAC. Rise, my charmer, go throw your snowy arms about his neck, and convince him you are——

1 *and Last*] 94, *F*, *NY*; *om. Rae*, *I* *A Grand Saloon*] 94, *I*, *NY*; *A Grand Saloon. Desert set out F*; *A Grand Saloon in* DON JEROME'S *House Rae* 2 LOPEZ, *and* SERVANTS] *Rae*, *F*, *NY*; SERVANTS *and* LOPEZ 94, *I* 12 Isaac] 94, *I*, *NY*, *Rae*; Isaac. | *Jerome*. Oh! *F* 19 *without*] 94, *I*, *NY*, *Rae*; *speaks without F* 20 *and* . . . JEROME] 94, *I*, *NY*; *and Duenna, she kneels, Jerome F*; *with* DUENNA; DON JEROME *Rae* *she kneels*] 94, *I*, *NY*, *Rae*; *om. F* 21 Come] 94, *Rae*, *I*, *NY*; Aye, come *F* my] 94, *Rae*, *I*, *NY*; thou *F* 27 nay] 94, *I*, *NY*, *Rae*; nay, hold up your sweet face *F* sweet] 94, *I*, *NY*, *Rae*; dear *F* 30 Duenna!] 94, *I*, *NY*, *Rae*; Duenna. | *Isaac*. The Duenna! you are out of your wits *F* 32 dear] 94, *F*, *NY*; *om. Rae*, *I*

DUENNA. O Sir, forgive me! [*Embraces him.*

JEROME. Help! murder! [*Servants come forward.*

SERVANTS. What's the matter, Sir?

JEROME. Why here, this damn'd Jew, has brought an old Harridan to strangle me.

ISAAC. Lord, it is his own daughter, and he is so hard hearted he won't forgive her.

Enter ANTONIO *and* LOUISA, *they kneel.*

JEROME. Zounds and fury what's here now? who sent for you, Sir, and who the devil are you?

ANTONIO. This lady's husband, Sir.

ISAAC. Aye, that he is I'll be sworn; for I left 'em with the Priest, and was to have given her away.

JEROME. You were?

ISAAC. Aye; that's my honest friend, Antonio; and that's the little girl I told you I had hamper'd him with.

JEROME. Why, you are either drunk or mad—this is my daughter.

ISAAC. No, no; 'tis you are both drunk and mad, I think—here's your daughter.

JEROME. Hark'ee, old iniquity, will you explain all this or not?

DUENNA. Come then, Don Jerome, I will—tho' our habits might inform you all—look on your daughter, there and on me.

ISAAC. What's this I hear?

DUENNA. The truth is, that in your passion this morning, you made a small mistake, for you turn'd your daughter out of doors, and lock'd up your humble servant.

ISAAC. O lud! O lud! here's a pretty fellow! to turn his daughter out of doors instead of an old Duenna.

JEROME. And, O lud! O lud! here's a pretty fellow to marry an old Duenna instead of my daughter—but how came the rest about?

DUENNA. I have only to add, that I remain'd in your daughter's place, and had the good fortune to engage the affections of my sweet husband here.

ISAAC. Her husband! why, you old witch, do you think I'll be your husband now! this is a trick, a cheat, and you ought all to be asham'd of yourselves.

ANTONIO. Hark'ee, Isaac, do you dare to complain of tricking—Don Jerome, I give you my word, this cunning Portugueze has brought all this upon himself, by endeavouring to over-reach you by getting your daughter's fortune, without making any settlement in return.

1 *Embraces*] *94, I, NY, Rae*; *Runs & embraces F* 2 *Servants come forward*] *F*; *om. 94, I, NY*; *Enter* SERVANTS *Rae* 9 Sir] *Rae, F, 94, I*; *om. NY* 13 her] *94, I, NY, Rae*; them *F* 20 iniquity] *Rae, I, 94, F*; antiquity *NY* not] *Rae, I, 94, F*; no *NY* 27 his] *Rae, 94, NY*; his own *F, I* 32 here] *Rae, 94, NY, I*; there *F* 33 do you think] *94, I, NY, Rae*; you, you don't think *F*

JEROME. Over-reach me!

ANTONIO. 'Tis so indeed, Sir, and we can prove it to you.

JEROME. Why, gad take me, it must be so, or he cou'd never have put up with such a face as Margaret's—so, little Solomon, I wish you joy of your wife with all my soul.

LOUISA. Isaac, tricking is all fair in love—let you alone for the plot.

ANTONIO. A cunning dog ar'n't you? A sly little villain, heh!

LOUISA. Roguish, perhaps; but keen, devilish keen.

JEROME. Yes, yes, his aunt always call'd him little Solomon.

ISAAC. Why, the plagues of Egypt upon you all—but do you think I'll submit to such an imposition?

ANTONIO. Isaac, one serious word—you'd better be content as you are, for believe me, you will find, that in the opinion of the world, there is not a fairer subject for contempt and ridicule, than a knave become the dupe of his own art.

ISAAC. I don't care—I'll not endure this—Don Jerome 'tis you have done it—you wou'd be so curst positive about the beauty of her you lock'd up, and all the time, I told you she was as old as my mother, and as ugly as the Devil.

DUENNA. Why you little insignificant reptile.

JEROME. That's right—attack him, Margaret.

DUENNA. Dares such a thing as you pretend to talk of beauty—a walking rouleau—a body that seems to owe all its consequence to the dropsy—a pair of eyes like two dead beetles in a wad of brown dough. A beard like an artichoke, with dry shrivell'd jaws that wou'd disgrace the mummy of a monkey.

JEROME. Well done, Margaret.

DUENNA. But you shall know that I have a brother who wears a sword, and if you don't do me justice—

ISAAC. Fire seize your brother, and you too—I'll fly to Jerusalem to avoid you.

DUENNA. Fly where you will, I'll follow you.

JEROME. Throw your snowy arms about him, Margaret.

[*Exeunt* ISAAC *and* DUENNA.

But Louisa, are you really married to this modest gentleman?

LOUISA. Sir, in obedience to your commands I gave him my hand within this hour.

JEROME. My commands!

3 never] *Rae*, *94*, *F*, *I*; not *NY* have] *94*, *I*, *NY*; *om. Rae*, *F* 10 plagues] *Rae*; plague *94*, *I*, *NY*, *F* upon] *94*, *I*, *NY*, *Rae*; on *F* I'll] *Rae*, *94*, *NY*, *I*; that I'll *F* 14 and ridicule] *94*, *I*, *NY*, *Rae*; *om. F* 17 it] *F*; this *Rae*, *94*, *I*, *NY* lock'd] *94*, *I*, *NY*, *Rae*; had lock'd *F* 33 Margaret.] *94*, *I*, *NY*, *Rae*; Margaret. | *Isaac*. O the devil!—Rape, rape. *F* 34 *Exeunt* . . . DUENNA] *94*, *I*, *NY*, *Rae*; *Exit Duenna after him.* | *Louisa*. Ha, ha, ha! He's justly serv'd, and I hope his punishment may overtake him. *F* 35 But] *94*, *I*, *NY*, *F*; But here *Rae*

ANTONIO. Yes, Sir, here is your consent under your own hand.

JEROME. How? wou'd you rob me of my child by a trick, a false pretence, and do you think to get her fortune by the same means? why s'life, you are as great a rogue as Isaac.

ANTONIO. No, Don Jerome, tho' I have profited by this paper in gaining your daughter's hand, I scorn to obtain her fortune by deceit, there Sir, [*Gives a letter*] now give her your blessing for a dower, and all the little I possess, shall be settled on her in return. Had you wedded her to a prince, he could do no more.

JEROME. Why, gad take me, but you are a very extraordinary fellow, but have you the impudence to suppose no one can do a generous action but yourself? Here Louisa, tell this proud fool of yours, that he's the only man I know that wou'd renounce your fortune; and by my soul, he's the only man in Spain that's worthy of it—there, bless you both, I'm an obstinate old fellow when I am in the wrong; but you shall now find me as steady in the right.

Enter FERDINAND *and* CLARA

Another wonder still! why, Sirrah! Ferdinand, you have not stole a nun, have you?

FERD. She is a nun in nothing but her habit, Sir—look nearer, and you will perceive 'tis Clara d'Almanza, Don Guzman's daughter, and with pardon for stealing a wedding, she is also my wife.

JEROME. Gadsbud,[1] and a great fortune—Ferdinand, you are a prudent young rogue and I forgive you; and ifecks you are a pretty little damsel. Give your father-in-law a kiss, you smiling rogue.

CLARA. There old gentleman, and now mind you behave well to us.

JEROME. Efecks, those lips ha'n't been chill'd by kissing beads—Egad, I believe I shall grow the best humour'd fellow in Spain—Lewis, Sancho, Carlos, d'ye hear, are all my doors thrown open? Our childrens weddings are the only hollidays that age can boast, and then we drain with pleasure, the little stock of spirits time has left us. [*Music within*] But see, here come our friends and neighbours.

1 hand] *94, I, NY, F*; hand and I thank you sincerely for your kindness *Rae* 2 How?] *94, I, NY, Rae*; *om. F* 7 *Gives a*] *94, I, NY, Rae*; *Returns the F* 11 suppose] *94, I, NY, Rae*; *think F* 18 Ferdinand] *94, I, NY, Rae*; Ferdinand, your dog *F* 20 habit] *94, I, NY, Rae*; habit, believe me *F* 23 Gadsbud] *94, I, NY, Rae*; Gad's me *F* 24 you] *94, I, NY, Rae*; you, boy *F* you are] *94, I, NY, Rae*; thou art *F* 26 now mind] *94, I, NY, Rae*; mind now that *F* 28 fellow] *94, I, NY, Rae*; old fellow *F* 30 that] *F*; our *Rae, 94, I, NY* 31 *Music within*] *94, I, NY, Rae*; *Horns & Clarinets F* 32 come] *94, I, Rae*; comes *F, NY*

[1] The oath associated with Sir Paul Plyant, 'an uxorious, Foolish, old Knight', in Congreve's *The Double Dealer*.

Enter MASQUERADERS.

And I'faith we'll make a night on't, with wine and dance, and catches—then old and young shall join us.

FINALE

JEROME.
Come now for jest and smiling,
Both old and young beguiling,
Let us laugh and play, so blyth and gay,
Till we banish care away.

LOUISA.
Thus crown'd with dance and song,
The hours shall glide along,
With a heart at ease, merry, merry glees,
Can never fail to please,

FERDINAND.
Each bride with blushes glowing,
Our wine as rosy flowing,
Let us laugh and play, so blythe and gay,
Till we banish care away,—

ANTONIO.
Then, healths to every friend,
The night's repast shall end,
With a heart at ease, merry, merry, glees,
Can never fail to please.

CLARA.
Nor while we are so joyous,
Shall anxious fear annoy us,
Let us laugh and play, so blythe and gay,
Till we banish care away.

JEROME.
For generous guests like these,
Accept the wish to please,
So we'll laugh and play, so blithe and gay,
Your smiles drive care away. [*Exeunt omnes.*

1 MASQUERADERS] *94*, *I*, *NY*, *Rae*; *Masks, all sides F* 2 on't] *94*, *I*, *Rae*, *NY*; of it *F* wine and] *Rae*, *94*, *I*, *NY*; wine *F* 7–8, 15–16, 23–24 Let us . . . away] *Rae*, *94*, *I*, *NY*, *F*, *Songs* (15th ed.); Fa, la, la, &c. | 'Till crown'd with dance and song | The hours shall glide along *Songs* (1st ed.) 9–12 Thus . . . please] *Rae*, *94*, *I*, *NY*, *F*, *Songs* (15th ed.); *om. Songs* (1st ed.) 17 healths] *94*, *I*, *NY*, *Rae*, *F*. *Songs* (15th ed.); a health *Songs* (1st ed.) 19–20 With . . . please] *94*, *I*, *NY*, *Rae*, *F*, *Songs* (15th ed.); Fa, la, la, &c. | 'Till crown'd with dance and song | The hours shall glide along. *Songs* (1st ed.) 27–28 So . . . away] *94*, *I*, *NY*, *Rae*, *F*, *Songs* (15th ed.); *om. Songs* (1st ed.) *For these changes in the Finale, see p. 210, above* 28 (*Exeunt omnes*)] *Rae*; *om. F*, *94*; THE END *I*; END OF THE DUENNA *NY*

THE SCHOOL FOR SCANDAL

A Comedy

THE SCHOOL FOR SCANDAL

COMPOSITION

SOON after the first performance of *The School for Scandal*, a writer in the *St. James's Chronicle* described the play as 'two or three Anecdotes in Sheridan's Life, which being tacked together made up the Fable . . .'[1] The statement is open to question, though it is obvious that two sets of events in his early life had taught him the power of gossip. His journey with Elizabeth Linley to France and the subsequent duels with Thomas Mathews certainly set tongues wagging. When he was convalescing after the second duel, the exaggerated reports in newspapers of his condition amused him, and a recollection of them may have provided some basis for Act v, Scene ii, of *The School for Scandal*.[2]

A year earlier he had some part in another scandal that engrossed Bath: the wooing of Elizabeth by the wealthy landowner Walter Long. A match had been arranged, then suddenly broken off. Sheridan contributed to the *Bath Chronicle*[3] a hundred lines of verse called 'Hymen and Hirco: A Vision', and satirizing Long as a billy-goat. Since Long was fifty-nine and Elizabeth sixteen, it was not difficult to hold him up to ridicule. He was held to have tarnished her reputation, and eventually had to make restitution in the form of three thousand pounds.[4]

The theme was taken up by Samuel Foote in his play, *The Maid of Bath* (1771). With his usual sharpness, Foote made fun of Long as the miserly Solomon Flint, who was to marry 'la petite Rossignole', Kitty Linnett. The lively young spark of the play, Major Tom Rackett, described Solomon in the same terms as Sheridan used of Hirco: 'He that enjoys—owns, I mean—half the farms in the country? . . . Why he is sixty at least. What a filthy old goat! But then, how does this design suit with his avarice? the girl has no fortune.'[5] Rackett and his friend, Sir Christopher Cripple, decide to frighten Flint out of the unnatural match, and since Flint is bent on winning the girl 'on easier terms than marriage' and proposes that she pass a night with him before the wedding, everyone sympathizes with her when she calls Solomon 'a despicable wretch'.

The early drafts[6] of *The School for Scandal* suggest that Sheridan remembered Foote's play when he came to compose his own. One of his central figures is Solomon Teazle, an old man who has married a young girl

[1] 13–15 May 1777.

[2] A. Lefanu, *op. cit.*, p. 406.

[3] 9 May 1771.

[4] See C. Price, 'Hymen and Hirco: A Vision', *T.L.S.*, 11 July 1958, p. 396, and 'Sheridan-Linley Documents', *Theatre Notebook*, xxi (1967), 165–7.

[5] II. i.

[6] See pp. 293–4.

and who echoes, in different phrases, Solomon Flint's mournful complaint, 'For my part, I can't see what pleasure pretty Misses can take in galloping to plays, and to balls, and such expensive vagaries.'[1] Sir Christopher Cripple ('one of the gazettes of Bath') has his counterpart in Sir Christopher Crab, the scandal-monger, later to become Crabtree. The resemblance is strengthened by the fact that, in a hasty jotting, Sheridan wrote

WOODWARD. You are not one of those who could convey a Libel in a frown—or wink a Reputation down.

The slip is of some significance for Henry Woodward was the player who took the part of Sir Christopher Cripple in Foote's production. It seems probable, therefore, that *The Maid of Bath* gave Sheridan some initial ideas and situations, though he was to develop them in a very different way.

One of the sheets of jottings, thought by Moore[2] to contain 'the very first hints', reads:

THE SLANDERERS.—*A Pump-Room Scene.*

Friendly caution to the newspapers.

It is whispered—

She is a constant attendant at church, and very frequently takes Dr. M'Brawn home with her.

Mr. Worthy is very good to the girl;—for my part, I dare swear he has no ill intention.

What! Major Wesley's Miss Montague?

Lud, ma'am, the match is certainly broke—no creature knows the cause;—some say a flaw in the lady's character, and others, in the gentleman's fortune.

To be sure they do say—

I hate to repeat what I hear.

She was inclined to be a little too plump before she went.

The most intrepid blush;—I've known her complexion stand fire for an hour together.

'She had twins,'—How ill-natured! as I hope to be saved, ma'am, she had but one! and that a little starved brat not worth remembering.

'Worthy' fleetingly calls to mind Vanbrugh's *The Relapse*, and 'the most intrepid blush' was to be turned in *St. Patrick's Day* into 'nothing on earth so impudent as an everlasting blush'.[3] The allusions to scandal-mongering and to the twins were to be developed later.

Another detached sheet[4] is more interesting in its possibilities, for it contains notes scribbled with different pens, one of them giving us the title of the play for the first time. The page reads:

Dodsley's Grey's Elegy—

we should make allowance for Age—

[1] II. i. [2] Moore, i. 210–11.

[3] See p. 167. It is noted by Sichel, i. 565, n. 1.

[4] In Mr. Robert H. Taylor's collection.

But if she drinks acid, and hurts[?] her fat sides every morning behind a coach Horse—to be sure she is to be pitied—

goes abroad to take care of her Character—

—The School for Scandal—

go you scandalous Toad—

Mrs. P. your servant Sir Benjamin—the world says scandalous things of you—but there is no minding what the world says—why it was but just now I heard that miss aircastle had gone off with—Captain Saunter

Maria—wasn't that the miss melville that they tal[k]'d

no Sir—Puppies might have talk'd—

Babble Bore

The Letter I forget to loose—

disap[p]ointed in marriage—she expects—

The Character of a Prude is hurt by a scandalous Tale as the strongest constitutions are most hurt by a Fever—but there is a kind of sickly Reputation—that holds up a long time—

—in the Dark—

She is a sort of valedudinaring—in Reputation being conscious how delicate the Character is [?]—she preserves it with great attention

He has taken your Brother's Name.

she indites the Letter.

to do wrong to become more cautious—loose her Virtue to preserve her Reputation

I have received an anonymous Letter—

The allusion to Gray's *Elegy* is something of a puzzle, but perhaps Sheridan had the following stanza in mind as a possible epigraph to his play:

The struggling pangs of conscious truth to hide,
To quench the blushes of ingenuous shame,
Or heap the shrine of Luxury and Pride
With incense kindled at the Muse's flame.

The jottings were obviously written at different times, with a view to future use. 'Miss Melville' was to appear in *The Rivals*, and the downright condemnation in 'Puppies might have talked' could have come happily from the mouth of Sir Anthony Absolute. The woman who lived on acid to reduce her bulk, the prude, and the valetudinarian, were all to be mentioned in similar—if not exactly the same—terms in the completed version of *The School for Scandal*. 'Go—go—you are a couple of provoking toads' was also there. The phrase, 'lose her virtue to preserve her reputation' appears on another sheet as 'You must get rid of your Virtue to preserve your Reputation', and is associated with the words, 'Sin in her own defence'. They were to provide a celebrated piece of casuistry in *The School for Scandal* (IV. i).

A few other phrases were to be picked up again in the drafts, but were not to find expression in the text of the first performance. 'In the dark' and the two allusions to the letter are expanded to read:

A man making Love to Aunt and Niece meeting wrong in the Dark—some one coming—locks up the Aunt—thinking it to be the Niece

not to drop the letter but take it from the maid.

The reference to 'Miss Aircastle' is also interesting because it occurs in slightly different form in a sheet of cancelled material, where it reads:

Her name is Lady Isabella Aircastle
Isabella Aircastle come forth.

Frances Sheridan's *A Journey to Bath* contains a haughty and patronizing character named 'Lady Bell Aircastle' but she is not involved in any incident of this kind.[1]

Just when he began to draft his comedy is difficult to judge. It seems likely that he had hit upon the title before the first performance of *The School for Wives* in December 1773. This play came out anonymously, and the *London Chronicle* suggested[2] that its author was either Sheridan or Major Addington, not knowing that it was really by Hugh Kelly. Since Sheridan was then only twenty-two and had made no name for himself as a dramatist, it is hard to understand why *The School for Wives* was attributed to him unless he had spread abroad in theatrical or newspaper circles the similar title of the play he was meditating.

His younger sister declared that she heard Sheridan speak about *The School for Scandal* long before it appeared:

many of the characters and incidents related to persons known to them both, and were laughingly talked over with his family.

. . . Before he put pen to paper, the fable, as perfectly conceived and matured in his mind, was communicated to his friends; and the expression he made use of, described at once the completeness and unity of his plan.—'The comedy is finished; *I have now nothing to do but to write it*.'[3]

There may be some exaggeration in this, either in Sheridan's attitude or in his sister's recollection of what had been said some fifty years earlier. What is certain from the extant manuscripts is that the writing of the play gave Sheridan considerable trouble.

The drafts themselves may be divided into a few sheets of jottings and some later but better-developed sketches and notes that concern the Teazles and the gossippers.

[1] Foote's *The Cozeners* (first performed on 15 July 1774) includes a character called 'Mrs. Aircastle'. This play also refers to a 'Lady Kitty Carmine, in her new vis-a-vis', and Lady Sneerwell in 'The Slanderers' says 'Sure you must confess our Friend Lady Carmine—is really beautiful.'

[2] 11–14 Dec. 1773. Cf. the *Monthly Miscellany* (1774), p. 27: 'given to the younger Mr. Sheridan'.

[3] A. Lefanu, *op. cit.*, pp. 408–10.

These jottings also contain some details that were afterwards abandoned. One of them is of 'Lady Margaret Macdonald of Glenalvon Castle', who may have been intended to resemble Lady Catherine Coldstream of *The Maid of Bath*. Yet another is a synopsis of a second act:

2d.—Scene 1st. all. 2d. Lady S. and Mrs. C.
3d. L. S. and Harr. Emm. and Mrs. C. listening.
4th. L. S. and Flor.—shews him into the Room—
bids him return the other way—L.S. and Emma
—Emma and Florival.—fits—maid—all
Faint to expose.[1]

The tone of this is clearly more exaggerated than anything to be found in later versions.

The two better-developed sets of sketches and notes may be conveniently known by names that have been given them before: 'The Slanderers' and 'The Teazles'.

The numbering of the thirty pages devoted to 'The Slanderers' is inaccurate, yet it is simple to reshuffle the sheets so that the dialogue becomes consecutive. In the new order,[2] the gossip is often close to that of the opening half of the first scene in the early performances. The remaining sheets[3] deal with the effects of scandal since they show Clerimont deceived by the story sedulously propagated by Lady Sneerwell and Spatter, that Maria is in love with Sir Benjamin.[4] This has a much vaguer connection with the finished version, and 'The Slanderers' is chiefly interesting in its scandalous chatter.

'The Teazles'[5] contributes far more to the fully formed plot and characterization. It begins with Old Teazle soliloquizing in a way that reminds the reader of Sir John Brute's opening remarks or Solomon Flint's statements, but after a couple of pages, Teazle's tone changes with his name and he becomes Sir Peter. His wife is much more uncouth than she is in the later version. As Moore remarked, their relationship at this stage shows 'a degree of glare and coarseness, which proves the eye of the artist to have been fresh from the study of Wycherley[6] and Vanbrugh'.[7] One passage may make this clear:

SIR PETER. If I were to die, what would you do?
LADY TEAZLE. Countermand my new Brocade.

[1] Sichel, i. 567, guessed that this was to be 'a conventional climax' to 'The Slanderers'.

[2] Reading pp. 4–7, 1–3, 25–8, 9–13.

[3] pp. 15, 17, 19, 21, 23.

[4] See the summary on pp. 293–4. Rhodes, ii. 138–9, mentions that Lady Alton in George Colman's *The English Merchant* (1767), employed a hack writer named 'Spatter' to vilify Amelia Douglas's character; and that Lady Riscounter in Foote's *The Bankrupt* (1773) paid a man to concoct a scurrilous paragraph.

[5] I accept Rhodes's name for it as likely to be less confusing than the title to be found on one of the copy-books, 'Act 3rd Sir Peter Teazle'.

[6] Though Moore (i. 256) also noted that Sheridan denied 'having ever read a line of Wycherley'.

[7] Moore, i. 231.

SIR PETER. You might have [been a] maid still but for me.

LADY TEAZLE. Well you made me a wife for which I am obliged to you and if you have a mind to make me more grateful still—make me a Widow.

This is another Miss Hoyden speaking. The stress is on directness and not on that delicate balance between country manners and town refinement found in the later version. Lady Teazle's bluntness can be cruel, as when she describes him as 'fatiguing his stiff face with an eternal senile grin'.

She goes to meet Young Pliant (afterwards Joseph Surface) and runs behind a screen when her husband calls. When Frank Pliant (Charles Surface to be) also comes in, Sir Peter steps behind another screen. The development of the action is very like that in the fully formed play, but Sir Peter's closing lines might well have been spoken by Sir Anthony Absolute:

[YOUNG PLIANT] Sir Peter, notwithstanding these appearances, Heaven knows—

[SIR PETER] That you are a Villain—and mark me, Sir, I'm not so old—but that I can hold a sword—I have given you your Name and if you are not [a] Coward—I shall hear of it— [*Exit.*

A duel is obviously suggested but the dramatist thought better of it, just as he subdued all the other exaggerated shadings in the drafts. Everything was to be more subtle in the later version. Manners softened all.

Nevertheless there are occasions even in the drafts, when a more delicate turn of raillery appears. The quarrel between Lady Teazle and her husband over her expenses provides a nice example:

SIR PETER. Well go to the Articles—Fruit for my Lady's monkey—5 *s.*[1] per week—five—for the monkey—why 'tis a Des[s]ert for an Alderman.

LADY TEAZLE. Why, Sir Peter, would you starve the poor animal? I dare swear He lives as reasonably as other monkeys do.

SIR PETER. Well, well, go on—

[LADY TEAZLE] —China for D[itt]o.—

SIR PETER. Hey—what does He eat out of China—

LADY TEAZLE. —Repairing China that He breaks—5—And I am sure no monkey breaks less—

It is a pity that this was eventually omitted, but Sheridan knew that he was luxuriant and that his humorous fancies might overburden the structure of his play.

A more muted tone, too, is to be found in the second draft of the interview between Lady Teazle and Joseph. In the first, Lady Teazle refers to her husband as 'an old curmudgeon', and Young Pliant speaks of Maria as 'a puling Idiot—without sense or spirit'. In the second, he alludes to the 'sprightly Attractions of this little Rustic [Lady Teazle]',

[1] Moore, i. 228, reads '£5'.

and she mentions her husband in a much more plaintive way: 'Now when I know the integrity of my own heart—and that I have never wrong'd him—to have him eternally suspicious, teazing, and dissatisfied—worse he could not be if I had served him as He merits.'

It is usually accepted that 'The Slanderers' and 'The Teazles' were originally intended to be separate plays,[1] but I am not altogether convinced that this is true. Maria is to be found in both of them. In 'The Teazles', Young Pliant says 'I am afraid the Insinuations we have spread for Frank have operated too strongly on him [Sir Peter]. We meant only to divert his suspicions to a wrong object.' In 'The Slanderers', Lady Sneerwell and Spatter are concerned to blacken Sir Benjamin's character in the same way, so as to increase Clerimont's jealousy. The effects of scandal-mongering are emphasized in both sketches, and are natural links between them. Consequently Moore's statement that 'the two plans are entirely distinct'[2] needs qualification, since it has misled editors who have not seen the original manuscripts and even some of those who have.

At this point, it is worth tabulating the material in the drafts wherever it bears some relationship to the version produced in the opening performances:

Completed version	*Drafts*
I. i.	['The Slanderers': my summary] Mrs./Lady Sneerwell encourages Spatter to print defamatory paragraphs in the newspapers, and hears from him the story of the Nova Scotia sheep. She says she is in love with Clerimont, but that since he is enamoured of Maria, she will 'poison both with jealousy of the other'. Lady Sneerwell pretends to be in love with Sir Benjamin and persuades Maria to see him and answer his letter, and hopes that this will inflame Clerimont's suspicions. Sir Benjamin is really in love with Maria but has been persuaded by her to make protestations to Lady Sneerwell. Mrs Candour enters and mentions a report of Clerimont's engagement to a lady in Norfolk. Maria is alarmed at this and seeks a word with Mrs. Candour. Cf. Moore's transcription, i. 211–18.
I. ii.	['The Teazles'] There are two pages of dialogue in which Old Teazle laments his third marriage and discusses his wife's extravagance with Jarvis. See Moore's transcription, i. 225–6.
II. i.	['The Teazles'] Eight pages of dialogue between Sir Peter and his wife on her expenses, and the company she keeps. See Moore's transcription, i, 226–30, and add on p. 229, after 'captivated me', 'and at Xmas to play at cross Questions or hunt the Slipper', and after 'Till death', 'Did you think age was catching?'

[1] The number of editors of the play who have seen these manuscripts, is minute, and most have been happy to follow Moore unquestioningly.

[2] Moore, i. 223, but cf. i. 227 n.

II. ii. ['The Slanderers'] Mrs. Sneerwell, Sir Benjamin, and Sir Christopher utter malicious remarks at the expense of their friends, much as in the finished version. Mrs. Candour does, too, but in a conversation with Maria. Clerimont enters and Sir Benjamin accuses him of looking grave. He replies that he has just received a letter from the country saying that his sister has left his uncle's house. She had been urged to marry a squire she did not like. He asks Sir Benjamin, who once paid addresses to his sister, if he was 'privy to her elopement'; but Sir Benjamin answers that he pays his devotions to another lady, 'one of your acquaintance'. Clerimont soliloquizes, wondering to himself if Sir Benjamin means Maria, and calls her 'a d——d deceitful wanton' when he overhears Sir Benjamin making protestations of love to her. Lady Sneerwell then enters for cards. See Moore, i. 219–23.

II. iii. ['The Teazles'] One sheet contains the following phrases and sentences:

universal Good Character.
I don't like everybody speaking well of him—
Keep a wench—
at his Age, I kept two.
every body speaks well of him—I'm sorry to hear it—for then he must have paid more homage to vice than merit—
He has too good—a character to be an honest Fellow

III. i. ['The Teazles'] Sixteen lines on the theme 'If you find him in great Distress—and want very bad you must ask double.'

Moore, i. 240, notes that 'there was a long scene, in which Rowley, by a minute examination of Snake, drew from him, in the presence of Sir Oliver and Sir Peter, a full confession of his designs against the reputation of Lady Teazle.' It is not now extant.

III. ii. ['The Teazles'] 'Bags and bouquets' were mentioned by Jarvis in the earlier scene with Old Teazle.

III. iii. ['The Teazles'] One sheet contains the following lines that were to be introduced in the completed play:

Come Sir—Here's success to Usury—fill the Gentleman [a] Bumper—

come no ceremony—I'm an extravagant young [Fellow] that want to borrow money[1]—You I take to be a usurer—old Fellow that have got money to lend—I am Block head enough to be willing to give fifty per Cent—and you I presume, are Rogue enough to take 100—if yould get it—now, Sir—I daresay we are acquainted at once—

The song is not in the drafts.

IV. i. There is no reference to the Auction scene.

IV. ii. ['The Teazles'] One jotting reads:

Sir O. and Pl[*iant*]. Like Birth Day Cloaths with the gloss on—

IV. iii. ['The Teazles'] Sixteen pages of dialogue involve Young Pliant, Lady Teazle, Sir Peter, and Frank, in action that follows the completed version fairly closely, though Sir Peter and Lady Teazle both go behind screens. A further three pages go over Lady Teazle's entrance,

[1] See p. 5 above.

again, but this time she talks to Joseph Surface. The dialogue in both versions was to be polished considerably before it was employed in performance. For a transcription of the opening three pages of the sixteen, see Moore, i. 232–4.

v. i. ['The Teazles'] Six pages of this scene are found in draft, so neatly written as to suggest a fair copy by Sheridan. However, Moore says (i. 241) that it 'was at first wholly different from what it is at present; and in some parts approached much nearer to the confines of caricature than the watchful taste of Mr. Sheridan would permit. For example, Joseph is represented in it as giving the old suitor only half-a guinea, which the latter indignantly returns, and leaves him; upon which Joseph, looking at the half-guinea, exclaims, "Well, let him starve—this will do for the opera."'[1]

v. ii. ['The Teazles'] Two jottings are of interest:
Bronze figure on chimney
Can't kill a man without a doctor.

v. iii. ['The Teazles'] One jotting is worth noting:
Let 'em marry—like oil and vinegar.

So it appears that Sheridan drafted, I. i, II. i, II. ii, and IV. iii, very fully, but that for a number of other scenes all that can be found is a comparatively brief run of dialogue or even as little as a central phrase or curtain-line. Unfortunately this conclusion can be only a tentative one since several drafts that were in existence soon after Sheridan's death have now disappeared.[2]

The most perplexing of these problems is the absence of any early manuscript of the Auction scene (IV. i). I wonder if the idea did not occur to Sheridan until late in 1775? On 23 December in that year, there was produced at the Grand Saloon of Exeter 'Change the following entertainment:

THE AUCTION ROOM;

A MORNING SCENE

Where will be exhibited and described a Number

of PAINTINGS

Particularly, several ALLEGORICAL FIGURES.

Principal Characters,

Mr. Simper (the Auctioneer), Dr. Anecdote, Lord Spindle, &c. &c. Lady Topple-Crown, Duchess of Feather-head, Lady Bridget Repartee,

Lady Rep., &c. &c.[3]

[1] The manuscript reads 'will serve for'.

[2] A. Lefanu, *op. cit.*, p. 409, says: 'in the first sketch, the character which now bears the name of Mrs. Candour, went by that of Lady Kitty Candour: a title which, I presume, Mr. Sheridan abandoned on account of its too great resemblance to one in a dramatic piece [*A Trip to Calais*] of Foote's—Lady Kitty Crocodile; which was supposed to be meant for the Duchess of Kingston.'

[3] *Morning Chronicle*, 23–28 Dec. 1775. It was a puppet-show.

The attention given to 'allegorical figures' and the implicit satire on lovers of 'vertù' does not appear in the auction scene in *The School for Scandal*, but Sheridan's play does contain, earlier, a reference to Lord Spindle. Some connection is just possible.

On 31 December 1775, Sheridan wrote to his father-in-law to say, 'I am finishing a two act comedy for Covent-Garden, which will be in rehearsal in a week.'[1] Moore guessed that this consisted of 'the quarrels of Old Teazle and his wife, the attachment between Maria and one of the Plausibles, and the intrigue of Mrs. Teazle with the other'.[2] A general statement seems to me more acceptable: the 'two act comedy' might have been a very much simpler form of the play afterwards developed into *The School for Scandal.* Once this is considered, we are compelled to ask ourselves why 'the two act comedy' was not completed in December 1775. One answer is that the idea of an auction scene may have made Sheridan pause to see how it could be worked in to advantage. Another is that he may have seen the performance of George Colman's revision of Jonson's *The Silent Woman* at Drury Lane on 13 January 1776, and so gained the idea of allusions to the 'Scandalous College'.[3] What is much less hypothetical is that he was busily engaged at this time in bargaining for control of Drury Lane Theatre, and had every reason to hold any new material until he became manager.

When the new season began in September 1776, he was part-proprietor and 'acting-manager' at Drury Lane, and was expected to produce a programme full of novelty. The months went by with stock plays, and little out of the ordinary except the revival of Congreve's *Love for Love* and *The Old Batchelor.*[4] Everyone was disappointed, and eventually 'empty benches, and the silent contempt and desertion of the town, seem to have electrified the manager in some degree'.[5]

On 8 February 1777, the *Morning Chronicle* reported: 'At Drury-Lane house an opera and two comedies are preparing for representation. The two latter come both from the pen of the acting Manager.' The first comedy was *A Trip to Scarborough*, performed on 24 February, but the other one was very much delayed. Drury Lane badly needed an attraction that would make Sheridan's first season distinctive, but the last three months of the theatrical year did not offer much opportunity since, by

[1] *Letters*, i. 95. [2] Moore, i. 224.

[3] Rhodes, ii. 141, made this suggestion, and found that its satirical target in 1776 was a ladies' club held at 'the Thatcht House in St. James's'.

[4] Sheridan himself was responsible for revising them for performance, and for removing 'the alloy of indecency': see p. 834 below. The savouring of Congreve's lines probably influenced the final phrasing of *The School for Scandal.*

[5] *London Magazine*, xlv (1776), 565. Later (xlvi 7), it had praised the revival of Congreve's plays at Drury Lane: 'the strength with which they were brought out, and the judicious, nay, masterly manner the parts were cast, as far as the insolence and caprice of a few capital performers would permit'.

custom, oratorio occupied the stage at Easter and benefit performances took up many nights before the playhouse closed for the summer. Sheridan was presented with a challenge to his mother wit, but he was as usual dilatory and it was not until nearly two months after its first announcement that the *Morning Chronicle* could make fuller reference to the new play:

By advices from the Meuse of Old Drury we learn that the slim foreign-bred *gelding* Orpheus (although the rider came post from Italy and is to receive £500, whether he performs or not) is ordered back to the stable; and will not start for the Town-plate this season. The jockey, like other foreigners, has not come to Old England for nothing. He received a £300 purse for riding over the short Oratorio course at Covent-garden; and is already engaged for the next races at Drury, at the handsome salary of £800.

Esquire Sheridan, Master of the Drury Race-ground, finding that the foreign horse Orpheus would not be sufficiently trained for a public race this season, spurred his *Pegasus* and came to town full speed last week, being determined to start his last young colt, *School for Scandal*, in less than a fortnight. Nothing, we hear, will delay the race longer, if the grooms are alert, and make the horse acquainted with the course.[1]

I interpret this as meaning that an unnamed Italian castrato[2] was unable to appear at Drury Lane, and that Sheridan would try to fill the gap with his new play.

The Gazetteer, 14 April, mentioned that a new comedy called *The School for Scandal* was in rehearsal at Drury Lane, and the *Morning Chronicle*, 16 April, provided (with irony) some of the details:

Contrary to the custom of past seasons, the theatrical business at Drury-Lane grows more languid on the stage, and more interesting in the cabinet, at a period when the former was wont to be almost wholly occupied by benefit performances, and the latter in a great measure had discharged its duty, and was rendered of little service. The New Manager, who proceeds entirely upon a system of his own, and disdains to conform to College rules, appears to be exceedingly alert, (just at the time when Managers are generally thinking of their *otium cum dignitate*) and is now actually busy in preparing a new Comedy of his own writing for representation. Each Actor in the Piece, it is said, is already in possession of a fourth part of his character; a second fourth, it is imagined, will be delivered to the Company this week, and unless a fit of indolence seizes the Author, or a fit of Gout the Prompter, the remaining half will be ready before the end of next week. God willing, therefore, this Comedy may probably be forward enough for representation the last week in May, or the first in June—a pretty time of year to produce a new piece at a WINTER THEATRE!

[1] 5 Apr. 1777. Garrick wrote to Lady Spencer on 10 Apr. to say, 'A New Comedy is preparing at Drury Lane call'd the *School for Scandal*, in which may be seen a variety of characters which will strike everybody with some resemblance of their friends. I am told there is a great deal of wit . . .' (*Letters of David Garrick and Georgiana Countess Spencer, 1759–1779*, ed. Earl Spencer and C. Dobson (Cambridge, 1960), p. 91).

[2] Possibly Giusto Tenducci, who sang at Covent Garden in March.

To this criticism of his encroachment on the normal time allotted to the summer programme at the Haymarket Theatre,[1] Sheridan is said to have replied

that his plan of management is purposely founded on novelty; and that if he pleases the town, he cares not either for method, or malice. The dog-trot observers of the first may preach again and again upon the threadbare text of theatrical custom, and the numerous votaries of the second may aim their random shafts from their cowardly concealments as often as their prevailing passion stimulates.[2]

Possibly Sheridan learnt the identity of his critics, for he suddenly changed the name of the person in the play who sends venomous paragraphs to the newspapers, from 'Miss Verjuice' to 'Snake'. The alteration was a very late one, and was not made until after the copyist who had to prepare a full text for the Lord Chamberlain's approval had begun his work.[3]

The newspapers of the day tell us nothing more about the actual composition of the comedy, but over two years later, the *Morning Chronicle* declared:

Writing managers generally take care to have their own pieces well played, tho' to say the truth, Mr. S. is of all authors the least anxious on this score, if we may judge from his preparation of the School for Scandal for performance, part of the fourth, and the whole of the fifth act of that admirable comedy being written on the stage during the rehearsals.[4]

To bring this into perspective, we need to note that the *Morning Post* reported on 23 April 1777, that 'the literary world, who have been indulged with a sight of Mr. Sheridan's new comedy of the *School for Scandal*, which is now in rehearsal, speak of it in the highest terms imaginable'. Five days later, the same newspaper mentioned that performances were deferred 'till Thursday se'ennight, as the benefits will all be over at that period'. So rehearsal went on for at least three weeks, and Sheridan's revisions and additions could have been handed out at any time during that period.

[1] It was followed by another in the *Morning Chronicle*, 19 Apr. 1777, which contrasted the situation of the '*little* man' (Colman), who was 'industrious to open with éclat' at the Haymarket, with the '*great* man' (Sheridan), who was 'busily employed in endeavouring to finish his season with something that will do him credit as a poet'.

[2] *Morning Chronicle*, 22 Apr. 1777.

[3] A correspondent of *The General Advertiser*, 12 May 1777, referred to the Revd. Henry Bate, editor of the *Morning Post*, as 'the Rev. Mr. Snake'. For his reputation at this period, see L. Werkmeister, *The London Daily Press, 1772–1792* (Lincoln, Nebr., 1963), pp. 19–34. R. C. Rhodes, *Harlequin Sheridan* (Oxford, 1933), pp. 71–2, noted that 'the tradition of dressing Snake in black is a legacy of his clerical occupation', and identified him with the Revd. William Jackson, editor of *The Public Ledger* and also Foote's 'Dr. Viper'.

[4] 11 Sept. 1779.

He took full advantage of the eighteenth-century actor's pride in being 'a quick study' and probably finished the comedy in fits and starts. When the desire to write came upon him or the demands of the theatre were urgent, he composed rapidly. W. T. Parke's description[1] of what happened at this period has not been noticed but deserves attention:

The fourth act of this admirable comedy, which is not only the longest but the best, was at the time stated to have been written in one day;[2] and the following fact, which came within my own knowledge, will in some measure confirm the truth of this rare instance of dramatic celerity: Mr. Sheridan, whilst writing 'The School for Scandal,' resided in Great Queen-street, Lincoln's Inn Fields, and it being intended to be brought out with great expedition, the under-prompter during the whole of that day was vibrating from the theatre to his house, and back again, like a pendulum; and, as Mahomet with the Alcoran, received it only a sheet at a time, to enable the copyist to get on with the parts destined to the actors to study from.

This was recorded many years after the event and must be treated with some reserve, as must a similar statement[3] by another writer:

Such is Mr. Sheridan's incurable indolence and procrastination that although to indulge it, and at the same time to raise the impatience of the public, he actually shut his theatre one night, yet it is a certain fact that half the last act was written after drawing up the curtain. If this exhibits his sloth in a high degree, it does no less his quickness.

David Garrick attended rehearsals 'and was never known on any former occasion, to be more anxious for a favourite piece'.[4] He was eager to assist not only because he still had a considerable amount of money invested in Drury Lane Theatre, but because he had read and admired the play and felt warmly towards its author. He wrote the prologue, and Colman the epilogue. Arthur Murphy, too, tried to be helpful. He thought the Auction scene would be flat with only one bidder, so he suggested that Sheridan bring in the scandal-mongers and make it a public occasion. Sheridan did not take his advice, and Murphy consoled himself with the reflection that the scene '*did* hang fire' on the first night.[5]

[1] *Musical Memoirs* (1830), i. 9–10.

[2] But earlier drafts are available of its last scene.

[3] *The Trial of Thomas Sheridan Esq. for Criminal Conversation with the Lady of Peter Campbell Esq. in the Sheriff's Court on July 7 1807. . . .* [1807], p. 7. Drury Lane was not closed on any week-night in the four weeks before 8 May.

[4] A. Murphy, *The Life of David Garrick* (1801), ii. 145. J. Cradock, *Literary and Miscellaneous Memoirs* (1828), iv. 257, prints Sir George Beaumont's letter saying that he met Garrick at the end of the first performance, 'and with darting eyes, I remember, he expressed his admiration of the play, and particularly praised the fourth Act'. He said, later, that Sheridan had 'Shewn a Wonderful Genius' (*The Letters of David Garrick*, ed. D. M. Little and G. M. Kahrl (Cambridge, Mass., 1963), p. 1164).

[5] See the extra-illustrated copy in the Widener Library of T. Moore, *Memoir of . . . Sheridan*, vi. 24.

When the fifth act was completed in all but the final verses, Sheridan scrawled on the last page a 'doxology'[1] on behalf of the prompter and himself:

——finis——

Thank God!
RBS——
Amen!
W. Hopkins

The prompter had to control the copying and distribution of the parts as well as arrangements for rehearsals. He, more than anyone, had had a very trying time, and Sheridan acknowledged a debt to his patience.

On 7 May, the day before the comedy was due to open, application was made for a licence,[2] but the Lord Chamberlain's office refused to grant one. Sheridan referred to the occasion many years later, in a Commons debate, and the passage is well known because it is reprinted in his *Speeches*.[3] Other versions have been ignored, but two of them contribute some new details. One[4] reads:

He once produced a piece called 'the School for Scandal', in which he introduced the character of a jew who lived by supplying extravagant young men with money at exorbitant interest, and thereby bringing them to ruin. The night before the piece was to be performed, he was much surprised to hear from the prompter that a licence had been refused. It happened at that time there was a contest in the city between two gentlemen, Mr. Wilkes and Mr. Hopkins. In the warmth of a contested election a story went about that the character of the jew was meant for Mr. Hopkins and the piece was represented as a factious and seditious opposition to a court-candidate. He, however, went to lord Hertford,[5] and explained the circumstance of the scene to be a matter of general satire, and not of personal obloquy or ridicule; lord Hertford laughed at the affair and gave the licence.

The other[6] says that Hopkins

was suspected to have lent money to young men in an usurious manner. This Mr. Hopkins being patronized by Government, the licence the Prompter said was refused. However the good sense of the Lord Chamberlain, on his (Mr. Sheridan's) going to him the next day, and laughing over the circumstance, prevented any such prohibition; the point was adjusted, and the play acted.

The subject is worth closer examination because of its bearing on some of the scenes and allusions in *The School for Scandal*.

[1] See p. 334 below.
[2] Printed in *Letters*, i. 110–11.
[3] Ed. 'A Constitutional Friend' [Sir John Phillipart?] (1816), iv. 188.
[4] *The Parliamentary History of England*, xxxii (1818), 441.
[5] Francis Seymour Conway, 1st Earl (later Marquis) of Hertford, Lord Chamberlain, 1766–82 and 1783.
[6] *The Times*, 4 Dec. 1795.

Benjamin Hopkins had already defeated Wilkes twice in contests for the office of Chamberlain of the City of London. He stood against him in the summer of 1777 and was once more successful, but the newspaper campaign against him at the time when Sheridan was writing the play made some very severe reflections on his granting an annuity on the life of Sir John St. Aubyn, a baronet who was only sixteen. 'An Aged Citizen and Father' is quoted in *The Gazetteer*[1] as saying

. . . It appears that Mr. Hopkins had agreed with a *Jew* broker to lend a certain sum of money upon an annuity bond of Sir John St. Aubin; that the execution of this business was adjourned from the place where the agreement was made, to the Guildhall of the City of London; and that Mr. Hopkins, when placed on the seat of cautious justice, declined complying with his engagement, *because he thought himself insecure from the nonage of the borrower*. The solid advantages of the transaction were not however to be foregone: the money was lent upon the bond of Mr. Baker, without any previous enquiry into his character, or circumstances in life, knowingly for the use of a minor. . . . The *Jew* acted in *his* vocation. But what apology can be made for a man grown hoary in the commerce of the world; a Director of the Bank, a Merchant, once a Senator, at the time of the transaction a Magistrate, and now Chamberlain of the City . . . ?

Another correspondent bluntly called Hopkins 'our Christian Shylock'.[2]

The Annuity Bill[3] that was discussed in April and passed on 12 May was aimed at Hopkins and his kind. By its terms anyone who took more than ten shillings per hundred pounds for obtaining money for annuities was to be fined or imprisoned, and contracts for the purchase of annuities by people under twenty-one were made void. All grants for life annuities had to be registered. Several references to these requirements occur in *The School for Scandal*, III. i and ii. Sir Peter asks Moses, 'Wouldn't you have him run out a little against the Annuity Bill?' Trip hopes to raise an annuity by insuring his life, and adds, 'But then, Moses, it must be done before this d——d register takes place—one wouldn't like to have one's name made public, you know.' The most cutting of them appears, however, only in the Frampton Court MS.:

[SIR PETER] Moses I suppose you would have him enquire if the borrower is a minor?
[MOSES] O yes—
[SIR PETER] And in that case his conscience will direct him—
[MOSES] To have the Bond in another Name to be sure.

These lines are not in the copy sent to the Lord Chamberlain, or any other text I have seen.

[1] 24 Mar. 1777.

[2] *The Gazetteer*, 15 Apr. 1777.

[3] 'An Act for registering the Grants of Life Annuities, and for the better protection of Infants against such Grants.'

The topicality of the allusions may be appreciated from a passage in the *London Evening Post*, 1–3 May 1777:

The Annuity Bill hangs like a sword over the heads of the many vultures who have for too long a time fed on the vitals of the distressed. The Jewish tribe (whether Heathenish or Christian, are equally unconscionable and rapacious) being informed the intended bill will have regard *to the past*, *as well as to the future*, happily for the public, are afraid of entering into fresh negociations with *beardless school boys*, and *brainless gamblers*, in the purlieus of St. James's. This truth is fully proved, by the discontinuance of almost every money broker's advertisement in the public prints. . . .

Sheridan makes their exorbitant demands very clear when Moses says that if any victim 'appears not very anxious for the supply, you should require only forty or fifty per cent, but if you find him in great Distress, and want the monies very bad—you may ask double'.

More particular satire is to be seen in the distinction made between Moses and the principal usurer, a shadowy figure in the background. Moses is described as 'a friendly Jew who to do him justice, has done every thing in his power to bring your Nephew to a proper sense of his Extravagance'. In his actions he is genially accommodating. Of the other all that is said is 'the Principal is Christian', and the irony is plain. Even though Hopkins's name was not mentioned, he had some ground for complaint, and it would be interesting to know how 'the point was adjusted' between Sheridan and Hertford.

What is certain is that the character of the Jew, Moses, was not 'meant for Mr. Hopkins'. In one of the earliest drafts of 'The Teazles', there is a note about a Jew who was to lend money and who had 'some of the annuities of his own Brother'. Sheridan seems to have begun with a stock type in mind, then to have called on his own personal knowledge of money-lenders to complete the portrait. Here, as elsewhere in the play, he softened the outline.

I believe he had a real person before him: Jacob Nathan Moses, who is described in *Kent's Directory for the Year 1776*,[1] as a merchant of 'No. 23, Bury-street, St. Mary-ax'.

This opinion is derived from a letter[2] written to Robert Langford, an auctioneer, by Willoughby Lacy, one of Sheridan's fellow proprietors of Drury Lane Theatre. Lacy's senselessly extravagant way of life was very like that of Charles Surface, and he had the same unpractical but cheerfully optimistic outlook. He was so short of money that in his letter of 2 August 1777 he gave Langford power of attorney to sell one moiety of Drury Lane Theatre for £20,000, then to use some of the money realized to pay two notes of £1,000 each (and a bond of judgement) to Jacob Nathan Moses.

[1] p. 127.
[2] Harvard College Theatre Collection MS. 49M—261F (11).

Moses also sued Sheridan for £2,000. This took place on 20 December 1777,[1] and reference is made to it in a Garrick Club MS.: 'A judgment in the Court of King's Bench between Jacob Nathan Moses Plaintiff and R. B. Sheridan defendant for £2,000 Debt and 63s. Costs Registered 23 Dec. 1777 Book 7, No. 385.'[2] The debt may have been Sheridan's from the start, or he may have become responsible for Lacy's two notes of hand. Though the record actually belongs to a period after *The School for Scandal* had been completed, it obviously refers to a transaction of an earlier date. Consequently we may assume that when Sheridan was finishing *The School for Scandal*, he had constant reminders of the plight of a good-natured man who is reckless with money and falls into the hands of usurers. Further, the stage Moses is so pleasantly portrayed that the real Moses would have been unwise to take offence.

So there seems to be evidence available to suggest that the play was completed rapidly, and that Sheridan threw in some interesting topical allusions. Of course, these were soon dated, and were omitted from later performances.

Much of the initial success of *The School for Scandal* was caused by perfect casting. That the abilities of the leading members of his company were very much in Sheridan's mind is revealed in his statement that he would have included a love scene for Charles and Maria 'but that the actors who played the parts were not able to do such a scene justice'.[3] Now, too, he seems to have accepted the advice given him at the beginning of his management, that he should call upon the full strength of the company.[4] It is worth looking at the cast in detail to see how it completed what Sheridan had in mind.

(*a*) SIR PETER TEAZLE

His development from 'Old Teazle' who had left off trade, to Sir Peter, has already been described.[5] The character, as it appeared to a contemporary,[6] is summarized in the following words: 'The second act opens with Sir Peter, a man of large fortune, who having lived a batchelor to the age of fifty-six, had then taken it into his head to marry . . . [He is] rendered perpetually unhappy by the capriciousness of his own peevish temper, yet is at bottom a man of honour.' The part was taken by Thomas King (1730–1805), who had played fops as well as men of strength of

[1] P.R.O. MS. IND 9647, King's Bench, p. 34: '20 December 1777/Middlesex Jacob Nathan Moses and Richard Brinsley Sheridan Esquire for £2000./c. 63s./Sante 2s.'

[2] 'Drury Lane General Abstract' (Garrick Club MS.), f. 43.

[3] Moore, *Journal*, ii. 191. For other examples, see Rhodes, ii. 16–18, and C. Deelman, 'The Original Cast of *The School for Scandal*', *R.E.S.*, N.S. xiii (1962), 257–66.

[4] By 'Old Stager' in the *Morning Chronicle*, 25 Sept. 1776, who said he had been acquainted with the stage for thirty or forty years and remembered only two plays in which the full strength of the company was shown.

[5] See pp. 291–2.

[6] *The Public Register*, 22–24 Jan. 1778.

character. In the previous season, he had been Witwoud and Lord Ogleby as well as Shylock and Archer. 'In Touchstone he's perfect, Malvolio, great.'[1] It was said of him that 'his peculiar sententious manner made him seek and require dialogue of the greatest point', and his 'rapid utterance' had been stressed.[2] The *Morning Post*, 9 May 1777, thought him excellent as Sir Peter, though the interpretation may surprise us: 'the old fretful dotard of a husband is finely pourtrayed'. There is evidence (at second hand and a much later date) to show that Sheridan himself was not entirely satisfied with it. In 1804 the dramatist volunteered to read the part to Charles Mathews:

> Mr. Mathews had many misgivings on this subject, and most embarrasing it proved in the result; for so totally unlike was Mr. Sheridan's reading of the character from every other conception of it, that it was next to impossible for the actor to adopt any one of his suggestions. Had it not been known that Mr. Sheridan was the author of the play, it would have been difficult to credit his acquaintance with the part in question. The consequence may be anticipated, Mr. Sheridan was dissatisfied with Mr. Mathews's performance when the night came (as, it was said in the green-room, he had been with every previous representative of it, including King) and, after a second night, Mr. Wroughton resumed the part, taken from him by Mr. Sheridan's desire, and given to Mr. Mathews. Mr. Sheridan grumbled with Mr. Wroughton's performance after the play was over, as much as he had done at that of Mr. Mathews.[3]

(*b*) LADY TEAZLE

It seems likely that Sheridan had Frances Abington (1737–1815) in mind when developing the part. The *Morning Post*[4] even claimed that he had 'made considerable alterations in Lady Teazle, at Mrs. Abington's suggestion'.

In the previous season she had played Mrs. Sullen and Olivia, as well as Beatrice to Garrick's Benedict. She could point her lines with humour and severity: 'There was, in truth, such a tartness in her pleasantry;—she was so fine a speaker of humour, like her friend Tom King, . . . that they each lost nearly half their soul in separation.'[5] The *Morning Chronicle*[6] said of her performance on the first night, 'Mrs. Abington, in Lady Teazle, gave a fresh proof of her easy, elegant manner, and her unrivalled vivacity'; and *The Gazetteer*[6] called her 'the incomparable'. There was a certain piquancy in the fact that she herself had appeared in a 'tête-à-tête' in *The Town and Country Magazine* earlier in the year, as Thalia, mistress of 'Malagrida' (Shelburne).[7]

1 'Anthony Pasquin', *Poems* [1789], ii. 25.
2 Boaden, *Kemble*, i. 59.
3 A. Mathews, *Memoirs of Charles Mathews, Comedian* (1838–9), ii. 6–7.
4 27 Apr. 1798.
5 Boaden, i. 83.
6 9 May 1777.
7 Noted by Rhodes, ii. 14, from the *Town and Country Magazine*. It is not impossible that Shelburne's reputation as a casuist influenced Sheridan in the development of Joseph Surface.

Her performances as Lady Teazle greatly increased her reputation, and the *Morning Chronicle*[1] referred to her as 'the only comic actress in our memory, that has given the graceful manners of a woman of breeding with ease and correctness in the theatre'.[2] She was so dazzling that it was little wonder a critic thought that 'if there was any seduction at either side, it seemed to arise on that of the lady'.[3] She was especially skilful at hinting an earlier frugal background to the studied elegance of this woman of *ton*. Her immediate successors stressed one or the other: Mrs. Jordan showed 'all the natural ingenuousness of an artless unsullied mind';[4] Miss Farren revealed 'the complete finished air of fashionable indifference'.[5] Sheridan presented any actress with a challenge when he combined the typical qualities of a traditional stage type, the country girl,[6] with those of the true lady of fashion, and in the process of shading suggested innocence and plain-dealing set against a knowledge of the polite world. When Lady Teazle values the integrity of her own heart, she exposes her country breeding. Her dilemma is expressed in lines[7] that Sheridan wrote and rewrote from the earliest drafts onwards: 'So—so—then I perceive your Prescription is that I must sin in my own Defence—and part with my virtue to preserve my Reputation.' They are central to any interpretation of the character, for her intelligence makes her debate the limits of sophistication. Good sense and good nature demand that she should deny Joseph, and she claims that if she 'could be perswaded to do wrong, it would be by Sir Peter's ill-usage sooner than your honourable Logic'. She is not saved merely by the accidental entry of the servant, for her acquiescence in Joseph's plans is always hypothetical.[8]

(*c*) JOSEPH SURFACE

Sheridan may have derived the idea for this character from a reading of Chesterfield's *Letters to his Son*. They were first published in April 1774, and were fiercely denounced for encouraging dissemblers. Sheridan wrote an essay on the subject,[9] and one of its sentences leads us, I believe,

[1] 16 Oct. 1780. A manuscript 'Biographical Sketch of Mrs. Abington' in the second volume of two extra-illustrated books, once owned by George Daniel, and called *The English Stage* (Folger Library) contains the following: 'Her success in the part, was eminent; the author acknowledged her merit in it, in the most handsome terms.'

[2] 16 Oct. 1780. A little earlier, she had acted in *The Rivals*, and was said to be 'easy and elegant in Lydia Languish, especially in the last act' (*Morning Post*, 17 Jan. 1777).

[3] *London Magazine*, xlvi (1777), 231.

[4] *The British Press*, 4 Jan. 1809.

[5] W. Hazlitt, *Complete Works*, ed. P. P. Howe (1930–4), v. 291.

[6] The best-known examples are Mrs. Pinchwife, Miss Prue, Miss Hoyden, Miss Peggy.

[7] IV. iii.

[8] She went 'to listen to his pretended Passion, if not to sacrifice your Honour to his Baseness'.

[9] Yale University MS. Cf. Moore, i. 134–5.

into the characterization of Joseph Surface: 'An Attention to take advantage of the weakness of others can neither be the characteristick of a great man—nor, the reserve he recommends consistent with a noble mind.' Similar criticism is to be found in *The Cozeners* (II. i), where Foote writes: 'Nothing but grace! I wish you would read some late Posthumous Letters; you would then know the true value of grace: Do you know, that the only way for a young man to thrive in the world, is to get a large dish of hypocrisy, well garnished with grace, an agreeable person, and a clear patrimonial estate?' In 'The Teazles', Frank Pliant says: 'Now there's Sobersides my Brother—I suppose he lives as chastely as [any] Cardinal—yet egad I don't know that He is the honester Fellow for that. . . . I don't believe he ever had an amour with any creature above a Housemaid—and so apprehensive of his good name.' Young Pliant, for his part, criticizes Frank because 'a Neglect of forms and of the opinion of the World has hurt him in the Estimation of all his poorer friends—and I have profited by his errors—practised to give a Character—which now serves me [as] a mask to lie under.'

Joseph Surface was taken by John Palmer (1742–98), and Sheridan seems to have had him in mind in moulding the finished character. He was described as possessing 'a sort of elaborate grace and stately superiority . . . with an accompaniment of the most plausible politeness. . . . [He] was an actor of infinite address.'[1] He is mentioned, too, as standing 'with an air of penitent humility; his head declined, the whites of his eyes turned upwards, his hands clasped together, and his whole air exactly that of *Joseph Surface* before Sir Peter Teazle'.[2] In the previous season, Palmer had played Edmund in *King Lear* and Sir Toby Belch, but he was better known for his acting of Stukely in *The Gamester*, and Iago. The insinuating and plausible[3] suited him perfectly, and he had no rival in the part of Joseph. Sometimes, however, he overplayed: 'In the discovery or screen scene, his hesitation yesterday was over-acted; it was unnatural and broke the comic delusion by being farcially ludicrous.'[4] After his day, no one equalled his success, but on one later occasion Hazlitt was moved by what he saw to write one of his most penetrating assessments of character:

> Wallack's[5] Joseph Surface wanted dignity and plausibility . . . he does not hit off the officious condescending solemnity of the character so well as Young.[6] He seems sulky and reserved, instead of being self-complacent and ostentatious; to shrink into a cautious contemplation of his own designs and villainy, instead of protecting others under the shadow of his assumed virtues, and covering their failings and defects with a veil of pompous sentiment.[7]

[1] Boaden, *Kemble*, i. 53–4.

[2] Ibid. i. 394.

[3] 'Plausible' was among the names Sheridan had thought of giving him, but he had changed it probably because it had already been used by Wycherley in *The Plain Dealer*.

[4] Newspaper cutting, dated 11 Nov. 1790, in the Folger Shakespeare Library.

[5] J. W. Wallack (1791?–1864).

[6] Charles M. Young (1777–1856).

[7] *Complete Works*, ed. P. P. Howe, xviii. 242–3.

As Sichel wrote,[1] 'Surface is the Iago of comedy, a polished schemer with a persuasive tongue. But he is more than plausible.'[2]

(*d*) CHARLES SURFACE

The good-natured man was much admired in the eighteenth century, and it has often been suggested that the contrast between Charles and Joseph was modelled on that between Tom Jones and Blifil. For expression of the character in drama, we need only look at Fielding's Boncour:

SIR GEORGE. You, brother, to obtain the character of a good-natured man, are content to be the bubble of all the world.

MR. BONCOUR. Well, I had rather be the bubble of other men's will than of my own; for, let me tell you, brother, whatever impositions knavery puts upon others, it puts greater on itself.[3]

Charles comes in quite naturally as the complement to Joseph, but the initial conception may be seen, perhaps, in *The Duenna*, II. iii:

FERDINAND. Antonio, sir, has many amiable qualities.

JEROME. But he is poor, can you clear him of that. I say—is he not a gay, dissipated rake, who has squander'd his patrimony?

FERDINAND. Sir, he inherited but little; and that his generosity, more than his profuseness, has stript him of—but he has never sullied his honor.

I have already suggested some resemblance between Charles Surface and Willoughby Lacy,[4] and others have seen a likeness to Charles Fox.[5]

The 'Frank Pliant'[6] of 'The Teazles' closely resembles Charles Surface,[7] but Clerimont[8] in 'The Slanderers' is more like one of Steele's heroes, grave and highly moral.

'Charles' was created by William Smith (1730–1819), better known as 'Gentleman Smith', partly from his fine manners and partly from his

[1] i. 555. Maskwell, in Congreve's *The Double Dealer*, is a more obvious parallel.

[2] For the bare possibility that 'Placidus' in the anonymous poem *Prometheus, or the Rise of Moral Evil* (1775) is Sheridan's earlier description of the type, see C. J. L. Price, 'The Completion of *The School for Scandal*', *T.L.S.*, 28 Dec. 1967, p. 1265. A more certain comparison is made by J. H. Hagstrum in *Samuel Johnson's Literary Criticism* (Minneapolis, Minn., 1952), p. 198: 'Fielding's Blifil and Sheridan's Surface are men of sentiment not because they are men of feeling (both are cold villains), but because they hypocritically mouth morality. Fielding and Sheridan were satirising that kind of moral sentiment which, without feeling, became hypocritical and vicious.'

[3] *Complete Works of Fielding*, ed. W. E. Henley (repr. 1967), xii. 187.

[4] See p. 303.

[5] Cf. *Blackwood's Magazine*, July 1826, p. 25.

[6] Sheridan also named him 'Florival' and 'Captain Harry'.

[7] The character is based on a favourite eighteenth-century idea. Sterne puts it clearly: 'In the naked temper which a merry heart discovered, he would say, there was no danger,—but to itself:—whereas the very essence of gravity was design, and consequently deceit.' (*Tristram Shandy*, Bk. I. Ch. II.)

[8] The name had already been used in Jonson's *Epicene*, and Cibber's *The Double Gallant*.

attendance at Eton and Cambridge. In the previous season he had played Townly (in *The Provoked Husband*) and Hamlet, but was best known for his acting of Kitely in *Every Man in his Humour*. 'Anthony Pasquin' wrote of him:

> With pleasure, with transport, the audience descry,
> The traits of benevolence beam in his eye;
> But that's to a Briton superior to art,
> 'Tis a comment which tacitly honors the heart.
> In the high paths of elegance who dare aspire,
> To walk as his compeer, or copy his fire.[1]

There were complaints, however, that Smith was 'too dignified and unyielding'[2] in the part of Charles, and the same criticism was levelled against J. P. Kemble. Though he was thought to be 'too sepulchral', Kemble argued that Sheridan had 'complimented him with having entirely executed his design'.[3]

Sichel's suggestion[4] that 'the real sentimentalist is Charles Surface' is supported by earlier criticism. Powell's interpretation of the role, drew the following comment: 'His animation in the Auction Scene was, if anything, too indiscriminate, some of the passages requiring a considerable degree of sentimental effect.'[5]

(*e*) SIR OLIVER SURFACE

He embodies two common stage types—the absent relative and the disguised watcher.[6] The part was given to the aged Richard Yates (1706?–96), whose 'manner was of the dry or grave humour, but perfectly natural; his speech slow; he knew he had his audience, and therefore took them at his leisure'.[7] After the first night, a critic said 'Mr. Yates was well in Sir Oliver, and when he is a little easier . . . will be still better.'[8]

(*f*) CRABTREE

In 'The Slanderers' he was Sir Christopher Crab, an elderly gossip like Foote's Sir Christopher Cripple,[9] and he is transferred to the completed version with few changes. Sheridan directed that he should 'wear

[1] *Poems*, pp. 39–40.

[2] From a newspaper cutting in the British Museum describing a performance at the Lyceum Theatre on 8 Nov. 1809.

[3] Boaden, *Kemble*, ii. 30. [4] Sichel, i. 556. [5] *Morning Herald*, 9 Jan. 1799.

[6] See B. Sprague Allen, *Tides of English Taste, 1619–1800* (New York, repr. 1958), ii. 10. I believe that Sheridan may have picked up a couple of ideas from Cumberland's *The West Indian.* Stockwell says: 'Before I publicly reveal myself, I could wish to make some experiment of my son's disposition' (I. i). There are references too, to 'Sir Oliver Roundhead', a name that Sheridan mentioned in his sketch, 'The Slanderers'. But Cumberland's Sir Oliver is puritanical, and Lady Rusport tells Charles, 'The distresses of your family, child, are quite out of the question at present; had Sir Oliver been pleased to consider them, I should have been well content' (I. vi).

[7] J. O'Keeffe, *Recollections* (1826), i. 85–6.

[8] *Morning Chronicle*, 9 May 1777. [9] See p. 288.

a muff',[1] and obviously intended that he should compete, as a macaroni, with his young nephew. The role was taken by William Parsons (1736–95), who played wheezy old men and, in the previous season, was Dogberry and Sterling. He was noted for his variety of facial expressions but was censured after the first night of *The School for Scandal*, for his 'hideous contortions of countenance' and 'horrid piece of playing'.[2] He created Sir Fretful Plagiary.

(*g*) SIR BENJAMIN BACKBITE

Sichel's statement[3] that Sir Benjamin 'makes love at the same moment to both aunt and niece' is not true, but it is clear that in 'The Slanderers' he had a more active part than in the completed play. His love for Maria is diminished as befits the egotistic macaroni, and from Sir Peter (who 'committed poetry' in 'The Teazles'), he takes up verse.

The part was created by J. W. Dodd (1740?–96), who had played Sir Andrew Aguecheek and Gratiano in the previous season. Boaden's description[4] of him is well known:

> one of the most perfect actors that I have ever seen . . . the prince of pink heels, the soul of empty eminence. As he tottered rather than walked down the stage, in all the protuberance of endless muslin and lace in his cravats and frills, he reminded you of the jutting motion of the pigeon. . . . He took his snuff, or his bergamot, with a delight so beyond all grosser enjoyments, that he left you no doubt whatever of the superior happiness of a coxcomb.

Hazlitt thought the character 'a foolish superfluity from the older comedy',[5] but there is no doubting that Dodd gave it much topical interest as a satirical portrait of a macaroni.

(*h*) ROWLEY

'Honest Rowley', the old steward, is a grave person whose judgement the audience can accept. It has been objected, however, that he is at times wittier than might be expected.[6] This may be accounted for, in general terms, by Anna Seward's remark:

> Sheridan . . . follows the track of Congreve. All Congreve's characters, and most of Sheridan's, are without much strict appropriation in the turn of their separate dialogue. Neither of these writers was able to restrain the torrent of their wit from flowing into every bay, channel, creek, or even gutter of the dramatis personae, where, perhaps, folly and insipidity . . . might have had a better effect.[7]

[1] Sichel, i. 586, notes this from a Sheridan MS. I have not seen. He also mentions (i. 11 n.) that Crabtree was a character in Sheridan's proposed magazine, 'Hernan's Miscellany'. Cf. Rae, *Sheridan*, i. 418.

[2] *London Magazine*, xlvi (1777), 232.

[3] Sichel, i. 566.

[4] Boaden, *Kemble*, i. 55.

[5] *Complete Works*, ed. Howe, v. 251.

[6] Rae, ii. 231.

[7] *Letters of Anna Seward written between . . . 1784 and 1807* (Edinburgh, 1811), i. 193.

A more particular reason is to be found in the way in which some of the dialogue was transferred from the draft to the completed play. Sir Oliver talks to a simple servant in 'The Teazles', but in the later version a few of the best lines are given to Rowley, and an ironical wit appears that was not obvious in the original.[1]

The part was taken by James Aikin (d. 1803), who had played Laertes and Subtle in the previous season. He was well cast as the honest steward.

(*i*) MOSES

I have already suggested that the character was partly based on Jacob Nathan Moses.[2] Robert Baddeley (1733–94) 'play'd the part . . . as a real Jew',[3] and from this we may assume that he took care not to exaggerate. Another critic said he was 'great' as Moses.[4] His general appearance is described by 'Anthony Pasquin':

> With crab-apple phiz, and a brow that's disdainful,
> See Baddely smile with fatigue that is painful;
> From his dissonant voice, and the form of each feature,
> You'd swear him the favourite child of Ill-nature.[5]

He had played Polonius and Petulant in the previous season.

(*j*) TRIP

Although Sheridan generally uses the name 'Trip' for this character in the Frampton Court MS., he forgets it at one point and writes:

CHARLES. Set Chairs Trim—Sit down Mr. Premium—Glasses Trim.

Sterne's Corporal resembled Sheridan's 'fop-servant' only in the fact that he 'loved . . . to hear himself talk'.[6]

The brief but telling part of Trip was taken by Philip La Mash (d. 1800), who had played Dapper in *The Alchemist* and Trippit in *The Lying Valet* in the previous season. Cooke said of him, 'In the fine gentlemen, (such as fine gentlemen *were*), he stood unequalled by any actor I ever saw.'[7] Bernard qualified this by saying that 'the gentleman's gentleman fitted him like his clothes'.[8]

[1] See Dr. J. R. de J. Jackson's acute examination of the lines in 'The Importance of Witty Dialogue in *The School for Scandal*', *Modern Language Notes*, lxxvi (1961), 603–4.

[2] See p. 302.

[3] *The Gazetteer*, 9 May 1777.

[4] *London Magazine*, xlvi (1777), 252. His portrait in the part was painted by Zoffany, and is now in the Lady Lever Art Gallery, Port Sunlight. A photograph of it is to be found in *Theatre Notebook*, vi (1951–2), 1, together with a note by Mr. Bertram Shuttleworth on the richness of the costume and the interesting background of pictures.

[5] *Poems*, ii. 73.

[6] L. Sterne, *Tristram Shandy*, Bk. 2, Ch. 5.

[7] W. Dunlap, *Life of G. F. Cooke* (2nd ed., 1815), i. 139.

[8] J. Bernard, *Retrospections of the Stage* (ed. W. B. Bernard, 1830), i. 319.

(*k*) SNAKE

He was born of 'Spatter' and 'Miss Verjuice'. In some manuscripts Sir Peter's last words about him are, 'There's a precious rogue—yet that fellow is a writer and a critic.' Some reference to Bate or Jackson may have been intended.[1] In other manuscripts the second half of the sentence is omitted.

The part was played by J. H. Packer (1729–1806), who possessed a certain unctuous stage authority. In the previous season he had acted Aimwell, Horatio, and Albany, but was better known for his performances as Prospero and Lodovico.

(*l*) CARELESS

Mellefont's ally in Congreve's *The Double Dealer* (1694) is 'Careless, his friend', but unlike Sheridan's character, he is 'weary of guzzling'. The role in *The School for Scandal* was taken by William Farren (1725–95). 'Anthony Pasquin' damned him:

> Hear Farren affright every muse from his station,
> By unqualified rant, and extreme intonation.[2]

In the Frampton Court and Lord Chamberlain's MSS. of the play, Careless was allocated the song, 'Here's to the maiden'. The texts read:

1ST GENT. Nay never Study Careless—we'll stand to the Toast—tho' your mistress should want an Eye,—and you know you have a song will excuse you—

CARELESS. Egad so I have—and I'll give him the Song instead of the Lady.— —*Song and Chorus*

In later manuscripts the lines spoken by the '1st Gent.' are recited by Careless, with appropriate changes. Those originally spoken by Careless are then given to Sir Toby or, in some manuscripts and a review in the *Public Advertiser* (9 May 1777), to Sir Harry. Probably the change was made because a better singer than Farren was available.

(*m*) SIR TOBY BUMPER

The character was not named in the early playbills.[3] When an authoritative version of the song was first published, it was described as having been sung by 'Mr. Vernon'. Joseph Vernon (?1738–82) was a well-known singer and actor at Drury Lane Theatre, and his rendering of Macheath's 'This best friend a brimmer' was much enjoyed; but the part of Sir Toby was first taken by J. S. Gaudry, a singer and music copyist there.[4]

[1] See p. 298 n. 3.

[2] *Poems*, ii. 171.

[3] It is interesting to notice that at the Bristol Theatre in 1779–80, 'Sir Toby' was introduced only when there was a good singer in the company. Otherwise the song was given to the actor (Griffin), who played Careless. See *Felix Farley's Bristol Journal*, 1 May, 4 Dec. 1779; 15 Apr., 20 May, 23 Sept. 1780.

[4] Folger Shakespeare Library MS. W. b. 279. Cf. p. 357 below.

(*n*) MARIA

Sheridan seems to have intended the part for the beautiful and talented Mary Robinson (1758–1800), who had taken Amanda in *A Trip to Scarborough*. She was pregnant, and refused the offer.[1] Priscilla Hopkins (1756–1845) accepted it, but was thought 'far from being striking'.[2]

(*o*) LADY SNEERWELL

The part was taken by Miss Sherry, who had played Dorinda and Mrs. Marwood in the previous season. The *London Magazine* thought her 'so so'. Lady Sneerwell speaks one very important line: 'There's no possibility of being witty without ill-nature.' The audience may accept it as being true to the characterization rather than true in itself, for throughout the play Sheridan reflects the attitude of Addison and Steele in suggesting that good nature is more admirable than wit, and that brilliant conversation should be warmed by humanity.

It has been suggested that the relationship of Lady Sneerwell to Charles is like that of Lady Wealthy and Young Valere in Mrs. Centlivre's *The Gamester* (1705).[3]

(*p*) MRS. CANDOUR

The part was taken by Jane Pope (1742–1818), character actress. She often played spinsters and 'Anthony Pasquin' remarked:

> See Fretfulness sits on the tip of her nose.[4]

The *London Magazine* reported that she 'was very well in Mrs. Scandal':[5] the slip in giving the name is significant, for Miss Pope became the stage embodiment of scandal, Mrs. Candour to the life.

RECEPTION

The *School for Scandal* is the production of Mr. Sheridan, and is an additional proof of that Gentleman's great abilities as a dramatic writer. The object of the satire is two-fold—Detraction and Hypocrisy, which are the prevailing vices of the times; by the first the good are reduced to a level with the worthless, and by means of the second the latter assume the appearance of men of virtue and sentiment. Nothing, therefore, could have been more seasonable than this comedy, which, in point of execution, is equal, if not superior, to most of the plays produced for the last twenty years. . . .

1 *Memoirs of the late Mrs. Robinson Written by Herself* (1801), ii. 6.

2 *London Magazine*, xlvi (1777), 232.

3 J. W. Bowyer, *The Celebrated Mrs. Centlivre* (Durham, N. Carolina, 1952), p. 66. Other resemblances between Charles and Valere are also mentioned.

4 *Poems*, ii. 48.

5 *London Magazine*, xlvi (1777), 228.

The dialogue of this comedy is easy, engaging, and witty. It abounds with strokes of pointed satire, and a rich vein of humour pervades the whole, rendering it equally interesting and entertaining. The fable is well conducted, and the incidents are managed with great judgment. There hardly ever was a better dramatic situation than that which occurs in the fourth act, where Sir Peter discovers Lady Teazle in Joseph Surface's study. It is almost the first time we ever saw a screen introduced and a closet used, without exclaiming against the incidents as poor devices. Mr. Sheridan, however, has so adroitly placed each, and made both so naturally of advantage to the conduct of the fable, that they appear by no means the instruments of art, or that kind of stage trick, which the French term *la fourberie du Théâtre*. The two characters of the brothers are finely contrasted, and those of the Scandal Club well imagined; the circumstances also of adding a duel to the report of the discovery made by Sir Peter, and making Snake beg, that his having, once in his life, done a good action, might be kept a profound secret, as he had nothing to depend on but the infamy of his character, are highly comic, and perfectly in Nature. The only objections we see to the play are, that it is somewhat too long; the satire upon the score of scandal is rather overcharged, and the last act appears to have been hastily made up. These objections, however, are easily done away; the two first in particular, by a few abridgements. Upon the whole, the SCHOOL FOR SCANDAL justifies the very great and cordial reception it met with; it certainly is a good comedy, and we should not at all wonder if it becomes as great a favourite as the *Duenna*, to which it is infinitely superior in point of sense, satire, and moral. . . . The play was ornamented with several new scenes, which did honour to the painters. The dresses were new and elegant. That of Mr. Yates, while personating the distressed Mr. Stanley, rather too rich—as Lord Mansfield said of the Jew bail, 'he would have burnt for the money he solicited'. (*Morning Chronicle*, 9 May 1777; reprinted *General Evening Post*, 8–10 May.)

. . . The Jew Broker's introduction of Sir *Oliver* to his nephew *Charles*, in the character of *Premium* the Usurer—the *Picture Auction*—and the *Screen* are three as natural, and comic situations as are to be met with in any comedy whatever—. The characters are drawn throughout with a masterly pencil, and contrasted with all the taste and judgment of a first-rate dramatist. . . . But the principal excellence of the Comedy will be found in the wit and elegance of the dialogue, with which it abounds. Indeed the spirited manner in which the author has seasoned the whole five acts, is astonishing. . . . If there is a part that the pen of criticism can justly point out as exceptionable, it will be found in the second act, where, in our opinion, the business of the piece is suffered to hang in compliment to a chain of *wit traps*, some of which seem rather too studiously laid to have the desired effect. (*Morning Post*, 9 May 1777.)

. . . The Persons of the drama have all of them something particular marked in their characters, and the Humour of each belongs to that character, and is admirably sustained throughout. The Satire is forcible and in many places as severe as Comedy can admit of, in order to produce what is called Stage Effect. . . . (*Public Advertiser*, 9 May 1777.)

. . . It is very easy to observe that the story of this piece is admirably suited to the present æra. Scandal indeed is quite coeval with the world, and has proved the bane of society in all ages, but never stared mankind in the face as in our modern times. Ancient scandal-mongers contented themselves with whispering their malice; but now, detraction is trumpetted out with the most daring assurance; and virtue, innocence and female weakness, are the usual victims sacrificed to the horrid monster. The business of plays is to *shoot folly as it flies*, to mend the heart, and improve the mind. This seems to have been forgot by modern authors, to the great prejudice of the stage. The genius, however, of Mr. Sheridan has made us ample amends in The School for Scandal; and has happily restored the English drama to those rays of glory, of which it was long shorn by a tedious set of contemptible scribblers. The compass of a newspaper intelligence will not allow us to point out all the beauties, nor to expatiate on the peculiar merit, of this most ingenious comedy; we shall therefore only observe that the perplexities of the plot are also not only contrived in the most striking, but regular manner;—a superior excellence scarcely known to the ancients, and attained by Molière alone among the moderns. The piece abounds with manly sentiments, intirely divested of affectation, and which are conveyed to the heart through the purest channels of wit. In this particular Congreve eclipsed the fame of all his predecessors, no nation excepted; for the wit of Aristophanes most generally lies in puns, Greek jingles, and local allusions, we know very little of, Plautus' *sales* are too low;—nor were *les bons mots* the great forte of Molière. They who have a sufficient knowledge of literature, will not offer to contest that Congreve sits unrivalled on the throne of dramatic wit;—and if any author has a right to dispute Congreve's royal supremacy, it is the writer of The School for Scandal.[1] (*The Gazetteer*, 10 May 1777.)

. . . Notwithstanding the Success of the *Rivals* and *Duenna*, there is a much greater Distance in their Merits, than in the difference of Time which produced them. The two first gave us great Promises, and true

[1] Charles Harold Gray, *Theatrical Criticism in London to 1795* (New York, 1931), p. 210, thinks this was probably written by 'Mr., or Captain, Cowley, husband of Mrs. Hannah Cowley'.

Genius, like unbounded Generosity, exceeds even the warmest Expectations. If *Dialogue* replete with Wit, yet as easy and natural as if there were none, and if that Wit, by being unaffected, is subservient to the Character, be the true Conversation of Comedy, Mr. Sheridan is most happy in that Part of the Drama. If *Characters* happily, but not too artfully contrasted, and distinguished by those nice Shadowings, which fly from common Observation, are Marks of true Genius, they will be found in the *School for Scandal.* If a *Fable* new and probable, clear, yet complicated in the Incidents, rising from Scene to Scene and Act to Act in Interest and Entertainment, employing in its Operations and unfolding the peculiar Humours and Passions of each Character, with an Art that not only occasions Bursts of Laughter, but an uncommon Agitation of Spirit in the Audience; if this, I say, is the grand Arcanum, the Philosopher's Stone of Dramatic Poetry, who bids more fair to find Gold at the Bottom of the Crucible, than our young Alchymist? The *Moral* is obvious, but not by throwing *Speeches*, *Observations*, and trite *Sentiments* among the Spectators, but it comes forth from a *certain Impression* made upon the Minds of the Audience, which arises from the Actions. . . .

That there may be Errors, and Negligences, some few Wants and Exuberances (ever attendant upon Genius) in this Comedy, I will not dispute, but I am at present so warmed with its Beauties, that I will not take from my present Pleasure by endeavouring to find them out, but leave that Task to the Gentlemen, Authors and Criticks by Profession. (*St. James's Chronicle*, 8–10 May 1777.)[1]

. . . Such is the outline of this excellent Comedy, which, to be a proper judge of its admirable effect, *must be seen*. . . . If the piece had any fault, it is the same which was attributed to Congreve, *that his wit flashed too often, and sometimes from characters that it could not be expected from*. . . .

. . . Mr. Sheridan, who, at the same time that he indulges his Muse in all the flights of *wit* and *fancy*, restrains it within the pale of *decency* and *morals*. Under this *poetical St. George*, we may expect to see the *Dragon* of *mere sentimental drama* entirely subdued, and the standard of *real comedy* once more unfurled. (*London Evening Post*, 8–10 May 1777.)

On Tuesday last Mrs. Sheridan, wife of R. B. Sheridan, Esq; was delivered of a child *still born*. And,

[1] At the American Art Galleries, 20 Mar. 1900, there was sold (as lot 1357), an extra-illustrated set of Boaden's edition of *The Private Correspondence of David Garrick* (1831–2), that contained five newspaper cuttings bearing notes in Garrick's hand. On a criticism of *The School for Scandal* printed three days after the first performance, he wrote: 'This critique by D.G.' Since he had a long connection with the *St. James's Chronicle*, and on 24–27 May contributed an ode to its columns, I hazard the suggestion that this is the 'critique'. For the 'ode', see pp. 317–18 below.

On Thursday night, at her house in Drury-lane, Mr. *Sheridan's* muse was delivered of a fine chopping female, *likely to live for ever.* (*London Evening Post*, 8–10 May 1777.)

. . . It is destitute of Fable, or has a very uninteresting one. It consists of several Groups of Characters freely drawn; but all marked with similar Features, and all more or less witty. It abounds with what are called Situations, Surprises, and Tricks . . . brought about by Improbabilities, yet they elevate and surprise the Audience. . . . The principal Surprise in it, that occasioned by the Fall of the Skreen, and the discovery of Lady Teazle, is brought about by a gross and palpable Improbability, that a cunning Rogue should leave the Room to a Husband whose Wife he had an Intrigue with, and who was separated only by a Skreen.—The Discovery is also made too soon, and renders the last Act heavy and tiresome. The Character of Joseph is but a Sketch, and a bad one. ('Theatrical Critic' in *St. James's Chronicle*, 13–15 May 1777.)

I have seen Sheridan's new comedy, and liked it much better than any I have seen since *The Provoked Husband*. There is a great deal of wit and good situations; but it is too long, has two or three bad scenes that might easily be omitted, and seemed to me to want nature and truth to character; but I have not read it, and sat too high to hear it well. It is admirably acted. (Horace Walpole to Mason, 16 May 1777, in *Walpole Corr.* xxviii (1955), 309.)

We hear it is Mr. Sheridan's intention not to publish the *School for Scandal*; in which case, as there will be but a small part of the town, comparatively, who will have an opportunity of seeing it this season, there is no doubt but its attraction, next winter, will operate as forcibly as it appears to do at present. (*Morning Chronicle*, 17 May 1777.)

The new comedy of the *School for Scandal* is now so much in fashion, that it is almost a matter of danger to offer a single objection to it. Truth, however, is able to stand against every argument; and after a repeated review of the performance, and a comparison of the several component parts of the play, with the established rules of the drama, an old theatrical correspondent ventures this opinion, which he the rather offers at present, because he always wishes to fill the humble post of the slave who rode behind the victor's chariot in a Roman triumph, and whose office it was, in the midst of the intoxicating plaudits of the populace, to exclaim 'Remember thou art but a man!' *The School for Scandal* is a work of great genius, but it is not perfect in point of fable, nor does it give the world a single character which has not been exhibited in some point of view by other writers. Several of the situations approach so very nearly to those in other plays, that nothing but the great skill of Mr. Sheridan, in giving an originality of dialogue to the characters, could have saved them from being deemed direct imitations. The grand situation in the fourth act, is founded in improbability, and though managed with a degree of art, which shews superior judgment, asks for great allowance from the spectators. Add to all this, the poet has adopted a double plot, when a single one would not only have been a sufficient groundwork, but, if well conducted, would have been essentially contributory to the roundness and perfection of the piece. The character of Joseph might, and indeed ought to have been amplified; the two first acts, which now have no great analogy to the fable, might then have been spared; and the comedy would have deserved the title of *The Man of Sentiment*, a title much more expressive than that it bears, and which, strictly speaking, is a gross misnomer. . . . In fine, Mr. Sheridan's *School for Scandal* is brilliant beyond example; but Mr. Sheridan is equal to a more correct comedy. (*Morning Chronicle*, 24 May 1777.)

ODE *to the Author of* The School for Scandal

It is a Shame, *young Sheridan*,
And ne'er will be forgot;
With more of *Wit* than falls to *Man*,
With *Character*, and *Plot*,

That you should dare to mount the Stage,
And fascinate the Town!
A suckling Poet of your Age,
To seize the Laurel Crown!

Though crouded Theatres applaud,
Our Hearts with Rapture beat,
And though thy Fame flies all abroad,
That Fame is not complete,

Till *Envy* and *Malevolence*
Begin their ranc'rous War,
And foaming *Rage* and *Impotence*
Attend the Victor's Car.

But hark! They hiss—See Envy wakes
The blooming Muse to seize!
You smile and crush two crawling Snakes*
An *Infant Hercules*!

Go on—Thy wondrous Pow'rs display,
Each Monster-Mode engage;
Each Hydra Vice and Folly slay,
And cleanse the *Augean Stage*.

DELIA[1]

(*St. James's Chronicle*, 24–27 May 1777: * This alludes to the two Writers who have shown their Malice in attacking our Author's Performance in the Daily Papers.)[2]

The New Comedy called, *The School for Scandal*, is to be acted this evening for the twentieth time, which is advertised as the last time of its being represented, or indeed of the Company's performing this season. The astonishing hold of the Publick which this Play has taken, is the best, and indeed an unquestionable proof of its excellence; no Comedy was ever so much flocked to at any part of the season, much more in the height of summer. (*Morning Chronicle*, 7 June 1777.)

Last night a phænomenon in the theatrical world made its first appearance at this House; that is, a modern comedy, unaided by the deceptions of scenery, or the absurdities of sing-song and pantomime, received by 'a brilliant and crouded audience,' with the most universal and continued marks of applause.

The piece is an assemblage of wit, sentiment, pointed observation, and improbabilities, unconnected by any grand principle of action. To give an account of the plot, where there is none, would be still a more difficult task than to write a good comedy.

. . . Besides the plot, and under plots, there is a groupe of figures worked into the body of the piece, which form a kind of club, whose sole delight is in propagating scandal, when they have materials; and when they have none, inventing, adding, and misrepresenting every thing they hear, or their rage, folly, malice, or prolific brains, can suggest. Lady Sneerwell, Mrs. Scandal, Sir Benjamin Backbite, and Crabtree, constitute this valuable society. Joseph and Lady Teazle, though now and then otherwise engaged, appear to be at least honorary members. It is a pity that the standing members of the club were not more directly engaged in the business of the piece; but in spite of this objection we do not recollect to have ever heard or read a more just or pointed satire; nor a dialogue fuller of wit than the conversation held up by this very respectable

[1] The manuscript of this poem by Garrick was sold at Sotheby's, 15 Apr. 1929, lot 868. It is now Berg Collection MS. 214342B at the New York Public Library.

[2] See p. 298, n. 3. Cumberland denied decrying it: see his *Memoirs* (2nd ed., 1807), i. 271. C. H. Gray, op. cit., p. 207, thought the review of 13–15 May was in the vein of George Steevens.

brotherhood and sisterhood of modern mohawks. Besides the general satire, which will hold good as long as the English language is read or understood, the particular application of it to a certain modern daily publication is logically true throughout, and ought to crimson with blushes every cheek which has encouraged such a butchery of male and female reputation.

Snake's character, though not so well known, is a character, we fear, but too frequent in this great town, and his fears lest he should lose it by telling truth, at the conclusion, is happily hit off.

The last scene of the scandal club in which [occur] the various reports relative to Sir Peter and Lady Teazle, it admirably wrought, finely conceived, and drawn by a masterly hand, while it exposes the general rage of scandal, it shews how matters are always exaggerated. The concealment behind the screen is turned into something worse than a bare concealment; the eclaircissement into a duel. The duel at first is a duel with swords. Pistols are introduced as an improvement, till at length Sir Peter Teazle, who is consigned to the dust, as having received a mortal wound in the Thorax, makes his appearance, and gives the lie to every syllable advanced by this seminary of combers and dressers.

Few who are capable of judging of this piece will speak the truth. The friends of the author, and other cotemporary playwrights, have their prejudices. We labouring under none of these impediments of partiality, rivalship, private pique, or an overflow of wit, we flatter ourselves that we are tolerably enabled to pronounce with critical truth on the merits and demerits of 'The School for Scandal'. The great objects of the satire are detraction and hypocrisy, which, according to character and situation, the author has very artfully blended, sometimes in the same person, and sometimes distinct. The person given to detraction is not always an hypocrite, though he often, nay generally, is one; when it is unaccompanied by hypocrisy it is certainly less noxious; the effects are seldom attended to, and seldomer felt in their consequences; whereas the malignant hypocrite scarcely ever deals in scandal, but to effect some sinister or dark purpose. Scandal is made to answer another very natural and obvious end between the extremes of slander aforethought, and the mere rage for tale-bearing, that of reducing every one to the level of the slanderer. This we repeat, as directed to the great end proposed by the author, is one of the keenest and best pointed satires in the English language.

The scene in Joseph's library, the *embarras* upon *embarras*, on the successive intrusion of Sir Peter Teazle and Charles, and the discovery of Lady Teazle behind the sentimental Joseph's screen, is a piece of as fine stage effect as can possibly be conceived.

The auction scene is happily imagined, and is rich in sentiment and nature.

The last scene of the scandalous club, as was before observed, has few equals in the whole circle of the English drama.

The mischief arising from usurious contracts, Moses's instructions to Sir Oliver, in the assumed character of Mr. Premium, and the mode of conducting money negotiations are strongly and faithfully delineated.

The dialogue abounds in wit throughout; the piece produces new and interesting situations in every scene; sentiments the most natural and elevated arise from those situations. Virtue and principle, operating on conduct, is strongly recommended. Vice is described in its most hideous garb; and yet neither one nor the other are effected in a disgusting sermonic stile. Virtue is judiciously blended with its failings and foibles, and even vice is only rendered hateful on account of its effects on society, and its contradiction to the first uncontaminated principles of our nature. These are a few out of innumerable beauties of a less striking nature, that are thickly strewed in every scene almost, in 'The School for Scandal.' Let us now perform a very disagreeable part of our duty, that of pointing out some of its leading defects, in which it is almost equally fruitful.

'The School for Scandal' is totally deficient in plot, and of the underplots or incidents, which all ultimately conduce to the *dénouement*, and are meant to constitute one complete action, we are still of opinion, that taking the whole business as referable to the end, the plot is still infinitely too complex and overcharged. There is no leading figure on the canvas, no great point seemingly in view. The figures all occupy equal spaces, the incidents equal attention, and the very marriage between the hero and heroine happens as it were by chance. Maria, till almost the very last scene, might be married to the witty Sir Benjamin Backbite, or any one else, as well as to Charles, and Charles to a nabob's daughter, whom he never saw before, as well as to Maria.

The means devised by Rowley and Sir Oliver, are too much dwelt and built on; a great part of that business might be well retrenched, which would have a double good effect; that of shortening the piece, and of melting, softening, and qualifying, the means made use of to depretiate Joseph, and raise Charles, in the esteem of his uncle.

To heap coals on poor Joseph's head, for seducing Lady Teazle, is in our opinion very unfair. If there was any seduction at either side, it seemed to arise on that of the lady. She was not won by his casuistical doctrines, but by something else. She controverted their truth, and the deductions drawn by him from them in his own favour. She was no convert at the time. Her conversion must have arisen previous to Joseph's sentimental sermon, from some more prevailing argument; but she is not the first lady, who made the first advances, and afterwards brought a charge of seduction against the party seduced.—On the whole, there is something very improbable in this love affair, nor can we at all reconcile Lady Teazle's going to see Joseph's library, to any thing which passed before or after.

Sir Peter Teazle's interview and consultation with Joseph, lies liable to the same objection; partly on his consulting a young man on so nice and delicate an affair; but more so, in his strange resolution, of settling an ample separate maintenance, and the reversion of his whole fortune on a woman, who had done every thing in her power to render herself disagreeable to him, and his life miserable and unhappy.

Charles's assisting to push Stanley out of Joseph's chamber, by no means accords with the idea held out of his generous and grateful nature, when in the very instant of this outrage he recognizes him, by the name of little Premium, who had acted so very generously in the purchase of the pictures.

Joseph and Charles, in point of character, are the principal figures in the groupe. Joseph, full of morality and sentiment, is always preaching up virtue and feeling; but is at bottom mean, mercenary, malignant, artful, and designing. Charles, on the other hand, is lively, giddy, profligate, and extravagant. His follies and vices are however qualified with openness and generosity; with an unstrung purse; a heart susceptible for others woes: he sympathizes with the unfortunate and miserable. He does not even confine himself to ineffective lamentation; he augments his own distresses to alleviate those of others. These two are indeed the great characteristic features of human nature, in the early stages of life. Every man under thirty is, in some measure, a Joseph or a Charles. He either acts up to some rules of prudential conduct, arising from native disposition, or dictated by art; or he gives way to his passions, and throwing off all restraint, stands confessed, the gay generous libertine, or the mere profligate sensualist. The characters afford no novelty, though they are newly dressed; and we are ready to allow, on the whole, well dressed. But we should have hardly troubled our readers with observations which are on a level with the meanest capacity, were it not to introduce others, of much more importance. What is the tendency of this piece? The author's friends will say; to promote active virtue; to disseminate true sentiment, and distinguish it from the counterfeit; to detect hypocrisy; and to encourage and deter by punishments and rewards. This may have been his intention, but we will appeal to common sense, to experience, and to a tolerable acquaintance with human nature, whether its incitements to a perseverance in vicious idle habits, and consequential injuries, are not much stronger than to the practice of virtues which cannot be models of imitation to him who does not recognize at least their seeds in his own breast. How will such a model probably operate on the real Charles's of the day? Ruminating in his own mind, says the spendthrift, 'I am extravagant; I have dissipated my patrimony, disposed of my younger brothers' and sisters' fortunes, because they loved and confided in me. I have ruined the too credulous tradesman. I have rendered myself despicable in the eyes of every sober intelligent man; but then, cannot I trace Charles Surface in every single circumstance almost in my conduct? When my father died, did not I spontaneously add to the provision made for younger children? Have not I exerted my interest as a member of parliament, to serve the deserving and distressed? Has not my pocket been always open to the application of the miserable? In fine, though ruined and undone myself, and having ruined and undone others, am not I Charles Surface?' Those observations might be multiplied beyond number, and extended to every stage, from seduction to total ruin; to prove that Charles Surface is rather a dangerous character to be held out to the youth of the present age. It reveals a villain, clothed with the outside trappings of morality and sentiment, a compound of hypocrisy and art; no uncommon sight in this designing tricking age; and it conveys pointed instructions to those who are apt to mistake appearances for realities . . . (*London Magazine* xlvi (1777), 228, 230–1.)

We may be led to condemn all appearances of honour, sentiment and virtue, because (in this instance) we see them only assumed; and we may be led to excuse every species of profligacy, debauchery and extravagance, because we behold an instance of these defects in Charles, united with a benevolent heart. . . . The Author insinuates into the minds of his audience wrong impressions which, if erected into general rules, will be highly injurious to men of real virtue, and make all outward appearances of it highly suspicious. (*The Public Register* (Dublin), 7–10 Feb. 1778.)

The fourth act though rich with incident and humour is rather long, and we think the scene of the discovery behind the screen should have been placed in the last act. (*Hibernian Journal*, 14–16 Jan. 1778.)

Apropos to the theatre, I have *read* the *School for Scandal*: it is rapid and lively, but is far from containing the wit I expected from seeing it acted. (Horace Walpole to Mason, 19 May 1780, in *Walpole Corr.*, xxix (1955), 35.)

We have more than once seen a dramatic piece from frequency of repetition sink into a state of careless representation, almost beneath contempt. . . . *The School for Scandal*, being acted under the author's eye, has never yet fallen into this disgrace, on the contrary, from the increasing merit of its several performers, it seems to rise in point of stage effect each time it is represented. On Saturday evening it was a rich treat to all who love the drama, and not more so, on account of its innate power as a comedy, than from its uncommon excellence as a stage exhibition. (*Morning Chronicle*, 16 Oct. 1780.)

By *The School for Scandal* the style of Congreve was again brought into fashion; and sentiment made way for wit, and delicate humour. That piece has indeed the beauties of Congreve's comedies, without their faults; its plot is deeply enough perplexed, without forcing one to labour to unravel it; its incidents sufficient without being too numerous; its wit pure, its situations truly dramatic. The characters however are not so strong as Congreve's; which may be regarded as the principal fault of this excellent piece. Lesser faults are Charles's sometimes blundering upon sentiments; nay sometimes upon what are the worst of all sentiments . . .: 'Justice is an old lame hobbling beldame, and I can't get her to keep pace with Generosity for the soul of me.' This sentiment, than which nothing can be more false and immoral, is always received by the silly audience with loud applause, whereas no reprobation can be too severe for it. ('Robert Heron' [i.e. John Pinkerton] in *The Universal Magazine*, lxxvii (1785), 120.)

This incomparable comedy perhaps in all but tendency, the best in the language, bore itself out as usual on Saturday [13th], notwithstanding some alterations, not for the better. (*The World*, 15 Oct. 1787.)

. . . The screen scene being introduced too soon, the plot is discovered in the fourth act--therefore the character of Joseph, that canting smiling hypocrite . . . is suddenly revealed.—The last act, which should be the best, is consequently the worst. The moral of this play is also bad—dissipation and extravagance being rewarded and thereby encouraged. The characters are admirably drawn, even the most insignificant in the piece—and the language abounds with genuine wit, which makes ample amends for the fable. (*The Thespian Magazine and Literary Repository*, i (1792), 42.)

It is very possible that a perusal of the novel [Fielding's *Tom Jones*] may have suggested the first idea of the comedy; but an author who can ennoble and exalt his primitive materials so splendidly, as is done in the present instance, is above every imputation of plagiarism. . . . (*Drakard's Paper*, 4 Apr. 1813.)

If some of the characters in the School for Scandal were contained in Murphy's comedy of *Know your own Mind*[1] (and certainly some of Dashwood's detached speeches and satirical sketches are written with quite as firm and masterly a hand as any of those given to the members of the scandalous club, Mrs. Candour or Lady Sneerwell), yet they were buried in it for want of grouping and relief, like the colours of a well-drawn picture sunk in the canvass. Sheridan brought them out, and exhibited them in all their glory. If that gem, the character of Joseph Surface, was Murphy's, the splendid and more valuable setting was Sheridan's. He

[1] Produced at Covent Garden Theatre, 22 Feb. 1777.

took Murphy's Malvil from his lurking-place in the closet, and 'dragged the struggling monster into day' upon the stage. That is, he gave interest, life, and action, or, in other words, its dramatic being, to the mere conception and written specimens of a character. This is the merit of Sheridan's comedies, that every thing in them *tells*; there is no labour in vain. . . . The School for Scandal is, if not the most original, perhaps the most finished and faultless comedy which we have. When it is acted, you hear people all around you exclaiming, 'Surely it is impossible for any thing to be cleverer.' The scene in which Charles sells all the old family pictures but his uncle's, who is the purchaser in disguise, and that of the discovery of Lady Teazle when the screen falls, are among the happiest and most highly wrought that comedy, in its wide and brilliant range, can boast. Besides the wit and ingenuity of this play, there is a genial spirit of frankness and generosity about it, that relieves the heart as well as clears the lungs. It professes a faith in the natural goodness, as well as natural depravity of human nature. While it strips off the mask of hypocrisy, it inspires a confidence between man and man. (W. Hazlitt, *Lectures on the English Comic Writers* (1819), pp. 334–6.)

With but little interest in the plot, with no very profound or ingenious developement of character, and with a group of personages, not one of whom has any legitimate claims upon either our affection or esteem, it yet, by the admirable skill with which its materials are managed,—the happy contrivance of the situations, at once both natural and striking,—the fine feeling of the ridiculous that smiles throughout, and that perpetual play of wit which never tires, but seems, like running water, to be kept fresh by its own flow,—by all this general animation and effect, combined with a finish of the details almost faultless, it unites the suffrages, at once, of the refined and the simple. . . .

The defects of The School for Scandal, if they can be allowed to amount to defects, are, in a great measure, traceable to that amalgamation of two distinct plots, out of which, as I have already shown, the piece was formed. From this cause,—like an accumulation of wealth from the union of two rich families,—has devolved that excessive opulence of wit, with which, as some critics think, the dialogue is overloaded; and which, Mr. Sheridan himself used often to mention, as a fault of which he was conscious in his work. (Moore, i. 245–7.)

CHOICE OF TEXT

The *Morning Chronicle* report[1] that Sheridan did not intend to publish *The School for Scandal* must have irritated many theatrical managers, but Sheridan knew only too well that the comedy would attract crowds for

[1] See p. 316 above: 17 May 1777.

some time to come and that he would be justified in keeping his masterpiece under his own control for as long as he could profitably do so. He could take example from Thomas Harris, who had bought the text of *The Duenna* and had carefully safeguarded his own interest in it by refusing to allow it to be published and by giving permission for performance outside Covent Garden only as a matter of personal favour. For example, when 'His Majesty's Comedians from the Theatres Royal, Drury Lane and Covent Garden' performed at Lewes in the summer of 1778, the Sussex manager was careful to advertise that *The Duenna* was not as yet published but was given with Harris's permission.[1] However, when J. B. Vandermere, a Dublin manager, presented the opera from a pirated text said to be provided by a London shorthand writer, Harris sent an attorney to Ireland to seek an injunction against him.[2]

The extraordinary success of *The School for Scandal* in London made Irish managers eager to put on a performance, and Irish readers anxious to obtain a copy. An Irish correspondent of the *Morning Post* declared: 'We are delighted with the public account of Sheridan's piece, and I believe was the copy to be purchased by the public, the subscription would be filled in a few minutes.'[3] The design was obvious: once a play was printed, it became public property. Sheridan showed no sign of acting upon the hint, but every appearance of using the play as a useful bargaining weapon, worth gold.[4] Ways of obtaining the text without his permission were therefore tried. Thomas Snagg, a leading member of Ryder's Dublin company, approached Joseph Gurney and other London shorthand writers with a view to their providing a text of *The School for Scandal*, only to meet with some little difficulty over payment for earlier work. Snagg and his friends decided, therefore, to make a longhand copy themselves during performances at Drury Lane Theatre: '. . . going into the two-shilling gallery, a party of five. By sitting together, two on one seat, two behind and two below, we composed a group and with paper and pencils each writing down the direct words of one of the characters in a scene and regulating the whole in a committee after each performance, in four or five nights we completed the whole.' Snagg says that this version, gained so laboriously, was not acted in Dublin, because Ryder had now bought a copy of the authentic text which Sheridan had sent to his sister, Alicia. 'The difference in the two copies was very trifling, the fair and the pirated, but we performed it from the original one.'[5] Ryder paid a hundred guineas for the difference,[6] and perhaps for immunity from possible prosecution. His advertisement[7] is full of virtue: 'Mr.

[1] *Sussex Weekly Advertiser*, 22 June 1778.

[2] *Morning Post*, 20 June 1777.

[3] Ibid.

[4] See p. 327.

[5] Thomas Snagg, *Recollection of Occurrences* (1951), p. 99. His stage name was Wilks.

[6] *Public Advertiser*, 31 Jan. 1778.

[7] *The Public Register: Or, Freeman's Journal* (Dublin), 1–3 Jan. 1778.

Ryder having procured from the Author a copy of the celebrated Comedy of *The School for Scandal* (as presented fifty nights, and now performing at the Theatre Royal in Drury Lane, London) it has been a considerable time in Rehearsal at the Theatre Royal in Crow-street, and will be performed for the first time on Thursday next, by Command of their Excellencies.'—Snagg thought that, by providing a copy in this way, Sheridan made a virtue of necessity. This is probably true, but we are bound to admire the neatness of Sheridan's solution to the problem: he gave his sister a good present and provided Ryder with every reason for keeping the text to himself. In fact, this text was not published in Ireland until 1799.

There was certainly a demand for reading copies. The *Freeman's Journal*, 16–18 July 1778, mentioned regretfully that the comedy was not published, and it is clear that the Irish public had to wait until 1780 before 'books of the play' were available. On 16 December the *Dublin Evening Post* announced that 'the Original SCHOOL for SCANDAL' was for sale, 'price a British sixpence'. The adjective 'original' was inaccurate, but this pirated version remains the first printed edition. It would be nice to think that the text put together by Snagg and his friends provided the copy, but Snagg does not claim that it did.

A number of other Irish editions were printed in the next few years[1] and news of them gradually reached England. Mary Delany remarked, in a letter of 19 May 1785: 'I hear the School for Scandal is to be got in Ireland. I beg you will obtain me two copies. It has not been published in England.'[2] Her last statement appears to be wrong: Bew published an edition in 1781[3] and Cadell brought out one in 1783.[4] Though they may have been suppressed, some note of their existence seems to have reached Edward Gibbon, who wrote to his bookseller on 26 September 1784, asking, 'Is not the School for Scandal at last published?'[5]

Some manuscript copies were available to friends and connections, and Horace Walpole read one before the play was even piratically published;[6] but, in general, Sheridan had too much to lose to allow manuscript versions to circulate freely. Few presentation copies are known to survive: the Georgetown Crewe manuscript alone is signed by the author.[7]

Some prompt copies must have been made for provincial companies, with or without Sheridan's consent. Those that he sanctioned seem to have

1 See B. Shuttleworth, 'Early Editions of *The School for Scandal*', *Theatre Notebook* vi (1951–2), 4–7.

2 *Autobiography and Correspondence of Mary Granville, Mrs. Delany*, ed. Lady Llanover (2nd ser., 1862), iii. 256.

3 B. Shuttleworth, 'The First London edition of *The School for Scandal*', *Theatre Notebook*, viii (1953), 23.

4 Rhodes, ii. 166.

5 E. Gibbon, *Letters*, ed. J. E. Norton, (1956), iii. 4.

6 *Walpole Corr.* xxix (1955), 35.

7 See p. 339 below.

been permitted as a bargaining weapon or mark of special esteem. When negotiating John Henderson's services, Sheridan agreed to present the comedy at Bath and did so on 4 November 1777.[1] Tate Wilkinson secured a copy for his own benefit night at York in April 1778,[2] and when Joseph Younger took a company to Liverpool and Manchester in the summer of 1778, he was glad to advertise that the comedy would be given 'By the particular permission of the Author'.[3] I do not know how Wilkinson secured his privilege, but Younger was to become deputy manager of Drury Lane Theatre and Sheridan was clearly anxious to be on good terms with him. Similarly, George Colman the elder reported,[4] in 1785, that Sheridan had 'kindly lent' the play to Miss Farren for a performance at the Haymarket Theatre.

There were, however, many companies that could not obtain favour so easily[5] so, like Snagg and his friends, they put their versions together as best as they could and without too great a reverence for the authentic text. John Bernard described the method used at Exeter in 1779:

Its success at Bath had dispersed its fame about the West of England, and it was highly probable that, if the play were produced at Exeter, it would run a number of nights to full houses. But the comedy was not yet published, and the managers, who had copies of it, had obtained them on condition that they did not permit the same to become the parents of others. This was a precaution of Sheridan's, not with any view of emolument, but in order to preserve his language from mutilation, and prevent the play being produced at any theatre where the proper attention could not be paid to its 'getting up.'

Under these circumstances, I offered to attempt a compilation of the comedy, if Mr. Hughes[6] would give me his word that the manuscript should be destroyed at the end of the season. This was agreed to, and I set about my task in the following manner:—I had played Sir Benjamin at Bath, and Charles at Richmond, and went on for Sir Peter one or two evenings when Edwin was indisposed;—thus I had three parts in my possession. Dimond and Blisset[7] (Joseph and Sir Oliver) transmitted their's by post, on conveying the assurance to them which Mr. Hughes had to me. Old Rowley was in the company, and my wife had played both Lady Teazle and Mrs. Candour. With these materials for a groundwork, my general knowledge of the play, collected in rehearsing and performing

[1] *Felix Farley's Bristol Journal*, 8 Nov. 1777; cf. *Morning Post*, 15 Sept., *London Evening Post*, 16–18 Sept. 1777.
[2] *York Courant*, 21 Apr. 1778.
[3] *Williamson's Liverpool Advertiser*, 26 June 1778.
[4] To J. Lefanu, 27 Aug. 1785 (Mr. W. R. LeFanu's collection of their correspondence, f. 115).
[5] Though one Glassington, manager of the players at the Stourbridge Fair in 1779, claimed 'to have purchased all the popular pieces at the winter theatres, including *The School for Scandal*, *The Duenna* and *The Camp*, none of which had been performed at the Fair before' (Sybil Rosenfeld, 'The Players in Cambridge, 1662–1800', *Studies in English Theatre History* (1952), p. 33).
[6] Manager of the Exeter and West of England Company.
[7] Dimond and Blissett were leading members of the Bath company.

in it above forty times, enabled me in a week to construct a comedy in five acts, called, in imitation of the original 'The School for Scandal.'

This comedy Mr. Hughes introduced to the public, (without any explanation of the above,) and it drew us crowded houses twice a-week, to the end of the season.[1]

Bernard's 'memorial reconstruction' and Snagg's compilation were two methods of making up a text. Others may have been employed. What is certain is that Sheridan was so successful in retaining the authentic version that these corrupt ones were current in the provinces right up to 1809.

Proof of this is to be found in an unexpected place: in preparations for a performance at Drury Lane Theatre, shortly before it was burnt down. Samuel Ryley, a country actor, sought permission in February 1809, to appear in the part of Lord Ogleby, but was told that

Mr. Sheridan had fixed upon Sir Peter Teazle for my debut. . . . One rehearsal was thought sufficient for an old play and a veteran actor; but what was my surprise, agitation, and alarm, when I found the manuscript from which this comedy was performed in provincial theatres, differed so materially from the original, it was utterly impossible to connect the speeches. Mrs. Jordan,[2] with a kindness peculiarly her own, endeavoured to reconcile the text, but 'twas impossible. Dowton[3] advised me to give it up, and Elliston[4] thought the difficulties insurmountable, unless I could get the performance postponed for a few days.

This I attempted, but in vain; the play was advertised for Monday, and must be done. Considering this as perhaps the only chance I should ever be allowed, I borrowed the original MS. and went home with a heavy heart and depressed hopes.—This was Friday; had the part, though very long, been entirely new to me, I could have studied it in the time; but in this case I had not only to learn, but to unlearn, the more difficult task of the two. I had to cut out a line or a speech here, and introduce a line or a speech there; in short, it was a complication of embarrassment.[5]

Ryley makes the difference between the pirated text and the Drury Lane prompt-book painfully obvious.

Bernard's statement that Sheridan refused to allow copies of the authentic text to be circulated because he wished 'to preserve his language from mutilation' may have some validity. It is also clear that the dramatist always intended to make the play more perfect, and that he toyed with the wording from time to time. Eventually he sold his copyright to James

[1] *Retrospections of the Stage*, ed. W. B. Bernard (1830), i. 208–9.

[2] Dorothy Jordan (1761–1816) was successful as Lady Teazle, though she more frequently played the tomboy.

[3] William Dowton (1764–1851) was celebrated for his Malvolio.

[4] Robert W. Elliston (1774–1831), a skilful tragic actor.

[5] S. W. Ryley, *The Itinerant, or, Memoirs of an Actor* (1816), iv. 124.

Ridgway, and promised to send him a corrected text.[1] Ridgway put out the following advertisement:

SCHOOL FOR SCANDAL

A GENUINE EDITION, from the Original Copy

By R. B. SHERIDAN, Esq.

Is in the Press, and will speedily by published.

JAMES RIDGWAY having purchased the Copy-right of the above celebrated Comedy, gives Notice, that the Venders of the *Spurious Copies* which been attempted to be imposed on the Public, will be prosecuted as the Law directs.[2]

If this is to be accepted at its face value, then Sheridan must have given him some corrected sheets. Ridgway certainly asked for some, and later 'expostulated pretty strongly' with Sheridan for being kept 'so long dancing after him'. To this Sheridan replied, 'The fact is, Mr. R., I have been nineteen years endeavouring to satisfy my own taste in this play, and have not yet succeeded.'[3] Ridgway ceased 'teasing him' for it, and never received the corrected copy. In November 1809, however, Sheridan agreed to sell the whole of his 'Dramatic and Poetical Works' to J. G. Raymond for publication. At the foot of the agreement, there appears a note asking Powell, the prompter, to deliver the manuscript of *The School for Scandal* to Raymond.[4] It is possible to read into this, the idea that Sheridan had given up hope of revising the play and was content to have it printed from the prompt copy.[5] However, Raymond did not go on with the project, and Sheridan failed to complete a revision before he died.

[1] Ridgway had joined with five others in contributing £600 towards the demands of the 'Old Renters' on Drury Lane Theatre, on 1 Oct. 1799. See Add. MS. 29710, f. 146 b.

[2] Printed in Sheridan's *Pizarro* (21st edn., 1799), p. [79]. Rhodes, iii. 86, says that it was first printed in the fifteenth edition, and I note a significant change in the wording; the earlier edition reads: '. . . Is in the Press, and will be published on *Monday*, 30*th Sept. instant*, 1799.'

[3] Moore, *Journal*, ii. 302.

[4] Egerton MS. 1975, f. 21; *Letters*, iii. 72.

[5] The fire at Drury Lane Theatre in 1809 may not have destroyed the old prompt-book of the play, for it is clear that, nine months later, a manuscript version was in the custody of William Powell, prompter at the old theatre and of the Drury Lane company then playing at the Lyceum. When Drury Lane Theatre was rebuilt, its 'Journal, 1812–1818' (Folger MS. W. b. 381) revealed that it borrowed the manuscript of *The School for Scandal* from the Lyceum. Surely this suggests that the manuscript had considerable authority among the players as an acting version. Cf. p. 837 below.

Since the printed texts have little authority, the manuscripts left behind by Sheridan and his copyists assume a particular importance, and require thorough examination.

I. OF 'THE PORTRAIT'

Frances Anne Crewe enjoyed a close friendship with the Sheridans for at least ten years. Her beauty and modest bearing impressed them both, and some verses by Sheridan describing his reaction appear to date from early in their acquaintance:

When young Philander fell a prize
To Amoret's all conquering eyes
He took his pipe, he sought the Plain
Regardless of his privy pain,
And resolutely bent to wrest
The barbed arrow from his breast.—
'Come gentle gales' the Shepherd cried—
Be Cupid and his bow defied!—
But as the gales obsequious flew
Bathed in the morning's richest dew
He did unconsciously repeat
'The breath of Amoret is sweet.'—[1]

The Portrait, too, seems to belong to this species of occasional complimentary verse. Moore mentioned[2] that when Mrs. Sheridan was on a visit to Bath, her husband went to a London party attended by some of the reigning beauties in the fashionable world, the Marchioness of Granby, the Duchess of Devonshire, Lady Craven, the Countess of Jersey, and Mrs. Crewe. His delight in their company provoked his wife to some pleasant lines 'To Silvio', in which she gently reproached him with his inconstancy to her and to them all. She wished his 'faithful *heart* shall beat for *her* alone'. It seems a little unlikely, therefore, that the response to her plea should have been a rhapsody on Mrs. Crewe.[3] Just what the occasion was remains uncertain.

No copy of *The Portrait* in Sheridan's hand has come to light, but Harvard College Library[4] contains a transcript that has been corrected in eight places by Sheridan. It is also endorsed by Garrick: 'These Verses were sent w[i]th the Comedy of the School for Scandal by the author.'

On 11 August 1777, Lord Camden thanked Garrick for a copy of the poem, saying:

. . . I have returned the Verses you were so good to lend me, and considering they are mere panegyric (the most insipid species of Poetry) are extremely

[1] Yale MS. in an extra-illustrated copy of Moore's *Memoirs of . . . Sheridan* (formerly at Frampton Court), viii. opp. 38. It is in William Linley's hand.

[2] Moore, i. 200–7.

[3] Rhodes, iii. 200, takes a different view.

[4] TS 1116/256.3, no. 61.

good. The Girls have taken a copy perhaps without leave, but if you think Mr. Sheridan may be displeased with this liberty, it shall be burnt. . . . Charles Fox . . . admires Sheridan's verses, and agrees with me in marking him for the first Genius of these times.[1]

On the following 8 October, Horace Walpole heard his grand-nephew, George Cholmondeley,[2] repeat 'part of a very good copy of verses from Sheridan to Mrs. Crewe', and declared 'I trust they will not long retain their MS-hood.[3]

They were not printed, however, for over thirty years. In a letter to his second wife written probably on 15 October 1814, Sheridan mentioned their unexpected appearance:

They are inaccurately printed. . . . From what Quarter they can have been sent to a Newspaper at this late date I cannot surmise—and I certainly have no means of furnishing the remainder of the Poem were I disposed to do it. . . . When I look at these ver[s]es Oh! how it reminds me what an ardent romantic Blockhead nature made me!

They were sent with a M.S. copy of the Play finely bound etc. N.B. I was not then 25—by the way She was in truth the Handsomest of the set.[4]

I have not been able to identify the newspaper that printed the verses in 1814, but a cutting from it is in Egerton MS. 1975, f. 169, and reads: 'Fragment of a Portrait, | By the Right Honourable R. B. Sheridan | (Never before Published) | Addressed to a Lady, with the Comedy of THE SCHOOL FOR SCANDAL.' The 'fragment' consists of thirty-seven couplets.[5] The full poem was not made available until Murray, Ridgway, and Wilkie printed it in *The Works of . . . Sheridan* (1821), ii. 3–7. This was the first occasion on which it was published with the text of *The School for Scandal.*

2. OF THE PROLOGUE

A late draft of the prologue in Garrick's hand is Folger MS. W. a. 154 (3). It contains corrections and gives some alternative versions: those on facing pages have been ignored in compiling the textual notes.

The Folger MS. has been collated with later versions of the text (in other hands) in both Crewe MSS., the Larpent MS., and the Countess of Buckinghamshire's copy of the play. It has also been compared with a transcript in the Harvard College Library,[6] and a text printed in *The Gazetteer*, 21 June 1777. The Folger MS. is used as copy-text.

To the versions of the prologue noted by Mary E. Knapp in *A Checklist of Verse by David Garrick* (Charlottesville, Va., 1955), p. 50, should be

[1] Folger MS. W. b. 478, opp. p. 254.
[2] See p. 51 above.
[3] *Walpole Corr.* xxxii (1965), 388.
[4] *Letters*, iii. 202–3. He must have been twenty-five.
[5] Mistakenly given as sixty-one in *Letters*, iii. 202, n. 1.
[6] TS 1116/256.3, no. 63.

added the Folger MS. mentioned above, and printed texts in the *General Evening Post*, 19–21 June 1777 and the *Sentimental Magazine*, v (1777), 285.

3. OF THE EPILOGUE

This was written by George Colman the elder, and I have been unable to locate any holograph manuscript. The earliest text is probably the copy sent to the Lord Chamberlain for licensing purposes, so I have collated this Larpent MS. with the texts found in both Crewe MSS., the Countess of Buckinghamshire's copy, and *The Gazetteer*, 21 June 1777.

4. OF THE SONGS

The four stanzas of 'Here's to the Maiden of bashful Fifteen' are omitted from the Frampton Court and Larpent MSS. of the play, and a small space is left in them to suggest the duration of the song. The full text appears in both Crewe MSS. and in the Countess of Buckinghamshire's copy, and is printed here from the Georgetown Crewe MS.

The song was the earliest piece of *The School for Scandal* to be printed, and the only part authorized by the writer. S. and A. Thompson of 75 St. Paul's Church Yard noted in the *Public Advertiser*, 17 November 1778, that the overture, songs, and marches in *The Camp* were that day published, and that 'the favourite Song in The School for Scandal is added at the End.'[1] A rather different text was printed in *Felix Farley's Bristol Journal*, 12 December 1778; and even more variants appear in the first edition of the play, a pirated version printed in Dublin in 1780. I have not seen the first Irish publication of the song, advertised in the *Hibernian Journal*, 12–14 January 1778. Stanzas 2 and 3 in Thompson's version are printed as 3 and 2 on p. 398 below, and line 27 there reads 'And e'en let us Toast all together' in Thompson.

Miss Duncan's Song

On 26 September 1804 Richard Wroughton wrote to Maria Duncan,[2] who was about to make her debut at Drury Lane Theatre, to say that 'Mr. Sheridan approves Lady Teazle for your first entrée, and will write a song for the occasion.'[3] *The Times*, 9 October 1804, reported on her performance of the previous evening that 'the introduction of a charming little air, which she sung without being accompanied, inspired the audience to a degree of admiration. . . .' It was published by Michael Kelly as 'sung by Miss Duncan with unbounded applause at the Theatre Royal,

[1] For further details, see p. 715 below.

[2] She (?1780–1858) became Mrs. Davison: see *D.N.B.* under her married name.

[3] Puttick and Simpson's sale catalogue, 14 June 1861, lot 361. The letter was also in Sotheby's Catalogue of 27 June 1956, lot 733.

Drury Lane, in R. B. Sheridan Esqr.'s Comedy of The School for Scandal'.[1] I am not sure that Sheridan wrote the words, but they have no great merit and have never been printed with the play. They read:

Feel, feel, the little flutt'rer feel,
My fond suspence so well reveal.
It beats, it throbs; no peace it knows,
But pit pat, pit pat, pit pat, goes.
Its ardent pulse I can't reveal.

Still, still, with hope and fear arise,
And still provoke my anxious sighs.
This tim'rous breast by doubt opprest,
This tim'rous breast will ne'er have rest,
Have rest, until I gain the prize.

5. OF THE PLAY

Although Sheridan never completed a final version of *The School for Scandal*, he left behind him a number of manuscripts of the work in its early and later forms. These are of the greatest interest, but to judge their relative value we must also compare them with certain playhouse and printed copies that are available.

(i) *The Preliminary Sketches*

'The Slanderers' consists of sixteen leaves[2] bound before the fuller manuscript of the play (the Frampton Court MS.), now owned by Mr. Robert H. Taylor and on deposit in Princeton University Library. Its theme has been summarized,[3] and it is clearly of lesser importance to the finished work of art than 'The Teazles'. On one of the sheets the handwriting in one section is different from that of another, and there may be some gap in time between them. A rather round, early script notes characters like 'Sir Oliver Roundhead', 'Frank', 'Spunge', and 'Miss Verjuice'. The later hand (both are Sheridan's) gives different names, and includes a list of the seven leading actors in the performance.

'The Teazles' has also been described in some detail, and is certainly a significant source of the play as we know it. The manuscript was given by Algernon Sheridan in 1918 to his daughter Sophie, and was sold at Sotheby's after her death.[4] It was catalogued as 'written on 46 pp. in two note books, each containing 26 leaves', and was acquired by Mr. Robert H. Taylor.[5]

Both are holograph manuscripts.

[1] From the title-page of a copy of Kelly's publication, owned by the present editor.
[2] In which there are twenty-five pages of handwriting.
[3] See p. 291 above.
[4] Sale catalogue, 24 May 1954, lot 269.
[5] Mr. Taylor also owns a contemporary manuscript of Sir Peter's lines, with a wrapper marked 'Mr. King'.

(ii) *The Frampton Court MS.*

The manuscript itself is first mentioned in Charles Sheridan's letter to Thomas Wilkie of 19 November 1817,[1] and it came eventually into the hands of R. B. Sheridan of Frampton. He noted: 'This manuscript of the play was also written in a series of copy books of different sizes. Each of the leaves, which were numbered, have been taken out and carefully inlaid in their present form. The abstraction of the last leaf of the copy book which concluded the play is deeply to be regretted.'[2] The one hundred and eight leaves of the manuscript were bound up in 1864, in a quarto volume lettered on the spine, 'Sheridan's School for Scandal and Original MSS. and Printed Text 1821'.[3] It remained at Frampton Court, Dorset, until 1929, when it was bought by Barton Currie.[4] It became Mr. Taylor's property in 1956, and is on deposit at Princeton University Library.

The last leaf has now been located in the Library of Congress.[5] The 'doxology' is rather differently worded from the quotation given by Moore, and he spoils the joke by describing it as 'in the handwriting of the respective parties'[6] when it is entirely in Sheridan's hand.

It seems to me highly unlikely that the Frampton Court MS. represents the next stage of composition after the preliminary sketches. It looks as if it is a fair copy written out after the intermediate versions had been completed. There are still changes to be made but the text is substantially settled. Besides, the opening is penned in Sheridan's neatest hand and is very easy to read. The largish penmanship of the first page and two lines of the second dwindles afterwards to a smaller and (what appears to be) an earlier hand. Though half the text of the third page is blocked off for deletion, most of the speeches in the first four pages contain comparatively few changes or insertions. As in the opening of the Frampton Court manuscript of *The Duenna*, Sheridan can be observed changing his mind about the names of some of the characters and about the lines that they were allocated. Lady Sneerwell discusses the scandalmongering paragraphs with Miss Verjuice and with the maid Lappet in attendance. They talk about Lady Clackit, gossip about the relations

[1] See p. 11 above.

[2] This memorandum is on the first page of the bound volume.

[3] The Frampton Catalogue, p. 136, describes it as 'The Author's first Sketch of the School for Scandal, and the original Manuscript of the Play, with the text from the edition of his works, by Thomas Moore, 1 vol. sm. 4to, *brown mor.*, illustrated with family portraits. 1864. Collected and arranged by his Grandson R. B. Sheridan.' See p. 21 above. The leaves measure 18×22·8 cm.

[4] See p. 23 above.

[5] See C. Price, 'Sheridan's Doxology', *T.L.S.*, 4 May 1962, p. 309. The sheet measures 19×25 cm., and is in the Batchelder Autogr. collection (II–11–D. 6), vol. 10, f. 1455. A similar leaf was listed in Sotheby's Catalogue, 10 Nov. 1931, lot 428, and was sold to Spencer for £32.

[6] Moore, i. 242.

between Frank and Maria, and refer later to poor Florival. Miss Verjuice soon becomes Snake; the maid is reduced to anonymity; Frank and Florival are combined in a new name, Charles.

Sheridan was aware of his own tendency to be luxuriant, and of a need to refine his suggestions with each rewriting. For instance, the opening page of this manuscript still includes a long speech by Verjuice that contained too much material of illustrative rather than central interest. It reads:

That is in as fine a Train as your Ladyship could wish.—I told the story Yesterday to my own maid with directions to communicate it immediately to my Hairdresser He I am informed has a Brother who courts a millener's Prentice in Pellmell whose mistress has a first cousin whose sister is Femme de Chambre to Lady Clackit—so that in the common course of Things it must reach Lady Clackit's Ears within four and twenty Hours and then you know the Business is as good as done.

Only five of these eleven lines were to be included in the text submitted to the Lord Chamberlain. Some of the speeches, too, that were blocked off for deletion in the third page were merely introductory, but Sheridan perceived that they could be used to advantage later in the play. The rejected piece of dialogue runs:

VERJUICE. I profess Scandal merely for amusement—I never feel any malice against the People I abuse—and I take it for granted they all speak in the same manner of me.—

LADY SNEERWELL. But Verjuice you haven't told me whether you find any difficulty with the innuendo of Miss Nicely's fondness for her own Footman—

VERJUICE. None in the world—She has always been so prudent and so reserved that every body was sure there was some reason for it at Bot[t]om—

LADY SNEERWELL. Yes a Tale of Scandal is as fatal to the Credit of a Prudent Lady of her Stamp, as a Fever is usually to those of the Strongest Constitutions but there is a sort of puny Sickly Reputation that is always ailing yet will outlive the Robuster Characters of a hundred Prudes.—

The first of these is very effectively transferred to Lady Teazle, to defend herself in her rally with Sir Peter (II. i).[1] The other three are allotted to the scandal-mongers in the first scene of the first act.[2] Similarly, Snake's lines expressing the pious hope that his good deed shall not be made known in case it spoils his evil reputation is found here in the first scene of the third act, before being moved to the last scene of the play.[3]

As we read through the Frampton Court MS. we gradually reach the conclusion that it consists of those sheets which he finally adopted out of the various drafts he had written. This idea is supported by the instruction that Sheridan gives himself in the last scene of the play: 'N. B. to be

[1] See p. 376 below. [2] See pp. 367–8.

[3] For a photograph of the first page of the last scene in the manuscript, and Sheridan's crude sketch of Snake, see Barton Currie, *Fishers of Books* (Boston, 1931), p. 320.

alter'd in the 4th Act.' It refers to Sir Oliver's statement: 'Sir Peter, do you know the Rogue bargain'd with me for all his Ancestors—sold me Judges and Generals by the Foot and Maiden Aunts as Cheap as broken China!' Presumably he then revised that particular leaf. A more certain example of one that has been rewritten may be seen in the page that contains the beginning of the description of Cousin Ogle's cosmopolitan collection of features (II. i). In this manuscript Sheridan has left plenty of space on the versos so that he can jot down ideas or snatches of dialogue as they occur to him, but he has crammed the rectos with his text. However, the particular page I have mentioned is blank for an inch at the bottom, and the lines end with

CRABTREE. Caledonian Locks—etc. etc.

Clear evidence of revision is to be seen also in a sheet of dialogue between Rowley and Sir Peter (I. ii). After Sir Peter asks 'Why has anybody told you she was dead', half a page is left blank, but with a line to link it to Rowley's answer 'Come—come.' Obviously half a page of dialogue—of a severe nature and at Lady Teazle's expense—has been omitted. The process of softening and amelioration was continuous.[1]

From the second act onwards, the handwriting is larger and less careful, though (for Sheridan) quite legible. The reader receives an impression of a writer who has a clear plan before him and firm developments in mind. Many corrections in wording and some in the positioning of speeches occur, and at one point the best part of five pages is removed; but the play, essentially as we know it, can be seen to be reaching completion.

It is impossible in an edition like the present one to reveal the adroitness of Sheridan in his revisions. I have given only a few examples of the playwright's skill in adding those subtle touches that go to form a great work of art. Nothing but a facsimile would bring out the manuscript's full complexity.[2] Fortunately Mr. Robert H. Taylor has in mind the idea of publishing it in this form in due course.

Three pages of the manuscript are not in Sheridan's hand. I propose to consider them below in the section dealing with a text prepared for the first performance.

(iii) *The Lord Chamberlain's Copy*

In a letter dated 7 May 1777[3] Sheridan applied to the Lord Chamberlain

[1] Moore, i. 241–2, makes a distinction between the last five scenes and the rest of the play in this respect: 'The manuscript, indeed, of the five last scenes bears evident marks of this haste in finishing,—there being but one rough draught of them, scribbled upon detached pieces of paper; while, of all the preceding acts, there are numerous transcripts, scattered promiscuously through six or seven books, with new delineations and memorandums to each.'

[2] Rae, pp. 147–220, prints the text rather carelessly and with some omissions.

[3] See *Letters*, i. 110–11. It is in the hand of William Hopkins, the Drury Lane Theatre prompter, but is signed by Sheridan.

for permission to present the comedy and enclosed a copy of the text for examination. It came into the hands of William Chetwynd, who was Examiner of Plays in the Lord Chamberlain's office from 1738 to 1778.[1] After his death[2] the manuscript was found by his solicitor with other plays at his house in Old Burlington Street. Nearly fifty-five years later, it was presented by the solicitor's eldest son to Chetwynd's grandson, Sir George Chetwynd of Grendon Hall, Warwickshire.[3] He sent it to be bound at Fairburn's, 10 Duke Street, Adelphi, but a serious fire broke out there on 26 February 1834,[4] affected the upper and outer margins of the pages, and removed a number of lines of text from the lower edges.

The manuscript then appeared at the sale of Augustin Daly's library at the American Art Galleries, New York, from 19 March 1900, as lot 3058, and made $1750. It came up for sale again in New York on 19 November 1946 at the Perke-Bernet Galleries as lot 537, and finally found a home in Yale University Library on 8 April 1947, when it was presented by the Class of 1912 in honour of George H. Nettleton.

The volume consists of eighty-three leaves. The text takes up seventy-nine, including prologue and epilogue. William Van Lennep distinguished four hands:[5] I note that the hand copying Act IV also transcribed Folger MS. Y. d. 105 for Garrick. For other details, see his article.[6]

(iv) *The Copy Prepared for the First Performance*

The Thespian Dictionary (1802) remarked that 'the copy of this play was lost after the first night's representation, and all the performers in it were summoned together early the next day, in order, by the assistance of their parts, to prepare another prompter's book.'[7] I have been unable to find any confirmation of this statement at a date nearer the event.[8] Even if the copy were not lost, it would probably have been worn to tatters before 1802 through over-use.

There are present, however, among the sheets of the Frampton Court MS., three that contain stage directions or textual changes that were written after the Lord Chamberlain's copy was transcribed. They appear to bring us closer to the text of the first night's performance.

[1] MacMillan, p. v, confuses him with W. R. Chetwynd, 3rd Viscount Chetwynd, who was an Under-Secretary of State, and died 3 Apr. 1770.

[2] 6 Oct. 1778.

[3] Sir George Chetwynd gave this information on the first page of the volume and dated his statement 10 Sept. 1834.

[4] From a cutting from the *Morning Herald*, 27 Feb. 1834, included in the volume.

[5] He mentions William Hopkins, prompter of Drury Lane Theatre, as responsible for most of it.

[6] 'The Chetwynd Manuscript of *The School for Scandal*', *Theatre Notebook*, vi (1951–2), 10–12. See also the photograph of the first page of the text, reproduced opp. p. 13.

[7] Leaf Hh.

[8] The statement is repeated in the anonymous *Memoirs of the late Rt. Hon. R. B. Sheridan* (1816), p. ix.

Two of them are corrected copies of sheets already represented in the Frampton Court MS. They contain part of the screen scene shortly before Lady Teazle is revealed. The Frampton Court and Lord Chamberlain's MSS. print:

SURFACE. Gentlemen—I beg Pardon—I must wait on you down stairs—Here is a Person come on particular Business.

Four lines later, Surface says 'I'll send this man away.' One of these corrected sheets[1] in the Frampton Court MS. is, however, in the hand of a Drury Lane copyist, and Sheridan has added his new readings in his own writing. Before 'Gentlemen—I beg pardon', he inserts:

(*to the servant*) Lady Sneerwell!—gad's life—she mustn't come here—

and, a little later, 'I'll send Lady Sneerwell away.'

A similar contrast can be made between the other two sheets. The uncorrected one,[2] entirely in Sheridan's hand, quotes Sir Peter as saying 'He'll hear of it', while the corrected one,[3] in the hands of two Drury Lane copyists as well as that of Sheridan, reads, 'He may chance to hear of it.' Sir Peter's next speech is brief in the uncorrected version, but considerably expanded in the revision. It is interesting to notice that the longer passage agrees in all but one respect with the reading in the Lord Chamberlain's copy: it adds 'whispering' at the end of Sir Peter's speech.

The third sheet cannot be compared with any original in Sheridan's hand. It is in the writing of William Hopkins, prompter at Drury Lane, and it clearly belonged to a prompt copy and was brought in to supply a deficiency in the Frampton Court MS. It prints the last lines of the fourth act with, at the very end, a direction to the stage-manager, 'Drop Hall.'

(v) *The Georgetown Crewe MS.*

I have already mentioned that Sheridan recollected sending 'The Portrait' to Mrs. Crewe 'with a M.S. copy of the Play finely bound'.[4] The date at which he did so is uncertain but since the verses themselves were being handed around between August and October 1777,[5] it seems probable that Sheridan sent play and poem to Mrs. Crewe in the late summer of 1777.

It was listed in the sale catalogue of the American Art Association, 16 April 1923, lot 841, and was described as belonging to '*c.* 1778' and containing 'about seventy inserted words' in Sheridan's hand. The volume was acquired by the Brick Row Bookshop, Inc., and then by Nicholas F. Brady. It passed to Mrs. Brady (later Mrs. W. J. B. Macaulay), and was presented by her to the Riggs Memorial Library, Georgetown University, in February 1935.

The volume (which does not now appear to be finely bound) consists of 362 pages, including blanks. The text of the play is written on the rectos

[1] Numbered '84' in some early hand.
[2] Numbered '118b'.
[3] Numbered '118a'.
[4] *Letters*, iii. 203.
[5] See p. 331 above.

of 168 numbered pages, and they are preceded by three unnumbered leaves for title-page, prologue, and dramatis personæ. The collation is:

> [i] title: 'The | School for Scandal | A | Comedy —' [Sheridan has written his signature below the title, and has added in the top right-hand corner of the page: 'To Mrs. Crewe | From the Author']; [i^v] blank; [ii–iii^r] Prologue | Spoken by Mr. King [Sheridan has added: 'written by D. Garrick Esqr.']; [iii^v] Dramatis Personae; 1–168 [numbered on rectos only], Text; [169–70] Epilogue [Sheridan has added: 'written by G. Coleman E[s]qr.'

The pages appear to be of Whatman paper of the sort current between 1764 and 1793. They measure 22·3 × 17·7 cm., and their watermark is given as figure 192 by Shorter.[1]

Nettleton (who first published this text) declared that it was 'transcribed by a professional copyist'.[2] William Hopkins quite definitely copied part of it: p. 44, for example, is in his hand. The other part, too, may be his, but written with a different pen. I hesitate about the identification because though some of the letter forms (e.g. 'N') are identical with those in the other part of the manuscript, some (e.g. 'T') are very different. I conclude that it is possible that two copyists were involved.

On one occasion Sheridan said that he had spent nineteen years revising the play and had not satisfied his taste even then. How thorough these revisions were remains open to question. Clearly Thomas Moore did not see them for he described the Georgetown Crewe MS. as 'the last, I believe, ever revised by himself'.[3]

(vi) *The Second Crewe MS.*

On 28 August 1855 Mrs. Thomas Moore presented a volume of plays to the Royal Irish Academy.[4] One of them was the Dublin edition of *The School for Scandal* (1799), and this contained Moore's full collations with the Crewe MS. When I compared them with Nettleton's text of the Crewe MS. and the readings in a Yale MS. copy on paper watermarked '1795',[5] I noted a number of discrepancies and came to the conclusion that Moore had examined not one, but two Crewe MSS.[6]

In 1963 Mr. R. C. Stretton lent me a manuscript of the play that proved to be a second Crewe MS. It had been acquired by his family after its

[1] A. H. Shorter, *Paper Mills and Paper Makers in England, 1495–1800* in *Monumenta Chartrae Papyraceae Historiam Illustrantia*, (Hilversum, 1957), p. 374.

[2] Nettleton and Case, p. 951.

[3] i. 260.

[4] It bears Moore's bookplate, and a note in his hand: 'The MS. copy given by Sheridan to Mrs. Crewe was evidently revised by himself, and agrees with the printed Copy, except in the few trifling instances marked here in the margin.' See also Moore, *Journal*, ii. 296.

[5] See Nettleton and Case, pp. 951–5.

[6] For further details, see C. Price, 'Another Crewe MS. of *The School for Scandal*?', *P.B.S.A.*, lvii (1963), 79–81.

sale at Hodgson's sale-rooms on 27 June 1918, and in due course came up again there on 16 December 1965 as lot 201. The manuscript consists of 218 leaves, of which one in the centre and three at both the beginning and end, are blank. The text is on the rectos only and is in an unidentified hand. Sheridan's writing is to be seen in some corrections, giving readings not to be found in either the Frampton Court or Georgetown MSS. In general, the text has a fairly close connection with the Countess of Buckinghamshire's version, and appears to be earlier[1] than that of the Georgetown MS. Both Crewe MSS. bear her label of ownership[2] on the pastedowns, but the coronet that is shown on the label over her initials, suggests that the two labels were not affixed until after February 1806, when John Crewe was raised to the peerage by the Ministry of All the Talents.

(vii) *The Buckinghamshire MS.*

The manuscript of 221 leaves contains the text of the play on the rectos only. Sheridan's hand appears only on the first leaf of the prologue where he has noted: 'written by Mr. Garrick'; and on the first leaf of the epilogue, on which he had added, 'written by Mr. Coleman'. The text itself is in an unidentified hand.

The fly-leaf contains the signature 'Albinia Buckinghamshire'. She was better known for many years as an enthusiast for amateur theatricals, and as the 'Hon. Mrs. Hobart' took the part of the Widow Belmour in a performance of *The Way to Keep Him* on 20 April 1788 at Richmond House before the Prince of Wales. She also presided at a faro-table patronized by the Prince, 'where on some evenings she gave her dramatic readings, in which she was assisted by that sprightly and witty barrister, the present Mr. Jekyll'.[3]

The London dealers, E. Parsons and Sons, sold the manuscript to James Tregaskis, whose catalogue 1019 (1936), included it (item 217) and printed the prologue. Yale University Library bought it from him.

(viii) *The Powell MS.*

Harvard MS. Thr. 5. 1 was acquired in 1948, and consists of the first four acts of *The School for Scandal.* Only the text of the first act is of importance to the present study: it is described on the cover as 'The

[1] See C. Price, 'The Second Crewe MS. of *The School for Scandal*', *P.B.S.A.*, lxi (1967), 351–6, where I have also argued that it may belong to a later date. In addition to the possibilities suggested there, it is worth noting that this manuscript omitted mention of 'the d——d register' (III. ii). The only watermark that I have been able to identify is that in the first two folios: no. 1846 in E. Heawood, *Watermarks, mainly of the 17th and 18th Centuries* (Hilversum, 1950). In the above article, I conjecture that a third Crewe MS. may also have been extant.

[2] There is nothing to suggest that Sheridan presented this one to her.

[3] Robert Huish, *Memoirs of George the Fourth* (1831), i. 238. For her husband, Robert Hobart, 4th Earl of Buckinghamshire, see *Letters*, ii. 201–2, 240, 259.

1st Act with the Prologue and Epilogue by Wm. Powell', and Sheridan has added in his own hand, 'A Good Fellow'.

Powell took up the post of prompter at Drury Lane Theatre after James Wrighten's death on 3 April 1793.[1] He was closely connected with Sheridan for the remainder of the playwright's association with the playhouse. In November 1809 Sheridan instructed him to deliver the manuscript of *The School for Scandal* to J. G. Raymond, who had agreed to publish all Sheridan's 'Dramatic and Poetical Works'.[2] We cannot be sure that the Drury Lane prompt copy of the play survived the fire in February 1809, but a manuscript of 1815 (quoted on p. 837 below) states that it was preserved because it was not in the theatre that night. If this is true, then Powell could have obeyed Sheridan's order by handing over the original or by giving up his (Powell's) own copy, of which the Harvard MS. appears to be a part. Its text breaks off in the second scene with Rowley's 'I came hither with news that will surprize you', but also includes the epilogue.

(ix) '*Two acts . . . prepared by Sheridan for publication*'

Rae, *Sheridan*, i. 332, states:

> I have been fortunate enough to find, among a mass of tattered and begrimed papers which had been put aside as worthless, two acts of *The School for Scandal* prepared by Sheridan for publication. The copy which he corrected had been made before the comedy was first represented, and in which some lines were suppressed. The insertions and alterations must have been executed in Sheridan's later life, as the dark ink of his pen is in striking contrast to the faded ink of the manuscript. Though the changes are few, they are all characteristic, and they testify to Sheridan's artistic striving after finish in expression. He did not neglect even the stage directions, and he improved them in every case.

He goes on to give eight examples of alteration. He added, 'I purpose printing the revised version of the comedy', but as far as I can discover, never did so.

The present whereabouts of these manuscripts is unknown.[3]

(x) *Manuscripts not inscribed by Sheridan*

Banbury MS.: owned by Mr. Robert H. Taylor.

This is a prompt copy, written throughout in the hand of William Hopkins. It is made up of 93 numbered leaves, with an inscription (not in Sheridan's hand) on the fly-leaf: 'From the Author. Catharine Banbury.' The volume was listed in Sotheby's Catalogue, 9 November 1954, lot 471. Its previous history is uncertain: Catharine Fox married Captain

[1] Earlier, he had been prompter and copyist at the Liverpool Theatre. In Oct. 1778, he was paid for 'writing Music and Parts' (Folger MS. W. b. 117); and in 1786 for 'Manuscript Copies' (Folger MS. W. a. 20).

[2] See pp. 7–8 above, and *Letters*, iii. 72.

[3] But see p. 837 below.

Banbury in 1807[1] but I have not been able to find a copy of her signature to compare with the one on the fly-leaf. The volume itself contains the following statement in an unidentified hand:

This Manuscript belonged to the late Frederick Duke of York, and was at his death given to B V[?] Stephenson; The words 'From the Author' at the top of one of the Blank Leaves, which are in His Royal Highness's own handwriting, shews it was presented to him by Mr. R: B: Sheridan, and was no doubt copied by an amanuensis, from the Author's original manuscript, and was probably intended for the Printer; this Comedy however was never printed by Mr. Sheridan in this Country; but by some very unaccountable means, and probably from the Theatre, a Manuscript Copy got over to Dublin, and was there printed and soon got into general circulation without the knowledge, and consent of the Author.

This is a very curious and valuable Manuscript.

The words 'From the Author' do not seem to me to be in the handwriting of Frederick, Duke of York.[2]

This is a good, early text, though it reveals some careless omissions. Possibly the insertion 'his hair' (p. 413, l. 24 below) is in Sheridan's hand.

Bates MS.: Harvard MS. Thr. 5. 4.

This is described in Catalogue 19 (1938) of George Bates, 13a Pall Mall, S.W. 1: 'A Manuscript on 70 leaves, 4to, original binding of boards and calf back . . . written in a neat copperplate hand with numerous corrections by the author. From the Frampton Court sale of Sheridan material.' Mr. Bates appends an argument to prove that this is 'the earliest and most authentic text of the play as first acted at Drury Lane, 8 May 1777'.

The corrections are not in Sheridan's hand. The fly-leaves bear the names 'Tom Sheridan' and 'Charles Brinsley Sheridan' in round, child-like penmanship that does not resemble the adult hands of either of Sheridan's sons.

The text is written on 135 pages, and is much closer to the pirated version printed in Dublin in 1780, than to any manuscript corrected by Sheridan or sanctioned by Drury Lane Theatre. It possesses no authority.

Columbia MS.: Brander Matthews Museum, Columbia University.

This is incomplete. Five hands are involved in the copying: not one of them is Sheridan's. Two of the watermarks are of paper belonging to the late eighteenth century, and one, to the early nineteenth century. The omission of the reference to the Annuity Bill and of the line, 'Has her

[1] Lord Granville Leveson Gower (First Earl Granville), *Private Correspondence, 1781 to 1821*, ed. Castalia, Countess Granville (1917), ii. 275. Cf. *Letters*, i. 163.

[2] Frederick Augustus, Duke of York and Albany (1763–1827), second son of George III.

ladyship discovered that she has an old husband', may also suggest a text compiled at a fairly late date. It is rather illiterate at times, and its variants lack authority. For further details, see C. Price, 'The Columbia Manuscript of *The School for Scandal*', *Columbia Library Columns*, xi (1961), 25–9.

Laurence MS.: Yale University Library, given by H. W. Liebert in honour of G. H. Nettleton, 1951.

The name of a former owner, Charles Laurence, is to be seen on the fly-leaf.

This is a manuscript copy on 199 folios, and in one unidentified hand. The good, early text shows affinity with the Buckinghamshire MS. and the version sent to the Lord Chamberlain. In fact, one of its readings, 'your own innocence' (p. 412, l. 14 below), is otherwise present only in the Lord Chamberlain's copy.

Lowell MS.: Harvard College Library MS. fms Lowell 2.

This appeared in Christie's Catalogue of 14 March 1906, lot 128A, and was described as: 'A manuscript prompt copy of the play, written and used before its publication in book form, with a note at the end stating that "The Prologue and Epilogue may be found in any of the Magazines for June 1777. The Music of the Song is publish'd." 78 pages, contemporary half binding (broken), small folio.' It is written in two unidentified hands. The 'Dramatis Personæ' suggests that the manuscript belonged to a small country company, since one actor was given Snake and Moses, another Sir Benjamin and Trip, and a third, Rowley and Careless. Many of the lines are transcribed from the Dublin pirated text of 1780. Others are rather garbled versions of Sheridan's text.

Mortieau MS.: Harvard College Library MS. Thr. 5. 2.

This is an equally unsatisfactory text, drawn from an unauthorized and undated Dublin edition of the play.[1] The manuscript is made up of eighty-two small quarto pages, and was listed in Sotheby's Catalogue of 2 December 1901 as lot 1398.

Paignton MS.: bought by Dr. M. L. Poston in Paignton about 1959.[2] For its later disposal, see Sotheby's Catalogue, 8 April 1968, lot 170.

This has an ownership signature on the title-page: 'J. Comyns's'. The cast list notes that Aikin played both Careless and Rowley. There are

[1] THE | SCHOOL FOR SCANDAL | A | COMEDY, | [double rule] | AS IT IS PERFORMED AT THE | *THEATRE ROYAL*, | IN | DRURY LANE. | [double rule] | *DUBLIN*: | PRINTED, AND SOLD BY THE BOOKSELLERS. A–F^6. 72 pp.

[2] Both (Paignton and Tonkinson) MSS. are mentioned in passing in the article on Dr. Poston's collection, 'Bibliotheca Medici', *The Book Collector*, xii (1963), 51.

fifty-nine leaves of text (twenty of them with a watermark like Heawood's no. 1846), and three other leaves. Its readings are close to those of the Laurence MS., though there are also differences. The copyist omitted some words rather carelessly, and was clearly not a skilled reader, but some of the errors were apparently caused by mishearing (e.g. p. 423, l. 24): 'it was so' for the more usual 'it was, sir.'

Scott MS.: Harvard College Library MS. Thr. 3, the gift of E. B. Blane, 1907.

The volume contains a bookplate reading 'John Fawcett, Theatre Royal, Covent Garden, 1791–1830. Presented [presumably to the Dramatic College] by his Son, The Rev. John Turner Colman Fawcett, Vicar of Kildwick in Craven, 1863.' A pencil note adds: 'Bought at Sale of Dramatic College Effects (Bond Street), 24 Feb. 1881 C.S.' Clement Scott's[1] bookplate is also included.

The text is written on 176 pages, and is in one hand throughout. Though it contains a reading ('every London wife' on p. 383, l. 3 below), that is otherwise to be found only in the Frampton Court MS., the Georgetown Crewe MS. and the Yale MS. derived from it, the Scott MS. seems generally to belong to an earlier phase in the composition of the comedy. This may be observed in some variants in the last scene of all: Sir Peter makes no pungent remarks immediately after Lady Sneerwell and Snake make their final exits, and when Joseph, too, goes, cries 'Moral to the last', not 'Moral to the last drop'.

Tickell MS.: owned by Mr. Leonard Schlosser in 1964.

'A neat transcript' by E. A. Tickell was among the books and manuscripts, formerly owned by Richard Tickell and his daughter and sold by Puttick and Simpson as lot 617 in their catalogue of 25 May 1869. It appeared again at auction on 12 May 1964[2] at Parke-Bernet's, given by Mr. Schlosser to be sold for the benefit of the Grolier Club's library endowment fund.

The fly-leaf contains the name 'E. A. Tickell' in an elaborate copperplate style of penmanship, and 'A Portrait addressed to Mrs. Crewe with the Comedy of the School for Scandal by R. B. Sheridan Esq.' fills the next eight pages. The title is found on f. 5^r: 'THE | SCHOOL for SCANDAL | A | COMEDY | in Five Acts | By The Right Honourable | Richard Brinsley Sheridan.' The honorific reveals that the manuscript was written in or after 1806, when Sheridan became a privy councillor. The watermark, however, proves that it must date from at least two years later: it is 'H. Willmott 1808'.

[1] Clement Scott (1841–1904), dramatic critic.

[2] I examined it in the previous month with Mr. Schlosser's permission and Dr. Robert F. Metzdorf's aid. It was lot 158.

The text begins on f. 7^r and is completed (with the epilogue) on f. 211. There are also nine blank leaves. The book itself measures 22·8 by 1·3 cm., and is bound in green straight-grain morocco, with a single gold fillet enclosing a row of blind tooled ornaments.

Elizabeth Ann Tickell (1781–1860) was the daughter of Richard and Mary Tickell and niece of Sheridan's first wife. Since her uncle, C. W. Ward, was secretary to the Board of Managers of Drury Lane Theatre from September 1808, she was in an advantageous position to see the playhouse copy. There is no proof that she did so, but the cast list given in the manuscript is that of the earliest performance, with one interesting addition—'Maid Mrs. Smith'. But Sir Toby Bumper is named Sir Harry, and Trip is listed as being played by 'Le Marsh'.

The text shows affinity with that in the Lord Chamberlain's copy, even printing 'Josepht' as that does. Its real importance, however, lies in its closeness to the Murray text of 1821. It has an unusual variant in I. ii, when Sir Peter says he 'committed matrimony', and a misreading in II. ii, (like that in the Lord Chamberlain's copy), where Maria's allusion to the 'intemperance' of the scandal-mongers becomes 'interference'.

Tonkinson MS.: bought by Dr. M. L. Poston, *c.* 1945, from the Tonkinson Library, Dorford Hall, near Nantwich, and owned by him until its disposal. See Sotheby's Catalogue, 8 April 1968, lot 171.

The manuscript is made up of fifty leaves, and the 'Dramatis Personæ' given on one of them is particularly significant because it names 'Spunge'. In the text itself, Rowley is once (I. i) called 'Rowland', just as he is in 'The Slanderers' sketch. This indicates that the text is an early one, something that becomes obvious when we collate it with other manuscripts. It contains a unique reading in 'Sir Harry Foxchase'[1] in place of 'Sir Twivy Tarrier' (III. i), and some evidence to show that the copyist was easily confused. He prints 'yonder pots' for 'beau pots' (III. iii), 'trickery' for 'treachery' (IV. iii), 'sly rogue' for 'silly rogue' (IV. iii). Some of the errors appear to be caused by mishearing: e.g. 'Grace cups' for 'race cups' (III. iii), and 'Eyes by? no sure' for 'Eyes my cynosure' (V. iii). Even so, the version is an interesting one written at about the same time as the Lord Chamberlain's copy.

Yale MS.: Yale University Library MS., given by Gabriel Wells.

This is an unbound folio manuscript, carefully copied out by a professional scribe on paper watermarked '1795'. It is made up of 141 leaves, with the text on the recto only. Nettleton declares: 'It remarkably attests the continued maintenance of the Crewe text in full authority, for its few and minor verbal variants are such as usually appear in manuscript transcripts by different copyists. . . .' He describes it in full, and notes that it bears Richard Brinsley Sheridan of Frampton Court's bookplate on the fly-leaf.[2]

[1] A character in Fielding's *Pasquin*.

[2] Nettleton and Case, p. 954.

Apart from these manuscript sources, there are three printed works that require study:

Printed by Hugh Gaine, New York, 1786

This contains an 'Advertisement'[1] reading: 'So many spurious Copies of The SCHOOL for SCANDAL having been obtruded on the Publick, has induced the Editor to lay before them, in its PROPER GARB, this most excellent Comedy, presented to him by RICHARD BRINSLEY SHERIDAN Esq.; the justly admired *Congreve* of the present Time.' William Dunlap records that 'Henry, an Irishman by birth, had been liberally educated, and made his *debut* in London, under the patronage of the elder Sheridan'.[2] He afterwards acted in Jamaica[3] and the United States,[4] and in 1785 became joint-manager of the American Company with Lewis Hallam. He himself played Sir Peter Teazle.

The title-page reads:

> THE | SCHOOL FOR SCANDAL. | A | COMEDY; | By *Richard Brinsley Sheridan*, Esq; | PERFORM'D WITH UNIVERSAL APPLAUSE | At the THEATRE IN *NEW-YORK*, | FROM A MANUSCRIPT COPY | IN THE POSSESSION OF | JOHN HENRY, *Esquire*, | *Joint Manager of the* AMERICAN COMPANY, *given* | *him by the* AUTHOR. | [Printer's ornament] | NEW-YORK: | PRINTED BY HUGH GAINE, AT THE BIBLE IN | HANOVER-SQUARE. | M,DCC,LXXX,VI.

Collation: [A^8] B–G^6.

Contents: [1] title; [2] blank; [3] Prologue; [4] Dramatis Personæ and Advertisement; [5]–86, text; 87–8, Epilogue.

Nettleton examined this publication in detail[5] and rightly pointed out that it is the first to print a text that is substantially closer to the versions that passed through Sheridan's hands than any other pirated copy. I do not altogether agree with him, however, when he scrutinizes the opening scene between the first entrance of Mrs. Candour and the entry of the servant, and allots nineteen speeches to the authentic text and eleven to a pirate. The latter do not accord with any pirated text that I have seen, and the phrasing in general is closest to what I have called the Paignton

[1] p. 4. [2] *A History of the American Theatre* (New York, 1832), p. 28.

[3] Richardson Wright, *Revels in Jamaica, 1682–1838* (New York, 1937), pp. 51–2, 100–1, 148, 203. Wright quotes a paragraph from the *Jamaica Mercury*, 22–29 Jan. 1780, concerning a performance of *Othello* at Drury Lane on 21 Oct. 1779 and 'bringing forward a young gentleman in the character of the Moor: we heard that his name is Henry.' A person of the same name took part in 'the new ballet of the Rural Chase' on 3 Oct. 1777: see *London Evening Post*, 2–4 Oct. 1777.

[4] George O. Seilhamer, *History of the American Theatre: During the Revolution and After* (Philadelphia, 1889), pp. 177–8.

[5] George H. Nettleton, '"The School for Scandal", First Edition of the Authentic Text', *T.L.S.*, 21 Dec. 1935, p. 876.

MS. When it does not follow this, it paraphrases it rather loosely and sometimes picks up or half-echoes lines that appear in the Scott and Tonkinson MSS. Occasionally the printer appears to be trying to improve on the accepted version: for example, 'Captain Quinze and Mr. Nickit' become, in this American version, 'Captain Queezy and Mr. Thicket'. Of course, the play does print some lines that are to be found in the pirated copies: for example, the opening stage direction 'discovered at a tea table' is also to be seen in the pirated copy from Dublin in 1793, and 'isn't it Josey?' comes closest to the same Dublin version's 'Is it not Joseph?' (IV. iii.). Altogether, the fairest conclusion might be that there are mongrel qualities in this text, but that the pedigree line is clear.

Dublin, 1799

Moore, i. 260, remarked:

> The edition printed in Dublin is, with the exception of a few unimportant omissions and verbal differences, perfectly correct. It appears that, after the success of the comedy in London, he presented a copy of it to his eldest sister, Mrs. Lefanu, to be disposed of, for her own advantage, to the manager of the Dublin Theatre. The sum of a hundred guineas, and free admissions for her family, were the terms upon which Ryder, the manager at that period, purchased from this lady[1] the right of acting the play; and it was from the copy thus procured that the edition afterwards published in Dublin was printed. I have collated this edition with the copy given by Mr. Sheridan to Lady Crewe (the last, I believe, ever revised by himself) and find it, with the few exceptions already mentioned, correct throughout.

At least twenty editions of the play were published in Dublin in the eighteenth century, but Rhodes was able to prove, from Moore's own copy now in the Royal Irish Academy library,[2] that his reference was to the edition of 1799.[3]

The title-page reads:

> The School for Scandal. | *A COMEDY*; | IN FIVE ACTS. | [rule] | By RICHARD BRINSLEY SHERIDAN, Esq. | [rule] | TAKEN FROM A CORRECT COPY, | PERFORMED AT THE THEATRES, LONDON AND DUBLIN. | [double rule] | *DUBLIN PRINTED*, | AND SOLD BY THE BOOKSELLERS. | [short swelled rule] | 1799

Collation:[4] 8vo: [A] B–H^6 I^2 [I]^3.

[1] Cf. Thomas Snagg, *Recollections of Occurrences* (1951), p. 99.

[2] Pressmark, 12 G 13.

[3] Rhodes, ii. 20, 154–8. Cf. Dowden, p. 476; and for the dating of the letter, R. B. Pearsall, 'Chronological Annotations to 250 Letters of Thomas Moore', *P.B.S.A.* lxiii (1969), 105–17.

[4] Signatures are printed in B–B3, C–C3, D–D3, E–E3, F–F3, G–G2, H–H2, I–I2; but it should be noted that D–D3 reads: D–D3 (recte D2)–D3.

Contents: pp. [1–2], 3–89, [90].

[1] Title; [2] Dramatis Personæ; 3–89, text; [90] blank.

This version contains a number of variants and seems to be a text that grew rather corrupt in the years before its printing. An illustration of this may be found at the end of the fourth act, where Sir Peter cries out 'Oh, damn your sentiment.' The texts that Sheridan approved read 'Oh!' only, and I think we may assume that the Dublin actors found Sheridan's one word insufficiently expressive and wanted a more forceful climax. In the pirated text of 1780, this was given as 'Oh, damn your sentiments—damn damn your sentiments.' In the Dublin text of 1799, the reading lies between the two extremes.

At times the text is close to the ones in the Paignton and Laurence MSS.: see, for example in the same act, 'I wish they were both well out of the room.' Some phrases are identical with those in the Scott MS.

Works: the Murray text

The version of *The School for Scandal* included in the *Works* in 1821 was long considered as the received text, and only lost its place when people realized that Thomas Moore had no hand in its editing.[1] It can now be seen to be based on an early manuscript that was corrected in the nineteenth century—but almost certainly not by Sheridan. It contains a number of variants, some of them without parallel elsewhere.

A few examples from the first scene of all may make plain the nature of the changes. Lady Sneerwell says, 'Snake has just been rallying me', though all the other versions of the authentic text agree on 'arraigning me'. Crabtree refers to prayers 'in all the synagogues', where the others read 'in the Synagogue'.

The most interesting relationship between this text and another is with the Tickell MS. They both read 'the tale makers' (instead of 'tale makers')[2] and 'the breeding Nova-Scotia sheep' (instead of 'the difficulty of breeding'). Sometimes the alterations seem dictated by the need for an ever greater moral delicacy of expression. 'Heav'ns!' (p. 361, l. 15 below) is omitted, and so is Lady Sneerwell's 'he generally calls about this time, I don't wonder at people's giving him to me for a Lover.'

Unexamined Material

There is some material (mentioned in sale catalogues) that I have not been able to see. In the following chronological list, I give the source of the information first, then particulars of the work itself:

Sabin Catalogue, New York, 8 October 1860, lot 1599.

The School for Scandal, interleaved, 18mo., sheep, 1786. 'This edition was privately printed; the present copy wants the last leaf but the matter is supplied in MS. by the author, Hon. R. B. Sheridan.'

[1] For the circumstances in which it was published. see p. 14 above.

[2] p. 366, l. 6.

American Art Galleries Catalogue, New York, 20 March 1900, lot 3059.

The School for Scandal. 'A prompt book used at the old Bath Theatre with the notations of a famous actor. A letter from Mr. H. Holl to Halliwell Phillips explains its probable history. 8vo. Half morocco.'

Bangs Catalogue, New York, 21 October 1901, lot 514.

The School for Scandal. Bound by Flack. MS. notes by Fawcett. Cf. John J. Anderson, Jr., Catalogue, New York, 16–17 April 1903, lot 513: 'Transcript from the Prompter's Book of the Theatre Royal, Drury Lane, made by John Fawcett, the actor, in 1815. Royal 8vo, scored Russia extra, by M. Flack, 1815. With Flack's bill for binding dated 4 July 1815 loosely inserted. From the library of Sir W. A. Fraser, with bookplate.' Also listed by Anderson Auction Co. Catalogue, New York, 3 October 1904, lot 663: old calf, 185 pages; and by the same company, 5 April 1909, lot 985.

Sotheby's Catalogue, London, 13 December 1911, lot 212.

A transcript of the fourth act, showing some 'divergences from the received text': fifteen leaves. Note also lot 227: MS. copy, 218 leaves, with 'variations from the printed copy' in Sichel's hand. See Sichel, i. 564.

Hodgson Catalogue, London, 12–14 December 1917, lot 40.

MS. prompter's copy of *The School for Scandal*, as used at the Theatre Royal, Birmingham, August 1813, with the autograph of R. W. Elliston.

Sotheby's Catalogue, London, 26–28 July 1926, lot 716.

The School for Scandal (1798). Interleaved with stage directions. Many textual cuts; alterations in an early nineteenth-century hand.

Hodgson Catalogue, London, 19 March 1964, lot 188.

The School for Scandal: 'manuscript Prompt Copy, with corrections and additions (most leaves loose and frayed), *cloth*. Watermark 1805.' The purchaser has not answered my inquiries concerning this item, but since it was from the library of 'the late Malcolm Letts, F.S.A.', I assume it is the one mentioned by Sichel, i. 565 n., as inspected by him through the kindness of Mr. Charles Letts. He seems to have found nothing in it worth noting.

Conclusion

Since the difference between a good and a bad text of *The School for Scandal* lies in a multitude of minor alterations of phrasing, I have decided to base this edition on the manuscripts (items ii, v, vi, vii, viii, above) that are in Sheridan's handwriting or bear some traces of it, and to collate the copy sent to the Lord Chamberlain with their readings. They show a very substantial measure of agreement.

Because the Frampton Court MS. was a draft containing a number of passages afterwards rejected, I have recorded its variants only when they were useful for the purposes of comparison. I have treated the 'Two acts . . . prepared by Sheridan for publication' (item ix) with reserve, but have indicated its few variants and have taken over one phrase as substantive.

I have used the Frampton Court MS., wherever possible, as copy-text, because its accidentals give us an accurate idea of Sheridan's rather wayward use of the conventions of his day. His punctuation is often interesting, even if unusual: it certainly suggests the way in which he intended the play to be spoken, and this may be found nowhere else. He usually begins a noun with a capital, but this is by no means invariable and he sometimes gives capitals to adjectives. He often omits exclamation and question marks. Where this manuscript is defective, I have printed the accidentals from the last fully revised copy that we have: the Georgetown Crewe MS. Its transcriber followed his own conventions, and readers may feel that it would have been better to normalize the whole text rather than interlard one system of punctuation and capitalization with another. I have resisted the temptation to do so on the ground that we gain by reading seven-eighths of the text in the way Sheridan wrote it, and would certainly lose something if we brought it into line with a twentieth-century usage that may soon be outmoded.

I have admitted into the text new readings from these five other manuscripts, particularly when they are in Sheridan's hand or correct errors. I have used the symbol '[S.]' in the textual footnotes to indicate phrases that Sheridan inserted in his own hand but omit it in any references to the Frampton Court MS. for the simple reason that he wrote out most of this himself.

The following abbreviations are used in the textual notes:

O Frampton Court MS.
Oa Corrected copies bound with the Frampton Court MS. See p. 338 above.
L Lord Chamberlain's copy.
Ca Georgetown Crewe MS.
Cb Second Crewe MS.
B Buckinghamshire MS.
P William Powell's transcript of part of Act I.

In addition to some of the above, I have used three abbreviations in the textual notes of the Prologue and Epilogue:

Fol. Folger MS. W. a. 154 (3), ff. 11–15.
Gaz. *The Gazetteer*, 21 June 1777.
Har. Harvard College Library MS.

In the textual notes to 'A Portrait', the following abbreviations are employed:

Eg. Egerton MS. 1975, f. 169.
Har. Harvard College Library MS. Copy text.
Mur. *Works*, ii. 3–7.

A PORTRAIT

Address'd to a Lady[1] with the Comedy of the School for Scandal

Tell me, ye prim Adepts in Scandal's School
Who rail by Precept, and detract by Rule,
Lives there no Character so tried—so known
So deck'd with Grace—and so unlike your own—
That even *you* assist her Fame to raise,
Approve by Envy, and by Silence praise?

Attend!—a model shall attract your view—
Daughters of Calumny[2]:—I summon YOU:—
You shall decide if this a *Portrait* prove,
Or fond Creation of the Muse and Love.

Attend!—Ye Virgin Critics shrewd and sage,[3]
Ye Matron Censors of this Childish age,—
Whose peering Eye, and wrinkled Front declare
A fix'd Antipathy to *Young* and *Fair*:
By Cunning cautious, or by Nature cold,
In maiden Malice virulently bold—

Attend—Ye skill'd to coin the precious Tale,
Creating Proof—where Innuendos fail!
Whose practic'd Mem'ries—cruelly exact—
Omit no Circumstance—except the Fact!
Attend!—All ye who boast—or Old or Young—
The living Libel of a Sland'rous Tongue!

4 prim] *Har.*, *Mur.*; prime *Eg.*   19 Malice] *Har.*, *Eg.*; madness *Mur.*

---

[1] Frances Anne Crewe (1748–1818), wife of John, later first Lord Crewe (1742–1829). *The Critic* was dedicated to her mother, Frances Greville.

[2] Harlan W. Hamilton, *Doctor Syntax*, *A Silhouette of William Combe*, *Esq.*, *1742–1823* (1969), pp. 58, 286, notes that in the *Morning Post*, 25 Feb., 31 Mar. 1777, the play was called *The School for Slander*. He suggests that Sheridan changed the title to achieve greater accuracy.

[3] Note also an eighteenth-century transcript of the poem, that I have read in a photographic copy kindly sent to me by Mr. Earle E. Coleman. The transcript belonged to Lord Palmerston, but is now owned by Mr. Robert H. Taylor, and is on deposit in Princeton University Library. Line 14 reads: 'Attend!—a model shall attract your view—'. Other variant readings are: p. 352, l. 2, 'whom'; l. 11, '*his* Art'; l. 19, 'nor'; p. 353, l. 1, 'frowns', '*moves* no *Queen*'; l. 2, 'Charm'; l. 8, 'divine . . . less'; l. 13, 'were'; l. 22, 'further'; l. 34, 'gentler'; p. 354, l. 12, 'Displays the tender'; l. 18, 'Candour'. It also prints the lines (p. 354, between 8 and 9) cancelled in the Harvard copy, but with the reading 'Millar's Dialect'.

So shall my Theme as far contrasted be
As Saints by Fiends—or Hymns by Calumny.

Come, gentle *Amoret*,[1] (—for 'neath that Name
In worthier Verse[2] is sung thy Beauty's Fame)
Come—for but *thee* whom seeks the Muse?—and while
Celestial Blushes check thy conscious Smile,—
With timid Grace, and hesitating Eye—
The perfect Model which I boast—supply!
Vain Muse,—could'st Thou the humblest Sketch create
Of *Her*—or slightest Charm could'st imitate,—
Could thy blest Strain, in kindred Colours, trace
The faintest Wonder of her Form, or Face—
Poets would study the immortal Line,
And *Reynolds*[3] own his *Art* subdued by *thine*!
That Art!—which well might added Lustre give
To Nature's best!—and Heaven's superlative!—
On *Granby's*[4] Cheek might bid new Glories rise,
Or point a purer Beam from *Devon's*[5] Eyes!—

Hard is the Task to shape that Beauty's Praise,
Whose Judgment scorns the Homage—Flatt'ry pays!
But praising *Amoret*—we cannot err:—
No Tongue o'ervalues Heav'n—or flatters *Her*!
Yet *She*—by Fate's Perverseness!—She alone
Would doubt our Truth—nor deem such Praise her *own*.

Adorning Fashion—unadorn'd by Dress—
Simple from Taste—and not from Carelessness.
Discreet in Gesture, in Deportment mild,
Not stiff with Prudence, nor uncouthly wild—
No State has *Amoret*!—no studied Mien!

5 whom] *Har.*, *Eg*; who *Mur.* 14 his *Art*] *Har.*; his art *Eg.*; *his* Art *Mur.*
22 or] *Mur.*; nor *Har.*, *Eg.*

[1] Mrs. Crewe. See pp. 330–1 above.

[2] See Rhodes, iii. 199–200, for the suggestion that Sheridan's first wife gave the name of Amoret to Mrs. Crewe in her poem 'Laura to Silvio', praising her 'gentle step and hesitating grace'. He adds that this poem is the 'worthier verse', and that Sheridan replied to it and echoed some phrases in 'A Portrait'. Charles Fox, however, also wrote verses to 'Amoret', which are mentioned by Horace Walpole in a letter of 27 May 1775, to William Mason.

[3] Sir Joshua Reynolds (1723–92) painted three portraits of Mrs. Crewe.

[4] Mary Isabella (Somerset), wife of Charles Manners, Marquis of Granby, and afterwards fourth Duke of Rutland. Cf. 'To Silvio' (Moore, i. 204).

[5] Georgiana (Spencer), first wife of William Cavendish, fifth Duke of Devonshire. The beauty of her eyes was constantly mentioned: cf. 'To Silvio' (Moore, i. 204). Iris Palmer, *The Face without a Frown* (1944), p. 85, mentions that the Devonshires were thought to be the originals of Sir Peter and Lady Teazle.

She apes no *Goddess*!—and she *moves* no *Queen*!
The softer Charm that in her Manner lies
Is fram'd to captivate, yet not surprise;
It justly suits th'Expression of her Face,—
'Tis less than Dignity—and more than Grace!

On her pure Cheek the native Hue is such,
That form'd by Heav'n to be admir'd so much,
The Hand that made her with such partial Care,
Might well have fix'd a fainter Crimson there,
And bade the gentle Inmate of her Breast,
Inshrined Modesty!—supply the Rest.

But Who the Peril of her Lips shall paint?—
Strip them of smiles—still, still all words were faint!
But moving—Love himself appears to teach
Their *Action*—tho' denied to rule her *Speech*!
And Thou,—who *seest* her speak—and dost not *hear*,
Mourn not her distant Accents 'scape thine ear,
Viewing those Lips—thou still may'st make pretence
To judge of what she says—and swear 'tis Sense;
Cloath'd with such Grace, with such Expression fraught,
They move in meaning, and they pause in Thought!
But do'st thou further watch, with charm'd Surprise,
The mild Irresolution of her Eyes?
Curious to mark—how frequent they repose
In brief Eclipse, and momentary close?
Ah!—see'st Thou not!—an ambush'd Cupid there—
Too tim'rous of his Charge!—with jealous care
Veils, and unveils those Beams of heav'nly Light,
Too full—too fatal else for mortal Sight!
Nor yet—such pleasing Vengeance fond to meet—
In pard'ning Dimples hope a safe retreat,
What tho' her peaceful Breast should ne'er allow
Subduing Frowns to arm her alter'd Brow,
By Love! I swear—and by his gentler wiles!—
More fatal still—the Mercy of her Smiles!

1 apes] *Har.*; frowns *Mur.*, *Eg.* *moves* no *Queen*] *Har.*; moves *no queen Mur.*; moves no Queen *Eg.* 8 that made her with such] *Har.*, *Eg.*; divine, with a less *Mur.* 13 were] *Har.*; are *Mur.*, *Eg.* 22 further] *Har.*, *Eg.*; farther *Mur.* 23 *Eg.* ends with this line, and adds 'Cetera desunt'. 34 gentler] *Har.*; gentle *Mur.*

Thus lovely!—thus adorn'd!—possessing all
Of bright, or fair—that can to woman fall,
The Height of Vanity might well be thought
Prerogative in her,—and Nature's Fault;
Yet gentle *Amoret*—in mind supreme
As well as Charms—rejects the vainer Theme;
And half mistrustful of her Beauty's store
She barbs with Wit—those Darts too keen before.

Grac'd by those signs—which Truth delights to own,
The timid Blush,—and mild submitted Tone—
Whate'er she says—tho' Sense appear throughout—
Bears the unartful Hue of female Doubt.
Deck'd with that Charm, how lovely *Wit* appears.
How graceful *Science* when that Robe she wears!
Such too her Talents, and her Bent of Mind
As speak a sprightly Heart—by Thought refin'd:
A Taste for Mirth—by Contemplation school'd;
A Turn for Ridicule—by Candour rul'd;
A Scorn of Folly—which she tries to hide;
An awe of Talent—which she owns with Pride.

Peace idle Muse!—no more thy Strain prolong,
But yield a Theme, thy warmest Praises wrong,
Just to her Merit tho' thou canst not raise
Thy feeble Verse—behold th'acknowledg'd Praise
Has spread Conviction thro' the envious Train,
And cast a fatal Gloom o'er Scandal's Reign!
And Lo! each pallid Hag, with blister'd Tongue,
Mutters Assent to all thy Zeal has sung,
Owns all the Colours just—the Outline true,
Thee my Inspirer—and my *Model*—CREWE!

Between lines 8 and 9, the following lines have been cancelled in *Har.*, presumably by Sheridan. They are printed by *Mur.*:

Read in all Knowledge that her sex should reach,
Tho' *Greville* or the Muse should deign to teach,
Fond to improve—nor tim'rous to discern
How far it is a Woman's Grace to learn;
In *Millar's* Catalogue she would not prove
Apollo's *Priestess* but Apollo's *Love*.

12 Bears the unartful] *Har.*; Displays the tender *Mur.* 18 Sheridan inserts 'Candour' in place of 'Judgment'. 20 Sheridan inserts 'An awe of Talent', in place of some words that have been heavily cancelled. 24 Sheridan inserts 'feeble' and 'acknowledg'd', in place of a word heavily cancelled, and 'feeble'.

PROLOGUE

Spoken by Mr. King

Written by D. Garrick, Esqr.

A School for Scandal! tell me I beseech you
Needs there a School this modish art to teach you?
No need of lessons *now* the knowing think:
We might as well be taught to Eat, and drink:
Caus'd by a Dearth of Scandal, should the Vapours
Distress our Fair ones,—let 'Em read the Papers—
Their pow'rful Mixtures such disorders hit
Crave what they will, there's *quantum Sufficit*.

'Lud' cries *my Lady Wormwood*, who loves Tattle,
And puts much Salt and pepper in her prattle;
Just ris'n at Noon, all Night at Cards when threshing;
Strong Tea and Scandal, 'bless me how refreshing!
Give me the Papers *Lisp*—how bold, and free—(*sips*)
Last Night Lord *L*— (*sips*) was caught with Lady *D*—
For aching heads what charming Sal Volatile! (*sips*)
If Mrs. B: will still continue flirting,
We hope she'll *draw*, or we'll *un*-draw the Curtain.
Fine Satire poz—in publick all abuse it—
But by Ourselves,—(*sips*) our praise we can't refuse it.
Now Lisp read *you*—there at that dash and Star'—(*sips*)
'Yes Ma'am—a certain Lord had best beware,
Who lives not twenty Miles from Grosv'nor Square
For should he *Lady W* find willing,
Wormwood is bitter'—'O that's me the villain

1 PROLOGUE] *L*, *Ca*, *Cb*, *B*; PROLOGUE *to the* New Comedy *of* The SCHOOL FOR SCANDAL *Gaz.*; Prologue for the School for Scandal *Fol.*, *Har.* 2 *Spoken . . . King*] *Ca*, *Gaz.*; *om. Fol.*, *L*, *Cb*, *B*, *Har.* 3 *Written . . . Esqr.*] *Ca* [S.], *B* [S.]; Written by Mr. Garrick *Gaz.*; *om. L*, *Fol.*, *Cb*, *Har.* 4 tell . . . you] *L*, *Ca*, *Cb*, *B*, *Gaz.*, *Har.*; Means our Bard t'impart *Fol.* 5 Needs . . . this] *L*, *Ca*, *Cb*, *B*, *Gaz.*, *Har.*; That you are Children in this *Fol.* modish] *Fol.*, *Ca*, *Cb*, *B*, *Har.*, *Gaz.*; modest *L* art . . . you] *L*, *Ca*, *Cb*, *B*, *Har.*, *Gaz.*; art? | Tell me, Good Sirs, and Ladies, I beseech you, | Wants there much Study this same Art to teach you *Fol.* 6 No . . . *now*] *Fol.*, *L*, *Ca*, *Cb*, *B*, *Gaz.*; Few Lessons may well serve *Har.* 11 they] *L*, *Ca*, *Cb*, *B*, *Gaz.*, *Har.*; you *Fol.* 12 Lud] *Fol.*, *L*, *Ca*, *Cb*, *B*, *Har.*; Lord *Gaz.* 17 *sips*] *L*, *Ca*, *Cb*, *B*, *Gaz.*, *Har.*; *om. Fol.* 22 But . . . it] *Fol.*, *Ca*, *Cb*, *B*, *Gaz.*, *Har.*; *om. L* 23 *sips*] *Fol.*; *om. L*, *Ca*, *Cb*, *B*, *Gaz.*, *Har.*

Throw it behind the fire, and never more,
Let that vile paper come within my door.'
Thus at our friends we laugh, who feel the Dart—
To reach *our* feelings, we ourselves must Smart.

Is our Young Bard so young to think that He
Can Stop *the full Spring-tide* of Calumny—
Knows he the World so little and Its trade?
Alas, the Devil is sooner *rais'd*, than *laid*—
So strong, so swift, the Monster there's no gagging;
Cut Scandal's head off—still the tongue is wagging.
Proud of your Smiles once lavishly bestow'd
Again our young Don Quixote takes the road:
To shew his Gratitude—he draws his pen,
And seeks this Hydra—Scandal in Its den
From his fell gripe the frighted fair to save
Tho he should fall—th'attempt must please the brave.
For your applause, all perils he would through,
He'll *fight*, that's *write*, a Cavalliero true,
Till Ev'ry drop of Blood, that's Ink, is spilt for *You*.

3 Thus . . . laugh] *L*, *Ca*, *Cb*, *B*, *Gaz.*, *Har.*; We laugh at Ev'n our friends *Fol.* 10 the] *L*, *Ca*, *Cb*, *B*, *Gaz.*, *Har.*; her *Fol.* 12 our] *Fol.*, *L*, *B*, *Har.*; your *Ca*, *Cb*, *Gaz.* *After 'road', insert*:

Come hither *King* says he—my trusty Squire
Let the House know, My Heart is all on fire, *Fol.*

13 his . . . draws] *L*, *Ca*, *Cb*, *B*, *Gaz.*, *Har.*; my gratitude I'll draw *Fol.* 14 seeks] *L*, *Ca*, *Cb*, *B*, *Gaz.*, *Har.*; seek *Fol.* 15 From . . . save] *Fol.*, *L*, *Cb*, *B*, *Gaz.*, *Har.*; *om. Ca* 16 Tho . . . fall] *L*, *Cb*, *B*, *Gaz.*, *Har.*; Tho with this feeble Arm *Fol.*; *om. Ca* th'attempt . . . brave] *L*, *Cb*, *B*, *Gaz.*, *Har.*; must please the brave *Fol.*; *om.* *Ca* 17 For . . . through] *L*, *Ca*, *Cb*, *B*, *Gaz.*, *Har.*; What is your pleasure, he will most pursue *Fol.* 18 a . . . true [*L*, *Ca*, *Cb*, *B*, *Gaz.*, *Har.*; like I Knight Errant true *Fol.*

DRAMATIS PERSONÆ

As acted at Drury Lane Theatre, May 1777[1]

SIR PETER TEAZLE	Mr. King
SIR OLIVER SURFACE	Mr. Yates
JOSEPH SURFACE	Mr. Palmer
CHARLES SURFACE	Mr. Smith
CRABTREE	Mr. Parsons
SIR BENJAMIN BACKBITE	Mr. Dodd
ROWLEY	Mr. Aickin
MOSES	Mr. Baddeley
TRIP	Mr. La Mash
SNAKE	Mr. Packer
CARELESS	Mr. Farren
SIR TOBY BUMPER	Mr. Gaudry
LADY TEAZLE	Mrs. Abington
MARIA	Miss P. Hopkins
LADY SNEERWELL	Miss Sherry
MRS. CANDOUR	Miss Pope

1 A report of the first performance, in the *Public Advertiser*, 9 May, noted that the 'gentlemen' (i.e. Charles's friends) were played by R. Palmer, Norris, and Chaplin. 'Sir Harry Bumper' was taken by Gaudry: cf. p. 311 above.

THE SCHOOL FOR SCANDAL

Act 1st

Scene 1st

LADY SNEERWELL'*s*[1] *House*

LADY SNEERWELL *at the dressing Table*

SNAKE *drinking Chocolate.*

LADY SNEERWELL. The Paragraphs you say, Mr. Snake, were all inserted?

SNAKE. They were Madam—and as I copied them myself in a feign'd Hand there can be no suspicion whence they came.—

LADY SNEER. Did you circulate the Report of Lady Brittle's Intrigue with Captain Boastall?

SNAKE. That is in as fine a Train as your Ladyship could wish.—In the common course of Things, I think it must reach Mrs. Clackit's[2] Ears within four and twenty Hours and then you know the Business is as good as done.

LADY SNEER. Why truly Mrs. Clackit has a very pretty Talent, and a great deal of industry.

SNAKE. True madam and has been tolerably successful in her day. To my Knowledge—she has been the cause of six matches being broken off, and three sons being disinherited, of four forced Elopements, as many close confinements, nine separate maintenances, and two Divorces.—nay, I have more than once traced her causing a Tête-à-Tête in the Town and Country Magazine[3]—when the Parties perhaps have never seen each other's Faces before in the course of their Lives.

4 LADY . . . *House*] *O*, *L*, *Cb*, *B*, *P*; *om. Ca* 5 *the*] *L*, *B*, *Ca*, *Cb*; her *O*; a *P* 7 Mr. Snake] *L*, *Ca*, *Cb*, *B*, *P*; *om. O* 11 Report] *O*, *Cb*, *P*; reports *L*, *B*, *Ca* 14 I think] *L*, *Ca*, *Cb*, *B*, *P*; *om. O* 17 and] *L*, *Ca*, *Cb*, *B*, *P*; *om. O* 19 SNAKE. True] *L*, *Ca*, *Cb*, *B*, *P*; *Lady Sneerwell* Yes-yes *O* tolerably] *O*, *L*, *Ca*, *Cb*, *P*; tolerable *B* day] *L*, *Ca*, *Cb*, *P*; way *O* 20–1 six . . . and] *L*, *Ca*, *Cb*, *B*, *P*; breaking off six matches—of *O* 21 of four] *L*, *Ca*, *Cb*, *B*, *F*; on *P*; and four Daughters being turn'd out of Doors—of three *O*

---

[1] There is a critic named Sneerwell in Fielding's *Pasquin* (1736), but he seems like Lady Sneerwell only when he says, 'Consider, sir, I am my own enemy.'

[2] Mrs. Clackit is a character in Gay's *The Distress'd Wife*. The name is also used in a story in the *Town and Country Magazine*, iii (1771), 242.

[3] This monthly periodical began in Jan. 1769, and in its first number declared, 'we flatter ourselves that the anecdotes we shall be able to furnish, will be the means of

LADY SNEER. She certainly has Talents, but her manner is gross.

SNAKE. 'Tis very true—she generally designs well—has a free tongue and a bold invention—but her colouring is too dark and her outline often extravagant. She wants that delicacy of Hint—and mellowness of sneer which distinguish your Ladyship's Scandal.

LADY SNEER. Ah! you are Partial Snake.

SNAKE. Not in the least—everybody allows that Lady Sneerwell can do more with a word or a Look, than many can with the most labour'd Detail even when they happen to have a little truth on their side to support it.

LADY SNEER. Yes my dear Snake, and I am no Hypocrite to deny the satisfaction I reap from the Success of my Efforts—wounded myself in the early Part of my Life by the envenom'd Tongue of Slander I confess I have since known no Pleasure equal to the reducing others, to the Level of my own injured Reputation—.

SNAKE. Nothing can be more natural—But Lady Sneerwell—There is one affair in which you have lately employ'd me wherein I confess I am at a Loss to guess your motives.

LADY SNEER. I conceive you mean with respect to my neighbour Sir Peter Teazle and his Family?

SNAKE. I do; here are two young men, to whom Sir Peter has acted as a kind of Guardian since their Father's death, the elder possessing the most amiable Character and universally well spoken of, the other the most dissipated and extravagant young Fellow in the Kingdom without Friends or Character—the former an avow'd Admirer of your Ladyship, and apparently your Favourite; the latter attached to Maria, Sir Peter's ward—and confessedly belov'd by her—now on the face of these circumstances it is utterly unaccountable to me why you, the

6 Ah] *L*, *Ca*, *Cb*, *B*; Oh *P* Snake] *Ca*, *Cb*, *B*, *P*, (*altered to Snake in L*); Verjuice *O* 11 Snake] *Ca*, *Cb*, *B*, *P*, (*changed to Snake in L*); Verjuice *O* 16 Lady] *L*, *Ca*, *Cb*, *B*, *P*; my dear Lady *O* 20 Family] *L*, *Ca*, *Cb*, *B*, *P*; Family.—Lappet.—*exit Maid. O* 21 I do] *L*, *Ca*, *Cb*, *B*, *P*; I do but *O* 22 a kind of] *O*, *L*, *Ca*, *Cb*, *B*, *P*; *om.* Rae, *Sheridan*, i. 332–4 elder] *Ca*, Rae, *Sheridan*, i. 332–4; eldest *O*, *L*, *Cb*, *B*, *P* 23 other] Rae, *Sheridan*, i. 332–4; youngest *O*, *L*, *Ca*, *Cb*, *B*, *P* 26 Ladyship] *L*, *Ca*, *Cb*; yours *O*; Ladyship's *B*, *P* 27 belov'd] *L*, *Ca*, *Cb*, *B*, *P*; favfour'd [?] *O* 28 circumstances] *O*, *L*, *Ca*, *Cb*, *B*, *P*; circumstances, which I am sure I state fairly Rae, *Sheridan*, i. 333–4.

---

handing down to posterity a lively idea of the prevailing beauties, and their most zealous admirers, of this aera'. These were the basis of the Tête-à-Tête, in which a scandalous intrigue between a man and woman in fashionable life was described in plausible detail, and illustrated with portraits of the parties concerned. Their identities were also suggested by pseudonyms or initials. The authors of these pieces were apparently men named Beaufort and Caracioli: see E. H. W. Meyerstein, *A Life of Thomas Chatterton* (1930), p. 404.

Widow of a City Knight with a good Jointure—should not close with the Passion of a man of such character and expectations as Mr. Surface—and more so why you should be so uncommonly earnest to destroy the mutual Attachment—subsisting between his brother Charles, and Maria.

LADY SNEER. Then at once to unravel this mystery—I must inform you that Love has no share whatever in the intercourse between Mr. Surface and me.

SNAKE. No!

LADY SNEER. His real attachment is to Maria or her Fortune—but finding in his Brother a favour'd Rival He has been obliged to mask his Pretensions—and profit by my Assistance.

SNAKE. Yet still I am more puzzled why you should interest yourself in his Success—

LADY SNEER. Heav'ns! how dull you are!,—cannot you surmise the weakness which I hitherto thro' shame have conceal'd even from you?—must I confess that Charles—that Libertine, that extravagant—that Bankrupt in Fortune and Reputation—that He it is for whom I am thus anxious and malicious and to gain whom I would sacrifice—everything?[1]

SNAKE. Now indeed—your conduct appears consistent—but how came you and Mr. Surface so confidential—

LADY SNEER. For our mutual interest; I have found him out a long time since—I know him to be artful selfish and malicious—in short, a Sentimental[2] Knave.

SNAKE. Yet, Sir Peter vows He has not his equal in England—and above all—he praises him as a *man of Sentiment*—

1 Widow . . . Knight] *L*, *Ca*, *Cb*, *B*, *P*; young Widow *O*   a good] *L*, *Ca*, *Cb*, *B*, *P*; no great *O*   5 Then] *O*, *Ca*, *Cb*, *B*, *P*; Than *L*   10 in] *O*, *L*, *Ca*, *Cb*, *P*; *om. B*   15 weakness] *O*, *L*, *Ca*, *Cb*, *B*, *P*; folly Rae, *Sheridan*, i. 334   15–16 you?—must] *O*, *L*, *Ca*, *Cb*, *B*, *P*; you? Where is the sagacity that should have almost anticipated my own consciousness of my weakness? Must Rae, *Sheridan*, i. 334.   20 consistent—but] *L*, *Ca*, *Cb*, *B*, *P*; consistent and I no longer wonder at your enmity to Maria—but *O*   21 Mr.] *Ca*, *Cb*, *B*, *P*; *om. O*, *L*   22 interest; I] *L*, *Ca*, *Cb*, *B*, *P*; interest but I *O*   23 since—I] *L*, *Ca*, *Cb*, *B*, *P*; since altho' He has contrived to deceive every body beside—I *O*   23–4 in . . . Knave] *L*, *Ca*, *Cb*, *B*, *P*; *om. O*   24 Knave] *Ca*; knave, while with Sir Peter, and indeed with all his acquaintance He passes for a youthful Miracle of Prudence—Good Sense and Benevolence *L*, *Cb*, *B*, *P*; *O omits* '*knave*'   25 Yet] *Ca*, *B*; Yes, I know him *Cb*; Yes, yes, I know *O*, *L*; Yes, yet *P*

---

[1] Cf. Mellefont's lines in Congreve's *The Double-Dealer* (1694), I. i: 'None besides you, and *Maskwell*, are acquainted with the Secret of my Aunt *Touchwood's* violent Passion for me. Since my first refusal of her Addresses, she has endeavour'd to do me all ill Offices with my Uncle. . . .'

[2] Given to moral reflections. See Erik Erämetsä, *A Study of the Word 'Sentimental' and of other Linguistic Characteristics of Eighteenth Century Sentimentalism in England* (Helsinki, 1951), pp. 27–39.

LADY SNEER. True and with the assistance of his Sentiments and Hypocrisy he has brought him entirely into his Interest with regard to Maria.

Enter SERVANT.

SERVANT. Mr. Surface.

LADY SNEER. Shew him up. [*Exit* SERVANT.
He generally calls about this Time—I don't wonder at People's giving him to me for a Lover—

Enter SURFACE.

SURFACE. My dear Lady Sneerwell—how do you do—to Day? Mr. Snake your most Obedient.

LADY SNEER. Snake has just been arraigning me on our mutual attachment but I have informed him of our real views—you know how useful he has been to us—and believe me the confidence is not ill placed.

SURFACE. Madam it is impossible for me to suspect a man of Mr. Snake's sensibility and discernment—

LADY SNEER. Well—well—no compliments now—but tell me when you saw your Mistress Maria, or what is more material to me your Brother—

SURFACE. I have not seen either since I left you—but I can inform you that they never meet—some of your Stories have taken a good effect on Maria.

LADY SNEER. Ah! my dear Snake the merit of this belongs to you—but do your Brother's Distresses encrease—?

SURFACE. Every—hour—I am told He has had another execution in the House yesterday—in short his Dissipation and extravagance exceed any thing I ever heard of—

LADY SNEER. Poor Charles!

SURFACE. True Madam—notwithstanding his Vices one can't help feeling for him—aye, poor Charles! I'm sure I wish it was in my Power to be of any essential Service to him—for the man who does not share in the Distresses of a Brother, even tho' merited by his own misconduct —deserves—

2 him] *L, Ca, Cb, B, P*; Sir Peter *O* into . . . regard] *L, Ca, Cb, B, P*; in his Interests with respect *O* 3 Maria] *Ca*; Maria—while poor Charles has no friend in the house, tho' I fear he has a powerful one in Maria's heart against whom we must direct our Schemes *O, L, Cb, B*; *P omits* '*a . . . in*' 6 *Exit* SERVANT] *L, Ca, Cb, B, P*; *om. O* 9 SURFACE] *O, L, Ca, Cb, B*; Joseph Surface *P* 10–11 Mr. Snake] *L, Ca, Cb, B, P*; Miss Verjuice *O* 12 Snake] *L, Ca, Cb, B, P*; She *O* 13 him] *L, Ca, Cb, B, P*; her *O* views—you] *L, Ca, Cb, B, P*; views and the Purposes for which our Genious at present co-operate—you *O* 14 he] *L, Ca, Cb, B, P*; she *O* 15 suspect] *L, Ca, Cb, B, P*; suspect that *O* man] *L, Ca, Cb, B, P*; Lady *O* 15–16 Mr. Snake's] *L, Ca, Cb, B, P*; Miss Verjuice['s] *O* 18 Maria] *L, Ca, Cb, B*; *om. O, P* 19 left] *L, Ca, Cb, B, P*; saw *O* 20 never meet] *L, Ca, Cb, B, P*; are at present at Variance *O* a] *O, L, Ca, Cb, B*; *om. P* 22 Snake] *L, Ca, Cb, B, P*; Verjuice *O*

LADY SNEER. O Lud you are going to be moral and forget that you are among Friends—

SURFACE. Egad that's true—I'll keep that sentiment 'till I see Sir Peter, however it is certainly a charity to rescue Maria from such a Libertine —who if He is to be reclaim'd can be so only by a Person of your Ladyship's superior accomplishments and understanding.—

SNAKE. I believe Lady Sneerwell here's Company coming, I'll go and Copy the Letter I mentioned to you.—Mr. Surface your most Obedient. [*Exit* SNAKE.

SURFACE. Sir, your very devoted.—Lady Sneerwell, I am very sorry you have put any further confidence in that Fellow.

LADY SNEER. Why so?

SURFACE. I have lately detected him in frequent Conference with old Rowley who was formerly my Father's Steward, and has never, you know, been a Friend of mine.

LADY SNEER. And do you think he would betray us?

SURFACE. Nothing more likely: take my word for't Lady Sneerwell, that Fellow hasn't Virtue enough to be faithful even to his own Villainy.—hah! Maria!

Enter MARIA.

LADY SNEER. Maria, my dear—how do you do—what's the matter?

MARIA. O there is that disagreeable Lover of mine Sir Benjamin Backbite has just call'd at my Guardian's, with his Odious Uncle Crabtree—so I slipt out and run hither to avoid them.

LADY SNEER. Is that all—?

SURFACE. If my Brother Charles had been of the Party, Ma'am, perhaps you would not have been so much alarmed.

LADY SNEER. Nay now—you are severe for I dare swear the Truth of the matter is Maria heard *you* were here;—but—my dear—what has Sir Benjamin done that you should avoid him so—

MARIA. Oh He has done nothing—but tis for what he has said—his conversation is a perpetual Libel on all his Acquaintance.

SURFACE. Aye and the worst of it is there is no advantage in not knowing

5 person] *O*, *L*, *Ca*, *Cb*, *P*; woman *B* 7–12 SNAKE. I believe . . . so?] *L*, *Ca*, *Cb*, *B*, *P*;

VERJUICE. 'Twould be a Hazardous experiment.

SURFACE. But—Madam—let me caution you to place no more confidence in our friend Snake the Libeller *O*

14 Rowley] *Ca*, *Cb*, *B*, *P*; Rowland *O*, *L* 14–15 you know] *L*, *Ca*, *Cb*, *B*, *P*; *om. O* 16 And] *Ca*, *Cb*, *B*; *om. O*, *P* 16–18 And . . . hasn't] *L*, *Ca*, *Cb*, *B*, *P*; I'm not disappointed in Snake, I never suspected the Fellow to have *O* 19 hah! Maria!] *L*, *Ca*, *Cb*, *B*, *P*; *om. O* 24 run] *O*, *L*, *Ca*, *B*, *P*; ran *Cb* 28 swear] *O*, *Ca*, *B*, *P*; say *Cb* 29 what] *L*, *Ca*, *Cb*, *B*, *P*; why *O*

him; for He'll abuse a Stranger just as soon as his best Friend—and his Uncle's as bad.

LADY SNEER. Nay but we should make allowance, Sir Benjamin is a Wit and a Poet.

MARIA. For my part—I own madam—Wit loses its respect with me when I see it in company with malice.[1]—what do you think Mr. Surface?

SURFACE. Certainly, Madam, to smile at the jest which plants a Thorn in another's Breast is to become a principal in the Mischief.

LADY SNEER. Pshaw!—there's no possibility of being witty—without a little ill nature—the malice of a good thing is the Barb that makes it stick—what's your opinion, Mr. Surface?

SURFACE. To be sure madam—that conversation where the Spirit of Raillery is suppress'd will ever appear tedious and insipid—

LADY SNEER. Well I'll not debate how far Scandal may be allowable—but in a man I am sure it is always contemptible;—we have Pride, envy, Rivalship, and a Thousand motives to depreciate each other—but the male-Slanderer—must have the cowardice of a woman before He can traduce one.

Enter SERVANT.

SERVANT. Madam Mrs. Candour is below and if your Ladyship's at leisure will leave her carriage—

LADY SNEER. Beg her to walk in—Now Maria however here is a Character to your Taste for tho' Mrs. Candour is a little talkative Everybody allows her to be the best natured and best sort of Woman—

MARIA. Yes with a very gross affectation of good Nature and Benevolence—she does more Mischief than the Direct malice of old Crabtree.—

SURFACE. 'Efaith 'tis very true Lady Sneerwell. Whenever—I hear the current running against the Characters of my Friends I never think them in such Danger as when Candour undertakes their Defence.

LADY SNEER. Hush here she is—

Enter MRS. CANDOUR.

MRS. CANDOUR. My dear Lady Sneerwell, how have you been this Century—Mr. Surface, what News do you hear? tho' indeed it is no matter, for I think one hears nothing else but Scandal—

1 him] *L*, *Ca*, *Cb*, *B*, *P*; them *O*   1–2 his Uncle's] *L*, *Ca*, *Cb*, *B*, *P*; Crabtree's *O*   7 the] *O*, *Ca*, *Cb*, *B*, *P*; a *L*   in] *L*, *Ca*, *Cb*, *B*, *P*; on *O*   12 To be sure] *L*, *Ca*, *Cb*, *B*, *P*; Certainly *O*   22 Beg . . . in] *O*, *L*, *Ca*, *Cb*, *B*, *P*; I shall be happy to see her Rae, *Sheridan*, i. 335   28 against] *L*, *Ca*, *Cb*, *B*, *P*; again *O*   Characters] *O*, *L*, *Ca*, *Cb*, *B*; Character *P*   33–4 Century . . . for] *L*, *Ca*, *Cb*, *B*, *P*; Century—I have never seen you—tho' I have heard of you very often. Mr. Surface—the World says scandalous things of you—but indeed it is no matter what the world says for *O*

[1] Cf. Steele's statement, 'I abhor . . . that kind of Wit which betrays hardness of Heart' (*Richard Steele's Periodical Journalism*, ed. R. Blanchard (Oxford, 1959), p. 35).

SURFACE. Just so, indeed Madam—.

MRS. CANDOUR. Ah! Maria Child—what is the whole affair off between you and Charles—His extravagance I presume—The Town talks of nothing else—

MARIA. I am very sorry Ma'am, the Town has so little to do.

MRS. CANDOUR. True—true Child but there is no stopping People's Tongues. I own I was hurt to hear it—as indeed I was to learn from the same quarter that your Guardian Sir Peter and Lady Teazle have not agreed lately so well as could be wish'd.

MARIA. 'Tis strangely impertinent for People to busy themselves so—

MRS. CANDOUR. Very true Child but what's to be done? People will talk—there's no preventing it.—why it was but yesterday, I was told that Miss Gadabout had eloped with Sir Filagree Flirt—but Lord! there is no minding what one hears—tho' to be sure I had this from very good Authority.—

MARIA. Such Reports are highly scandalous—

MRS. CANDOUR. So they are Child—shameful! shameful! but the world is so censorious, no character escapes—Lud now!—who would have suspected your Friend Miss Prim of an Indiscretion yet such is the ill nature of People that they say her Uckle stopt her last Week just as she was stepping into the York Diligence with her Dancing master.

MARIA. I'll answer for't there are no grounds for the Report—

MRS. CANDOUR. Oh no foundation in the world I dare swear, no more probably than for the story circulated last month—of Mrs. Festino's[1] affair with Colonel Cassino—tho' to be sure that matter was never rightly clear'd up.

SURFACE. The Licence of invention some People take is monstrous indeed.

MARIA. 'Tis so—but in my opinion those who report such things are equally culpable.

MRS. CANDOUR. To be sure they are—Tale Bearers are as bad as the Tale makers—'tis an old observation and a very true one—but what's to be done as I said before—how will you prevent People from talking? —to Day Mrs. Clackit assur'd me Mr. and Mrs. Honeymoon—were at last become mere man and wife like the rest of their acquaintances —she likewise hinted that a certain widow in the next street had got

3 and] *L*, *Ca*, *Cb*, *B*, *P*; *om. O* His] *O*, *L*, *Ca*, *Cb*, *B*; he is *P* 7 as indeed] *O*, *L*, *Ca*, *Cb*, *B*; and indeed *P* 21 the York Diligence] *L*, *Ca*, *Cb*, *B*, *P*; a Postchaise *O* 23 world] *O*, *L*, *Ca*, *B*, *P*; World Child *Cb* 24 Festino] *L*, *Ca*, *B*, *P*; Festiono *O* 31 they] *O*, *Ca*, *Cb*, *B*, *P*; there *L* 35 the rest of] *L*, *Ca*, *Cb*, *B*, *P*; *om. O*

[1] The seventh meeting of the 'Subscription Festinos' (Italianate entertainments) in Hanover Square, were advertised in the *Public Advertiser*, 25 Apr. 1776.

rid of her Dropsy and recover'd her shape in a most surprising manner —and at the same time Miss Tattle who was bye affirm'd that Lord Buffalo had discover'd his Lady at a house of no extraordinary Fame— and that Sir Harry Bouquet[1] and Tom Saunter were to measure swords on a similar Provocation, but Lord! do you think I would report these Things? No—no Tale Bearers as I said before are just as bad as tale-makers.

SURFACE. Ah! Mrs. Candour—if everybody had your Forbearance and Good nature!

MRS. CANDOUR. I confess Mr. Surface I cannot bear to hear People Attack'd behind their Backs and when ugly circumstances come out against one's acquaintances I own I always love to think the best—by the bye I hope 'tis not true;—that your Brother is absolutely ruin'd—

SURFACE. I am afraid his circumstances are very bad indeed—Ma'am.

MRS. CANDOUR. Ah! I heard so—but you must tell him to keep up his Spirits—every body almost is in the same way—Lord Spindle,[2] Sir Thomas Splint, Captain Quinze, and Mr. Nickit[3]—all up I hear within this Week! so if Charles is undone He'll find half his Acquaintances ruin'd too—and that you know is a consolation—

SURFACE. Doubtless Ma'am—a very great one—

Enter SERVANT.

SERVANT. Mr. Crabtree and Sir Benjamin Backbite. [*Exit* SERVANT.

LADY SNEER. Soh! Maria, You see your Lover pursues you. Positively you shan't escape—

Enter CRABTREE, *and* SIR BENJAMIN BACKBITE.

CRABTREE. Lady Sneerwell—I kiss your hands—Mrs. Candour I don't believe you are acquainted with my Nephew Sir Benjamin Backbite— egad Ma'am—He has a pretty Wit—and is a pretty Poet too isn't He Lady Sneerwell?—

SIR BENJ. O fie Uncle—

CRABTREE. Nay egad it's true. I'll back him at a Rebus[4] or a

2 and] *L*, *Ca*, *Cb*, *B*, *P*; *om. O* at] *O*, *Ca*, *P*; *om. L*, *Cb*, *B* time] *L*, *Ca*, *Cb*, *B*, *P*; *om. O* 8 had] *L*, *Ca*, *Cb*, *B*, *P*; had had *O* 11 Attack'd] *L*, *Ca*, *Cb*, *B*, *P*; traduced *O* circumstances] *L*, *Ca*, *Cb*, *B*, *P*; circumstance *O* 17 and] *L*, *Ca*, *Cb*, *B*, *P*; *om. O* Nickit] *L*, *Ca*, *Cb*, *B*; Nick-it *O* Nicket *P* 18 Acquaintances] *O*, *Ca*, *B*, *P*; Acquaintance *Cb* 22 *Exit* SERVANT] *Ca*, *P*; *om. O*, *L*, *B*, *Cb*

[1] He appears again in *The Camp*: see p. 745 below.

[2] See pp. 295–6.

[3] 'Nick' was a winning throw at dice. To 'nick it' was to guess correctly.

[4] Condemned by Addison in one of his papers on 'false wit': 'I find likewise among the Ancients that ingenious Kind of Conceit, which the Moderns distinguish by the Name of a Rebus, that does not sink a Letter but a whole Word, by substituting a Picture in its place' (*The Spectator*, ed. D. F. Bond (Oxford, 1965), i. 250).

Charade[1] against the best Rhymer in the Kingdom—has your Ladyship heard the Epigram He wrote last week on Lady Frizzle's Feather catching Fire? do Benjamin repeat it—or the Charade you made last Night extempore at Mrs. Drowzy's conversazione—come now your first is the Name of a Fish, your second a great Naval Commander—and

SIR BENJ. Uncle—now—prithee—

CRABTREE. Efaith Ma'am—'twould surprise you to hear how ready He is at these Things.—

LADY SNEER. I wonder Sir Benjamin you never publish any-thing.

SIR BENJ. To say truth Ma'am 'tis very vulgar to Print, and as my little Productions are mostly Satires and Lampoons on particular people I find they circulate more by giving copies[2] in confidence to the Friends of the Parties—however I have some love-Elegies[3] which when favour'd —with this Lady's smiles I mean to give to the Public.

CRABTREE. 'Fore Heav'n Ma'am they'll immortalise you—you'll be handed down to Posterity like Petrarch's Laura or Waller's Sacharissa.[4]

SIR BENJ. Yes Madam I think you will like them—when you shall see them on a beautiful Quarto page where a neat rivulet of Text shall murmur thro' a meadow of margin.—'fore Gad they will be the most elegant Things of their Kind.

CRABTREE. But Ladies that's true have you heard the news?—

MRS. CANDOUR. What Sir, do you mean the Report of—

CRABTREE. No ma'am that's not it.—Miss Nicely is going to be married to her own Footman.

MRS. CANDOUR. Impossible!

CRABTREE. Ask Sir Benjamin.

11 on particular people] *L*, *Ca*, *Cb*, *B*, *P*; *om. O* 18 on] *Ca*, *Cb*, *B*, *P*; in *O* where] *Ca*, *Cb*, *B*, *P*; how *O*

---

[1] Cf. R. Tickell, *The Wreath of Fashion* (1777), p. 7:

With *chips* of wit, and mutilated lays,
See *Palmerston* fineer his *Bout's Rhimées*.
Fav'rite of ev'ry Muse, elect of Phoebus,
To string Charades, or fabricate a Rebus.

[2] Cf. *Poetical Amusements at a Villa near Bath* (2nd edn., 1776), i. p. v: 'The Editor does not apprehend private confidence wounded in the present publication, as the greatest part of these poems were acknowledged by their Authors in numerous assemblies, and with their approbation copied and dispersed through every quarter of England.'

[3] The *Love Elegies* (1743) of James Hammond (1710–42) were very well known, but Sheridan may have intended a more personal jest at the expense of the author of *Nuptial Elegies* (1774). A copy of this work is listed in Sotheby's Catalogue of 15 July 1929, item 288, as follows: '*Nuptial Elegies*, vignette on title, two leaves containing a manuscript poem, "Sonnet to Mrs. Sheridan with *Nuptial Elegies*," in six six-line stanzas, bound before title, on verso of the second leaf (facing the title) "From the Author" in a contemporary hand. . . .'

[4] Edmund Waller (1606–87) wrote verses to 'Sacharissa', Lady Dorothy Sidney (1617–84), afterwards Countess of Sunderland.

SIR BENJ. 'Tis very true Ma'am—everything is fix'd and the Wedding Livery bespoke.

CRABTREE. Yes and they *do* say there were pressing Reasons for't.

LADY SNEER. Why I *have* heard something of this before.

MRS. CANDOUR. It can't be—and I wonder any one should believe such a story of so prudent a Lady as Miss Nicely.

SIR BENJ. O Lud ma'am that's the very reason 'twas believed at once,—she has always been so cautious and so reserved that every Body was sure there was some reason for it at bottom.

MRS. CANDOUR. Why to be sure a Tale of Scandal is as fatal to the Credit of a prudent Lady of her Stamp as a Fever is generally to those of the strongest Constitutions, but there is a sort of puny sickly Reputation that is always ailing yet will outlive the robuster Characters of a hundred Prudes.

SIR BENJ. True Madam there are Valetudinarians in Reputation as well as constitution—who being conscious of their weak Part avoid the least breath of air and supply their want of Stamina by care and circumspection.

MRS. CANDOUR. Well but this may be all a mistake—you know Sir Benjamin very trifling circumstances often give rise to the most injurious Tales—

CRABTREE. That they do I'll be sworn Ma'am—did you ever hear how Miss Piper came to lose her Lover and her Character last Summer at Tunbridge?—Sir Benjamin you remember it—

SIR BENJ. O to be sure the most whimsical Circumstance—

LADY SNEER. How was it Pray?

CRABTREE. Why one Evening at Mrs. Ponto's Assembly the conversation happen'd to turn on the difficulty of breeding Nova-Scotia Sheep in this Country—says a young Lady in company, 'I have known instances of it for Miss Letitia Piper, a first cousin of mine, had a Nova-Scotia Sheep that produc'd her Twins.'—'what!' cries the old Dowager Lady Dundizzy (who you know is as deaf as a Post) 'has Miss Piper had twins?' this Mistake as you may imagine threw the whole company into a fit of Laughing;—however 'twas the next morning everywhere reported and in a few Days believ'd by the whole Town, that Miss

3 *do*] *L*, *Ca*, *Cb*, *B*, *P*; *om. O* 4 Why . . . before.] *L*, *Ca*, *Cb*, *B*, *P*; *om. O* 6 Lady] *O*, *L*, *Ca*, *B*, *P*; Woman *Cb* 7 that's . . . 'twas] *O*, *L*, *Ca*, *Cb*, *B*, *P*; you have mentioned the very circumstance that made it be Rae, *Sheridan*, i. 335. 8 she] *O*, *L*, *Ca*, *Cb*, *B*, *P*; Yes—she Rae, *Sheridan*, i. 335 10 Why to be sure] *L*, *Ca*, *Cb*, *B*, *P*; Yes *O* Credit] *L*, *Ca*, *Cb*, *B*, *P*; Reputation *O* 13 a] *L*, *Ca*, *Cb*, *B*, *P*; an *O* 16 avoid] *O*, *L*, *Ca*, *Cb*, *B*; avid *P* 19 a] *L*, *Ca*, *Cb*, *B*, *P*; *om. O* 29 young] *O*, *L*, *Ca*, *Cb*, *P*; *om. B* 23 & 30 Piper] *Ca*, *Cb*, *B*, *P*; Shepherd *O* 31 old] *O*, *Ca*; *om. L*, *Cb*, *B*, *P* Dowager Lady] *O*, *L*, *Ca*, *B*, *P*; Lady Dowager *Cb* 32 who] *O*, *L*, *Ca*, *Cb*, *P*; whom *B* Piper] *Ca*; Laetitia Shephard *L*; Letitia Shepherd *O*; Letitia Piper *Cb*, *B*, *P* 34 morning everywhere] *O*, *Ca*, *Cb*, *P*; day *B*

Letitia Piper had actually been brought to Bed of a fine Boy and a Girl —and in less than a Week there were People who could name the Father, and the Farm House where the Babies were put out to Nurse.

LADY SNEER. Strange indeed!

CRABTREE. Matter of Fact I assure you—O Lud Mr. Surface pray is it true that your Unkle Sir Oliver is coming home—

SURFACE. Not that I know of indeed Sir.

CRABTREE. He has been in the east Indies a long time—you can Scarcely remember him—I believe—sad comfort whenever he returns to hear how your Brother has gone on.—

SURFACE. Charles has been imprudent Sir to be sure but I hope no Busy People have already prejudiced Sir Oliver against him—he may reform—

SIR BENJ. To be sure He may—for my Part I never believed him to be so utterly void of Principle as People say—and tho' He has lost all his Friends I am told no body is better spoken of—by the Jews.

CRABTREE. That's true egad nephew—if the old Jewry were a Ward I believe Charles would be an alderman—no man more popular there —foregad I hear He pays as many annuities[1] as the Irish Tontine[2] and that whenever He's sick they have Prayers for the recovery of his Health in the Synagogue—

SIR BENJ. Yet no man lives in greater Splendour:—they tell me when He entertains his Friends—He can sit down to dinner with a dozen of his own Securities, have a score Tradesmen waiting in the Anti-Chamber and an Officer behind every Guest's Chair.

SURFACE. This may be entertainment to you Gentlemen but you pay very little regard to the Feelings of a Brother.

1 Piper] *Ca*, *Cb*, *B*, *P*; Shephard *L*; Shepherd *O* 5 Lud] *O*, *L*, *B*, *P*; Lord *Cb* 8 Indies] *O*, *Cb*, *B*, *P*; Indias *Ca* 9 whenever . . . returns] *L*, *Ca*, *Cb*, *B*, *P*; on his arrival *O* 14 him to be] *O*, *L*, *Ca*, *Cb*, *P*; him *B* 15 his] *O*, *L*, *Ca*, *Cb*, *B*; his Christian *P* 16 of] *O*, *L*, *Ca*, *B*, *P*; off *Cb* 17 were] *Ca*; was *O*, *L*, *Cb*, *B*, *P*

---

[1] 'My Lord Winterbottom . . . though he is little more than thirty years of age, pays to Jew Annuitants the moderate sum of 5700 l. only out of an estate of 9000 l. per Annum.' (Robert Bage, *Barham Downs* (1784), i. 119.)

[2] Lorenzo Tonti, a seventeenth-century Neapolitan banker, invented the scheme named after him, by which contributors to a loan were paid an annuity during their lifetime and it grew in size as the number of subscribers died. The last to remain took the whole. The Irish government set up a tontine to help pay off its debts. An advertisement of the 'English Tontine Annuities' in the *London Evening Post*, 28–30 Sept. 1775, claimed that its benefits were greater than those of the 'Irish Tontine': 'A subscription of 100 l. in the Irish Tontine (which filled with such rapidity) produced only 100 l. a year, and 883 lives must drop before that sum could be obtained; whereas, in this Tontine, five guineas will produce 100 l. a year, or fifty guineas 1000 l. a year, after the fall of 499 lives only.'

MARIA. Their Malice is intollerable.—Lady Sneerwell I must wish you a good morning—I'm not very well— [*Exit* MARIA.

MRS. CANDOUR. O dear she chang'd colour very much—!

LADY SNEER. Do Mrs. Candour follow her—she may want assistance.

MRS. CANDOUR. That I will with all my soul. Ma'am—poor dear Girl—who knows—what her situation may be! [*Exit* MRS. CANDOUR.

LADY SNEER. 'Twas nothing but that she could not bear to hear Charles reflected on notwithstanding their difference.

SIR BENJ. The young Lady's Penchant is obvious.

CRABTREE. But Benjamin—you mustn't give up the Pursuit for that—follow her and put her into good humour—repeat her some of your own Verses—come I'll assist you.

SIR BENJ. Mr. Surface I did not mean to hurt you—but depend upon't your Brother is utterly undone— [*going.*

CRABTREE. O Lud! aye—undone as ever man was—can't raise a guinea. [*going.*

SIR BENJ. And every thing sold—I'm told that was moveable.— [*going.*

CRABTREE. I have seen one that was at his house—not a thing left but some empty Bottles that were over-look'd, and the Family Pictures which I believe are framed in the Wainscoat.— [*going.*

SIR BENJ. And I'm very sorry to hear also some bad stories against him. [*going.*

CRABTREE. O He has done many mean things—that's certain!

SIR BENJ. But however as He's your Brother— [*going.*

CRABTREE. We'll tell you all another opportunity. [*Exeunt* CRABTREE *and* SIR BENJAMIN.

LADY SNEER. Ha, ha! ha! 'tis very hard for them to leave a subject they have not quite run down.

SURFACE. And I believe the Abuse was no more acceptable to your Ladyship than to Maria.

LADY SNEER. I doubt her Affections are farther engaged than we imagin'd but the Family are to be here this Evening so you may as well dine where you are and we shall have an opportunity of observing farther, in the meantime I'll go and Plot mischief and you shall study Sentiments— [*Exeunt.*

2 MARIA] *O, Ca, Cb, B, P*; *om. L* 3 chang'd] *O*; changes *L, Ca, Cb, B, P* 13 upon't] *Ca*; on't *O, L, Cb, B, P* 14 *going*] *O, Ca* [S.], *Cb, P*; *om. L, B* 16 *going*] *O, Ca* [S.]; *om. L, Cb, B, P* 18 *going*] *O, Ca* [S.]; *om. L, Cb, B, P* 19 I . . . that] *L, Ca, Cb, B, P*; I *O* 21 *going*] *O, Ca* [S.]; *om. L, Cb, B, P* 27 *Exeunt*] *O, Ca, Cb*; (*Exit*) *L, B, P* CRABTREE *and* SIR BENJAMIN] *Ca, P*; (*Sir Benjamin and Crabtree*) *B*; *om. O, L, Cb* 31 to] *Ca*; *om. O, L, Cb, B, P* 36 *Exeunt*] *O, L, Ca, P*; (*Exit &c*) *B*; (*Exit*) *Cb*

Scene 2d

SIR PETER'*s House*

Enter SIR PETER.

SIR PETER. When an Old Bachelor takes a young Wife—what is he to expect!—'Tis now Six Months since Lady Teazle made me the happiest of Men—and I have been the miserablest Dog ever since that ever committed wedlock:—we tift a little going to church—and came to a Quarrel before the Bells were done ringing—I was more than once nearly choak'd with gall during the Honeymoon—and had lost all comfort in Life before my Friends had done wishing me Joy—yet I chose with caution—a Girl bred whol[l]y in the country—who never knew Luxury beyond one silk Gown nor Dissipation above the annual Gala of a Race-Ball—yet now she plays her Part in all the extravagant Fopperies of the Fashion and the Town with as ready a Grace as if she had never seen a Bush nor a grass Plat out of Grosvenor-Square—! I am sneer'd at by my old acquaintance—paragraph'd—in the news-Papers—She dissipate[s] my Fortune, and contradicts all my Humours: —Yet the worst of it is I doubt I love her or I should never bear all this —However I'll never be weak enough to own it.

Enter ROWLEY.

ROWLEY. Oh, Sir Peter your Servant—how is it with you Sir—

SIR PETER. Very bad—Master Rowley—very bad. I meet with nothing but crosses and vexations—

ROWLEY. What can have happen'd to trouble you since yesterday?

SIR PETER. A good—question to a married man.—

ROWLEY. Nay I'm sure your Lady Sir Peter can't be the cause of your uneasiness.

SIR PETER. Why has anyone told you she was dead?

ROWLEY. Come—come Sir Peter you love her notwithstanding your tempers do not exactly agree.

SIR PETER. But the Fault is entirely hers Master Rowley—I am myself the sweetest temper'd Man alive and hate a teizing Temper—and so I tell her a hundred Times—a day—

ROWLEY. Indeed!

SIR PETER. Aye and what is very extraordinary in all our disputes she is always in the wrong! but Lady Sneerwell and the Set she meets at her House encourage the perverseness of her Disposition—then to

6–7 that ever committed wedlock] *O*, *Ca*; *om. L*, *Cb*, *B*, *P*   7 came] *O*, *L*, *Ca*, *B*, *P*; come *Cb*   9 Honeymoon] *L*, *Ca*, *Cb*, *B*, *P*; Honewmoon *O*   21 Oh] *Ca*, *Cb*, *B*; *om. O*   26 your . . . Peter] *O*, *L*, *Ca*, *Cb*, *P*; Sir Peter your Lady *B*   28 anyone] *Ca*; anybody *O*, *L*, *Cb*, *B*, *P*   33 her] *L*, *Ca*, *Cb*, *B*, *P*; *om. O*

complete my vex[a]tions—Maria—my Ward—whom I ought to have the Power of a Father over—is determined to turn Rebel too—and absolutely refuses the man whom I have long resolved on for her husband—meaning I suppose to bestow herself on his profligate Brother.

ROWLEY. You know Sir Peter I have always taken the Liberty to differ with you on the subject of these two young Gentlemen.—I only wish you may not be deceiv'd in your opinion of the elder—for Charles—my life on't—He will retrieve his Errors yet—their worthy Father, once my honour'd master, was at his years nearly as wild a Spark—yet when he died, he did not leave a more benevolent heart to lament his loss.

SIR PETER. You are wrong Master Rowley—on their Father's Death you know I acted as a kind of Guardian to them both—'till their unk[l]e Sir Oliver's eastern liberality gave them an early independance—of course no Person could have more opportunities of judging of their Hearts, and I was never mistaken in my Life. Joseph is indeed a model for the young men of the Age. He is a man of Sentiment—and acts up to the Sentiments he professes—but for the other take my word for't if he had any grains of Virtue by descent—he has dissipated them with the rest of his inheritance.—Ah! my old Friend Sir Oliver will be deeply mortified when he finds how Part of his Bounty has been misapplied—!

ROWLEY. I am sorry to find you so violent against the young man because this may be the most critical Period of his Fortune—I came hither with news that will surprise you.

SIR PETER. What!—let me hear—

ROWLEY. Sir Oliver *is* arrived and at this moment in Town.

SIR PETER. How!—you astonish me. I thought you did not expect him this month!—

ROWLEY. I did not—but his Passage has been remarkably quick.

SIR PETER. 'Egad I shall rejoice to see my old Friend—'tis Sixteen Years since we met—we have had many a Day together, but does He still enjoin us not to inform his Nephews of his Arrival—?

ROWLEY. Most—strictly—he means before it is known to make some trial of their Dispositions.—

SIR PETER. Ah there needs no art to discover their merits—! however he shall have his way—but pray does he know I am married?

ROWLEY. Yes and will soon wish you joy.

3 absolutely] *L*, *Ca*, *Cb*, *B*, *P*; obstinately *O* 7 these] *O*, *Ca*, *Cb*, *B*, *P*; those *L* 8 Charles] *L*, *Ca*, *Cb*, *B*, *P*; Florival *O* 10–11 yet . . . loss] *L*, *Ca*, *Cb*, *B*, *P*; *om.* *O* 14 liberality] *L*, *Ca*, *Cb*, *B*, *P*; Bounty *O* independance] *Ca*, *B*, *P*; dependance *Cb* them] *L*, *Ca*, *Cb*, *B*, *P*; it *O* 20 deeply] *L*, *Ca*, *Cb*, *B*, *P*; deeple *O* 32 Nephews] *O*, *Cb*; Nephew *L*, *Ca*, *B* 33 it is] *L*, *Ca*, *Cb*, *B*; he makes it *O* 34 Dispositions] *L*, *Ca*, *Cb*, *B*; dispositions and we have already plann'd something for the Purpose *O*

SIR PETER. What as we drink health to a Friend in a Consumption—ah Oliver will laugh at me—we used to rail at matrimony together—but He has been steady to his Text.—well He must be at my house tho' —I'll instantly give orders for his Reception—but Master Rowley—don't drop a word that Lady Teazle and I ever disagree.

ROWLEY. By no means—

SIR PETER. For I should never be able to stand Noll's Jokes—so I'd have him think, Lord Forgive me, that we are a very happy couple.

ROWLEY. I—understand you—but then you must be very careful not to differ while He's in the House with you.

SIR PETER. 'Egad—and so we must—and that's impossible—ah! Master Rowley when an old Batchelor marries a young wife—He deserves—no the Crime carries the Punishment along with it— [*Exeunt.*

END OF ACT 1ST

Act 2d

Scene 1st.—SIR PETER TEAZLE'*s House*

Enter SIR PETER *and* LADY TEAZLE.

SIR PETER. Lady Teazle—Lady Teazle I'll not bear it.

LADY TEAZLE. Sir Peter—Sir Peter you—may bear it or not as you please, but I ought to have my own way in every thing, and what's more I will too—what! tho' I was educated in the country I know very well that women of Fashion in London are accountable to nobody after they are married.

SIR PETER. Very well!—Ma'am very well! so a husband is to have no influence, no authority?

LADY TEAZLE. Authority! no to be sure—if you wanted authority over me you should have adopted me and not married me I am sure you were Old enough.

SIR PETER. Old enough!—aye there it is—well—well—Lady Teazle tho' my Life may be made unhappy by your Temper—I'll not be ruin'd by your extravagance.

LADY TEAZLE. My extravagance!—I'm sure I'm not more extravagant than a woman of Fashion ought to be.—

SIR PETER. No no Madam you shall throw away no more sums on such unmeaning Luxury—'slife to spend as much to furnish your Dressing

1 What . . . Consumption] *L*, *Ca*, *Cb*; You may tell him 'tis too late *O* 13 carries the] *O*, *Ca*, *B*; carries Its *L*, *Cb* 14 *Exeunt*] *O*, *L*, *Ca*, *B*; *Exit Cb* 17 SIR . . . *House*] *Ca*; *om. O*, *L*, *B*, *Cb* 18 *Enter*] *Ca*; *om. O*, *L*, *B*, *Cb* 20 bear . . . please] *L*, *Ca*, *Cb*, *B*; scold me or smile according to your Humour *O* 29 were] *O*, *L*, *Ca*, *Cb*; are *B*

Room with Flow'rs in winter, as would suffice to turn the Pantheon[1] into a Green-house and give a Fête-Champêtre at Christmas!

LADY TEAZLE. Lord! Sir Peter am I to blame because Flow'rs are dear in cold weather? you should find fault with the Climate and not with me. For my part I am sure I wish it was Spring all the year round—and that Roses grew under one's feet!—

SIR PETER. Oons! Madam—if you had been born to this I shouldn't Wonder at your talking thus.—but you forget what your situation was when I married you.

LADY TEAZLE. No—no—I don't—'twas a very disagreeable one or I should never have married you—

SIR PETER. Yes—yes madam you were then in somewhat an humbler Style—the Daughter of a plain country Squire—recollect Lady Teazle when I saw you first—sitting at your tambour in a pretty figured Linnen gown—with a Bunch of Keys by your side, your hair comb'd smooth over a Roll, and your apartment hung round with Fruits in worsted of your own working—

LADY TEAZLE. O Yes, I remember it very well, and a Curious life I led! My daily occupation to inspect the Dairy, superintend the Poultry, make extracts from the Family Receipt book and Comb my aunt Deborah's Lap-Dog.

SIR PETER. Yes, yes, Ma'am, 'twas so indeed.

LADY TEAZLE. And then you know my evening amusements—to draw Patterns for Ruffles which I had not the Materials to make—to play Pope Joan with the Curate—to read a Novel to my Aunt—or to be stuck down to an old Spinnet—to strum my Father to sleep after a Fox chase.

6 one's] *O*, *Ca*, *Cb*; our *L*, *B*   7 this] *L*, *Ca*, *Cb*, *B*; those Fopperies *O*   14 saw you first] *O*, *L*, *Ca*, *B*; first saw you *Cb*   15–16 your hair . . . Roll] *L*, *Ca*, *Cb*, *B*; *om. O*   18–19 O Yes . . . led] *Ca*, *Cb*, *B*; O horrible!—horrible!—don't put me in mind of it! *O*   19–21 My daily . . . Dog] *L*, *Ca*, *Cb*, *B*;

SIR PETER. Yes yes—madam and your daily occupation to inspect the Dairy, superintend the Poultry, make extracts from the Family Receit book and comb your Aunt Deborah's Lap Dog *O*

22 Yes . . . indeed] *L*, *Ca*, *Cb*, *B*; Abominable! *O*   23–6 And then . . . chase] *L*, *Ca*, *Cb*, *B*;

SIR PETER. Yes madam and what were your Evening amusements?—to draw Patterns for Ruffles which you hadn't the materials to make—to play Pope Joan with the Curate—to read a Sermon to your Aunt—or be stuck down to an old Spinet—to strum your Father to sleep after a Fox Chase—

LADY TEAZLE. Scandalous—Sir Peter not a word of it true *O*

25 Novel] *Ca*; Sermon *O*, *L*, *Cb*, *B*

[1] 'The much-talked-of Receptacle of fashionable Pleasure the Pantheon. . . . The whole Building is composed of a Suite of 14 Rooms, . . . each affording a striking Instance of the Splendour and Profusion of modern Times' (*The Public Advertiser*, 29 Jan. 1772). See the view of the interior by C. Brandoin included in *Johnson's England*, ed. A. S. Turberville (Oxford, 1933), i. 344; and compare the supper room at The Oaks erected by Robert Adam for the *fête-champêtre* there, ii. 112.

SIR PETER. I am glad you have so good a Memory,—Yes—Madam—These were the Recreations I took you from.—But now you must have your Coach, Vis-à-Vis,[1] and three powder'd Footmen before your Chair—and in summer a pair of white Cats[2] to draw you to Kensington gardens—no Recollection I suppose when you were content to ride double behind the Butler on a dock'd Coach Horse.

LADY TEAZLE. No—I swear I never did that—I deny the Butler, and the Coach Horse.

SIR PETER. This madam was your Situation—and what have I not done for you?-I have made you a woman of Fashion, of Fortune, of Rank—in short I have made you my Wife—

LADY TEAZLE. Well then and there is but one thing more you can make me to add to the obligation—and that is—

SIR PETER. My widow I suppose?

LADY TEAZLE. Hem! hem!

SIR PETER. Thank-you Madam—but don't flatter yourself for—tho' your ill conduct may disturb my Peace it shall never break my Heart I promise you:—however I am equally oblig'd to you for the Hint.

LADY TEAZLE. Then why will you endeavour to make yourself so disagreeable to me, and thwart me in every little elegant expence?

SIR PETER. 'Slife—Madam I say had you any of these Elegant expences when you married me?

LADY TEAZLE. Lud Sir Peter would you have me be out of the Fashion—?

SIR PETER. The Fashion indeed!—what had you to do with the Fashion before you married me?

LADY TEAZLE. For my Part—I should think you would like to have your Wife thought a Woman of Taste.

1 I . . . Memory] *L*, *Ca*, *Cb*, *B*; *om. O* 2 *After 'from'*, *insert*: and now—no one more extravagantly in the Fashion—every Fop[p]ery adopted—you forget Lady Teazle when a little wire and gauze with a few Beads made you a fly Case not much bigger than a blew-bottle, and your Hair was comb'd smooth over a Roll—| *Lady Teazle.*—horrible! Roll! *O* 3 Footmen] *O*, *L*, *Ca*, *B*; footman *Cb* 5 I suppose] *Ca*, *Cb*, *B*; *om. O* 7–8 No . . . Horse] *L*, *Ca*, *Cb*, *B*; Horrid!—I swear I never did—*O* I deny] *L*, *Ca*, *B*; no I deny *Cb* 10 a] *L*, *Ca*, *Cb*, *B*; *om. O* 13 and that is] *L*, *Ca*, *Cb*, *B*; *om. O* 14 My . . . suppose] *L*, *Ca*, *Cb*, *B*; What's that pray *O* 15 Hem! hem!] *Ca*, *Cb*, *B*; Your widow—*O*; No! No! *L*

[1] Cf. p. 592, n. 1, below.

[2] Short for 'cattle'? Or possibly suggested by Colman's prologue to Garrick's *Bon Ton* (1775):

> Nature it [*Bon Ton*] thwarts, and contradicts all reason;
> 'Tis stiff French stays, and fruit when out of season;
> A rose, when half a guinea is the price;
> A set of bays, scarce bigger than six mice.

SIR PETER. Aye, there again—Taste!—zounds Madam you had no Taste when you married me—

LADY TEAZLE. That's very true indeed Sir Peter and after having married you I am sure I should never pretend to Taste again!—But now Sir Peter if we have finish'd our daily Jangle I presume I may go to my Engagement at Lady Sneerwell's—

SIR PETER. Aye—there's another Precious circumstance, a charming set of acquaintance—you have made there.

LADY TEAZLE. Nay Sir Peter They are People of Rank and Fortune—and remarkably tenacious of Reputation.

SIR PETER. Yes 'egad they are tenacious of Reputation with a vengeance, for they don't chuse any body should have a Character—but themselves—such a crew! ah! many a wretch has rid on a hurdle[1] who has done less mischief than those utterers of forg'd Tales, coiners of Scandal,—and clippers of Reputation.

LADY TEAZLE. What would you restrain the freedom of speech?

SIR PETER. O! they have made you just as bad as any one of the Society.

LADY TEAZLE. Why—I believe I do bear a Part with a tolerable Grace——But I vow I have no malice against the People I abuse, when I say an ill natured thing 'tis out of pure Good-Humour—and I take it for granted they deal exactly in the same manner with me but Sir Peter you know you promised to come to Lady Sneerwell's too.

SIR PETER. Well well I'll call in just to look after my own character.

LADY TEAZLE. Then indeed you must make Haste after me or you'll be too late—so good bye to ye. [*Exit* LADY TEAZLE.

SIR PETER. So—I have gain'd much by my intended expostulations[2]—yet with what a charming air she contradicts every thing I say—and how pleasingly she shews her contempt of my authority—well tho' I can't make her love me there is a great Satisfaction in quar[r]elling with her and I think she never appear[s] to such advantage as when she's doing every thing in her Power to plague me. [*Exit.*

3 and] *Ca*, *Cb* [S.], *B*; *om. O*, *L* 4 I am sure] *Ca* [S.]; *om. O*, *L*, *Cb*, *B* again] *Ca*; again I allow *O*, *L*, *Cb*, *B* 6 at] *O*; of *L*, *Ca*, *Cb*, *B* 13 a hurdle] *L*, *Ca*, *Cb*, *B*; hurdles *O* 14 those] *Ca*, *Cb*; these *O*, *L*, *B* 17 O!] *L*, *Ca*, *Cb*, *B*; Aye *O* 19 I believe I do] *O*, *Ca*, *B*; I do I believe *Cb* 22 exactly in] *O*, *L*, *Ca*, *B*; just in *Cb* 26 ye] *O*, *L*, *Ca*; you *Cb*, *B* *Exit* . . . TEAZLE] *Ca*, *Cb*, *B*; *Exit O*, *L* 27 So] *O*, *L*, *Ca*, *B*; *om. Cb* expostulations] *Ca*, *B*; expostulation *O*, *L*, *Cb* 30 is a] *Ca*, *Cb*; is certainly a *O*; is *L*, *B*

[1] Criminals were drawn on a rough sledge to the place of execution.

[2] Cf. Clerimont Senior in Steele's *The Tender Husband* (1705), I. i: 'Now I can neither Mortify her Vanity, that I may Live at ease with her, or quite discard her, till have catched her a little enlarging her Innocent Freedoms, as she calls 'em.'

Scene 2d. LADY SNEERWELL'*s*

LADY SNEERWELL—MRS. CANDOUR—CRABTREE—SIR BENJAMIN —*and* SURFACE.

LADY SNEERWELL. Nay positively we will hear it—

SURFACE. Yes—yes the Epigram by all means.—

SIR BENJ. Plague on't Unkle—'tis mere nonsense.

CRABTREE. No no—'fore gad very clever for an extempore—

SIR BENJ. But Ladies you should be acquainted with the circumstance, you must know that one day last week as Lady Betty Curricle—was taking the Dust[1] in Hyde Park, in a sort of duodecimo Phaeton—She desir'd me to write some verses on her Ponies—upon which I took out my Pocket-Book—and in one moment produc'd—the following[2]—

Sure never were seen two such beautiful Ponies
Other Horses are Clowns—and these—macaronies.
Nay to give 'em this Title I'm sure isn't wrong—
—Their Legs are so slim—and their Tails are so long.[3]

CRABTREE. There—Ladies—done in the smack of a whip—and on Horseback too—

SURFACE. A very Phœbus mounted—indeed, Sir Benjamin.

SIR BENJ. O dear Sir Trifles—Trifles!—

Enter LADY TEAZLE *and* MARIA.

MRS. CANDOUR. I must have a Copy.

LADY SNEERWELL. Lady Teazle—I hope we shall see Sir Peter—

LADY TEAZLE. I believe He'll wait on your La'ship—presently.

LADY SNEERWELL. Maria my Love you look grave—come you shall sit down to Cards with Mr. Surface—

MARIA. I take very little Pleasure in Cards—however I'll do as your Ladyship pleases.

1 LADY SNEERWELL'*s*] *Ca*, *Cb*, *B*; At Lady Sneerwell's *L*, *O*   2–3 SIR... SURFACE] *Ca*; *Surface* and *Sir Ben. Backbite L*; Sir Benjn. & *Surface* (*Discover'd*) *B*, *Cb*; *Sir Benjamin Backbite and Surface O*   6 Plague] *Ca*; O plague *O*, *L*, *Cb*, *B*   10 Hyde] *L*, *Ca*, *Cb*, *B*; High *O*   13 were] *O*, *Ca*, *Cb*, *B*; was *L*   two] *L*, *Ca*, *Cb*, *B*; too *O*   19 A] *O*, *Ca*, *Cb*; O *B*   24 La'ship] *O*; Ladyship *L*, *Ca*, *Cb*, *B*   26 Cards] *Ca* [S.], *Cb* [S.]; Picquet *O*, *L*, *B*   27–8 as ... pleases] *Ca*, *Cb*, *B*; as you Please *O*

---

[1] Cf. the prologue to *The Miniature Picture*, and *Pizarro*: p. 654, lines 12–13 below.

[2] For an earlier form of these lines, see Rae, *Sheridan*, i. 330–1.

[3] Cf. the article on macaronis in the *Town and Country Magazine*, iv (1772), 243: 'They do indeed make a most ridiculous figure . . . with about two pounds of fictitious hair, formed into what is called a club, hanging down their shoulders as white as a baker's sack. . . . Their legs are at times covered with all the colours of the rainbow; even flesh-coloured and green silk stockings are not excluded.'

LADY TEAZLE. I am surprised Mr. Surface should sit down with her—I thought He would have embraced this opportunity of speaking to me before Sir Peter came—

MRS. CANDOUR. [*Coming forward*] Now I'll die but you are so scandalous I'll forswear your society.—

LADY TEAZLE. What's the matter Mrs. Candour—?

MRS. CANDOUR. They'll not allow our Friend Miss Vermillion to be handsome.

LADY SNEERWELL. O surely she's a pretty woman—

CRABTREE. I am very glad you think so Ma'am—

MRS. CANDOUR. She has a charming fresh Colour—

LADY TEAZLE. Yes when it is fresh put on—

MRS. CANDOUR. O fie I'll swear her Colour is natural—I have seen it come and go—

LADY TEAZLE. I dare swear you have, ma'am—it goes of a Night and comes again in the morning.

MRS. CANDOUR. Ha! ha! ha! how I hate to hear you talk so—but surely now her Sister is or was very Handsome.

CRABTREE. Who, Mrs. Evergreen?—O Lud she's six and fifty if she's an hour—

MRS. CANDOUR. Now positively you wrong her fifty-two or fifty-three is the utmost—and I don't think she looks more—

SIR BENJ. Ah there is no judging by her Looks unless one could see her Face.

LADY SNEERWELL. Well—well—if Mrs. Evergreen does take some pains to repair the Ravages of Time—you must allow she effects it with great ingenuity—and surely that's better than the careless manner in which the Widow Ocre—caulks her wrinkles.

SIR BENJ. Nay now Lady Sneerwell—you are severe upon the Widow—come—come it is not that she paints so ill—but when she has finish'd her Face she joins it on so badly to her Neck that she looks like a mended Statue in which the Connoisseur sees at once that the Head's modern tho' the Trunk's antique.—

CRABTREE. Ha! ha! ha! well said Nephew!

MRS. CANDOUR. Ha! ha! ha! well you make me laugh but I vow I hate you for't—what do you think of Miss Simper?

SIR BENJ. Why she has very pretty Teeth.

2 this] *O*, *L*, *Ca*, *B*; the *Cb* 4 *Coming forward*] *Cb* [S.]; *om. O*, *L*, *Ca*, *B* 15 of a] *O*, *Ca*; off at *L*; of at *Cb*, *B* 16 *After* '*morning*', *insert*: SIR BENJ. True Unkle it not only comes and goes but what's more egad her maid can fetch and carry it. *O*, *L* 19 Evergreen] *L*, *Ca*, *Cb*, *B*; Stucco *O* Lud] *O*; Lord *L*, *Ca*, *Cb*, *B* 23 could] *L*, *Ca*, *Cb*, *B*; was to *O* 25 Evergreen] *L*, *Ca*, *Cb*, *B*; she *O* 26 effects] *L*, *Ca*, *Cb*, *B*; does *O* 28 caulks] *Ca*, *Cb*, *B*; chaulks *O*, *L* 29 Lady Sneerwell] *L*, *Ca*, *Cb*, *B*; *om. O*

LADY TEAZLE. Yes and on that account when she is neither speaking nor laughing (which very seldom happens)—she never absolutely shuts her mouth, but leaves it always on a Jar as it were.

MRS. CANDOUR. How can you be so ill natur'd?

LADY TEAZLE. Nay I allow even that's better than the Pains Mrs. Prim takes to conceal her losses in Front. She draws her mouth 'till it positively resembles the aperture of a Poor's-Box, and all her words appear to slide out edgeways.

LADY SNEERWELL. Very well Lady Teazle I see you can be a little severe—

LADY TEAZLE. In defence of a Friend it is but justice but here comes Sir Peter to spoil our Pleasantry—!

Enter SIR PETER TEAZLE.

SIR PETER. Ladies your most obedient—Mercy on me, here is the whole set! a character dead at every word[1] I suppose. [*aside*]

MRS. CANDOUR. I am rejoic'd you are come Sir Peter—they have been so censorious—they will allow good Qualities to nobody—not even good-nature to our Friend Mrs. Pursy.—

LADY TEAZLE. What the Fat Dowager—who was at Mrs. Codille's last Night.—

MRS. CANDOUR. Nay—her bulk is her misfortune and when she takes such Pains to get rid of it you ought not to reflect on her.

LADY SNEERWELL. That's very true indeed.

LADY TEAZLE. Yes I know she almost lives on acids and small whey—laces herself by pullies and often in the hottest noon of summer you may see her on a little squat Poney with her hair platted up behind like a Drummer's—and puffing round the Ring[2] on a full Trot.

MRS. CANDOUR. I thank you Lady Teazle for defending her.

SIR PETER. Yes a good Defence truly.

MRS. CANDOUR. But Sir Benjamin is as Censorious as Miss Sallow.

CRABTREE. Yes and she is a curious Being to pretend to be censorious —an aukward Gawky without any one good Point under Heaven!

7 positively] *L*, *Ca*, *Cb*, *B*; *om. O* 13 SIR PETER TEAZLE] *Ca*; Sir Peter *O*, *L*, *Cb*, *B* 14 most] *Ca*, *Cb*, *B*; *om. O* 14–15 Mercy . . . suppose] *L*, *Ca*, *Cb*, *B*; *om. O* 15 (*aside*)] *Ca* [S.]; *om. L*, *O*, *Cb*, *B* 17 censorious—they] *Ca*, *Cb*, *B*; censorious and Lady Teazle as bad as anyone —

SIR PETER. It must be very distressing to you Mrs. Candour I dare swear.

MRS. CANDOUR. O they *O*, *L*

23 That's] *L*, *Ca*, *Cb*, *B*; 'tis *O* 30 But . . . is] *L*, *Ca*, *Cb*, *B*; But for Sir Benjamin He is *O*

[1] Cf. A. Pope, *The Rape of the Lock*, iii. 16: 'At ev'ry word a reputation dies.'

[2] The fashionable drive in Hyde Park, shut in by railings and fine trees.

MRS. CANDOUR. Positively you shall not be so very severe. Miss Sallow is a Relation of mine by marriage and as for her Person great allowance is to be made—for let me tell you a woman labours under many disadvantages who tries to pass for a girl at six and thirty.

LADY SNEERWELL. Tho' surely she is handsome still—and for the weakness in her eyes considering how much she reads by candle light it is not to be wonder'd at.

MRS. CANDOUR. True, and then as to her manner—upon my word I think it is particularly graceful considering she never had the least Education for you know her Mother was a Welch millener and her Father a Sugar-Baker at Bristow.—

SIR BENJ. Ah! you are both of you too good natur'd!

SIR PETER. Yes damn'd good natur'd!—this their own Relation!—mercy on me! [*aside*]

SIR BENJ. And Mrs. Candour is of so moral a turn—she can sit for an hour to hear Lady Stucco talk Sentiment.

LADY TEAZLE. Nay, I vow Lady Stucco is very well with the Des[s]ert after dinner for she's just like the French Fruit one cracks for mottos[1]—made up of Paint and Proverb.—

MRS. CANDOUR. Well I never will Join in ridiculing a Friend—and so I constantly tell my Cousin Ogle—and you all know what pretentions She has to be critical in Beauty—

CRABTREE. O to be sure she has herself the oddest countenance that ever was seen—'tis a collection of Features from all the different Countries of the Globe.

SIR BENJ. So she has indeed.—An Irish front

CRABTREE. Caledonian Locks—

SIR BENJ. Dutch nose—

CRABTREE. Austrian lip—

1 very] *O*, *L*, *Ca*, *Cb*; *om. B* 5 still] *O*, *Ca*, *Cb*, *B*; *om. L* 6 in] *O*, *L*, *Ca*, *B*; of *Cb* 11 Bristow] *O*; Bristol *Ca*, *Cb*, *B* 12 Ah] *O*, *Ca*, *B*; Ay *Cb* 13 Yes] *O*, *L*, *Ca*, *B*; O yes *Cb* Relation] *O*, *L*, *Ca*, *B*; relation too *Cb* 14 *aside*] *Ca*; *om. O*, *L*, *Cb*, *B* 15–16 SIR BENJ. . . . Sentiment] *Ca*; Well Mrs. Candour is of so moral a turn *B*; *om. Cb*;

MRS. CANDOUR. For my part, I own I cannot bear to hear a Friend ill spoken of.
SIR PETER. No, to be sure.
SIR BENJ. Ah, you are of a Moral turn; Mrs. Candour and I can sit for an hour to hear Lady Stucco talk Sentiments *L*;

MRS. CANDOUR. For my Part I own I cannot bear to hear a friend ill spoken of.
SIR PETER. No, to be sure—!—
SIR BENJ. Ah you are of a moral turn Mrs. Candour and can sit for an hour to hear Lady Stucco talk Sentiments. *O*

17–19 Nay . . . Proverb] *O*, *L*, *Ca*; *om. Cb*, *B* 20 and so] *O*, *L*, *Ca*, *B*; so *Cb*

[1] Cf. Horace Walpole to Lady Ossory: 'Paragraphs of news . . . are like mottoes too wrapped in sugar, which everybody breaks, finds nothing worth reading, and yet goes on cracking' (*Walpole Corr.* xxxiii (1965), 213).

SIR BENJ. Complexion of a Spaniard—

CRABTREE. And Teeth à la Chinoise[1]—

SIR BENJ. In short her Face resembles a Table d'hôte at Spaw where no two guests are of a nation—

CRABTREE. Or a Congress at the close of a general War—wherein all the members even to her eyes appear to have a different interest and her Nose and Chin are the only Parties likely to join issue.

MRS. CANDOUR. Ha! ha! ha!

SIR PETER. Mercy on my life! a Person they dine with twice a Week. [*aside*]

MRS. CANDOUR. Nay but I vow you shall not carry the Laugh off so—for give me leave to say that Mrs. Ogle—

SIR PETER. Madam—madam—I beg your Pardon—There's no stopping these good Gentlemen's Tongues—but when I tell you Mrs. Candour that the Lady they are abusing is a particular Friend of mine—I hope you'll not take her Part.

LADY SNEERWELL. Well said Sir Peter, but you are a cruel creature—too Phlegmatic yourself for a jest and too peevish to allow wit on others.

SIR PETER. Ah! Madam true wit is more nearly allied to good Nature than your Ladyship is aware of.

LADY TEAZLE. True Sir Peter I believe they are so near akin that they can never be united—

SIR BENJ. Or rather Madam suppose them man and wife because one so seldom sees them together.

LADY TEAZLE. But Sir Peter is such an Enemy to Scandal I believe He would have it put down by Parliament.

SIR PETER. 'Fore Heaven! Madam if they were to Consider—the Sporting with Reputation of as much importance as poaching on manors[2]—

3 Spaw] *O, L, B, Cb*; Spa *Ca* 7 to] *L, Ca, Cb, B*; *om. O* 10 *aside*] *Ca*; *om. O, L, Cb, B* *After 'aside', insert*: LADY SNEERWELL. Go—go—you are a couple of provoking Toads—*O, L* 16 her] *O, Ca, Cb, B*; their *L* 17 Well said] *Ca, Cb, B*; Ha! ha! ha!—Well said *O, L* 18 on] *O, Ca*; in *L, Cb, B* 19 allied] *L, Ca, Cb, B*; allow'd *O* 21 akin] *O*; a Kin *L, Ca, Cb*; of kin *B* 23 Or] *Ca, Cb*; O *O, L, B*

[1] Cf. *The Citizen of the World*: 'And first the beauties of China appeared . . . Their black teeth and plucked eye-brows were however alleged by the Genius against them' (*Collected Works of Oliver Goldsmith*, ed. A. Friedman (Oxford, 1966), ii. 442).

[2] Cf. Miss Walsingham's speech in Hugh Kelly's *The School for Wives*, 4th edn. (1774), p. 63: 'And yet if the laws against it [duelling], were as well enforced as the laws against destroying the game, perhaps it would be equally for the benefit of the kingdom.' See, also, the *Public Advertiser*, 22 Apr. 1776: 'The Noblemen and Gentlemen of the Association for the Preservation of Game all over England, are desired to meet To-morrow at Eleven o'Clock, at the St. Alban's Tavern in St. Alban's-street: WHEREAS the said Noblemen and Gentlemen have prosecuted and convicted several Poulterers, Higlers, Carriers, Stage Coachmen, Masters of Vessels, Night Netters, Snarers and others, for destroying the Game and carrying and selling the same. . . .'

and pass An Act for the Preservation of Fame—I believe there are many would thank them for the Bill.

LADY SNEERWELL. O Lud! Sir Peter would you deprive us of our Privileges—

SIR PETER. Aye Madam—and then no Person should be permitted to kill characters, or run down Reputations but qualified old Maids and disap[p]ointed Widows.—

LADY SNEERWELL. Go—you Monster—

MRS. CANDOUR. But sure you would not be quite so severe on those who only report what they hear.

SIR PETER. Yes Madam I would have Law Merchant[1] for them—too—and in all cases of Slander currency whenever the Drawer of the Lie was not to be found the injured Party should have a right to come on any of the indorsers.

CRABTREE. Well for my Part I believe there never was a Scandalous Tale without some foundation—

LADY SNEERWELL. Come Ladies shall we sit down to Cards in the next Room—

Enter SERVANT *and Whispers* SIR PETER.

SIR PETER. I'll be with them directly!—[*Exeunt*]—I'll get away unperceiv'd.

LADY SNEERWELL. Sir Peter you are not leaving us?

SIR PETER. Your Ladyship must excuse me—I'm called away by particular Business—but I leave my Character behind me.—

[*Exit* SIR PETER.

SIR BENJ. Well certainly Lady Teazle that Lord of yours is a strange being—I could tell you some stories of him would make you laugh heartily if he wasn't your Husband—

LADY TEAZLE. O pray don't mind that.—come do let's hear 'em.

[*They join the rest of the Company all talking as they are going into the next room.*

SURFACE. [*rising with* MARIA] Maria I see you have no satisfaction in this society.

MARIA. How is it possible I should?—if to raise malicious smiles at the infirmities and misfortunes—of those who have never injured us be the

11 have] *L, Ca, Cb, B*; of *O* Law Merchant] *O, Ca, Cb, B*; Law-Merchants *L* them] *L, Ca, Cb, B*; that *O* 13 on] *O, L, Ca, B*; upon *Cb* 19 *and*] *Ca, Cb, B*; *om. O, L* *Whispers*] *O, L, Ca, Cb*; *whisper B* 20 *Exeunt*] *O*; *om. L, Ca, Cb, B* 25 SIR PETER] *Ca, Cb, B*; *om. O, L* 27 him] *O, L, Ca, B*; his *Cb* 30 *They*] *L, Ca*; *om. O, Cb, B* *all . . . are*] *Ca*; *om. O, L*; talking etc. *Cb* [S.]; all talking *B* 32 *rising with* MARIA] *Ca* [S.]; *om. O, L, Cb, B*

[1] Privileges peculiar to merchants, differing from Common Law but the same as the Law of the Staple.

province of wit or Humour Heav'n grant me a double Portion of Dullness—

SURFACE. Yet they appear more ill natur'd than they are—They have no malice at heart—

MARIA. Then is their conduct still more contemptible for in my opinion —nothing could—excuse the intemperance of their tongues but a natural and ungovernable bitterness of Mind.

SURFACE. But can you Maria feel thus for others and be unkind to me alone—is hope to be denied the tenderest Passion?—

MARIA. Why will you distress me by renewing this subject—

SURFACE. Ah! Maria you would not treat me thus and oppose your Guardian's Sir Peter's wishes—but that I see that profligate Charles is still a favour'd Rival.

MARIA. Ungenerously urged—but whatever my sentiments of that Unfortunate young man are—be assured I shall not feel more bound to give him up because his Distresses have lost him the regard even of a Brother.— [LADY TEAZLE *returns.*

SURFACE. Nay but Maria do not leave me with a Frown—by all that's honest I swear—Gad's life here's Lady Teazle. [*aside*]—you must not—no you shall not—for tho' I have the greatest Regard for Lady Teazle—

MARIA. Lady Teazle—!

SURFACE. Yet were Sir Peter to suspect—

LADY TEAZLE. [*Coming forward*] What's this Pray—do you take her for me!—Child you are wanted in the next Room— [*Exit* MARIA. what is all this pray—

SURFACE. O the most unlucky circumstance in Nature. Maria has somehow suspected the tender concern which I have for your happiness and threaten'd to acquaint Sir Peter with her suspicions—and I was just endeavouring to reason with her when you came.

LADY TEAZLE. Indeed but you seem'd to adopt—a very tender method of reasoning—do you usually argue on your knees—?

SURFACE. O she's a Child—and I thought a little Bombast—but Lady Teazle when are you to give me your Judgment on my Library as you promised?

6 intemperance] *O*, *Ca*, *Cb*, *B*; interference *L* 8 But] *Ca*, *Cb*, *B*; Undoubtedly, Madam; and it has always been a Sentiment of mine—that to propagate a malicious truth wantonly—is more despicable than to falsify from Revenge; but *O*, *L* feel thus] *O*, *L*, *Ca*, *B*; thus feel *Cb* 9 is] *L*, *Ca*, *Cb*, *B*; nay is *O* 11 Maria] *O*, *L*, *Ca*, *B*; Madam *Cb* 12 Guardian's] *O*, *L*; Guardian *Ca*, *Cb*, *B* wishes] *O*; will *L*, *Ca*, *Cb*, *B* that . . . Charles] *L*, *Ca*, *Cb*, *B*; my profligate Brother *O* 16 lost him] *L*, *Ca*, *Cb*, *B*; sunk him so low as to deprive him of *O* 17 LADY . . . *returns*] *Ca* [S.]; *om.* *O*, *L*, *B*, *Cb* 19 *aside*] *Ca*; *om.* *O*, *L*, *Cb*, *B* 20 shall not] *L*, *Ca*, *Cb*, *B*; shall *O* 23 *Coming forward*] *Ca*; (*Comes forward*) *Cb*; *om.* *O*, *L*, *B* 24 *Exit* MARIA] *L*, *Ca*; *om.* *O*, *Cb*, *B* 25 what is] *Ca* [S.]; what's *O*, *L*, *Cb*, *B*

LADY TEAZLE. No—no I begin to think it would be imprudent—and you know I admit you as a Lover no further than Fashion requires.—

SURFACE. True—a mere Platonic Cicisbeo[1]—what every London wife is entitled too.

LADY TEAZLE. Certainly one must not be out of the Fashion—however I have so much of my country Prejudices left—that—tho' Sir Peter's ill humour may vex me ever so—it never shall provoke me to—

SURFACE. The only revenge in your Power—well I applaud your moderation.

LADY TEAZLE. Go—you are an insinuating Wretch—but we shall be miss'd—let us join the company.

SURFACE. But we had best not return together.

LADY TEAZLE. Well don't stay—for Maria shan't come to hear any more of your Reasoning I promise you— [*Exit* LADY TEAZLE.

SURFACE. A curious Dilemma truly my Politics have run me into.—I wanted at first only to ingratiate myself with Lady Teazle that she might not be my enemy with Maria—and I have I don't know how—become her serious Lover.—Sincerely I begin to wish I had never made such a Point of gaining so very good a character—for it has led me into so many curs'd Rogueries that I doubt I shall be exposed at last.

[*Exit.*

Scene 3d. SIR PETER'*s*

Enter SIR OLIVER *and* ROWLEY.

SIR OLIVER. Ha! ha! ha! and so my old Friend is married hey?—a young Wife out of the Country!—ha! ha! ha!—that he should have stood Bluff[2] to old Batchelor so long and sink into a Husband at last!—

3 True] *L*, *Ca*, *Cb*, *B*; True—true *O* London] *O*, *Ca*; *om.* *L*, *Cb*, *B* 7 never shall] *O*, *Ca*, *B*; shall never *L*, *Cb* 10 Wretch] *L*, *Ca*, *Cb*, *B*; Hypocrite *O* 12 But] *L*, *Ca*, *Cb*, *B*; True but *O* 14 *Exit* LADY TEAZLE] *Ca*, *Cb*, *B*; *Ex.* *O* 18 Lover.—Sincerely] *L*, *Ca*, *Cb*, *B*; Lover, so that I stand a chance of committing a Crime I never meditated—and probably of losing Maria by the Pursuit:—*O* 22 SIR PETER'*s*] *Ca*; At Sir Peter's *O*, *L*; Sir Peter Teazle's *Cb*, *B*; At Sir Peter Teazle's *L* 23 *Enter* . . . ROWLEY] *Ca*;—Rowley and Sir Oliver *O*, *L*, *Cb*, *B* 24 hey?] *O*, *Cb*, *Ca*, *B*; ha! *L*

[1] The privileges of the cicisbeo are described in Frances Sheridan's *A Journey to Bath*: see Rae, pp. 296–7: 'I may come in when you are dressing. I am to put essence into your handkerchief, reach you your combs, your pins . . . I am never to be from your elbow if you command me. I am to help you tea, coffee, and fruit before any other lady in the company, and give it you on my knee. . . . I am to attend you to all publick places and home again, and to see you up to your chamber door.'

[2] Sheridan may have picked up the phrase from some satirical verses on him by 'Philo-Musa', that appeared in the *Morning Chronicle*, 2 Apr. 1777:

Between us we'll monopolize,
Monopolies are now the fashion,

ROWLEY. But you must not rally him on the subject Sir Oliver—'tis a tender Point I assure you tho He has been married only seven months.

SIR OLIVER. Then He has been just half a year on the stool of Repentance—Poor Peter! But you say he has entirely given up Charles? never sees him hey?

ROWLEY. His Prejudice against him is astonishing—and I am sure greatly encreas'd by a Jealousy of him with Lady Teazle—which He has been industriously led into by a scandalous Society in the neighbourhood—who have contributed not a little to Charles's ill name. Whereas the truth is I believe if the Lady is partial to either of them his Brother is the Favourite.

SIR OLIVER. Aye—I know—there are a set of malicious prating prudent Gossips both male and Female, who murder characters to kill time and will rob a young Fellow of his good name before He has years to know the value of it.—but I am not to be prejudic'd—against my nephew by such I promise you. No! no—if Charles has done nothing false or mean[1] I shall compound for his extravagance.

ROWLEY. Then my life on't you will reclaim him. Ah Sir—it gives me new life to find that your heart is not turned against him—and that the son of my good old master has one friend however left.

SIR OLIVER. What! shall I forget Master Rowley—when I was at his years my self?—egad my Brother and I were neither of us very prudent youths—and yet I believe you have not seen many better Men than your old master was.

ROWLEY. Sir, 'tis this reflection gives me assurance that Charles may yet be a Credit to his Family—but here comes Sir Peter—

SIR OLIVER. 'Egad so He does—mercy on me—He's greatly alter'd—and seems to have a settled Married look—one may read husband in his Face at this Distance.—

1 'tis] *O, L, Ca, B*; *om. Cb* 3 Then] *L, Ca, Cb, B*; Ah then *O* 18–19 me new life] *L, Ca, Cb, B*; my old life new vigour *O* 23 believe] *L, Ca, Cb, B*; believe Master Rowley *O*

Your [Thomas Linley's] care our *harmony* supplies,
And *Van's* [Vanbrugh's] old scenes I now am slashing.

No matter whether new or stale,
I'll furnish *Comedy* enough,
The *whoreson authors* may turn pale,
'Gainst their intrusion we'll stand bluff.

The School for Scandal reference is the earliest usage given in the *O.E.D.*

[1] Cf. Marvell's 'Horatian Ode Upon Cromwell's Return from Ireland', stanza 15, of Charles I:

He nothing common did or mean
Upon that memorable scene.

Enter SIR PETER TEAZLE.

SIR PETER. Hah! Sir Oliver—my Old Friend:—welcome to England—a thousand Times!

SIR OLIVER. Thank you—thank—you Sir Peter—and—'efaith—I am as glad to find you well, believe me—

SIR PETER. Ah! 'tis a long time since we met—sixteen years I doubt, Sir Oliver—and many a cross accident in the Time—

SIR OLIVER. Aye I have had my share—but what I find you are married—hey my old Boy—well—well it can't be help'd—and so I wish you joy with all my heart.—

SIR PETER. Thank—you—thank you Sir Oliver—yes I have enter'd into the happy state but we'll not talk of that now.

SIR OLIVER. True true Sir Peter, Old Friends should not begin on Grievances—at first meeting—no—no—no.

ROWLEY. [*to* SIR OLIVER] Take Care pray Sir—

SIR OLIVER. Well—so one of my Nephews I find is a wild Rogue—hey?

SIR PETER. Wild!—ah! my old Friend—I grieve for your disap[p]ointment there—He's a lost Young Man indeed—however his Brother will make you amends. Joseph is indeed what a youth should be—every body in the world speaks well of him—

SIR OLIVER. I am sorry to hear it—he has too good a character to be an honest Fellow.—Every body speaks well of him! Psha! then He has bow'd as low to Knaves and Fools—as to the honest dignity of Genius or Virtue.

SIR PETER. What Sir Oliver do you blame him for not making Enemies—?

SIR OLIVER. Yes—if He has merit enough to deserve them.

SIR PETER. Well—well—you'll be convinc'd when you know him—'tis edification to hear him converse—he professes the noblest—Sentiments.

SIR OLIVER. Ah plague on his Sentiments—if He salutes me with a Scrap of morality in his mouth I shall be sick directly.—but however don't mistake me Sir Peter—I don't mean to defend Charles' Errors—but before I form my judgement of either of them I intend to make a trial of their Hearts—and my Friend Rowley and I have plann'd something for the Purpose—

ROWLEY. And Sir Peter shall own he has been for once mistaken.

SIR PETER. O—my Life on Joseph's Honour!

SIR OLIVER. Well come give us a bottle of good wine—and we'll drink the Lads Healths and tell you our scheme.—

1 TEAZLE] *Ca*; *om. O, L, Cb, B* 6 met] *L, Ca, Cb, B*; meet *O* 11 you Sir Oliver] *L, Ca, Cb, B*; thank Sir Peter *O* 14 no—no—no] *L, Ca, Cb, B*; no—no *O* 15 *to* SIR OLIVER] *Ca* [S.]; *om. O, L, Cb, B* 23–4 Genius or] *L, Ca, Cb, B*; *om. O* 30 on] *O*; of *Ca, Cb, B* 39 Lads] *O, B*; Lad's *L, Ca, Cb* Healths] *O, Cb*; health *L, Ca, B*

SIR PETER. Al[l]ons then—

SIR OLIVER. And don't Sir Peter be so severe against your old Friend's son—Odds—my Life—I am not sorry that He has run out of the course a little—for my Part I hate to see Prudence clinging to the green Succours of Youth—'tis like Ivy round a sapling and spoils the Growth of the Tree. [*Exeunt*.

END OF ACT 2

Act 3d

Scene 1st.—SIR PETER'*s*

SIR PETER—SIR OLIVER—*and* ROWLEY.

SIR PETER. Well then—we will see this Fellow first and have our wine afterwards.—but how is this—Master Rowley—I don't see the Jet[1] of your Scheme—?

ROWLEY. Why Sir—this Mr. Stanley whom I was speaking of—is nearly related to them by their mother. He was once a merchant in Dublin—but has been ruined by a series of undeserved misfortunes—He has applied by Letter since his confinement both to Mr. Surface and Charles.—from the former—He has received nothing but evasive promises of future Service—while Charles has done all that his extravagance has left him power to do—and He is at this time endeavouring to raise a sum of money—part of which in the midst of his own distresses I know he intends for the service of poor Stanley.

SIR OLIVER. Ah! He is my Brother's Son—

SIR PETER. Well—but how is Sir Oliver personally to—

ROWLEY. Why Sir I will inform Charles—and his Brother that Stanley has obtain'd Permission to apply in Person to his Friends—and as they have neither of them ever seen him let Sir Oliver assume his Character—and he will have a fair opportunity of judging at least of the

3 son—Odds] *L*, *Ca*, *Cb*, *B*;
SIR OLIVER. . . . son.
SIR PETER. Tis his Vices and Foibles have made me his Enemy.
ROWLEY. Come—come—Sir Peter consider how early He was left to his own guidance—Odds *O*

9 SIR PETER'*s*] *L*, *Ca*, *B*; At Sir Peters *O*, *Cb* 11 this Fellow] *L*, *Ca*, *Cb*, *B*; the Fellows *O* 17 since his confinement] *L*, *Ca*, *Cb*, *B*; *om.* *O* 18 former—He] *L*, *Ca*, *Cb*, *B*; former—I speak with some certainty—I believe that *O* 20 do—and] *L*, *Ca*, *Cb*, *B*; do—I have more than once carried him a present relief from him—and *O*

[1] Cf. R. Cumberland, *The West Indian* (1771), III. x: 'the jet of the story is . . . .' The sense is 'gist'.

Benevolence of their Dispositions, and believe me Sir, you will find in the youngest Brother—one who in the midst of Folly and Dissipation—has still as our immortal Bard expresses it—'a Tear for Pity and a Hand open as Day for melting Charity.'[1]

SIR PETER. Pshaw! what signifies his having an open Hand or Purse either when He has nothing left to give!—Well—well—make the Trial if you please—but where is the Fellow whom you brought for Sir Oliver to Examine relative to Charles's Affairs?

ROWLEY. Below, waiting his commands, and no one can give him better intelligence;—This Sir Oliver is a friendly Jew who to do him justice has done every thing in his power to bring your Nephew to a proper sense of his Extravagance.

SIR PETER. Pray let us have him in—

ROWLEY. Desire Mr. Moses to walk upstairs.—

SIR PETER. But why should you suppose He will speak the Truth.

ROWLEY. O I have convinced him that he has no chance of recovering Certain Sums advanced to Charles, but thro' the Bounty of Sir Oliver, who he knows is arriv'd; so that you may depend on his fidelity to his Interest; I have also another Evidence in my power, one Snake—whom I have detected in a Matter little short of Forgery, and shall shortly produce to remove some of your prejudices Sir Peter, relative to Charles and Lady Teazle.

SIR PETER. I have heard too much on that Subject.

ROWLEY. Here comes the honest Israelite.

Enter MOSES.

This is Sir Oliver—

SIR OLIVER. Sir—I—understand you have lately had great dealings with my Nephew Charles.

MOSES. Yes Sir Oliver—I have done all I could for him, but He was ruin'd before He came to me for Assistance.

SIR OLIVER. That was unlucky truly—for you have had no opportunity of shewing your Talents.—

MOSES. None at all—I hadn't the Pleasure of knowing his Distresses—'till He was some thousands worse than nothing.

1 and . . . Sir] *Ca*, *Cb*, *B*; and believe me *L*; Then Sir believe me *O* 4 as Day] *Ca*, *Cb*; as the day *O*, *L*, *B* 5 Pshaw!] *L*, *Ca*, *Cb*, *B*; Pshaw (*Aside*) *O* 7–8 the Fellow . . . Affairs] *L*, *Ca*, *Cb*, *B*; these two Fellows you were to bring to confession before us? *O* 9 his] *L*, *Ca*, *Cb*, *B*; your *O* 14 Moses] *L*, *Ca*, *Cb*, *B*; Snake *O* 15 But why] *Ca*; But pray why *L*, *Cb*, *B*; *om.* *O* 19 Interest] *O*, *Ca*; own Interest *L*, *Cb*, *B* 20 have detected . . . and] *Ca*, *Cb*, *B*; *om.* *O*, *L* 32 Talents] *O*, *L*, *Ca*, *B*; Parts *Cb* 34 'till . . . nothing] *L*, *Ca*, *Cb*, *B*; 'till it was impossible to add to them *O*

[1] 2 *Henry IV*, IV. iv.

SIR OLIVER. Unfortunate indeed! but I suppose you have done all in your Power for him honest Moses?

MOSES. Yes he knows that.—This very Evening I was to have brought him a Gentleman from the city who doesn't know him and will I believe advance him some money.

SIR PETER. What one Charles has never had money from before?

MOSES. Yes Mr. Premium of Crutched-Friars[1]—formerly a Broker.

SIR PETER. Egad Sir Oliver a Thought strikes me—Charles you say doesn't know Mr.—Premium—

MOSES. Not at all.—

SIR PETER. Now then Sir Oliver you may have a better opportunity of satisfying yourself than by an old romancing tale of a poor Relation.—go with my Friend Moses and Represent Mr. Premium and then I'll answer for't, you will see your Nephew in all his Glory.—

SIR OLIVER. Egad I like this Idea better than the other and I may visit Joseph afterwards as old Stanley.

SIR PETER. True so you may—

ROWLEY. Well this is taking Charles rather at a disadvantage to be sure—however Moses—you understand Sir Peter and will be faithful.—

MOSES. You may depend upon me—this is near the Time I was to have gone.

SIR OLIVER. I'll accompany you as soon as you please, Moses, but hold—I have forgot one thing—how the Plague shall I be able to pass for a Jew?

MOSES. There's no need—the Principal is Christian.

SIR OLIVER. Is He—I'm sorry to hear it—but then again—an't I rather too smartly dress'd to look like a money-Lender?—

SIR PETER. Not at all—'twould not be out of character if you went in your own carriage—would it Moses—?

MOSES. Not in the least.

SIR OLIVER. Well—but—how must I talk? there's certainly some cant of usury—and mode of treating that I ought to know—

SIR PETER. O there's not much to learn—the great point as I take it is to be exorbitant enough in your Demands, hey Moses?

MOSES. Yes, that's a very great Point—

SIR OLIVER. I'll answer for't I'll not be wanting in that—I'll ask him eight or ten per cent on the loan—at least.

MOSES. If you ask him no more than that, you'll be discovered immediately.

5 him] *L*, *Ca*, *Cb*, *B*; *om.* *O* 6–7 SIR PETER. . . Friars] *O*, *Ca*, *Cb*, *B*; *om.* *L* 7 formerly a Broker] *Ca*, *Cb*, *B*; *om.* *O*, *L* 15 this] *O*, *Ca*, *Cb*, *B*; that *L* 20 this] *L*, *Ca*, *Cb*, *B*; and this *O* 24 There's] *O*, *L*, *Ca*, *B*; O there is *Cb* 25 sorry] *Ca*; very sorry *O*, *L*, *Cb*, *B* 28 carriage] *L*, *Ca*, *Cb*, *B*; Character *O* 34 a] *Ca*, *Cb*, *B*; *om.* *O* 37 If] *Ca*, *Cb*, *B*; You'll be found out directly—if *O*, *L*

[1] A continuation of Jewry Street, running from Aldgate to Mark Lane.

SIR OLIVER. Hey—what the Plague! how much then?

MOSES. That depends upon the Circumstances, if he appears not very anxious for the supply—you should require only forty or fifty per cent—but if you find him in great Distress and want the monies very bad—you may ask double.

SIR PETER. A good Honest Trade you're learning Sir Oliver—

SIR OLIVER. Truly I think so—and not unprofitable—

MOSES. Then you know—you haven't the monies yourself—but are forced—to borrow them for him of a Friend.

SIR OLIVER. Oh I borrow it of a Friend do I?

MOSES. Yes—and your friend is an unconscionable Dog,—but you can't help it.—

SIR OLIVER. My Friend is an unconscionable Dog is he?

MOSES. Yes—and He himself hasn't the moneys by him—but is forced to sell stock at a great Loss—

SIR OLIVER. He is forced to sell stock is he—at a great loss is he—well that's very kind of him.

SIR PETER. Efaith Sir Oliver, Mr. Premium, I mean, you'll soon be Master of the Trade—but Moses—wouldn't you have him run out a little against the annuity Bill[1] that would be in character I should think—

MOSES. Very much—

ROWLEY. And lament that a young man now must be at years of discretion before He is suffered to ruin himself—

MOSES. Aye—great Pity!

SIR PETER. And abuse—the Public—for allowing merit to an act whose only object—is to snatch Misfortune and imprudence—from the rapacious Relief of usury! and give the minor a chance of inheriting his estate, without being undone by coming into Possession.—

SIR OLIVER. So—so—Moses shall give me further instructions as we go together—

SIR PETER. You will not have much time for your Nephew lives hard bye—

SIR OLIVER. O Never fear—my Tutor appears so able that tho' Charles lived in the next street it must be my own Fault if I am not a compleat Rogue before I turn the corner.— [*Exeunt* SIR OLIVER *and* MOSES.

SIR PETER. So—now I think Sir Oliver will be convinced—you are partial Rowley—and would have prepared Charles for the other Plot.

1 the] *O*, *L*, *Ca*, *Cb*; a *B*
2 depends] *L*, *Ca*, *Cb*; depend *O*, *B*
14 moneys] *Ca*; monies *Cb*, *B*; money *O*, *L*
16 He] *L*, *Ca*, *Cb*, *B*; O—He *O*
stock, is he] *O*, *L*, *Ca*, *B*; Stock *Cb*
19 him] *L*, *Ca*, *Cb*, *B*; him also *O*
24 great] *O*, *Ca*, *Cb*, *B*; a great *L*
25 allowing] *L*, *Ca*, *Cb*, *B*; giving *O*
29 further] *O*, *Ca*, *B*; farther *Cb*
35 *Exeunt*] *O*, *Ca* [S.]; *Exit* *L*, *Cb*, *B*
37 the other] *L*, *Ca*, *Cb*, *B*; t'other *O*

[1] See p. 301.

ROWLEY. No upon my Word Sir Peter—

SIR PETER. Well go bring me this Snake, and I'll hear what he has to say presently—I see Maria and want to Speak with her—[*Exit* ROWLEY] I should be glad to be convinced, my Suspicions of Lady Teazle and Charles were unjust—I have never yet open'd my mind on this subject to my—Friend Joseph—I'm determined I will do it—He will give me his Opinion Sincerely.—

Enter MARIA.

So—child—has Mr. Surface returned with you?

MARIA. No Sir—He was engaged—

SIR PETER. Well—Maria—do you not reflect the more you converse with that amiable young man, what return his Partiality for you deserves?

MARIA. Indeed Sir Peter—your frequent importunity on this subject—distresses me extremely—you compell me to Declare that I know no man who has ever paid me a particular attention whom I would not prefer to Mr. Surface.

SIR PETER. Soh! Here's Perverseness!—no—no—Maria—'tis Charles—only whom you would prefer—'tis evident his Vices and Follies have won your Heart.

MARIA. This is unkind Sir—you know I have obey'd you in neither seeing nor corresponding with him—I have heard enough to convince me that He is unworthy my regard—Yet I cannot think it culpable—if while my understanding severely condemns his Vices—my Heart suggests some Pity for his Distresses.—

SIR PETER. Well well Pity him as much as you please but give your Heart and Hand—to a worthier object.

MARIA. Never to his Brother—

SIR PETER. Go—perverse and obstinate! but take care Madam—you have never yet known what the authority of a Guardian is—don't compel me to inform you of it.—

MARIA. I can only say you shall not have just reason—'tis true by my Father's will I am for a short period bound to regard you as his substitute, but must cease to think you so, when you would compel me to be miserable. [*Exit* MARIA.

SIR PETER. Was ever Man so cross'd as I am!—everything conspiring to fret me!—I hadn't been involv'd in matrimony a fortnight before her Father—a hale and hearty man—died on purpose I believe—for the Pleasure of plaguing me with the care of his Daughter.—but here comes my Helpmate!—She appears—in great good-humour—how happy I should be if I could teaze her into loving me tho' but a little.—

2 go . . . Snake] *L*, *Ca*, *Cb*, *B*; go to Snake *O* what] *L*, *Ca*, *Cb*, *B*; what more *O*
4–5 I should . . . unjust] *L*, *Ca*, *Cb*, *B*; *om.* *O*
33 must] *L*, *Ca*, *Cb*, *B*; I must *O*
34 *Exit* MARIA] *Ca*, *Cb*, *B*; *Exit* *O*, *L*

Enter LADY TEAZLE.

LADY TEAZLE. Lud! Sir Peter—I hope you haven't been quarrelling with Maria—it isn't using me well to be ill-humour'd when I am not bye—!

SIR PETER. Ah! Lady Teazle you might have the Power to make me good humour'd at all times.—

LADY TEAZLE. I am sure—I wish I had—for I want you to be in charming sweet Temper at this moment—do be good humour'd now—and let me have two hundred Pounds will you?

SIR PETER. Two hundred-Pounds—! what an't I to be in a good humour without paying for it—but speak to me thus—and efaith there's nothing I could refuse you. You shall have it—but seal me a bond for the repayment—

LADY TEAZLE. O no—there my Note of Hand will do as well—

SIR PETER. [*kissing her hand*] And you shall no longer reproach me with not giving you an independent settlement—I mean shortly to surprise you—but shall we always live thus—hey?

LADY TEAZLE. If you—please—I'm sure I don't care how soon we leave off quarrelling provided you'll own you were tired first—

SIR PETER. Well—then let our future contest be who shall be most obliging.

LADY TEAZLE. I assure you Sir Peter Good Nature becomes you—you look now as you did before we were married!—when you us'd to walk with me under the Elms and tell me stories of what a Gallant you were in your youth and chuck me under the Chin—you would—and ask me if I thought I could love an Old Fellow who would deny me nothing—didn't you?

SIR PETER. Yes—yes—and you were as kind and attentive.

LADY TEAZLE. Aye so I was—and would always take your Part when my acquaintance used to abuse you and turn you into ridicule—

SIR PETER. Indeed—!

LADY TEAZLE. Aye—and when my cousin Sophy[1] has call'd you a stiff peevish old batchelor and laugh'd at me for thinking of marrying one who might be my Father—I have always defended you—and said I didn't think you so ugly by any means and that I dared say you'd make a very good sort of a Husband.

SIR PETER. And you prophesied right—and we shall certainly now be the happiest couple.

11 but] *O*, *L*, *Ca*, *B*; *om. Cb* 15 *kissing . . . hand*] *Ca* [S.]; *om. O*, *L*, *Cb*, *B* 16 I . . . to] *L*, *Ca*, *Cb*, *B*; I shall shortly *O* 17 you—but] *L*, *Ca*, *Cb*, *B*; you—and you'll not call me ungenerous—but *O* 19 provided] *L*, *Ca*, *Cb*, *B*; if *O*

[1] Cousin Sophy in *St. Patrick's Day*, I. ii, 'married an officer': see p. 170, l. 29.

LADY TEAZLE. And never differ again—

SIR PETER. No never—tho' at the same time—indeed my dear Lady Teazle—you must watch your Temper very narrowly—for in all our little Quarrels—my dear—if you recollect my Love you always began first—

LADY TEAZLE. I beg your Pardon—my dear Sir Peter—indeed you always gave the provocation.

SIR PETER. Now—see my—Angel take care—contradicting isn't the way to keep Friends.

LADY TEAZLE. Then don't you begin it, my Love!

SIR PETER. There now—you—you are going on—you don't perceive my Life that you are just doing the very thing which you know always makes me angry.

LADY TEAZLE. Nay—you know if you will be angry without any reason—

SIR PETER. There now you want to quarrel again—

LADY TEAZLE. No—I am sure I don't—but if you will be so peevish—

SIR PETER. There—now who begins first—

LADY TEAZLE. Why you to be sure. I said nothing but—there's no bearing—your Temper—

SIR PETER. No—no—Madam—the Fault's in your own temper—

LADY TEAZLE. Aye you are just what my cousin Sophy said you would be.

SIR PETER. Your cousin Sophy—is a forward impertinent Gypsey—

LADY TEAZLE. You are a great Bear I'm sure to abuse my Relations[1]—

SIR PETER. Now may all the Plagues of marriage be doubled on me if ever I try to be Friends with you any more—

LADY TEAZLE. So much the Better—

SIR PETER. No—no madam 'tis evident you—never cared a Pin for me—and I was a madman to marry you—a Pert rural Coquet that had refused half the honest Squires in the neighbourhood.

LADY TEAZLE. And I am sure I was a Fool to marry you—an Old dangling Batchelor who was single at fifty only because He never could meet with any one who would have him.

SIR PETER. Aye—aye—Madam—but you were pleased enough—to listen to me—you never had such an Offer before.

7 Angel] *L*, *Ca*, *Cb*, *B*; Love *O* 10 you—you] *Ca*, *Cb*, *B*; you *O*, *L* 11 thing] *L*, *Ca*, *Cb*, *B*; thing my Love *O* 13 reason] *Ca*, *B*; reason my Dear *O*, *L*, *Cb* 19 Madam] *Ca*, *Cb*, *B*; my dear *O*, *L* 22 You . . . to] *L*, *Ca*, *Cb*; Go you great Bear how dare dare you *O*; And you a great Bear I'm sure to *B* 27 to] *L*, *Ca*, *Cb*, *B*; ever to *O* that] *L*, *Ca*, *Cb*, *B*; who *O* 29 marry] *L*, *Ca*, *Cb*, *B*; marrow *O*

[1] Charles Reade's mother related that Sheridan stopped Mrs. Abington in rehearsal and said: 'No, no, that won't do at all. It mustn't be *pettish*. That's shallow—shallow. You must go up stage with, "You are just what my cousin Sophy said you would be," and then turn and sweep down on him like a volcano. "You are a great bear to abuse my relations! How *dare* you abuse my relations!"' See Ellen Terry, *The Story of my Life*, 2nd edn. (1908), p. 49.

LADY TEAZLE. No! didn't I refuse Sir Twivy Tarrier—who every body said would have been a better Match—for his Estate is just as good as yours—and He has broke his Neck[1] since we have been married!

SIR PETER. I have done with you Madam—you are an unfeeling—ungrateful—but there's an end of every thing—I believe you capable of anything that's bad—yes Madam—I now believe the Reports relative to you and Charles—Madam—yes Madam you and—Charles are not without Grounds—

LADY TEAZLE. Take—care Sir Peter—you had better not insinuate any such thing! I'll not be suspected without cause I promise you.—

SIR PETER. Very—well, Madam—very well—a separate maintenance—as soon as you Please—yes Madam or a Divorce—I'll make an example of myself for the benefit of all old Batchelors. Let us separate Madam—

LADY TEAZLE. Agreed—agreed—and now—my Dear Sir Peter we are of a Mind once more we may be the happiest Couple—and never differ again you know; ha! ha!—well you are going to be in a Passion I see—and I shall only interrupt you—so, bye, bye! [*Exit.*

SIR PETER. Plagues and Tortures! can't I make her Angry neither! O I am the miserablest Fellow—But I'll not bear her presuming to keep her Temper—No she may break my Heart but she shan't keep her Temper. [*Exit.*

Scene 2d. CHARLES'*s House*

Enter TRIP—MOSES *and* SIR OLIVER.

TRIP. Here Master Moses—if you'll stay a moment—I'll try whether Mr.—what's the Gentleman's Name?

SIR OLIVER. Mr.——. Moses—what *is* my name? [*aside*]

MOSES. Mr. Premium—

TRIP. Premium—very well. [*Exit* TRIP *taking snuff.*

SIR OLIVER. To Judge by the Servants—one wouldn't believe the master was ruin'd—but what—sure this was my Brother's House?

MOSES. Yes Sir Mr. Charles bought it of Mr. Joseph with the Furniture

1 Twivy] *O, Ca, B*; Tivy *Cb* 13 old] *O, L, Ca, B*; *om. Cb* 15 once more] *L, Ca, Cb, B*; again *O* 16 well] *L, Ca, Cb, B*; O lud *O* 17 so, bye, bye] *L, Ca Cb, B*; so good bye bye *O* *Exit*] *O, L, Ca, B*; *om. Cb* 18 Tortures] *L, Ca, Cb, B*; Tortures!—She pretends to keep her Temper *O* 19 presuming] *L, Ca, Cb, B*; daring *O* 20 No] *O, L, Ca, B*; *om. Cb* 22 CHARLES'*s*] *L, Ca, Cb, B*; *At Charles's O* 24–5 whether Mr.] *O*; whether *L, Ca, Cb*; whither *B* 26 Mr.—] *O, L, B*; Mr. Moses *Ca, Cb* *aside*] *Ca* [S.]; *om. O, L, Cb, B* 28 TRIP *taking*] *O, Ca, Cb, B*; taking *L*

[1] Cf. Garrick's *Bon Ton*, Act I: '*Lady Minikin*: He's a colonel: his elder brother, Sir Tan Tivy, will certainly break his neck, and then my friend will be a happy man.'

Pictures—etc.—just as the old Gentleman left—it—Sir Peter thought it a great Piece of Extravagance in him!

SIR OLIVER. In my mind the other's œconomy in selling it to him was more reprehensible by half.—

Re-enter TRIP.

TRIP. My Master says you must wait Gentlemen. He has Company and can't Speak with you yet.—

SIR OLIVER. If He knew who it was wanted to see him perhaps He wouldn't have sent such a Message.

TRIP. Yes—yes—Sir—He knows you are here—I didn't forget little Premium—no, no, no—

SIR OLIVER. Very well—and I pray Sir what may be your Name?—

TRIP. Trip Sir—my Name is Trip at your Service.

SIR OLIVER. Well then Mr. Trip—you have a pleasant sort of a place here I guess.

TRIP. Why yes—here are three or four of us pass our time agreeably enough—but then our wages are sometimes a little in arrear—and not very great either—but fifty Pounds a year and find our own Bags[1] and Bouquets[2]—

SIR OLIVER. [*Aside*] Bags and Bouquets!—Halters and Bastinadoes!—

TRIP. But à propos Moses—have you been able to get me that little Bill discounted?

SIR OLIVER. Wants to raise Money too!—mercy on me—has his distresses I warrant like a Lord—and affects Creditors and Duns!

MOSES. 'Twas not to be done indeed Mr. Trip—[*gives the Note.*]

TRIP. Good lack—you surprize me—my Friend Brush has indorsed it and I thought when he put his Mark on the Back of a Bill 'twas as good as cash—

MOSES. No 'twouldn't do—

TRIP. A small—sum—but twenty Pounds—hearkee Moses do you think you couldn't get it me by way of annuity?

5 *Re-enter*] *Ca*; *Enter O*, *L*, *Cb*, *B* 6 says . . . Gentlemen] *L*, *Ca*, *Cb*, *B*; Gentlemen says you must wait *O* 11 no, no, no] *L*, *Ca*, *Cb*, *B*; no—no *O* 12 I] *L*, *Ca*, *Cb*, *B*; *om. O* 14 Trip] *L*, *Ca*, *Cb*, *B*; Trip—I presume your Master is seldom without company.

TRIP. Very seldom Sir—the world says ill-natured things of him but 'tis all malice—no man was ever better beloved. Sir he seldom sits down to dinner without a dozen particular Friends—

SIR OLIVER. He's very happy indeed—well—master Trip *O*

20 *Aside*] *Ca*; *om. O*, *L*, *Cb*, *B* 25 Mr. Trip] *L*, *Ca*, *Cb*, *B*; *om. O* *gives . . . Note*] *L*, *Ca*, *B*; *om. O*, *Cb* 31 couldn't] *Ca*, *Cb*, *B*; could *O*, *L*

[1] A pouch of silk for the tail of a bag-wig.

[2] The English fop in Paris 'tops the mode with a white feather, red heels, and an immense *bouquet*' (*Town and Country Magazine*, v (1773), 261).

SIR OLIVER. An annuity! ha! ha! ha! a Footman raise Money by annuity—well done Luxury egad!

MOSES. But you must ensure your Place.

TRIP. O with all my Heart—I'll ensure my Place and my Life too if you Please—

SIR OLIVER. It's more than I would your neck.

TRIP. But then, Moses, it must be done before this d——d register[1] takes place—one wouldn't like to have one's Name made public you know.

MOSES. No certainly, But is there nothing you could deposit.

TRIP. Why, nothing capital of my master's wardrobe has dropp'd lately—but I could give you a mortgage on some of his winter Cloaths with equity of redemption before November—or—you shall have the reversion—of the French Velvet—or a post Obit on the Blue and Silver—These I should think Moses—with a few Pair of Point Ruffles as a collateral security—hey my little Fellow—?

MOSES. Well, well. [*bell rings.*

TRIP. Gad I heard the Bell—I believe Gentlemen I can now introduce you—don't forget the annuity little Moses; this way Gentlemen, ensure my place! you know—

SIR OLIVER. If the man be a shadow of his Master—this is the Temple of Dissipation indeed! [*Exeunt.*

Scene 3d

CHARLES—CARELESS—*etc. etc.*

at a Table with Wine etc.

CHARLES. 'Fore heaven, 'tis true—there's the great Degeneracy of the age—many of our acquaintance have Taste, spirit, and Politeness—but plague on't they won't drink.

3 But] *Ca*, *B*; Well but *Cb*

MOSES. Who would you get to join with you?

TRIP. You know my Lord Applicit [*O* = Applice] you have seen him however.

MOSES. Yes.

TRIP. Very well. You must have observ'd what an appearance he makes—nobody dresses better—nobody throws off faster—very well—his own Gentleman will stand my security.

MOSES. Well—but *O*, *L*

6 would] *Ca*, *B*; would do *O*, *L*, *Cb* 7–9 But . . . certainly] *L*, *Ca*, *B*; *om. O*, *Cb*
14 as] *O*, *Ca*, *B*; is *L*, *Cb* 16 *bell rings*] *Ca* [S.], *Cb*; *om. L*, *B*; We'll talk presently—we detain the Gentleman—

SIR OLIVER. O pray dont let me interrupt Mr. Trip's Negotiation.—*O*

17 Gad] *L*, *Ca*, *B*, *Cb*; Hark *O* 18–19 this way . . . know] *L*, *Ca*, *Cb*, *B*; *om. O*
19 ensure] *L*, *Ca*, *B*; *om. O*; I ensure *Cb* 24 *a*] *L*, *Ca*, *Cb*, *B*; *om. O* *with*] *O*, *L*, *Ca*, *Cb*; *drinking B*

[1] See p. 301.

CARELESS. It is so indeed Charles—they give into all the Substantial Luxuries of the Table—and abstain from nothing but wine and wit—

CHARLES. O certainly Society suffers by it intolerably—for now instead of the social spirit of Raillery that used to mantle over a glass of bright Burgundy their conversation is become just like the Spa water they drink which has all the Pertness and flatulence of Champaine without its Spirit or Flavour.—

1ST. GENT. But what are they to do who love Play better than wine?

CARELESS. True—there's Harry diets himself—for Gaming and is now under a Hazard—Regimen—

CHARLES. Then He'll have the worst of it—what you wouldn't train a horse for the course by keeping him from corn—for my Part egad I am now—never so successful as when I am a little—merry—let me throw on a Bottle of Champaine and I never lose—at least I never feel my losses which is exactly the same thing.

2D. GENT. Aye—that I believe.

CHARLES. And then what man can pretend to be a Believer in Love who is an abjuror of Wine—tis the Test by which the Lover knows his own Heart, fill a dozen Bumpers to a dozen Beauties—and she that floats at top is the Maid that has bewitch'd you—

CARELESS. Now then Charles—be honest and give us your real favorite—

CHARLES. Why I have withheld her only in compassion to you—if I toast her you must give a round of her Peers which is impossible! on earth!

CARELESS. O then we'll find some canonized Vestals or heathen Goddesses that will do I warrant—

CHARLES. Here then—Bumpers—you Rogues—Bumpers!—Maria——Maria—[*drink*]

1ST. GENT. Maria who?

CHARLES. O damn the Surname! 'tis too formal to be register'd in Love's Calendar.—but now Sir Toby Bumper beware—we must have Beauty superlative.

CARELESS. Nay never Study Sir Toby—we'll Stand to The toast—tho' your mistress should want an Eye—and you know you have a song will excuse you—

5 Spa] *O*, *L*, *Ca*, *Cb*; Spaw *B* 7 its] *O*, *L*, *Ca*, *B*; the *Cb* 11 of it] *O*, *L*, *Ca*, *B*; on't *Cb* 13 now] *O*, *L*, *Ca*, *B*; *om.* *Cb* 16 I believe] *L*, *Ca*, *Cb*, *B*; may be—but it is as impossible to follow wine and Play—as to unite Love and Politics *O* 17 And then what] *L*, *Ca*, *Cb*, *B*; Pshaw you may do both.—Caesar made Love and Laws in a Breath—and was liked by the Senate as well as the Ladies—but no *O* 18 the Lover] *Ca*, *Cb*, *B*; Love *L*; a Lover *O* 19–20 at top] *Ca*, *B*; atop *O*, *L*; a Top *Cb* 21 your . . . favorite] *L*, *Ca*, *Cb*, *B*; yours *O* 22 if] *O*, *L*, *Ca*, *B*; and if *Cb* 27 *drink*] *Ca* [S.]; *om.* *O*, *L*, *Cb*, *B* 30 Sir Toby Bumper] *Ca*; Careless *O*, *L*; Sir Harry *Cb*, *B* Beauty] *Ca*; Beauty's *O*, *L*, *Cb*, *B* 32 CARELESS.] *Ca*, *Cb*, *B*; 1ST. GENT. *O*, *L* Sir Toby] *Ca*; Careless *O*, *L*; Sir Harry *Cb*, *B*

SIR TOBY. Egad so I have—and I'll give him the Song instead of the Lady.—

Song[1] *and Chorus*

Here's to the maiden of Bashful fifteen
Here's to the Widow of Fifty
Here's to the flaunting, Extravagant Quean,
And here's to the House Wife that's thrifty.

CHORUS. Let the toast pass—
Drink to the Lass—
I'll warrant She'll prove an Excuse for the Glass!

2d.

Here's to the Charmer whose Dimples we Prize!
Now to the Maid who has none Sir;
Here's to the Girl with a pair of blue Eyes,
—And Here's to the Nymph with but one Sir!

CHORUS. Let the Toast pass etc.

3d.

Here's to the Maid with a Bosom of Snow,
Now to her that's as brown as a berry:
Here's to the Wife with a face full of Woe,
And now for the Damsel that's Merry.

CHORUS. Let the Toast pass etc.

4th.

For let 'Em be Clumsy or let 'Em be Slim
Young or Ancient, I care not a Feather:
—So fill a Pint Bumper Quite up to the Brim
—And let us E'en toast 'Em together!

CHORUS. Let the Toast pass etc.

ALL.—Bravo. Bravo!

1 SIR TOBY] *Ca*; Careless, *O*, *L*; Sir Harry *Cb*, *B* 3 *and Chorus*] *O*, *Ca*, *Cb*, *B*; *om. L* 4–22 Here's to . . . Toast pass etc.] *Ca*, *Cb*, *B*; *om. O*, *L* 23–9 4th/For . . . Bravo!] *Ca*, *Cb*, *B*; *om. O*, *L* 29 ALL.—Bravo. Bravo!] *Ca*, *B*; Bravo *Cb*;
2ND GENT. Bravo Careless—there's Toast and Sentiment too.
1ST GENT. Efaith there's infinite charity in that Song *O*, *L*

[1] Sichel, i. 576, denies that its source was a song in *The Goblins*:

A health to the nut-brown lass,
With the hazle eyes, let it pass,
She that has good eyes
Has good thighs:
Let it pass, . . . let it pass.

(*The Works of Sir John Suckling* (1770), ii. 313.) See, too, p. 804 below.

Enter TRIP *and Whispers* CHARLES.

CHARLES. Gentlemen you must excuse me a little—Careless take the Chair will you?

CARELESS. Nay prithee Charles—what now—this is one of your Peerless Beauties I suppose—has dropt in by chance.

CHARLES. No—Faith—to tell you the Truth 'tis a Jew—and a broker who are come—by appointment.

CARELESS. O damn it let's have the Jew in—

1ST. GENT. Aye and the Broker too by all means—

2ND. GENT. Yes yes the Jew and the Broker.

CHARLES. Egad with all my Heart—Trip—bid the Gentlemen walk in—tho' there's one of them a Stranger I can tell you—

CARELESS. Charles—let us Give them some generous Burgundy—and perhaps they'll grow conscientious.

CHARLES. O Hang 'em—no—wine does but draw forth a man's natural qualities and to make them drink would only be to whet their Knavery.—

Enter TRIP—SIR OLIVER *and* MOSES.

CHARLES. So—honest Moses—walk in—walk in, pray Mr. Premium—that's the Gentleman's name isn't it Moses?

MOSES. Yes Sir.

CHARLES. Set Chairs—Trip—sit down Mr. Premium—Glasses Trip—Sit down Moses.—come Mr. Premium I'll give you a sentiment[1]—Here's Success to Usury—Moses fill the Gentleman a Bumper.

MOSES. Success to Usury—

CARELESS. Right Moses—Usury is Prudence and industry and deserves to succeed—

SIR OLIVER. Then Here is all the success it deserves.

CARELESS. No, no—that won't do Mr. Premium, you have demur'd to the Toast, and must Drink it in a Pint Bumper.

1ST. GENT. A Pint Bumper at least.

1 *and*] *L*, *Ca*, *Cb*, *B*; *om. O* 8 let's] *L*, *Ca*, *Cb*, *B*; lest's *O* 11 Gentlemen] *O*, *Ca*, *Cb*, *B*; Gentleman *L* 13 Charles] *Ca*, *Cb*, *B*;
TRIP. What Sir would you chuse Mr. Premium to come up with—
1ST GENT. Yes—Yes—Mr. Premium certainly—
CARELESS. To be sure Mr. Premium by all means—Charles *O*, *L*
18 Moses . . . pray] *O*, *L*, *B*; Moses, walk in, walk in, pray walk in *Cb*; Moses, walk in—pray *Ca* 19 it] *L*, *Ca*, *Cb*, *B*; *om. O* 21 Trip] *Ca*, *Cb*, *B*; Trim *O*, *L*
27 *After* '*deserves*', *insert*:
CHARLES. Mr. Premium you and I are but Strangers yet but I hope we shall be better acquainted by and bye.
SIR OLIVER. Yes Sir I hope we shall—more intimate perhaps than you'll wish (*aside*) *O*, *L*. *There is a gap in O MS. from this point to p. 409, l. 18.* 28 to] *Ca*, *B*; at *L*, *Cb*

[1] Cf. Edward Bull's statement in Frances Sheridan's *A Journey to Bath*: 'I have drunk sentiments very often, we give them for toasts' (Rae, p. 281).

MOSES. O Pray Sir consider Mr. Premium's a Gentleman.

CARELESS. And therefore loves good Wine.

2D. GENT Give Moses a Quart Glass—this is Mutiny, and a High contempt of the Chair.

CARELESS. Here—now for't—I'll see Justice done to the last drop of my Bottle.

SIR OLIVER. Nay pray Gentlemen—I did not Expect this Usage.

CHARLES. No—hang it—Careless—you Shan't: Mr. Premium's a Stranger.

SIR OLIVER. Odd—I wish I was well out of this Company.

CARELESS. Plague on 'Em then—if they won't Drink—we'll not Sit down with 'em; come Harry the Dice are in the next Room; Charles you'll Join us—when you have finish'd your Business with these Gentlemen—

CHARLES. I will. I will.—[*Exeunt*] Careless—!

CARELESS. Well—

CHARLES. Perhaps I may want you.

CARELESS. O you know I am always ready—Word, Note—or Bond 'tis all the same to me. [*Exit.*

MOSES. Sir—this is Mr. Premium, a Gentleman of the Strictest honour and Secrecy—and always performs what he undertakes—Mr. Premium this is—

CHARLES. Pshaw have done!—Sir, my Friend Moses is a very honest fellow, but a little Slow at Expression, he'll be an Hour giving us our Titles—Mr. Premium—the Plain State of the Matter is this—I am an Extravagant young Fellow, who want[s] Money to Borrow,[1] you I take to be a Prudent old Fellow, who has got Money to lend—I am Blockhead enough to give Fifty per Cent. sooner than not have it, and you I presume are Rogue Enough to take a hundred if you could get it,—Now Sir, you See we are acquainted at once, and may proceed to Business without farther Ceremony.

SIR OLIVER. Exceeding frank upon my Word—I see Sir, you are not a Man of many Compliments.

CHARLES. O No Sir—plain Dealing in Business I always think best.

SIR OLIVER. Sir—I like you the better for't—however you are Mistaken in one thing—I have no Money to lend. But I believe I could procure some of a Friend; but then he's an unconscionable Dog isn't he Moses? and must sell Stock to accom[m]odate you—mustn't he Moses?

6 Bottle] *Ca*, *Cb*, *B*; wine *L* 10 this] *Ca*; their *L*, *Cb*, *B* 13 these] *Ca*, *B*; the *Cb*
14 *Exeunt*] *Ca*, *Cb*, *B*; 1 GENT. And do Moses—let Charles bring in a few Notes in his pocket for egad he'll win his thousands, and pay you like a Nabob. *L*
18 *Exit*] *Ca*; (*Exit Careless*) *B*; *om.* *L*, *Cb* 20 performs] *L*, *Ca*, *Cb*; perform *B*
26 has] *B*; have *L*, *Ca*, *Cb* 28 could] *L*, *Ca*, *B*; can *Cb*

[1] See p. 5 above.

MOSES. Yes indeed!—you know I always speak the truth, and Scorn to tell a lie.

CHARLES. Right! People that Expect truth Generally do—but these are Trifles Mr. Premium—What—I know money isn't to be bought without paying for't.

SIR OLIVER. Well but what Security could you give—you have no Land I suppose?

CHARLES. Not a Mole-hill—nor a Twig, but what's in beau pots out at the Window.

SIR OLIVER. Nor any Stock I presume.

CHARLES. Nothing but live stock—and that's only a few Pointers and Ponies. But pray Mr. Premium are you acquainted at all with any of my connections—

SIR OLIVER. Why to say truth I am.

CHARLES. Then you must know that I have a devilish rich Uncle in the East Indies—Sir Oliver Surface—from whom I have the greatest Expectations.

SIR OLIVER. That you have a Wealthy Uncle I have heard—but how your Expectations will turn out is more I believe than you can tell.

CHARLES. O no—there can be no doubt of it—they tell me I'm a prodigious Favorite—and that he talks of leaving me every thing.

SIR OLIVER. Indeed this is the first I've heard on't.

CHARLES. Yes, yes—tis just so—Moses knows 'tis true—don't you Moses?

MOSES. O yes—I'll swear to't—

SIR OLIVER. Egad they'll persuade me presently I'm at Bengal.

CHARLES. Now I propose Mr. Premium if it's agreeable to you to Grant you a Post Obit on Sir Oliver's Life tho' at the same time the Old Fellow has been so liberal to me that I give you my word I should be very Sorry to hear any thing had happen'd to him.

SIR OLIVER. Not more than I should I assure you; But the bond you mention happens to be Just the worst Security you could Offer me—for I might Live to a hundred and never recover the Principal.

CHARLES. O yes you would—the moment Sir Oliver dies you know you'd come on me for the Money.

SIR OLIVER. Then I believe I should be the most unwelcome Dun you Ever had in your Life.

CHARLES. What I suppose you are afraid now that Sir Oliver is too good a Life.

SIR OLIVER. No indeed I am not—tho' I have heard he is as hale and healthy as any Man of his years in Christendom.

CHARLES. There again you are misinformed—No, no, the Climate has

1 Scorn] *Ca*, *Cb*, *B*; I scorn *L* 8 at] *Ca*, *B*; of *L*, *Cb* 20 of it] *Cb* [S.]; *om.* *L*, *Ca*, *B* 32 a] *L*, *Ca*, *Cb*; an *B* 41 again] *Ca*, *B*; again now *L*, *Cb* No, no] *L*, *Ca*, *B*; No *Cb*

hurt him considerably—Poor uncle Oliver—yes he breaks apace I'm told—and so much alter'd lately that his nearest Relations don't know him—

SIR OLIVER. No!—ha! ha! ha! so much altered lately that his Relations don't know him, ha! ha! ha! that's droll egad—ha! ha! ha!—

CHARLES. Ha! ha! you're glad to hear that little Premium.

SIR OLIVER. No—no—I'm not.

CHARLES. Yes, yes, you are—ha! ha! ha!—you know that mends your Chance.

SIR OLIVER. But I'm told Sir Oliver is coming over—nay some say he is Actually Arrived.

CHARLES. Pshaw! Sure I must know better than you whether He's come or not—no, no, rely on't, he is at this Moment at Calcutta, isn't he Moses?

MOSES. O yes certainly.

SIR OLIVER. Very true, as you Say—you must know better than I; tho' I have it from pretty good Authority—hav'nt I Moses?

MOSES. Yes—most undoubted—

SIR OLIVER. But Sir—as I understand you want a few hundreds immediately—is there nothing you would dispose of?

CHARLES. How do you mean?

SIR OLIVER. For instance now—I have heard—that your Father left behind him a Great Quantity of Massy old Plate—

CHARLES. O Lud that's gone, long ago—Moses can tell you how better than I can—

SIR OLIVER. Good lack! all the Family Race cups and Corporation Bowls! [*aside*]—then it was also Suppos'd that his Library was one of the most Valuable and compleat—

CHARLES. Yes—yes. So it was—vastly too much so for a private Gentleman—for my part I was always of a Communicative disposition, So I thought it a Shame to keep so much knowledge to myself—

SIR OLIVER. Mercy on me! Learning that had run in the Family like an Heir Loom! Pray what are become of the Books?

CHARLES. You must Enquire of the Auctioneer, Master Premium, for I don't believe Even Moses can direct you there.

MOSES. I never Meddle with Books.

1 uncle] *L*, *Ca*, *B*; *om. Cb* yes] *L*, *Ca*, *B*; Yes, yes *Cb* 5 egad—ha! ha! ha!] *L*, *Ca*, *B*; egad *Cb* 12–13 Pshaw! . . . or not] *Ca*, *Cb*, *B*; No such thing depend on't. You must not mind what People say—if he had been come, you must know I must have heard on't *L* 14 *After 'certainly', insert*:

SIR OLIVER. Well but I have been positively told.

CHARLES. Pshaw! Sure I must know better than you whether he's come or not. *L*

21 that] *L*, *Ca*, *B*; *om. Cb* 24 can] *L*, *Ca*, *Cb*; *om. B* 26 *aside*] *Ca* [S.], *Cb* [S.]; *om. L*, *B* 28 Yes—yes] *Ca*, *Cb*, *B*; Aye, yes, yet *L* 30 myself] *Ca*, *Cb*, *B*; one's self *L* 31 me] *L*, *Ca*, *B*; us *Cb* had] *L*, *Ca*, *B*; has *Cb* 35 MOSES. . . . books] *Ca*, *Cb*, *B*; *om. L*

SIR OLIVER. So—so—nothing of the Family Property left I suppose.

CHARLES. Not much Indeed, unless you have a mind to the Family Pictures[1]—I have got a Room full of Ancestors above—and if you have a Taste for old Paintings Egad, you shall have 'Em a Bargain.

SIR OLIVER. Hey! and the Devil! Sure you wouldn't Sell your Forefathers—would you?

CHARLES. Every man of 'Em to the best bidder—

SIR OLIVER. What your great Uncles and Aunts?

CHARLES. Aye, and my Great grand Fathers and Grandmothers too.

SIR OLIVER. Now I give him up!—[*aside*]—what the plague have you no Bowels for your own kindred?—Odds Life—do you take me for Shylock in the Play, that you would raise Money of me, on your own Flesh and Blood?

CHARLES. Nay, my little Broker—don't be angry—what need you care, If you have your Money's worth?

SIR OLIVER. Well—I'll be the purchaser—I think I can dispose of the Family—Oh I'll never forgive him—this—never!

Enter CARELESS.

CARELESS. Come Charles—what keeps you?

CHARLES. I can't come yet a'faith! we are going to have a Sale above—here's little Premium will buy all my Ancestors—

CARELESS. Oh burn your ancestors—

CHARLES. No, he may do that afterwards if he pleases: Stay Careless we want you, Egad you shall be Auctioneer. So come along with us.

CARELESS. Oh, have with you, If that's the Case—I can handle a hammer as well as a Dice Box!

SIR OLIVER. Oh the Profligates!

CHARLES. Come Moses—you shall be appraiser if we want one, gads Life, little Premium, you don't seem to like the business.

SIR OLIVER. Oh yes I do vastly—ha, ha, yes, yes, I think it a rare Joke to Sell one's Family by Auction, ha! ha! Oh, the prodigal!

CHARLES. To be Sure! when a man wants money, where the plague should he get Assistance,—If he can't make free with his own Relations. [*Exeunt*.

END OF THE THIRD ACT

9 Aye] *L*, *Ca*, *B*; Yes *Cb* 10 *aside*] *Ca* [S.]; *om. Cb*, *B* 11 own] *L*, *Ca*, *Cb*; *om. B* 17 Family] *Ca*; Family canvass *L*, *Cb*, *B* this—never] *L*, *Ca*, *B*; this No—never *Cb* 25 Oh] *L*, *Ca*, *B*; *om. Cb* 28–9 gads Life] *L*, *Ca*, *B*; *om. Cb* 31 ha! ha!] *L*, *Ca*, *B*; *om. Cb*

[1] Cf. Sir Jeremy's statement in Frances Sheridan's *A Journey to Bath*: 'Why the land and the Mansion house has slippd thro' our finger's boy; but thank heaven the family pictures are still extant' (Rae, p. 312).

Act 4th. Scene 1st

Picture Room at CHARLES'*s*

Enter CHARLES, SIR OLIVER, MOSES *and* CARELESS.

CHARLES. Walk in Gentlemen, pray walk in!—here they are, the family of the Surfaces up to the Conquest.

SIR OLIVER. And, in my opinion a goodly Collection.

CHARLES. Aye, Aye, these are done in the true spirit of Portrait-Painting—no Volunteer Grace, or Expression—not like the Works of your Modern Raphael,[1] who gives you the strongest resemblance[2] yet contrives to make your own Portrait independent of you[3]—So that you may Sink the Original and not hurt the Picture—no—no, the merit of these is the Inveterate likeness[4]—all Stiff and Aukward as the Originals and like nothing in human Nature beside!

SIR OLIVER. Ah! we shall never see such Figures of men again.

CHARLES. No, I hope not, you See Master Premium what a domestic Character I am—here I sit of an Evening Surrounded by my Family—But come get to your Pulpit Mr. Auctioneer—here's an old Gouty chair[5] of my Grandfather's—will Answer the purpose.

15 No . . . not] *Cb* [S.]; I hope not; well *L*, *Ca*, *B*

---

[1] A cutting (in the Folger Library) from an unnamed newspaper, but dated 14 Apr. 1779, describes an Opera House masquerade, at which were present 'our modern Raphael and his lovely companions, Sir Joshua, with his three Graces'. Sheridan also made the comparison in *Verses to the Memory of Garrick*, lines 25–6 (p. 459 below).

[2] Cf. Edmond Malone's opinion: 'The two portraits which Sir Joshua Reynolds has lately painted of Mr. William Windham of Norfolk and Richard Brinsley Sheridan are so like the originals, that they seem almost alive and ready to speak to you. Painting, in point of resemblance, can go no farther' (James Prior, *The Life of Edmond Malone* (1860), p. 388).

[3] Sir Joshua showed thirteen pictures at the Royal Academy exhibition of 1777, and the *Morning Chronicle*, 25 Apr. 1777, remarked of them: 'As the face of every portrait is the speaking part of the picture, Sir Joshua is particularly happy in giving all his figures such force of expression, that scarce a person looks at them without entering into a kind of colloquy with the picture.'

[4] Cf. Wycherley, *The Plain Dealer*, II: 'I find one may have a collection of all ones acquaintances Pictures, as well at your house, as at Mr. *Lely's*; only the difference is, there we find 'em much handsomer than they are, and like; here much uglier, and like' (*Complete Works*, ed. M. Summers (1924), i. 123).

[5] Paraphrased in *The Public Register: or Freeman's Journal*, 27–29 Jan. 1778, as 'an old easy chair', but this may still have meant one particularly adapted for sufferers of gout, as is evident in Horace Walpole's letter to Mann, 3 Jan. 1778 (*Walpole Corr.*, viii. 346). See for 'a gouty stool', plate 15 from Hepplewhite's *Cabinet Maker and Upholsterer's Guide* (1788), reproduced in John Gloag, *Georgian Grace* (1956), p. 163. Some verses on 'The Gouty Chair, and Chimney Corner', by 'Lister Esq.', are printed in *Poetical Amusements at a Villa near Bath* (2nd edn., 1776), iv. 105–11.

CARELESS. Aye—aye—this will do—but Charles I have ne'er a Hammer and what's an Auctioneer without his Hammer?

CHARLES. Egad, that's true, What parchment have we here? [*takes down a roll*] *Richard Heir to Thomas*—our genealogy in full! Here Careless you shall have no Common bit of Mahogany—Here's the Family Tree for you, you Rogue—this shall be your Hammer, and now you may knock down my Ancestors with their own Pedigree.

SIR OLIVER. What an unnatural Rogue! an ex post facto Parricide!

CARELESS. Yes, yes, here's a list of your Generation indeed.—faith Charles—this is the most Convenient thing you could have found for the Business, for 'twill Serve not only as a Hammer, but a Catalogue into the Bargain—but come begin—a going—a going—a going!—

CHARLES. Bravo! Careless—well here's my Great uncle Sir Richard Raviline[1]—a Marvellous good General in his Day I assure you—He served in all the Duke of Marlborough's Wars; and got that cut over his Eye at the Battle of Malplaquet;[2] What say you Mr. Premium—look at him—there's a Hero for you! not cut out of his Feathers, as your Modern clipt Captains are[3]—but enveloped in Wig and Regimentals as a General should be—what do you bid?

MOSES. Mr. Premium would have you Speak—

CHARLES. Why then he shall have him for ten Pounds and I am Sure that's not Dear for a Staff Officer.

SIR OLIVER. Heaven deliver me! his famous uncle Richard for Ten pounds! Very well Sir—I take him at that.

CHARLES. Careless, knock down my uncle Richard—Here now is a Maiden Sister of his, my Great Aunt Deborah done by Kneller thought to be in his best Manner;[4] and a very formidable Likeness—There She is you See—A Shepherdess feeding her flock—you shall have her for five pounds Ten—the Sheep are worth the Money.[5]

SIR OLIVER. Ah! poor Deborah—a woman who set such a Value on herself!—Five pound ten! She's mine.

3–4 *takes . . . roll*] *Ca* [S.]; reading a Roll *Cb* [S.]; *om. L, B*   4 our] *Ca, Cb*; O our *L, B*   12 but come begin] *Ca, Cb, B*; *om. L*   16–17 look at him] *L, Ca, B*; *om. Cb*   17 for you] *Ca* [S.]; *om. L, Cb, B*   31 pound] *Ca, Cb, B*; pounds *L*

---

1 A ravelin was a fortification with two faces at an angle to the main structure.

2 The English and allied troops were commanded by Marlborough and Prince Eugène at this battle, fought on 11 Sept. 1709, in the War of the Spanish Succession.

3 Without the plumes, but (as paraphrased in the *Public Register*, 27–29 Jan. 1778) 'with the *friseur* of the modern officer'.

4 Sir Godfrey Kneller (1646–1723). For his 'thinly painted method', see C. H. Collins-Baker, *Lely and Kneller* (1922), pp. 104–5.

5 Cf. *The Vicar of Wakefield*: 'Sophia was to be a shepherdess, with as many sheep as the painter could put in for nothing' (*Collected Works of Oliver Goldsmith*, ed. A. Friedman (Oxford, 1966), iv. 83).

CHARLES. Knock down my aunt Deborah! Here now are two that were a Sort of Cousins of theirs—you see Moses these Pictures were done some time ago—when Beaux wore Wigs,[1] and the Ladies wore their own Hair.

SIR OLIVER. Yes truly Head dresses appear to have been a little lower[2] in those Days.

CHARLES. Well take that Couple for the same.

MOSES. Tis good Bargain.

CHARLES. Careless!—This now is a Grandfather of my Mother's, a learned Judge, well known on the Western Circuit—What do you rate him at Moses?

MOSES. Four Guineas.

CHARLES. Four guineas! Gads Life, you don't bid me the Price of his Wig! Mr. Premium—you have more respect for the Woolsack—do let us knock his Lordship down at fifteen.

SIR OLIVER. By all means—

CARELESS. Gone.—

CHARLES. And there are two Brothers of his William and Walter Blunt Esquires both Members of Parliament and Noted Speakers, and what's very Extraordinary, I believe this is the first time they were ever bought and Sold.

SIR OLIVER. That's very extraordinary Indeed! I'll take them at your own Price for the Honour of Parliament.

CARELESS. Well said Little Premium—I'll knock 'em down at forty.

CHARLES. Here's a Jolly Fellow—I don't know what Relation—But he was Mayor of Manchester,[3] take him at Eight pounds.

SIR OLIVER. No, no—six will do for the Mayor.

CHARLES. Come make it Guineas and I'll throw you the two Aldermen there into the Bargain.—

SIR OLIVER. They're mine.

CHARLES. Careless—knock down the Mayor and Aldermen—but Plague on't we shall be all Day—retailing in this manner, do let us deal Wholesale—what say you little Premium—give me three hundred pounds, for the Rest of the family in the Lump.

9 on] *Ca*, *Cb*, *B*; in *L* 25 Manchester] *Ca*; Bristol *L*; Norwich *Cb*, *B* 31 in this] *Ca*, *Cb*, *B*; thus *L* 33 for . . . family] *L*, *Ca*; and take all that Remains on each side *Cb*, *B*

---

[1] Cf. Garrick's prologue to *A Trip to Scarborough* (p. 570 below), lines 19–22.

[2] 'The female head dress had now reached the highest degree of ridicule. It was time for the stage to lay hold of such extreme folly . . .' (*Chester Chronicle*, 12 Feb. 1776). Garrick derided it when playing Sir John Brute at this date, and Foote, as Lady Pentweazle, wore a head-dress a yard wide and full of ostrich feathers.

[3] The name of the town may have been varied to satisfy local prejudices. The comedy was such a success at Manchester that 'the theatre was in danger of being destroyed by the crowd who pressed for places' (*Morning Chronicle*, 19 June 1778).

CARELESS. Aye—aye—that will be the best way.—

SIR OLIVER. Well, well, any thing to accommodate you, they are mine. —but there is one Portrait, which you have always passed Over—

CARELESS. What, that ill looking little Fellow over the Settee

SIR OLIVER. Yes Sir I mean that, tho' I don't think him so ill looking a little Fellow by any means.

CHARLES. What that? Oh that's my unkle Oliver, 'twas done before he went to India—

CARELESS. Your Uncle Oliver! Gad! then you'll never be friends Charles, That now to me is as Stern a looking Rogue as Ever I saw—an Unforgiving Eye, and a damn'd disinheriting Countenance! an Inveterate Knave depend on't, don't you think so little Premium?

SIR OLIVER. Upon my Soul Sir, I do not; I think it is as honest a looking Face as any in the Room—dead or alive; but I suppose your Uncle Oliver goes with the rest of the Lumber

CHARLES. No hang it, I'll not part with poor Noll—The Old Fellow has been very good to me, and Egad I'll keep his Picture, while I've a Room to put it in.

SIR OLIVER. [*aside*] The rogue's my nephew after all!—but, sir, I have Somehow taken a fancy to that Picture.

CHARLES. I'm sorry for't, for you certainly will not have it—Oons! haven't you got enough of 'Em?

SIR OLIVER. I forgive him everything! [*aside*]—but Sir when I take a Whim in my Head I don't Value Money—I'll give as much for that as for all the rest—

CHARLES. Don't teize me, Master Broker, I tell you I'll not part with it—And there's an End on't—

SIR OLIVER. How like his Father the Dog is! [*aside*] well, well, I have done; I did not perceive it before but I think I never Saw such a Resemblance [*aside*]—well Sir—Here is a Draught for your Sum.

CHARLES. Why 'tis for Eight hundred pounds!

SIR OLIVER. You will not let Oliver go?

CHARLES. Z——ds! no I tell you once more.

SIR OLIVER. Then never mind the Difference; we'll Ballance another time, but give me your hand on the Bargain—you are an Honest Fellow Charles—I beg pardon Sir for being so free,—come Moses,—

CHARLES. Egad this is a Whimsical old Fellow—but hearkee Premium, you'll prepare Lodgings for these Gentlemen.

SIR OLIVER. Yes, Yes, I'll send for them in a Day or two—

4 Settee] *Ca*, *Cb*, *B*; door *L* 13 is] *Ca*; *om. L*, *Ca*, *B* 19 *aside*] *Ca* [S.], *Cb* [S.]; *om. L*, *B* 21 you certainly will] *L*, *Ca*, *B*; you'l certainly *Cb* 23 *aside*] *Ca* [S.]; *om. L*, *Cb*, *B* 27 there's] *Ca*, *Cb*; there *B* 28 *aside*] *Ca* [S.]; *om. L*, *Cb*, *B* 30 *aside*] *B*; *om. L*, *Ca*, *Cb* your] *L*, *Ca*, *Cb*; the *B*

CHARLES. But hold—do now—Send a Genteel Conveyance for them, for I Assure you they were most of them used to Ride in their own Carriages.

SIR OLIVER. I will, I will, for all but—Oliver—

CHARLES. Aye all, but the little honest nabob.[1]

SIR OLIVER. You're fixed on that—

CHARLES. Peremptorily.

SIR OLIVER. A Dear extravagant Rogue! Good day come Moses,—let me hear now who dares call him Profligate!

[*Exeunt* SIR OLIVER *and* MOSES.

CARELESS. Why this is the Oddest Genius—of the Sort I ever Saw.

CHARLES. Egad he's the Prince of Brokers I think, I wonder how the Devil Moses got acquainted with so honest a fellow—hah! here's Rowley, do Careless; Say I'll join the Company in a Moment—

CARELESS. I will,—but don't now let that old Blockhead persuade you—to Squander any of that Money on old Musty debts, or any such Nonsense for tradesmen—Charles, are the most Exorbitant Fellows!—

CHARLES. Very true, and paying them is only Encouraging them.

CARELESS. Nothing else.

CHARLES. Aye—Aye—never fear.—[*Exit* CARELESS] Soh—this was an Odd old Fellow Indeed! Let me See, two thirds of this is mine by Right; five hundred and thirty pounds 'Fore Heaven, I find one's Ancestors are more Valuable Relations than I took 'Em for!—Ladies and Gentlemen, your most Obedient and very Grateful humble Servant,—[*Enter* ROWLEY]—hah! old Rowley, Egad, you are Just come in Time, to take leave of your Old Acquaintance—

ROWLEY. Yes I heard they were going—but I wonder you can have such Spirits under so many Distresses.

CHARLES. Why there's the point,—my Distresses are so many that I can't afford to part with my Spirits, but I shall be rich and Splenetic all in good time; however I suppose you are Surprized that I am not more sorrowful at parting with so many near Relations, to be Sure 'tis very affecting—but rot 'Em you See they never move a muscle, So why should I.

5 honest] *Ca*; *om. L*, *Cb*, *B* 10 *Exeunt . . . Moses*] *Ca* [S.]; Exit *Sir Oliver* & Moses *Cb*, *B*; *Exit with Moses L* 13 hah]! *L*, *Ca*, *Cb*; But hah! *B* 16 on] *Ca*, *B*; in *L*, *Cb* 21 this is] *L*, *Ca*, *Cb*; this five hundred and thirty odd Pounds are *B* 22 five . . . pounds] *Ca*; *om. B*; Five Hundred and thirty odd Pounds *Cb*; five hundred and sixty *L*

[1] A civil or military official of the East India Company, who made a fortune during his stay in India. It is interesting to find that the word 'honest' appeared in the text presented to Mrs. Crewe: the reputation of the 'nabobs' grew steadily worse between 1760 and 1785. For a full discussion, see James M. Holzman, *The Nabobs in England. A Study of the Retired Anglo-Indian, 1760–85* (New York, 1926).

ROWLEY. There's no making—you Serious a Moment.

CHARLES. Yes faith: I am so now—here my honest Rowley here get me this chang'd, and take a hundred pounds of it immediately to old Stanley—

ROWLEY. A Hundred pounds—Consider only—

CHARLES. Gad's Life don't talk about it poor Stanley's wants are pressing—and if you don't make haste we shall have some one call that has a better Right to the Money—

ROWLEY. Ah! there's the point.—I never will cease Dunning you with the Old Proverb—

CHARLES. 'Be Just before you're Generous' hey!—why so I would if I could—but Justice is an Old lame hobbling Beldame—and I can't Get her to keep pace with Generosity, for the Soul of Me.[1]—

ROWLEY. Yet, Charles, believe me—one hour's reflection—

CHARLES. Aye—Aye—its all very true—but hearkee, Rowley while I have, by heaven I'll give—so Damn your economy—and now for hazard . . . . [*Exeunt.*

Scene 2d: the Parlour

Enter SIR OLIVER *and* MOSES.

MOSES. Well Sir I think as Sir Peter said you have seen Mr. Charles in high Glory—'tis great Pity He's so extravagant.

SIR OLIVER. True—but He wouldn't Sell my Picture—

MOSES. And loves wine and women so much—

SIR OLIVER. But He wouldn't Sell my Picture.

MOSES. And game so deep—

SIR OLIVER. But He wouldn't Sell my Picture.—O—here's Rowley!

Enter ROWLEY.

ROWLEY. So—Sir Oliver—I find you have made a Purchase.

SIR OLIVER. Yes—yes—Our young Rake has parted with his Ancestors like Old Tapestry.

ROWLEY. And here has he commission'd me to redeliver you Part of the purchase Money I mean tho' in your necessitous Character of old Stanley—

3 chang'd] *Ca*; chang'd directly *L*, *Cb*, *B* 7 if . . . haste] *Ca*. [S.], *Cb*, *B*; *om. L* 15 all] *L*, *Ca*, *Cb*; *om. B* 17 *Exeunt*] *Cb* [S.], *L*, *B*; (*Exit*) *Ca* 18 *The text of O MS. recommences with this scene.* 30 Tapestry] *Ca*, *Cb*, *B*; Tapestry—sold judges and Generals by the Foot—and maiden Aunts as cheap as broken—China.—*O*, *L* 31 redeliver] *O*, *Ca*, *Cb*, *B*; deliver *L*

[1] Cf. Christopher Smart, *Jubilate Agno*, ed. W. H. Bond (1954), p. 97: 'For Tully says to be generous you must be first just, but the voice of Christ is distribute at all events.'

MOSES. Ah! there is the Pity of all! He is so damn'd charitable.

ROWLEY. And I have left a Hosier and two Tailors in the Hall—who I'm sure won't be paid, and this hundred would Satisfy 'em!

SIR OLIVER. Well—well—I'll pay his Debts—and his Benevolences too—but now I am no more a Broker and you shall introduce me to the elder Brother as Old Stanley.

ROWLEY. Not yet awhile—Sir Peter I know means to call there about this time.—

Enter TRIP.

TRIP. O Gentlemen I beg Pardon for not shewing you out—this way—Moses a Word [*Exeunt* TRIP *and* MOSES.

SIR OLIVER. There's a fellow for you—would you believe it! that Puppy intercepted the Jew, on our coming and wanted to raise money before he got to his master—

ROWLEY. Indeed!—

SIR OLIVER. Yes—they are now planning an annuity Business—ah! Master Rowley in my Day Servants were content with the Follies of their Masters when they were worn a little Thread-Bare but now they have their Vices, like their Birth-Day Cloaths with the Gloss on.— [*Exeunt.*

Scene 3d: A Library

SURFACE *and* SERVANT.

SURFACE. No Letter from Lady Teazle?

SERVANT. No Sir—

SURFACE. I am surprised she hasn't sent if she is prevented from coming—? Sir Peter certainly does not suspect me—yet I wish I may not lose the Heiress, thro' the scrape I have drawn myself in with the wife—However Charles's imprudence and bad character are great Points in my Favour.— [*Knocking.*

SERVANT. Sir—I believe that must be Lady Teazle—

SURFACE. Hold see—whether it is or not before you go to the Door—I have a particular Message for you if it should be my Brother—

SERVANT. 'Tis her Ladyship Sir, She always leaves her Chair at the millener's in the next Street.

SURFACE. Stay—stay—draw that Skreen before the Window—that will do—my opposite Neighbour—is a maiden Lady of so curious a

1 Ah] *O*, *L*, *Ca*, *B*; Ay *Cb* Pity] *O*, *L*, *Ca*, *B*; great pity *Cb* 2 have] *Cb*, [S.]; *om.* *O*, *L*, *Ca*, *B* 5 too—but] *Ca*, *Cb*, *B*; too I'll take care of old Stanley—myself:—but *O* 6 Old] *L*, *Ca*, *Cb*, *B*; *om.* *O* 10 way] *O*, *L*, *Ca*, *Cb*; way Gentlemen *B* 11 *Exeunt*] *O*, *Ca*; (*Exit*) *L*, *Cb*, *B* 12 There's] *L*, *Ca*, *Cb*, *B*; There *O* 17 Day] *O*; Days *L*, *Ca*, *Cb*, *B* 21 *3d:*] *O*, *L*, *Cb*, *B*; *4th Ca* 29 *Knocking*] *Ca* [S.], *B*, *Cb*; (*Knock*) *L*; *om.* *O*

temper!—[*Servant draws the Screen and Exit*] I have a difficult Hand to play in this Affair—Lady Teazle has lately Suspected my Views on Maria—but She must by no means be let into that secret, at least not 'till I have her more in my Power.

Enter LADY TEAZLE.

LADY TEAZLE. What Sentiment in Soliloquy—have you been very impatient now?—O lud! don't pretend to look grave—I vow I couldn't come before—

SURFACE. O Madam Punctuality is a species of constancy, a very unfashionable quality in a Lady.

LADY TEAZLE. Upon my word you ought to pity me, do you know that Sir Peter is grown so ill-temper'd to me of Late!—and so jealous! of Charles too that's the best of the Story isn't it—?

SURFACE. I am glad my scandalous Friends keep that up—[*aside*]

LADY TEAZLE. I am sure I wish He would let Maria marry him—and then perhaps He would be convinced—don't you—Mr. Surface?

SURFACE. Indeed I do not.—[*aside*] O Certainly I do—for then my dear Lady Teazle would also be convinced how wrong her suspicions were—of my having any Design on the silly Girl—[*sit*]

LADY TEAZLE. Well—well I'm inclined to believe you—But isn't it provoking to have the most ill natured Things said to one? and there's my friend Lady Sneerwell has circulated I don't know how many Scandalous Tales of me and all without any Foundation too—that's what vexes me.—

SURFACE. Aye Madam to be sure that is the Provoking circumstance—without Foundation.—yes yes—there's the mortification indeed—for when a slanderous Story is believed against one—there certainly is no comfort—like the consciousness of having deserv'd it—

LADY TEAZLE. No to be sure—then I'd forgive their Malice—but to attack me who am really so innocent—and who never say an ill natured thing of anybody—that is of any Friend—! and then Sir Peter too—to have him so peevish and so suspicious—when I know the integrity of my own Heart[1]—indeed 'tis monstrous.

SURFACE. But my dear Lady Teazle 'tis your own fault if you suffer it—when a Husband entertains a groundless suspicion of his Wife, and

2 on] *O*, *Ca*, *Cb*, *B*; with *L* 3 that] *O*, *L*, *Ca*, *B*; the *Cb* not] *Ca* [S.]; *om.* *O*, *L*, *Cb*, *B* 12 temper'd] *O*, *L*, *Ca*, *Cb*; natur'd *B* 13 best] *O*, *L*, *Ca*, *B*; Jest *Cb* it] *Ca*, *Cb*, *B*; *om.* *O*, *L* 19 *sit*] *Cb* [S.]; *om.* *O*, *L*, *Ca*, *B* 20 it] *L*, *Ca*, *Cb*, *B*; *om.* *O* 21 said to] *O*, *L*, *Ca*, *B*; said of *Cb* 27 slanderous] *O*; scandalous *L*, *Ca*, *Cb*, *B*

[1] Cf. 'The integrity of her own heart makes her liable to be imposed on by a plausible outside; and yet the dear good woman takes a sort of pride in her sagacity' (Frances Sheridan, *Memoirs of Miss Sidney Bidulph* (Dublin (1761), i. 82).

withdraws his confidence from her—the original compact is broke and she owes it to the Honor of her sex to endeavour to outwit him.

LADY TEAZLE. Indeed—so that if He suspects me without cause, it follows that the best way of curing his Jealousy is to give him reason for't.

SURFACE. Undoubtedly—for your Husband should never be deceived—in you—and in that case it becomes you to be frail in compliment to his discernment.

LADY TEAZLE. To be sure what you say is very reasonable—and when the consciousness of my own Innocence—

SURFACE. Ah! my Dear—Madam there is the great mistake—'tis this very conscious Innocence that is of the greatest Prejudice to you—What is it makes you negligent of Forms and careless of the world's opinion?—why the consciousness of your Innocence[1]—what makes you thoughtless in your Conduct and apt to run into a thousand little imprudences?—why the consciousness of your Innocence—what makes you impatient of Sir Peter's Temper and outrageous at his suspicions?—why the consciousness of your own Innocence—

LADY TEAZLE. Tis very true.

SURFACE. Now my dear Lady Teazle if you would but once make a trifling Faux-Pas—you can't conceive how cautious you would grow—and how ready to humour and agree with your Husband.

LADY TEAZLE. Do you think so—

SURFACE. O I'm sure on't—and then you would find all Scandall would cease at once—for in short your Character at Present is like a Person in a Plethora absolutely dying of too much Health.

LADY TEAZLE. So—so—then I perceive your Prescription is that I must sin in my own Defence—and part with my virtue to preserve my Reputation.—

SURFACE. Exactly so upon my credit Ma'am.

LADY TEAZLE. Well certainly this is the oddest Doctrine—and the newest Receipt for avoiding Calumny.

SURFACE. An infallible one—believe me—Prudence like experience must be paid for—

LADY TEAZLE. Why if my understanding were once convinced—

14 your] *O*, *Ca*, *Cb*, *B*; your own *L* makes] *L*, *Ca*, *Cb*, *B*; make *O* 15 in] *O*, *L*, *Ca*, *B*; of *Cb* 20 would] *L*, *Ca*, *Cb*, *B*; *om.* *O* 24 you would] *Ca*; You'd *O*, *B*; you'l *Cb* would] *O*, *Ca*, *B*; will *Cb* 28 preserve] *O*, *L*, *Ca*, *B*; secure *Cb*

[1] 'A collection of Toasts to reform the manners of the Times' (printed in *Bath Chronicle*, 19 Dec. 1771) includes the following: 'May the consciousness of our own innocence ever afford us that pleasure which the lewd man never enjoyed, and the guilty never felt.'

SURFACE. O certainly madam your understanding *should* be convinced—yes—yes—Heav'n forbid I should perswade you to do any thing you *thought* wrong—no—no—I have too much honor to desire it—

LADY TEAZLE. Don't—you think we may as well leave Honor out of the Argument?

SURFACE. Ah—the ill effects of your country education I see still remain with you.

LADY TEAZLE. I doubt they do indeed—and I will fairly own to you that If I could be perswaded to do wrong it would be by Sir Peter's ill-usage—sooner than your honourable Logic after all—

SURFACE. Then by this Hand which He is unworthy of—

Enter SERVANT.

Sdeath, you Blockhead—what do you want—

SERVANT. I beg Pardon Sir but I thought you wouldn't chuse Sir Peter to come up without announcing him—?

SURFACE. Sir Peter—oons and the Devil—

LADY TEAZLE. Sir Peter! O Lud! I'm ruin'd—I'm ruin'd—

SERVANT. Sir twasn't I let him in.

LADY TEAZLE. O I'm undone—what will become of me now Mr. Logick?—O mercy He's on the Stairs—I'll get behind here—and if ever I am so imprudent again— [*Goes behind the Screen.*

SURFACE. Give me that—Book!—

[*Sits down*—SERVANT *pretends to adjust his Hair.*

Enter SIR PETER.

SIR PETER. Aye, ever improving himself!—Mr. Surface—Mr. Surface!—

SURFACE. Oh!—my Dear Sir Peter—I beg your Pardon—[*gaping and throws away the Book*][1] I have been dozing over a stupid Book! well—I am much obliged to you for this Call—you haven't been here I believe since I fitted up this Room—Books you know are the only Things I am a Coxcomb in—

16 oons and] *O, Ca, Cb, B*; ons *L* *'I'm ruin'd' (l. 17) and 'Mr. Surface' (l. 26) are not repeated in O* 19 O] *O, Ca, B, L*; *om. Cb* 22 that] *O, L, Ca, Cb*; a *B* 29 well] *O, Ca, Cb, B*; *om. L* 30 Call] *O, Ca, Cb, B*; visit *L*

[1] Mary Linley described the successful Bath performance of *The School for Scandal* in a letter to her sister, Mrs. Sheridan, of 14 Nov. [1777], and added, 'I particularly observed that instead of throwing the Book to the other end of the Room as Palmer does he [Dimond] very carefully pulled down the Page he was reading and gave it to his Servant w[hi]ch is certainly more consistent with his Character' (*Sheridan Correspondence*, viii. 44, in the Widener Library, Harvard University).

SIR PETER. Tis very neat indeed—well well that's proper—and you make even your screen a source of knowledge—hung I perceive with Maps—

SURFACE. O yes—I find great use in that Screen.

SIR PETER. I dare say you must—certainly—when you want to find anything in a Hurry—

SURFACE. Aye or to hide any thing in a Hurry either—(*aside*)

SIR PETER. Well I have a little private Business—

SURFACE. You needn't stay—[*to* SERVANT]

SERVANT. No, sir— [*Exit.*

SURFACE. Here's a chair—Sir Peter—I beg—

SIR PETER. Well now we are alone—there *is* a Subject—my dear—Friend—on which I wish to unburthen my Mind to you—a Point of the greatest moment to my Peace—in short—my good Friend—Lady Teazle's Conduct of late has made me extremely unhappy.

SURFACE. Indeed I'm very sorry to hear it—

SIR PETER. Yes 'tis but too plain she has not the least regard for me—but what's worse—I have pretty good Authority to suspect that she must have formed an attachment to another.

SURFACE. You astonish me.

SIR PETER. Yes—and between ourselves—I think I have discover'd the Person.

SURFACE. How—you alarm me exceedingly!

SIR PETER. Ah! my Dear friend I knew you would sympathize with me.—

SURFACE. Yes—believe me Sir Peter—such a discovery would hurt me just as much as it would you—

SIR PETER. I am convinced of it—ah!—it is a happiness to have a Friend whom one can trust even with one's Family Secrets—but—have you no guess who I mean?

SURFACE. I haven't the most distant Idea.—it can't be Sir Benjamin Backbite.

SIR PETER. O No—what say you to Charles?

SURFACE. My Brother—impossible!—

SIR PETER. Ah! my dear Friend—the goodness of your own Heart misleads you—you judge of others by—yourself—

SURFACE. Certainly Sir Peter—the Heart that is conscious of its own integrity is ever slow to credit another's Treachery—

1 well well] *O*, *L*, *Ca*, *B*; well *Cb* 5 find] *L*, *Ca*, *Cb*, *B*; find out *O* 7 *aside*] *Cb* [S.], *B*; *om. O*, *L*, *Ca* 8 little . . . Business] *L*, *Ca*, *Cb*, *B*; little Business—if we were alone *O* 9 *to* SERVANT] *Ca* [S.]; *om. O*, *L*, *Cb*, *B* 10 *Exit*] *L*, *Ca*, *Cb*, *B*; (*Exit Servant*) *O* 14 Peace] *L*, *Ca*, *Cb*, *B*; Peace—which makes me extremely unhappy *O* 17 plain] *O*, *Ca*, *Cb*, *B*; true *L* 18 suspect] *O*, *L*, *Ca*, *Cb*; suppose *B* 20 You] *Ca* [S.]; Indeed! you *O*, *L*, *Cb*, *B* 27 ah!] *O*, *Ca*, *Cb*, *B*; *om. L* 32 O] *O*, *L*, *Ca*, *B*; *om. Cb* 35 others] *L*, *Ca*, *Cb*, *B*; other *O*

SIR PETER. True but your Brother has no sentiment—you never hear him talk so.—

SURFACE. Yet I can't but think that Lady Teazle herself has too much Principle—

SIR PETER. Aye—but what's her Principle—against the flattery of a handsome—lively young Fellow—

SURFACE. That's very true—

SIR PETER. And then you know the difference of our ages makes it very improb[ab]le that she should have a great affection for me—and if she were to be frail and I were to make it Public—why the Town would only laugh at me, the foolish old Batchelor who had Married a Girl.—

SURFACE. That's true—to be sure—they *would* laugh—

SIR PETER. Laugh!—aye—and make Ballads—and Paragraphs and the Devil knows what of me—

SURFACE. No—you must never make it Public—

SIR PETER. But then again that the Nephew of my old Friend Sir Oliver should be the Person to attempt such a wrong—hurts me more nearly—

SURFACE. Aye there's the point; when Ingratitude barbs the Dart of Injury—the wound has double danger in it—

SIR PETER. Aye, I that was in a manner left his Guardian—in whose House he had been so often entertain'd—who never in my Life denied him my advice—

SURFACE. O 'tis not to be credited—There may be a man capable of such Baseness to be sure—but for my Part 'till you can give me positive Proofs—I can not but doubt it. However if this should be proved on him He is no longer a Brother of mine! I disclaim kindred with him—for the Man who can break thro' the Laws of Hospitality—and attempt the wife—of his Friend deserves to be branded as the Pest of Society—

SIR PETER. What a difference there is between you—what noble sentiments!—

SURFACE. Yet I cannot suspect Lady Teazle's Honor—

SIR PETER. I am sure I wish to think well of her—and to remove all ground of quarrel between us—She has lately reproach'd me more than once—with having made no settlement on her—and in our last Quarrel she almost hinted that she should not break her Heart if I was Dead.—

3 Yet] *L, Ca, Cb, B*; Well there certainly is no knowing what men are capable of—no—there is no knowing—yet *O* 9 a] *Ca*; any *O, L, Cb*; any very *B* 11 me] *L, Ca, Cb, B*; *om. O* the] *O, L, Ca*; a *Cb, B* 12 they] *L, Ca, Cb, B*; People *O* 17 a wrong] *L, Ca, Cb, B*; an injury *O* 19 Aye . . . point] *L, Ca, Cb, B*; Undoubtedly *O* 21 whose] *L, Ca, Cb, B*; his *O* 26 I . . . doubt it] *Ca, Cb, B*; you must forgive my withholding my Belief *O* 33 Yet] *L, Ca, Cb, B*; But *O* 37 she almost] *L, Ca, B*; almost *O, Cb*

now as we seem to differ in our Ideas of Expence I have resolved she shall be her own Mistress in that Respect for the future—and if I were to die she shall find that I have not been inattentive to her Interest while living—Here my Friend are the Draughts of two Deeds which I wish to have your opinion on: by one—She will enjoy eight hundred a year independent while I live—and by the other the Bulk of my Fortune after my Death—

SURFACE. This Conduct Sir Peter is indeed truly Generous!—I wish it may not corrupt my Pupil—[*aside*]

SIR PETER. Yes I am Determined she shall have no cause to complain—tho' I would not have her acquainted with the latter Instance of my Affection yet awhile—

SURFACE. Nor I—if I could help it—[*aside*]

SIR PETER. And now my Dear Friend if you please we will talk over the situation of your hopes with Maria—

SURFACE. No—no—Sir Peter—another Time if you Please—[*softly*]

SIR PETER. I am Sensibly chagrined at the little Progress you seem to make in her affection—

SURFACE. I beg you will not mention it—what are my Disap[p]ointments when your Happiness is in Debate! [*softly*] 'sdeath—I should be ruin'd every way—[*aside*]

SIR PETER. And tho' you are so averse to my acquainting Lady Teazle with your Passion—I am sure she's not your Enemy in the Affair—

SURFACE. Pray Sir Peter—now oblige me.—I am really too much affected by the subject we have been speaking on to bestow a thought on my own concerns—The Man who is entrusted with his Friend's Distresses can never—well Sir?

Enter SERVANT.

SERVANT. Your Brother, Sir, is—speaking to a Gentleman in the Street—and says He knows you are within—

SURFACE. Sdeath, Blockhead—I'm not within—I'm out for the Day—

SIR PETER. Stay—hold—a thought has struck me—you shall be at home—

SURFACE. Well—well—let him up—[*Exit* SERVANT] He'll Interrupt Sir Peter—however—

SIR PETER. Now my good Friend—oblige me I entreat you—before Charles comes—let me conceal myself somewhere—Then do you tax him on the Point we have been talking on—and his answers may satisfy me at once—

3 Interest] *L*, *Ca*, *Cb*, *B*; Interests *O* 5 on] *O*, *L*, *Ca*, *Cb*, *B*; of *Cb* 13 *aside*] *L*, *Ca*; *om.* *O*, *Cb*, *B* 14 if . . . please] *O*, *Ca*, *Cb*, *B*; *om.* *L* 19 it] *O*, *L*, *Ca*, *Cb*; it Sir *B* 20 should] *Ca*; shall *O*, *Cb*, *B* 21 *aside*] *Ca*, *Cb* [S.]; *om.* *O*, *B*

SURFACE. O Fie Sir Peter—would you have me join in so mean a Trick—to trepan[1] my Brother to—

SIR PETER. Nay you tell me—you are *sure* He is innocent—if so you do him the greatest service in giving him an opportunity to clear himself—and—you will set—my Heart at rest—come you shall not refuse me—here behind this Screen will be [*goes to the Screen*]—hey! what the Devil—there seems to be one list'ner here already—I'll swear I saw a Petticoat.—

SURFACE. Ha! ha! ha!—well this is ridiculous enough—I'll tell you Sir Peter—tho' I hold a man of Intrigue to be a most despicable Character—yet you know it doesn't follow that one is to be an absolute Joseph[2] either.—hearkee—'tis a little French Millener—a silly Rogue that Plagues me—and having some character, on your coming she ran behind the Screen—

SIR PETER. Ah! you Rogue—but 'egad she has overheard all I have been saying of my Wife.

SURFACE. O 'twill never go any further—you may depend on't.

SIR PETER. No!—then—'efaith, let her hear it out.—Here's a Closet will do as well.—

SURFACE. Well go in then—

SIR PETER. Sly Rogue—sly Rogue— [*Goes into the Closet*[3]

SURFACE. A very narrow escape indeed!—and a curious situation I'm in!—to part man and wife in this manner.

LADY TEAZLE. [*Peeping from the screen*]. Couldn't I steal off?—

SURFACE. Keep close my Angel—

SIR PETER. [*Peeping out*]. Joseph—tax him home—

SURFACE. Back—my dear Friend!

LADY TEAZLE [*Peeping*]. Couldn't you Lock Sir Peter in?

SURFACE. Be still—my Life.

SIR PETER [*Peeping*]. You're sure—the little Millener won't blab?

SURFACE. In! in! my good Sir Peter—foregad—I wish I had a Key to the Door.—

6 *goes to the Screen*] *Ca* [S.]; *om. O, L, B*; (*goes towards the Screen*) *Cb* 11 one] *L, Ca, Cb, B*; a man *O* 13 ran] *Ca, Cb, B*; run *O* 17 further] *Ca, Cb*; farther *O, L, B* you] *L, Ca, Cb, B*; you—you *O* 21 *Goes . . . Closet*] *L, Ca, Cb, B*; *om. O* 22 A . . . indeed] *Ca*; a narrow escape indeed *L, Cb, B*; Gad's my Life what an Escape—*O* 24 *Peeping . . . screen*] *Ca* [S.]; (*peeps out*) *O*; (*peeping out*) *L, Cb, B* 28 Couldn't] *L, Ca, Cb, B*; can't *O* 30 *Peeping*] *Ca* [S.], *Cb* [S.]; *om. O, L, B* 31 good] *O, L, Ca, Cb*; dear *B*

---

[1] Decoy or beguile. Cf. *The Beggar's Opera*, II. xiii: 'Force or cunning | Never shall my heart trapan.'

[2] Resisting Potiphar's wife: Genesis 39: 7 seq.

[3] Cf. *A Trip to Scarborough*, IV. iii (p. 609 below): *Exit Loveless into the Closet.*

Enter CHARLES.

CHARLES SURFACE. Hollo! Brother—what has been the matter? your Fellow wouldn't let me up at first—what have you had a Jew or a wench with you?

SURFACE. Neither Brother I assure you.

CHARLES SURFACE. But—what has made Sir Peter—steal off—I thought He had been with you.

SURFACE. He *was* Brother—but hearing you were coming He did not chuse to stay—

CHARLES SURFACE. What was the old Gentleman afraid I wanted to borrow money of him!—

JOSEPH. No Sir—but I am Sorry—to find Charles—that you have lately given that worthy man grounds for great Uneasiness—

CHARLES SURFACE. Yes they tell me I do that to a great many worthy men—but How so Pray?

JOSEPH. To be plain with you Brother He thinks you are endeavouring—to gain Lady Teazle's Affections from him.

CHARLES SURFACE. Who I—O Lud! not I upon my word. Ha! ha! ha! so the old Fellow has found out that He has got a young wife—has He? or what's worse has her Ladyship discover'd that she has an old Husband?

JOSEPH. This is—no subject to jest on Brother—He who can laugh—

CHARLES SURFACE. True Brother as you were going to say—then seriously I never had the least idea of what—you charge me with, upon my honour—

SURFACE. Well, it will give Sir Peter great satisfaction to hear this—[*aloud*]

CHARLES SURFACE. To be sure I once thought the Lady seem'd to have taken a fancy to me—but upon my soul I never gave her the least encouragement.—besides, you know my Attachment to Maria—

SURFACE. But sure Brother even if Lady Teazle had betray'd the fondest partiality for you—

CHARLES SURFACE Why—lookee Joseph—I hope I shall never deliberately do a dishonourable Action—but if—a pretty woman were purposely to throw herself in my way—and that pretty woman married to a man old enough to be her Father—

SURFACE. Well!—

6 But] *O*, *L*, *Ca*, *Cb*; and *B* 18 not I] *L*, *Ca*, *Cb*, *B*; no—not I *O* 20 or . . . Ladyship] *L*, *Ca*; or what's worse has she *O*; *om.* *Cb*, *B* 20–1 discover'd . . . Husband] *O*, *L*, *Ca*; *om.* *B*, *Cb* 22 on] *O*, *L*, *Ca*, *Cb*; upon *B* 23 True Brother] *Cb*. [S.]; True, True *O*, *L*, *Ca*, *B* 29 to me] *L*, *Ca*, *Cb*, *B*; *del.* *O* her] *O*, *L*, *Ca*, *Cb*; *om.* *B* 30 besides] *Ca*; beside *O*, *L*, *Cb*, *B* 34 were] *L*, *Ca*, *B*; was *O*, *Cb*

CHARLES SURFACE. —Why I believe I should be obliged to borrow a little of your Morality—that's all.—but Brother—do you know now that you surprize me Exceedingly by naming *me* with Lady—Teazle—for faith I always understood *you* were her Favourite—

SURFACE. O—for Shame Charles—this retort is Foolish

CHARLES SURFACE. Nay I swear I have seen you exchange such significant Glances—

SURFACE. Nay—nay—Sir—this is no jest—

CHARLES SURFACE. Egad—I'm serious—don't you remember—one Day when I call'd here—

SURFACE. Nay—prithee—Charles

CHARLES SURFACE. And found you together—

SURFACE. Zounds—Sir—I insist—

CHARLES SURFACE. And another time when your Servant—

SURFACE. Brother—Brother a word with you—gad I must stop him—[*aside*]

CHARLES SURFACE. Inform'd—me I say that—

SURFACE. Hush!—I beg your—Pardon but—Sir Peter has overheard all we have been saying—I knew you would clear yourself or I should not have consented—

CHARLES SURFACE. How Sir Peter!—where is He—?

SURFACE. Softly—there—[*points to the Closet*]

CHARLES SURFACE. O—'fore Heav'n I'll have him out—Sir Peter come forth—

SURFACE. No—No—

CHARLES SURFACE. I say Sir Peter—come into Court.—[*pulls in Sir Peter*] What—my old Guardian—what turn inquisitor and take evidence incog.—

SIR PETER. Give me your hand—Charles—I believe I have suspected you wrongfully—but you mustn't be angry with Joseph—'twas my Plan—

CHARLES SURFACE. Indeed!—

SIR PETER. But I acquit you.—I promise you I don't think near so ill of you as I did—what I have heard has given me great satisfaction—

CHARLES SURFACE. Egad then 'twas lucky you didn't hear any more—wasn't it Joseph? [*half aside*]

SIR PETER. Ah! you would have retorted on him—

CHARLES SURFACE. Aye—aye—that was a Joke—

SIR PETER. Yes—yes I know his Honor too well

CHARLES SURFACE. But you might as well have suspected him as me in this matter for all that, mightn't He Joseph? [*half aside*]

3 Exceedingly] *L*, *Ca*, *Cb*, *B*; exceeding *O* 16 *aside*] *O*, *L*, *Ca*, *B*; *om. Cb* 17 I say] *L*, *Ca*, *Cb*, *B*; *om. O* 23 O] *L*, *Ca*, *Cb*, *B*; In the Closet! O *O* 26 I say] *L*, *Ca*, *Cb*, *B*; *om. O* 34 then 'twas] *O*, *L*, *Ca*, *B*; it was then *Cb* 35 *half aside*] *Ca* [S.]; *om. O*, *L*, *Cb*, *B* 40 *half aside*] *Ca* [S.]; *om. O*, *L*, *Cb*, *B*

SIR PETER. Well well I believe you—

SURFACE. Would they were both well out of the Room! [*aside*]

Enter SERVANT *who Whispers* SURFACE

SIR PETER. And in future perhaps we may not be such Strangers.

SURFACE. Lady Sneerwell!—stop her by all means—[*exit* SERVANT] Gentlemen—I beg Pardon—I must wait on you down stairs—Here is a Person come on particular Business.—

CHARLES SURFACE. Well you can see him in another Room, Sir Peter and I haven't met a long time and I have something to say to him.—

SURFACE. They must not be left together.—I'll contrive to send Lady Sneerwell away, and return directly. [*aside to him*] Sir Peter not a Word of the French milliner. [*Exit* SURFACE]

SIR PETER. O not for the world! Ah—Charles if you associated more with your Brother, one might indeed hope for your reformation—He is a man of Sentiment—well! there is nothing in the world so noble as a man of Sentiment!

CHARLES SURFACE. Pshaw—He is too moral by half—and so apprehensive of his good Name, as he calls it, that I suppose He would as soon let a Priest into his House as a Girl—

SIR PETER. No—no—come come—you wrong him—no—no Joseph is no Rake but He is not such a Saint in that Respect either—I have a great mind to tell him—we should have a Laugh—[*aside*]

CHARLES SURFACE. Oh hang him! He's a very Anchorite—a young Hermit—

SIR PETER. Hearkee—you must not abuse him—He may chance to hear of it again I promise you—

CHARLES SURFACE. Why you won't tell him—

SIR PETER. No—but—this way—egad! I'll tell him!—hearkee! have you a mind to have a good Laugh at Joseph?

CHARLES SURFACE. I should like it of all things—

2 *aside*] *B*; *om. O, L, Cb, Ca* 3 *Enter* . . . SURFACE] *Ca*; Enter Servant, whispers Surface *O*; Enter Servant and whispers Surface *L*; *Enter Servant* (To Surface) Sir Lady Sneerwell is below and says she will come up *Cb, B* 5 Lady Sneerwell!] *Oa* [S.], *Ca, Cb, B*; *om. O, L* stop . . . means] *Ca*; *om. O, L*; (to the Servant) Gad's life she mustn't come here *Oa* [S.] *Cb, B. See also p. 338 above* *exit* SERVANT] *Ca* [S.]; *om. O, Oa, L, Cb, B* 10 I'll . . . send] *Cb* [S.]; I'll send *O, Oa, L, Ca, B* 10–11 Lady Sneerwell] *Oa, Ca, Cb, B*; this man *O, L* 11 *aside to him*] *Cb* [S.]; (*aside*) *Ca*; *om. O, Oa, L, B* 11–12 Sir Peter . . . the] *L, Ca, Cb, B*; *om. O, Oa* 12 French] *L, Ca, B*; little French *Cb*; *om. O, Oa* *Exit* SURFACE] *Ca*; *om. Oa, Cb*; *Surface goes out O, L* 13 O . . . world] *Ca, Cb, B*; Not for the world *L*; *om. O, Oa* Ah—] *Ca*; (*Exit Surface*) Ah *Cb, B*; *om. O, Oa, L* 21 no . . . a] *Oa, L, Ca, Cb, B*; *om. O* not . . . a] *Ca* [S.]; no such *O, Oa, L, Cb, B* 22 *aside*] *Ca* [S.], *Cb* [S.]; *om. O, Oa, L, B* 25 He . . . to] *Oa, L, Ca, Cb, B*; he'll *O* 28–line 2, page 421 this way . . . me] *Oa, L, Ca, Cb, B*; You'll laugh heartily *O* 29 at] *Ca*; against *Oa, L, Cb, B*

SIR PETER. Then efaith we will—I'll be quit with him for discovering me—[*aside*] He had a Girl with him when I call'd—[*Whispering*]

CHARLES SURFACE. What—Joseph! you jest—

SIR PETER. Hush!—a little—French Millener—[*whispers*] and the best of the Jest is—she's in the Room now

CHARLES SURFACE. The Devil she is—

SIR PETER. Hush—I tell you—[*points*]

CHARLES SURFACE. Behind the Screen—'slife let us unveil her—

SIR PETER. No—no! He's coming—you shan't indeed—

CHARLES SURFACE. O egad! we'll have a peep at the little Millener—

SIR PETER. Not for the world—Joseph—will never forgive me—

CHARLES SURFACE. I'll Stand by you—

SIR PETER. [*Strug[g]ling with* CHARLES] Oods! here he is . . .

[*Surface enters just as* CHARLES *throws down the Screen.*]

CHARLES SURFACE. Lady Teazle! by all that's wonderfull!

SIR PETER. Lady Teazle! by all that's Horrible!

CHARLES SURFACE. Sir Peter—This is one of the smartest French Milliners I ever saw!—egad you seem all to have been diverting yourselves here at Hyde and Seek—and I don't See who is out of the Secret!—Shall I beg your Ladyship—to inform me!—not a word! Brother!—will you please to explain this matter?—what—Morality Dumb too?—Sir Peter—tho' I found—you in the Dark—perhaps you are not so now—all mute—!—well tho' I can make nothing of the Affair I Suppose you perfectly understand one another—so I'll leave you to yourselves—[*going*] Brother I'm Sorry to find you have given that worthy man so much uneasiness!—Sir Peter—there's nothing in the world so noble as a man of Sentiment!— [*Exit* CHARLES.

[*Stand for some time looking at each other*]

SURFACE. Sir Peter—notwithstanding I confess that appearances are against me—If you will afford me your Patience I make no doubt but I shall explain everything to your Satisfaction.

SIR PETER. If you please—

SURFACE. The Fact is Sir—that Lady Teazle, knowing my Pretensions to your ward Maria—I say Sir Lady Teazle—being apprehensive of the Jealousy of your Temper—and knowing my Friendship to the Family—

2 *aside*] *Ca* [S.]; *om. O, Oa, L, Cb, B* *Whispering*] *Oa, B*; (*Whispers*) *Cb*; *om. O, L, Ca* 4 *whispers*] *Cb* [S.]; *om. O, Oa, L, Ca, B* 8 'slife] *L, Ca*; Ad's life *Cb*; Odds-life *B, O, Oa* 9 He's . . . indeed] *Oa, L, Ca, Cb, B*; upon my Life—you shan't *O* 13 *Strug[g]ling with Charles*] *Ca*; (*struggling*) *Cb*; *om. O, L, B* Oods] *Ca*; Ons *L*; Odds *Cb*; Odds-life *O, B* he is] *L, Ca, Cb, B*; he's coming *O* 21 what—Morality] *Ca*; What is Morality *L, Cb, B*; What is Honesty *O* 24 Suppose] *L, Ca, Cb, B*; make no doubt by *O* one another] *O, Ca, Cb, B*; each other *L* 26 so] *O, Ca*; grounds for so *Cb, B* 27 CHARLES] *Ca, B*; *om. O, Cb* 28 *each*] *L, Ca, Cb, B*; one *O* 32 please] *Ca*; please—Sir—*O, L, Cb, B*

She Sir I say call'd here—in order that I might explain those Pretensions—but on your coming—being apprehensive—as I said of your Jealousy—she withdrew—and this you may depend on't is the whole Truth of the Matter.

SIR PETER. A very clear account upon my word and I dare swear the Lady will Vouch for every article of it—

LADY TEAZLE. [*Coming forward*] For not one word of it Sir Peter.

SIR PETER. How! don't you even think it worth while to agree in the lie—

LADY TEAZLE. There is not one syllable of Truth in what that Gentleman has told you—

SIR PETER. I believe you upon my Soul Ma'am—

SURFACE. 'Sdeath madam will you betray me—[*aside*]

LADY TEAZLE. Good Mr. Hypocrite by your leave I will speak for myself—

SIR PETER. Aye—let her alone Sir—you'll find she'll make out a better story than you without Prompting.

LADY TEAZLE. Hear me Sir Peter—I came hither—on no matter—relating to your Ward and even ignorant of this Gentleman's Pretensions to her—but I came seduced by his insidious arguments, at least to listen to his pretended Passion, if not to sacrifice your Honour to his Baseness—

SIR PETER. Now I believe the Truth is coming indeed—

SURFACE. The Woman's mad—

LADY TEAZLE. No Sir—she has recover'd her Senses, and your own Arts have furnish'd her with the means. Sir Peter—I do not Expect you to credit me—but the Tenderness you express'd for me when I am sure you could not think I was a witness to it, has penetrated to my Heart and had I left the Place without the Shame of this discovery—my future Life should have Spoke the sincerity of my Gratitude.—as for that smooth tongue Hypocrite—who would have seduced the wife of his too credulous Friend while he affected honourable addresses to his ward—I behold him now in a light so truly despicable—that I shall never again respect myself for having listen'd to him— [*Exit.*

SURFACE. Notwithstanding all this Sir Peter—Heav'n knows—

SIR PETER. That you are a Villain!—and so I leave you to your Conscience—

SURFACE. You are too Rash Sir Peter—you shall hear me! the Man who shuts out Conviction by refusing to—

6 article] *O*, *L*, *Ca*, *B*; tittle *Cb* 7 *Coming forward*] *Ca* [S.], *Cb*, *B*; *om.* *O*, *L* 20–1 at . . . Passion] *L*, *Ca*, *Cb*, *B*; and pretended Passion at least to listen to his dishonourable Love *O* 25 and] *L*, *Ca*, *Cb*, *B*; *om.* *O* 28 to my] *Ca*; so to my *O*, *L*, *Cb*, *B* 29 and] *Ca* [S.]; that *O*, *L*, *Cb*, *B* 31 tongue] *Ca*; tongu'd *Cb*; tongued *O*, *L*, *B* 32 affected] *L*, *Ca*, *Cb*, *B*; pretended *O*

SIR PETER. Oh! [*Exeunt*, SURFACE *following and Speaking*.

END OF ACT 4TH

Act 5th

Scene 1st. The Library

Enter SURFACE *and* SERVANT.

SURFACE. Mr. Stanley! why should you think I would see him? you must know he comes to ask something!

SERVANT. Sir—I should not have let him in but that Mr. Rowley came to the Door with him.—

SURFACE. Pshaw!—Blockhead to Suppose that I should now be in a Temper to receive visits from poor Relations!—well why don't you shew the Fellow up—?

SERVANT. I will—Sir—why Sir—it was not my Fault that Sir Peter discover'd my Lady—

SURFACE. Go—Fool—! [*Exit* SERVANT] Sure Fortune never play'd a man of my Policy—such a Trick—before—my character with Sir Peter! my Hopes with Maria!—destroy'd in a moment!—I'm in a rare Humour to listen to other People's Distresses!—I shan't be able to bestow even a benevolent sentiment on Stanley.—So! here—He comes and Rowley with him—I *must* try to recover myself—and put a little Charity into my Face however.— [*Exit*.

Enter SIR OLIVER *and* ROWLEY.

SIR OLIVER. What! does He avoid us?—that was He—was it not?

ROWLEY. It was Sir—but I doubt you are come a little too abruptly—his Nerves are so weak, that the sight of a poor Relation may be too much for him—I should have gone first—to break you to him.

SIR OLIVER. A Plague of his Nerves—yet this is He whom Sir Peter extolls as a Man of the most Benevolent way of thinking!—

ROWLEY. As to his way of thinking—I can't pretend to decide for to do him justice He appears to have as much speculative Benevolence as any private Gentleman in the Kingdom—tho' He is seldom so sensual as to indulge himself in the Exercise of it.—

1 SIR PETER. Oh! [*Exeunt . . . Speaking*] *O*, *Ca* [S.]; (*Exit Sir Peter*) *Surface following and speaking*. *Cb*; (*Exit following and Speaking to Sir Peter*) *B*; (*Exit following him and Speaking*) *L* 6 why] *Ca*; and why *O*, *L*, *Cb*, *B* 22 OLIVER] *O*, *L*, *Ca*, *B*; Oliver as Old Stanley *Cb* 26 have] *L*, *Ca*, *Cb*, *B*; I have *O*

SIR OLIVER. Yet has a string of charitable Sentiments I suppose at his Fingers' ends!—

ROWLEY. Or rather at his Tongue's end Sir Oliver—for I believe there is no sentiment He has more faith in than that 'Charity begins at Home'.

SIR OLIVER. And his I presume is of that domestic sort which never stirs abroad at all.

ROWLEY. I doubt you'll find it so—but He's coming—I mustn't seem to interrupt you—and you know immediately—as you leave him—I come in to announce—your arrival in your real Character.—

SIR OLIVER. True—and afterwards you'll meet me at Sir Peter's.

ROWLEY. Without losing a Moment.— [*Exit* ROWLEY.

SIR OLIVER. So—I don't like the Complaisance of his Features.

Re-Enter SURFACE.

SURFACE. Sir—I beg you ten thousand Pardons—for keeping—you a moment waiting—Mr. Stanley—I presume—

SIR OLIVER. At your Service—

SURFACE. Sir—I beg you will do me the honor to sit down—I entreat you Sir—

SIR OLIVER. Dear Sir there's no occasion.—too civil by half!—[*aside*]

SURFACE. I have not the Pleasure of knowing you Mr. Stanley—but I am extremely happy to see you look so well—you were nearly related to my Mother—I think Mr. Stanley.

SIR OLIVER. I was Sir—so nearly that my present Poverty I fear may do discredit to her Wealthy Children—else I should not have presumed to trouble you.—

SURFACE. Dear Sir—there needs no Apology—He that is in Distress tho' a stranger has a right to claim kindred with the Wealthy.—I am sure I wish I was of that Class, and had it in my Power to offer you even a small relief.

SIR OLIVER. If your Unkle Sir Oliver were here—I should have a Friend.

SURFACE. I wish He were Sir with all my Heart—you should not want an advocate with him believe me Sir—

SIR OLIVER. I should not need one—my Distresses would recommend me.—but I imagined—his Bounty had enabled you to become the agent of his Charity.

SURFACE. My dear Sir—you were strangely misinformed. Sir Oliver is a worthy man—a very worthy sort of Man—but—avarice Mr. Stanley is the vice of age—I will tell you my good Sir—in confidence!—what—

4 than] *O*, *Ca*; then *Cb*, *B* 11 a] *L*, *Ca*, *Cb*, *B*; *om. O* *Exit* ROWLEY] *Ca*, *Cb*, *B*; (*Exit*) *O*, *L* 12 I don't like] *Ca*, *Cb*, *B*; I see he has [*L* = had] premeditated a Denial by *O*, *L* 13 *Re-Enter*] *Ca*; *Enter O*, *L*, *Cb*, *B* 14 ten] *O*, *Cb*, *Ca*, *B*; a *L* 19 *aside*] *L*, *Ca*, *Cb*, *B*; *om. O* 31 were] *Ca* [S.]; was *O*, *L*, *Cb*, *B* 36 were] *Ca*, *L*, *Cb*, *B*; are *O* 37 sort of Man] *O*, *Ca*, *Cb*, *B*; sort of a man *L* 38 of age] *O*, *Ca*, *Cb*, *B*; of the age *L*

he has done for me has been a mere—nothing, tho' People I know have thought—otherwise and for my Part I never chose to contradict the Report.

SIR OLIVER. What!—has He never—transmitted—you—Bullion!—Rupees!—Pagodas![1]—

SURFACE. O Dear Sir—Nothing of the kind—no—no—a few—Presents—now and then—China—shawls—Congo[2] Tea—Avadavats[3]—and Indian Crackers—little more, believe me—

SIR OLIVER. Here's Gratitude for twelve thousand Pounds!—avadavats—and Indian Crackers!

SURFACE. Then my dear Sir—you have heard I doubt not of the extravagance of my Brother.—There are very few would credit what I have done for that unfortunate young man!—

SIR OLIVER. Not I for one! [*aside*]

SURFACE. The Sums I have lent—him!—indeed—I have been exceedingly to blame—it was an amiable Weakness!—however—I don't pretend to defend it—and now I feel it doubly culpable—since it has deprived me of the Power of serving *you* Mr. Stanley as my Heart directs—

SIR OLIVER. Dissembler!—Then Sir—you cannot assist me?

SURFACE. At Present it grieves me to say I cannot, but whenever I have the ability you may depend upon hearing from me.

SIR OLIVER. I am extremely sorry.

SURFACE. Not more than I am believe me—to pity without the Power to relieve is still more painful than to ask and be denied—

SIR OLIVER. Kind Sir—your most obedient humble Servant.

SURFACE. You leave me deeply affected Mr. Stanley—William—be ready to open the door—

SIR OLIVER. O Dear Sir—no ceremony—

SURFACE. Your very obedient—

SIR OLIVER. Sir your most obsequeous—

SURFACE. You may depend upon hearing from me—when ever I can be of service—

SIR OLIVER. Sweet Sir—you are too good—

SURFACE. In the mean time—I wish you Health and Spirits—

SIR OLIVER. Your ever grateful—and perpetual humble Servant.

2 for] *O*, *L*, *Ca*, *Cb*; *om. B* chose] *O*, *Ca* [S.]; chuse *L*, *Cb*, *B* 8 Indian] *O*, *Ca*; India *Cb*, *B* 10 Indian] *O*, *Ca*, *Cb*, *B*; India *L* 11 I . . . not] *L*, *Ca*, *Cb*, *B*; *om. O* 12 Brother] *L*, *Ca*, *Cb*, *B*; Brother—Sir *O* 14 *aside*] *Ca* [S.], *Cb* [S.]; *om. O*, *L*, *B* 32 upon] *L*, *Ca*, *Cb*, *B*; on *O*

[1] Zelida, in Kelly's *The Romance of an Hour* (1774), p. 5, is 'ballasted with rupees and pagodas': Indian coins.

[2] Chinese.

[3] Small red and black singing birds from India. Sheridan gave some to his first wife and wrote a mock elegy on the death of one of them: see Sichel, ii. 98.

SURFACE. Sir—yours as sincerely—

SIR OLIVER. Now I am satisfied!— [*Exit.*

SURFACE. [*Solus*] This is one bad effect of a good Character, it invites applications from the unfortunate and there needs no small degree of address to gain the reputation of Benevolence without incurring the expence.—The silver ore of pure Charity is an expensive article in the catalogue of a man's good Qualities—whereas the sentimental French Plate I use instead of it, makes just as good a shew—and pays no tax.—

Enter ROWLEY.

ROWLEY. Mr. Surface—your Servant—I was apprehensive of interrupting you—tho'—my Business demands immediate attention—as this Note will inform you—

SURFACE. Always Happy to see Mr. Rowley—[*reads*] how!—'Oliver—Surface!'—my Unkle arrived!

ROWLEY. He is indeed—we have just parted—quite well—after a speedy voyage—and impatient to embrace—his worthy Nephew—

SURFACE. I am astonish'd!—William—stop Mr. Stanley if He's not gone—

ROWLEY. O—He's out of reach—I believe.

SURFACE. Why didn't you let me know this when you came in together—?

ROWLEY. I thought you had particular—Business—but I must be gone to inform your Brother—and appoint him here to meet his Uncle—He will be with you in a quarter of an hour—

SURFACE. So He says—well—I am Strangely overjoy'd at his coming—never to be sure was any thing so damn'd unlucky! [*aside*]

ROWLEY. You will be delighted to see how well He looks.

SURFACE. O—I'm rejoiced to hear it—just at this time! [*aside*]

ROWLEY. I'll tell him how impatiently—you expect him—[*Exit* ROWLEY.

SURFACE. Do—do—pray—give my best duty and affection—indeed I cannot—express the sensations I feel at the thought of seeing him!—certainly—his coming just as this Time is the cruellest Piece of ill Fortune—! [*Exit.*

Scene 2d. at SIR PETER'*s*

Enter MRS. CANDOUR—*and* MAID.

MAID. Indeed Ma'am my Lady will see nobody at Present.

2 Now . . . satisfied] *Ca*, *Cb*, *B*; Charles—you are my Heir *O*, *L* Exit] *O*, *L*, *Ca*, *Cb*; (*Exit Sir Oliver*) *B* 3 *Solus*] *O*, *Ca*, *Cb*, *B*; *om. L* This] *L*, *Ca*, *Cb*, *B*; Soh! This *O* 5 of] *O*, *L*, *Ca*, *B*; of the *Cb* 13 *reads*] *Ca* [S.]; (*Reading*) *Cb*; *om. O*, *B* 23 coming] *O*, *B*; coming (*aside*) *L*, *Ca*, *Cb* 24 *aside*] *Ca*, *B*; *om. O*, *L*, *Cb* 26 *aside*] *Ca*, *B*; *om. O*, *L*, *Cb* 27 *Exit* ROWLEY] *B*; (*Exit*) *Cb*; *om. O*, *L*, *Ca* 31 *Exit*] *Ca*, *Cb*, *B*; (*Exeunt*) *O*, *L* 32 *at*] *O*, *L*, *Ca*, *Cb*; *om. B* 33 *Enter*] *O*, *L*, *Ca*, *B*; *om. Cb* MAID] *L*, *Ca*, *Cb*, *B*; Madam-Servant *O*

MRS. CANDOUR. Did you tell her it was her Friend Mrs. Candour—

MAID. Yes Ma'am, but she begs you will excuse her—

MRS. CANDOUR. Do go again—I shall be glad to see her if it be only for a moment—for I am sure she must be in great Distress [*Exit* MAID. —Dear Heart—how provoking!—I'm not mistress of half the circumstances!—we shall have the whole affair in the news Papers with the Names of the Parties at Length before I have dropt the story at a dozen houses.—

Enter SIR BENJAMIN.

O Dear Sir Benjamin you have heard I suppose—

SIR BENJAMIN. Of Lady Teazle and Mr. Surface—

MRS. CANDOUR. And Sir Peter's Discovery—

SIR BENJAMIN. O the strangest Piece of Business to be sure—

MRS. CANDOUR. Well I never was so surpris'd in my life!—I am so sorry for all Parties, indeed I am.

SIR BENJAMIN. Now I don't Pity Sir Peter at all—He was so extravagantly partial to Mr. Surface—

MRS. CANDOUR. Mr. Surface—why 'twas with Charles Lady Teazle was—detected

SIR BENJAMIN. No such thing—Mr. Surface is the gallant—

MRS. CANDOUR. No—no—Charles—is the man—'twas Mr. Surface brought Sir Peter on purpose to discover them—

SIR BENJAMIN. I tell you I have it from one

MRS. CANDOUR. And I have it from one

SIR BENJAMIN. Who had it from one who had it—

MRS. CANDOUR. From one immediately—but here's Lady Sneerwell—perhaps she knows the whole affair—

Enter LADY SNEERWELL.

LADY SNEERWELL. So—my dear Mrs. Candour Here's a sad affair of our Friend Lady Teazle—

MRS. CANDOUR. Aye!—my Dear Friend who could have thought it.

LADY SNEERWELL. Well there is no trusting appearances. Tho'—indeed she was always too lively for me—

MRS. CANDOUR. To be sure her manners were a little too—free—but she was very young—

LADY SNEERWELL. And had indeed some good Qualities—

MRS. CANDOUR. So she had Indeed—but have you heard the Particulars?

LADY SNEERWELL. No—but every body says that Mr. Surface—

10 Dear] *L*, *Ca*, *Cb*, *B*; *om.* *O* 15 I am] *Ca* [S.]; *om.* *O*, *L*, *Cb*, *B* 16 Now] *L*, *Ca*, *Cb*, *B*; now indeed *O* so] *L*, *Ca*, *Cb*, *B*; always so *O* 16–17 extravagantly] *L*, *Ca*, *Cb*, *B*; extravagant *O* 30 Lady] *Ca* [S.]; *om.* *O*, *L*, *Cb*, *B* 31 Aye] *O*, *Ca*, *Cb*, *B*; Ah *L* 36 and 37 had] *O*, *Ca*, *Cb*, *B*; has *L*

SIR BENJAMIN. Aye there I told—you Mr. Surface was the Man.

MRS. CANDOUR. No—no—indeed—the assignation was with Charles.

LADY SNEERWELL. With Charles!—you alarm me Mrs. Candour.

MRS. CANDOUR. Yes—yes—He was the Lover—Mr. Surface—do him justice—was only the Informer—

SIR BENJAMIN. Well I'll not—dispute with you Mrs. Candour—but be it which it may—I hope that Sir Peter's wound will not—

MRS. CANDOUR. Sir Peter's wound!—O Mercy! I didn't hear a Word of their Fighting—

LADY SNEERWELL. Nor I a syllable!

SIR BENJAMIN. No—what no mention of the Duel—

MRS. CANDOUR. Not a word—

SIR BENJAMIN. O Lord—yes—yes—they fought before they left the Room.

LADY SNEERWELL. Pray let us hear.

MRS. CANDOUR. Aye do oblige—us with the Duel.

SIR BENJAMIN. Sir—says Sir Peter—immediately—after the Discovery—you are a most ungrateful Fellow.

MRS. CANDOUR. Aye to Charles—

SIR BENJAMIN. No—no—to Mr. Surface—a most ungrateful Fellow and old as I am Sir says He I insist on immediate satisfaction.

MRS. CANDOUR. Aye that must have been to Charles for 'tis very unlikely Mr. Surface should go to fight in his own House.

SIR BENJAMIN. 'Gad's Life Ma'am not at all—giving me immediate Satisfaction—on this—Madam—Lady Teazle seeing Sir Peter in such Danger—ran out of the Room in strong Hysterics—and Charles after her calling out for Hartshorn and Water! Then Madam—they began to fight with Swords—

Enter CRABTREE.

CRABTREE. With Pistols—Nephew—I have it from undoubted authority.—

MRS. CANDOUR. O Mr. Crabtree then it is all true—

CRABTREE. Too true indeed Ma'am and Sir Peter's Dangerously wounded—

SIR BENJAMIN. By a Thrust in Séconde[1]—quite thro' his left side.

CRABTREE. By a Bullet lodged in the Thorax—

11–13 No . . . Lord] *O, Ca, Cb, B*; *om. L* 21 on] *L, Ca, Cb, B*; on your giving me *O* 23 own] *O, B*; *om. L, Ca, Cb* 24 at] *Ca, Cb, B*; at at *O* 33 Peter's] *Ca, Cb, B*; Peter *O, L*; 35 Thrust] *O, L, Cb, B*; Thurst of *Ca* Séconde] *Ca, B*; sécond *O*; second *Cb*; a second *L*

[1] A 'thrust in *seconde*' is one delivered under one's opponent's blade, and with the knuckles upwards, the wrist turned downwards.

MRS. CANDOUR. Mercy—on me Poor Sir Peter—

CRABTREE. Yes ma'am—tho' Charles would have avoided the matter if He could.—

MRS. CANDOUR. I knew Charles was the Person.

SIR BENJAMIN. O my Unkle I see knows nothing of the matter—

CRABTREE. But Sir Peter tax'd him with the basest ingratitude—

SIR BENJAMIN. That I told you you know.

CRABTREE. Do Nephew let me Speak—and insisted on an immediate—

SIR BENJAMIN. Just as I said.

CRABTREE. Odds! life! Nephew allow others to know something too—a Pair of Pistols lay on the Bureau—for Mr. Surface—it seems had come the Night before late from Salt-Hill where He had been to see the Montem[1] with a Friend who has a Son at Eaton—so unluckily the Pistols were left Charged—

SIR BENJAMIN. I heard—nothing of this—

CRABTREE. Sir Peter forced Charles to take one and They fired—it seems pretty nearly together—Charles's Shot took Place as I told you—and Sir Peter's miss'd—but what is very extraordinary the Ball struck against a little Bronze Pliny that stood over the chimney piece—grazed out of the window at a right angle—and wounded the Postman, who was just coming to the Door with a double letter from Northamptonshire—

SIR BENJAMIN. My Unkle's account is more circumstantial I must confess—but I believe mine is the true one for all that.—

LADY SNEERWELL. I am more interested in this Affair than they imagine—and must have better information. [*Exit* LADY SNEERWELL.

SIR BENJAMIN. [*after a pause looking at each other*] Ah! Lady—Sneerwell's alarm is very easily accounted for—

CRABTREE. Yes, yes, they certainly *do* say—but that's neither here nor there.

MRS. CANDOUR. But pray where is Sir Peter at present—

CRABTREE. Oh! they—brought—him home and He is now in the House tho' the Servants are order'd to deny it—

MRS. CANDOUR. I believe so—and Lady Teazle I suppose—attending him—

CRABTREE. Yes yes—I saw one of the Faculty enter just before me—

SIR BENJAMIN. Hey—who comes here—

CRABTREE. O this is He—the Physician depend on't

8 an] *O*, *Ca*, *Cb*, *B*; *om*. *L* 17 told] *Ca*; tell *O*, *L*, *Cb*, *B* 19 Bronze] *L*; Bronce *O*; Broonze *Ca*, *Cb*, *B* chimney piece] *L*, *Ca*, *Cb*, *B*; Fire Place *O* 26 *after . . . other*] *Ca* [S.]; *om*. *O*, *L*, *Cb*, *B* 36 Hey] *O*, *L*, *Ca*, *B*; Hah! *Cb*

[1] This was the procession, on Whit Tuesday, by Eton boys to Salt-hill. On the way they collected money for the senior collegers: see John Brand, *Popular Antiquities of Great Britain*, ed. W. C. Hazlitt (1870), i. 240–5.

MRS. CANDOUR. O certainly, it must be the Physician and now we shall know—

Enter SIR OLIVER.

CRABTREE. Well Doctor—what Hopes?

MRS. CANDOUR. Aye Doctor how's your Patient?

SIR BENJAMIN. Now Doctor isn't it a wound with a small sword?

CRABTREE. A Bullet lodg'd in the Thorax—for a hundred!

SIR OLIVER. Doctor!—a wound with—a small sword! and a Bullet in the Thorax! oons are you mad good People?

SIR BENJAMIN. Perhaps Sir you are not a Doctor.

SIR OLIVER. Truly I am to thank you for my Degree If I am.

CRABTREE. Only a Friend of Sir Peter's then I presume; but Sir you must have heard of this Accident—

SIR OLIVER. Not a Word!

CRABTREE. Not of his being dangerously Wounded?

SIR OLIVER. The Devil he is!

SIR BENJAMIN. Run thro' the Body—

CRABTREE. Shot in the Breast—

SIR BENJAMIN. By one Mr. Surface—

CRABTREE. Aye the younger.

SIR OLIVER. Hey! what the Plague! you seem to differ Strangely in your Accounts—however you agree that Sir Peter is dangerously wounded—

SIR BENJAMIN. Oh, yes, we agree there—

CRABTREE. Yes, yes, I believe there can be no doubt of that.

SIR OLIVER. Then upon my Word, for a person in that Situation he is the most imprudent Man alive—For here he comes Walking as if nothing at all were the Matter.

Enter SIR PETER.

Odd's heart Sir Peter—you are come in good time I promise you, for we had Just given you Over.

SIR BENJAMIN. 'Egad Uncle this is the most Sudden recovery!

SIR OLIVER. Why Man what do you do out of Bed with a Small Sword thro' your Body, and a Bullet lodged in your Thorax!

SIR PETER. A Small Sword and a Bullet—

SIR OLIVER. Aye these Gentlemen would have kill'd you, without Law, or Physic—and wanted to dubb me a Doctor—to make me an accomplice.

SIR PETER. Why what is all this?

SIR BENJAMIN. We rejoice Sir Peter that the Story of the Duel is not true—and are Sincerely Sorry for your other misfortunes—

5 Aye] *O*, *Ca*, *Cb*, *B*; Ah *L* 11 Truly] *L*, *Ca*, *B*; Truly Sir *O*, *Cb* *O MS. ends with 'for', and recommences on p. 432* 13 this] *Ca*; his *L*, *Cb*, *B* 27 were] *aC* [S.]; was *L*, *Cb*, *B* 32 Bed] *L*, *Ca*; your Bed *Cb*, *B* 39 misfortunes] *aC*, *B*; misfortune *L*, *Cb*

SIR PETER. So So—all over the Town already—[*aside*]

CRABTREE. Tho' Sir Peter, you were certainly vastly to blame to Marry at all, at your years.

SIR PETER. Sir, what Business is that of yours?

MRS. CANDOUR. Tho' indeed as Sir Peter made so good a Husband He's very much to be pitied!

SIR PETER. Plague on your Pity Ma'am, I desire none of it:

SIR BENJAMIN. However Sir Peter, you must not mind the Laughing and Jests, you will meet with on this Occasion—

SIR PETER. Sir, I desire to be Master in my own House.

CRABTREE. 'Tis no uncommon case, that's one comfort.

SIR PETER. I insist on being left to myself, without ceremony, I insist on your leaving my House directly!

MRS. CANDOUR. Well, well, we are going and depend on't we'll make the best report of you we can—

SIR PETER. Leave my House—

CRABTREE. And tell how hardly you have been treated.

SIR PETER. Leave my House.

SIR BENJAMIN. And how Patiently you bear it.

SIR PETER. Fiends—Vipers!—Furies!—Oh that their own Venom would choak them— [*Exeunt* MRS. CANDOUR, SIR BENJAMIN, CRABTREE, *etc.*

SIR OLIVER. They are very provoking Indeed Sir Peter.

Enter ROWLEY.

ROWLEY. I heard high Words—what has ruffled you Sir Peter?

SIR PETER. Pshaw what Signifies asking, do I ever pass a Day without my Vexations?

SIR OLIVER. Well I'm not inquisitive—I come only to tell you that I have seen both my Nephews in the Manner we proposed—

SIR PETER. A precious couple they are!

ROWLEY. Yes and Sir Oliver is convinced—that your Judgment was right Sir Peter—

SIR OLIVER. Yes, I find Joseph is indeed the Man after all—

ROWLEY. Yes as Sir Peter Says, He's a Man of Sentiment.

SIR OLIVER. And Acts up to the Sentiments he professes.

ROWLEY. It certainly is Edification to hear him talk

SIR OLIVER. Oh He's a Model for the young Men of the Age!—but how's this Sir Peter—you don't Join in your Friend Joseph's Praise as I Expected.

1 *aside*] *Ca* [S.]; *om. L*, *Cb*, *B* 9 this] *Ca*, *Cb*; the *L*, *B* 14 Well, well] *L*, *Ca*, *B*; Well *Cb* 21 *Exeunt*] *Ca* [S.]; (*Exit*) *L*, *Cb*, *B* 22 CRABTREE, *etc.*] *Ca*; and Crabtree *L*, *Cb*, *B* 29 we proposed] *Ca*, *Cb*, *B*; I proposed, a precious couple they are *L* 30 A . . . are] *Ca*, *B*; Yes, a precious couple they are *Cb*; *om. L* 32 Sir Peter] *L*, *Ca*, *B*; *om. Cb* 34 Yes] *Ca*, *Cb*; Aye *B*; *om. L*

SIR PETER. Sir Oliver, we live in a damn'd wicked World, and the fewer we praise the better.

ROWLEY. What do *you* say so, Sir Peter—who were never mistaken in your Life?

SIR PETER. Pshaw—Plague on you both—I see by your sneering you have heard—the whole affair—I shall go mad among you!

ROWLEY. Then to fret you no longer Sir Peter—we are indeed acquainted with it all—I met Lady Teazle coming from Mr. Surface's—so humbled that she deigned to request *me* to be her advocate with you—

SIR PETER. And does Sir Oliver know all too?

SIR OLIVER. Every circumstance!

SIR PETER. What of the—Closet—and the screen—hey

SIR OLIVER. Yes yes—and the little—French Millener—O I have—been vastly diverted with the story—ha! ha!

SIR PETER. Twas—very Pleasant—!

SIR OLIVER. I never laugh'd more in my Life—I assure you, ha! ha!

SIR PETER. O vastly diverting—ha! ha!

ROWLEY. To be sure Joseph—with his Sentiments—ha! ha!

SIR PETER. Yes yes his sentiments—ha! ha!—a hypocritical Villain!

SIR OLIVER. Aye—and that Rogue Charles—to pull Sir Peter out of the Closet—ha! ha!

SIR PETER. Ha! ha! 'twas devilish entertaining to be sure—

SIR OLIVER. Ha! ha! egad Sir Peter I should like to have seen your Face when the Screen was thrown down, ha! ha!

SIR PETER. Yes yes my Face when the screen was thrown down, ha! ha! O I must never Shew my head again!

SIR OLIVER. But come—come it isn't fair to laugh at you neither my old Friend—tho' upon my soul I can't help it—

SIR PETER. O pray don't—restrain your—mirth on my account—It does not hurt—me at all—I laugh at the whole affair myself—yes—yes—I think being a standing Jest for all one's acquaintances—a very happy—situation—O yes—and then of a morning to read the Paragraphs about Mr. S—— Lady T—— and Sir P—— will—be so entertaining!—

ROWLEY. Without affectation Sir Peter you may despise the ridicule of Fools—but I see Lady Teazle—going towards the next Room—I am sure you must desire a Reconciliation as earnestly as she does—

3 *O MS. recommences with 'What'* 9 deigned] *O*, *L*, *Ca*, *B*; design'd *Cb* 14, 20 & 31 Yes yes] *O*, *L*, *Ca*, *B*; Yes *Cb* 23 Ha! ha! . . . sure] *O*, *L*, *Ca*, *B*; 'Twas devilish entertaining to be sure Ha! ha! *Cb* 28 come—come] *O*, *L*, *Ca*, *B*; come *Cb* 28 at] *L*, *Ca*, *Cb*, *B*; to *O* 32 acquaintances] *Ca*; acquaintance *O*, *L*, *Cb*, *B* 33–4 O . . . so] *O*, *L*, *Ca*, *Cb*; *om.* *B* 34–5 entertaining] *Ca*, *B*; entertaining. I shall certainly—leave town tomorrow and never look mankind in the Face again! *O*, *L*, *Cb*

SIR OLIVER. Perhaps my being here—prevents her coming to you—well I'll leave honest Rowley to mediate between you.—but he must bring you all presently to Mr. Surface's—where—I am now returning—if not to reclaim a Libertine—at least to expose Hypocrisy—

SIR PETER. Ah!—I'll be present at your discovering yourself there with all my heart.—tho' 'tis a vile unlucky Place for discoveries—

ROWLEY. We'll follow— [*exit* SIR OLIVER.

SIR PETER. She is not coming here you see Rowley—

ROWLEY. No but she has left the Door of that Room open you perceive. —see She is in Tears—!

SIR PETER. Certainly a little mortification appears very becoming in a wife—don't you think it will do her good to let her Pine a little.

ROWLEY. O this is ungenerous in you—

SIR PETER. Well I know not what to think—you remember Rowley the Letter I found of hers—evidently intended for Charles?—

ROWLEY. A mere Forgery Sir Peter—laid in your way on Purpose—this is one of the Points which I intend Snake shall give you conviction on—

SIR PETER. I wish I were once satisfied of that—she looks this way—what a remarkably elegant Turn of the Head she has!—Rowley I'll go to her—

ROWLEY. Certainly.

SIR PETER. Tho' when—it is known that we are reconciled People will laugh at me ten times more!

ROWLEY. Let—them laugh—and retort their malice only by shewing them you are happy in spite of it.

SIR PETER. Efaith so I will—and if I'm not mistaken, we may yet be the happiest couple—in the country.

ROWLEY. Nay, Sir Peter—He who once lays aside suspicion—

SIR PETER. Hold my dear Rowley—if you have any Regard for me—never let me hear you utter any thing like—a Sentiment. I have had enough of *them* to serve me the rest of my Life. [*Exeunt.*

4 Hypocrisy] *Ca*; Hypocricy (*Exit*) *Cb*; hypocrisy (*Exit Sir Oliver*) *B*; Hypocracy *O* 6 *After* '*discoveries*', *insert*: SIR OLIVER. However it is very convenient to the carrying on of my Plot that you all live so near one another! *O*; *L adds*: (*Exit*) 7 *exit* SIR OLIVER] *O*; *om. L*, *Ca*, *Cb*, *B* 10 see] *O*, *L*, *Ca*, *B*; *om. Cb* *After* '*Tears*' *insert*:

SIR PETER. She seems indeed to wish I should go to her—how dejected she appears.
ROWLEY. And will you refrain from comforting her. *O*, *L*

19 remarkably elegant] *O*, *Ca*; remarkable elegant *L*, *B*; remarkable *Cb* 27 couple] *O*, *L*, *Ca*, *B*; people *Cb* 29 my dear] *Ca* [S.]; Master *O*, *L*, *Cb*, *B* 31 *Exeunt*] *O*, *L*, *B*; (*Exit Sir Peter and Rowley*) *Ca*; (*Exeunt Sir Peter and Rowley*) *Cb*

Scene the Last

The Library

SURFACE *and* LADY SNEERWELL.

LADY SNEERWELL. Impossible—! will not Sir Peter immediately be reconciled to *Charles*? and of consequence no longer oppose his union with *Maria*?—the thought is Distraction to me!

SURFACE. Can Passion furnish a Remedy?

LADY SNEERWELL. No—nor Cunning either—O I was a Fool! an Ideot—to league with such a Blunderer!—

SURFACE. Sure Lady Sneerwell I am the greatest Sufferer—yet you see I bear the accident with Calmness.

LADY SNEERWELL. Because the Disap[p]ointment—doesn't reach your *Heart*—your interest only attached you to Maria—had you felt for her —what I have for that ungrateful Libertine, neither your Temper nor Hypocrisy could prevent your shewing the sharpness of your Vexation.

SURFACE. But why should your Reproaches fall on me for this Disap[p]ointment?

LADY SNEERWELL. Are not you the cause of it?—what had you to do— to bate in your Pursuit of Maria to pervert Lady Teazle by the way?— had you not a sufficient Field for your Roguery in blinding Sir Peter and supplanting your Brother?—I hate such an avarice of Crimes—'tis an unfair monopoly and never prospers.

SURFACE. Well I admit I have—been to blame—I confess I deviated from the direct Road of wrong but I don't think we're so totally defeated neither.

LADY SNEERWELL. No!

SURFACE. You tell me you have made a trial of Snake since we met—and that you Still believe him faithful to us—

LADY SNEERWELL. I do believe so—

SURFACE. And that He has undertaken should it be necessary—to swear and prove that Charles is at this Time contracted by vows and Honor to your Ladyship—which some of his former Letters to you will serve to support.—

LADY SNEERWELL. This indeed might have assisted—

SURFACE. Come—come it is not too late yet [*Knocking*]—but Hark! this is probably my unkle Sir Oliver—retire to that Room—we'll consult farther when He's gone.—

LADY SNEERWELL. Well!—but if He should find you out too—

3 SURFACE] *O*, *L*, *Ca*, *Cb*; *Enter Surface B*
19 pervert] *O*, *L*, *Ca*, *B*; prevent *Cb*
24 we're] *L*, *Ca*, *Cb*; we are *B*; we *O*
27 me you] *L*, *Ca*, *Cb*, *B*; me that you *O*
35 *Knocking*] *Cb* [S.], *B*; *om.* *O*, *L*, *Ca*
38 too] *Ca*, *Cb*; to *O*, *L*, *B*

SURFACE. O I have no fear of that—Sir Peter will hold his tongue for his own credit sake—and you may depend on't I shall soon Discover Sir Oliver's weak side!—

LADY SNEERWELL. I have no diffidence of your abilities—only be constant to one roguery at a time— [*Exit.*

SURFACE. I will—I will—so 'tis confounded—hard after such bad Fortune to be baited by one's confederate in evil.—well at all events my character is so much better than Charles's that I certainly—hey! what! —this is not Sir Oliver—but old Stanley again!—Plague on't! that He should return to teize me just now—we shall have Sir Oliver come and find him—here—and—

Enter SIR OLIVER.

Gad's life—Mr. Stanley—why have you come back to plague me just at this time?—you must not stay now upon my word!

SIR OLIVER. Sir—I hear your unkle Oliver is expected here—and tho' He has been so penurious to you I'll try what He'll do for me—

SURFACE. Sir 'tis—impossible for you to stay now—so I must beg—come any other Time and I promise you you shall be assisted—

SIR OLIVER. No—Sir Oliver and I must be acquainted—

SURFACE. Zounds Sir then I insist on your quitting the—Room directly—

SIR OLIVER. Nay Sir!

SURFACE. Sir—I insist on't—here William Shew this Gentleman out.—since you compell me Sir—not one moment—this is such insolence [*going to push him out.*

Enter CHARLES.

CHARLES SURFACE. Heydey! what's the matter now?—what the Devil have you got hold of my little Broker here! Zounds—Brother don't hurt little Premium—what's the matter—my little Fellow?

SURFACE. So! He has been with you too has He?

CHARLES SURFACE. To be sure He has!—why 'tis as honest a little—but sure Joseph, you have not been borrowing money too, have you?

SURFACE. Borrowing—no!—but Brother—you know here we—expect Sir Oliver every—

CHARLES SURFACE. O Gad! that's true—Noll mustn't find the little Broker here to be sure—

SURFACE. Yet Mr. Stanley insists—

CHARLES SURFACE. Stanley—why his name's Premium—

SURFACE. No—no—Stanley—

CHARLES SURFACE. No—no—Premium—

SURFACE. Well no—matter—which but—

5 *Exit*] *O, L, Ca, Cb*; (*Exit Lady Sneerwell*) *B* 17 beg] *O, L, Ca, Cb*; beg you *B* 20 I] *L, Ca, Cb, B*; *om. O* 24 *going . . . out*] *O, L, Ca, B*; (*pushing him out*) *Cb* 31 too] *O, L, Ca, B*; *om. Cb* 32 here] *O, L, Ca, B*; *om. Cb*

CHARLES SURFACE. Aye—aye Stanley or Premium 'tis the same thing as you say—for I suppose He goes by half a hundred Names—besides A.B.'s at the Coffee-Houses— [*knock.*

SURFACE. Death—here's Sir Oliver—at the Door.—[*knocking again*]—now I beg—Mr. Stanley—

CHARLES SURFACE. Aye and I beg Mr. Premium—

SIR OLIVER. Gentlemen—

SURFACE. Sir By Heav'n you shall go—

CHARLES SURFACE. Aye out with him certainly—

SIR OLIVER. This Violence—

SURFACE. 'Tis your own Fault—

CHARLES SURFACE. Out with him to be sure—

[*Both forcing* SIR OLIVER *out.*

Enter SIR PETER, LADY TEAZLE, MARIA, *and* ROWLEY.

SIR PETER. My old Friend Sir Oliver!—hey—what in the name of wonder!—Here are dutiful Nephews!—assault their Uncle at the first Visit—

LADY TEAZLE. Indeed Sir Oliver 'twas well we came in to rescue you—

ROWLEY. Truly it was—for I perceive Sir Oliver the character of Old Stanley was no Protection to you

SIR OLIVER. Nor of Premium—either—the necessities of the former couldn't extort a shilling from that benevolent Gentleman and now—egad!—I stood a Chance of faring worse than my Ancestors—and being knock'd down without being bid for.—

[*af*[*t*]*er a Pause*—JOSEPH *and* CHARLES *turning to each other.*

SURFACE. Charles—!

CHARLES SURFACE. Joseph!

SURFACE. 'Tis now compleat!—

CHARLES SURFACE. Very.

SIR OLIVER. Sir Peter—my Friend and Rowley too—look on that elder Nephew of mine—you know what He has already received from my Bounty,—and you know also—how gladly I would have regarded half my Fortune as held in trust for him—judge then my Disap[p]ointment in discovering him to be destitute of Truth—Charity—and Gratitude—

2 half a hundred] *O*, *L*, *Cb*, *B*; half hundred *Ca* 3 A.B.'s] *O*, *Ca*; A.B. *L*, *Cb*, *B* Houses] *O*, *Ca*; House *L*, *Cb*, *B* *knock*] *O*; (*knocking*) *Cb*; *om. L*, *Ca*, *B* 4 Death] *Ca*; O death *L*; Sdeath *O*, *Cb*, *B* *knocking again*] *Ca* [S.]; (*Knock*), *L*, *Cb*, *B*; *om.* O 6 Aye and] *O*, *Ca*; Aye aye and *B*, *Cb*; Aye aye *L* 20 Truly] *O*, *L*, *Ca*, *B*; Truly so *Cb* 26 *af*[*t*]*er . . . other*] *Ca* [S.]; *om. O*, *L*, *Cb*, *B* 27 Charles (*aside*)] *Cb* [S.]; Charles *O*, *L*, *Ca*, *B*; 29 now] *Ca*, *Cb*, *B*; *om. O*, *L* 31 too] *O*, *Ca*, *Cb*, *B*; *om. L* 33 regarded] *Ca*, *Cb*, *B*; look'd on *O*, *L*

SIR PETER. Sir Oliver—I should be more Surprized at this Declaration if I had not myself found him selfish—treacherous and Hypocritical—

LADY TEAZLE. And if the gentleman pleads not guilty to these—pray let him call *me* to his Character—

SIR PETER. Then I believe we need add no more—if He knows himself He will consider it as the most perfect Punishment that He is known by the world—

CHARLES SURFACE. [*aside*] If they talk this way to Honesty—what will they say to *me* by and bye!

SIR OLIVER. As for that Prodigal—his Brother there—

CHARLES SURFACE. [*aside*] Aye now comes my Turn—the damn'd Family Pictures will ruin me—

SURFACE. Sir Oliver! Unkle!—will you honor—me with a hearing?

CHARLES SURFACE. [*aside*] Now if Joseph would make one of his long Speeches I might recollect myself a little—

SIR OLIVER. I suppose you would undertake to justify yourself entirely.

SURFACE. I trust I could.

SIR OLIVER. Pshaw!—well Sir! and *you* [*to* CHARLES] could *justify* yourself too I suppose—

CHARLES SURFACE. Not that I know of Sir Oliver.—

SIR OLIVER. What little Premium—has been let too much into the secret I presume.

CHARLES SURFACE. True—Sir—but they were Family Secrets and should never be mention'd again you know.

ROWLEY. Come Sir Oliver I know you cannot Speak of Charles's Follies with anger.

SIR OLIVER. Odds heart no more I can—nor with Gravity either. Sir Peter, do you know the Rogue bargain'd with me for all his Ancestors—sold me Judges and Generals by the Foot and Maiden Aunts as Cheap as broken China!

CHARLES SURFACE. To be Sure Sir Oliver I did make a little free with the Family Canvass that's the Truth on't—my Ancestors may certainly rise in Evidence against me there's no denying it—but believe me sincere when I tell you, and upon my soul I would not Say it if I was not—that if I do not appear mortified—at the exposure of my Follies—it is because I feel at this moment the warmest satisfaction—in seeing you—my *liberal* Benefactor.

2 him] *Ca* [S.]; him to be *O, L, Cb, B* 8 *aside*] *Ca* [S.]; *om. O, L, Cb, B* 9 say] *O, L, Ca, B*; do *Cb* 11 *aside*] *Ca* [S.]; *om. O, L, Cb, B* 14 *aside*] *Ca* [S.], *B*; *om. O, L, Cb* Now if Joseph] *Ca, Cb, B*; I wish Joseph now *O, L* 15 I] *Ca, Cb, B*; and I *O, L* 16 I] *L, Ca, Cb, B*; and I *O* justify] *Ca, Cb, B*; vindicate *O, L* 18 Pshaw] *Ca*; Nay if you desert your Roguery in its Distress—and try to be justified—you have even less principle than I thought you had—*O, L, Cb, B* *to* CHARLES] *Ca* [S.]; *om. O, Cb, B* 24 know] *Ca, Cb, B*; know, Sir *O, L* 33 rise] *O, L, Cb, B*; raise *Ca* 33 it] *O, L, Ca, Cb*; *om. B* 34 it if I] *O, L, Ca, Cb*; it if it *B*

SIR OLIVER. Charles—I believe you—give me your hand again. The ill-looking little Fellow over the Settee has made your Peace, Sirrah!

CHARLES SURFACE. Then Sir—my Gratitude to the original is still encreased.

LADY TEAZLE. [*pointing to* MARIA] Yet I believe Sir Oliver, here is one whom Charles is still more anxious to be reconciled to.

SIR OLIVER. O I have heard of his Attachment there—and with the young Lady's Pardon if I construe right that Blush—

SIR PETER. Well—Child—speak your sentiments—

MARIA. Sir—I have little to say—but that I shall rejoice to hear that He is happy—for me—whatever claim I had to his Affection—I willingly resign it to one who has a better Title.

CHARLES SURFACE. How Maria!

SIR PETER. Heydey—what's the mystery now?—while He appear'd an incorrigible Rake you would give your hand to no one else and now that He's likely to reform I warrant you won't have him!—

MARIA. His own Heart—and Lady Sneerwell know the Cause.

CHARLES SURFACE. Lady Sneerwell—

SURFACE. Brother, it—is with great concern—I am obliged to speak on this Point but my Regard to Justice compells me.—and Lady Sneerwell's—Injuries can no longer—be concealed— [*goes to the Door.*

Enter LADY SNEERWELL.

SIR PETER. Soh! another French milliner egad!—He has one in every Room in the House I suppose—

LADY SNEERWELL. Ungrateful Charles!—well may you be surprised and feel for the indelicate situation which your Perfidy has forced me into.

CHARLES SURFACE. Pray Unkle is this another Plot of yours? for as I have Life I don't understand it.

SURFACE. I believe Sir there is but the evidence of one Person more necessary to make it extremely Clear.

SIR PETER. And that Person—I imagine is Mr. Snake—Rowley—you were perfectly—right to bring him with us—and pray let him appear.

ROWLEY. Walk in Mr. Snake—

1 again] *Ca, Cb, B*; *om. O, L*   2 Settee] *Ca, Cb, B*; Couch *O, L*   Sirrah] *Cb* [S.]; *om. O, L, Ca, B*   5 *pointing to* MARIA] *Ca* [S.]; *om. O, L, Cb, B*   7–8 O... Blush] *O, Ca, Cb, B*; *om. L*   8 Pardon] *O, Ca, B*; consent *Cb*   9 sentiments] *Ca, Cb, B*; sentiments—you know—we are going to be reconciled to Charles *O, L*   10 that He] *O, L, Ca, B*; He *Cb*   11 had] *O, L, Ca, B*; once had *Cb*   Affection] *O, Ca, Cb, B*; affections *L*   willingly] *L, Ca, Cb, B*; willing *O*   12 it] *Ca* [S.]; *om. O, L, Cb, B*   20 compells] *Ca* [S.]; obliges *O, L, Cb, B*   21 *goes to the Door*] *O, L, Ca, B*; *om. Cb*   24 in] *L, Ca, B*; of *O, Cb*   33 and] *O, L, Ca, B*; *om. Cb*

Enter SNAKE.

I thought his Testimony might be wanted—however it happens unluckily that he comes to Confront Lady Sneerwell and not to support her.

LADY SNEERWELL. Villain!—treacherous to me at last!—[*aside*] speak Fellow have you too conspired against me?

SNAKE. I beg your Ladyship—ten thousand Pardons, you paid me extremely Liberally for the Lie in question—but I have unfortunately been offer'd double to speak the Truth.[1]—

SIR PETER. Plot and Counterplot Egad—I wish your Ladyship Joy of the Success of your Negotiation.

LADY SNEERWELL. The Torments of Shame and Disap[p]ointment on you all!—

LADY TEAZLE. Hold—Lady Sneerwell—before you go let me thank you for the trouble you and that Gentleman have taken in writing Letters to me from Charles and answering them yourself—and let me also request you to make my—Respects to the Scandalous College—of which you are President—and inform them—that Lady Teazle Licentiate—begs leave to return the Diploma they granted her—as she leaves off Practice and kills Characters no longer.

LADY SNEERWELL. You too Madam—provoking—insolent!—may your Husband live these fifty years! [*Exit.*

SIR PETER. Oons what a Fury—

LADY TEAZLE. What a malicious creature it is!

SIR PETER. Hey—not for her last wish—?

LADY TEAZLE. O No—

SIR OLIVER. Well, Sir, and what have you to say now?

SURFACE. Sir, I am so confounded to find that Lady Sneerwell could be guilty of suborning Mr. Snake in this manner to impose on us all that I know not what to say—however lest her Revengeful Spirit should prompt her to injure my Brother I had certainly better follow her directly— [*Exit.*

SIR PETER. Moral to the last drop!

5 Villain] *Ca* [S.]; A Villain *O*, *L*, *Cb*, *B* *aside*] *Ca* [S.]; *om.* *O*, *L*, *Cb*, *B* 6 too] *O*, *Ca*, *Cb*; *om.* *B* 10 Plot and Counterplot] *Ca*, *Cb*, *B*; *om.* *O*, *L* 10–11 Egad . . . Negotiation] *Ca*; *om.* *O*, *L*, *Cb*, *B* 19 Licentiate] *Ca* [S.]; Licentiante *O*, *Cb*; Licentiant *L*, *B* return] *O*, *L*, *Ca*, *B*; return her *Cb* 20 off] *Ca*, *Cb*; of *O*, *L*, *B* 22 *Exit*] *L*, *Ca*, *Cb*; (*Exit Lady Sneerwell*) *B*; *om.* *O* 24 What . . . is] *Cb* [S.]; A Malicious Creature indeed *O*, *L*, *Ca*, *B* 32 *Exit*] *O*, *L*, *Ca*, *Cb*; (*Exit Mr. Surface*) *B*

---

[1] Cf. T. Smollett, *The Adventures of Sir Launcelot Greaves* (1762), Ch. 24: 'Perhaps his fidelity to his employer, reinforced by the hope of many future jobs of that kind, might have been proof against the offer of fifty pounds; but double that sum was a temptation he could not resist.'

SIR OLIVER. Aye and marry her Joseph if you can—Oil and Vinegar egad!—you'll do very well together.—

ROWLEY. I believe we have no more occasion for Mr. Snake at Present—

SNAKE. Before I go—I beg—Pardon once for all, for whatever uneasiness I have been the humble Instrument of causing to the Parties present.

SIR PETER. Well—well you have made Atonement by a good Deed at last—

SNAKE. But I must Request of the Company that it shall never be known—

SIR PETER. Hey!—what the Plague—are you ashamed of having done a right thing once in your life?

SNAKE. Ah! Sir—consider I live by the Badness of my Character!—I have nothing but my Infamy to depend on! and if it were once known that I had been betray'd into an honest Action I should lose every Friend I have in the world.

SIR OLIVER. Well—well we'll not traduce you by saying anything in your Praise never fear. [*Exit* SNAKE.

SIR PETER. There's a precious Rogue—yet that Fellow is a Writer and a Critic!

LADY TEAZLE. See Sir Oliver there needs no Persuasion now to reconcile your Nephew and Maria— [CHARLES *and* MARIA *apart*.

SIR OLIVER. Aye—aye that's as it should—be and egad we'll have the wedding tomorrow-morning.

CHARLES SURFACE. Thank you my dear Unkle.

SIR PETER. What! you rogue don't you ask the Girl's Consent first?

CHARLES SURFACE. O I have done that a long time—above a minute ago—and She has look'd yes—

MARIA. For Shame—Charles—I protest Sir Peter there has not been a word—

SIR OLIVER. Well then the fewer the Better—may your love for each other never know—abatement

SIR PETER. And may you live as happily together as Lady Teazle and I—intend to do.

CHARLES SURFACE. Rowley my old Friend—I am sure you congratulate me and I suspect that I owe you much.

SIR OLIVER. You do indeed Charles.

ROWLEY. If my Efforts to serve you had not succeeded you would have

1 Oil and Vinegar] *O, Ca*; *om. Cb, B* 6 Well—well] *O, L, Ca, B*; Well *Cb* 12 Ah] *O, L, Ca, B*; Ay *Cb* 15 world] *O, L, Ca, B*; world (*Exit*) *Cb* 16 in] *Ca, Cb*; to *O, L, B* 17 *Exit* SNAKE] *O, L, Ca*; *om. Cb, B* 18 There's . . . Rogue] *O, L, Ca*; *placed by Cb and B between lines 15 and 16* 18–19 yet . . . Critic] *O, L, Ca*; *om. Cb, B* 21 CHARLES . . . *apart*] *L, Ca*; *om. O, Cb, B* 26 O] *O, L, Ca, Cb*; *om. B* above] *O, Ca* [S.]; *om. L, Cb, B* 35 and] *O Ca, B*; *om. L, Cb* suspect] *L, Ca, Cb, B*; suspect too *O*

been in my Debt for the attempt—but deserve to be happy—and you overpay me—

SIR PETER. Aye honest Rowley always said you would Reform.

CHARLES SURFACE. Why as to Reforming Sir Peter I'll make no Promises—and that I take to be a proof that I intend to set about it—But Here shall be my monitor—my gentle Guide[1]—ah! can I leave the Virtuous path those Eyes illumine?

Tho'—thou, dear Maid; should'st wa[i]ve thy Beauty's Sway,
—Thou Still must Rule—because I will obey;
An humbled Fugitive from Folly View,
No Sanctuary near—but Love and—YOU;

[*to the Audience*

You can indeed each Anxious Fear remove,
For even Scandal dies if you approve.

—finis.—

5 set] *O*, *Ca*, *Cb*, *B*; sit *L* 6 Guide] *Ca*, *Cb*, *B*; Pilot *O*, *L* 6–7 leave . . . path] *Ca*, *Cb*, *B*; wander and *O*, *L* 7 illumine] *Ca*, *Cb*, *B*; my Cynosure! *O*, *L* 8–14 Tho' . . . approve] *Ca*, *Cb*, *B*; *om.* *O*, *L* 8 wa[i]ve] *Ca*, *Cb*; leave *B* 12 *to . . . Audience*] *Ca*; *placed after 'approve' in Cb and B.*

[1] Cf. Faulkland's 'my future guide and monitress' in *The Rivals*, v. i: p. 133 above.

EPILOGUE

Written by G. Coleman, Eqr.[1]

Spoken by Mrs. Abington in the Character of Lady Teazle

I who was late so volatile and gay,
Like a Trade-wind must now blow all one way,
Bend all my Cares, my Studies, and my vows,
To one old rusty weather-cock my spouse;
So wills our virtuous Bard!—the Motley Bayes[2]
Of crying Epilogues[3] and laughing Plays.

Old Bachelors, who marry smart young Wives,
Learn from our Play to regulate your lives!
Each bring his Dear to Town—all Faults upon her—
London will prove the very Source of Honour;
Plung'd fairly in like a cold Bath, it serves,
When Principles relax—to brace the Nerves.
Such is my Case—and yet I might deplore
That the gay dream of dissipation's o'er;
And say, ye fair, was ever lively Wife,
Born with a genius for the highest Life
Like me, untimely blasted in her bloom,
Like me condemn'd to such a dismal doom?
Save money—when I just knew how to waste it!
Leave London—just as I began to taste it!
Must I then watch the early-crowing Cock?
The melancholy Ticking of a Clock?
In the lone rustic hall for ever pounded,
With Dogs, Cats, Rats, and squalling Brats surrounded?

1 EPILOGUE] *L*, *Ca*, *Gaz.*; Epilogue for Lady Teazle *Cb*; *Epilogue by Lady Teazle B* 2 *Written . . . Eqr.*] *Ca* [S.]; *Written by George Colman, Esq. Gaz.*; written by Mr. Coleman *B* [S.]; *om. Cb*, *L* 3 *Spoken . . . Abington*] *L*, *Ca*; *om. Cb*, *B*; *And spoken . . . Abington Gaz.* *in . . . Teazle*] *L*, *Gaz.*; *om. Ca*, *Cb*, *B* 8 the Motley] *Ca*; a motley *B*; his Motley *Cb*; the pye-Ball'd *L*, *Gaz.* 16 might] *Ca*, *Cb*, *B*; must *L*, *Gaz.* *Lines 21 and 22 are burnt away in L, and are supplied from The Gazetteer.*

[1] George Colman the elder (1732–94), manager of the Haymarket Theatre and author of *The Jealous Wife* (1761) and, with Garrick, of *The Clandestine Marriage* (1766).

[2] Cf. p. 472, below.

[3] Colman is laughing at Sheridan's epilogue to George Ayscough's tragedy, *Semiramis* (1776). See p. 823 below.

With humble curates can I now retire
(While good Sir Peter boozes with the Squire)
And at Back-gammon mortify my Soul,
That pants for Lu,[1] or flutters at a Vole?[2]
Seven's the Main![3]—dear sound!—that must expire,
Lost at hot-cockles[4] round a Christmas Fire!
The Transient Hour of Fashion too soon spent,
'Farewell the tranquil mind, farewell Content!
Farewell the plum'd Head—the cushion'd Tete,
That takes the Cushion from its proper seat![5]
The spirit stirring Drum!—Card Drums[6] I mean—
Spadille,[7] odd Trick, Pam,[8] Basto,[9] King and Queen!
And you, ye knockers, that with Brazen Throat
The welcome Visitor's Approach denote,
Farewell!—all Quality of high Renown,
Pride, Pomp, and Circumstance of glorious Town!
Farewell! your revels I partake no more,
And Lady Teazle's occupation's o'er!'[10]
—All this I told our Bard—he smil'd and said 'twas clear
I ought to play deep Tragedy next year:
Meanwhile he drew wise morals from his play,
And in these solemn Periods stalk'd away.
'Blest were the Fair, like you her Faults who stopt,
And clos'd her Follies when the Curtain dropt!
No more in vice or error to engage,
Or play the Fool at large on Life's great Stage.'

15 all . . . Renown] *L, Ca, B, Gaz.*; *om. Cb* 16 Pride . . . Town] *Ca, B, Gaz.*; *om. L, Cb* 17 Farewell] *Ca, B, Gaz.*; *om. L, Cb* your . . . more] *Ca, Cb, B, Gaz.*; *om. L*

---

[1] Loo was a fashionable card game, played with three or five cards. In 1775 Lady Spencer recommended her daughter to satisfy herself with whist or backgammon, and not to indulge in the more expensive forms of gaming, 'quinze, lou, brag, faro' (*Georgiana* (ed. The Earl of Bessbororough), 1955, p. 24).

[2] Winning all the tricks in a deal.

[3] The main was the number (five to nine) called by the caster in hazard, before the dice were thrown. 'If seven is thrown for a Main, and four the Chance, it is two to one against the Person who throws' (*Hoyle's Games Improv'd*, rev. Thomas Jones (1778), p. 210).

[4] One of the innocent amusements enjoyed by the family in Goldsmith's *The Vicar of Wakefield* (*Collected Works*, ed. A. Friedman (Oxford, 1966), iv. 60): a blindfolded player guessed who had hit him in the back.

[5] Cf. p. 571, ll. 3–6.

[6] Card parties at private houses.

[7] The Ace of Spades in ombre and quadrille.

[8] The Knave of Clubs in loo.

[9] The Ace of Clubs.

[10] The eleven lines, ending here, form a parody of Othello, III, iii:

Farewell the tranquil mind; farewell content!
Farewell the plumed troop and the big wars.